MOON OVER AJALON

JOSHUA PRAYED ALOUD,
"LET THE SUN STAND STILL OVER GIBEON,
AND LET THE MOON STAND IN ITS PLACE
OVER THE VALLEY OF AJALON!"

ROBERT SIKKENGA

Pleasant Word
A Division of WINEPRESS PUBLISHING

ISBN 1-4141-0093-0
Library of Congress Catalog Card Number: 2003115237

Acknowledgment

I am grateful to the Lord for the inspiration and
perseverance that enabled me to write this book.
The labor itself was reward beyond gold.

I am deeply indebted to my wife for her love,
patience, advice, support, and the many tedious
hours of proofreading and editing. She is a
priceless mate.

I sincerely appreciate the encouragement
and counsel of my friendly critics.

And I am thankful to the good people at
Pleasant Word for their commitment
to give of their best to the Master.

Welcome

*W*hen Jesus broke the bonds of death on that first Easter Sunday, another wonderful thing happened: he opened the doors of heaven and bequeathed to all believers *"an inheritance incorruptible and undefiled, and that fadeth not away . . ."* (1 Peter 1:4 KJV). That heavenly inheritance is a free gift given to us by the grace of God. Though we can do nothing to earn it, God calls us to work as though we could earn it. One of our many assignments is to *"study to shew thyself approved unto God, a workman that needeth not to be ashamed, rightly dividing the word of truth"* (2 Timothy 2:15 KJV).

Paul taught us that *"All scripture is given by inspiration of God, and is profitable for doctrine, for reproof, for correction, for instruction in righteousness: that the man of God may be perfect, thoroughly furnished unto all good works"* (2 Timothy 3:16–17 KJV). Simply put, Paul was telling us that the Bible is God's Word, and that from it we can learn what God is like and how he wants us to live.

As I was growing up, my father read the Bible to us several times over, and I know from experience that just reading it did little to inspire me to live righteously or to devote my life to doing God's will. Merely *reading* God's Word is not enough. We have to *study* it. That means we have to set aside sufficient time to pore over it, struggle with it, ingest it, digest it, and "hide it in our hearts." We have to meditate and contemplate, begging the Holy Spirit to counsel us and instruct us in righteousness and understanding.

If you commit yourself to this series of devotional studies, in order to gain the most you will have to place your open Bible on your table next to this book and read the main scripture as well as the suggested reading before you turn to the meditation.

We begin at the beginning when God created the universe and placed us in our garden paradise with the command to be obedient and diligent overseers of all that he had made. We watch ourselves fail to live up to our Maker's expectations, and we see a just and loving God judge us, condemn us, punish us, pardon us, and give us another chance. We conclude our series of devotions when the army of the Lord conquers the pagan armies of Canaan, and Joshua sends the children of Israel to their inheritance in the Promised Land.

As we study, we must see ourselves as characters in the drama of Israel. We must open our minds and hearts to understand the designs of our creator, cross over Jordan into holy ground, and commit ourselves to living as God would have us live. If we do, his gift to us will be like his gift to Israel: the opportunity to live an abundant life in a spiritual promised land, an inheritance in a kingdom abloom with the fruit of the Spirit and flowing with the milk and honey of God's grace. But if we fail, Israel's doom will be our doom, a fate horrible beyond imagination.

We must understand the metaphor that is Israel. Only then can we begin to understand the extent of God's genius, his passion for obedience, his uncompromising insistence upon justice, the depth of his love, his gift of salvation, and the bountiful inheritance he has promised us.

When we cross the Jordan for the last time, God will look into our hearts, and if he finds his Word properly hidden there he will approve of our work, declare us innocent and say, ". . . *well done, thou good and faithful servant, . . . enter thou into the joy of the Lord*" (Matthew 25:21 KJV).

The Beginning

Welcome to a pilgrimage from the Garden of Eden, through the mountains and the valleys and the rough places, and on to the kingdom of heaven. I am truly blessed to be your traveling companion.

Our walk with Christ is a journey that begins when God first breathes into us the fresh breath of his new life and continues through our final victory over the forces of Satan as we struggle to secure our inheritance in the spiritual promised land, the kingdom of heaven. These meditations are designed as daily walks through the Bible, beginning on the day God knelt down and breathed life into Adam's nostrils, and culminating with the revelation of the mystery hidden for the ages, the spiritual promised land that we can possess if we die to self and are reborn into a new life with Jesus living in us.

As we walk day by day and step by step with Adam, Noah, Abraham, Isaac, Jacob, Joseph, Moses, and Joshua, we will see how their collective travels parallel our journey from paradise to apostasy, to repentance, and on to sanctification. The lessons that God teaches us along the way, some bitter, others sweet, can transform us from enslaved sinners into priestly citizens of the kingdom of heaven who, as children of the King, inherit his divine nature, dine sumptuously on the fruit of the Spirit, and enjoy the abundant life our Lord came to give us.

When Joshua fought a battle against the Amorites at Gibeon, God stopped the sun in the sky and gave Joshua daylight for as long as he needed to gain the victory. When we think of how God made the sun stand still, we remember how he gives us strength for the day and the resources to accomplish the tasks he has set before us.

But we must remember that when the sun stood still, the moon stood still too, over the valley of Ajalon. Our lives are filled with battlefields and with valleys, and just as God's sun illumines the arenas in which we fight our daily wars against the forces of evil, the warm glow of his moonbeam pierces the darkness of our deep places. And sometimes when our abyss begs for more of his light, he makes the moon stand still as long as necessary for us to find our way and keep from stubbing our toes on the rocks.

When the Syrian king, Ben-hadad and his pagan coalition lost a battle to an inferior Israelite army in the hills of Samaria, his prophets told him that Israel's God was only a God of the mountains, and that he could defeat Israel's King Ahab if he fought him in the lowlands. So in the spring he sent his hoards against Ahab's tiny forces in the valley of Jezreel, where, with God at their side, the Israelites slew a hundred thousand Syrians in the rout over Ben-hadad, while God slew another twenty-seven thousand by burying them under the walls of the city of Aphek. In that victory over evil, God proved that he is the God of the valleys as well as the God of the mountains.

Many inspirational meditations and hymns have been written detailing the wonders of God's brilliant presence in the lives of people who were constant companions to pain and challenge. But not so much has been made of the little streams of God's moonbeams that light our way as we grope through the valleys of our lives, struggle with our doubts and raise our rebellious sighs of discontent. As the inspired songwriter George Crowly knew, our God is not only the Sinai God of earthquake, wind, and fire who can fill our lives with ecstasy by ripping through our veil of clay, opening the skies and sending angels to minister to us, but he is also the lowlands God, the God of the still, small voice who can take the dimness of our soul away and teach us to love him as we ought to love.

I've Just Seen Jesus

Scripture: Genesis 1:1
Suggested Reading: John 1:1–8

When I was a boy I loved to look up at the fluffy clouds floating overhead and imagine that I could see whales, giant birds and big white rabbits soaring through space. Perhaps one of the vestiges of our vivid childhood ability to imagine and create remains with us today as we look into the clouds and see more than just colossal puffs of vapor. That is exactly the faculty we need to employ if we are to appreciate the Old Testament to its fullest; we have to be able to look behind the obvious and see the mysteries that hide there.

That's exactly what John did with the aid of the Holy Spirit, when he read the first chapter of Genesis. In those mists that swirled over the firmament, he saw Jesus. In the Spirit that hovered over the face of the deep, he saw Jesus. In the shadows that separated the light from the darkness, he saw the silhouette of Jesus. And in the voice that said, "Let there be light," he heard the voice of Jesus.

Jesus didn't come into being at that moment when time was divided into two histories. He always was. He was there in the first magnificent moment of creation. He was there when the triune godhead said, "Let us make man in our image." He was there in that moment of eternal horror when Adam and Eve disobeyed the voice of God and ate the forbidden fruit. He was there from the beginning of eternity, and he knew our names.

When I was a sophomore in college, the wonder of creation lay in wondering just how God did it. Did he do it, as some say, in the twinkling of an eye? Was the land barren one moment and lush with greenery the next? Or did he do it, as others say, over eons of time, letting cells slowly evolve and multiply in accordance with the laws of nature that he built into the system?

In my mind, that debate has long since been deposited into that thick notebook of mysteries that I hope will unravel when our creator calls me to my eternal home. The wonder of creation now lies in the simple fact that somehow he did it, and that when he did it, the Jesus who left his eternal home to walk among us, the Jesus who taught us how to live, the Jesus who laid down his life before a just and loving God as the ultimate sacrifice for sin, was there, creating the universe, planning its destiny, and knowing all about me and how much I would need him.

When Jesus was a boy he studied the writings of Moses and the other prophets. He read about the opening of the Red Sea, about the fall of the walls of Jericho and about the sun standing still at Gibeon and the moon over the valley of Ajalon while his name-sake, Joshua, fought a decisive battle against the Amorites. Did it amuse him to read history that he caused to happen? To read about himself as he stood in the midst of the sea and parted the waters? As he stomped his foot and shook the walls of Jericho? As he reached into the sky and stopped the sun and the moon in their tracks? Does he look down with amusement today on us as we wonder just how he did it?

"I and the Father are one," he told us, and as we read the older of the two Testaments we must always remember that Jesus is there. Sometimes, as we shall see, he leaps off the page at us, but usually his presence is more subtle, more in the background as he awaits his moment of singular attention later in history.

But he is always there.

. . . And You Were There

Scripture: Genesis 1:2
Suggested Reading: Matthew 25:34–40; Ephesians 1:1–4;
Revelation 13:8

One of the debates that raged at the onset of the twenty-first century was the debate between the so-called pro life and pro choice movements regarding abortion. The pro choice people argued that life does not really begin until some point at which the newly formed being begins to have feelings and experiences. The pro life people, on the other hand, argued that life begins at conception.

Since voluntary abortion was not a moral issue back when the Bible was written, its inspired authors had no grounds for entering the debate between pro lifers and pro choicers or for directly answering the question of whether or not abortion is murder. But fortunately, they did not avoid the question of when life begins. They told me very clearly that God knew me from before the beginning of time and had my name written in his book even before he laid the foundations of the earth. As surely as I exist in this age, my biography was etched in the genes of my father, and his in his father's. We can trace our roots back to the day when the breath of God first blew upon the dark face of the deep and churned up ripples that swell across eternity to break some glorious morning on the shores of the Crystal Sea.

But where was I before I was born? Where was I when Noah emerged from the ark to mark the dawn of a new history, or when Jesus came forth from the tomb to mark the end of slavery under the law? Some would fancy that my life surged through the veins of a beast or a bird, while others surmise that I might have been a Caesar or a Napoleon, that the residue of those prior beings still lingers somewhere in the recesses of my subconscious memory and that I might become someone else when I cease being me. What memory will I have of my temporal life when someday I sit and ponder my past in the house he's built for me in glory? The possibilities are amusing and mysterious, and on that great some-day, all amusing and mysterious questions will finally be joined to their elusive answers.

The only thing that matters now is what I do with this present life. When the gates of the heavenly kingdom swing open to me, I may or may not be able to reflect on the tent in which I dwelled during the seasons of my sojourn, but I will be able to reflect on the fact that my name appeared on the citizenship rolls of that kingdom long before pterodactyls glided through the heavens or Noah floated over the face of the earth. And I will be able to reflect on the fact that it was written there by the creator who knew me before he began to brood over the formless deep, written in the blood of the lamb who had to be slain to seal my inheritance in that kingdom.

How then should I live? What should I do each day as I go my way? I have no choice, for since I am an heir to the kingdom of God I must go on my way feeding the hungry, giving water to the thirsty, welcoming the stranger, clothing the naked, visiting the sick, minis-tering to the prisoner and confessing the name of Jesus Christ.

Why? Because in doing so I am ministering to the needs of the one who knew me and loved me before time began, who knew me so well and loved me so much that when he saw me stumble in my sin, he left his home in glory, sought me in the wild places, picked me up, carried me on his shoulders, suffered and died to earn my pardon, and made me a blood brother worthy to be called a son of God.

Let There Be Light

Scripture: Genesis 1:3–23
Suggested Reading: Matthew 5:14–16; Luke 23:44; John 1:4–9; 8:12; 12:36; Romans 12:4–8; Revelation 21:10–27

One night after touring the old city of Jerusalem, we stood by the fountain outside our hotel and watched a total eclipse of the moon. When we began watching, the moon was full and the ripples in the pond shimmered in the shower of cascading water. Buildings on the hillside gleamed white.

As the crescent of the earth's shadow slowly edged its way over the face of the moon, the sparkle faded from the pond, the white buildings retreated into the obscurity of night, and for the next few hours, the city of Jerusalem cowered in cold, dark shadows.

As I stood there in the gloom, I remembered a time when another cosmic event shrouded the old city in darkness. When the children of the night nailed the King of the Jews to the cross, the sun failed to shine, and darkness prevailed over the land for three hours. They thought they had extinguished the Light of the world.

Physically, the sun illuminates our globe, but spiritually its light is Jesus. When the sons of Israel rejected and crucified their Messiah, they plunged the nation and its capitol city into spiritual darkness, a darkness that will not be overcome until Jesus returns to claim his kingdom.

Those who follow Jesus are children of light, and those who follow Satan are children of darkness. Disciples of the Lord reflect his light; he has commissioned them to be the light of the world, to let their light shine so others may see his glory. But children of darkness try to eclipse the light of the world and plunge the earth into the shadows of evil.

Followers of Jesus let their light shine in many ways. They are suns and moons and stars. God has gifted some of his lights to shine brightly by preaching, teaching, and singing to millions on radio and television. Some are moons who light the way in someone's dark valley. And some are stars, twinkling with the joy they bring to the sick, the imprisoned, and the lonely. However bright the light God has bestowed on each of his luminaries, they may not hide it, but must use their gifts of light in his service.

And the "lesser lights," as we view them from our perspective, cannot be jealous of the power with which God has endowed his "greater lights." As we see it, one sun is brilliant, while millions of tiny stars merely twinkle in the black vault of the heavens. But from where God sits, all stars are suns.

God's first act after creating light was to separate the light from the darkness. And one of God's final acts at the end of time will be to separate the light from the darkness once again. As he separates the sheep from the goats, he will separate the children of light from the children of darkness. The children of darkness will be plunged into the eternal abyss of hell, while the children of light will dwell in the eternal brilliance of the New Jerusalem.

And on that glad day, the glory of the Lord will illuminate the Holy City. Jesus will be its lamp and there shall be no night there.

Are you a child of the light? Will you be there?

... *In Our Image*

Scripture: Genesis 1:24–26a
Suggested Reading: Genesis 2:7 (KJV); 2 Peter 1:4; 1 John 3:1–10

What does it mean to be made in God's image? Do we look like him? Do we have his personality traits? Do we share his attributes?

As for appearance, most of us have much in common with the ape. As for character, I believe my dog Duke to be more capable of unconditional love than I am. As for cleverness and creativity, the virus that attacks our bodies seems able to outthink the most brilliant of our scientists.

The old Greeks saw their gods as beautiful and athletic, but prone to most human weaknesses. Satan told Eve that being like God meant knowing the difference between good and evil. Most pagan religions created their gods in the image of people, animals, or monsters. All religions see some sort of similarity between creator and creatures, but not all have struggled to define clearly that elusive likeness.

Our resemblance to God cannot be found in biology, character, behavior, personality trait, or attribute. If it could, all creatures would bear his image in some way. I think old Duke knows the difference between good and evil. Why else does he wait until my back is turned to run off and violate the boundaries I've trained him to observe? And why does he tuck his tail between his legs, hang his head and whimper when he comes slinking back? And why does his repentant countenance seem to beg for forgiveness rather than punishment?

So, like the father in the parable, I welcome him home, teach him his boundaries all over again, and give him a treat.

The likeness of God is a spiritual thing that the human race possesses apart from the rest of creation. When God formed man of the dust of the earth, he did something he didn't do to dogs and apes: he "breathed into his nostrils the breath of life, and man became a living soul." A living *soul!*

As a father and mother infuse their own lives into the lives of their children, so God has infused his life into us. We bear his likeness because we are his children, and his children are in his will to inherit his eternal kingdom.

But, we are wayward children. When we lived in his garden, we used to walk and talk with him in the cool of the day. But, like my disobedient dog, we violated his trust, crossed the line, and alienated ourselves from the master who loves us.

And like the son in the parable, we long to return home. We long to escape from our waywardness and from the corruption of the flesh. When we are finally fed up with our life of dissipation, we yearn to go back to our father and beg his forgiveness. And when he runs to meet us, "we shall be like him, for we shall see him as he is." Only then will we regain our original status and "become partakers of the divine nature."

Anyone who has ever heard an evangelist preach knows the formula: repent of your sins, be crucified with Christ, die to self, be raised with him in newness of life, be born again, and, as a repatriated child created in the image of the Father, claim your inheritance in the kingdom of heaven.

Dominion Over All . . .

Scripture: Genesis 1:26b
Suggested Reading: Genesis 37:8; Exodus 16:4; Numbers 24:19;
Daniel 7:13–14; Psalms 8:5–6; Revelation 20:6

*I*t is both interesting and compelling that God used the word *dominion* to define the relationship between humans and the rest of his creation. As the dominant creatures, we are to dominate the earth. It is our domain. We are its lords.

Back in my youth, we called our pastor *dominie*, not to be funny, but to pay him genuine respect and to recognize the position to which God had appointed him: the lord of the church, or the agent supervising the church in the Lord's place.

The word *dominion* appears often in the Bible. When Joseph shared his dream with his brothers, they asked, "Are you to reign over us . . . to have dominion over us?" Israel's total destruction of pagan Canaanite cities in accordance with God's judgment was described as exercising dominion. As king of the Israelite empire, Solomon had dominion over many nations. The psalmist David described having dominion over the works of God's hands as being "a little less than God" himself. But in the end, dominion belongs to the Lord because God will give Jesus dominion over all the earth.

So, our dominion over the earth is a temporary assignment, a charge God has given us, an agency of divine authority that carries with it a grave responsibility.

It is clear that when God used the word *dominion* to define our role in his creation, he was giving us divine authority, a kingship, a vast amount of power to govern anything we could develop the skill and knowledge to govern.

How are we to exercise the dominion God has entrusted to us? He ordered us to subdue the earth, to take command of it, to control all of its resources. Such dominion seems to assume that we have the authority to use the resources of nature for our benefit and comfort. He has given us the worlds of animal, vegetable, and mineral to be our domains, and he has endowed us with the skill and power to harness those worlds.

But by clothing us with the mantle of authority over the works of his hands, did he also give us license to do anything we want to do with his creation? Are we entirely free to use and abuse the heavens and the earth for our gratification? Is dominion synonymous with ownership? Or will we be someday called to account for what we have done with the world? At the end of time when God turns that dominion over to his Son, will he hold us responsible for the condition of the domain he's entrusted to our care?

I believe so. Just as God gave manna to the Israelites in the wilderness to test them to see if they would obey his commandment regarding the Sabbath, so he gave the universe into our keeping to test our stewardship, to see if we will be worthy to sit next to the new ruler of the new creation.

When Jesus returns in glory, the redeemed saints will return with him and will sit beside him on his throne to rule the nations.

When that day comes, will we qualify?

... *In His Own Image*

Scripture: Genesis 1:27
Suggested Reading: Genesis 11:6–7; Proverbs 31:10–31

In our church service one Sunday morning, Pastor Don's wife, Sharmin, presented a children's sermon I thought was amazing. Opening her usual picnic basket that contained her props, she removed three containers. The first was a thermos filled with ice, the second a cup of water, the third a thermos of hot water with steam wafting into the air from the top. The children clearly understood that ice was frozen water and that the steam was hot water turning to vapor. Using their knowledge that water exists in three forms, she unfolded to them the mystery of the trinity; that God could exist in three forms: Father, Son and Holy Spirit.

When God contemplated the crowning glory of his creation, he used the plural form *us* to refer to the deity. Most commentators believe that he intended to reveal to us a pluralistic godhead. And when God spoke in heaven as he watched the men build the tower intended to reach to the skies, he said, "Let *us* go down . . . ." In addressing the other aspects of the deity, he most certainly confirmed the existence of the trinity.

The object lesson further blesses me when I extend the metaphor.

Ice is firm and powerful. Moses, David, and other prophets refer to God as the Rock. Rock is as old as creation itself, and, like God, it is hard and powerful. Fill any container with water and put it in your freezer. If the container can't stretch, it will break. Ask anyone who's ever had to deal with frozen water pipes.

Jesus called himself the living water. Water quenches thirst. Jesus told the woman at the well that if she would drink the water he gave her, she would never thirst again.

And Jesus described the Holy Spirit as moving like the wind to give us counsel, courage, and comfort.

We have been created in the image of the triune God. And the question is, how do we behave having been created in the likeness of the Father, the Son, and the Holy Spirit?

Molded in the image of the ideal Father, men must not only be strong, firm, and just, but also compassionate and making rules; not only chastising children when they fail to obey, but rewarding them when they do. God has made for us an eternal home, and though we may stray, he will always welcome us back with open arms. We should be as forgiving with our children. And the Spirit inspired Solomon to describe the woman whose life clearly reflects the image of God. She is more precious than fine stones. The scripture provides true models for the kind of godly men and women we are called be.

As creatures shaped in the image of Christ, our duty is to pour out water for those who thirst, and share the Living Water with all who come to the fountain.

As creatures formed in the image of the Holy Spirit, we must rush like the wind to inspire and comfort whomever God sends us: to minister to the sick, to encourage the depressed, to feed the hungry, to clothe the naked, give aid to the poor, rest to the weary and good counsel to the prisoner.

God created us in his image, and in doing so commissioned us to do that likeness justice.

Do we?

The Nick of Time

Scripture: Review Genesis 1
Suggested Reading: Joshua 24:14–15

Life is full of choices that must be made within a defined period of time. We must make some, as they say, on the spur of the
moment, while others can simmer until we've carefully weighed
every option. A baseball player has only a fragment of a second to
decide whether or not to swing at a fastball coming toward him at
ninety-some miles an hour. Judges, on the other hand, can mull
over a case for what seems an eternity before rendering a decision.

Sometimes we are forced to make choices more quickly than
necessary, as when high pressure salespeople bully us into quick
decisions. And sometimes we linger over alternatives until our
options have vanished, as when we ponder the purchase of a
house while someone more decisive comes along and buys it
while we're mulling.

When is the right time to choose to serve the Lord? Can we
brood over that choice, weighing the alternatives or just procrasti-
nating until a more convenient time? Is it a choice that demands
an immediate answer, or do we have plenty of time to reflect?

God knew us before he laid the foundations of the earth, and
we shall exist for an eternity after the foundations of the earth
have crumbled. Our existence began an eternity ago in the mind
of God, and shot through time until it collided with this planet. At
any moment it may glance off the earth and head into the eternal
future. In the tiny nick of time between those two infinities, we
touch the earth for one brief but very decisive moment.

Time is relative. When the dentist is drilling our teeth, a few seconds seems to be endless. On the other hand, time, they say, flies when we're having fun. To God, a day and a thousand years are the same. In the grand endless continuum of eons, one person's lifetime is a mere notch in the measuring stick of time, a notch that separates two eternities. Whom we shall serve? That one choice we make in our brief moment on this globe determines which way we bounce, into eternal bliss or eternal damnation.

My neighbor down the road has a sign on his gatepost proclaiming, "As for me and my house, we will serve the Lord." No one can fault him for that. He is not a closet Christian. He has painted the blood on his doorpost. My daughter, Kyle, has a little plaque hanging next to the coat rack just inside her back door, right at eye level, which she can't help but see every time she leaves her house, "Choose you this day whom you will serve . . . ." My neighbor continuously reminds the passing world that he has chosen to serve the Lord. My daughter reminds herself.

The point is not whom we tell. The point is that we make the choice. Oh yes, we have a duty to tell others and to urge others, as Joshua did, to make the choice for themselves. But at the same time, we need to remind ourselves every day that we belong to the Lord. Joshua didn't simply tell Israel, "Choose whom you will serve." He made it an urgent matter, "Choose *this day* whom you will serve."

The choice to serve the Lord is not a decision that we make just one time. Nor is it a choice that we can mull for a lifetime. Serving the Lord is a way of life that we must confirm every morning when we rise from our beds. Living for him is a commitment that we must constantly renew. Each moment in our lives is a nick in time, a crucial moment in which we make a crucial decision that will last forever.

. . . And Hallowed It

Scripture: Genesis 2:1–3
Suggested Reading: Mark 2:23–28

In our home when I was growing up, our folks laid down very strict rules about what we could not do on Sunday. We always went to church and Sunday school, and always came home to a big dinner of roast beef and potatoes. After eating our fill, we always took a Sunday afternoon nap, ate a light supper and returned to church for the evening service. Whenever we groaned, our parents, in boasting about how hard they had it as kids, faithfully reminded us that they had to go to church in the afternoon as well as in the morning and evening.

Since Sunday was our Sabbath, and God had hallowed the Sabbath, we were not allowed to do any kind of work. Buttons that fell off remained off until sewing day during the week. Tools remained in the toolbox, and the baseball glove remained stashed in the corner with the bat, the broom, and the fat old yardstick. The radio stayed off, except for religious broadcasts. If we couldn't sleep in the afternoon, we were permitted the pleasure of reading, providing it was literature that would, in some way, benefit us spiritually.

We've come a long way since then. Or have we?

We've discarded many of the practices of our parents as Pharisaical. We've quoted the words of Jesus, "The Sabbath was made for man, not man for the Sabbath." Since we slave at our jobs fifty to sixty hours each week and since Saturday is saturated with errands and other domestic chores, we fill our Sundays with self-indulgence. Since we love the Tigers, the Lions, the Pistons, and the Red Wings, and since it is "restful" to relax in our recliners in front of the television, we justify spending our Sabbath worshipping at those altars.

Somewhere there has to be a holy compromise. Just as our employer knows that we must take a rest from the rigors of our jobs so that we can return and serve him more productively on Monday, God knows that we have to step back and take a weekly sabbatical from the rigors of the labor he has called us to do so we may return and serve him more faithfully the next week. He never intended a seven-day workweek, and he never intended a Sabbath full of anxiety, distraction, or hedonistic pleasures. It is a holy day.

On the seventh day God rested from his labors, not because he needed to relax, but as an example for us to go and do likewise. After he rescued us from the tyranny of bondage under the Egyptians, he commanded us to remember the Sabbath day and keep it holy. When we perverted his commandment into an unmanageable library of do's and don'ts, Jesus stepped in to remind us that the purpose of the day of rest was to benefit us, not God. But perhaps in using Jesus' words as our guide, after giving God his token hour in the pew, we've become too self-serving and too self-indulgent, claiming that the rest of the day was made for us to do as we wish. Perhaps we've forgotten that it should be set aside for holy use and to refresh us so on Monday we are better able to serve our Lord, our loved ones, and our employer.

I've never ceased to thank God that he didn't call me to be a judge or a lawmaker because I'm not very good at making up rules and enforcing them. I'm thankful that I'm only called upon to serve him and love my neighbor. For that purpose he's given me a special day, a day in which I can do things that will make me a better Christian, a better neighbor, a better husband, and a better father and grandfather.

The Breath of Life

Scripture: Genesis 2:4–7
Suggested Reading: Ephesians 2:1–6; John 10:10;
1 Corinthians 15:22

Once at a public beach on Lake Michigan I watched a young man swim bravely through the waves out into deep water to rescue a swimmer who was frantically thrashing around in surf well over his head. The victim vanished beneath the surface for a few moments and bobbed up again a little further from shore. Then he went under and did not reappear.

When the rescuer reached the spot where the boy last went down, he dived beneath the waves, and after what seemed like a hopeless eternity, reappeared with a strong arm locked around the lad's neck. Then he swam back to shallow water, dragged the limp body of the boy through the lapping waves, laid him on the shore, and began to administer mouth-to-mouth resuscitation. Finally the boy's sand-caked body began to twitch, and soon he was breathing on his own, having been snatched from the grip of death by a caring and gifted stranger.

On the drive home, my mind wandered to the passage in Genesis that describes God forming man of the dust of the earth and breathing into his nostrils the breath of life. After witnessing that dramatic scene, I had a new understanding of what happened as God blew the essence of his own being into the lump of dirt he had shaped from the sands of Eden, and a new understanding of what happens as our Savior rescues us from the flood of sin.

I don't know what became of the lad who received new life that day on the beach, but I do know what happened to Adam. God told him that his disobedience would mean death, and the errant creature lost the divine life that God had given him.

There's life, and then there is Life. When God created the birds and the beasts, he gave them life. But when God created Adam and Eve, he not only gave them biological life, he also gave them spiritual Life, a gift from his own being that he did not bestow on the animals. When our first parents sinned, they not only began to die physically, but they instantly lost that gift of divine Life that the creator had breathed into them. As the corpses of possums and raccoons decay along the roadway with the life crushed out of them, the body I inherited will also return to the dust from which it was formed. But what about the Life?

When Adam and Eve succumbed to the waves of temptation that swept them far from shore, I went under with them. But, praise God, a brave and gifted young man saw me floundering in the surf and swam out to rescue me. He plucked me from the deep, carried me to the shore, placed his face against mine, and, just as God breathed into Adam's body ages ago, Jesus, my savior, breathed into my nostrils the breath of his divine Life! Rich in mercy, he gave this dead child of wrath new Life and invited me to sit with him in heavenly places. Now I shall live forever!

> Breathe on me, breath of God,
> Fill me with life anew
> That I may love what thou dost love,
> And do what thou wouldst do.
>
> Breathe on me breath of God,
> So I shall never die,
> But live with thee the perfect life
> Of thy eternity.

Edwin Hatch 1886

An Age of Innocence

Scripture: Genesis 2:8–17
Suggested Reading: Isaiah 51:1–3

In the valley behind my childhood home ran a crystal clear "crick" with a clean, sandy bottom. It wove through the underbrush and past frog ponds filled with tadpoles and skimmers. A footpath followed the stream, which in some places grew wide and shallow and in other places narrow, deep, and quick. About a hundred yards before the creek reached the celery flats, it opened up into the finest swimming hole any group of neighborhood boys ever knew. The pool was about thirty feet in diameter, cool, and clear as rainwater.

On the horizontal limb of a big tree growing on the bank, some boys from a prior generation had tied a fat, knotted old manila tow rope that was perfect for swinging and jumping into the water. On hot summer days we would slip "down the crick" and spend the afternoon skinny dipping and splashing in the cool water. It was truly an age of joy and gladness.

Sometimes after our swim we would follow the footpath to the muck flats and walk barefoot between the rows of celery, letting the rich black soil ooze up between our toes. If harvest was near, we could snitch a stalk from the corner of the field, wash it in the creek, and wander back down the path munching on a crisp piece of celery.

In my adult years I've tried to go back, but the celery flats are deserted. The swamp has reclaimed the fallow farmland, and the creek has become a clogged and contaminated waste. The old swimming hole is fouled with scum. The footpath has vanished beneath years of undergrowth. The big tree with its frayed rope, dead and bare of bark, still stands as grotesque testimony to a paradise lost. The shouts of happy children echo only in an old man's memory.

I treasure my recollection of those childhood days, because it is as close as I can come to imagining what the Garden of Eden must have been like. It seems almost sacrilegious to think that God's notion of bliss was to plop us naked and shameless into a lush garden and fill it with "cricks" for us to swim about in, plant it full of good things for us to eat, then sit back and watch us splash around, walk its shaded paths, and nibble on its tasty fruits. But that's the picture I get when I read the scripture and mingle its words with my memories.

As I look with sadness upon what my childhood Eden has become, I can also understand more clearly what happened to God's Garden when we became disobedient. But as I recall with great joy what my garden was like in that wonderful age of innocence, I can also more clearly comprehend the mission of Jesus.

The prophet Isaiah told us that Jesus will make the foul creeks of our wilderness clear, like the streams of Eden, and make our wilderness bloom like the Garden of the Lord. He told us that joy and gladness will be found there once more and that the lost songs of thanksgiving will again echo through the trees. I believe I am enjoying that promise as I live the abundant life in God's kingdom today.

There are as many theories about heaven as there are theologians. Some see pearly gates, streets of gold, and a river flowing from the throne of God into a crystal sea. Some see a mansion with beautiful, spacious rooms and angels strumming golden harps. Others see a more ethereal, spiritual place flooded with the brilliant presence of God. Nobody's wrong, I suppose, but when I think of paradise, I think of that age of innocence and our old swimming hole, "down the crick."

It Is Not Good . . .

Scripture: Genesis 2:18–23

I am a rather private person. As a child I played alone a lot, building imaginary cities on the sand pile with my toy steam shovel and peopling them with my version of our neighborhood's more amusing characters. I beat Babe Ruth's home run record by swatting sixty-one stones over Uncle Si's garage with my scarred up baseball bat, and I torpedoed German submarines under Mr. Medendorp's berry patch from the deck of the lumber pile behind our garage. I was alone with my imagination, but my mother was in the house, just a shout away.

Even today, I am content spending hours by myself, working at my desk, reading a book, solving a crossword puzzle, or watching a football game. One of my favorite pastimes is mowing the lawn, when I can spend three hours on the garden tractor plotting a new pattern of attack on the grass, meditating, stopping for a drink of cold water at the old hand pump, sitting at the top of the hill surveying the bounds of my domain, trimming the walking paths through the woods, or just pausing to watch my neighbor's horses watching me work. I enjoy being alone . . . that is, if Mary Ann, my wife, is just a shout away.

It baffles me that the hermit enjoys the lonely life. God seems to have created in each of us the need for companionship, and he enforces that need by making loneliness miserable, as if to force us to find a friend. I can enjoy solitude if Mary Ann is somewhere around, even outdoors or in the living room, playing her piano. But if she is away, emptiness fills the house and magnifies every sound. If she is gone overnight, I hardly sleep, and I leap out of bed to investigate every little noise.

I did live alone for a few years, and it was the most miserable time of my life. I worked long hours, went to every movie Hollywood produced, played golf every summer evening until dark, and went to every meeting and business event my expense account could bear and then some. At the end of every long day I flopped into bed, dead tired, and lay awake for hours. I understand loneliness.

God understands loneliness too. He declared that it was not good for man to be alone. That's why he created a companion for Adam, a helper fit for him. Not just to share the workload around the house or even to be in business together, but to fill the emptiness.

My heart aches for lonely people. Widowed and divorced folks who live alone seem to seek companionship at every turn. They create singles groups and take bus tours and cruises just to be with people or to find a new and special friend. Loneliness is so rampant that evil people have created a whole industry designed to prey upon those who live solitary, unhappy lives.

I'm not going to suggest that friendship with the Lord will cure the pain of isolation. Whether we are Christians or not, human companionship seems to be a fundamental need that almost all of us have in common. Even though he walked and talked with Adam, God noticed Adam's isolation before his first disobedience, suggesting that even a world free from sin may not be free from loneliness.

And it is possible to be lonely in a crowd. Even in a crowd of Christians. Husbands and wives can be together and still be alone if their hearts are not joined in Christ. But if their hearts are joined in Christ, the time they spend together is blessed beyond mere human joy, and the time they spend apart is less painful. I know.

The End of Innocence

Scripture: Genesis 3:1–8
Suggested Reading: Luke 15:3–7

In a coffee shop back in my hometown, I ran across Billy, one of my childhood playmates. He was living in an adult foster home, never having progressed mentally beyond the age of eight. I have no idea how he recognized me behind this old battered face and gray beard, but he did. He saw me as clearly as though these last six decades had never happened.

I didn't recognize him; I had to be told his name. Once told who he was, I could see the youthful Billy slowly emerge through the wrinkles of his adult face. We visited for a while, recalling old friends and the adventures of our youth. He had a remarkable memory for details that the years had not erased.

"But we can't go down the crick no more," he sputtered with a regretful tone. "It's all just prickers and quicksand now." When his chaperone called him to leave, he said, "We can't find my dad. If you see him, tell him I'm at Ed's. He's looking for me to take me home."

Sometimes now in my fancy I wonder what life might have been like if time had suddenly stopped when we were eight. Might the "crick" still be clear? Might the footpath still be free of prickers? Might the sun still sparkle on the ripples of the old swimming hole as an innocent gang of happy, naked boys splashed innocently about? And what about us? Would we have ever comprehended what it meant to have to work for a living and worry about our jobs and our security? Would we ever have understood the bliss and banes of marriage or the terrors of raising children? Would we have known what is like to live in a world full of want and temptation?

Sometimes in my fancy I wonder what life might have been like had Adam and Eve never eaten of the forbidden fruit. Would they have grown into a nation of innocents still splashing joyously in the sparkling waters of the Garden of the Lord? And what about me? Would I ever have existed?

Such thoughts tease us to the edge of our capacity to think, and we are inevitably beaten back to the fact that what is, is. We yielded to the serpent's goading. Even though God told us what the outcome of our disobedience would be, we consciously chose to offend him. And each generation of us has done it over and over again ever since. Over and over we have traded our innocence for sordid knowledge, our comfort for pain, and our clear waters for murky.

Although the third chapter of Genesis is one of the saddest stories in the scriptures, a chapter on which the balance of history turns, one especially wonderful thing happened. After we sinned and went off into the bushes to hide our shame, it would have been easy for God, in his anger, just to abandon us. But he didn't. He came looking for us! When he found us, he executed proper punishment upon us, because as a just God he had to. But as a loving just God, he wrapped us in warm clothing and promised that he would never leave us or forsake us.

Through the millennia that have followed, he has always kept that promise. Whenever you or I or my old friend Billy stray from that path of innocence, some memory from a former age speaks to us and lets us know that our Father is looking for us and is coming to carry us home on his shoulders rejoicing!

Hallelujah!

Where Are You?

Scripture: Genesis 3:9–15
Suggested Reading: John 4:5–18; 10:30

One of the many memorable flannelgraph scenes I remember from Mrs. Hooker's first grade Sunday school class is the picture of Adam and his long haired wife Eve slinking behind the waist-high shrubs playing hide-and-seek with God, who was on the footpath shouting, "Adam, where are you?" Now, I wasn't exactly an intellectually precocious little boy, but the fact that an all-knowing, all-seeing God couldn't find them baffled me.

Didn't God know where they were? Couldn't he see through the trees? And the rest of the questions: "Who told you that you were naked . . . have you eaten of the tree?" Didn't God know how they knew they were naked? Didn't he know they had eaten of the forbidden tree? Why ask such questions? Isn't he supposed to know all the answers?

Ironically, the very questions that challenged my childish theology also strengthened it. As I began to understand the fundamentals of education, I began to understand why God asked those questions. Teachers ask students questions, not because they don't know the answers themselves, but because they want to find out if the students know the answers. And lawyers ask witnesses questions to which they already know the answers just to get them to voice those answers. So, God asked Adam and Eve questions to which he already knew the answers just to get them to confess with their mouths what they had done to cause them to flee into the bushes.

These very questions leaped back into my mind as I read John's description of Jesus' encounter with the woman at the well. "Go, call your husband," he said to her, knowing full well that she had no husband. In fact, never having met her before, he knew that she'd had five husbands and was presently living in sin with a man to whom she was not married. If he knew her marital state, why did he ask her to call her husband? Again, the answer is simple: to get her to confess with her mouth that she had no husband.

In a movie I once saw, an old Jewish man sauntering through New York's Central Park spied another old man sitting on a bench feeding the birds. The old bird feeder had a strange habit of tearing a portion of bread from a loaf, rolling it into a ball in the palm of his hands, tossing it into the air and chuckling with glee as he watched the hungry birds fight over the single morsel.

Suddenly the movie flashed back to a black and white scene in a concentration camp during the Holocaust and showed an arrogant German guard in identical fashion tearing bread from a loaf, rolling it into a ball, and tossing it to the birds outside the barbed wire fence while emaciated Jews watched in pain. Every now and again he tossed a scrap to the center of the group of prisoners and chuckled in glee as they fought over it.

Back in the present, in a stunning moment of illumination, the old Jewish man suddenly realized that the man feeding the birds was the Nazi guard who had tortured him decades before in the prison camp. A small personal trait had given him away.

I had a similar moment of illumination when I read the story of the woman at the well. When Jesus asked questions to which he already knew the answers, I suddenly realized that the Jesus of the gospels is the same person as the God of creation. A small personal trait had given him away, had unveiled his identity and confirmed to me that "I and the Father are one."

Birth Pangs

Scripture: Genesis 3:16

My mother once told me that the greatest pain she ever suffered was the pain of giving me birth. Now I never knew for sure if she was telling me the clear truth. Maybe she was trying to make me feel guilty for having been born, maybe she was suggesting that I be more grateful to her for having given me life, or maybe she was telling me that the whole business of being my mother caused her great anguish. She often said one thing and meant another, so I've never quite known how to take what she said about childbirth. But I'm sure she went to her tomb convinced I hadn't thanked her enough for all she had done for me. And I really don't blame her.

It has occurred to me, however, that when I came into this life, someone else bore the birth pangs, but when I depart from this life, I must bear the pain of dying. I don't remember feeling anything when I entered this world, but I'll probably suffer a bit leaving it. That's OK, because I know where I will be when the pain goes away.

Just as my mother suffered giving me temporal life, Jesus suffered giving me eternal life. And I'm sure the pain he suffered on the cross was more intense than my mother's pain on the birthing bed.

My teachers and my parents never tired of telling me that Jesus died a horrible death that I might live forever. And every time I read about it or remember the messages from the past, I come to realize that I've never expressed to him the level of gratitude his selfless act deserves.

I wince as I watch children thoughtlessly unwrap and quickly set aside gifts we have purchased for them with great care and considerable expense, just to get to the next one. And I wonder if Jesus winces when we casually accept and disregard the gift of salvation he purchased for us with the cruel pain of crucifixion.

And if we recklessly receive his gift of eternal life, do we live our new lives with equal abandon, often lapsing into old patterns of sin, failing to be the salt of the earth, and often failing to let our light shine as we ought? Do we fail to confess him before men as we expect him to confess us before his Father in heaven?

Though my mother suffered great anguish giving me birth, Jesus suffered greater anguish giving me rebirth. I know I caused my mother grief as she watched me grow up and do the things she taught me not to do, and I also know I cause Jesus grief as he watches me live at a level of sanctification I know to be far below his expectation.

My sisters, Carol and Wilma, would confirm that hugs and kisses were rare in our Dutch Calvinistic home, but we knew for certain that our parents loved us. We felt it when Mother sat by our sick bed all through the long night and bathed our heads with cool water as we burned with fever, and we felt it as well when we transgressed and Dad applied that thick old yardstick to our "seat of learning." In a similar way we feel the love of Jesus both in his grace and his chastening. He gives us unfathomable peace to endure the tragedies of our lives, and smites our conscience when we stray from the paths of righteousness.

The pain of giving life doesn't begin or end with the delivery. It begins and ends with love. I know my mother loved me even before she gave me birth. How else could she have tolerated the pain I caused her? And I know that Jesus loved me even before I was formed in my mother's womb. How else could he have borne the agony of the cross and the pain of my waywardness?

To Guard the Way

Scripture: **Genesis 3:17–24**
Suggested Reading: Romans 8:37; Revelation 2:7; 22

*W*hen God planted that glorious garden at the dawn of human history, he planted trees that bore a variety of fruit, enough to satisfy the palates of his creatures forever. And he planted two very special trees: the tree of life and the tree of death. Moses recorded no advice from the creator regarding the tree of life, but did record God's stern warning that eating of the tree of knowledge of good and evil would result in certain death. I've often wondered if God said anything at all to Adam and Eve about that wonderful tree of life and the rewards of eating its fruit.

They must have suspected that eating of the tree of life would benefit them in some way, because when God expelled them from the paradise they had spoiled, he had to set a guard at the gate to keep them from returning and eating the fruit that would give them eternal life, a guard that presumably remained there until God washed the remnants of Eden away in the flood. But was the tree of life lost forever?

None of the writers of scripture mentioned it again until God gave John his vision of heaven as he languished on the Isle of Patmos. John wrote that to the conqueror, the Lord would "grant to eat of the tree of life, which is in the paradise of God." And after he had watched all the horrors of the great tribulation pass, an angel carried John to a great, high mountain and showed him the tree of life growing in the New Jerusalem, spanning the river that flows from the throne of God!

Paradise restored!

My sojourn among the thorns and thistles that the ground brought forth after the tempter seduced us has lasted nearly the three score and ten years that the Lord has allotted. If I eat right, exercise, and take my pills, the Lord may grant me another five, or ten, or maybe more before I return to the ground from which I was taken. And then I'll just lie there, resting from my labors, until the trumpet blast wakens me and I am raised up on that day of rapture to meet him in the air.

Then, if I'm rightly dividing his Word, he'll put me back to work for a thousand years helping him run the world. But after the millennium I'll get to retire again from my labors and go to live in that city of light, singing hymns of gladness, splashing joyously in the river of life and nibbling forever on the fruit that grows on the tree of life!

And what did I do to earn the right to such a glorious retirement? Did I live a saintly life walking steadfastly in the steps of the savior? Did I give all I had to the poor and spread the good news to the four corners of the earth? Am I a conqueror? Did I battle Satan and put him down for the count?

Sadly, I have to answer *no* to all of the above. My name will never be inscribed with the names of the martyrs who gave their blood for their beliefs. I will never be listed among the contemporary heroes of faith. My biography will never be shelved among those of the reformers and the great evangelists, or even summarized to the *Who's Who* of the saints. But my name does appear in the most important book of all, God's *Book of Life*.

How so? Simply because I took the stained robes of my life to the foot of the cross and washed them in the blood of the Lamb. On that cross Jesus conquered Satan for me, and through his victory I have become more than a conqueror, I have become a son of God, an inheritor of the kingdom of heaven!

A Parent's Pain

Scripture: Genesis 4:1–8
Suggested Reading: Luke 15:10

When Adam and Eve disobeyed God, they ushered the grim face of death into a lovely society that had known no death. Not only would they have to die, they would have to live in a world in which death would become commonplace. I have often wondered if, as the first consequence of their sin, God made them stand by and watch as he killed and skinned the animal from whose hide he made the clothes to replace the inadequate fig leaves they had sewn together.

Most likely, when God told them that they were going to die, they assumed that they would be the first humans to go to the grave, and that their children would probably bury them in some quaint spot in a glen beside a brook. They could hardly have begun to comprehend the consequences they would have to suffer because of their actions, and the torrent of consequences that would deluge all who came after.

When Eve brought forth her firstborn, little did she know that the travail of birth would be but the beginning of the pain her children were to bring her. Surely she and Adam loved their two boys, played with them in their youth, and cared for them.

My one son, Cameron, is alive and well. So, only by knowing parents whose children died or brought them terrible grief, can I begin to imagine how our first parents must have felt when they discovered that one of their sons had murdered the other. Only by having stood at the grave with parents who were returning a child to the earth, can I begin to imagine Adam and Eve's misery as they dug the grave in which to bury their beloved son, Abel. Only the joy that Eve expressed when Seth was born is offered to suggest to us that they grieved the loss of Abel for a long time. And even if they hated their outcast son for his crime, that hate had to be expressed at the price of great pain.

Many people since Cain have committed horrible acts against children that have brought great sorrow to mothers and fathers. Many parents since Adam and Eve have lost children they loved to disease, accident, treachery, perversion, or war. The bearing of the children is often only the beginning of the pain.

When Adam and Eve disobeyed God, they pronounced a heavy sentence of grief upon themselves and upon all mortal parents who followed. They pronounced a particularly heavy sentence of grief upon a lovely young lady who was to live several thousand years later. When they ate the forbidden fruit, they not only condemned their own God-fearing son to his grave, but they also doomed Mary's God-fearing son to that terrible march up Golgotha's hill, and they sentenced her to stand and watch as he suffered and died and was carried to his tomb.

When God pronounced judgment upon Adam and Eve for their disobedience, he also pronounced judgment upon himself. As a result of their sin, Jesus, the only begotten Son of the Father, suffered the same deadly end as their son, Abel, and the Father suffered the same torment that those first parents suffered, the torment of losing the son he loved to the murderous hands of others he called his children.

In this dark valley of sorrow, does even the slightest glimmer of hope shine through? Oh, yes! God looked down upon the suffering of Eve and blessed her with another son, Seth. And God's own grief turned to joy on Easter morning when his Son broke the bonds of death. That day the angels around the great throne must have shouted for joy the way they do when a sinner repents!

. . . My Brother's Keeper?

Scripture: Genesis 4:9–11
Suggested Reading: Matthew 22:34–40; Luke 10:25–37

*W*hen the voice of the Lord rumbled from heaven asking Cain, "Where is your brother?" Cain responded first by lying, then by asking the first recorded question ever asked by any man, ". . . am I my brother's keeper?"

Had I been a member of the first family to inhabit this earth, I could have thought up a lot of questions to ask God. "Wow! Look at those stars! How did you do that?" Or, "That fruit looks mighty good, why don't you want me to eat it?" Perhaps those first humans did ask God a lot of questions that didn't get written down, but it seems very important that the first question asked by man and recorded in the Bible is the question Cain raised, ". . . am I my brother's keeper?"

When Cain asked that question, he certainly didn't ask in the mood of honest inquiry, seeking an answer to a problem that had been plaguing him. In the context in which he asked it, his question had to have been posed in a surly, defensive manner. He was angry, not inquisitive. And God obviously didn't think Cain's question deserved the dignity of a response at that time. Its answer is obvious. Being our brother's keeper is an inherent demand of our very existence as members of the human family.

What does it mean to be our brother's keeper?

A lot of nosey people have justified their snooping into the affairs of others on the ground that their curiosity was really an essential part of their being their brother's keeper. My dear old grandmother believed that she was called by God to sit at her window and monitor the comings and goings of her neighbors and relatives and report to the rest of the family. Many paternalistic employers justify their meddling in the lives of their employees, claiming to be doing so in the best interest of the workers. Even prying pastors have been known to engage in indiscriminate spying among their parishioners on the pretext of being their brother's keeper.

When God asked Cain where his brother was, he didn't ask in order to discover the whereabouts of Abel. He knew where Abel was. He put the pointed question to him in order to convict him that he had failed in his duty to his brother and to impress clearly upon us that we have a duty to our brother.

What is that duty?

The Lord told us very clearly and very simply what that duty is. It is to love our brother as we love ourselves, and to do unto our brother as we would have our brother do unto us. We are to afford our brother the privacy and independence we want for ourselves. We are to treat our brother with the dignity and respect with which we would like to be treated. If our brother has a need, we are to fill that need as if it were our own. If he needs a sandwich, we are to make him one. If he needs a coat, we are to give him one of ours. If he needs a ride, we are to let him use our car. If he needs companionship, we are to be his friend. If he is suffering, we are to soothe him by sharing his torment.

And who is our brother? The kid we shared a room with? The neighbor next door? The relative? Jesus answered that question for us too. Our brother is any person God puts in our path who is hungry, cold, sick, stranded, or lonely. And if ever we pass him by as did the priest and the Levite, we do to our brother as Cain did to his. We murder him.

. . . *Fugitive and Wanderer*

Scripture: Genesis 4:12–14
Suggested Reading: Genesis 6:1–4; 2 Chronicles 7:14;
Psalms 27:8–10; Matthew 5:21–24

The Fugitive, a very popular old movie and television series about a man falsely accused of murder and on the run from police, played on the networks for many years, was syndicated, continued to run on specialty stations, then was remade with a new cast and modernized. Both versions remain popular yet today. For countless episodes, the fugitive eluded police, bounty hunters, and bloodhounds. Why is the saga of a man on the run such compelling entertainment? Do we, in some way, see ourselves as fugitives? Are we all trying to escape from something? Why do we cheer each time he evades the net?

The terms *fugitive* and *wanderer* are not synonymous. A fugitive is being chased. He is fleeing, trying to elude capture. A wanderer is one who moves about aimlessly. About all they have in common is that they make no one place their home. Cain was a fugitive in that someone was hunting him, and a wanderer in that he was driven from the ground that yielded his produce. But he didn't remain a wanderer long; soon he built a city and named it for his son, Enoch.

But even in his city, did he remain a fugitive? Was he always looking over his shoulder in fear that someone wanted to kill him? Were avengers after him? Were those mysterious fathers of "the daughters of men" or even the Nephilim out for the murderer's blood? Or did some other intimidating force lurk in every shadow?

The story never came out, for Cain vanished from the pages of history after he moved eastward to the land of Nod, sired a son, and built his city.

But I'll bet his guilt continued to haunt him. Guilty men with a conscience always look over their shoulder, fearful that their sin will somehow be avenged. Even though the Lord put a mark of protection on Cain and warned prospective killers that they would suffer sevenfold vengeance at the hand of God if they raised their hand against him, my guess is that fear tormented him until the day he died.

Living away from the presence of the Lord, hidden from his face, is a terrible thing for a sinner who knows that God is real and that he is just. Cain himself declared that it is unbearable punishment. Though he may have rued the fact that he slew his brother, there is no evidence that he was remorseful or that he was forgiven. Later scripture writers refer to him only as a murderer and an evil person. Perhaps he died unaware that God forgives repentant sinners.

Though Cain's life is tragic, it didn't earn God's sympathy. Unlike the fictional fugitive, Cain was not falsely accused. He is an icon of evil. We are not to cheer for him. We can only assume that he is spending a well-deserved eternity in hell. Although his death is unrecorded, we know that God put his mark of protection on him and preserved him from the hand of the avenger, but perhaps for his sin God sentenced him to a long, unhappy life of terror, and then eternal damnation. And perhaps Cain died never knowing that he could have repented, sought the face of the Lord, and received forgiveness.

We, like Cain, are murderers, but we don't have to be fugitives. Maybe we've never literally shed our brother's blood, but we have killed him with anger, insult, and neglect. We know that the God of our salvation will forgive us when we come forward and confess our sin, seek his face and turn from our wicked ways, but does our brother know?

And how will he know if we don't tell him?

Vengeance Is Mine

Scripture: Genesis 4:15–26
Suggested Reading: Mark 16:17–18; Romans 9:14–24; 12:19

Even though God exiled Cain to Nod and sentenced him to be a fugitive and a wanderer in the land for the murder of his brother, he protected him from anyone who sought to slay him by putting a mark on him and promising that anyone who did succeed in killing him would become the victim of sevenfold vengeance.

Now for his own protection, Cain must have spread the word about that promise with such great vigor that it remained a saying among his descendants for at least five generations. His great, great grandson Lamech echoed God's words of promise to Cain when he bragged to his wives about killing a young man who had struck him.

These two verses about Lamech's boast seem to be an interjection into the Bible, almost as a trivial afterthought to conclude forever the chronicling of the line of Cain. And that little narrative is neither explained nor referenced again in the scriptures, nor does this Lamech ever reappear.

But nothing in the scripture is trivial. Everything recorded there was recorded by inspiration and serves to teach us about God and how God wants us to live. So, what can we learn from that little moment?

Did Lamech think that God's promise to protect Cain extended to every murderer? And since his attack on the young man who wounded him may have been in self-defense, or at least more justified than Cain's killing of Abel in jealousy, did Lamech think that such justification automatically multiplied God's promised vengeance by the symbolic seven? Why is this little episode recorded? Certainly it is there to teach us something.

Obviously Lamech's understanding of the way God works was seriously flawed. His arrogant boast was clearly erroneous and apparently recorded to teach us not to follow his example. He intended a personal promise made to someone else to apply to himself.

Well meaning Christians also often fall into the trap of applying to themselves promises or directives God gave to others in the scripture. I wonder how many believers have died horrible deaths from drinking poison or playing with deadly rattlesnakes. I know I'm not going to tempt God with such foolishness.

Perhaps those signs once accompanied certain believers for a specific purpose, but I'm not going to interpret that passage to imply that all believers throughout the entire history of the church can safely drink poison and toy with snakes. God gave that rattler fangs and venom for self-protection, and I plan to go through life assuming that it intends to protect itself from me if I get too close. Amen?

God has made many wonderful promises and has given blessed gifts to his children. We should believe the promises and exercise the gifts with humility. The boastful Christian who flaunts God's blessings and tempts providence sets a bad example and repels the unbeliever. Such arrogance is a sin. If we boast at all, we should boast in the things that show our weakness and reveal the power of God.

Let us learn from Lamech's error that God does reserve some of his grace for certain of his creatures, and some of his wrath for others.

. . . *For God Took Him*

Scripture: Genesis 5:1–24
Suggested Reading: 2 Kings 2:11; 1 Thessalonians 4: 15–17;
Hebrews 11:5

*I*spent some time studying at a Christian College where it was the habit of the "intellectual" to gather in the back room at Louie's for discourse and libation. One of our many topics was the manner in which the godly Enoch ended his sojourn on this earth.

The debaters who claimed a miracle had an unfair advantage, because the inspired writer to the Hebrews declared that when God translated Enoch from flesh to spirit, he did not experience death as his fathers had. They suspected that he might have had the same kind of whirlwind ride that Elijah had some few thousands of years later.

The pragmatists among us, on the other hand, claimed that because he was such a godly man, he probably just keeled over dead one day of a swift, providential heart attack without suffering in the least. They allowed that one might die without actually seeing death just as one might pass through some tiny town on the highway without really seeing it. No one ever won or lost those debates. In the haze of that room, one topic simply blurred into the next.

How Enoch made the leap from time into eternity is not nearly as important as how you and I make that leap. And *how* we get there is not nearly as important as *where* we go. We all will somehow make the transition from this life to the next. Some of us may die slowly and painfully from injury or disease. For those who do, we pray that God will provide peace and the courage to endure such suffering. Some of us may have the good fortune to slip gently into the next life. And some of us may not die at all, but like Enoch and Elijah be taken up in the manner Paul described. Since I've always liked roller coasters, I'm hoping for the thrill of a chariot ride on the whirlwind.

I love God's sense of the dramatic and the particular spirit he employed to inspire the great narratives of the Bible. We will notice from time to time that those narratives are usually written in colossal simplicity. For example, God said, "Let there be light, and there was light." Another example is the description of Enoch's death, ". . . and he was not, for God took him." The severe economy of words contributes greatly to the majesty of the statement. Unlike our feeble attempt to express ourselves, God's words do not clutter his message.

If we ponder why God left such a vacuum of detail, we might find our answer in the words, "Enoch walked with God." Perhaps God wants us to focus in the *why* rather than on the *how*. Perhaps he wants to tell us that the *how* of Enoch's translation is irrelevant in the face of the *why*. That isn't surprising when we consider that the fundamental message in God's lectures to the patriarchs was that his primary desire was that they walk with him.

The main focus of all we do, the substance of our every thought, should be our walk with God. Whether we are striding over the mountains on our way to fame and glory or struggling to survive in the valleys below, our singular concern should be if we are walking with God. If we are climbing mountains, are we bathed in the sunlight of God's victories rather than our own? If we are groping our way through valleys, are we bravely edging forward in the miracle moonlight that lit the valley of Ajalon?

When we come to our "was not," how will we answer the question, "With whom did you walk?"

The Song of Lamech

Scripture: Genesis 5:25–32
Suggested Reading: Luke 1:26–55; Colossians 3:12–14

I'm grateful that the Bible has two Lamechs. The earlier one, the descendant of Cain, is an example of how we ought not apply God's Word to our lives. But the second, a descendant of Seth, is a man who correctly understood the mind of God.

Now I don't know exactly what this second Lamech perceived, but it is clear that he had a vision of God's plan of redemption. He knew that as a result of our sin God cursed the ground and condemned the human race to a life of sweat, toil, tears, and pain. And through some marvelous revelation, he discovered that through his son, Noah, God was preparing to send someone to deliver us from the grief that our sin had brought upon us. And as his soul filled to bursting with that majestic truth, with quiet restraint he uttered the simple but solemn words, ". . . and this one shall bring us relief . . . ."

What must it have felt like to receive such a powerful revelation?

When Gabriel revealed to Mary that she would be the mother of the Messiah, she flew to the home of her kinswoman to share the good news. And when Elizabeth heard her announcement, the Holy Spirit filled her, the babe in her womb leapt for joy, and she burst into inspired poetry, voicing a prayer that has survived the centuries. And Mary responded with joyous and lofty words that are still sung every year when Christian churches celebrate the birth of the Lord.

The Song of Mary also proclaims relief from the miseries of this world. As she peered through the tunnel of time and saw the vision the Spirit had given her, she perceived the mercy of God, she perceived deliverance from oppression, she perceived joy for the downtrodden, and she perceived the bread from heaven that would satisfy the longing of a hungry soul. She saw relief from the bondage of sin, and the glorious sight of it inspired her to lively song.

The ecstasy that goes with the realization of salvation has brought the Christian church a bit of grief. Some denominations express that joy with the unbridled enthusiasm of a Mary, while others celebrate it with the calm reserve of a Lamech.

Many congregations today have two worship services, one contemporary and the other traditional. In the contemporary services, the worshippers clap and sing joyous songs of praise with their hands in the air, accompanied by drums, guitars, synthesizers, and keyboards. In the traditional service they sing the grand old hymns of the church accompanied by the soaring strains of an organ. Unfortunately, in some of our churches the Marys and the Lamechs have been somewhat unkind to each other.

The people who worshipped at the Christian church in Colossae also had issues that caused them to be unkind to each other. Paul instructed them to be tolerant of their differences and to "put on love, which binds all things together."

No denomination or group within a church has the exclusively righteous way of responding to God's grace. God has given each of us a different personality. I, as Lamech, might be overcome with joy but respond in simple, solemn, and restrained words. And you, as Mary, might burst into joyous song. But if we let love abound, we can all experience the joy of the Lord, each in his own way, and each happy for the ecstasy the other feels.

The Wickedness of Man

Scripture: Genesis 6
Suggested Reading: Romans 3:9–12

The first thing God told us was that we may not eat of the tree of the knowledge of good and evil. Now if I had been the creator and was about to have my very first conversation with the creature I had fashioned, I might have begun our relationship with some of the usual trivial amenities. I might have asked him how he liked being here or if there were anything else I could do for him. But not God. First things first. The most important thing we needed to know was that he was our Lord and that we were to be unconditionally obedient to him. All else in our relationship with God comes second. He is the Potter and we are the clay. The clay must always do as the Potter says.

It sounds easy. I have apple, plum, and peach trees on my property whose fruit I have never tasted nor have ever been tempted to taste. I leave it for the birds, the bugs, and the worms. But then, if some attractive siren were to come along and tell me that if I were to touch that fruit to my lips I would be like God, I just might be tempted.

Might nothing! I did it. My sin was that I couldn't stand being submissive to God. Then after he threw me out of the Garden I became even worse. I couldn't stand being second to my brother so I killed him. Then it got to the point that every imagination and thought of my heart was evil continually. Had I been the creator, and had my creatures done as we did, I, too, would have been sorry that I made them.

The thought contained in verse five is a central thought in the scriptures. Back home they called it total depravity. As we progress through the patriarchs and the leaders of the nation of Israel, we shall see that, with few exceptions, the thoughts and imaginings of man are continually evil. We shall come to the inevitable conclusion that man, left to his own ability to obey, will surely fail. From the day he fell into sin he was doomed to be a creature who needed the power of Christ, who needed the power of the Holy Spirit in his heart if he were even to begin to live righteously. And even with all that power, Jesus would still have to stand his judgment for him if he were to be found spotless before the assembly of the elect in life eternal.

I can remember some of the thunderstorms we had when I was young. On the day after the storm I would go out to the driveway, with its cracks and uneven surfaces, and watch the various colonies of ants trying to rebuild. I would see twigs, worms, and leaves plastered to the concrete, corrupting the pavement. Then I would have great pleasure wielding the garden hose, washing the driveway clean. I would start at the garage and wash everything downward toward the gutter, out into the street and finally down the storm sewer. Sometimes I had to adjust the nozzle into a powerful stream, and sometimes into a splashing flood. I always enjoyed washing the driveway after a thunderstorm. It gave me a feeling of great power.

Ever since those days, I have wondered how God felt as he sent the torrents of rain that washed all living creatures into the gutters of the earth. I know he was angry. He said so many times. But I also believe he was sad. He didn't cleanse the earth with the childish glee of a youngster washing worms and twigs from the driveway. He did it, not only with the bitter disappointment of a Potter whose clay had refused to be molded according to the design of his hands, but with the deep sorrow of a loving father who knew that the only way he could ultimately save his dying creation would be to send his own beloved Son down to earth to be mocked, abused, and finally murdered by those wayward creatures he had fashioned in his own image.

A Righteous Man

Scripture: Genesis 7:1–5
Suggested Reading: 2 Corinthians 5:17–21

To me, Noah is one of the Bible's great mysteries. In the previous chapter we were told that Noah was a righteous man, blameless in his generation, that he walked with God, and that he found favor in the eyes of the Lord. What was required in his day to be blameless, to walk with God and to find favor in his eyes?

So far, the only precise commands that God had given to the human race in general were to be fruitful and multiply and not to eat of the tree of knowledge. The first, of course, we obeyed with great relish, but the second we violated at great cost both on earth and in heaven. There were no other commandments to obey, no other rules to follow. With no principles laid out, how did Noah get classified as a righteous man? Did God talk to him directly? Did God give him specific rules regarding his behavior? Regarding his relationship with others? Regarding his relationship with God?

This chapter begins to clear up the mystery. Here God tells us that Noah did all the things God told him to do. God did speak directly to him and told him to do something very specific: build an ark and gather mated pairs of all creatures for survival. That must have been a challenging command indeed. We have often speculated that Noah must have been the laughing stock of his generation, doing something so absurd as building a huge ship on dry ground. Although the Bible tells us nothing about Noah's suffering during the time it took him to build the ark, we have painted our own pictures of Noah's neighbors ridiculing him as he hauled timber, carved pegs, and mixed pitch.

Our scholars calculate that Noah's ark was about 450 feet long, 75 feet wide, and stood three stories tall. And since scripture doesn't suggest that Noah had any supernatural help in building the gigantic vessel, we are led to conclude that he and his boys must have built it all by themselves, probably with one eye to the sky. While the men were busy at the shipyard, the women and children were probably gathering the pairs of birds, snakes, rabbits, and giraffes, and baling the hay and the straw for the cargo hold.

It was no easy task. I often wonder if even godly Noah sometimes despaired in the face of the challenge, and if the Lord ever stepped in to renew his faith or restore his energy. I hope so, because that is the essence of our daily walk with him. Even Jesus, when he stood at the brink of the most difficult task of his human life, pleaded with God to lift his burden. When Noah shaped the beam of the ark, he must have been walking in a valley, brooding over the vastness of his task. And as Jesus knelt in Gethsemane, he knew that he was bowing his head in the valley of the shadow of death. As we struggle through our valleys, our loving father is there, not making any brilliant splash of light, but simply making the moon stand still so that we know he is watching over us as we gather our courage for the tasks we face.

Noah's life's work was to build his refuge in the time of storm. Our life's work should be the same. Jesus is our ark, our refuge, not only from the storms of death and hell, but also from the storms of life. As we live our lives, we must constantly be shaping and molding our relationship with our Lord, our ark. We should listen for his Word, bring him our cares, and strive to walk with him and do all that he commands, as Noah did.

Then, when God gathers in the last of his harvest, he might say of us as he said of Noah, "There stands a righteous person."

Our God Cares

Scripture: Genesis 7:6–24

*I*once had the privilege of listening to a series of lectures about the pagan deities the ancients created. Those old myths not only tell stories of the creation of the earth and its creatures, the entrance of sin into the world, and a great flood with few survivors, but they are rife with tales of territorial gods who were strong, but not bright, who fought and schemed, who had no sense of justice, and, most of all, cared about no one but themselves.

In one account of the great flood, the chief god became annoyed with the people of the earth because they kept begging him to give them a better life. In frustration, he decided to eradicate the human race with a flood. But one lesser god, in an act of rebellion against his chief, went below and warned one of the people that a great deluge was on the way, and the fortunate man who got the warning built a boat so he and his family could escape a watery grave.

The kinds of gods that Abraham knew when he lived with his parents in the land of the Chaldeans were terrifying and whimsical beings that cared nothing for people. Those were the kinds of gods the Israelites learned about as they slaved in Egypt. Their knowledge of history was warped as they discovered gods who were to be feared but not trusted, worshipped but not loved. Is it any wonder that Abraham was reluctant to trust his destiny to this "new god" who called him out of Haran? Can we blame those early Israelites for their inability to trust this "new god" who plucked them out of Egypt and led them to a far country they couldn't begin to comprehend?

So, God gave his people the book of Genesis, not only to set the record straight about how the universe and its inhabitants came into being, but also to reveal to them the truth about himself. They needed to know that their God was the only God, that he was all powerful and that he was just, loving, and merciful. They needed to know that their God cared for them and that they could trust him to keep his promises.

But God didn't write the book of Genesis simply to reveal himself to that tattered band of chosen people who had escaped the barbs of the slave master's whip, he gave it to reveal himself to us.

So now, as we land Noah and his family safely on the top of Mount Ararat and see the rainbow appear in the sky as a sign of God's promise of a new beginning, we can begin to comprehend how wondrous our God really is.

Oh, he's strict, and he's laid down some pretty tough rules for us to follow, but he's also given us some good teaching and some exemplary role models who can inspire us to be obedient. And speaking of inspiration, he's even empowered us with the presence of his Holy Spirit in us to resist temptation. He's told us in no uncertain terms what our punishment will be for our disobedience, and he's explained very clearly the consequences of our misbehavior, but he's also proven that he will be with us as we suffer those consequences, and that he will help us bear our load.

But most of all, being both just and merciful, he's absorbed our punishment for us, and he's promised us that if we simply accept his offer of atonement, he'll wipe the slate clean with his own blood and treat us as though we'd never sinned at all!

Our God cares!

The Promise of Springtime

Scripture: Genesis 8
Suggested Reading: 1 Corinthians 15:35–54

God made a lot of promises. Some we appreciate, some we don't, and too many we take for granted.

God's first promise to the human race was that if we were to disobey him we would surely die. Then after we did disobey, he promised us that from that day forth our lives would be miserable in many ways. He has kept those promises.

But after he washed the world clean with a flood, he made a promise that we were happy to receive. He not only promised that he would never again curse the ground because of man's sin and that he would never again flood the earth, but he also promised that springtime would always come!

The last verse of the chapter is one of the take-for-granted verses of the Bible. We focus on many other wonderful promises and many other very comforting words of scripture, but to my mind, the promise of verse twenty-two is a promise to live by.

Can you imagine what life would be like if we were not able to count on the sun rising every morning and setting every evening? Can you imagine what life would be like if we were not able to count on the tulips budding every spring, and the leaves turning to gold and flame every fall? Can you imagine what life would be like if we could not count on planting our crops every May and harvesting them every September? What would happen if the sun suddenly decided to shine all night or if the snow decided to cover the ground all summer? A scientist might assert that if the heavenly bodies did not spin and revolve in a repetitious and consistent manner, our planet would be unable to sustain life, particularly human life.

So the promise of consistency of sun and season is not merely a promise made for our pleasure or convenience, nor a promise we should casually shrug off. It is the promise of life! The promise of perpetual seasons and perpetually recurring springtime is also the promise upon which God communicates to us the promise of our resurrection and the promise of eternal life. Because we have been able to depend on the seed kernel dying in the earth, springing through the crust of soil, blooming and yielding its fruit in due season, we can also be certain that God will not leave us in the earth, but that we too will break from our tombs and live again.

It gets even better. The body that is sown in the ground is a perishable thing, sown with clogged arteries, cancerous parts, broken bones, and befuddled brains. But the body that will be raised will be imperishable and incorruptible! That which was flesh will become spirit; that which was terrestrial will become celestial.

I have always loved Keats' *Ode on a Grecian Urn*. Because the engravings on the urn are timeless, the piper's song will ever be new, the lover will love eternally, and the bride will be forever beautiful and forever young. By comprehending that, I can comprehend how this battered old body will be planted down the road in our little country cemetery and will spring forth on that promised day, healed of all its diseases, bursting with the vigor of eternal youth, and forever full of praise and thanksgiving!

Hallelujah!

A Plan Brews

*Scripture: **Genesis 9***
Suggested Reading: Galatians 3:29; Hebrews 11:7

In its epic narrative simplicity, the Bible tells us that Noah became a farmer, planted a vineyard, pressed the grapes, drank the wine, got drunk and fell asleep in his tent, naked. No other adjectives add any color to the moment. There is no moral implication or divine judgment about Noah's drunkenness or his nakedness. It simply happened, and a few verses later Noah died at a ripe old age, qualified to be enshrined in the hall of the heroes of faith. The only judgmental thing God ever said about him was that he was a righteous man who walked with God and did all that God commanded him to do.

Any honor or any guilt spilling from Noah's drunkenness and nakedness falls upon his boys, Shem, Ham, and Japheth. Ham's reaction was one of mockery, while that the other sons was one of respect and modesty. The degree to which they honored their father was the striking difference between them, and upon that difference hangs the balance of history and the rest of scripture. In that seemingly insignificant moment in the saga of man, God laid the first stones for the foundation of his plan to redeem humanity from eternal death.

In Ham's action we see that the imaginings of man's heart are continually evil and that he deserves the terrible judgment that God has reserved for him. As we will learn in subsequent chapters, the sons of Ham, particularly Canaan, lived lives of such indescribable evil that there are some passages of scripture we hope our children don't discover until they become adults with a solid spirit of discernment. Thus it is that God gave them a land to inhabit and the opportunity to repent until their iniquity matured to the full, then he tore the land from them and gave it to select descendants of Shem, Abraham's seed, making the sons of Canaan their slaves.

Japheth was as deserving as Shem, so God promised him that someday he would dwell in Shem's tents as an equal inheritor of the blessings he reserved for his chosen people. Thus the Gentiles, or the non-Jewish people who are in Christ are to be considered equal with Jacob's children as heirs to the kingdom of heaven.

Had Noah not got drunk and had his sons not treated him as they did, the basis for the rest of scripture would not exist. God would have had to devise some other way to justify subsequent history. But the question that nags me is *why* God authored the episode of Noah's drunkenness and his sons' conduct as the footing on which to build the rest of the story. Is this a story from which we should learn something beyond the fact that it is a peg on which God's plan of salvation hangs?

As I look back over my years, I stand amazed at the number of seemingly insignificant events and decisions that have turned the course of my life. A simple twist of the steering wheel at one corner rather than the next changed my life forever. A rash decision to add an elective to my class schedule altered my destiny. Hasty consent to serve on a particular committee turned my life in a whole new direction.

Noah, Ham, Shem, and Japheth made simple decisions that changed the course, not only of their own lives, but also of both history and eternity. God gives us the same opportunity. In every day and every moment of our lives we face tiny decisions that may have a gigantic impact, most particularly the moment-by-moment decisions of whether or not to walk with God and do what he commands us to do. We can judge no action, no matter how small, to be insignificant.

A Different Book

Scripture: Genesis 10
Suggested Reading: Genesis 12:3; Philippians 4:3;
Revelation 7:9–10

*S*ince I've read ahead, I know what happens. For whatever reason, God gave us a census of the sons of Shem, Ham, and Japheth, scattered their peoples over the face of the earth, and then focused his attention on one descendant of Shem ten generations down the road. The rest of the book is mostly about Abraham and his seed, from Isaac to Jacob, to Joseph and his brothers, then on to David and finally to Jesus. *Finally* to Jesus? Well, not quite *finally*.

What about me? I descended from Japheth. I've had friends and neighbors who trace their lineage back to Shem and Ham, but did God lose interest in the rest of us after the tenth chapter of Genesis and concern himself only with the children of Abraham?

It almost appears so. He gathered Japheth's progeny up into five short verses and packed my ancestors off to various ports on the coastlands, declared them to be migrant sailors, and floated them out to sea, never to be seen again . . . or almost never. He did the same for the sons of Ham, except he sent them mainly south. Doesn't he love us? It seems at this point that that one distant descendant of Shem, Abraham, is, for no apparent reason, his favorite, and the rest of us are left to fare for ourselves.

But wait just one moment. Did he send us off in disarray? No, of course not. He made a list. In addition to naming the sons of Shem, he also named each of the sons of Ham and Japheth and their earliest descendants in genealogical order; you can bet that as the ages rolled on he kept a running inventory of all succeeding generations. He didn't ignore us, nor did he put us on a shelf until a more convenient time. He kept track of each of us and numbered the hairs of our heads just as he kept track of Abraham, Isaac, and Jacob.

We're just in a different book.

Do we ever show up again in the Bible? To be sure, and in various ways.

We appear right after he counted us and sent us off to our careers. Then when God promised Abraham that he would bless him, make his name great, and make of him a great nation, he also promised him that someday, in some way, he would be a blessing to *all* the families of the earth. And that includes us!

We appear during Paul's journeys as objects of grace as he and his fellow missionaries launched from those same ports from which the sons of Japheth set sail, carrying the story of salvation to the Gentiles in Asia Minor, Greece, and Italy.

We appear from time to time, both in narrative and in prophecy, as enemies of Israel, chosen by God to carry out some of the terrible judgments he inflicted upon them for their disobedience.

And finally we appear again at the end of the story, gathered up from our forays over the seas. And, praise God, I'm there too, wearing my white robe and carrying in my hand a white stone bearing my name. I'm there among that great innumerable throng from every nation, tribe and tongue, singing praises before the throne because my name is written in the other book . . . the Lamb's Book of Life!

A Very Small Rudder

Scripture: Genesis 11:1–9
Suggested Reading: Acts 2:1–8; James 3:1–12

What people say to one another determines the course God allows history to take. Nations rise and fall on the strength of what people say. A few simple words, well or poorly chosen, may alter the relationship between individuals or countries. The tongue is such a powerful instrument that James likens it to a tiny rudder that turns a great ship.

In our infancy on the plain of Shinar we gave each other some very bad advice. We talked ourselves into a foolish project that was to become our undoing as a unified race of beings. We talked ourselves into making "a name for ourselves." In a moment of unbridled conceit we decided that we wanted to "be somebody." Not content to be clay in the hands of our divine Potter, we decided to become molders of clay ourselves and make bricks with which to build a tower to invade the sanctity of heaven and become equals with God. We showered ourselves with powerfully persuasive words that determined the destiny of the entire population.

Our triune God looked down upon us, took counsel with himself, and decided to put an end to our arrogance.

I've often imagined myself a little mouse, if heaven has mice, sitting in my little hole in the mopboard of God's ivory palace listening to the debate between the Father, Son, and Holy Spirit as they developed their plan to undo the upstarts of Shinar.

Perhaps the Father wanted to send down fire and brimstone to destroy that silly tower, but the other two persuaded him to defer that disaster to sometime in the future.

Perhaps the Son wanted to go down there himself and walk among them, teaching humility and living an exemplary life before the people in hopes that they would repent of their evil ways, but the other two persuaded him to save that remedy for another occasion.

The Holy Spirit's idea must have been the counsel they settled on, since the godhead had put him in charge of tongues. Perhaps they gave him this opportunity to practice the art of controlling what people say and what others understand or fail to understand in order to perfect it for that great day in Jerusalem just a few millennia down the road. Then again, maybe they settled on the Babel plan simply to show us early on what power they had put in our tongues, what power they had over our tongues, and what power they had reserved unto themselves.

The tongue is a wondrous instrument. It does more than just talk. Sometimes, as I've just done and as I do from time to time in these meditations, we can put it in our cheek, and if we have a twinkle in our eye we can take the harm out of our words.

When God didn't like what we were doing at Shinar, he changed it all by taking charge of our tongues. When he decided to change the course of history at Pentecost, he did it by taking charge of the tongues of the apostles and filling the ears of the listeners with powerful and persuasive words that dictated the behavior of thousands of souls.

We lay many things on the altar for God's use: our time, our talent, our money. But if we are to commit to the Lord's keeping the most powerful of our members, we must lay down our tongues.

Something There Is . . .

Scripture: Review Genesis 11:1–9

Something there is, said Robert Frost, "that doesn't love a wall." When the ground beneath a wall freezes and thaws, it heaves and spills the rocks. And hunters and vandals dislodge the stones. But we keep building and mending our walls, unsure of what we're walling in or walling out, and unsure to whom we might be giving offense.

Had Frost written about both ancient and modern events, he might have said, "Something there is that doesn't love a tower." To be sure, it's not the tower itself that goes unloved, but rather the purpose of the tower and the motivation behind the building of it.

The men of Babel tried to build a tower whose top was in the heavens in order to deify themselves and draw attention to their power and prosperity. But heaven took offense. The godhead conferred and passed judgment, determining that the tower and the city around it could not stand. But they didn't knock it down right then, they let it stand for a time as a monument to man's arrogance, and simply confused the tongues of the builders and forced them to abandon their grandiose project. Some scholars believe that the rubble of that tower is still strewn on the banks of the Euphrates River near Babylon.

Some four thousand years later on the other side of the world, an international group of very prosperous and intelligent people overcame their language barriers and built a pair of towers side by side. They were probably ten or twelve times as tall as the tower of Babel and their tops vanished into the mists on days when the heavens hung low. Over fifty thousand people worked in those twin towers, conducting commerce and controlling the world's trade. The concrete, glass and metal edifice stood as a monument to prosperity.

But "something there was" didn't love those towers. Some force with mission and commitment far beyond our comprehension took offense at all they stood for, and one calm summer day violently reduced those skyscrapers to a giant heap of smoking rubble on the banks of the Hudson River. Thousands perished.

In an instant the righteous governments of the earth declared war against the forces of evil and vowed vengeance on the dark powers that had destroyed their enormous towers, murdered their people, and botched their grandiose plans. Those who struck the blow claimed to have inflicted mortal injury on the great Satan. Nations revved up their engines of war, determined to avenge the assault and rid the earth of such terrors.

In the background, as gas-masked rescue workers sifted through the rubble in a grim search for victims, various voices shook the airwaves with an acrid mixture of anger and prayer. One circumspect commentator expressed the hope that when our tremors of rage ceased, we would all turn our thoughts inward to assess the extent to which, by our pride and selfishness, we might have brought this horrible judgment down on ourselves.

To fulfill God's call to do justice in this unjust world, Christians on my right urged government to exact revenge and rid civilization of terrorists and all who abet them. Christians on my left urged government to reach out and tear down the walls that offend the poor and powerless and to destroy the roots of terrorism by feeding the hungry and clothing the naked.

And I prayed for Jesus to come quickly and claim his kingdom.

Go

Scripture: Genesis 11:10–12:3
Suggested Reading: Matthew 4:18–22; Mark 10:17–31

The Lord said to Abram, 'Go from your country and your kindred and your father's house . . .' So Abram went, as the Lord had told him. What a remarkable moment in scripture! This moment has become a prototype for many to follow. God called Abram from the security of his father's house and family business to leave it all and follow him by faith alone into a new and strange territory.

In a similar manner God called Moses from the security of his father-in-law's sheep business to lead Abram's descendants out of Egypt, through the Red Sea, across the wilderness to the brink of the Promised Land. God used Samuel to call David from his pasture to the throne of a nation on the brink of becoming the greatest power on earth. God used Elijah to call Elisha from his farm to follow him into a life of unspeakable fulfillment walking with God. And Jesus called his disciples to leave the security of their family businesses and follow him into a ministry filled with miracles and healing, and finally death.

Could any of the called have said, "No, I won't go. I'm going to stay right here where it is safe and secure"? Had Abram declined God's call, presumably there would have been no Israel, no Moses, no commandments, no David, and no Jesus. Had David stayed with his sheep, there would have been no psalms and no Solomon. Had Elisha said no, there would have been no floating axe heads. Had Peter said no, he would have missed seeing Lazarus come forth, he would have missed walking on the water, he would have missed bursting into Jesus' empty tomb, he would not have preached his great Pentecost sermon, and he would never have been given the keys to the gates of heaven.

Seeing what these great servants of God would have missed had they responded negatively to their call makes us wonder what the rich young ruler missed by saying no to Jesus. He went back to his successful business never to know the joy of walking in the steps of the savior. He missed seeing blind Bartimaeus receive his sight. He missed the palm branches and the children shouting "Hosanna!" He missed the cleansing of the temple. He missed kneeling with Jesus in the Garden. He missed the crucifixion and the resurrection, and he may have missed countless other memorable moments. But most of all he missed, in the age to come, eternal life!

The call of the Lord comes to each of us in different ways. Some of us are knocked down by a bright light as we are on our way to a place God doesn't want us to go. Some of us are stung by guilt when we end up someplace we shouldn't be, doing things we shouldn't do. Some of us are prodded to answer God's call as we sit in the presence of a persuasive evangelist. Some of us feel the gentle nudging of the Spirit, and we change the course of our lives. Some of us hear God's voice bellowing through the earthquake, wind, or fire, and some of us hear his still, small voice at every turn in the road whispering, "Go," or "Follow me."

Many of us have experienced the joy of walking with the Lord, with persecutions, to be sure. Some of us have experienced ecstasy that defies the telling, and some of us have simply had the dimness of our soul taken away. But I wonder what some of us might have missed because of the times we have not responded to his daily call to follow him. Might we have missed a moment of splendor? Might we have missed eternal life?

The Promised Land

Scripture: Genesis 12:4–9
Suggested Reading: Mark 10:28–31; Galatians 3:29

God promised that he would give the land of the Canaanites to Abram's descendants. What does that mean to me? For centuries Abram's children dreamed of their Promised Land, and at last God delivered it to them. They conquered it, possessed it, built in it a great kingdom, sinned greatly in it, and because of their sin, lost it back to the pagans. What is that to me? So what if I am an heir to the promise that God made to Abram almost four thousand years ago? For Abram's seed, the promise was fulfilled, but today it is only history. Or is it?

I can find two reasons to pay attention to the promise God made to Abram.

First of all, my eternal destiny rides on it. In its dying gasp, just before it passed into centuries of oblivion, the nation of Israel raised a perfect son who is the ultimate fulfillment of the promise. As the lamb without blemish he became the sacrifice that paid for my sin and earned my entry into heaven. That's the mountaintop of Christian experience.

The other reason is that my study of that promise and the manner of its fulfillment can teach me how I should live and what I can expect as I walk through the valleys of life as one who has an inheritance that was promised at the dawn of history.

How may I view this Promised Land and my share in it? Certainly as much more than dry historical fact. From the mountaintop I can see my eternal promised land lying on the opposite shore of the Jordan. When this feeble life is over, I am assured that my Lord will lead me through that river to the other shore and bring me safely to the land where there is no night, nor pain, nor tears.

But there is also a promised land here and now. After Jesus told the rich young ruler what he had to do to gain eternal life, he turned to his own disciples and told them that anyone who leaves all and follows him will receive "now, in this time," a multitude of blessings, including lands and loved ones, with persecutions, of course. Study and experience dictate that we must take this promise as we take a parable, a literal statement with a metaphorical meaning, for we know that after he was sent out to carry the gospel to the ends of the earth, Peter never actually possessed lands and houses.

We used to sing a great old hymn of the church that proclaimed, "I am dwelling in Beulah land!" What did we mean by that? What's Beulah land? Beulah is the name given to the Promised Land after the exile when it was restored to God's favor.

How can I be dwelling there? If I have been crucified with Christ by dying to self, if I have been raised with him in newness of life, and if it is no longer I who live but Christ who lives in me, then I have inherited that part of the promised land that Jesus said he would give me "now, in this time."

The promised land that we can inhabit in this lifetime is a spiritual promised land. It is the land we can walk in when we walk in the steps of our savior. It is a land where we are never alone because he is always there, walking beside us and living within us. It is a land of delight, full of giants and enemies, to be sure, but a land flowing with milk, honey, and very satisfying spiritual fruit!

A Famine in the Land

Scripture: Genesis 12:10
Suggested Reading: 2 Kings 8:1; Amos 8:11–12;
Revelation 6:8; 18:1–8; 19:1–9

Here the word *famine* appears in the Bible for the first time. But it is far from the last. If you sort through the books of the Bible, you will find that many famines occurred in and around Israel, not only during Old Testament times, but also during the life of the early church. Famine must have been a fairly common phenomenon since Jesus even based the parable of the prodigal son on it.

We in America have little comprehension of famine. The closest we come is when we see television pictures of bloated, scrawny children with tin cups standing in line for gruel in some far off land. A few of us dash off a small check to the Red Cross, then, grateful that we live in a land of plenty, we head for the pantry to get another handful of chocolate covered peanuts.

It appears that nearly every generation in Israel suffered the ravages of famine. Abraham, Isaac, and Jacob each lived through one. Since they had no huge cargo planes to carry food into their dry and thirsty land, they either had to migrate to a country that had food, or caravan their way to a food source and back. Egypt seemed the likely place to go for provisions, but during Joseph's time, even that lush land endured seven years of drought.

Since we believe in an omnipotent God, and since scripture directly attributes at least one famine to the hand of God, we must suppose that God either causes or permits famines to occur, and that at his word a famine may end. Sometimes God punished his wayward children by withholding rain for a long period, and sometimes, when they repented, he again blessed their land with fruitfulness.

Famines are horrible things. They uproot families, they cause deadly conflicts over food morsels, they bring untold suffering and horrible death. Yet the misery that dry fields cause is nothing compared to the misery that will come crashing down when we suffer, "not a famine of bread, . . . but of hearing the words of the Lord."

Some of my friends say the famine that Amos prophesied is happening right now. I don't profess to know. Where I live a lot of churches faithfully preach God's Word every Sunday. And when I surf my TV channels, I always find, among the smut, one or two stations spreading the good news of salvation. On the other hand, it sometimes seems that Satan's voice is drowning out God's.

John prophesied that famine would continue to the end of time. Now I don't presume to know whether the famine that the pale horse will bring in his wake will be a famine of bread or some other kind of famine, but I'm quite sure that the famine the bright angel will bring upon Babylon will be a dearth of whatever Satan needs to survive. Babylon is the symbolic essence of evil, the source of everything from idolatry in the world to heresy in the church, and in the end, with the skies echoing with a shout of great victory, God will starve her out and burn her to death. Sin will cease to exist.

Then will come that grand moment history has awaited since the fall of our first parents: God and man will be reconciled, and we will feast with our savior at his banquet table.

The great famine will be over!

Little White Lies

Scripture: Genesis 12:11–20; 13:1–4

One thing that gives me much comfort is that the portraits of the great heroes of the Bible are painted clearly before our eyes with a brush of realism dipped in the true colors of their lives. There is no divine cover up or attempt to whitewash the reputations of the people to whom God entrusted his blessing and his plan of salvation. Of all the heroes of scripture, only one made it through life without ever yielding to the wiles of Satan. The rest were sinners. Among them were liars, connivers, adulterers, and murderers. Not that any of that mitigates or justifies my sin in any way, it just gives me the comfort of knowing that as a sinner, I am in good company.

When the Lord appeared to Abram and told him he was standing on the ground his descendants would inherit, Abram celebrated the good news by building altars, one by the oak of Moreh, and another on the mountain east of Bethel, a spot that grows to great significance later in the story. Abram was on speaking terms with God himself, and by building altars he demonstrated that he was subservient to the God he worshipped.

That makes me wonder why, when famine came to Canaan, Abram didn't call on the Lord to get directions. He simply took it upon himself to follow the tradition of the day and go to Egypt where there was an abundance of food and where Canaanites were welcome. His failure to secure the Lord's blessing on his plan for survival was a mistake that got him into trouble.

What might have happened had he sought God's will for his life at that point? God may have sent him to Egypt, or God may have provided for him in any number or miraculous ways. After receiving God's blessing and promise of protection, it was sinful of him to strike out on his own, and it resulted in his having to compound his wrongdoing to dig himself out of the mess he made.

Abram lied to Pharaoh and compromised his marriage to save his own skin. His lie, though it may have been "only a little white lie" because Sarai was his half-sister, was the act of a coward who had lost faith in God's promise to bless him, and to bless those who bless him and curse those who curse him. Only by divine intervention did God preserve the sanctity of Abram's relationship with his wife.

What was the end result of Abram's little foray into Egypt? He came out with more wealth than he had when he arrived, including an Egyptian maid who later played a pivotal role on the stage of history. He deserved to be punished, but God blessed him instead.

We cannot be too harsh on Abram lest in the process we judge ourselves. Abram's faith in God was a brand new thing for him. He was still learning how to relate to his new God and how to be a faithful, obedient follower. He had a long way to go.

It is less important to note that Abram sinned than to note what he did after he sinned. He could have gone anywhere, but he chose to return to Bethel, to return to the land of promise, to return to the altar he had built to the Lord and to reaffirm his commitment.

We all sin. We all fall short of what God wants of us. We all sometimes go our own headstrong way without securing God's blessing. But it is less important to note that we are sinners than to note what we do after we sin. Do we come to our senses and return to the place in our lives where we first met God and where we built our altar of commitment to him? Do we go back to our Bethel?

... And There Was Strife

Scripture: Genesis 13:5–18
Suggested Reading: Genesis 19:30–38; Hebrews 11:8–10

We celebrate Abraham as a man whose actions epitomized obedience to God. The writer of Hebrews honors him as one of the heroes of faith, perhaps the most distinguished of all. When we consider that he turned his back on his career, his family, and the comforts of home to spend his life camping in the desert for a promise that he only "glimpsed afar off," we, too, must recognize him as a monument of obedience. In fact, we are so awed by the extent to which this man responded to God's call that we nearly fail to note another small flaw in his conduct.

God said to him, "Go from your country *and your kindred* and your father's house . . . ." Then we read, "So Abram went *and Lot went with him.*" That's not exactly leaving one's kindred.

When Abram left his home with his nephew in tow, God had a number of choices. He could have simply turned his back on Abram's failure to be one hundred percent obedient, and let the two of them live happily or unhappily ever after. If he were determined that they should not be together, he could have simply tapped Abram on the shoulder and said, "When I said 'Leave your kindred,' I meant Lot too. There's not enough room for both of you out there, so you have to leave him behind." But that's not how God works. He lays down the rules, and if we disobey we must suffer the consequences and learn the lessons. Sin has its own rewards.

In Abram's case, as God was blessing him by multiplying his material wealth, he was blessing Lot too. God's blessing got so big that the land couldn't hold it all. And when a land is too small for two people and all their stuff, conflict inevitably breaks out. When their flocks suffered the effects of over population, discord erupted in their household, and the only way to settle the matter was to split the household in two and send one half packing.

If the matter had ended with their separation, Abram's disobedience would have had little consequence. They would have simply gone their separate ways. They might have stayed in touch as close relatives usually do, and might have got together every now and again for a family reunion. Eventually, their families might have lost contract with each other as distant relatives tend to do.

But the matter didn't end with their separation. God would not let Abram's sin sink into the sea of his forgetfulness without consequence. Abram, or rather his descendants, had to pay a steep price for his one small sin. If we look far into the future, we will find that Lot's offspring, begotten in another grievous sin, the Moabites and the Ammonites, bedevil Israel for centuries to come. The soil of Canaan is soaked with blood from Abram's veins that was drawn by the swords of the sons of Lot.

Fortunately for us, our God is not just a God of punishment. He covenants with us, and his promises always contain two parts: the punishment he will pour out on us if we violate his rules, and the blessings he will pour out on us if we do as he says.

In our age we have another advantage. From Adam on we all failed to walk the proper path, so at Calvary God meted out one punishment for all sinners. Those who choose to accept Christ's sacrifice as the punishment for their sins will inherit, through father Abraham, the blessing God promised to all the families of the earth.

The Giver's Gain

Scripture: Genesis 13:1–16
Suggested Reading: Philippians 2:3–11

On first reading, it would appear that Abram made a rather unwise move when he offered his nephew first choice of the land. After all, since it was the land that God had promised to *him* and *his* descendants, what right did he have to give any of it away? And if Lot were any kind of elder-respecting nephew, he'd have responded to Abram's generous offer by saying, "No, Uncle Abram, you choose first, and I'll take what is left." But, had Abram acted the way he had a right to act, and had Lot behaved as a good nephew should behave, we would not have had the opportunity to witness one of the most fundamental principles of Christian life in action.

True followers of Christ never argue about what their rights are. They always look for an opportunity to give up their rights, to sacrifice, to contribute first to the welfare of others. Their primary concern is selflessness, emptying themselves of self, and humbly serving those in need.

That's all right, you say, with that which is mine, such as my stuff and my money, but the land is the land God promised to Abram's descendants. What right did he have to give it away?

That is precisely the point! God demands that we be willing to give our everything away to others, *especially* the promises he has made to us. The essence of the great commission is to give unto others the land that flows with spiritual milk and honey.

What amazes me is that so far back in history, God infused into his chosen man a measure of the spirit that didn't become generally available to the rest of his chosen people until Pentecost, the spirit of selflessness, the spiritual state that allows us to empty ourselves of self and live to serve others.

Given the chance to choose first, what choice did Lot make and on what ground did he make it? He "lifted up his *eyes* and *saw* . . . ." He made his choice according to what pleased his eyes! What a tragic error! He looked at external appearance and saw that he might gain comfort and prosperity, but he failed to see what other consequences his choice might have.

I had a friend back in the sixties who quit a job because the scheduled wage rose beyond twenty thousand dollars, a fairly generous wage back then. He explained to me that he was afraid to live in that income bracket, that so much money might become a temptation he couldn't withstand. He preferred a simpler life. Most of us adopt a lifestyle appropriate to our income, but my friend had his priorities straight. He set his lifestyle first, then sought appropriate employment.

God warns us over and over of the lure of comfort and prosperity in this life. It carried Lot to an evil destiny, and it kept the rich young ruler from following Christ. Lot's temporal gain might have condemned him to eternal loss, while Abram's temporal sacrifice brought him eternal gain. Christ emptied himself, humbled himself, and became obedient even unto death. Therefore, God exalted him.

The same promise holds for us. If we seek only to serve, God promised us that he will bless us and reward us beyond measure.

Arise, Walk . . .

Scripture: Genesis 13:17–18

We once owned a beautiful six-acre piece of real estate that had a crystal clear creek cutting a jagged path across the middle of it. The land was hilly and I had built my house on the highest rise of the north side of the property. As I sat on the back deck I could look down on the creek and the three acres beyond.

We tamed the north half by fencing off part of it as pasture for Kyle's horse and by landscaping the rest of it, around the house and down to the banks of the creek. Cam and I built a plank bridge over the creek and set a picnic table in the small clearing just on the other side. But we never picnicked there, nor did we ever explore the land beyond the bridge. We looked at it from our house on the hill, just as we looked at the forests and fields that composed the view from our deck, but we never walked the length and breadth of it.

As I look back over those years, I realize that we really possessed only a three-acre parcel of land. Although we paid for six acres and held the deed to six acres, we had only laid claim to three.

Reflecting on that during these latter years of my life, it has become obvious to me that a land is never yours until you've walked it. You can't *possess* a piece of land with your eyes. You've got to plant your feet in its soil. You've got to walk the length and breadth of it. And when you've finished your walk and you sit down to take off your shoes and massage your aching feet, only then have you begun to possess the land.

You don't own life's valleys until you've walked through them. You can't know hunger until you've craved a crust of bread. You can't know grief until you've wept beside the casket of one you've loved. You can't know loneliness until you've been a stranger in a friendless land.

You don't own the mountains until you've climbed them. You can't know plenty until you've bought everything you want. You can't know love until you are folded securely in the arms of one who truly cares. You can't know hunger, grief, or love by reading books or looking at pictures. You've got to walk the length and breadth of those lands of feeling.

When God directed Abram to walk the length and breadth of the land of Canaan, he was also telling us how to claim his promises and live our Christian life to its fullest and most rewarding potential. Just as he ordered his chosen people to go in and possess the land of promise, he is ordering us to step out and possess every grain of the Christian landscape.

A passive Christian cannot be a fulfilled Christian. We must cast our bread upon the waters if it is to return to us multiplied. We must love generously if we hope to be generously loved. We must give to our neighbor with an open hand if we expect God to open his hand of blessing to us. We must explore all of God's promises and possibilities if we are ever to feel what the apostles felt the day the wind roared around them and the tongues of fire danced on their heads.

Jesus paid for the whole six acres and gave us the deed to the whole six acres. Now he wants us to cross the bridge and walk the length and breadth of the land of promise, possessing it in its fullness.

Not a Thread

Scripture: Genesis 14
Suggested Reading: Joshua 6:15–26; Psalms 110; Hebrews 7:1–3

When America celebrated the fiftieth anniversary of the Normandy invasion, troops staged a reenactment of the D-Day battle. Paratroopers floated from the skies, old bombers rumbled overhead, landing craft assaulted the beach, and soldiers scaled the cliffs. Vintage tanks and jeeps rolled over the landscape and bands played homage to the fallen heroes who lay under endless rows of white crosses in the cemetery overlooking Omaha Beach. From the podium, heads of state praised the courage of the victors while wrinkled veterans in the audience wept in remembrance of the pals they lost in the bloody horror of that battle. A few of the circumspect expressed appreciation for the peace that the battle eventually wrought.

The war of the kings is the first of many armed conflicts into which God led his people. In that campaign, God taught his people not only how to fight a battle, but also how to celebrate a victory. He reminded them that it is God, not the army, who wins the war by delivering the enemy into their hand. God inspired Abram to celebrate victory, not by taking the spoils of battle for the enhancement of his own possessions, but instead to celebrate the peace by offering a sacrifice from his own possessions to his priest in thanksgiving. And, after the hostilities ended, rather than gloriously praising the "king of war" by reenacting battle scenes, Abram sat down and communed with the "king of peace."

About a month ago we noted that Jesus was present at the creation and remained involved in the lives of God's people down through the scriptural ages. As part of the godhead, he first led Abram's troops into battle against the evil kings, and afterward appeared through the presence of Melchizedek to receive Abram's tithe, to break bread with him, and to bless him. This same Christ, the priest forever after the order of Melchizedek, is present in our lives today, not only to lead us into battle against the forces of evil that surround us, but also to commune with us after the battle and celebrate the peace his victory has earned.

I once met a man who gave his life to Christ after having made a fortune in the liquor business. Before he became a Christian, his opulent home was filled with trophies of success, such as plaques and awards from distillers honoring him for his sales. But once Jesus stepped in and led him to victory over the forces of evil, like Abram, he vowed that he would not take a thread of the old life into the new lest he be constantly reminded what had made him rich. He got rid of everything that represented his past. He sold his business and his home. He carefully calculated a tenth of his cumulative profits and earnings and gave the tithe to the Lord. With what remained he bought a modest home and established the first of a chain of small restaurants. Today a tenth of his profit goes to the Lord as a thank offering for the covenant of peace the Lord has given him.

In spirit, the man sets a wonderful example for us to follow. When our commander leads us to victory over our Sodom, we should take none of its trophies with us. Victory over sin can come only after we've completely divested ourselves of everything that continues to remind us what we once were. We are to take no prisoners; we are to take no spoils of war. As true victors we come away from the battle empty handed, possessing only the joy he's given us and celebrating only with the Prince who has won for us our everlasting peace.

A Royal Priesthood

Scripture: Review Genesis 14
Suggested Reading: Exodus 19:5–6; 1 Peter 2: 4–5,9;
Revelation 5:9–10

The thought of being a priest never appealed much to me. I'm thankful that the Lord called me into different profession, one in which I could serve others, yet one I found both rewarding and fulfilling. My greatest earthly joy is the companionship of my lovely wife who shares my comfortable retirement. My children are life's most satisfying blessings, and now my grandchildren fill me with immeasurable happiness. I enjoy having a nice home in which to live and entertain my friends and family. The priesthood might have required sacrifice beyond my capacity to give. I'm grateful that the Lord never called me into such service.

It's sad to note that a multitude of priests recorded in our histories, whether in the Bible or in the newspapers, should also have chosen a different line of work, perhaps one that lifts up deceit and self-indulgence as desirable traits. Some Old Testament priests were notorious for abusing the temple and the worshippers, and for turning the people's sacrifices into succulent servings for their own tables. Some modern priests have made the news by absconding with the people's tithes and by abusing children. Jesus told a parable about a priest who refused to help a man in desperate need. And we may not forget that it was a priest who condemned our Lord to die.

Now before I get into trouble with the clergy, I want it known that history is also blessed with innumerable good priests, those who honor their calling and devote their lives to the service of the Lord. They are the soldiers of the cross whose selfless labor has served to advance the kingdom of God. They are the true priests who have never soiled the cloth.

Clearly there are two orders of the priesthood: the order of Levi and the order of Melchizedek. Since so many of the priests belonging to the order of Levi have brought dishonor to their profession, it's no wonder that the prophets of the Old Testament named Jesus to the order of Melchizedek. And I believe that most of today's clerics bring the honor of Melchizedek to their vestments rather than the shame of Levi.

But we, too, are called to be priests, whether we like it or not. The church of Jesus Christ is a kingdom of priests, a holy and royal priesthood destined to reign with our Lord forever. To which order do we belong? The order of Levi, or the order of Melchizedek?

By their fruits ye shall know them. The emblem of either Levi or Melchizedek hangs symbolically around the necks of the priests who presided over the altars in the ancient temple or who serve the sacraments in the modern church, and reflects the character of their calling. So our service reflects ours. What fruit do we bear?

Fortunately we have a role model. Our prototype wears the mantle of a prophet, the collar of a priest, and the crown of a king. Yet he didn't make his home in palaces or temples. He had nowhere to lay his head. He was a man of the streets, reaching out, touching the untouchable and pardoning sinners. And what's his word to us?

Go and do thou likewise.

Choices

Scripture: Review Genesis 14
Suggested Reading: Hebrews 2:8; 4:15

As you've probably noticed, we are having a little trouble getting past chapter fourteen. Every time I begin to contemplate a new meditation, my natural sense of anxiety and my love for Abram's next experience tug my eye toward the next chapter, but something in my spirit pulls me back to the story of Abram's war and his encounter with Melchizedek. Why did Moses give us such a brief and matter-of-fact account of Abram's great military expedition, and such a detailed account of his brief meetings with the kings of Sodom and Salem?

My thoughts go back to the fundamentals of scripture that I learned in school. The main reason God gave us his Word was to reveal himself to us and to teach us how he wants us to live our lives. For the most part, he leaves science to the scientists and history to the historians to make what they can of nature and the course of human events. In the Bible, historical accounts and natural phenomena serve only a secondary purpose.

Twenty-four years will have passed from the day we first met Abram and the day Isaac is born. During that quarter century, only a few of the events in Abram's life are recorded. Many important things must have happened to the man that the Lord found unnecessary to relate to us. I'm thinking of such things as the alliances with Mamre, Eschol, and Aner and of the military force they built and trained. The Lord was very economical in selecting the events of Abram's life that he preserved on the written record. It seems that he chose to reveal to us those events that convey a message or that reveal either his own character or his expectations for us. Thus, the message of this chapter is not to be found so much in the story of the war of the kings, but in the episode that followed in which Abram seemingly had to make a choice between accepting the offer of either the good king or the evil king.

But was the choice so simple? Did he have to choose one over the other? Couldn't he have communed with Melchizedek *and* have taken the spoils of war from the King of Sodom? In contrast, Adam and Eve had a simple decision: to eat or not to eat. Do the choices get more complicated as we progress from the simplicity of Eden to the complexity of Canaan?

And what about our choices today? Do the intricacies of the seventh millennium offer us shades of gray that the citizens of the first millennium couldn't have begun to comprehend? Adam and Eve were formed into a black and white world. By Abram's day the decisions had become significantly more difficult. The founders of the early church faced grave issues such as the continuance of circumcision and the eating of food that had been sacrificed to idols. And they lived two thousand years ago when there were no automobiles, television, or the world wide web.

Our children seem to scorn our moral standards much as we scorned those set by our parents when we were young. As the pace of life speeds up, issues of right and wrong emerge, mature, and vanish in the course of one brief lifetime. Do we have any consolation as we flounder in this bewildering confusion surrounding abortion, euthanasia, and human cloning?

Of course we do. Jesus struggled too. He knows our frame; he knows that we are dust. He understands our weaknesses and sympathizes with us as we face the great moral dilemmas of our day.

Sassing God?

Scripture: Genesis 15:1–8
Suggested Reading: Luke 1:5–20; Revelation 3:19

One of the glorious moments of my youth was the night our high school basketball team won the district championship. The heroes of the hardwood rode the school bus back into town with a police escort, lights blinking and sirens wailing. Back in our own gym, the fans almost deified the team with chants and oratory. We had overcome! So I know how Abram must have felt as he returned from his great victory over his enemies and his greater victory over his own greed that he won by rejecting Sodom's goods and communing with Melchizedek.

Or do I know? The next episode in his life begins with the word of the Lord coming to him and saying, "Fear not, Abram, I am your shield." What does he have to be afraid of? With God's help he has just obliterated his political enemies and has advanced one giant step in his relationship with his Lord. So why the fright? Was he afraid that the kings he vanquished would recoup and return to make war anew? Was he afraid that he might not be able to overcome the next temptation? Did he have doubts about the reliability of God?

Although Abram was growing in faith, his understanding of God had not yet matured to the point that he was willing to trust him unconditionally. Shadows of the whimsical, capricious old pagan deities still lurked in the recesses of his memory and hindered his spiritual development. So in the quiet time that followed the storm of success, Satan slithered in and began to sow the seeds of doubt. And Abram became afraid.

In Abram's moment of misgiving, the Lord stepped in to reassure him that he stood as Abram's shield against all enemies, whether in the flesh or in the spirit. But Satan had established such a foothold that Abram challenged God's integrity by saying, in effect, "You promised me a son years ago and you haven't delivered, so why should I trust you to shield me from my enemies in the future?" Good point? Is this where God should have become angry with him and chastised him for his unbelief? No. A gentle and patient God repeated his promise of an heir, and Abram believed. And God "reckoned it to him as righteousness."

Would God be as patient with mature Christians who, in a moment of temptation or weakness, would question God's integrity as Abram did? Old Zechariah sure got chastised when he asked God essentially the same question Abram asked, "How am I to know that you will keep your promise?" Without a moment of hesitation or any forbearance at all, God struck the old priest dumb for his doubt. What is the difference? Is our God as capricious as those old deities of myth? Do I have to be careful what I ask when I'm speaking to him? Is there room in my relationship with him to express my doubts and fears? Does he tolerate honest questions from honest, but very human, believers?

In a way it's unfortunate that Zechariah and I have been blessed with a more detailed revelation of God that Abram had. By our standards, Abram got away with murder by sassing God as he did. If I were to ask the same question, I think God would throw me over his knee and give me the thrashing of a lifetime for being so impudent.

So what's my consolation in all this? God will most certainly answer my questions as he answered Zechariah's, but my answer might come in the woodshed. Why? Because he loves me!

. . . *Go to Your Fathers*

Scripture: Genesis 15:9–21
Suggested Reading: John 14:1–3

The fifteenth chapter of Genesis one of the most majestic passages of the scripture. It reveals a God who makes magnificent promises and keeps them. It reveals a God who renders awful judgment on man for his sins, and who keeps a tally of man's acts of faithfulness and righteousness. It reveals a God of justice who demands blood as the price for sin. It reveals a God who has complete control over his whole creation, both in time and in eternity. Then it reveals a man who, after communing with God in celebration of a great victory over a multitude of enemies, became fearful of his future and demanded proof of God's promises. It reveals a man destined to become the father of the greatest nation on earth reduced to the role of scarecrow, shooing the birds away from the carcasses he has laid out. The page on which this chapter is written is one of the most worn out pages of any teacher's Bible.

There is much in the chapter that fills me with great awe and much that gives me great comfort. But of all the much-studied promises and events packed into this chapter, there is one promise hidden in the cracks that gives me more solace than any other: ". . . you shall go to your fathers in peace."

Scores of people have entered and departed this world in the preceding chapters. One of them, Enoch, escaped into eternity without tasting death, but all the others simply died. Chapter five is a good example. Eight of the forefathers simply sired children and died. Until God made these promises to Abram, there is nothing in the scripture to give us any assurance of what happens to us after we die, or that there is any life at all after death. For all we know at this point, Enoch is going to be the only mortal to pass through the portals of heaven. But here God told Abram that when he dies he will go to be with his fathers. This is God's first indication to us that when we die we will be reunited with those who have gone before.

Sometimes when our mind gets in the way of our faith, this revelation raises some difficult and awkward questions about loved ones who were unbelievers or about believers who have been married more than once. But when we grow mature enough to become like little children in our faith, we simply trust God that heaven will be a wonderful place, without fears, without tears, without embarrassment, without jealousy, and without any sense of loss. As we continue through the Bible, we find the promise repeated over and over again.

The Bible is full of wonderful promises. God promised Abram that his seed would be as numberless as the stars of the sky and the sands of the sea. He promised them a land flowing with milk and honey, he promised that they would be a great nation, and he promised that by them all the families of the earth would be blessed. He has kept those promises.

God also made promises to us. He promised that whatsoever we ask in his name we would receive, he promised to reward our faithful obedience by pouring down blessings upon us, and he promised us his light and warmth as we walk through the valleys of our life.

But when this life is over, the best promise yet awaits those who believe: they shall go to be with the ones they have loved on this earth, and together they shall sit at the feet of Jesus and be with him evermore!

. . . Go in unto My Maid

Scripture: Genesis 16:1–3

Apastor in my home town once led his congregation in such a special weekend of music, messages, testimony, and prayer that one of his parishioners was led to call it a mountaintop experience, an experience that made him feel that he had been in the very presence of the Lord. On Monday the pastor ran off with one of the women of the church.

Devilish things have a way of happening right on the heels of mountaintop experiences, and that is no coincidence. As we descend from the holy hill, Satan is lurking in the bushes along the way and will leap out to tempt us, sometimes beyond our ability to resist. In the flush of victory we are most vulnerable to a new attack by our enemy. And Satan knows that.

Abram had just been in the presence of God. In response to his question, "How am I to know?" the Lord condescended to meet with his chosen man and entered into a covenant to provide not only an heir, but also a nation with a land of its own and an eternal destiny. And the deal was not sealed by a simple handshake or the exchange of a sandal, as the custom later came to be, but it was sealed by the shedding of innocent blood. As the father of the nation slept, God himself appeared to him in the form of fire and smoke, and he walked up and down among the slain animals to memorialize his solemn agreement.

But poor Abram had no idea what dangers hid in the shadows at the bottom of the mountain. While he was in the presence of the

Lord, Satan was in his tent slipping insidious thoughts into the mind of his wife, Sarai. And just as the devil hid behind the skirts of the woman to tempt Adam, so he used the God-given maternal instincts of Sarai to seduce Abram.

Now before we make enemies of the women, we must be quick to point out that women do not have a greater weakness than men for Satan to exploit. Quite the contrary. It's men's weakness that Satan exploits: men's weakness for women. Why do some faiths require women to be covered in public? Because there is something inherent in the flesh of the woman that is evil and deserves to be hidden from public view? No, because there is something inherently evil in the eye of the man, and in order to protect himself from his own lustful nature he puts the object of his lust out of his sight.

We have no evidence that Abram came back to his home aglow from his time spent with God. We have no evidence that he told his wife and the other members of his household of the wonders that befell him on that divine night. Perhaps he withheld from sharing because he was afraid they might think him to be just a crazy old man. After all, he bore a name that meant he was an "exalted father," and now in his mid eighties not only had no children, but had no obvious prospects of having any. And he still had the temerity to hang on to that silly old name? No, sharing his experience might only invite ridicule.

So, Sarai said, "Behold now, the Lord has prevented me from having children; go in unto my maid that I shall obtain children by her." What should he do? Hagar was a young, pretty Egyptian girl and his wife had made the offer. He was only a man. What could go wrong? Maybe this is God's way of fulfilling his promise?

Wrong.

. . . And Abram Hearkened

Scripture: Genesis 16:1–3
Suggested Reading: Proverbs 7:1–3; Isaiah 30:20–22;
John 14:15–20

When I was a young man trying to decide what God wanted me to do for a living, I sought free advice from a number of people who worked at different kinds of jobs to see if their line of work appealed to me. I visited with preachers, teachers, electricians, lawyers, and bricklayers, but I never had the benefit of advice from anyone who called himself a career counselor. In those days no one could make a living by simply giving advice to young people who were trying to figure out what kind of work they might be suited to do. At least I didn't know of anyone.

Today things are different. It seems that there is a good living to be made by selling advice on almost any subject. High schools have academic counselors. Colleges have career counselors. Financial advisors hang their shingles in nearly every office complex in town. Consultants have sprung up to give advice on every subject imaginable, from education to nutrition, health, marriage, child rearing, taxes, finances, travel, and retirement.

This is not bad, of course. The complexity of our human endeavors today almost demands that we receive expert advice on how to be good stewards of the many blessings God has given us. The problem is that there are so many different voices speaking at once that the noise confuses us. Most of those who seek to advise us have self-serving motives, as did Sarai. Most of the people who want to advise us on how we should invest our money, for example, are driven by the desire to get some of it for themselves.

To which voices should we hearken? Adam hearkened to the voice of Eve, and they plunged the whole world into the darkness of sin and eternal wrath of God. Abram hearkened to the voice of Sarai and not only got himself into trouble, but caused immeasurable grief for the rest of human history. Often God's people have hearkened to voices that have led them astray. Now, I'm not suggesting for one moment that people ought not listen to their spouses, quite to the contrary. If marriages are to succeed, partners should discuss all matters thoroughly and make prayerful, informed consensus decisions. I know that, and I'm not even a marriage counselor.

Ever since any of us first set foot into a church, we have known that we are always to seek God's will for our lives. But, even then, how do we sort out the myriad of voices that seek to counsel us? How do we separate the voice of God from the voices of quacks and con artists?

Often God's will comes pouring out to us from the pages of scripture. I've known people who go to the Bible when they have a decision to make and read until something leaps out at them and tells them what to do. Those folks are confident that the choices they make are God's will for their lives. I've known people who isolate themselves in prayer and fasting until they are satisfied that they have distinguished the voice of God from the other voices. And, if we have fully yielded our lives, we have the assurance that the Counselor, God's Holy Spirit, the Spirit of truth, lives within us, walks with us, and at every turn in the road whispers, "This is the way, walk in it."

But, we are still sinful humans. I haven't met any saints yet who boast that they have always sought the Lord in making decisions. The best have always said that as they mature in Christ they hope to do better than they did when they were babes. And they always seem to add that they get some comfort from the fact that the great heroes of faith also made some bad moves.

. . . *With Contempt*

Scripture: Genesis 16:4–6
Suggested Reading: Mark 9:33–41

We've all experienced it at some time or other. The *A* in math when Buddy got a *B*. The only homer in the game we won by one run. The sale that put us a notch above any of our colleagues. The landscape job that made our house the attraction of the neighborhood. The dish that ran out first at the potluck. There's a special feeling that comes with having something wonderful that others do not have.

How do we celebrate our special blessings? When we won the war we went downtown and mingled with the jubilant throng. When we got married we drove downtown blowing our horn and towing a string of clattering tin cans. Winning something or gaining something wonderful fills us with a desire to shout our joy to the rooftops. I've heard it said jokingly by old saints that there is nothing as obnoxious as a newly redeemed Christian. Filled with something they've never felt before, they stand up tall and blow the heat of their fresh zeal into the faces of others who are simply bearing their crosses and following as best they can.

Sometimes people win things and others fail to see joy in it. Most of us shake our heads in disbelief when we see homosexuals parading in the streets celebrating their escape from the closet and campaigning for special recognition and rights. When the other team won the World Series, maybe we smirked a little when we saw television reports of their riotous fans destroying their city.

In sports they speak of being a good winner or a good loser. Good winners don't look with contempt upon those they have defeated. They shake their hands, pat them on the back, and wish them well. Good losers don't pout or make excuses. They commend the winners for their outstanding play, accept defeat with grace, and hope for a brighter future.

Hagar experienced something new and wonderful that set her a notch above all of the other women in her circle. She was carrying the only child of the patriarch. How did she celebrate her blessing? As a good sport? No. She looked with contempt upon her mistress!

Sometimes our zeal in the midst of blessing gets a little puffed up, as did Hagar's, and we celebrate by looking with contempt upon those who are not as blessed as we. We create classes of people on the basis of the extent to which God has distributed his gifts. We socialize with those who have the resources to go to restaurants we can afford to patronize. We visit with those whose conversation reflects a level of education consistent with our own. We travel with those who like to go, and can afford to go, to the places we like to go.

In our efforts to live the abundant life, we sometimes forget that God calls us to be simple folk, unconcerned with greatness. Jesus didn't mingle with the great nearly as much as he mingled with the simple, or with the rich as much as he mingled with the poor. If God has blessed us with two coats, Jesus doesn't call us to hobnob with others who have two coats; rather, he calls us to seek out the person who has none and to give him one of ours.

How we celebrate our blessings reflects the manner of our walk with Christ. If we look with contempt upon those we think less blessed, we are like Hagar, puffed up and proud. But if we carry our blessings in an open hand, we are like Jesus, humble and generous.

The Angel of the Lord

Scripture: Genesis 16:7
Suggested Reading: 2 Kings 6:11–19; Hebrews 1:5–14;
Matthew 4:11

We don't speak much of angels today. Every now and again people tell stories about the sudden appearance of mysterious strangers who save them from some sort of devilment. Then they vanish, unseen by others. Since there is no plausible explanation for such events, we sometimes believe the strangers to have been angels sent by God.

When I was a boy, one such story emerged. Two men from our church council lay in wait for our pastor one night after a contentious meeting. When the minister left the building, he was accompanied by two husky men who appeared to be bodyguards. The presence of the strangers prevented an attack. Later, when the would-be attackers confessed their intent and mentioned the deterring presence of the strangers, the pastor responded that he had left the church alone that night, and that when he left he felt an overwhelming sense of peace in spite of the fact that he had just conducted a tempestuous meeting in which he had been threatened with bodily harm. Ever after, those repentant brothers have confessed that the bodyguards were angels sent by God to protect the pastor.

While some of the brothers and sisters in the church accepted the angel story without question, some disagreed and suggested that the two rowdies were "just seeing things," or were making up a story to get attention. Some, with superior education in the ways of God, declared that angels quit plying their trade when "Bible times" ended.

Others, with equal vigor, declare that angels are still alive and well, doing the things that angels have always done, but perhaps not quite so overtly. Still others just shrug in bafflement.

There seems to be plenty of suggestion in the scriptures that angels are permanent inhabitants of the eternal cosmos. We can expect them to welcome us into eternity with trumpets blaring, and we can expect to stand side by side with them, raising songs of praise on the shore of the crystal sea. But what about now, when we need them? Are they here?

I've never seen one. At least not that I know of. But I think that if my eyes could be opened, like Elisha's servant, I would be able to see them all around me, fending off demons, stopping me in my tracks just short of disaster, gently nudging me in the direction God wants me to go, and preparing tables before me in the presence of my enemies.

I can't see them, but Jesus could. After Satan tormented him with temptation, angels came and ministered to him. For Jesus, that must have been a moment of agony and ecstasy, the agony of the fast and the battle, and the ecstasy of victory over the devil. In his pain and exhaustion, he needed tender loving care, and he got it from the angels.

The writer of Hebrews convinces me that angels are present in my life to minister to me as they ministered to Jesus. When I am weary, when I have fought the devil, when my faith has been tested, when all the forces of evil seem to be surrounding me as the Syrians surrounded Elisha, when I am cowering in fear in some dark valley, I am confident that the angels are there with me, sheltering me under their wings.

After the Ecstasy

Scripture: Genesis 16: 8–16
Suggested Reading: John 7:4–29; James 4:7–10; 1 Peter 5:6–9

*M*any evangelicals who write books about the Bible believe that the angel of the Lord who appeared to Hagar by the spring of water in the wilderness was really Jesus making an early appearance on the earth. They call the event a Christophany. If this is the case, Hagar is the first "woman at the well" to drink of the living water that only Christ can provide, and was the first Christian missionary to return to her people to tell them the good news. If this assertion is true, it's no wonder that Jesus opened his dialog with her just as he did with Adam after the Fall and with numerous other people in the Bible—with a question to which he knew the answer.

Then what I find fascinating is that in two successive chapters two different people are blessed with the presence of the Lord in mountaintop experiences: the chosen hero of faith, Abram, in the vision of the covenantal sacrifice, and the pagan exile, Hagar, at the well in the wilderness. But what I find disconcerting is that the chosen hero of faith returned to his home and faithlessly leapt into bed with the maid, while the pagan returned to the same home, a glowing, born again person, sharing her blessed experience with her mistress and her master.

How else could an arrogant maid who had been driven out of her home for her haughty behavior return to the mistress she had injured and submit to her authority? How else could she have persuaded Abram to name her son Ishmael, which meant that the

Lord had given heed to her in her affliction? Abram must have come home from his mountaintop experience quite unconvinced, wondering out loud just how God was going to keep his promise of an heir. But Hagar must have returned home shouting, "I've just seen the Lord!"

And just as the woman of Samaria went out after meeting Jesus to testify to the people of her village, so Hagar must have witnessed to Abram's household.

Is the Lord telling us something here? Amid the brilliant main theme of Abram's taking God's promise into his own hands and unwittingly siring the whole Arab world, populating all of North Africa and the Middle East, creating eternal enemies for Isaac's sons, and programming the time machine for Armageddon, is there a lesser light to illuminate for us a narrower path?

What are we supposed to do after we descend the mountain after being in the presence of God? To me the answer is clear: tell others. If we wipe the name of Jesus off our lips after we reenter the secular world, we open the door for Satan to take our holy moment and pervert it to his evil purpose, as he did with Abram and the pastor we wrote about a few days ago. Satan is lurking in the bushes on the downward slope of the mountain, and while we are walking on air, he is trying to trip us.

This time, instead of taking our cue from the hero of faith, we must imitate the women at the well. Both of them. We must resist the devil by humbling ourselves and submitting to our Master. Then we must put his name on our lips, return to the place where he's put us and tell the others. And when he gives us a drink of his wonderful living water, it must become a spring that flows from us and quenches the thirst of others.

That will send Satan running!

What's in a Name?

Scripture: Genesis 17:1–8
Suggested Reading: Revelation 2:17; 3:12

One of my old college friends named Burkowitz changed his name to Burke when he became a professional and hung out his shingle. I never questioned him about it, but I assume he believes that prospective clients might shun him because of whatever they think the suffix on his name might imply.

In my family, names don't mean nearly as much as they do in other circles. I'm "named after" my father. My grandson, Collin Thomas, is named after his father, Tom. My other grandson, Caleb Robert, is named after me. Their sister, Krista Lynne, is named after her aunt. Why? Simply to honor and perpetuate the memory of one who is loved. It's a nice gesture and it is truly appreciated, but it has no significance beyond honor. I've never considered changing my name either for business reasons or for what my name might signify to someone else. I've never considered my name to have any significance other than to honor the memory of my father.

Entertainers have been known to change their names because the names they were born with were funny, or because they were associated with deprecatory characteristics that plague the minds of bigots. Perhaps they selected new names that suggest human qualities that the public might pay to experience. People have all sorts of reasons for changing their names, especially if they attach meaning to those names.

When people convert to Islam, they are given new names to signify that they have become new beings, reborn into a new faith.

Christians don't make a practice of doing that, even though the idea has a sound scriptural basis.

In the day of the patriarchs, a name meant something. Abram meant "exalted father." His new name, Abraham, meant "the father of multitudes," which, when you think about it, must have got some laughs around the compound because, as yet, he was the father of just one son, and at his age, unlikely to become the father of any more.

God gave Isaac and Ishmael their names, and he changed Jacob to Israel. Later, Simon became Peter, and Saul changed his name to Paul after his conversion because back then, in the Holy Land, names had meaning that our culture doesn't appreciate.

As a father, I had a pet name for both my son and my daughter. They're both grown now, but sometimes in nostalgic moments I still use those childish names. When two people fall in love and get married, often the bride changes her name and address to match the groom's, suggesting for her a whole new identity. And often lovers give each other secret pet names that have a joyful, private meaning, known only to themselves.

The Bible tells me that as a member of the church, I am engaged to be the bride of Christ. When he comes with trumpets blaring to claim the love of his life, I will be transformed into a new being. My master will have fulfilled his covenant with me and I will get a new name and a new address. His home will become my home, and his identity my identity. Besides that, because he loves me he will give me my own secret name, a name known only to him and to me, a name with a private meaning that gives us both joy!

There's a new name written down in glory, and it's mine, oh yes, mine!

All the Men of His House

Scripture: Genesis 17:9–27
Suggested Reading: Acts 11:1–18

My upbringing was very sectarian. We went to a Dutch school and learned that we shouldn't mingle with outsiders. We learned songs that disparaged other races, nationalities, and beliefs. We learned that since it was sinful to be "unequally yoked together," we should not date or marry someone outside our nationality or denomination. I'm sure that our parents and our teachers taught us those things without malice in their hearts. They loved us and only wanted what was right and good for us. They sincerely believed that they were doing God's will and raising us as God wanted us raised.

Perhaps my attitude today is still tainted a bit by rebellion against the old restrictive standards of our faith. I don't know. But I am very sensitive to the moments in the scriptures when the Jews, who were raised as sectarian as I, were forced to accept outsiders into their circle. Peter is a good case in point. He was raised to have nothing to do with Gentiles. Anyone who was uncircumcised could not sit at his table, go to his school, or date his sister.

That kind of upbringing is the parent of the sort of bigotry that has left children crying in the bloody streets of cities ravaged by war. Two stars of the National Basketball Association who were friends and teammates in the former Czech Republic, quit speaking to each other during the civil war over there because one was Serbian and the other Croatian. In Ireland, men ambushed each other because one was Catholic and the other Protestant. In Alabama, bigots burned a school because a white boy wanted to take his black girlfriend to the prom. All over our globe, people fight and destroy because one has one heritage and someone else another.

That's not how our God wants us to act. The Jews didn't really have to wait until Peter had his dream to discover that God was an inclusive rather than exclusive God. They should have learned that from Father Abraham. When God gave Abraham the seal of his covenant, circumcision, Abraham did not hesitate to share it with all the men of his house, even foreign slaves who may have been of another race, another culture, or another heritage. Abraham was not motivated by a "better than thou" attitude, rather he was driven to share with others the good things that God had given him, regardless of their origins or persuasions.

Abraham had an outward symbol of his citizenship in the kingdom of heaven. But rather than flaunt it in nationalistic or selfish pride like many of us who wave our flags, he chose to share his blessing with others. Many Jews of Peter's day viewed their symbol of citizenship in God's covenant kingdom not as an open door that let them in, but as a closed door that kept others out. They had their badge of citizenship and slammed the door of salvation in the face of others who didn't wear that badge, just as we who have our United States citizenship papers slam the door of freedom in the face of the huddled masses who didn't get to this land of opportunity as quickly as our grandparents did.

Fortunately, as someone said, churches are not museums for saints, but hospitals for sinners, even misers, racists, and hypocrites. Thank our generous God that "to the Gentiles also he has granted repentance unto life," and that we can go to our knees, beg forgiveness for our selfishness and bigotry, and pledge to live our lives with an open hand, an open mind, and an open heart.

A Matter of the Heart

Scripture: Review Genesis 17:14
Suggested Reading: Galatians 3:29; Deuteronomy 10:16;
Jeremiah 4:4; Psalms 51:10; Acts 15; Romans 2:29;
Colossians 2:11–14

Circumcision is a crucial requirement for membership in the kingdom of God. Now hold on! Don't go running out to that old butcher rock yet because I'm not talking about the flesh. The Lord requires much more of us than he did of Abraham. Circumcision only cost Abraham his foreskin, but it costs us our hearts.

I can only imagine what it must have been like in Canaan on that bloody day Abraham circumcised all the men of his house. I have no idea how many men lined up at the rock to have their foreskins severed. We are told that he had over three hundred men in his security force, and if you add all his servants, herdsmen, and administrative assistants to that train of soldiers, you can imagine that Abraham's circumcision line stretched out for quite a distance.

Paul told us that if we belong to Christ, we are Abraham's seed and heirs to the promise. And if we are heirs to the covenant promise, we must be obligated to wear the sign of that covenant. God told Abraham in no uncertain terms that the uncircumcised have broken the covenant and are cut off from his people. Where does that put us Gentiles?

Fortunately for some of us there was a big squabble during the first century over the question of circumcision. Gentile converts from Rome and Asia Minor balked at the prospect of being circumcised because it would make them appear to be despised Jews, and they certainly didn't want people to think that. In those days, nudity, especially at athletic events, was quite common and men who were circumcised were ridiculed. When the issue became an impediment to the spread of the gospel, the council at Jerusalem decided after strenuous debate that circumcision of the flesh was not necessary for salvation.

But the whole idea of severance of self from the flesh is too good a principle to discard with the minutes of a meeting that took place two thousand years ago. And perhaps it was God's plan that the amputation of the foreskin became a symbol for a separation of much greater consequence: the separation of the Christian from the ways of the flesh.

Back in the Old Testament, even as far back as the days of Moses, God was talking to his people about a different kind of circumcision: circumcision of the heart. Jeremiah prophesied it, David prayed for it, and Paul explained it.

Once, while browsing in the drug store, I noticed that Valentine's Day cards were on prominent display in preparation for the coming day of festivity for lovers. As I searched for an appropriate message to reaffirm to Mary Ann that I was once again giving her my heart, it occurred to me that it would be just as appropriate to reconfirm to Christ that my heart belongs to him too.

We live in a world that constantly seduces us with its attractiveness and tries to lure us away from our first love. Jesus suffered our physical circumcision for us by putting his flesh on the cross. As his bride, it is now our duty to respond by putting off the body of flesh that entices us and by making our love for him a matter of the heart.

A New Creation

Scripture: Genesis 18:1–8
Suggested Reading: Genesis 19:1–3

The Lord doles Abraham's life out to us in snippets, almost like a series of film clips that comprise a movie preview. We see him at the age of eighty-six becoming a father for the first time, then we don't see him again until the Lord comes to him thirteen years later and orders the circumcisions. At eighty-six he seemed a rather contentious and doubtful man, demanding that God give him a sign to signify that his promise was sincere. Then at ninety-nine we see a man of quite different character. He appears to have gone to the rock of circumcision without a whimper to make his sacrifice of blood to God, and following his circumcision, he is the model of the Spirit-filled, fully submitted believer, anxious to serve his Lord with the very best he has to offer.

What happened to him in the interval? Was he overwhelmed by the exuberant testimony of Hagar after she had been in the presence of the Lord? Did the specific promise of a son to be named Isaac lift him to new heights of conviction? Did circumcision make him a new man? Was his circumcision more than just a matter of the flesh? Did he become circumcised in his heart?

As he basked in the shade of the oaks of Mamre in the heat of the day, the Lord appeared to him in the form of three men who were actually angels. Why three? The three dwindled to two by evening when they came to Sodom. Does this manifestation of the Lord to Abraham in the form of three persons suggest the presence of the triune God? Does the reduction to two at Sodom suggest the absence of the Holy Spirit in that perverse city? Because of his association with his uncle Abraham, Lot certainly knew of the creator God, and because of his rescue from the Mesopotamian kings, he understood the concept of redemption. But did his lack of circumcision deny him the presence of the Holy Spirit in his life? Some think so.

The Lord came to Abraham in the middle of the day, when most men's minds are on their work. Even during business hours, Abraham turned his thoughts away from his flocks and commerce to dwell solely on God. The angels waited until city hall closed to talk to Lot, knowing that during the business day, he would be preoccupied with the politics of Sodom, his new home town. During the day, Abraham's mind was available to the Spirit, while Lot's mind was consumed by the carnal things of life.

When the angels appeared to Abraham, he ran to meet them, then bowed in their presence. Lot merely rose before he bowed. Both Abraham and Lot lavished hospitality on their angelic guests. The angels readily accepted Abraham's invitation to dinner, but rejected Lot's offer of hospitality. He had to urge them strongly before they would finally accept.

Abraham ran and hastened and his servants hurried. Sarah baked bread quickly. Lot merely prepared a feast without running and hastening. Abraham's relationship with the ambassadors of heaven was filled with zest and mutual joy. Lot's was slow and laborious.

What kind of Christian am I? If the Lord came to visit me right now, would I run to meet him? Would I hasten to kill the fatted calf? Or would the Lord wait until evening when I am at rest, knowing that during the day I am preoccupied with my business?

Have I truly gone to the Rock of my salvation? Have I been crucified with Christ? Have I circumcised my heart? Am I a new creation, reborn in the Holy Spirit?

To Charge His Children

Scripture: Genesis 18:9–21
Suggested Reading: John 15:15

One Sunday afternoon at a certain point in my growing up, my father took me for a long walk and explained that it was time for our relationship to grow to a new level. Since I was beginning to approach manhood, he explained that he wanted to begin to relate with me man to man. No longer was I simply to obey without question, but I could, in a respectful manner, seek reasons and express my opinion. I could become a member of the family cabinet and consult with the adults on matters that involved me and the rest of the household.

But, as my status changed within the family, I could no longer hide behind the cloak of childhood. I had to begin to assume responsibility for my actions. If I were going to relate with adults as equals, I also had to accept the duties of manhood. I had to begin to behave as a man. I had to behave as my father behaved. After all, someday I would be a father too, and I had to learn to set an example for my own children, just as he did for his. I had to get a part-time job, pay room and board, join the church, take holy communion, pledge a tenth of my income to the Lord, treat my parents with respect, and love my siblings as myself.

For years I wondered why chronologically the conception and birth of Isaac is so intertwined with the destruction of Sodom and Gomorrah. The answer to the question leaps out at us from verses seventeen to twenty.

Abraham and the Lord were about to enter a new stage in their relationship. Abraham was no longer going to be as a child enjoying his membership in the family of God without the attendant responsibilities. God was bringing Abraham into the inner counsels, into the cabinet, to discuss such important things as righteousness and justice. God was going to let Abraham know what he intended to do about sin in the world. After all, Abraham was to become a father, not just the father of a child, but the father of a nation. As the father of Isaac and of Israel, he would have to charge his own children to keep the way of the Lord and to set an example of righteousness in order that the promise of God might be fulfilled.

God is a God of justice. People who do not keep their end of the covenant, people who do not walk in obedience, will not enjoy the benefits of the promise. They will not enjoy citizenship in the kingdom of heaven. God will destroy them.

When God became the man Jesus, he treated his disciples in somewhat the same manner he treated his early disciple, Abraham. They too, at a certain point in their relationship with their master, graduated from a childish, servile status to the status of friend. Jesus brought his friends into the cabinet and began to tell them what he intended to do about sin in the world. He also taught them what their responsibilities would be in his kingdom, that they were to go out and bear fruit.

Our walk with the Lord must reflect the walk of Abraham and the disciples. We cannot hide forever in a babbling, unproductive, self-serving, childish relationship with God. We've got to grow up. We've got to assume our responsibilities. We've got to set an example for babes in Christ. We've got to bear fruit. We've got to keep the way of the Lord by doing righteousness and justice, and we've got to charge our children to walk in our footsteps so that the Lord may bring to his church all that he has promised.

Banging on the Table

Scripture: Genesis 18:22–32
Suggested Reading: Matthew 26:26–28; Ephesians 5:22–33

There are times when I get a little heady and would like to rewrite certain parts of the Bible. For example, back in the second chapter of Genesis when God ordered Adam not to eat of the tree of knowledge of good and evil, I would have had Adam ask, "Why not?"

Then I would have had God give him an answer that would help us all understand the mystery of original sin and how it was, according to McGuffey, that "In Adam's fall, we sinned all." I may have had God and Adam enter into a debate about the pitfalls of knowing and understanding good and evil. I may have even allowed Adam to persuade God to let him have just one harmless little bite of the forbidden fruit just to see what it tasted like, so he would understand clearly why it would be better for him to avoid it. But, fortunately, I did not write the scriptures, and I suppose Christendom is the better for it.

Back there in the infancy of the human race, Adam's relationship with God was like a tot's relationship to his parent. Even though the tot may not be able to comprehend the concept of danger or of drowning, he is simply ordered not to play in the traffic or jump into the deep end of the pool. I recall as a small child sometimes asking my father, "Why?" He would firmly respond, "It is not yours to wonder why." In retrospect, I realize that at the time I was too young to understand the whys and wherefores, and that it was best for me just to be unquestioningly obedient.

But as I began to grow up, my father began to respect my curiosity. He even began to encourage my need to know and often engaged me in debates which led to understanding. And although he sometimes tolerated disagreement, he never tolerated disobedience or insubordination. On rare occasions, he even allowed me to change his mind.

In Adam we see our childlike self, the time in our lives when we were to keep our mouths shut and do as we were told. In Abraham we see ourselves maturing to the point where we dare ask our Father the reason for his judgments, and even to bargain a bit over his dispensation of justice. As we continue to read, we see man maturing even more in his relationship with his heavenly Father. Moses often stood toe to toe with God, banging on the bargaining table and battling with him over the destiny of Israel. David poured out his heart to God in anger, fear, love, and praise. But after the outpouring, both Moses and David always recognized their proper place in relation to God: he was their Potter, they were his clay.

What kind of relationship does our God want to have with us? Does he want us simply to be unquestioning children? Does he want a little give and take? Does he want to be our father, our brother, our friend, our Potter, or what?

Jesus himself began to hint at the answer to that question when he asked his disciples to eat the bread and drink the wine that symbolized his body and his blood. He wants to live *in* us. He wants to be one flesh with us. He wants us to be his bride! He wants us to share all things with him, including our doubts, our fears, and our temptations. He wants an open and honest relationship with us, without ever forgetting that his bride, the church, is subject to her husband and that he is forever the Potter and we are forever the clay.

And the best part is that all we have to do is say, "I do!"

The Sojourner

Scripture: Genesis 19:1–9
Suggested Reading: Ephesians 2:11–22; 2 Peter 2:6–10

Being raised in a very fundamental home and church has its advantages. You get to know words and understand notions that the rest of the world can't comprehend. Not that the rest of the world doesn't understand sojourning. They understand the concept well, if not the word.

The families who live with soldiers know that wherever they go they are only sojourners, not citizens of the land where they have gone to serve their country. Pastors, too, know by experience the meaning of sojourning, being only temporary residents of the parish they serve. But what the rest of the world doesn't comprehend as we Christians comprehend is that we are only sojourners on this earth, and that our true home is . . . well, the hymn writer E. T. Cassel said it best:

> I am a stranger here, within a foreign land;
> My home is far away, upon a golden strand;
> Ambassador to be of realms beyond the sea,
> I'm here on business for my King.

We thought that Lot left Abraham to dwell, not sojourn, in the lush Jordan valley. Lot thought so too, but to the people of Sodom he was only a sojourner whom the native sons resented because he judged them and found them to be wicked. For one brief moment the righteous but self-serving nephew of Abraham was a stranger in a foreign land, an ambassador to Sodom, there on business for his King, condemning their sinful ways and trying to set them straight.

God calls us to be sojourners on this planet. We must be *in* the world, but not *of* the world, knowing full well that the natives here resent and despise us.

But what is the role of a sojourner?

Isabella Baumfree understood her role so well that when she went out to preach love for God and love for others, she renamed herself Sojourner Truth. She separated herself from a world that disregarded God and his command to love our neighbors as ourselves; she viewed herself as an ambassador from another land bringing a message of truth to the land of her sojourn.

And that is our task today. We are here to teach others that this world's store of goods and pleasures is nothing more than lies and empty promises, and to teach them that they can restore a right relationship with God and become fellow citizens of the kingdom of heaven and members of the household of Christ.

Again Cassel said it best:

My home is brighter far than Sharon's rosy plain,
Eternal light and joy throughout its vast domain;
My Sovereign bids me tell how mortals there may dwell,
And that's my business for my King.

This is the message that I bring,
A message angels fain would sing:
O be ye reconciled—thus saith my Lord and King—
O be ye reconciled to God!

Weary with Groping

Scripture: Genesis 19:10–11
Suggested Reading: Job 12:24–25; Psalms 107:40–43; Isaiah 9:2;
John 1:1–13

I subscribe to the *Biblical Archeology Review*. Even though that good publication is fairly scholarly in nature and often tromps about in intellectual territories that the Ph.D.'s have greedily reserved unto themselves, I sometimes get edified by certain discoveries and insights described in its articles. Often after I have read about things unearthed by the shores of Galilee, I feel that I have truly walked where Jesus walked.

But as often as they edify me, they disappoint me. Many of them delve with relentless tedium into the trifles of scripture as they try to disprove a point long accepted by faith as the truth of God. They weary themselves groping in the blindness of unbelief.

We all know what it is to weary ourselves groping. We've all had those moments when we've driven up to the toll booth and tried to find the right coins in a pocket strapped shut by a seat belt. We've had those moments when we've tried to find the car keys when we're already five minutes late leaving for work. We've had those moments when we've hunted for a gift for the friend who has everything. We've had those moments, as amateur scholars ourselves, when we've plundered the books on the library shelves or scanned the infinite sea of cyberspace searching for information for a paper we were assigned to write for a high school or college class. We've even had those moments when we've tried to come to grips with such mysteries as creation, eternity, or the virgin birth.

Lot's Sodomite brothers wearied themselves groping in the darkness after God took away their sight to keep them from having their way with his angels. Some scholars weary themselves groping in the dark caves of academia when God takes away their understanding and makes them wander in a pathless waste, groping in their darkness without a light. And sadly, multitudes of people in this world grope and grope in a futile search for a faith that works.

The good news is that we need not grope. The simple truth is that the light of God came into this world two millennia ago and taught us how to walk this earth and seek fulfillment with our eyes opened to the truth. Jesus, the Word, is the lamp unto our feet. He didn't tell us that in order to understand salvation we had to go to Israel and dig holes looking for shards of broken lamps that would light our way to the doorstep of God. He didn't tell us that we had to enroll in a seminary and study Hebrew, Greek, hermeneutics, and apologetics in order to bask in the sunlight of God's truth. He told us that in order to comprehend clearly the kingdom of God we had to become as little children, our minds unclouded by too much learning and our faith unpunctured by the darts of doubt that learning invariably hurls at us. We must only pray the simple prayer,

> Open my eyes that I may see
> Glimpses of truth thou hast for me;
> Place in my hands the wonderful key
> That shall unclasp and set me free.
>
> Silently now I wait for thee,
> Ready my God, thy will to see
> Open my eyes, Illumine me,
> Spirit divine!
>
> (Clara H. Scott, 1896)

Then, with the eyes of our souls wide open, we can dig our holes, pore through our books, and study to show ourselves approved by God, rightly dividing the Word of Truth.

... *Being Merciful to Him*

Scripture: Genesis 19:12–16
Suggested Reading: Isaiah 64; 1 Corinthians 12:1–10

Amazing grace!

We've all known bad people. I mean very bad people. We do our best just to love and leave the judging to God, but sometimes we encounter people who are so bad that we simply shake our heads in disbelief and silently consign them to hell.

If we limit our reading to the book of Genesis, we might be tempted to place Lot in that category of people. Imagine a man whose two virgin daughters were engaged to marry young men of the city. When the handsome angels spent the night at Lot's house, the perverts in the street banged on his door demanding that the angels come out and sport with them. Instead Lot offered them his two daughters to do with as they pleased.

How much of a wretch can a man become? And even after witnessing the miracle the angels performed in striking the Sodomites blind, he refused to accept them as agents of heaven and would not take their warning seriously. When he went with his sons-in-law to the people and urged them to leave the city, they thought he was joking. Then, in the morning, he still lingered. He wouldn't leave! He was so attached to his evil city that the angels had to seize him by the hand and drag him to safety!

Did he want to go? No, he wanted to remain an elder, sitting in the city gates, but the ministering angels wouldn't let him stay. They gripped his hand all the tighter and "brought him forth and set him outside the city." Why? Simply because the Lord had mercy on him.

Recently I was browsing in my local family bookstore looking for a book about grace. I was overwhelmed. There were books on prevenient grace, saving grace, justifying grace, irresistible grace, sanctifying grace, and any kind of grace a thoughtful mind might imagine. It was as if modern scholars had snipped at the Bible and the intellectual probings of Wesley, Calvin, Luther and other reformers, had cut grace up into little pieces, pasted them to the wall, and created a huge collage portraying the many facets of God's wonderful, marvelous, matchless grace.

One thing we are sure to discover when we study grace: our own sinfulness. And if we read enough books and articles about grace, we are sure to come to the conclusion that we are really not much better than old Lot himself. Even though we may never have offered our daughters to the wolves banging on our doors, reflection on our past reveals that we've made other offerings just as vile, and we cannot escape the conclusion that any righteousness we can conjure up for ourselves is nothing more than filthy rags to God.

It is then that we feel the angels tugging at our hand, pulling us away from the life of sin that has become our focus. We linger, but they tug a little harder, and we find that we cannot resist that tug. That's grace. That's God's simple, merciful, saving grace. That's . . .

> Amazing Grace, how sweet the sound
> That saved a wretch like me!
> I once was lost, but now am found;
> Was blind, but now I see.
>
> (John Newton)

And why? Simply because our God is a merciful God!

Flee to the Hills!

Scripture: Genesis 19:17–23
Suggested Reading: 1 Corinthians 1:4–9

*Y*esterday we saw God pour out a full measure of his saving grace upon Lot as he literally took him by the hand and dragged him out of Sodom. But even though Lot had experienced things that would have transformed normal people into obedient believers, he was so entrenched in his self-imposed mission to make his world a better place, that he still resisted God's call to flee to the hills, preferring instead to dwell in Zoar, another city on the plain.

Now, had I been God, I would have thrown up my hands in angry disgust and said, "OK then, foolish man, go to Zoar and see what happens!" Then I would have destroyed Zoar with Lot in it. After all, he had nothing more productive to do in life than sire people who would become thorns in the flesh to Abraham's children.

The world can be mighty thankful that I'm not God!

If I were God, a lot of things would have been done differently. When Adam and Eve violated my order by eating of the forbidden fruit, I would have simply struck them dead on the spot as I had threatened to do, then I would have created two new people and given them another chance to do it right. And I certainly would not have bothered sparing Israel when she heeded the advice of the ten foolish spies. I would have simply left them in the wilderness to be destroyed, either by nature or by savage men. The world can be mighty thankful that I'm not God.

In fact, *I'm* thankful that I'm not God. Were I God, I'd have consigned myself to the flames of hell long ago. When I think about it, I find that I'm a lot like Adam or the Israelites. Aren't we all? Haven't we all nibbled at forbidden fruit at one time or another just to see what it's like? Haven't we all gone where we wanted to go rather than where God told us to go? Haven't we all turned our backs on our land of promise because we feared to go there? Haven't we all made golden calves for ourselves and bowed down to them? Haven't we all played God just a little bit? Aren't we all thankful that God continues to love us and care for us in spite of our waywardness?

Lot is a real lesson in grace. First, God showered his grace on him by warning him of the impending destruction of the city. Then God continued to be gracious to him by taking him by the hand and leading him from the city. Then God poured more grace on him when he resisted going where God wanted him to go, and for his sake spared Zoar from the fire of heaven.

The scholars who fight and write about God's grace have invented terms such as *saving* and *irresistible*. In Lot's case we see both at the same time. God responded generously by permitting Lot to go to Zoar rather than to the hills. Whenever Lot acted outside the will of God, God responded by gracing him anyway. Lot could not resist or escape from God's grace no matter what he did. Even when he went his own foolish way, God's grace followed him and was there to care for him and to rescue him from his own stubbornness.

And the Israelites. Even though they resisted going where God wanted them to go, they spent forty years in the wilderness under his gracious protection. They couldn't resist his safekeeping no matter how hard they tried.

Thankfully, our gracious God is more faithful to us than we are to him.

What Was Their Sin?

Scripture: Genesis 19:24–26
Suggested Reading: Leviticus 18:22; Micah 6:8

In my youth, I never felt the need to apply the moral of the Sodom and Gomorrah story to myself. After all, I am not homosexual, nor have I ever tried to force my affections on someone who was unwilling. I have never felt that God would weigh me in the same balance with the Sodomites because I've never committed the kinds of sins they committed. Sure, I had plenty of sins of my own that I confessed and for which I've received forgiveness, but I was sure mine fell into the category of lesser infractions, rather than abominations.

I was confused, though, by one element of the story: the angels told both Abraham and Lot that the reason God was going to destroy Sodom was because there was a great "outcry" against the wicked people of that city. Did their neighbors cry out to God because the Sodomites were perverts or because they worshipped idols? No, all of their pagan neighbors did the same. Why would they cry out?

The Hebrew word translated in Genesis as "outcry" is used in other instances in the Bible to describe a cry of torment from an oppressed person or a painful plea from a victim of injustice. But who were the victims of the Sodomites? Whom were they abusing? The revelation of their true sin came as quite a shock to me. Though I had read the book of Ezekiel before, what he had to say about the sin of Sodom had never quite registered with me:

Behold, this was the guilt of your sister Sodom. She and her daugh-
ters had pride, surfeit of food, and prosperous ease, but they did not
aid the poor and needy. They were haughty and did abominable
things before me, therefore I removed them. (Ezekiel 16:49–50)

Their sexual abominations are mentioned almost as an after-thought. The real reason God destroyed their city was because he had blessed them with plenty, but in their pride they refused to share their blessings with their needy neighbors.

The people of Sodom lived in a lush, well-watered valley that reminded Moses of the Garden of Eden. Their crops always flour-ished and their livestock was always well fed. The people pros-pered in a community that had an abundance of food, but outside their green valley the nomads roamed the territory trying to feed their flocks on the scanty grasses that struggled to grow in the arid hills. And their neighbors were not nearly as prosperous. They and their herds often suffered from lack of food and water. When their land was parched, they could look down into the Valley of Siddim and see the greenery below, but when they begged for aid, they were turned away. It was these victims of famine who uttered the cries of anguish that were heard in heaven. They were the vic-tims of injustice who shouted their painful pleas to the skies above. The people of Sodom heard those desperate pleas, but turned a deaf ear to their needy neighbors.

The pantry of my country home is well stocked, and I know that there are children in the city who are going to bed without supper. I know that they cry out in hunger during the night, and that their cries ascend to heaven. Like the Sodomites, I live in prosperous ease, but I am doing precious little to aid the poor and needy.

Will the Lord judge me as he judged them? Am I as guilty?

The Smoke of the Land

Scripture: Review Genesis 19:27–29
Suggested Reading: Review Ezekiel 16:49–50

Hollywood turned the story of Sodom and Gomorrah into a spectacular movie. Near the end, as fire and brimstone poured from the sky, sinners scurried in all directions to escape the flaming debris that was falling all around them. Billowing fireballs engulfed the tall towers of Sodom as bodies, bricks, and fiery timbers came crashing to the ground. When the terror ended, the great cities of the plains lay reduced to piles of smoldering rubble. And Abraham stood on a hill far away and watched the smoke of the land rising to heaven like the smoke of a furnace.

Images from that movie painted themselves on the backdrop of my mind as I watched television the morning the terrorists took down the twin towers of the World Trade Center. I couldn't help but draw a parallel between the two events. The cameras caught glimpses of bodies falling to the ground and people dodging the flying debris and fleeing the giant clouds of dust that chased them through the corridors of Gotham. Later the long lens zoomed in from its perch on a distant hill and gave us the same view of New York that Abraham had of Sodom, and for weeks we watched the smoke of the city rise like the smoke of a furnace.

Is the greatest city in the United States a twenty-first century Sodom? Was the outcry that brought the wrath of God down on the cities of the plain the same outcry that sent our great towers crashing to the ground?

From the slums of Chicago to the villages in Rwanda and the filthy streets of Calcutta, starving people cry out for a crust of bread as we fat Americans sit in theaters swigging overpriced root beer and devouring five dollar sacks of popcorn while we watch sordid scenes of violence and human carnage leap from the big screen to entertain us. We lounge by our heated pools, sip martinis and drive our expensive cars to flashy malls while the disenfranchised of the world hurl stones at their oppressors. The hungry and the landless have labeled us "the great Satan" because, among other things, we have "pride, surfeit of food, and prosperous ease" but do not do enough to aid the poor and needy.

Those who study such matters agree that there is enough food in the world to feed everyone, if only we would distribute it properly and not hoard it. Intelligent observers know that if Catholics and Protestants, Jews and Palestinians, blacks and whites, Hutus and Tutsis, Muslims and Christians, and all other groups would abandon their bigotry, the peoples of the earth could live together in peace, harmony, and comfort.

We have labeled the terrorists who flew the planes into our towers as cowards and savages. Perhaps they were. But killing them one by one or in lots of a hundred will only breed more of them unless we eradicate the root cause that drives them to such barbaric acts.

When we weary of war and when the last wisp of smoke from our burning cities has stained God's beautiful blue skies, we may look inside our souls and ask if we have committed the sin of Sodom and brought the wrath of God down upon ourselves.

In the great battle between the forces of good and evil, are we sure we're on the right side? Do we judge ourselves to be righteous, when in the eyes of God we are selfish sinners who have wallowed in our blessings to the anguish of our hungry neighbors?

The Consequences of Sin

Scripture: Genesis 19:30–35

A fine Christian brother once confided to me that in the folly of youth he violated God's ordinances by taking to bed a woman not his wife, and as a result contracted a venereal disease. Through God's blessing of medicine he was cured of the disease, and through God's good grace he was forgiven, healed of the nagging guilt, and assured his place in heaven. But the consequences of his sin remained: he became sterile and went through life childless.

Tears come to his eyes when he talks of it. He often thinks about the little boys and girls who never sat on his lap to listen to stories or be rocked to sleep. He knows that though God has drowned his sin in the sea of forgetfulness, the awful consequences of his action remain his to bear. If only the tempter had never come to him. If only he'd restrained himself. If only . . . If only . . .

God warned us of that principle long ago. If only Abraham had left Lot in Haran as God directed him. If only Lot had approached his sons-in-law in a serious rather than a joking mood when warning them of the destruction approaching Sodom. If only Moab and Ben-ammi had never been born, the destiny of Israel may have been very different. If only . . .

We are all inclined to look back on the course of our lives and dwell on the multitude of "if onlys" that plague us. Many of our bad decisions have nothing to do with morality or with the laws of God: if only I'd put my money in Polaroid or IBM. Some are trivial events with serious results: If only I'd turned on Division Street as I usually do rather than going to Monroe, the terrible accident that crippled my friend may never have happened. But whether or not they are moral decisions, or whether or not they are major decisions, we have to live with the results. Forgiveness does not mean that the consequences are taken away. The sin may be erased, but the after effects continue to plague us.

Not only do the results of our forgiven iniquities continue to plague us, but they often impact our innocent loved ones. When God said that he would visit our iniquities upon others, he wasn't kidding. My Christian brother's good wife also went childless because of his sin. And since they were both only children, their parents were never blessed with grandchildren.

He used to ask me, "If God forgives sin, why doesn't he also erase its consequences?" But as he grew in wisdom, he came to understand that just as by God's grace his sin is forgiven, by God's grace the effects linger on. Think of what would happen if the consequences of sin would vanish with its forgiveness. All criminals who repented would be freed. All adulterers with persistent venereal diseases would be cured when they fell to their knees to seek forgiveness. This would be good? Think further. What a cheap bargain repentance would become, and sin would be worth the price.

When we repent, we are empowered by the Holy Spirit to turn our back on sin and begin to walk righteously before God. Sanctification is the great premium of repentance and forgiveness. God's plan is for us to live in a spiritual promised land, forgiven yet scarred with the effects of our waywardness, graced to learn how to "go and sin no more." But the scars of our sin stand as mute warning to ourselves and to others that even though God forgives us and opens heaven's eternal doors, on this earth we always reap what we have sown.

Turning Evil into Good

Scripture: Genesis 19:36–38
Suggested Reading: Ruth 1:1–5; Matthew 1:1–16; Romans 3:5–8

*R*ecently in a Bible Study I led, a young man testified that in his life God had turned evil into good. He and his wife of sixteen years had failed to preserve their marital bliss, and each could serve up only misery to the other. When one of their two children became troublesome, each blamed the other, and as they compounded their blame, the child compounded his troublesomeness. When they reached their human limit of tolerance, they separated and eventually divorced. Since the divorce, the entire family has built new lives. He and his former wife are both happily remarried and both children are faring well. To an amazing extent, relationships have been mended and animosity has evaporated.

How wonderful it is that our loving God has a way of turning evil into good. The original sin of Adam and Eve has resulted in God's gracious plan of salvation and the opportunity to have Christ living in our hearts. Some have even come to call it the "fortunate fall." As we look out through the opening of that little cave in the hills beyond Zoar, in the distance we can see the sin of Lot and his daughters transforming itself into the wonderful story of Ruth, the life of David, and eventually the birth of Jesus. All of them traced their roots back to the sin in that cave. And later in our meditations we will see how the sins of Israel resulted in many good things, especially the coming of the Messiah. We could go on and on with this theme. God does turn evil into good.

Although it is wonderful that God does that, we should beware lest we turn that great truth into an excuse for sinning. The fact that Jesus emerged from a lineage whose seed was planted in that notorious cave does not justify the behavior of Lot and his daughters. The world of good that came from Israel's Diaspora does not justify her history of sin. The good that resulted from my friend's troubles does not justify his divorce.

Paul pointed out to the Romans that our wickedness reveals the *justice* of God. What is God's justice? Simple. God's justice is the punishment of our sin in the crucifixion of Jesus and the reconciling power of the Holy Spirit in our hearts. God's justice is the ultimate good in this evil world, and if we had never sinned, we could never know the wonder of his justice.

Yesterday we noticed that God in his mercy has found a way to forgive the guilt of our sin, but that we still have to suffer the consequences. Adam's sin has had grave consequences for our world. Lot's sin plagued the Israelites for generations, and the effect of Abraham's sin still tortures the world today. God may well forgive Adam, Abraham, Lot, my young friend, me and you for the sins we commit, but the consequences linger. The justice and the good come only because we have a merciful God who loves us.

It will always be better if we had never sinned in the first place. If Lot's daughters had not enticed their father into that cave, the Moabites would have not been there to harass Israel, and though we would have missed the beautiful story of Ruth, the psalms of David and the wisdom of Solomon, God would certainly have planned another lineage for the Savior. And if Adam had not been disobedient in the Garden, we would never have needed a Savior, God would not have had to watch his beloved Son die on a cross, and the human race might still be living in an unblemished paradise.

School of Hard Knocks

Scripture: Genesis 20:1–7
Suggested Reading: Hebrews 11:8–10

If experience is the master teacher, we must be awfully poor learners!

After I've devoured more than my share of pizza and prime rib, I show high numbers on the bathroom scale and my cholesterol level hits a new peak. I experience discomfort and shortness of breath. My doctor shakes his finger at me and predicts my doom unless I repent. So, I suffer self-denial at the dinner table and the agony of exercise until the numbers are back down where they belong. Experience has taught me a valuable lesson.

But what do I do with that lesson? If I am at all intelligent, I continue to eat moderately and exercise responsibly, holding those numbers within a reasonable range. But am I a good student of that greatest of all teachers? No, fool that I am, I reward my accomplishment by returning to those tables of abundance where those luscious morsels again lure me to overeat. Then what happens? Those numbers slowly edge back up, and eventually I start the whole painful process over again.

It's somewhat of a comfort to know that other poor students sometimes fail to learn the lessons experience teaches. Especially when it comes to spiritual matters. More than that, it is very comforting to know that even the great heroes of faith failed to learn from the error of their ways and repeated their mistakes. So, as a sinner who has often failed to learn from experience, I am in good company.

Back when we first met Abraham, he escaped from a famine by retreating to the land of plenty on the banks of the Nile. The Pharaoh saw and desired Abraham's wife, Sarah, and in order to escape the possibility of death, Abraham told a little white lie and passed his wife off as his sister and gave her to the king. Serious error in judgment. Serious lack of faith in the God who had promised him fatherhood, longevity, and prosperity. okay, so he made one mistake. His loving heavenly Father mercifully minimized the consequences and taught him, by the experience of a mistake, to trust in God.

But did he learn from that mistake in Egypt? Obviously not, because when he met the king of Gerar down in the Negev, faith again yielded to fear and he offered Abimelech his "sister" in exchange for his life. The same foolish mistake he made before, but now it is less forgivable, because he should have learned from the lesson God tried to teach him back in Egypt. Were there unhappy consequences? The Bible doesn't tell us, but his relationship with his wife must have suffered. I know mine would if I didn't treasure her honor as much as I treasure my life.

But hold on. I've got to be careful drawing comfort from the fact that our heroes of faith had their foibles and that God went easy on them. I don't think that's the lesson God is trying to teach us. In the lives of many giants of the scripture including Abraham, Sarah, Jacob, Rebecca, David, and Solomon, God is trying to teach us what we should *not* do. He uses their experience to give us many good examples to follow, but also shows us the consequences of their sin.

Abraham was a novice in walking with God, so God gave him a little latitude. David, on the other hand, had much revelation to rely on for guidance, so his sin cost him dearly. Today we have both the scriptures and the power of the Holy Spirit living in our hearts.

So, what level of obedience is required of us?

Prayer Power

Scripture: Genesis 20:8–18
Suggested Reading: James 5:13–18; Matthew 6:5–8;
1 Thessalonians 5:17

few years ago when I went through a serious surgery, a call went out from my church to the prayer warriors asking God to guide the hands of the surgeon and to give me the strength to survive.

I missed one Sunday service and was back in my pew the second week after the operation, feeling pretty good under the circumstances. I thanked my brothers and sisters and testified that I felt the power of their prayers surging through my body as I rapidly recovered.

The next week I felt so good that I started doing things I shouldn't have done. I exerted myself beyond the doctor's recommendation and resumed normal activity too soon. I felt so good that I dragged my bag of clubs out to the driving range and started blasting the ball as far as I could, slicing it way out into the eighteenth fairway. As a result of my excess energy, I suffered a mild setback.

But instead of getting grumpy, I made a joke of it. I laughingly blamed the prayer warriors for "over praying" me, for praying me more full of good health than my system could handle. I've since warned them, again with tongue in cheek, that when praying for others they should use the vast power of prayer gently, lest God deliver too much healing power all at once.

But, setting levity aside, there is a basic truth here. James tells us that the prayer of a righteous person "availeth much." In other words, when God's people kneel to pray, he stoops to listen. He isn't deaf. We don't have to shout. We are told not to pray loudly or proudly or to use pretty words. We're told simply to shut ourselves up in the presence of God and to pray gently, without ceasing. As with the art of golf, if we reach back with all our strength and try to blast our prayers to heaven, they may go far in the wrong direction and take us where we dread to go. Just as God speaks to us in a still, small voice, we can speak to him in like manner. The hour of prayer should be sweet and gentle.

One of the nicest things about prayer, besides the joy of abiding in sweet communion with our Lord, is what it does for our relationships. We develop our relationships by sharing experiences. We have golfing partners, fishing cronies, teammates, classmates, colleagues, and army buddies. They are our friends because we share with them some of our more meaningful moments. But the common experience that can weld our friendships together into an unbreakable loving bond is the fellowship of prayer.

Look what it did for Abraham and Abimelech. At the beginning of their relationship they were rivals in a love triangle. It was the basest of all relationships in that one almost became an adulterer and the other a cuckold. But after confessing their sin and joining together in a prayer of faith, their hearts were bound together and they became good neighbors, sharing the healing that God effects only through the prayers of the righteous.

Blessed be the tie that binds
Our hearts in Christian love;
The fellowship of kindred minds
Is like to that above.

Before our Father's throne
We pour our ardent prayers;
Our fears, our hopes, our aims are one,
Our comforts and our cares.

(John Fawcett, 1782)

What Troubles You?

Scripture: Genesis 21:1–19
Suggested Reading: Matthew 10:32–33; Romans 10:8–10

The Lord often comes to us asking a question to which he already knows the answer.

He certainly knew where Adam was when he asked, "Where are you Adam?" When the glorified, risen Jesus appeared to the ten startled disciples and asked, "What troubles you?" he certainly knew what their problem was.

It's no secret why he does this: he wants us to verbalize an answer. From Adam he wanted a confession of guilt, from the disciples he wanted an expression of their conviction, and from Hagar he wanted a confession of faith in the promise he made when he first came to her and promised to make her son Ishmael into a nation so great it could not be numbered.

It is important to the Lord that we confess him with our lips. He made that point early in the scripture and again near the end.

I have friends who have attended church with me for many years. They are faithful, as far as I know, in their giving. To the best of my knowledge they don't steal things, commit adultery, lie, or hurt others. They go to church regularly, serve on committees, and receive holy communion. They are really nice people, and I am flattered that they call me their friend.

Yet, in all the time I've spent with them, I've never heard them confess, except when they are singing a hymn or reciting a creed in the worship service, that Jesus Christ is Lord. I have never heard them say with their lips that they love the Lord, that he is their

Savior, or that they belong to him. That troubles me. My job is just to witness and to love, and I'm happy to leave the judging to God, but it concerns me that they do not witness for him verbally even though they are fully aware of his warning that if we fail to confess him before men he will not confess us before his Father on Judgment Day.

Many wonderful people I know say that it just isn't their gift to get up and talk before others. They declare that their lives are their sermons and that they let their behavior talk for them. Now it's true that our actions should be silent confessions of our faith, but it bothers me that these very same people who find it impossible to declare their allegiance to the Lord have no trouble declaring their allegiance to their favorite football team on New Year's Day or to their *Alma Mater* each year when March madness comes around. They have no trouble voicing their opinion on politics, the economy, the trouble with the Tigers, rumors about their neighbors, or the latest judgmental gossip in the church. But when the talk turns to faith, their religion suddenly becomes a private matter not to be discussed with others.

Unfortunately, the threat of eternal damnation isn't motivation enough to get some people to open their mouths for the Lord. I understand that. For a long time it wasn't motivation enough for me. I, too, was one of the silent believers even though I knew those verses well that told me that if I kept my mouth shut, my advocate at the judgment would not vouch for me before that court. But, fortunately for me, the Lord engineered a moment in my life that literally forced me to confess my faith publicly. Once I broke the initial barrier, it became easy to keep talking for him.

I pray that the Lord blesses my friends as he blessed me.

An Expert with the Bow

Scripture: Genesis 21:20–21
Suggested Reading: Romans 9:6–24

We learned a little about Ishmael even before he was born. Back when the pregnant Hagar fled from the angry mistress she had offended with her arrogance, the angel of the Lord came to her and prophesied that her son would be "a wild ass of a man" who would live his life at war with all of his relatives. Doesn't our sense of justice cringe at that prophecy? It just doesn't seem fair that a little boy would have no choice but to grow up and, through no choice of his own, be destined by God to be a "wild ass of a man," in constant conflict with his kin and his neighbors.

And it doesn't end with Ishmael. Later, we will see that there are certain people who are given life by God for the specific purpose of being bad people and presumably to spend eternity in hell. God hated Esau even before he was born. God raised Pharaoh up purely for the purpose of enslaving the children of Israel, for suffering the torment of the plagues, and for ultimate death in the Red Sea. Later Judas came to life for just one purpose: to betray his Lord and Master.

To top it off, God even equips his "evil" ones to do their dirty work. God was "with" Ishmael and gave him the talent to become an expert archer so he could more effectively shoot his brothers. God protected Esau until his seed could become the savage nation that constantly harassed Israel. God gave Pharaoh his power and later empowered Nebuchadnezzar, whom he called his deputy, to destroy his holy city and tear down his magnificent temple. Why would a just, loving God act like that? It just doesn't seem right.

Paul gives the answer.

Who am I, a mere man, to sass God like that? He is the creator of the universe and everything in it. Where was I when he harnessed the unimaginable power of a million suns and molded a million solar systems into a beautiful, intricate, unified machine? He is the Potter, and I am his clay, to be molded into anything he chooses, whether it be a thing of beauty to grace a shelf in an exquisite gallery or a pot to transport waste to the dunghill.

The sooner I learn that, the better.

Recently I heard of an art exhibit that featured a clay chamber pot that Napoleon used when he was in exile on Elba. I'll bet that if that clay had had a mind of its own when it was still wet on the wheel, it would have chosen to be anything but a chamber pot. And the same potter probably crafted any number of other chamber pots that ended up as shards in the trash. Only one survived to become a priceless object of admiration.

We never know what God has in store for us. The drunk had to be the drunk before God could use him in the mission, but he may have always remained the drunk. The choice is God's.

It's not our business to second guess our maker. It's only our business to sing sincerely:

Have thy own way Lord, have thine own way!
Thou art the Potter, I am the clay:
Mold me and make me after thy will,
while I am waiting, yielded and still.

(Adelaide A. Pollard, 1906)

With You in All You Do . . .

Scripture: Genesis 21:22–34
Suggested Reading: Matthew 28:20; Hebrews 13:5

*G*od is with you in all that you do. . . . What an astonishing thing for Abimelech to say! He observed the hand of God in Abraham's life. Not just in the big things, not just in the good things, but in *all* things. Even bad things. Stop and think about it.

Some years before, Abraham did a bad thing: he sold his wife to Pharaoh. But contrary to all human logic, she came out of Pharaoh's house untainted and Abraham came out rich. It shouldn't have happened that way. God should have punished Abraham for his faithlessness and mendacity, and Pharaoh should have had his vengeance on the trickster. But, God was with Abraham.

And since that little ruse worked so well in Egypt, he decided to try it again in Gerar of Canaan. He sold her to King Abimelech. Again she was not violated. Again he gained a lot of wealth. Again, it should not have happened that way, and it could not have happened that way unless God had taken command of the moment and controlled the heart of Abimelech and filled him with fear and respect for Abraham's God. Again, God was with Abraham.

Now these are not tricks we should try at home. God did not preserve these moments in the scripture with an implicit command for us to go and do likewise. If I were to pull the stunt that Abraham pulled, I'm sure I would incur the everlasting wrath of my wife as well as the wrath of God. And I'm equally sure I would not emerge with great blessings.

So, what should we learn from these events? The answer lies in the words of Abimelech, "God is with you in all that you do."

Now, I'm living in a different age, so God is not going to be as lenient with me as he was with Abraham. I have the full revelation of scripture that Abraham did not have, and, in addition, I have the Holy Spirit dwelling in me showing me the way I should live. So, if I commit a faithless act, I'm sure to be punished and possibly held up to the world as an example of how not to behave. And my life is not being recorded in the scripture either as a life to be emulated or a life to be scorned, so I'm sure to suffer the natural consequences of my behavior.

But wouldn't it be nice if someone would look at me and say, "God is with him in all that he does"? Wouldn't it be nice if I, like Enoch, walked with God? Wouldn't it be nice if I, like Noah, found favor in the eyes of the Lord, was reckoned as righteous, and did all that God commanded me to do? Wouldn't it be nice if I, like Abraham, turned my back on all I possessed in obedience to his call? Wouldn't it be nice if I were as loyal as Ruth to my family and as attentive as Mary to my Master's words? And wouldn't it be nice if I, like Jesus, loved even the least of my brothers enough to die for them? Maybe if I pleased God as the heroes of faith did, people would be able to say of me, "God is with him in all that he does."

The truth is that I am a sinner. But do you know what? God *is* with me in all that I do. Not because I qualify as a hero of faith, and not because he's using me as an example for others, but just because he loves me, has accepted me, has forgiven me, and has promised he would always be with me. He loves me enough to bless me when I need blessing and to let me suffer the consequences of my errors when I have been disobedient. But in all that I do, in blessing, and in suffering, I am never alone. Abimelech's witness to a monumental truth stands as solid testimony that God is always with me and will never forsake me.

Early in the Morning

Scripture: Genesis 22:1–3
Suggested Reading: Luke 9:57–62

God has blessed me with an extraordinary ability to enjoy sleep. Particularly in the morning when everyone else is rising and shining. I've never felt any fondness for the garbage collector who raises a clatter at dawn clanging garbage cans against his truck, nor for the happy bugler who reviles sleepers with that intrusive tune he calls reveille. I am motivated to get out of bed early only if some monumental pleasure awaits me.

Not Abraham. The day before God had ordered him to take his son, the son of promise that he had waited a lifetime to sire, and go up the mountain to offer him as a burnt offering.

I don't know what Abraham did during that long night. God has allowed Abraham to keep that a secret. So I don't know how many times he went to the lad's room just to look at him as he slept. I don't know how long he sat at his son's bedside, stroking his head. I don't know how he anguished at the thought of what he had to do, though I do know that he loved his son, and, if he were at all like me, was tormented at the prospect of losing him. God only tells me that Abraham got up early in the morning to do the business that he had called him to do, no matter how unpleasant.

Abraham must have been a morning man. He got up early in the morning to climb the hill and see the smoking ruins of Sodom and Gomorrah. He got up early in the morning to send Hagar off into exile. Whenever Abraham set his mind to do something or was ordered by God to do something, he didn't procrastinate. He got right to it. Such a morning man stands tall as a role model for us. Especially for me.

Jesus must have loved Abraham because he was a morning man too. He got up early in the morning to go to his favorite place of prayer. In fact, he railed against procrastinators. He said that anyone who set his hand to the plow ought to turn his whole attention to plowing immediately. If he paused to look back he wasn't fit for the kingdom of God.

Now, the Lord isn't against resting. He enjoyed taking time off from his ministry just to relax and refresh himself. In fact, when he created the universe, he took the seventh day off to rest and *ordered* us to follow his example. He created us to wear out. Rest is a necessity, but it has to be earned. And its purpose is not primarily for enjoyment; its purpose is restoration so we can get back to our work and do it better, with more vigor, spirit, and competency.

Our Lord wants us to be task oriented, not pleasure oriented. He put us here for a purpose. He gave us the work that we do for a living, and he called us to be his disciples. In everything we do, he wants us to be like Abraham; he wants us to get up early in the morning and . . .

> Work, for the night is coming,
> Work through the morning hours;
> Work while the dew is sparkling,
> Work mid springing flowers.
> Work when the day grows brighter,
> Work in the glowing sun;
> Work, for the night is coming,
> When man's work is done.
> (Anna Walker Coghill, 1854)

... And God Will Provide

Scripture: Genesis 22:4–8
Suggested Reading: John 1:29; Hebrews 11:8–10

A really mysterious thing happens at my house. Whenever I slip into my big leather recliner in the loft to sneak a short nap in the afternoon, just as I begin to drift off a signal goes out from somewhere to someone informing them that they should call me on the phone. And when the sudden, loud ring of the phone jars me out of my reverie, I clench my fists and shout, "How do they know?" The phone may lie silent for three days, but as soon as I nod off, someone gets the inspiration to call me. It could be my son or just some peddler breaking the news to me that I have been pre-approved for a wonderful, low-interest credit card. But some devious mind out there knows that I've just snuggled down and should be awakened.

Knowledge comes to us in unfathomable ways. Mary Ann will watch me wire a new light switch or countersink a screw into a piece of wood. "How do you know how to do that?" she asks. And I confess that I don't know how I know. "I don't remember my dad ever teaching me," I say, "and I don't remember reading it in a book. Maybe it just comes with being a guy. Maybe it's knowledge that has been programmed into my genes from before the foundations of the earth."

How did Abraham know that the Lord would provide the lamb for the offering? The record states that God only told him that he was to offer his only son on the altar as a sacrifice. Was he lying to young Isaac so the boy wouldn't know until they got to the top of

Mount Moriah that he was to be the offering? No use causing the lad undue stress at this point. Maybe he would rebel and run off? Then where would Abraham be?

No, I doubt that he was just being facetious or trying to cover up the truth of the plan. Though the Bible doesn't tell us what Abraham knew or didn't know, I think he had some premonition that something wonderful was going to happen.

God had promised him that through Isaac his descendants would be named, and I think he expected God to honor that promise. God promised him that through his descendants all the families of the earth would be blessed, and I think he expected a miracle. Then again, maybe God gave him some hazy vision of wonders yet to come because we know, although he lived in tents, he looked forward to living in a city with foundations, a city built by God himself. I have no idea how he knew that. Maybe God programmed that insight into his genes before history began.

I'm very grateful that God gave some people prophetic visions of the future. Without the visions he gave to Isaiah, Ezekiel, Daniel, Paul, John, and the other seers, how would we know of the rapturous wonders we will experience in the future, of our resurrection, of our being taken up to the New Jerusalem, of our wedding feast, of our place in the hallelujah choir, and of our eternal inheritance?

Now I don't really believe that when I lie down to sneak an afternoon nap a signal goes out from some mysterious source that inspires someone out there to give me a ring. It just seems like that. The coincidence is uncanny. And I'm sure I learned somehow from someone how to wire a switch and countersink a screw. I've just forgotten how I've come to know those things.

But I do know by the power of the Holy Spirit within me that the Word of God is true, that his promises are sure, and that the visions of his prophets will someday come to pass.

In the Shade of the Tree

Scripture: Genesis 22:9–24
Suggested Reading: John 6:31–35

I doubt if anything can be added to the myriad of sermons that have been preached and the multitudes of books and articles that have been written on this chapter. Abraham has been nearly deified as a godly man for his willingness to offer his only son as an atonement for sin. Isaac has been lifted up as an early hint of the sacrifice that is to come under the new covenant. The chapter has been hailed as prophetic for picturing the promised Messiah as the Lamb of God.

Historians have pointed out that Mount Moriah is one of the hills upon which Jerusalem was built, and had Abraham been able to see through time he might have seen Solomon's temple on the very spot where he built his altar and the hill of Calvary just a stone's throw away. Poets have pondered the unrecorded thoughts of father and son as they trudged up that mountain on their way to becoming heroes of faith, and about the relief each must have felt as they returned to Beersheba with the renewed promise ringing in their ears.

Beersheba must have been a wonderful place. A well watered pastureland at the southern edge of Palestine, Beersheba has been billed throughout history as the border town of the Promised Land and a safe haven for embattled refugees from the north. Today it stands in our memory as an altar, a judgment seat, a sanctuary, a fort, and a religious center. But to Abraham it was a cool drink of water and a tamarisk tree in whose shade he could sit and watch his son grow.

Out in my yard I have an old hand pump that draws icy water from the well. An old tin cup hangs from a chain fastened to the pump. Next to the pump is a comfortable old Adirondack chair where I sit in the shade of an oak tree in the heat of the day sipping cold water from that tin cup. With the sun behind me, I can see tiny insects streaming through its rays as the breeze stirs them from their perches in the trees and bushes. Sometimes I wonder if old Abraham ever sat beside his well under the tamarisk tree that he had planted there and listened to it whisper in the breeze as he watched the cicadas and other insects feed on its sweet exudations. If he did, he may have witnessed the beginning of one of the most significant miracles of the age.

Some people who get paid for figuring out how miracles happen believe that the manna the Israelites ate in the wilderness somehow traces its beginnings back to the tamarisk trees that grow in abundance in Palestine. Billions of little bugs, they say, ate the sweet substance that oozed from those trees, then flew south to the Sinai Peninsula and secreted their precious cargo of honeydew that evaporated into little flakes and covered the ground in an amount sufficient to feed the tribes of Israel on their march to the Promised Land. Now I don't know if that is true or not. As far as I'm concerned, God might just as well have created that manna out of nothing, like he did the earth, and thrown it down in handfuls right in the people's path. But there's something touching and compelling about the possibility that Abraham, fresh from his monumental experience on Mount Moriah in which he caught a fleeting glimpse of the Bread of Life, could now sit under his tree and catch a glimpse of the marvelous manna that was to feed his family generations later as they suffered for their faithlessness in the desert.

And I wonder if God gave him a faint vision of the future the day he planted that tree and let him look down the tunnel of history and watch its sap transformed into bread from heaven in the wilderness, and finally into the Bread of Life on which I am privileged to feed every day.

. . . To Mourn for Sarah

Scripture: Genesis 23
Suggested Reading: Hebrews 11:11; 1 Peter 3:1–6

If Christian historians have anything to feel guilty about, they should feel guilty about forgetting Sarah. We have so much to feel guilty about that we really don't need anything new, but perhaps we should mourn the fact that we have relegated memory of Sarah to the service entrance of our minds when we should have cast her as one of the heroes of our faith, worthy of a special statue in the front vestibule. Sarah had her foibles, it's true, but God didn't forget her.

Neither did Peter. Nearly two thousand years after she died, God inspired Peter to remember her to the Christian world as a holy lady worthy of serving as a role model for the rest of redeemed womanhood.

When she made her vow to be a loving wife to Abraham, she had no idea that he would one day take her by the hand and lead her from her comfortable apartments in Ur and Haran to the dusty tents of Palestine. I can't believe that she didn't set up some kind of howl when he uprooted her from her life as the wife of a successful city businessman and dragged her into the rugged world of the nomadic goat herder; most women would, probably with some justification. But in the end she followed, obedient even to Abraham's most foolish and faithless demands.

When she married Abraham, she undoubtedly had well-founded expectations for the kind of life they were to live, and when her husband informed her of the shocking new plans laid out by a brand new God she had never heard of, she was probably disappointed. Maybe even mad.

But God rewarded her in the end for giving up the good life she had come to know. He memorialized her in a whole chapter of scripture, an honor that had never before nor would ever again be accorded to any other woman, not even the mother of Jesus. She is the only woman whose age is recorded in the Bible. She is the only woman whose death and burial consumes an entire chapter.

Sarah is the Mary of the Old Testament. She gave miraculous birth to a promised son. Not even the blessed virgin who bore the Son of God had her age or death recorded. She simply vanished from the pages of scripture without fanfare.

Sarah must have been a wonderful mother. Her son Isaac loved her so much that after she died he refused to be comforted until the lovely Rebekah came to be his wife.

It was important for men of Abraham's time to maintain the tradition of their fathers. They built family burial vaults and preserved the succession of generations by preserving the bones of the sons next to the bones of the fathers. Abraham broke that tradition and established a new order and a new nation by opening a new burial ground in a new land.

He bought his first and only piece of property in the Promised Land solely to have a place to bury his beloved wife. Sarah was the first to be laid to rest in that new land, but she would not be the last. Next to her would eventually lie her husband, her son, and even grandchildren and great grandchildren. But she lived a full life, she finished the work God gave her to do, and it was time for her to pass the maternal torch to a new generation of women.

May the hero of faith rest in peace.

A Bride for Isaac

Scripture: Genesis 24:1–9

Isaac had grown to the age of thirty-seven, and was of proper age to take a wife. His mother had recently died and he was still mourning her death. He and his father needed a woman around the tent to tend to the womanly things of the household, and, if God's promise of a nation was to come true, they needed a woman to mother the children of Isaac who would be heir to that promise.

Too bad Sarah had already died. How helpful she would have been in teaching her daughter-in-law the art of being a proper wife for her beloved son! Certainly she would not, in any way, have come between Isaac and his wife or have meddled in their relationship or their parenting. The babies would need a grandma. God might have left her here for a few years yet, at least until the new wife got her household firmly established. Oh well, God does know best.

If any of us were to find ourselves in Abraham's position today, we would simply urge the lad to go out and find a good wife for himself, one of whom his mother would have been proud. We would be more interested in her potential than her background, though we certainly could not ignore the traits she might carry in her genes. We would be more interested in her character than her looks, though we certainly could not ignore the physical traits she might pass on to our grandchildren. The question of her national origin could wait. It wouldn't be important. We could raise the question in a moment of idle curiosity when the conversation needed prodding.

But with Abraham it was different. In those days the parents chose mates for their children. Although we have no record of God telling him not to mingle his Semitic blood with the blood of Ham, the touch of prophet in him knew that someday in the future it would be important to God's plan that his heirs be identified as purely Jewish. So, he had to pick a wife for Isaac from among his own people.

But how? Should he go himself? Out of the question. He was too old to travel the six hundred miles to Haran. Anyhow, if he were to go on such a long trip, who would tend to the business? Besides, he had no will to go back to his people now that he had separated himself from them. He had set his "hand to the plow," as one of his future heirs would put it. Occasional news of their well being was good enough for him.

Should he send Isaac? Also out of the question. A compelling spirit in him declared that Isaac should not set his foot outside the Promised Land for any reason. What if he liked the old country? What if his wife would urge him to stay? After all, it was common to pay for a wife with labor. What if he were to die while Isaac was away? Besides, boys just don't go out and get their own wives. He had to send someone else. But whom should he send?

Could he spare his head man, Eliezer, his Syrian servant? After all, he was a Semite who knew the traditions. And since he was with the family back in Haran, he would know the people and they would know him. Yes, Eliezer was the man for the job. But wait! Could he be trusted? After all, he was now disinherited. Had Isaac never been born, Eliezer would have been heir to all that Abraham owned. Of course he could be trusted! Let the thought perish! He'd been with the family all his life. Look how he tended so carefully to the boy when he was small. Yes, he was the man for the job.

So, the trusted servant was sent to court a bride for the father's only son. Ring a bell?

A Little Gift...

Scripture: Genesis 24:10–53
Suggested Reading: Matthew 10:37–38; Mark 10:29–30

As we've noticed before, God has wonderful ways of letting us peek for a moment at the future he has planned for us. He uses models of prior times as prototypes of events to come. Often, as we read in the Old Testament, we are able to close our eyes and, with a little imagination, see the New.

Often Jesus jumps out at us from the ancient pages as prophetic proof of his existence and his purpose. In a symbolic way, Isaac got to play the role of Jesus twice: once when he willingly went to the altar to serve as the sacrifice, and again as he stood at the altar as the groom awaiting his bride.

We know that God has a good reason for everything he has preserved in his Holy Word and we know that his singular purpose since the original corruption of the human race has been to restore us to himself, to restore us to the righteousness he intended for us in the first place.

So, a chapter such as this does more than simply teach us to pray when we face major hurdles, to do our best when our master gives us a task to perform, or to secure quality brides for our sons. After we read a chapter such as this, we should close our eyes and see if we can see Jesus going to the altar to claim his bride.

The Lord loves metaphors and parables. So do I. Figures of speech are the very soul of successful communication and language art, and God masterfully uses such figures to communicate to us. In fact, most of the Old Testament can be viewed as a parable that symbolizes the Christian's journey from the bondage of sin to his life as a free man in the Promised Land. And within the big parable are smaller, but no less significant, parables such as the courting of a bride for Isaac.

We, the church, the body of believers, have been called the bride of Christ. It is a beautiful metaphor. Like Isaac, Jesus didn't first see us and then decide to love us. No, he loved us first, then he came courting. He didn't do the courting himself because God had already chosen his bride for him. God sent his trusted servant, the Holy Spirit, bearing the gift of grace to woo us.

I recently attended a sales presentation in which a company was trying to sell me a membership in a vacation club. The first thing the sales people did was to offer me a small gift to make me feel beholden enough to buy the bigger thing they wanted to sell me. If I accepted the gift, I was obligated to listen to their pitch. The little gift came first, then the commitment, then the joys and responsibilities of membership.

Rebekah first accepted the small gifts, but when she made her promise to become the bride of Isaac, Abraham's servant opened his chests and poured out for her many beautiful gifts so she would be a proper bride for his master's son. Yet, after becoming Isaac's wife, Rebekah's life was not all sweetness. In serving her lord, she suffered much anguish.

Once we have made the commitment to become the bride of Christ, the Holy Spirit opens his chest of gifts and bestows them on us in abundance. Jesus also told us that once we have accepted him as our groom, we often must bear our cross and suffer persecutions for his sake, just as he suffered for us. But he first gives us the gifts that we need to live righteous lives, to serve him as we should, and to sustain us through the times of suffering that lie ahead.

Do Not Delay

Scripture: Genesis 24:54–61
Suggested Reading: Hebrews 11:24–25

One of the common practices of the men and women of our time is to have a "bachelor" party the night before the wedding. They get together with old friends and have one last fling before settling down to the routine of married life. One last sowing of the wild oats. Enjoy the pleasures of the past one last time.

Supposedly, this party so satisfies them that they no longer have a desire to run with the old gang or cavort with old lovers. They get a final purging before their wedding day so they can focus all their attention on their new mates.

In retrospect, we know that the bachelor party is a lie. Rather than purging, it tightens the grip on the past and makes the new future look less attractive. In a sense, it's looking back after setting their hand to the plow. If they enjoy that night too much, the pleasure might entice them to change their minds, or at least taint their view of what is to come.

Rebekah's family tried to throw a big "bachelor" party for her before she went off to become Isaac's bride. They begged Eliezer to let her remain for ten days so they could have one last fling with her before she left Haran to settle down to the routine of married life with Isaac.

But Eliezer knew the pitfalls of such a proposition. He knew that it was necessary for her to leave immediately upon making her commitment, or the enjoyment of the celebration of the past might entice her to change her mind, break the engagement, and return to her old life.

One of the difficulties we face when we give our lives to Christ is the question of how to respond to the bidding of our old habits and our old friends who want us to stick around for a while and celebrate the old days. Our sinful past wants to throw a bachelor party for us, hoping we will change our minds and return to our former ways. Eliezer taught us how to respond to that invitation. We must turn to those voices and say, "Do not delay me . . . let me go that I may go to my new master!"

As we learned in earlier meditations, we must turn our back completely on our past. We must not even look back and see what is happening in those cities of sin from which we have fled. We must leave the dead to bury the dead. Once we have taken the plow in hand, we must never look back. If we turn our heads, we are not fit to be citizens of the kingdom of God. We are not fit to be the bride of Christ.

Rebekah serves as our model. When the invitation went out for the party, the servant objected, but the invitation was presented directly to the bride for her RSVP. "Will you stay for the party, or will you go with this man?" Her answer qualifies her to be enshrined in the hall of the heroes of faith: "I will go."

When the follies of our past call to us like the sirens or the Lorelei, the Holy Spirit is first to intervene. Like Eliezer, he shouts, "Do not delay us! Be gone! Our new master is waiting for us at the altar! We've got to leave now!"

But in the end, we must answer the invitation ourselves. We can tell the tempter that we will stay and enjoy the pleasures of sin for a season, or like Rebekah, we can answer, "I will go."

. . . *And He Loved Her*

Scripture: genesis 24:62–67
Suggested Reading: Isaiah 40:1–2

*I*t stands to reason that Sarah would spoil Isaac. After all, though she was his mother, she was old enough to be his grandmother. Probably nurses and nannies saw to his basic needs, giving Sarah the privilege of playing a different role. She certainly didn't expect to live long enough to have grandchildren of her own, and Isaac would never know a grandmother of his own, so why not take advantage of the opportunity to play the part herself?

Those of us who were fortunate enough to have had a grandmother nearby know what a blessing it can be. When we thought our parents were maltreating us, we could always run away to grandma's house to have our bruised egos nursed, our tummies filled with special cookies, and be cuddled in her loving arms. She could speak to us so peacefully that our torment vanished.

The day my grandmother died was a day of great loss. As we stood by her casket we remembered the cookies, the reassurance, the gentle touch, and the soft voice. We wept as we remembered the fondest days of our youth and the love only a grandmother can give.

As we walked away from the cemetery, we were so overwhelmed with emptiness and loss that we reached out and wrapped our arms around others we loved and pulled them close in an effort to be comforted after our dear grandmother had gone to be forever with the Lord.

After Sarah died, Isaac felt the loneliness of his loss. In apparent despondency, he packed up his tent and went out into the wilderness to mourn the death of his mother. Like David, he refused to be comforted.

But what's that in the distance? Camels? Are they bringing my bride to me? Yes! "Then Isaac brought her into the tent, and took Rebekah, and she became his wife; and he loved her. So Isaac was comforted after his mother's death."

What a glorious verse! Do we treasure our mates as Isaac treasured his? Does the love that we share comfort us as we face our losses? It should. God gave us our loved ones because it is not good to be alone. It is not good to brood over loss and refuse to be comforted, so God has blessed us with the bond of marriage, not just to preserve the race, but to give us a balm in our Gilead, a comfort in the time of sorrow.

So, on your way home from work tonight, stop and pick up that little gift, those roses or that box of candy that says, "I love you."

But we must take one more step up the spiritual ladder. We are, first and foremost, brides of Christ. He is our divine comforter. When no light on earth can pierce the awful darkness of our valley of grief, when no power on earth can lift our heavy load of sorrow, when there is no mate's or mother's or grandmother's voice to turn our torment into peace, we can turn to him who was ordained by his father to . . .

Comfort ye my people, speak ye peace, thus saith our God;
Comfort those who sit in darkness, mourning 'neath their sorrow's load.

Speak ye to Jerusalem of the peace that waits for them;
Tell her that her sins I cover, and her warfare now is over.
(Johannes Olearius, 1671)

Another Wife

Scripture: Genesis 25:1–6, 12–18
Suggested Reading: Review Genesis 12:1–3; Galatians 3:29

I know a lawyer who works for a large firm that specializes in estate law. She explained to me that when a person dies, the children often fight over the property and the valuables that their parents leave behind. Brothers and sisters become foes in the litigation that determines how much of what each is to inherit. Surprisingly, many people die intestate, that is, without a will, assuming that the children will unselfishly divide the estate when they are gone.

Her cases become more complicated when one of the surviving parents has remarried, particularly if that parent has remarried someone else who is widowed and also has an estate and children. Often estates are challenged because the parents didn't clearly or legally specify what was to become of their holdings. And at times, grandchildren and relatives other than direct descendants get involved in the fight. Whether or not there is plenty for everyone is immaterial. Each wants more than the others.

My lawyer friend was once so frustrated that she declared that there ought to be specific laws governing remarriage and the division of estates, or at least laws requiring people to plan the distribution of their estates in a clear and legally sound manner.

Abraham stands before us as good evidence that an old man should not get married again after the wife of his youth dies. The folly of the father's old age, as well of the folly of his youth, haunt the son of promise forever. When Isaac was born, Abraham sent Ishmael, the son of the servant girl, away to the east to become the founder of the Arab nations. Then he also sent six sons that his second wife bore him to the east to become the fathers of other nations, such as the Midianites, who would, in addition to the sons of Ishmael, make perpetual war against Isaac's descendants.

Abraham could have used the services of an estate planner. Had he made out a proper will, perhaps today his children would not be battling over that one little piece of land that the Lord promised to give to him and his descendants forever. Though there is enough for all, both argue that under the terms of the covenant, they are the rightful sole heirs. They have even enlisted the descendants of Ham and Japheth as allies in their family squabble.

The saddest thing about some of my friend's cases is that the heirs fight only over tangible things, things with monetary or sentimental value. They seem to neglect the spiritual values their ancestors have left behind. They fight about who will get grandpa's walking stick, but care nothing about inheriting his close walk with the Lord, his kindness, or his charitable spirit. Perhaps when our parents die and we are taking inventory of the material things they leave behind, we should also take inventory of the personal traits and spiritual heritage they have spent their lives trying to give us.

The same is true of the eight sons of Abraham. Their great ancestor left behind a tiny piece of rugged land that has become the focus of their greed. The land has served its purpose and is no longer Abraham's most valuable bequest. The most valuable thing God gave to Abraham to pass on to his heirs was the promise that by him all the families of the earth might be blessed, the promise of Jesus' ultimate sacrifice, the forgiveness of sins, and eternal life in the kingdom of heaven. We who are in Christ are heirs to that great promise.

He who inherits the earthly kingdom inherits dust, but he who inherits the heavenly kingdom inherits eternal glory.

Gathered to His People

Scripture: Genesis 25:7–8
Suggested Reading: 2 Samuel 12:22–23

The Bible contains many beautiful promises. Some of them are stated openly while some seem almost to be written between the lines. After Abraham had lived to a grand old age, he breathed his last and was *gathered to his people*. Did his children carry his body back to Mesopotamia or Haran so he could be buried next to his parents, his grandparents, and other relatives? No, they buried him next to his wife Sarah in the cave that he had bought from the Hittite, Machpelah. His own people were buried far away.

How can it be said, then, that he was *gathered to his people*? Is it just a nice figure of speech the Bible uses to avoid saying that he *died*? Is it nothing more than a euphemism?

No, the Bible is telling a truth that constitutes one of the most beautiful promises we can ever hope to hear. It is the promise that gave David the hope of someday being in heaven with his son who died in infancy. It is the promise that widows and widowers hold dear when they get out the old photo albums and stir up beautiful but painful memories of a husband or wife who has gone to be with the Lord. It is the promise that brings a measure of peace to grieving parents as they stand by the little white casket and ask why.

The promise that we will be gathered to our people when we die is the promise that makes all of scripture worthwhile. If it weren't for that promise, there would be little point in going to Sunday school or spending time in God's Word. If when we die we do something other than enter into eternal life with our Lord and our loved ones, then all of the scriptures are false. If that promise of God holds no truth, how can any other?

But what if our spouse or one of our beloved children dies without confessing Christ as savior? Won't heaven be a little lonely when we see the mates of our friends there and not our own? Or if our children aren't there with us? The answer to that is easier than we sometimes think. When the Lord comes, he is going to separate the sheep from the goats. The sheep he will place at his right hand and the goats at his left. I doubt that any of the sheep will mourn if there are no goats among them. If heaven is the place of perfect, tearless bliss, there can be no recollection at all that someone we hoped was a sheep turned out to be a goat.

The Holy Spirit gave S. F. Bennett the knowledge that beyond the sunset of our lives . . .

There's a land that is fairer than day,
and by faith we can see it afar,
For the Father waits over the way,
to prepare us a dwelling place there.

We shall sing on that beautiful shore,
the melodious song of the blessed,
And our spirits shall sorrow no more,
not a sigh for the blessings of rest.

In the sweet bye and bye,
we shall meet on that beautiful shore
In the sweet bye and bye,
we shall meet on that beautiful shore.

Amen!

Welcome Home, Son

Scripture: Genesis 25:9–18
Suggested Reading: Galatians 3:29

When Hagar and her alienated son Ishmael wandered off into the wilderness of Paran some years ago, we probably thought we would never see him again. He had a quiver of arrows slung on his back and the grim look of anger and revenge pasted on his face as he trudged off to fulfill his destiny as the ancestor to a race of people hostile to his brother's heirs. Frankly, I am quite surprised to see him standing at one end of the bier as he and Isaac commit their father's body to its grave.

And I wonder what went on in Ishmael's mind as he was greeted with the news of his father's death. Did he still claim him as father? Why should he? Abraham disinherited him and sent him away so his presence would not taint the character of his favorite son. As boys they quarreled. Ishmael, of course, was the instigator because his mother set the mood for him with the contemptuous attitude that finally got her thrown off the premises. If it weren't for God's promise to Abraham that Ishmael, too, would become the father of a great nation, we would have every reason to believe that God abandoned him in the desert, perhaps to die.

Why should he make that long trip back "home"? It really wasn't his home anymore although his descendants would always claim it in their eternal grudge against the sons of Isaac. Could it be that he wanted to take the opportunity to perform one last act of decency before placing the destiny of his family in the thoughtless hands of history? Or did he want to look Isaac in the eye one last time and shake his hand, as boxers glare and greet at the beginning of the match, before round one of their endless conflict began? What thoughts and feelings possessed him as he and his estranged brother buried their father? What did they say to each other? When they parted after the funeral, did they embrace? Did they wish each other well? Did they have a premonition of things to come?

I think they did. Oh, I don't know what suspicions they might have had about such mundane matters as land, war, and empires, but I think their coming together to bury their father bears witness to the fact that they both looked beyond time and saw a glimmer of the eternity into which they believed they would once again be gathered as a family. I think they knew that death was an event that overshadowed the temporal trivia of history. I think they knew that the follies of this life would vanish in the glory of the great reunion that would occur when the Lord would gather them unto their people. I believe their vision of the meaning of life transcended the boundaries of time.

When Hagar and her son wandered off into the wilderness, God could have banished them from the pages of scripture until Ishmael's seed declared war against the sons of Isaac. But he didn't. Almost as a parenthetical statement, God informed us that when the exiled son died, he was gathered to his kindred just as his father before him. To whom were they gathered? Who are their people? Who are their kindred?

Does it surprise you that we will be part of that reunion? If we are in Christ, we are Abraham's seed and heirs to the promise. And I'm convinced that on that glorious day of reunion we, too, will be gathered unto our people: Sarah, Abraham, Ishmael, Isaac, Jacob, Moses, and all the rest of the redeemed family of God!

What Use Is a Birthright?

Scripture: Genesis 25:19–34
Suggested Reading: 2 Kings 6:28–29; Daniel 3:1–7;
Matthew 10:32–33; 26:69–75

Literature and life are full of stories about people who give up very valuable possessions in order to survive a crisis. Doomed travelers on a cruise ship have paid thousands of dollars for a seat in a lifeboat. Poor parents have sold prized possessions to buy Christmas gifts for their children. Even in Jerusalem, God's chosen people ate their own babies when the city suffered famine during a siege. When severe crises loom, that which we once thought precious loses its value.

Does it make sense to devalue the precious when a crisis strikes? After all, what good would money and possessions be if one might be dead tomorrow? If all it takes is wealth to stay alive, why not give up wealth rather than die?

Of course, others have seen it differently. When the specter of poverty suddenly appears, some people, such as those who plunged from skyscraper windows the day the Great Depression hit, prefer to die rather than live as paupers.

However they are juxtaposed, wealth and life are trading partners.

During rational moments, most people will reason that life is more valuable than wealth. But during times of terror, the value of each becomes distorted. Sometimes life is dear, sometimes it is cheap. Sometimes wealth is precious, sometimes it is worthless. If your inheritance is of great value, it is usually worth protecting at great cost. But if the breath of life may go out of you tomorrow, its value depreciates. Sometimes it makes sense to trade a birthright for a bowl of pottage. Of what use is an estate when you are starving?

But what if the birthright has value that cannot be measured in dollars? What if the birthright is your eternal destiny? What if it is your birthright to be numbered among the redeemed of the Lamb? What if your birthright is the kingdom of heaven?

Many have traded that birthright for a few more breaths of life. Before the time of Christ, many Jews gave up their inheritance in the kingdom of heaven by bowing to idols in order to avoid torture or death. Some first century Christians, rather than face the flames or the lions, denied their Lord in exchange for the promise of survival on the earth. Some modern day Christians might well be trading their heavenly inheritance for a few comforts.

It is uncomfortable to stand up for Jesus when someone whose respect you treasure is blaspheming his name. In places where one is ridiculed for being a follower of Christ, it is easy to pretend you don't know him. Peter knows all about that.

Pretending not to be a child of the King is to deny your inheritance in the kingdom of God. Fortunately for Peter, he had a warning sign, the crowing of the cock. After the cock crew, he had the opportunity to weep the bitter tears of repentance. In his remorse, he could turn to the Lord, beg forgiveness, and be redeemed.

But for us, there might not be the crowing of the cock. There might be no warning sign at all. We've been privileged to have the experiences of Esau and Peter held up as red flags for us. But if we ignore them, we might easily sell our birthright and wake up in hell.

Passing the Torch

Scripture: Genesis 26
Suggested Reading: Deuteronomy 6:6–7; Luke 1:42; Galatians 3:29;
Hebrews 11:20

*B*asketball players measure their importance to the team by
how many minutes of playing time the coach gives them in a game.
I'm happy that the saints of God don't measure their significance
to the plan of salvation by how many chapters of scripture God
has devoted to their exploits.

So far, Abraham has dominated about a dozen chapters of holy
writ. Next, his grandson Jacob will be the star feature of another
dozen or so. In between there is Isaac. Isaac's early years were overshadowed by the adventures of his father. His declining years were
obscured by the saga of his son. Then the story of his grandson
Joseph occupies another twelve chapters. Poor Isaac doesn't get
much more than one chapter. Although his playing time is much
shorter than that of the other patriarchs, he still earned his niche
in the hall of fame. Why? What was it that made him great? What
earned him recognition as one of the heroes of faith?

Certainly he is to be remembered for his miraculous birth, although it was not of his doing. His mother was well beyond her
childbearing years when he was conceived, in accordance with the
promise of God. What other figure in history was conceived in a
miraculous manner in accordance with the promise of God? As
the baby Isaac entered the world, he was unmistakably the figure
of the baby Jesus lying in the manger at Bethlehem.

Certainly he is to be remembered for his obedient climb up Mount Moriah and his willingness to be the sacrificial lamb on the altar. What other figure in history was so obedient to the will of his father, even unto death? When young Isaac toiled up that steep hillside carrying the firewood on his back, he was unmistakably the figure of Jesus carrying his heavy cross up the hill of Calvary, just one peak away from Moriah.

Certainly he is to be remembered as the only patriarch who loved just one wife from their wedding day until the day death parted them. Could Isaac's marriage have become a symbol of Christ's marriage with his church if he were to have indulged himself with more than one woman as did his father before him and his sons after him?

In his short time on the court, Isaac performed a number of memorable acts, but when the final summation is entered into the record on the hall of heroes, he is remembered for just one thing: the blessing he passed on to his children.

The most important legacy we parents can leave to this world is children who inherit our walk with the Lord. It's nice if we leave them a comfortable estate. It's nice if we provide them with an education so they can be successful in society's workplace. It's nice if they inherit their mother's eyes or their dad's stately frame.

But every bit of material inheritance shrinks in worth when placed next to our duty to raise our children in the faith and to teach them the way of the Lord. That is a blessing that relegates money, education, and looks to the back page of the will and the family album. If we fail to pass the birthright of salvation on to our children, they may not be in Christ, they may not be Abraham's seed, they may not inherit the kingdom of heaven, and they may not be at the reunion when we are finally all gathered to our people.

To Love the Unlovable

Scripture: Genesis 27
Suggested Reading: Matthew 8:1–3; John 8:1–11

Esau was an unlovable son. He went against the principles his parents taught him by marrying pagan women who made life bitter for Isaac and Rebekah. Undoubtedly his wives worshipped idols and practiced rituals that made their in-laws sick with revulsion. And Esau probably condoned his wives' conduct, to the distress of his parents.

The wickedness of the Edomites, his progeny, suggests that he did nothing to teach his children the way of the Lord. He was not only a wayward son, but he scorned the traditions that his family had established. With all the land before him, what was a mere birthright to the self-sufficient great hunter? He became so unlovable that even his mother turned her back on him.

Isaac and Rebekah knew that God had rejected Esau as an heir to the promise and had ordained that the inheritance pass on to the second son, Jacob. Even though Jacob and his mother turned out to be schemers, Jacob must have been a fairly lovable young man. We learn that later in his life he loved his wives, that he was kind to his family, and that he honored his word.

We aren't sure why he found it necessary to practice deceit in order to gain the birthright that God had promised to him, but it is not unusual for members of this family to take matters into their own hands rather than to allow God to work out his promises in his own way and in his own time. After all, father Abraham had tinkered with God's plan by taking Hagar to bed when God had promised that Sarah would be the mother of the heir. It seems only characteristic that his grandson would follow in his footsteps and map out his own plan to get what God said he would give him. Jacob was just another cut from the family cloth. But Esau was different. He was a nonconformist, a rebel. He deserved to be the outcast.

It would seem logical for *both* Isaac and Rebekah to favor Jacob, the son of promise, and turn their backs on Esau, whose behavior did nothing but bring them torment. But if Isaac had followed his wife and turned his affection away from Esau, he would have lost his image as a type of Christ and would have tainted every other comparison to Jesus that we have cited. If Isaac had failed to love his wayward son, no matter how unlovable he became, he could not have been a true representation of the Son of God.

All through their history, the sons of Jacob acted more like their uncle Esau than their father. They, too, sacrificed to idols and turned their backs on the traditions God had established for them. Their sins were grievous, but God kept on loving them. Oh, he often got very angry with them, and justifiably so, but he never quit loving them.

When Jesus walked this earth, he loved the unlovable and touched the untouchable. He loved the shunned prostitute who had earned a death sentence under the law of Moses. He laid loving, healing hands on the decaying flesh of lepers no one else could stand to be near. He loved and died for the likes of you and me, and for other sinners whose slate is so covered with transgression that even their church disowned them.

If Isaac was to be at all like the Lord whose coming he portrayed by his miraculous birth, by being the obedient sacrifice on Moriah, and by being faithful to his only bride as Christ is faithful to his church, he had to love his wayward and unlovable son. And if we are to be heirs to the promise, we too must learn to love the unlovable and touch the untouchable as Isaac and Jesus did.

The Man Needs a Moon!

Scripture: Genesis 28:1–11

The man's in trouble! He has just outwitted his brother and deceived his father in order to obtain the family blessing. His brother is irate and wants to kill him. His parents have schemed to get him out of the country on the pretext that he go to Haran to get a wife. For all he knows, his angry brother is chasing him through the valley, blade in hand. He is scared. The terrain is rocky. He can barely see where he is going, partly because it's dark, partly because tears and sweat are blinding his eyes.

Sure, he has been named heir to the family estate and has received his father's blessing. But what good is all that to a man on the run with a sword to his back? Sure, he remembers what his grandpa and his dad told him about God's promise; that his descendants would become a great nation inhabiting the very land in which he is now a hunter's prey, and that someday that nation would be the source of blessing for all the people of the earth. But today he is a fugitive, not a prince. Is that wonderful promise mere fancy? The sun has set. He is in the dark. The heir to the promise needs a moon to light his darkness, to show him the way he should go.

As he laid his exhausted body down to sleep with a rock for a pillow, he must have thought about the treachery that got him there. Because of his scheming, he had to forfeit his nice soft bed in his father's tents. Deception built upon deception. First he tricked his older brother out of the birthright by cooking a pot of savory stew and holding it under his nose while his stomach rumbled with hunger pangs. Then while his disinherited brother and his father were scheming to steal the blessing back, he masqueraded as a hairy man and tricked his father as treacherously as he had tricked his brother.

Now it is Mother's turn to play the trickster. Esau is threatening to kill Jacob out of jealousy. The lovely Rebekah is about to become another Eve, mourning the murder of one son by the other. How does she avoid burying her beloved son? Sure . . . go to Isaac and plead with him to send Jacob to Mesopotamia to take a wife!

So back to their roots he goes, but this time it is not such a pretty story. This time we have no broken-hearted son who needs the companionship of a lovely lady to ease the pain of his mother's death. This time we have no beautiful allegorical story about a loving father sending his trusted servant on a long journey, bearing gifts to lure the bride to the tent of the grieving son. This time we have a deceitful son conniving with his deceitful mother to flee from the murderous anger of the brother he had duped. How ironic that the lovely bride of the first story becomes the Molly Maguire of the second.

Oh, what wonderful fiction the Lord gives us to read! Fiction? Wait just a minute. I've been out there, haven't you? Have you ever been out in a rock-strewn valley, stumbling aimlessly about and stubbing your toe in the darkness? Have you ever heard the cold steel sword of your disinherited brother clanging in the distance as you tried to sleep? Have you ever turned out your lights at night in terror of what the morning might bring? Has your pillow ever felt like a rock and your bed like the hard ground?

Then you know how Jacob felt as he closed his eyes in the valley near Luz. Tired, unloved, and afraid, he desperately needed a soft light from heaven to shine on him and warm his heart.

And guess what . . .

A Certain Place

Scripture: **Genesis 28:12–15**
Suggested Reading: *Joshua 1:5; Matthew 28:20; Philippians 1:6; Hebrews 13:5*

We have no reason to believe that Jacob had a good personal relationship with God. We know that his grandfather Abraham was on speaking terms with God and that God had appeared to his father, Isaac. But so far we have seen nothing similar with Jacob.

Since Jacob was just a lad of fifteen when his grandfather died, we might imagine that the old man sat with his young grandson and told him of his own walk with the Lord and of the divine promises to which the boy was heir. Perhaps his father, too, if he was not too busy buttering up to Esau, told him about the time God appeared to him. Undoubtedly his mother explained to him that God had spoken with her and had told her that he, the younger son rather than the elder, stood to inherit the treasure that God had promised to Abraham. But as yet the Lord had not taken Jacob into his confidence.

As a matter of fact, Jacob didn't seem to have much respect for the God of his fathers. When he went into his old, blind father's tent made up as Esau in an effort to dupe the old man into giving him the blessing, he lied to his father about being "home from the hunt" so soon. The reason he gave was that "the Lord *your* God granted me success." First of all, he didn't claim the Lord as his own God, but only as the God of his father. Second, he included God in his lie. Now I've heard many definitions of taking the Lord's name in vain, but here Jacob gives us a classic biblical example of the vain use of the name of God. So far, this man has given no member of his family any reason ever to trust him or to have any respect for him. And certainly he has given God no reason to care for him.

But there he was, bottomed out, alone, on the run, confused about his relationship with both God and his family, and fearing for his life. As he lay down in exhaustion, he must have believed, as did the prodigal son, that his life had come to nothing and that he fully deserved every bit of torment he was suffering. It was at that low moment, and in that *certain place*, that God came to him. He did not go to God; God came to him!

God let him see what he has allowed very few people to see: the army of angels that is commissioned to minister to God's beloved people. Perhaps he saw the very angels that put on people clothes and visited Cousin Lot in Sodom! Perhaps he saw the very angels that would minister to Jesus after he resisted the temptation of Satan! He saw the angels, and he knew from that day on that he was a man of destiny and that the hosts of heaven were guarding him.

But look beyond the angels to the top of the ladder. There stood God himself, looking down on that poor sinner lying out in the wilderness, and promising him a prosperous future. In that *certain place*, the Lord became *his* God, and his God promised him that he was with him and would remain with him to protect him and bring to completion the good work that he had begun in him. And what was that good work? A great earthly nation? Much more than that, a great kingdom composed of all the saints of the Most High, with Jesus himself sitting on the throne.

And the promise of God's continuing presence and protection is not reserved solely for the likes of Jacob, Moses, Joshua, and Peter. That promise is there for you and for me once we come to our *certain place* and lie down on our rock, knowing that by our own design we will come to nothing. Only then can we look up and see our God and sense the presence of his army of angels.

A House for God?

Scripture: Genesis 28: 16–21
Suggested Reading: Psalms 32:1–5; 1 Kings 8:12–13; Ezra 1:2;
Galatians 2:20

God's people have an obsessive need to build him a house. The classic stone wonders of Europe, the great cathedrals that men have built as houses for God, stand as monumental evidence of that need. In America there are architectural firms and building contractors whose exclusive business is the building of churches we are inclined to call the house of God.

Soon after they escaped from Egypt, God's people built a tabernacle which was to be his dwelling place. Once in the Promised Land, a main aim of the kings was to build a temple grand enough to be a house in which God could abide. As the Psalms attest, David was particularly obsessed about building a dwelling place for the most high God. When Solomon finally got the opportunity, he built a temple that was the envy of the world. The Bible devotes several chapters just to describing it and telling the story of its being built. When it was finished, Solomon held a solemn dedication for his great masterpiece and declared, "I have built thee an exalted house, a place for thee to dwell in forever."

Over the years that followed, God saw fit to let Israel's enemies destroy their temple twice. Each time it was destroyed, it became their obsession to rebuild it. God even inspired a pagan foreign tyrant to rebuild it. The Romans destroyed it last in A.D. 70 and some Bible expositors interpret the prophecies as declaring that it will be rebuilt again in the last days.

When Jacob awoke from his dream, he looked around and sensed how awesome was the place where he was lying, and he declared it to be the house of God. He didn't notice the awesomeness of the place when he laid his head down there the night before, but now that God had been there, the place took on a new significance. So, he set up a stone as an altar, poured oil on it, and named the place Bethel, which means "House of God." So, God has his first house. His first house on earth, that is.

Where does God really live? Is he in an ornate box, long since lost to the world, but which some believe may show up again some day? As Bob Benson put it, is he under the lid of a mayonnaise jar on the lower shelf of the pulpit which the preacher opens from Sunday to Sunday and lets God out so he and his people can get acquainted again? Has he chosen the finest cathedral of France to be his home? Or is he homeless, waiting for the glorious day his chosen people will rebuild Solomon's temple on that hill in Jerusalem?

During the children's sermon, when asked where God lives, the little ones say he lives up in heaven, and the bigger ones say that he is everywhere all the time. In catechism we learned that God is omnipresent.

In a sense, you might be right if you say God is homeless, because the truth is that he is looking for a home. He wants our bodies to be his temple and our hearts to be his Holy of Holies, his mercy seat, where we can meet with him and tell him that we love him, tell him how good he is, and share with him all the things that trouble us and thank him for the things that bring us joy.

My body is not a thing of physical splendor, but because God is alive in me it is a glorious spiritual thing. Is he alive in you?

I Will Give a Tenth . . .

Scripture: Genesis 28:22
Suggested Reading: Leviticus 27:30; Malachi 3:7–11; Luke 6:38;
Luke 11:42

Purely out of gratitude for what the Lord had done for Jacob, Jacob promised to give a tenth of everything back to him. His pledge was voluntary: the Lord had not yet commanded his people to return to him a tenth of everything they gained from his hand. Where did he get the idea that he ought to do that? Why a tenth rather than a fifth or a fifteenth?

The tithe can be a confusing thing. Today we hear disputes among God's people about whether the tithe is still a divine requirement. And if they conclude that it is, the next thing they argue about is whether it comes out of the paycheck before or after taxes. I even knew a man who subtracted all of his taxes as well as his house payment, car payment, utilities, and grocery bills before he calculated his tithe. Then, once the issue of deductions is settled, they argue about how to divide it between the church, civic charities, and the poor.

We get more confused when we look to the ancients for answers. Abraham gave a tithe to Melchizedek, a priest of "God Most High," after God had granted him a military victory over a conspiracy of kings. Jacob's tithe was also promised out of gratitude.

Victorious kingdoms, long before Abraham and long after David, exacted tithes from nations they conquered. The required tithe of Leviticus went to a variety of causes: the support of the priests, the maintenance of the temple, feasts, and to feed the poor, but it was sufficient to meet all needs. But sometimes, probably more often than not, God's people failed to tithe and it brought them grief.

It's easy to be perplexed about the rules of tithing. But it's easier not to be. If we refuse to be weighed down by detail, but rather be buoyed up by principle, we should easily discover that God wants us to live with an open hand, responding generously to the needs he brings to our attention, whether it be the minister's salary, the church building program, the disabled, or the poor.

God never told us to give to him because he and his kingdom need our money if they are to survive on the planet he created. The idea is preposterous! To the contrary, God's kingdom seems to have flourished more during times of oppression than during times of plenty. God never told us to give to the poor so the poor will be poor no more. He told us that the poor will always be with us. He gives us only one reason and one reason only for tithing, and that reason is repeated over and over again in the scriptures: *give so that you may be blessed.*

We should thank God for the gift of money, not because it can buy us things or give us security. We should thank God for the gift of money because through it he can teach us to live generously, trusting him to supply all our needs. And if we put our trust in him rather than in the money he has given us, and if we bring our tithes into his storehouse as he has commanded, he has promised to open the windows of heaven and pour down blessings upon us.

But how much is a tithe? Before taxes or after? The answer to that is easy. Give until the blessings start rolling in. And when your many blessings come to you in a package that's been shaken together, packed down, and running all over your lap, you'll know that you've got it right!

Angels Rolled the Stone . . .

Scripture: Genesis 29:1–20
Suggested Reading: Exodus 2:15–17; Matthew 28:1–6; John 4:5–15

For one brief moment in his young life, the exiled scamp had an opportunity to be an angel. Not a fallen angel, but an angel of mercy. There was a damsel in mild distress. Her sheep were ready to be watered, but the young men of the town refused to roll the stone away from the mouth of the well until all the flocks of the community had arrived. So, Jacob rushed to her aid and rolled away the stone so she could water her sheep. This was not only a way to impress the lovely lady that God had picked to be his bride, but also an act of significant symbolic value.

Dramatic events at wells involving brides-to-be is a theme that God saw fit to weave through the scriptures. God led Abraham's faithful servant Eleazar to the well and revealed to him Rebekah, Isaac's future wife. Later Moses intervened at Jethro's well to protect the Midianite maidens from a renegade gang of shepherds who were harassing them; one of them turned out to be the woman he later married. But Jacob's act at Haran was the only one in which someone rolled away a stone so the water could flow.

It's probably pretty far fetched to presume that God intended any symbolic connection between this moment at Haran and an incident that occurred about sixteen hundred years later when the angels rolled the stone away from the tomb in which Jesus' body had been laid. But we do know that God prophesies and teaches through spirit, metaphor, symbolism, and a variety of figures of speech. So, if my spirit senses a connection, who is to tell me with any authority that there is none?

Now we all know that the angels didn't roll the stone away from the mouth of the tomb to let Jesus out. He didn't need that kind of help. He was out already, even before the stone was moved. The angels removed the stone so his followers could look in and see that the tomb was empty. And when they saw that the tomb was empty, living water flowed from the well of truth that had been a tomb, gave life to those who drank it, and became in them a "spring of water welling up to eternal life."

Just as Jacob rolled the stone away from the well so his bride's sheep could be watered, angels rolled the stone away from the mouth of the tomb so the bride of Christ and all his sheep could drink of the living water of truth and never die.

Even the incident at Jacob's well in Samaria fits the pattern in its own way. Jesus gave substance to the symbol by clearly stating that the water he provides is the water of eternal life. And even though the adulterous woman to whom he ministered had been a bride seven times, the moment she received his living water she became his bride, a member of his church, a disciple.

Christ's bride, the church, is gathered with her flock at the mouth of that well of truth, the empty tomb. Some members of the flock still thirst for the water that gives eternal life. Jesus has commissioned us to be angels who, like Jacob, roll rocks away so those thirsty sheep might drink.

We are called to spread the good news of the resurrection to the ends of the earth, to tell others that Jesus is the Christ, the Son of the living God, the Rock of truth upon which the church is built, the once-for-all sacrifice for the sins of the world, the living Lord who has gone to prepare a place for us.

And when they look for him among the dead, we are called to declare with conviction, "He is not here, he is risen!"

The Swindler Swindled

Scripture: Genesis 29:21–30
Suggested Reading: Proverbs 24:17–18; 1 Corinthians 13:6

*L*ast winter in the early morning dusk Mary Ann and I were driving on the freeway through about four inches of fresh, mushy slush. The line of cars patiently drove single file in the two tracks carved by tires into the driving lane, no one daring to be first to cut through the untracked slush of the passing lane. Well, almost no one.

I heard some honking behind me, and as I looked in my side mirror, I saw him coming, a little white four-by-four in the passing lane, going about ten miles an hour faster than anyone else. As he passed me he splashed a blinding torrent of the soggy stuff onto my windshield that took several passes of the wiper blades to brush away. In displeasure, I joined the honking, and as he continued the cars ahead of me honked their horns in outrage as he doused everyone he passed.

A mile down the road the honking began anew. But this time they blared out tones of delight. There in the median, the lone occupant standing beside the wreck looking forlorn, the four-by-four lay on its top, apparently having caught more slush than it could handle, sliding off the road out of control and overturning. No one stopped to help. We all just passed by, blowing our horns in disdainful pleasure, happy that the offensive driver was properly rewarded for the disservice he'd done to his fellow travelers. He deserved no better.

That's the kind of feeling I got when Jacob was tricked into marrying Leah. While my friends ponder the mechanics of how such a deception could possibly have been perpetrated without the knowledge of the victim, I secretly rejoice that the great deceiver of others has finally been deceived himself. I've always considered this to be one of the finest moments of retributive trickery in the Bible.

Had I ended my reading of the scriptures with the book of Genesis, I might have had the pleasure of going through life never having had to repent of that attitude. But as my education in the ways of the Lord became more complete, I learned that I was not to rejoice when my enemy has fallen lest my pleasure displease the Lord and he turn his anger on me. But even beyond that, I learned that I am supposed to love others as Christ loves me. Since he loved me when I was unlovable and forgave me when I did not deserve to be forgiven, I am supposed to go out and do likewise. Each Sunday, when I pray "forgive us our trespasses as we forgive those who trespass against us," I think of Jesus on the cross forgiving the very men who nailed him there.

But I also think of that Jehu in the four-by-four whose upending gave me so much pleasure. When I think that I joined in the chorus of horns to convey to the offender that I shared the world's sense of satisfaction and joy at his plight, I stand embarrassed before my dying Lord who forgave me for hammering the nails into his hands. If God would but grant me the opportunity to relive that moment of my life, I would stop my car, get out, bite my tongue, and offer the man a ride to town, slowly.

I've done so many times in fantasy. The shivering stranger gets into my warm car, grateful that someone would have compassion on such as him. It would be a perfect moment to share my walk with the Lord and perhaps bring a wandering lamb back into the fold. But it is only fantasy. I missed a perfect opportunity. Now one golden opportunity to be like Christ is gone forever.

Sands of the Seashore

Scripture: Genesis 29:31–30:43
Suggested Reading: Matthew 5:1–11

God truly works in mysterious ways. Back when God told Abraham that his descendants would be as numerous as the sands of the seashore, we, recalling life on the farm, smiled and said, "That's nice, a big family with a lot of strong boys to do the work." Well, three generations later it is finally coming to pass. We're seeing the hand of God open and the first few grains of sand fall out.

The sons of promise are not being born in the land of promise. They are not being born into a nice, loving family. This isn't quite how we imagined that the strand would begin to grow. One wave of the great sand dune is developing in the desert where cousin Ishmael is building his belligerent nations. Another wave is developing in Canaan, but with wives unfit to be the mother of the son of promise. Another is growing in the east country where Abraham sent Keturah's sons. Yet another is developing in exile in Mesopotamia. Isaac and Rebekah are wasting into old age, probably wondering just how God plans to do what he said he would do. If God hadn't made the promise directly to Isaac himself, perhaps they might begin to doubt the promise and write Abraham off as a fanciful dreamer. Yet, God is in charge, is doing things his way, and is teaching us lessons in the process.

The schemer is enrolled in the school of hard knocks, getting a degree in husbandry, both human and animal. So far he hasn't done anything right since leaving Bethel. God promised him the birthright and the blessing, so he took God's plan into his own hands and wrangled the family heritage out of his brother and father. And now, because he was not patient enough to allow God to work out his plan, he's in a foreign land, slaving for and playing con games with his uncle Laban while his dysfunctional family is suffering severe growing pains. Let's not deceive ourselves into thinking that being married to two women and bedding with two others while swindling your father-in-law makes for pleasant living. He should have learned from his grandfather that all that comes from such an arrangement is stress and conflict. Today's reading gives us a little taste of it.

But let's not be too hard on Jacob. The rules for managing life God's way have not yet been laid out. At this point God has only given the patriarchs a dim view of what the future holds. There is no way we can hold them accountable for knowing what constitutes the kind of life that God will reward. Lying, stealing, cheating, and even killing to get your way seem to be the ingredients of the formula for positioning yourself to inherit that little plot of rocky ground that lies between the Mediterranean Sea and the Jordan River. Jacob is totally unaware of any godly character traits that will earn him either divine favor or the promised inheritance. All he knows is that he has to outwit even the members of his own family to get what God has promised him.

But amid all the bungling and bullying, God's purposes are being accomplished. Though unconventional and far outside our standards of morality, life is being given to the boys whose sons will someday comprise the tribes of Israel.

And much mischief, torment, and disobedience later, one of those grains of sand, a descendant of the fourth son of the unloved girl with weak eyes, will stand on a hill and tell the world that it will not be the one who schemes, cheats and lies, but the one who is meek and merciful, the one who hungers and thirsts for righteousness who will inherit, not a strip of rocky, war-weary land, but the whole glorious kingdom of heaven!

Enemies at Peace

Scripture: Genesis 31
Suggested Reading: Proverbs 16:7; Romans 9:13

*I*sn't it amazing how the wonder of God even shines through an episode in the life of a man whose heart was filled with nothing but treachery, mendacity, and malice? This moment in the life of our son of promise shows man at his worst and God at his best.

The possessive Laban, a poor man who became rich purely as a side effect of the blessing God bestowed on Jacob, still wanted to keep Jacob and use him as his means to gain greater wealth. The beautiful but untrustworthy Rachel deceived both her husband and her father by stealing his idols in the expectation that possession of his gods would entitle her to lay claim to his estate. Jacob, even though God had ordered him to leave Laban and promised him that he would protect him, faithlessly fled from Laban while his back was turned. Are these the kinds of people God chooses to love and bless?

It once baffled me that the murderous and adulterous David was called "a man after God's own heart." Though God punished David severely for his sins, he obviously still loved him and cared for him by spreading a table before him in the presence of his enemies. God had decided early on that this son of Jesse would hold a special place in his heart in spite of the evil he would do. He decided the same for Jacob. Before he laid the foundation of the earth, he had decided that he would love Jacob. And since God had decided to be pleased with Jacob, he intervened in his enemy's attitude toward him and inspired the shifty pair of belligerents to fashion a pact of peace, once again proving that the destiny of all things is in his hand.

If this chapter were to have ended with verse fifty-two, I would have no more faith in their peace treaty than in a handshake agreement with Jack the Ripper. So far neither of these men has given us any reason whatsoever to trust him. Had I been Jacob, before heading south I would have stationed a solid rear guard at the end of my caravan to intercept Laban's sneak attack.

But as usual, God was in charge. He softened Laban's heart and the hearts of his sons. The boys who jealously accused Jacob of stealing their inheritance were now at peace with him. They sat around a campfire in the dead of night breaking bread with the cousin they had accused of driving their herds southward to Canaan. Perhaps as they listened to Jacob's lambs bleating in the background, they realized that their own herds back home had flourished because of Jacob's presence, and that if he had not come into their lives, they would certainly be much poorer than they were before he arrived twenty years earlier. Yes, they had spent twenty years together, but they didn't become friends until that night.

Jacob's ways pleased the Lord, so the Lord made his enemies to be at peace with him. And why would Jacob's ways please the Lord? Did it please him that Jacob was an accomplished swindler? No, of course not. At this point, it was not what Jacob *is* that pleased the Lord, but rather, he was pleased because of what Jacob *would become*. At that point in his life, Jacob was a working piece of clay trying to be obedient. The Potter was not finished with him yet.

Even though we know we are sinners, we can lay claim to the promise that if our ways please the Lord he will make our enemies to be at peace with us. We don't have to be finished saints to claim that promise if we are willing, as Jacob, to trust that the God who made us and called us will continue to walk with us and preserve us until he has shaped us into the obedient servants he wants us to become and has finished the good work he began in us.

The Winner Is the Loser!

Scripture: Genesis 32.
Suggested Reading: 2 Corinthians 12:7–10

*J*acob had defeated one enemy by making him his friend, but now another old enemy, his brother Esau, waits on the other side of the river. His recent enemy was marching northward toward home, while his old enemy was marching toward him from the south. One crisis had ended, but another loomed.

Jacob had passed this way before. Twenty years earlier, with only his staff in his hand, he had taken lonesome flight from the brother he had betrayed. Then at Bethel, God had revealed himself to Jacob in a dream. There the Lord promised him that during his period of alienation he would be surrounded by angels, and that one day he would return to claim the land of promise.

Now Jacob, wealthy beyond description, is about to cross the Jordan at the ford of Jabbok, near Bethel, and plant his feet back in the land that God had sworn to him and his children. And again God had to make his presence known in Jacob's life.

When the Lord brought the crisis with Laban to a peaceful resolution, Jacob responded by offering a sacrifice of thanksgiving. He took the initiative in his relationship with God by stepping into God's presence with an offering. God responded again by showing him that the great army of angels was on his side and that he need not be afraid.

But the spirit that God had planted in Jacob let him know that he could not return to his homeland as a brazen, strutting nabob.

No conniving cheat could inherit the kingdom of God. He had to have his battle with God, and God had to kick the self out of him.

The fight was a classic. All through the night they fought, toe to toe, no holds barred, neither winning, neither losing. As the morning sun rose on the fighters the mysterious challenger landed a decisive blow that hurt Jacob. With the instinct of boxers we watch on television today, Jacob responded to the devastating punch by falling into a clinch and hanging on for dear life. There was no referee to separate them, so Jacob hung on and would not let go until the man who beat him would give him a blessing. Then the winner said something amazing. He said in effect, "Jacob, you've lost this fight to me, but in losing you've won. By clinging to me you have surrendered your old self, and by surrendering you have become a new creation."

What a sight it must have been as Jacob limped past Penuel that morning! I can almost visualize the scene as though from an old Ingmar Bergman movie. The hero, silhouetted against the rising sun, exhausted from his struggle, leans on his staff as he hobbles across the rocky terrain dragging his lame leg behind him. Every few painful steps he stops, looks up with a gleam of hope in his eye, and at last smiles joyously as the mist lifts and reveals the Jordan River snaking through the valley below.

In sharp contrast to the arrogant schemer who had laid crisp and heavy words on his uncle Laban just a few days before, he is now a cripple, a man with a thorn in his flesh that keeps him from walking as a man living in his own strength ought to walk. He wrestled with God and lost, but from that defeat emerged a victor over the forces that made him the type of man he had been. The new Jacob, Israel, had been humbled, but through that humbling had become a true son of God, an inheritor of the kingdom of heaven!

Back to Bethel

Scripture: Genesis 33
Suggested Reading; Proverbs 16:7; Matthew 5:21–26

The next step for Jacob was to make peace with his brother. Had he not had the experience at Penuel, he might have sent a detachment on ahead to confront Esau's forces. But now he knew that he had an army of angels out in front of him who were going to assure victory, not in his way, but in God's way. So, the Spirit spoke again, "Don't send an army of soldiers, send gifts. Come humbly into the presence of your angry brother, with a peace offering in your hand. Come in your weakness, and you will experience the power of God!"

Hold on! It's not in man's nature to drop his sword and approach his enemy with an olive branch in his hand. What if that enemy, seeing him unarmed, should pounce on him in his defenselessness and win an easy victory? Even Jacob, rather Israel, after his personal conversion experience, took precautionary measures to keep his family from being annihilated by the enemy that pursued him.

Unlike us, he did not have the wisdom of Solomon or the teachings of Jesus to guide him. No one had told him that if a man's ways please the Lord he will make his enemies to be at peace with him. No one had taught him that he should make peace with his brother before coming into the presence of God. He was plowing new ground in the relationship between man and his Maker without the experience and teachings of others to guide him. Thus he became the classic example of the forgiven sinner finding peace with both God and man.

Obviously God was as much at work in the heart of Esau as he was in the heart of his brother. Their moment of meeting is one of the Bible's beautiful passages. After twenty years of estrangement, anger, and fear they fell into each other's arms in warm embrace. The sins of the past were forgiven and the brothers were reconciled.

But is it all that simple? Is there more here than meets the eye? Our hero had not yet crossed the Jordan. He had not yet returned to the land to which God told him to return. Bethel should be the next stop on his travel plan as he returned to Canaan, *west* of the river, the land of his birth.

The brother with whom he is now at peace is heading to Seir, a region *east* of the Jordan, outside the Promised Land, and Jacob has told Esau that he will follow him to Seir. No, no Jacob! That's the wrong way. Go back to Canaan, don't go to Seir. Hold on, he's not going down. He is turning west. Good. But wait, he's stopping at Succoth instead of crossing the Jordan, and it looks as if he's planning to settle there for a while. Did he lie to his brother? We'll never know because they never talked on the record again, and to our knowledge they didn't meet again until old Isaac died and they got together to bury him.

Ah, finally we see him pull up stakes, cross the river and go . . . where? To Bethel? No! To the city, to Shechem! Not a good place, Jacob, not a good place at all. There's trouble there. Go back to where you encountered God in the first place, go back to Bethel!

What a lesson for the wandering Christian. So often we fail to go where God leads us and we find ourselves in strange and troublesome places. We should go back in our spiritual walk to where God came to us in the first place rather than trying to find him in some new way. If we don't, as we shall soon see, God will find a way to uproot us. And it may hurt.

An Ugly Turn

Scripture: Genesis 34
Suggested Reading: Genesis 18:19; Proverbs 22:6

When we read this chapter, it seems as if Bethel and Penuel had never happened. We seem to be reading about people who have never had the Lord touch their lives in any way. Just when we think we're growing in grace, we suddenly plunge into a morass of rape and murder.

What a letdown. We have just crossed over into the Promised Land after a twenty year exile during which our life was filled with deceit and treachery. We have found the Lord, and now that we're back home where we know he wants us to be, we expect life to be calmer and gentler. What is wrong?

Does God promise us that once we've had our wrestling match with him and lost that our life will be a sumptuous feast of blessing? Does he promise us that the sins of the past will not come back to haunt us or that we will not have to suffer the effects of the bad decisions we have made? Quite the contrary. God has always made it plain to us that our behavior will have consequences, and that nothing short of a miracle will change the course of events we set in motion by our conduct. A transforming moment in our lives will bury our sins forever in God's sea of forgetfulness, allowing us passage into the kingdom of heaven, but it is not likely to change the course of natural history. Even after we've entered the kingdom of heaven, we still have major duties to perform, enemies to face, and the obligation to do our best to live righteously.

So, where did Jacob fail?

Back in Paddan-aram, his boys must have got a great education in malevolence watching their father and grandfather do business. Why should anyone be surprised when they imitate their father's special form of treachery? Nowhere in all the detailed chapters about Jacob's life and his exploits do we read that he ever took his sons aside and testified to them about his walk with God, teaching them how to live righteous lives. Even after his own special divine touch, no mention is made of his bringing his sons to the Lord or consulting with the Lord when he has a decision to make.

Once we've come into the kingdom, God's corrective touch becomes more severe. The closer we get to God and the more he blesses us with gifts and responsibilities, the graver the chastisement when we fail to do his will. If you question the truth of that, examine the life of David. As for Jacob, he will still reap future consequences for his failings as a father.

But, you say, what about those innocent Canaanites who fell to the swords of Simeon and Levi? As we continue in our meditations we will learn that they are not so innocent. In fact, one of the reasons that God chose the land of Canaan to be an inheritance for the sons of Abraham was the terrible wickedness of the Canaanites. We will find that they were guilty of unspeakable sin, and as punishment God used the nation of Israel to bring his horrible judgment down upon them.

So, where do we go from here? Our family is scarred. Our daughter bears the indignity of rape, and our sons the guilt of deception and murder. What can we do? There's one simple answer: turn away from sin and turn back to God. Repent and go back to Bethel. There's an old altar there where God came to us once before, and now that we need another healing touch he is calling us back to be with him in that holy place where we first met him.

Oaks, Idols and Tombs

Scripture: Genesis 35–36
Suggested Reading: Genesis 12:6–7; Isaiah 30:19–22

What do we do with our old idols? Do we defile them and scatter them as dust when we've heard our master tell us to turn from them? Or do we hide them somewhere under a tree? In spite of his apparently good intentions, our man Jacob seems to have a problem parting with the unclean things of the past. In burying the idols under the old oak at Shechem, he probably insulted both his ancestry and the Lord by stashing them on the same spot where his grandfather Abraham once built an altar to memorialize the promise that God made to him there.

And even before the insulting image of his hiding the idols under the oak fades from our memory, we find him burying his mother's beloved nurse, Deborah, under an oak near Bethel. And after we've paid proper respects to Deborah, one of the few women whose death is recorded in the Bible, our minds have to go back to those idols and assume that he hid them under the oak for safekeeping, thinking he might possibly have use for them in the future. So, in spite of the wonderful things he is doing to mend his ways, purify his garments, and enter into fellowship with the Lord, there is still the uncomfortable sense that he is holding back a little.

Once we've completed our pilgrimage to Bethel, it's back to the brutal realities of life. The happy cry of a newborn gave way to sobbing as his mother, Rachel, Jacob's beloved wife, died in childbirth. Reuben leaped into bed with his father's concubine, Bilhah, the mother of his brothers Dan and Naphtali, and by doing so forever lost his birthright as the eldest of Jacob's sons. Then the family returned to Hebron and Grandfather Isaac was gathered to his people after a long life. A messenger went to Seir and Esau returned home to help Jacob lay him to rest in the family plot.

I'd love to have given the eulogy at Isaac's funeral. Of course we would have glossed over his shortcomings and weaknesses with patronizing humor and focused on those attributes for which he should be honored. At a time when tradition allowed promiscuity, he loved just one wife. When the world around him, even his own family, was worshipping Canaanite idols, he remained faithful to the Lord. When the rest of the family pitched its tents over the length and breadth of the land, he maintained the family home at Hebron and preserved the family cemetery. As a type of the Christ to come, he loved an unlovable son and a perfidious bride.

I've often wondered what the reunion was like when Jacob and Esau met at Isaac's funeral. Did Esau ever ask Jacob why he didn't go to Seir as he had promised? Did Jacob ever explain why he lied? I suspect that there wasn't much conversation between them, and that soon after the funeral Esau returned to Seir, never to see his brother again.

The focus of history is about to shift once more. Esau will go his way to plant the seeds of a mighty nation that will be a bane to Israel right up to the day it is scattered to the four corners of the earth. Esau could never have guessed that his role in blessing all the families of the earth would be to sire a son who would play a major role in nailing Christ to the cross. And Jacob will retire to his easy chair and leave the running of the farm to his sons, except to meddle just enough to trigger one of the most fortunate tragedies of Hebrew history: the selling of Joseph into slavery.

One thing is certain in all of man's bungling: God is in control of his people's destiny.

More Mysterious Ways

Scripture: Genesis 37
Suggested Reading: Genesis 15:13

*T*he great hymn writer, William Cowper, put it so well:

God moves in a mysterious way,
his wonders to perform;
He plants his footsteps in the sea
and rides upon the storm.

When God was making promises to Abraham about a son, a nation, and blessings for all the families of the earth, he slipped in a caveat that must have made Abraham wince. He told him that his descendants would be slaves in a foreign land. But to soften the prophecy he added that they would emerge after four hundred years with great wealth.

As Abraham grew old and watched his sons and grandsons fight, he must have wondered how his children could ever come to be a great nation. He must have wondered even more as Jacob fled to Padan-aram and Esau took foreign wives and lived among the pagan tribes as if he were one of them. Jacob and Esau were just thirty-five years old when Abraham died, so he may never have seen the sons that Jacob brought back to Canaan after he parted company with Laban. He must have died wondering just how God was going to go about fulfilling the promises he had made to him.

But if he watched from heaven, he began to see it all unfold. He watched the eleven schemers, who had learned their craft so well from their scheming father, sell their brother to the Ishmaelites who in turn sold him to the Egyptians. Then as Jacob mourned the loss of his beloved son, old Abraham must have peered down the corridors of time and seen all things work out for humanity's ultimate gain, and he understood that

> Deep in unfathomable mines
> of never failing skill,
> He treasures up his bright designs
> and works his sovereign will.

And as Jacob mourned, Abraham might have wished to cross the great divide to tell him

> Ye fearful saints, fresh courage take;
> the clouds ye so much dread
> Are big with mercy and shall break
> in blessing on your head.

Who could imagine that the egoism, jealousy, and trickery that Jacob's sons carried in their genes would all fit into a marvelous plan to build a nation? As Jacob, in accordance with God's plan, stole an inheritance that tradition had reserved for the elder, he passed the same notion to his young son Joseph by giving him the clothing that tradition had reserved for the brother who by birth had the right to be the boss of the family crew. And he passed to his older sons the character to rebel against Joseph and to plot his death.

Suddenly a seventeen year old lad, only moments before puffed up with self-importance, found himself in irons, walking behind a camel on his way to a culture in which he could hope to be nothing more than an outcast and a slave.

But in God's mysterious way, the door of blessing was about to open.

Exporting the Balm

Scripture: Genesis 37:25
Suggested Readings: Genesis 14:10; 43:11; Jeremiah 8:22;
Ezekiel 27:17

When Joseph was carried away to become a slave in Egypt, included in the cargo the caravan carried was a very special item, balm, perhaps from Gilead, the land that lay east of the Jordan River. The balm was wonderful stuff. It was a resinous substance that oozed from small evergreen trees and was shipped all over the world as salve to ease the discomfort of skin ailments or to soothe aching joints and muscles. The Egyptians also used it as an embalming agent to preserve the bodies of the dead.

Before Joseph ultimately revealed his true identity to his brothers, they told their father Jacob that there was a "man" in Egypt holding Simeon hostage but promising to provide food for the family during the famine. In order to impress him, Jacob sent "the man" a gift of some prize dainties, including some balm. The slave traders were the first biblically recorded exporters of the balm, and Jacob was the second. In both cases, the balm was on its way to Egypt for use both as a healing agent and as a preservative.

From Ezekiel we learn that the balm of Gilead was a major export during the kingdom period when the tribes of Reuben, Gad, and Manasseh occupied the land east of the Jordan. In reflecting on the volume of commerce that passed through the great port city of Tyre, he noted that the balm of Gilead was a product that Israel exported to the whole world.

The trees that produced the balm no longer grow in Gilead, and Gilead is no longer part of Israel, but Israel still exports a balm of a different kind. When we visited Qumran by the Dead Sea, one item we found in the souvenir store was Dead Sea black mud, a slimy natural substance that is found in pits in the "Vale of Siddim" and packaged and sold as a balm "very effective for a wide range of rheumatic ailments . . . for stimulating the blood circulation . . . helping to relieve painful joints . . . removing grime . . . and for restoring the skin's vitality."

Undoubtedly the pits that produce the black mud are the same bitumen slime pits that swallowed up the soldiers of Sodom as they fled at night from Abraham's army. Along the road by the Dead Sea coast yet today, the Israeli government has posted signs warning people to stay away at night lest they stumble into the open pits.

When Judah was falling to the invading armies of the Babylonian Empire, the inspired prophet Jeremiah plaintively asked, "Is there no balm in Gilead?" Since the tribes east of the river had fallen earlier to the Assyrians, Israel no longer had access to the balm. So, in poetic figure of speech, there was no balm to heal the pain that the wounded nation was suffering.

Hundreds of years later another inspired poet, an anonymous slave in the cotton fields answered Jeremiah's question. "There is a balm in Gilead," he said, "to make the wounded whole; there is a balm in Gilead to heal the sin sick soul." That balm, of course, is Jesus, the great physician, who eases our suffering, removes our grime of sin, defeats our enemies, and preserves us for eternity.

Paul and the other missionaries exported that balm from Israel to the entire world. All Christians have a plentiful supply, and it is our duty to share our balm with brothers and sisters who are still slaves to sin or who are suffering the afflictions of this world.

. . . *To Whom It Belongs*

Scripture: Genesis 38
Suggested Reading: Genesis 49:10–12; Matthew 1:1–16

His purposes will ripen fast,
    unfolding every hour;
The bud may have a bitter taste,
    but sweet will be the flower.

(William Cowper 1772)

For a giddy youngster of seventeen bloated with ego to find himself in chains walking behind a camel on his way to some unknown place is, most certainly, a bitter tasting bud. And now another of Jacob's sons, one who is in the eternal record of events with reasonable favor for having saved Joseph from certain death and for siring kings, stands in the showcase of history and not only commits adultery with his own daughter-in-law, but gets caught at it by doing something so stupid one wonders what ever happened to the scheming instincts he should have inherited from his father.

As we work our way through the scriptures we marvel at some of God's mysterious ways. We are amazed that the master plan has Lot falling into drunken incest with his own daughters. We are stunned to see Judah sinning with Tamar. And we shake our heads in shame as we watch David lusting for Bathsheba. The road from Abraham to Jesus is strewn with bitter buds, but the ultimate blossom, the blessing of salvation for all the families of the earth, is the sweetest flower that ever bloomed on the vine of life.

People who do not have Jesus living in them are sure to look at the Savior's ancestry and raise a mocking brow. But those of us who know that to our eternal King belongs all honor, glory, and praise, also know that the ancestry of the Lion of Judah is the tree *on* which he died and *for* which he died. He was born *of* sinful people, and he died *for* sinful people. His own tree has branches which deserve to be cut off and thrown into the fire, just as all of us deserve the eternal flames, but Jesus loved the most wretched of us enough to bear the guilt of murder and adultery on the cross so that we might inherit the eternal kingdom of heaven.

Jesus is the choice vine, and history ties him to many ass's colts. And if Jesus was willing to have his lineage linked to some of the greatest sinners that history has to offer, how can any of us have the audacity to look down on anyone for his lineage or the error of his ways? Our duty as Christians is not to scorn others either for their heritage or for their sin, but to love them just as Jesus loved us and to be willing not just to feed and clothe them, but to lay down our lives for them as he laid down his life for us. If we are unwilling to do for others as he did for us, we can lay no claim to the kingdom.

God's ways are mysterious. It is not our business to divine the reasons why God does as he does, it is simply our business to be pliable clay in the Potter's hands, willing to be what he wants us to be and to do what he wants us to do without question and without the need for answers. Lot never comprehended his contribution to God's great plan, Judah had no way of knowing that the fruit of his whore mongering would be a scepter for the King of kings, Jacob never understood that his scheming nature ultimately served God's purpose, and David never knew that his savior would be the son of his lust.

As we serve God according to our calling, we may never understand how our sin and suffering might fit into his plan, but . . .

Blind unbelief is sure to err,
     and scan his work in vain;
God is his own interpreter,
     and he will make it plain.

Brothers

Scripture: Genesis 39:1–12
Suggested Reading: John 1:1–3

Back in the days of my youth, I knew a pair of brothers who were so opposite they didn't even claim each other as kin.

Bill was a good boy. He worked hard in school, got good grades, did what his parents told him to do, and selected friends from among other young people of good reputation. He delivered the daily newspaper faithfully, dry and on time. He was always polite and good natured. He didn't smoke, drink, or curse.

Alfred, on the other hand, was devilish. He didn't care about school, cheated, did everything his parents and teachers told him not to do, and ran with a crowd of troublemakers. He often got into trouble for stealing, and spent at least one night in jail for being drunk and disorderly. He smoked, swore, fought, and had a bad temper. Whenever his parents made him substitute for Bill on the paper route, we could be sure that the paper would arrive late and end up lying in a mud puddle.

We always wondered how parents could have two boys who were so different. Sometimes we even surmised that Alfred wasn't really theirs, that he had been adopted, or there had been some mix up at the hospital.

That's how it seems with Judah and Joseph. How could Jacob have two sons who were so different? How could one brother casually satisfy himself with a harlot while the other brother, in the prime of his youth, seemingly be stamped with a moral code that made him reject the advances of an attractive lady of the leisure class?

If we had lived back then and had the opportunity to choose one or the other of them as friends, which would we have chosen? Would we have chosen to run with Judah and his crowd, enjoying the fruits of lascivious living? Or would we have chosen to be friends with the man who was determined to live a virtuous life?

Or if we were descendants of Jacob and had the privilege of choosing our ancestry, would we choose to trace our heritage back to the illegitimate son of a whoremonger and an adulteress, or would we find it more dignified to follow our roots back to a man of good taste, a man of honor and integrity?

Well, Jesus had that choice. When in the beginning he devised his master plan he could have chosen to come into this world through a line of pristine saints, claiming righteousness as his heritage and living an exemplary life.

But he didn't. He chose to hang his earthly existence on a family tree flowing with sour sap and full of diseased branches and rotten fruit.

He chose to be one of us in every sense, to live among us, to love us, to be our brother, to walk with us, to teach us, to tell us, among other things, not to scorn our ancestry or someone else's, to show us that we could rise above our lineage, that we need not be tainted by the character of our father or our brother, and that in spite of our genes we could, with him dwelling in us, live a righteous life and carry out our divine calling.

Then, in the ultimate demonstration of our faith, our Christian character and our inheritance, with God's grace we could be like him, and love our errant brother enough to lay down our life for him.

Shattered Dreams

Abraham had a dream. In accordance with God's promise, he dreamed that he would father a son. He waited. And he waited. He was approaching a hundred years old and God seemed to be reneging on his promise. So he took the dream into his own hands and sired a son with his servant girl. When Sarah, his wife, became pregnant, the error of his judgment must have leaped up and struck him in the face. And later, when strife once more arose in his home, he must have repented bitterly for his mistake. But now he had a true son, Isaac, who was the fulfillment of God's promise to him. His dream had come true! Then God came to him with that awful demand to take the son he loved to the mountain and offer him on the altar as a sacrifice. As he trudged up that mountain in obedience, his dream must have shattered with every step.

Isaac had a dream. In accordance with God's promise, he dreamed that his sons would prosper and possess the land. Imagine how his dreams shattered when one son fled for his life to a foreign country, and the other son began taking wives from among his pagan neighbors.

Jacob had a dream. He dreamed that his beloved son Joseph would be a prince among men, so he bought him a prince's coat. Then his other sons brought him the bloody coat and reported to him that Joseph had been slain. Another dream shattered.

Joseph had a dream. He dreamed that he would rise to glory and that his brothers would bow down and worship him. Then those very brothers sold him into slavery and he languished in an Egyptian prison. Yet another dream shattered.

Jesus' disciples had a dream. In accordance with their understanding of the scriptures, they dreamed that their Messiah would become king of Israel and restore the greatness of the nation. They dreamed of being seated on his right and on his left when he came into his kingdom. Imagine the pieces of their dream lying crushed at the foot of the cross when he cried out, "It is finished," and gave up the ghost.

If they watched from heaven, Abraham and Isaac saw their dreams come true in a measure they could not possibly have imagined in the flesh. When Jacob appeared in Egypt and saw his son wearing the signet of royalty, his shattered dream reappeared, more glorious than he had envisioned. Joseph dreamed that only his brothers would pay him homage, but when the pieces of his shattered dream came back together, not only his brothers but all of Egypt bowed the knee to him. And when the disciples saw the empty tomb and met their risen Lord in all his glory, their shattered dream took on a dimension so magnificent that only a disciple of Jesus who is filled with the Holy Spirit can begin to comprehend it.

The Lord gives us dreams, but through the example of the patriarchs and the disciples warns us not to meddle in nor anticipate their fulfillment, or to interpret them through the dim eye of a frail human being.

The Lord's vision for us far exceeds our ability to comprehend the scope of it. The blurred picture we are capable of painting in our tiny minds needs to be shredded. Any hope we have of fulfilling it in our way and in our time needs to be dashed. We must take the dream God gives us and return it to him with the expectation that he will make it come true according to his will and in his time.

Then we need to stand back in full submission to the Holy Spirit within us and watch his vision for our lives unfold in astoundingly glorious measure.

But I'm Innocent!

Scripture: Genesis 39:13–23
Suggested Reading: I Peter 2:18–25

What a raw deal! Our spirits rebel when we see a person treated as unjustly as Joseph was treated. Potiphar should have rewarded him for his faithfulness and integrity, not thrown him in jail for something he didn't do.

Oh yes, we've known the whole story since we were children and we can understand that God planned Joseph's sojourn in Egypt as he did, having him put in prison, bringing him to the attention of the king through the interpretation of dreams, and placing him in a position of power so the rest of the story could develop the way it did. But why did he have to treat him so unfairly? Sure, maybe his arrogance as a youth had earned him the wrath of his brothers, but why did his integrity as a young man in that awfully tempting situation have to be rewarded with such gross injustice? Is there a lesson in that for us?

Once when I was in elementary school I was sent home for setting off the fire alarm. It was an accident. I explained to the principal that I had tripped on the top stair wearing my sloppy winter boots and had inadvertently stumbled against the box, triggering the alarm with my elbow. Perhaps if I had had a better reputation, he might have believed me, but I had become known as a prankster. Not a malicious one, but simply as a jokester. One result of my clumsiness was that the student body had to stand out in the cold for twenty minutes while the teachers sniffed around the school for signs of fire. The other result was that I was expelled for a week and had to bring my parents in for a conference with the principal.

I was certain that my father would believe me, plead my innocence, and get me back in school with an unblemished record. But instead he hauled out the family Bible and read to me the story of Joseph and the passage from Peter. By the time he was finished instructing me, I was actually glad that I had been unjustly punished. I could sense God's approval as I sat home and did my lessons, and because Jesus had also suffered unjustly, I felt rather Christlike in my humiliation.

In a world in which it is commonplace for people to escape from judgment for the evil deeds they have done and for others to suffer unjustly, the truly great reward comes not in exoneration, whether guilty or innocent, but in patiently walking with confident strides down the path that God has laid down for us.

How can we do that? Just as Joseph did. In this narrative we don't hear Joseph loudly protesting his innocence, and we don't see him being dragged, kicking and screaming, into a jail cell. The picture we get is the picture of a man whose face radiates honesty and whose posture professes the presence of God in his life. With full expectation that what he was suffering was for the glory of God, he could walk into that prison confident that the Lord was with him and would give him the strength to endure whatever anguish lay ahead.

We can never be so bold as to presume that our misery will be a door that opens to greatness, nor can we ever presume to know the reason, purpose, or end of our suffering. But we can know that we are innocent and we can know for a certainty that the Lord will walk with us through our valleys, shine the soft light of his moon on our path, and provide the courage we need to endure with patience and grace.

Mittens

Scripture: Genesis 40:1–41:13
Suggested Reading: Matthew 25:31–46

Our Lord has given us work to do. He has made it plain that until he returns we are to busy ourselves with the business of feeding the hungry, clothing the naked, tending the sick, welcoming the stranger and visiting the prisoner. Of course, that is our task if we have clothes and food to give, if we are not sick ourselves, or are not locked up in jail. Certainly God would not expect us to serve those in need if our needs were as pressing as theirs, would he?

So, here's Joseph, stuck in this prison, having done nothing to deserve it. He had every human right to be angry and sullen, yet when he saw the hurt etched in the faces of the other prisoners, he set his own misery aside and asked them "Why are your faces downcast today?" Only after he had listened patiently to each and had ministered to their needs by interpreting their dreams did he ask to have his own need remembered.

Jesus taught us the same lesson. Often the hungry and the sick pursued him when he was weary, and every time he met people in need, their needs took precedence over his own.

I had an aunt like that. Although her limbs were twisted with crippling rheumatoid arthritis that she had suffered as a child, each year Aunt Catherine knitted mittens for all of the grandchildren. As the years passed her knuckles became more and more knotted and her fingers more and more twisted, but the family kept growing and she kept on knitting more and more mittens.

The neighborhood began to change and poor children began moving in. As she sat by the window and watched the youngsters walk to school through the snow, she noticed that many of them had bare hands. Her concern for her own relatives spread to the neighborhood, and soon she was knitting mittens for every shivering little urchin who passed by her door. Though they were happy to receive them, none had the social grace to thank her. But she kept right on knitting anyway. Sometimes the people Jesus healed didn't return to thank him either, but he kept right on healing anyway.

When the butler returned to Pharaoh's court, he forgot Joseph, but I imagine that Joseph kept right on being compassionate to the other prisoners who had downcast faces. The Lord does not reward our obedience with the thanks of those we help along the way. He is planning to reward us later, in other, more wonderful ways.

After waiting two more years, Joseph received his reward by being called into Pharaoh's court to interpret Pharaoh's dream. God had not forgotten him, but had prepared him for his future work. Probably all Joseph wanted was to be let out of jail and allowed to return home to his father. He had no idea what God had in store for him. True Christians who humbly serve the Lord by feeding the hungry, ministering to the sick, or putting mittens on shivering little hands do not look for a reward in this life, but the Lord has promised them that their reward in heaven will be great.

Probably Aunt Catherine had no desire greater than that her hands be made whole so she might serve the Lord even better. But I remember looking at her hands as she lay in her casket and thinking how powerfully God had used those twisted fingers to preach a sermon to everyone blessed with healthy hands. And I shed a tear when it struck me that now she has a new and glorified body with pretty hands and straight, agile fingers. But then I smiled when it also struck me that she probably kept right on knitting mittens for the angels.

Discrete and Wise

Scripture: Genesis 41:14–57
Suggested Reading: James 4:10

Years ago I was a school teacher. Though memory of those long-gone days has dimmed, I still remember some of the kids who sat in my high school classes. A decade after he had dropped out of school, a despondent and hopeless Jimmy turned up on my television set as a dapper, bright eyed contender for the national billiards championship. And about ten years after her graduation, chubby, retiring Rosie smiled beautifully at me from her New York studio as she anchored the evening news. People change as they mature from youth to adulthood. Things happen to them that mold their character.

The thirty-year-old man who changed his clothes and shaved before being brought into the presence of the King of Egypt was not the same person as the seventeen-year-old big shot who had been thrown into the pit by his jealous brothers. The arrogant kid with the fancy coat and fancier dreams had been transformed into a humble, discrete, and wise adult.

God had given Joseph a dream of greatness, but with Jacob's misguided assistance he flaunted his dream before his brothers and got into great trouble for his brashness. He misunderstood the dream. He reduced a sacred revelation to self-serving babble and paid the price for it with thirteen years of slavery and imprisonment. So much for belittling the great vision God gives us.

But the mysterious ways of God confound us. The consequences of Joseph's haughty behavior were the very tools God used to change not only a man, but the whole course of human history. During that long period of humiliation, God honed an impertinent young man into the meek and humble servant he needed him to be to play his role in shaping the destiny of the world.

As he served his sentence, he learned to be a servant to others. All the egocentricity of his youth vanished and God became the center of his being. When he interpreted the king's dream, he took no credit for the marvelous powers that God had vested in him, but rather gave all the glory and credit for the working of the gifts to the Lord. Suffering had filled him with the Spirit of God, and the fear of the Lord that he learned truly became the beginning of his wisdom.

Most of us have to wait until we get to heaven to receive our reward for the good works we do. Few of us are rewarded in this life. Joseph is an exception. We cannot deny him his earthly reward because by our standards he suffered unjustly in earning it, but we must remember that even the earthly reward can be part of God's plan whereby we serve those around us.

After being exalted to sit at the right hand of the king and to have full royal power, Joseph remained a servant, fully aware that God was still using him for some kingdom purpose he didn't yet understand. Not until he meets his brothers in the future will he begin to comprehend that what his brothers meant for evil, God intended for good.

My thoughts go back to my aunt with the knitting needles. She never had a reward in this life except to look out the window and see children wearing her mittens and playing happily in the snow. Perhaps that was reward enough in this life for her years of physical suffering and privation, but I expect that the Lord she served saved the greatest rewards for later, and in my fancy I imagine the hosts of heaven gaping in awe as she clicks her golden needles fashioning mittens fit for angels.

Food for Foreigners

Scripture: Genesis 42
Suggested Reading: Matthew 15:32–38; John 6:30–35, 48–51

Suddenly Joseph became the number two man in the Egyptian monarchy. His clear duty was to preserve a grain surplus during the seven years of plenty and manage its use during the famine. Although Egypt had historically opened its gates to foreigners when famine struck their lands, it seems that the current grain reserve was intended just for Egyptians, since this time it was their own nation that suffered a dearth of food. In fact, Egypt might well have been inclined to close her borders to aliens lest her own people go hungry in the end.

So when Jacob told his sons that there was grain in Egypt and that they should go down there to buy some, people who read this story for the first time might well think that such a mission might be foolish, for certainly the crafty Egyptians had no plan to share their food with anyone. But we must remember that there was someone special in charge of the Egyptian grain supply, someone whose spirit was greater than any spirit of nationalism or racism, someone, in fact, whose spirit led him to have compassion on "all the families of the earth," a phrase that undoubtedly echoed through his memory from the stories handed down from his great grandfather, Abraham.

It would be rather far fetched to presume that Joseph expected that his brothers would be coming to Egypt to buy grain. Probably for genuine security reasons he had all foreign buyers brought to him. Perhaps he was keeping an eye out for his brothers just in case they might be coming, but I'm convinced that the head man in charge of Egypt's food supply didn't open the country's gates to foreigners only on the hunch that his brothers might come in. If we are to see and understand this event as a symbol of the story of salvation, we must understand that the grain of Egypt's harvest was sufficient to save anyone who would come and ask for it. And just as the bread that Jesus brings is sufficient to feed multitudes and redeem all sinners who eat of it, Joseph intended to feed all the hungry of the world.

When Joseph was "gathered to his people" at the end of his part in the saga, he must have been delighted to discover that the role in which he had been cast was that of a type of the Christ to come. Like Jesus, he came from a far country and took citizenship in his adopted land in order to provide the bread of life for all the peoples of the earth. The Lord, too, was treated cruelly by his brothers and unjustly punished. After being cast into the pit, he was also considered dead, but he returned from the dead to give life to those who had abused him. When his brothers confessed their sin, Joseph, like Christ, forgave them. Finally his youthful dream came true in a measure that he could not have comprehended as a child when not only his brothers, but all the people of the earth bowed their knee to him.

What price did Jacob's sons pay for the bread of life? The same price we all have to pay: everything and nothing.

First, we must confess the wrong we have done and put our trust fully in the savior who provides the bread. We must be willing to give up to him everything in our lives that is precious, including the family members we love the most. And just as Simeon went into the same tomb of a prison that Joseph had been in, we must be willing to be crucified with Christ, go down into the pit with him, to die unto self, and be raised again with him.

Then when we open the sacks of our new, born-again being, we will find that the Lord has not only given us the bread of life, but has given back to us the life we gave to pay for it.

That We May Live . . .

Scripture: Genesis 43
Suggested Reading: Genesis 42:2; Ezekiel 18:21–23 ;
Matthew 15:32–38; John 6:48–51; 11:25–26.

"Send the lad with me," said Judah, "that we may live and not die."

Now Judah didn't go to the same junior high school that I went to. If he had, he would have learned that living is the same as not dying, and that when he speaks he would incur the wrath of his English teacher if he were to speak redundantly.

Perhaps he was simply echoing his father, who had just told him that he and his brothers should go to Egypt to buy grain so that "we may live and not die." Speech patterns do run in families, and neither Jacob nor his sons were educated men. So we'll forgive the error of their tongues.

But Ezekiel was an educated man. He was a member of a priestly family and was learned in both law and letters. He was a prolific writer, living among the educated of Babylon and writing to the Jews in Jerusalem. So, what's an educated man doing using such redundancies?

Or is the expression a redundancy at all? Perhaps living is not the same as not dying. Perhaps not dying is more than simply living. Perhaps living is more than simply being alive.

Did Jesus know that somebody in modern times would question the syntax of his ancestors? Is that why he went into such detail to explain just how one may "live and not die?" Unlike those who ate the bread in the wilderness, and he might have included the bread of Egypt, those who eat of the bread he offers will live forever. The Old Testament people who received Joseph's bread in Egypt or the manna in the wilderness lived and later died, but he who eats of the bread of life that Jesus gives, "though he die, yet shall he live." So, who is going to question Jesus when he says that one may die and still live? What Christian doesn't know today what it means to live forever, and that living forever is much more than simply being alive?

Through the inspiring power of the Holy Spirit, the Lord gave his prophets an understanding of the concept of redemption and eternal life, and in their writings they attempted to prepare the Jews of a latter day to understand the offer of life that Jesus would make to them.

No, the patriarchs weren't educated men, and certainly they didn't understand the symbolic significance of the words that passed their lips, but God gave them expressions that echo through the corridors of time and carry a meaning that blesses us today more than they could ever comprehend.

Benjamin was Jacob's beloved son, and Judah, the ancestor of Jesus, was his big brother. Together they projected an image of the mission of Christ when Judah said to his father, "Let the lad come with me, and we will arise and go, that we may live and not die, both we and you and also our little ones."

Jesus, God's beloved son, came down to the Egypt of this world holding on to the hand of Judah. With his father's blessing he arose from the grandeur of heaven and came to this earth where he suffered and died for our sins, so that we may live forever with him!

Instead of the Lad . . .

Scripture: Genesis 44
Suggested Reading: Revelation 5:5

If we hadn't read the recent chapters of the book of Genesis, we might be inclined to think that Judah was a pretty good man. After all, for many years the nation bore his name and yet today his name stands as the root word used to describe the offspring if Israel, the Jews. Of all the twelve sons of Jacob who might have begot kings, the Lord picked Judah to sire the royal line that once ruled the world, the great kings David and Solomon. But more significantly, he is ancestor to Jesus the conqueror, the Son we call the Lion of Judah, the eternal King to whom every knee shall bow. What a reputation this man has throughout all of history, from the days of the patriarchs of Genesis to the eternity that John described in the Revelation.

Does he deserve the applause of history? When he was a young man he schemed to kill his younger brother and deceive his father into believing Joseph was dead. Later he committed adultery with his daughter-in-law, thinking she was a prostitute. To that point in his life he had not been the kind of man whose character reflected honor upon the royalty that would emerge from his lineage, the nation that would bear his name, or the Messiah who was to come. To that point in his life he deserved only the scorn of the world and the terrible judgment of his God. But people can change. The pews and pulpits of our churches are filled with people whose sins equal or exceed the sins of Judah. Some of our greatest evangelists have testimonies that even an open-minded adult audience can hardly bear to hear. I'm sure that paradise is filled with people who have been forgiven for sins that most of the inhabitants of heaven and many of the inhabitants of hell would never have dreamed of committing. God uses sinners to fulfill his purposes, and God forgives sinners who confess and repent.

That's what Judah did. He confessed his sin against God and his brother, and he repented of his evil deeds. Having done that, he submitted to the will of God, and God used him in a mighty way. Judah's words and actions in this episode are words and actions that even Jesus can look to with pride.

By offering himself as a substitute sacrifice for his brother, he prophesied the sacrifice that Jesus would later make in our stead, and thus he became a symbol of the Christ to come. Though Benjamin was charged with an offense that would justify his spending the rest of his life in slavery, Judah stepped forward and offered himself *instead of the lad* to pay with his life for the crime of which his brother stood accused.

Because of Judah's offer, Benjamin was able to return to his father. Because of Jesus' offer, we are able to return to our Father.

Without Judah's offer, Benjamin would have been doomed to spend the rest of his life in slavery to the Egyptians, separated from his father. Without Jesus' offer, we would be doomed to spend the rest of our lives in slavery to sin and our eternity in hell, separated from our heavenly Father.

Just as Judah declared that he would give his life in Benjamin's place, Jesus declared that he would give his life as a ransom for many.

Thank you Lord for changing Judah and for using him to open our eyes to the salvation you had planned for us from before the foundation of the earth.

Do Not Quarrel . . .

Scripture: Genesis 45:1–24
Suggested Reading: Colossians 3:1–17

After all the hugging and weeping and kissing that led up to the brothers' departure to a barren Canaan with wagonloads of Egypt's provender, Joseph might have pronounced any of a hundred benedictions to spur them on their way. He might have sung to them an ancient equivalent of "God be with you till we meet again," or he might have simply said, "Be careful." We don't know if he said anything else or not, because the only parting words God chose to preserve for us in scripture are the words, "Do not quarrel on the way."

Did the brothers have anything to quarrel about? To be sure. As they began to brainstorm ways to break the good news of Joseph's survival to their father, they certainly had to revise the story they had made up twenty-two years earlier when they brought that bloody coat back to Jacob.

But how? Should they now claim innocence before their father and suggest that Joseph must have somehow escaped the clutches of the imaginary wild beast that bloodied him and tore his coat? Might Joseph later tell their father that they had sold him to the slave traders? Should they confess their sin of long ago and its continuous cover up, and beg their father's forgiveness? How should they handle this new situation? The best among them might argue for total penitence, while the worst might favor some face saving explanation. They were in a dilemma.

Joseph knew his brothers. He knew that they were not a single-hearted family that feared the Lord. He knew that Reuben was a lusty man who lacked malice, and he knew that Judah had set his moral house in order. But he may have suspected that Simeon or Levi might not be contrite enough to confess their guilt and beg their father's forgiveness. He knew that they were proud, deceitful, contentious men to whom repentance was a disagreeable alternative. Since the brothers were not of one mind, his parting advice to them was, "Do not quarrel on the way."

We have no record of whether or not they explained to their father how it came to pass that Joseph landed in Egypt and became the grand potentate of the granaries. God didn't write the Bible to satisfy our curiosity about such things. He merely determined that it was important for us to know that Joseph dismissed them with the simple exhortation, "Do not quarrel on the way."

If we look at the story of Israel as a metaphor defining our journey from the rocky valley of sin to the glorious heights of paradise, we might apply Joseph's advice to our travels.

Do we have occasion to quarrel along the way? The opportunities are numberless. We quarrel about the jots and tittles of theology until we divide the congregation. We quarrel about whether it is best to feed a hungry brother so he can work, or whether to make him work so he can eat. As we quarrel about doctrine, music, morality, politics, economics, education, and fashions, we drive wedges that split brotherly love into slivers and cut the ties that bind everything together in the perfect harmony that Christ desires. We push compassion, justice, and tolerance aside and replace our holiness with anger and malice.

The words of Joseph are as applicable to us today as they were to his brothers over three thousand years ago, "Do not quarrel on the way."

. . . *Before I Die*

Scripture: Genesis 45:25–28
Suggested Reading: Philippians 1:6

*G*od has a plan for each of his people. Sometimes that plan is obscured from our understanding by facts and situations we cannot grasp. Sometimes that plan is obscured by events that seem to drive us to despair.

When Jacob and his family returned to the Promised Land with the wealth he had gained in Padan-aram, he must have expected life in Canaan to be good. He had returned to his father, he had made peace with his brother, he had sired twelve sons, he had plenty of land and cattle, and he had God's promise of an abundant life for his heirs. What could possibly go wrong?

But something was going wrong that he didn't understand and it must have caused him great confusion. After the incident with Dinah, he was despised by his neighbors. His favorite son had been killed by a beast in the wilderness, or so he thought. And now a famine was threatening his family's very existence. What had become of the promises that had been handed down to him from his grandfather, Abraham? What was happening to the land and the people of promise? The marvelous vision was fading.

And now some wonderful but confusing news: his precious son Joseph was alive! Not only alive, but thriving in a land of plenty, and he had invited his whole family to join him in Egypt.

All of that was astonishing and wonderful, but also baffling. Canaan, not Egypt, was the Promised Land. Why was necessity uprooting him from the land of his fathers and relocating him in

Egypt? As he walked through that emotional valley, one bright, full moon shined down on him, comforting and inspiring him. "Joseph my son is alive," he said. "I will go and see him before I die."

That was a happy but bewildering moment in Jacob's life. The son he thought to be dead had come alive, but the vision of the land he thought belonged to him and his sons faded in the dry dust of their wagon train as they headed southward into alien territory. Did all of his expectations regarding Canaan crumble as he left that arid and unyielding land and turned his face toward Joseph? Was seeing his lost son once more before he died the only faint hope he had left?

God had a plan for Jacob's family that he set into motion the day Jacob sent Joseph out into the fields wearing that famous coat of many colors. In fulfilling his plan, God used all of the evil forces in the heart of man in a way that even the most faithful could not possibly have understood.

As they packed for the trip to Egypt, Jacob was a weary man. Sorrow and the struggle for survival might have clouded his vision for the future of his family. He might have thought that God had abandoned him, but deep in his being a spark remained, and God spoke to him, gave him the confidence and faith he needed to make the journey, and opened his mouth to prophesy the destiny of his sons and the coming of the kingdom that God had promised to Abraham.

God has a plan for all of his people, and though sometimes we walk through the valley of despair, we can walk in the moon glow of his love with the assurance that our loving, almighty God will complete his plan in his own way, in his own time.

Do Not Be Afraid

Scripture: Genesis 46–47:12

The word *fear* is used in our English Bible in two distinctly different ways. God often reminds us that we are to fear him, but also reminds us that we are to fear nothing when we are doing his will. To fear the Lord means to respect him because of his greatness. And if we truly fear him, we have nothing else to fear.

Often when God sends us on a mission, we have good reason to be afraid. Sometimes we don't think we have the ability or the stamina to do what he wants us to do. Sometimes the task is so daunting that we despair. Sometimes he sends us to places boiling with hostility.

Many of my friends fear being the liturgist in the Sunday service, praying before the congregation, delivering food baskets to the poor at Thanksgiving, or participating in the jail ministry. They fear that they might stumble over words or be caught in a threatening or uncomfortable situation.

Jacob feared going to Egypt. He was an old man, and traveling would take its toll on his frail body. He remembered that God had warned his father, Isaac, not to go down to Egypt. Besides, the Egyptians were a fearsome people who despised shepherds. But Joseph was there and the people were starving in Canaan. He was in a bind. He needed a special touch. He needed assurance.

So, he went back to Beersheba and offered sacrifices to God. Then God spoke to him. He called him by name, telling him not to be afraid to go to Egypt. Jacob was quick to respond because he had a desperate need for the reassuring hand of God in his life.

Then God reminded him of the basic principle of fear. 'I am God," he said, reminding Jacob that the only fear a son of promise need entertain is the fear of the Lord. "Do not be afraid to go down to Egypt," he continued, reminding Jacob that when he was doing what the Lord wanted him to do, the Lord would protect him and see the event to its completion.

And once again Jacob needed confirmation that his heirs were to be the founders of a great nation. He must have begun to wonder what had become of that promise. After all, it seemed only logical that if they were to become a great nation, they ought to become great right there in Canaan. After all, Canaan was the land of promise and it only made sense that they should grow and prosper right there. The prospect of going off to Egypt derailed that expectation.

But God's ways are not men's ways. Sometimes God's people are better off in a land where they are despised. There they will not mingle with the natives of the land. There they can maintain their purity and preserve their identity and their culture for the number of generations necessary for them to grow into the kind of nation God wants them to become. Sometimes God's people are better off suffering hardships. Then they recognize their dependence on God and through adversity grow strong enough to do the work God wants them to do.

Sometimes it is good for God's people to stumble over words or to tremble in a threatening situation. A little embarrassment is a good pin to puncture an inflated ego. A little terror is sure to bring one scurrying back to the protection that can be found only in the shelter of his wings. We learn again to fear him and know for a certainty that the Lord is our God. We learn again we have nothing to fear, and we can be confident that he is building us into what he wants us to be so he can fulfill his glorious promise through us.

More Mysterious Ways

Scripture: Genesis 47:13–26
Suggested Reading: 2 Timothy 3:16

For years I wondered why God inspired Moses to include in the scriptures the section we've entitled *The Land Policies of Joseph*. Certainly what is recorded is true, but how is it profitable for doctrine, reproof, correction, or training in righteousness? I sometimes wished it had been left out of the Bible because it disappointed me that a man as wonderful as Joseph made slaves of a nation of poor people.

I've learned lately that in biblical days slavery was looked upon differently than it is today. We consider America's heritage of slavery to be as ugly a blight on our record as the ethnic cleansing we perpetrated on the native Americans shortly after our arrival. We are no more proud of life in the cotton fields as modern Germans are of the Holocaust. But in Bible times, slavery was as common as home mortgages are today.

When one group conquered another, the vanquished became their slaves. When depression or famine struck, people often sold themselves to their creditors. What Joseph did to the Egyptians who had spent all they had was quite normal and practical for his time. And the people who sold themselves, though they probably did it unhappily, did it voluntarily. Had it not been for such slavery, great cultures might not have flourished, and wonders such as the pyramids might not have been built.

But slavery in Egypt has an interesting twist to it. The Semitic Hyksos immigrants who saturated the power structure of Egypt in

Joseph's day eventually ascended to the throne. As Pharaohs, they owned the whole nation of Hamitic Egyptian slaves that Joseph had bought for them. Though those Egyptians were content to be slaves during the famine and the rest of the lean years, when prosperity returned they began to resent their slave status, especially when they looked toward Goshen and saw the Hebrews enjoying their freedom and abundance. In fact, they resented their slavery so much that they eventually rebelled and dethroned the Hyksos Pharaoh. Thus arose a new Pharaoh, an anti-Semitic Egyptian who "knew not Joseph" and in retaliation and fear enslaved the Hebrews.

God's truth lurks in the old expression, "what goes around, comes around." It was the Hebrew Joseph who enslaved all of Egypt, and in the natural evolution of human affairs, the Egyptians enslaved his people.

So where is the doctrine, the reproof, the correction, or instruction in righteousness? Who inspired Jacob to dote on his favorite son and give him a coat of many colors? God. Who made the brothers jealous enough to conspire to sell Joseph into slavery? God. Who gave the dreams and the interpretations? God. Who caused the years of famine and the years of plenty? God. Who elevated Joseph to the position of prime minister? God. Who dictated the enslavement of the Egyptians? God. Who restored the land and inspired the popular uprising against the slave masters? God. Who gave and fulfilled the prophecy that Abraham's seed would become slaves and suffer the bread of affliction in this foreign land so they could grow into a strong nation? God. God, God, God.

The cornerstone of Christian doctrine is the sovereignty of God. His will *will* be done on earth as it is in heaven, and his ways are inscrutable. He is the Potter, and the world and everything in it is his lump of clay. He can fashion of that lump anything he chooses.

Would you have a God who is less?

. . . *With My Fathers*

Scripture: Genesis 47:27–31
Suggested Reading: 1 Thessalonians 4:13–18

Each year Mary Ann and I visit the family burial plots in the old hometown cemeteries. There in the shadows of the monuments bearing familiar surnames stand markers identifying dead friends, ancestors, relatives, and other family members. Some are war veterans who died in foreign lands and whose bodies were brought home to lie with their fathers.

I remember waiting for the body of a man from our church to be brought home after he had been killed in Korea. The book of his life could not be closed until his bones were safely buried next to his father who had been killed in World War II. Another son of the old neighborhood, Eddie, died in the navy and was buried at sea. Their family plot is just north of ours and has a marker in his memory, but when his sisters come to the cemetery with flowers to honor their dead, there is a hollow spot in their hearts because his grave is empty.

We call these plots "our final resting place." Every branch of every family we know has one, and as new generations evolve and people move from one part of the world to another and establish new families, they also establish new family burial plots and erect new monuments bearing their names. Sometimes we callously assert that we don't care what happens to our flesh after we die, and some of us have our bodies cremated and our ashes strewn in some nostalgic place, but yet there is something in most of us that demands that our remains be preserved in a location known to our survivors.

That something is the expectation of resurrection. My parents believed that cremation was immoral, that we were supposed to preserve our bodies so that God can open our graves and raise us up when the last trumpet sounds. When as a youth I asked how Eddie could be raised if his body had disintegrated in the ocean, they replied that the Lord, being the creator of the universe, could do anything, but that we were not to test him by purposefully scattering our remains to the winds. I've pondered the thought at length and still don't know if it is valid. But I'm not going to argue with my parents.

What I do know is valid is the fact of resurrection. Jesus will return and the saved who've died will rise up to meet him. The Bible says so. We have fond expectations of our family having a glorious reunion right there in the old hometown cemetery and rejoicing together as we meet our Lord and await the fiery chariots that will carry us to heaven.

The picture is crystal clear. Those brothers and sisters who have died in Christ whether they be buried in Abraham's tomb, in the hometown cemetery or scattered in the deep, will be caught up together with those who remain to meet the Lord in the air. The Bible says so.

Final resting place? The family plot is *not* our final resting place. Our embalmed flesh may lie there until the great and glorious day of the Lord, or it may return to the earth from whence it came, ashes to ashes and dust to dust. But when the archangel calls, we will be miraculously gathered together and carried to our true final resting place in the mansions of glory.

Tears come to my eyes when I fancy standing by our tombstone on that blessed day singing hymns of praise with my parents, my wife, my children, my grandchildren and my sisters. And I know that when I turn my head and look to the north, I'll see Eddie and his parents and his sisters dancing together joyously among the flowers.

A Real Man

Scripture: Genesis 48
Suggested Reading: Philippians 1:6

As I look back over recent meditations, I cannot help but notice that we have disparaged the character of Jacob more than we have praised it. We should not let this great patriarch go to his grave with a reputation worse than he deserves. Not that all the things we've said about him aren't true. They are. He will always be remembered as the cunning twin who deceived his brother, his father, and his uncle. But the man changed. Or rather, God changed the man. And as with our own friends and family, we should be generous and forgiving enough to remember the man at his best as we carry him to his grave.

Even the consequences of his early sins serve to bring him honor. The traits that his sons developed as they watched their father in action in Padan-aram are traits that eventually backfired, causing Jacob untold grief. Yet he bore his grief with patience, confessing the sins of his youth, repenting of them, recognizing God as his redeemer, and accepting the inevitable consequences of his conduct. That is the finest definition of a real man that anyone could pen.

He was capable of great affection. He loved his wife Rachel and mourned her death until the day he died. She, too, brought him grief just as Rebekah brought grief to Isaac, yet he loved her and in the context of his culture remained faithful to her all his life. He also loved Rachel's sons to a fault and fawned over them to excess.

But when they had grown into men, he honored them only to the extent God allowed.

God gave Jacob the insight to comprehend one of the most outstanding of his attributes that he revealed to us in the book of Genesis. God does not follow man's inclination to give honor according to rank or bias, but rather according to his own sovereign will. Man systematically honored the firstborn or his favorites, but God often chose the younger or the weaker for distinction, going all the way back to Adam's time.

It was Seth, not Cain whom God selected to father the line leading to his chosen people. Subsequently it was Shem rather than Japheth, Isaac rather than Ishmael, and Jacob rather than Esau. And rather than following man's tradition, Jacob followed God's. Instead of giving a double portion of inheritance to his eldest son, Reuben, he gave it to his eleventh son, Joseph, by blessing Joseph's sons, Ephriam and Manasseh. Even then he bypassed the elder Manasseh and gave the dominant blessing to the younger Ephriam.

With God's grace, Jacob somehow preserved in his sons the faith of his fathers while he endured their deceit and infidelity. With God's grace, Jacob overcame the character conditioned by a life of guile and emerged from ancient history as one of the heroes of faith with the prophetic insight to bless each of his children with a vision so keen that it spanned forty generations and melded into the same visions that Daniel and John saw of the end of time. God's grace surpasses human understanding. He loves sinners and patiently molds them into what he wants them to become.

Jacob was a real man, and the course of his life is one we can understand and appreciate. He was a sinner who let God take him as he was on that terrible day long ago when he fled, wretched and lonely, from a brother who wanted to kill him, and to the best of his ability gave his life to the God who would complete and perfect the good work that he began in him.

In Days to Come . . .

Scripture: Genesis 49
Suggested Reading: Ezekiel 21:26–27; Daniel 7:13–14;
Hebrews 11:21; 2 Peter 1:20; Revelation 5:5

*J*acob must have had mixed feelings as he sensed the cold hand of death reaching toward him. He was overjoyed to look once again upon the face of the beloved son he thought he had lost, and upon the faces of the two young grandsons he didn't know he had, Ephriam and Manasseh. His family was safe and satisfied in the land of Egypt, and his sheep grazed contentedly on the lush grass of Goshen. But he was alienated from Canaan, the land that God had promised to him and his children. God was blessing his family, yet the dream God had given him was slipping away with his breath. He wouldn't be human if such a predicament didn't bewilder him a little.

So, as he was stumbling about in his dark valley of confusion, God beamed a full moon on him and gave him a prophetic vision that reached not only through the forty generations of history between him and the Messiah, but also peered into the eternity that latter seers envisioned and recorded for us. Thus he could call his sons together and tell them what should befall them in the days to come.

What he revealed for his sons was not a fate that he had determined for them; it was God's plan for them as God allowed Jacob to see it and express it. When he spoke, he didn't speak in his own words, but he opened his mouth and God spoke through him, using the lofty language that the Holy Spirit planted on his lips, the same language that he gave to Moses, Isaiah, and the other prophets when they uttered the pronouncements of the Lord. And when his sons heard those majestic words they had to know that God was revealing to them their destiny, bad as it was for most of them.

Reuben was punished for his sin of incest by losing the firstborn's share of the inheritance and being doomed to pitch his tent outside the land of promise. Levi was destined to shed his brothers' blood in a holy cause, losing his status as a landed tribe, but gaining the distinction of priesthood. Simeon eventually lost his identity, being swallowed up by his brother Judah. Zebulun became an international trader. Issachar became a slave to the Canaanites because he was afraid to fight them. Dan defended the nation from invaders from the northeast before mingling with the Philistines. Gad was stationed east of the Jordan with his brother Reuben and provided the first line of defense against invaders from the desert. Asher was blessed with a life of plenty in the coastal region. Naphtali's sons became leaders in the land. And Benjamin gave us Saul, Jonathon, the slingers of military fame, and the apostle Paul.

The highest praise of all was reserved for Joseph. His sons, Ephriam and Manasseh, were given the heart of Israel, and not only enjoyed its best lands, but also produced the greatest warriors. The ultimate blessing for Ephriam was that Bethlehem lay within its borders.

But the greatest blessing of all went to Judah, though he had done little to earn it except to offer his life in place of his little brother's. He was not the firstborn, nor did he receive the double share of blessing, yet he became the father of kings and of the King of kings. To be sure, his line was abased after the glory of David and Solomon so that Jesus could claim a humble origin, but to the Lion of Judah, Jesus Christ, came the right to grasp the great scepter, to open the scroll and its seven seals, and to have eternal dominion over all the nations of the world! How happy that displaced old sojourner, Jacob, must have been to peer down the vast corridors of time and see the salvation of the Lord for his family and all the families of the earth!

... And the Egyptians Wept

Scripture: Genesis 50:1–14
Suggested Reading: Luke 2:52

When Jacob died, the *Egyptians* wept for him for seventy days. Some commentators believed that the old patriarch so endeared himself to the natives of the land that they genuinely mourned for him when he died. Others believe that the government declared an official state of mourning out of respect for his son Joseph who had saved the nation from death by famine. It suits me best to believe that the mourning was sincere, and I believe that the seven day lamentation at Atad supports the notion that his death was indeed a very grievous cause of mourning for the Egyptians.

The sadness of the Egyptians comes as somewhat of a surprise. First of all, Jacob was a foreign immigrant living among people who did not particularly like foreigners. Secondly, he was a shepherd, an occupation generally despised by the agricultural Egyptians, even though the nation's governors had no such animus for keepers of livestock. But in any case, old Jacob earned such respect from his hosts that they were deeply grieved by his passing.

Symbolically, we were aliens in Egypt too, before we escaped from our slavery to sin and migrated to our spiritual promised land. Can we take a lesson from Jacob and learn how we should get along with the people of Egypt? Of course we know that we are to love our neighbors and try to win them to Christ, but in fulfilling that mission we can easily make ourselves odious to them and incur their disrespect, as many of us do. We can also walk at arm's length from them, quietly minding our own business, and when we die, perhaps none of them will even know, much less mourn for us. But is there a way to relate to the people of the world in a way that neither offends them nor distances us from them?

When Jesus was young, he grew in favor with both God and man. What he did pleased his heavenly Father and earned the respect of his neighbors as well. Now, unless the only people he pleased were people "of the church," he did a pretty fancy job of tightrope walking to make both God and man happy. Although the Jews of Jesus' day were homogeneous in religion, there is no reason to believe that most of them spent most of their time trying to please God. It is more likely that when it came to worldly things, they were much like us, stretching the rules and living in a less than righteous manner. Yet, Jesus increased in favor with them.

I've known wonderful people of the church who died, and only people of the church attended their funeral. No one else, not even their next door neighbors knew who they were. They were fine members, serving the church well by teaching Sunday school or singing in the choir, but their lives were limited to the affairs of the church. I've known other members of the church who died, and when eulogy time came people from all walks of life came forward to testify that the person in the casket was one who had earned their lasting admiration. They were people of the world we would probably never see again, but along the way a saint had blessed them in some special way and had gained their favor.

I find it remarkable that Egypt mourned when Jacob died. In spite of the fact that he served a different God, worked at a different occupation and lived apart from them, he found a way to touch their lives in such a way that when he died, they mourned his death.

May we all have the grace to grow in such favor with both God and man.

A Coffin in Egypt

Scripture: Genesis 50:15–26

Even in death, Joseph was a symbol of the Christian sojourner.

Although he lived and worked in Egypt, he was never in his heart a citizen of that country. Even as he rose to a position of power in the Egyptian world, he always remembered that he was a citizen of another world, and when he looked to his eternal future, he was determined that someday his remains would be borne to Canaan, his true homeland.

My mother used to sing as she did her housework,

"I am a stranger here,
Within a foreign land;
My home is far away,
Upon a golden strand . . .,"

and

"This world is not my home,
I'm just a passin' through;
my treasures are laid up
somewhere beyond the blue . . . ."

And she was very fond of advising me as a youth that I must be "*in* the world, but not *of* the world."

The same spirit must have persevered in Joseph, reminding him that he was a stranger in a foreign country, and although he lived and labored in Egypt, he was a citizen of the land of promise. As one who knew his destiny lay elsewhere, Joseph prepared for eternity by arranging to have his bones taken out of Egypt when the day of exodus arrived, and delivered to his faraway home where he could enter into rest with his people. What a beautiful lesson for us.

I know my people are in heaven with the Lord while I labor here in Egypt storing up grain and other things. Sometimes when I get to feeling comfortably at home here, which is easy to do when things are going well, as they usually do, the haunting strains of my mother's songs and admonitions sail into my spirit and chide me for being so content.

We make a lot of arrangements for earthly matters. We budget our time and our money. We try to be good stewards of all that God has given us, balancing our checkbooks, monitoring our investments, and maintaining our properties. We try to take care of our bodies by exercising and eating the right things. We make sure our children are educated so they can be satisfied contributors to our economy and our culture rather than a burden on others. In fact, we spend most of our lives making arrangements for our sojourn in this strange land and preparing for our futures here.

To a reasonable extent, all of that is necessary. God has advised us many times that we are to be responsible citizens in this temporal world, just as Joseph was in his, multiplying the talents he has given us, planning before we build, laying a firm foundation, raising our children properly, loving our neighbors as ourselves, and being charitable to the poor.

But do we take equal pain to make arrangements for our eternal destiny? All of the same principles apply to salvation that apply to our sojourn here, and just as we plan for the things of earth, we must plan for the things of heaven. No . . . we should take far more pains planning for our eternal destiny, because the things of earth pale in significance compared to the things of eternity.

As Joseph's, our bones will be put in a coffin here in Egypt, but we also must make firm arrangements to have them carried on the day of exodus to our land beyond the blue.

The End of the Beginning

*W*hen the momentum of World War II began to shift to the Allies' favor, Winston Churchill said, "This is not the end, this is not even the beginning of the end, it is only the end of the beginning."

When Joseph died and left his sons and brothers tending their flocks on the lush plains of Goshen, the preface for God's Book of Life had been written. Joseph's death is the last scene of the first act of God's great drama of paradise lost and paradise regained.

Like the Allies, we have a long way to go before we get to the beginning of the end. Oh, it is only one page in the Bible, the short step from the end of Genesis to the beginning of Exodus, but that one page covers twice the amount of time it took the United States to get from the shot heard 'round the world at Concord to the guns of D-day, the beginning of the end of our war with Germany.

The disobedience of our first parents started the human race on a downward spiral of sin that is like the downward spiral of the sons of Jacob, living peacefully with their flocks one day in a delta paradise, then suddenly being plunged into brutal slavery under the new Pharaoh of Egypt, the synonym for all that is evil.

Just as Adam and Eve's sojourn in the lush Garden of Eden began with their being the favored guests of a friendly God, so the Israelites' sojourn in the delta plains began with their being the favored guests of a friendly Pharaoh. And as Adam and Eve's being forced to work by the sweat of their brow and not only to bear children in pain but also to watch them die, so the Israelites labored under the whips of their Egyptian taskmasters and anguished at the sight of their babies being thrown into the Nile.

We allude to World War II because it is also a part of the big picture. Before God invited the Israelites to enter the Promised

Land, he took them to the foot of Mount Sinai and taught them how they were to live as a nation. The core of his instruction was that they were to love and obey him and never bow their knee to idols. He promised them that if they obeyed, they would live in security and abundance, but if they abandoned him and turned to the worship of foreign gods, the consequences would be catastrophic. But even before they arrived in Canaan, they saw the fleshly pleasures of the pagan fertility rituals, lusted, and soon found themselves violating God's primary rule and rushing headlong toward holocaust.

The book of Deuteronomy details the curses that would befall them if they were to continue to disobey his commands. God promised to drive them from the land he had sworn to their fathers and scatter them abroad in the world to be abused by foreign nations in the most horrible ways imaginable. They did and he did. But he also promised to bring them back when their punishment was complete and promised that he would open their eyes and melt their hearts so they would be faithful to him.

In the last half of the twentieth century, some of the pundits of prophecy who used adding machines counted the years of promised exile and found 1948 to be the predicted year of return. Whether those pundits figured correctly or manipulated their calculations is not for me to say. But the Jews did begin their prophesied return to the Promised Land in 1948, they did build a new nation, and God restored their fortunes as he had promised. The Nazis executed the last of the curses on a disobedient people and God used World War II, the United States and its allies, and the United Nations to fulfill his promise to return them to their land.

In our travels from the promise to the fulfillment, we have come to the end of the beginning, but the end is still a long way off.

The First Step

Our walk with the Lord began at Calvary. His Passover sacrifice broke the bonds of our slavery to sin and set us free. At the first Passover, the angel of death broke the iron will of Pharaoh and delivered the Israelites from the bonds of slavery to the Egyptians. Our exodus from Satan's captivity is the beginning of a new life, walking with Jesus at our side. It is the beginning of our return to paradise.

The journey from slavery to the Promised Land is an eventful trip with two separate levels of meaning: physical and spiritual.

On the physical level, we are saved by the blood of Christ; by being baptized we pass through the Red Sea, and there, by the grace of God, the forces of evil that enslaved us die in the flood of his redeeming water. Then we sit at the feet of the Lord at Sinai and learn how he wants us to live. Next, we pass through the wilderness of this life, ravaged by its droughts and the barbarians who roam freely in it, but blessed by the daily Bread from heaven and the water from the Rock. Finally we cross the Jordan and enter paradise to be with our Savior forever.

The spiritual level is different. After being saved by the blood of Christ and learning how he wants us to live, he invites us to experience a second birth, to be filled with the Holy Spirit and to become citizens of the kingdom of heaven.

Being by nature curious, we spy out the land and find it to be a pleasant land full of fine houses, flowing with milk and honey, and lush with the fruit of the Spirit. But we also discover that there are giants in that land, demonic forces that oppose our entry. And although a small fraction of our being has the faith that we could conquer those foes, the loudest voice within us tells us to fear that land and its awful inhabitants. So we wander in the wilderness until the "old man" in us, the freed slave, wears out and dies, and tired of the arid desert, we long for green pastures and still waters.

Then a new generation arises, a generation that looks forward instead of backward, a generation willing to die to self, to be crucified with Christ and raised up with him in newness of life, willing to plunge into the Jordan and emerge on Canaan's side ready to follow the Commander of the army of the Lord into battle against the enemies that would keep us from possessing the land of promise.

In Christ we become the seed of Abraham, heirs to the promises. But inheriting the kingdom of heaven is not an easy task. We possess our inheritance by conquest. Conquest means war, and war means sacrifice, pain, and bloodshed.

The enemies in that spiritual promised land are not enemies of flesh and blood, but dark spiritual forces that have infested our beings and penetrated our minds and hearts. Battling those forces requires both courage and faith that the battle is the Lord's and that he will keep his promise to give us the victory.

So, there are two ends, the physical and the spiritual. Our physical life begins in the delivery room and ends in a death that delivers us to our eternal reward. Our spiritual life begins with our deliverance from sin, our rebirth, and culminates in a glorious life of communion with the saints and being named conquerors over the forces of the evil one.

The people who write the catechism books call it sanctification. Just as the old Israelites never totally eradicated paganism from their midst, we never achieve absolute perfection. But just as they scored victory after victory over the Canaanites under the leadership of Joshua, we can score victory after victory over Satan's armies under the leadership of the new Joshua, Jesus Christ.

A New King

Scripture: Exodus 1:1–14
Suggested Reading: Genesis 15:13; Isaiah 30:19–22;
Jeremiah 27:4–7

A look behind the pages of scripture confirms that God is totally in charge of the nations of this world.

When God promised Abraham that he would make of him a great nation, he also warned him that his descendants would be sojourners in a foreign land for four hundred years and would be slaves in that country. That prophecy came true.

When Joseph went into Egypt, its political structure was rife with Semitic Hyksos who liked shepherds even though the agricultural Hamitic Egyptians despised them. The hospitable Hyksos gave Jacob and his sons a warm welcome and a good piece of grassland separate from the local Egyptians. But some time after Joseph died, native rebels deposed the Hyksos Pharaoh and restored power to the Egyptians who had good reason to believe that the Hebrews would be sympathetic to foreign invaders, particularly if those invaders were Semites like themselves.

So, this "new king" had neither love for the sons of Jacob nor respect for the memory of Joseph who had enslaved them. So, fearing Hebrew complicity in a possible invasion, he made slaves of them, fulfilling the prophecy God gave to Abraham and building them into a unified nation with a desire to escape from Egypt, capable of enduring the hardship of the wilderness.

Is this old fragment of Egyptian history just coincidental to the destiny of the Jews and the rest of the human race? Of course not.

God, the creator of this earth and everything that lives and breathes in it, rules the kingdoms of men and fashions history to suit his divine purposes. Over and over he confirms in his Word that he controls the nations.

If you are like me, you probably have a hard time seeing the providence of a loving God in the events of history. Sometimes he blesses us and sometimes he chastens us. Sometimes he rewards the good that we do, and sometimes he gives us the bread of adversity and the water of affliction so our character might be strengthened for the work he gives us.

On the day Joseph's brothers sold him into slavery, I doubt if he felt the hand of God in his life. And beyond his callow dreams, we have no record of God giving Joseph any assurances that all would turn out well. When the revolution in Egypt toppled the government that was sympathetic to the sons of Jacob, I doubt if even the most devoted Hebrews felt that the hand of God was moving providentially in their nation. As yet they had received no revelation from God that he was in control of all nations and that he would one day turn their adversity to advantage. We could say the same thing for young Daniel and his friends and for many other Bible people we've yet to meet. Even the dying Jesus felt that God had abandoned him.

But we in modern times have the benefit of scripture and the Lord's promise that he will never leave us nor forsake us. We have the guarantee that our loving God holds the reins of every government that man invents. And whenever a new king comes along who seems to be operating outside the will of God, we have a faith that confirms that whatever that new king does to us, even if he fills our lives with misery, that he is nothing more and nothing less than an agent of the living God, serving his divine purpose and playing his part in fulfilling a divine destiny.

The Midwives Feared God

Scripture: Exodus 1:15–22
Suggested Reading: Genesis 12:3; Deuteronomy 28:36–68

Idoubt that many Sunday school children could give the right answer in the Bible quiz if they were asked to name the Egyptian midwives who feared God so much that they disobeyed their king when he ordered them to kill the Hebrew baby boys. That's not surprising since in the epic drama with many great heroes, they play rather minor roles. But what is surprising is that even the most authoritative biblical scholars can't give the right answer when asked to name the Pharaoh who ordered the death of those babies.

From the time Moses penned the first chapter of the book of Genesis until the Holy Spirit inspired the most recently written word of scripture, many people have managed to get their names in the Bible, some for doing great good, others for doing great evil. Some people's exploits cover many chapters, while others are barely noticed. Some are named just because they appear on a family tree, or just for begetting sons, others because their lives changed the course of history.

Shiphra and Puah were named just once in a single tiny paragraph of scripture for being a blessing to Abraham's descendants. They risked severe punishment to save the Jewish people from history's first recorded case of ethnic cleansing.

God had told Abraham that he would bless the people who blessed him and curse the people who cursed him. Because the two midwives blessed the Israelites, God blessed them by giving them families of their own. Presumably they served as midwives because they were barren, but after they served the Lord by letting the Hebrew boys live, God rewarded them, not just by opening their wombs, but by recording their names and their bravery for all of history.

What curse awaited the nameless king who cursed the seed of Abraham? Although his name undoubtedly occurs somewhere in secular history, no one today can tell us for sure which of the Pharaohs ordered the massacre. And God has excluded his name from the Book.

Throughout succeeding ages, the Jews have been mightily oppressed wherever they have gone. From the Middle East to Europe and Asia, God has raised up barbaric tyrants who have laid heavy hands upon his people. From the great ancient empires to the Third Reich and the Soviet Union, the Jews have been victims of savage attempts to erase them from the human family, but following all the adversity, God has kept his promise and has cursed the oppressor to eventual destruction.

God has also blessed nations and individuals who have been a blessing to Israel. As a Christian nation with a substantial Jewish population, it has been the policy of the United States to protect the civil rights of all ethnic groups and to ally with the nation of Israel. I cannot help but believe that somewhere behind that policy lies God's declaration that he would bless those who bless Abraham and curse those who curse him.

Two ladies who blessed him over three thousand years ago, Shiphra and Puah, not only had babies of their own, but also had their names recorded in the greatest book on earth.

If we bless the one Son of Abraham before whom all the nations of the earth will someday bow, we will be blessed by having our names recorded in the greatest book in heaven, the Lamb's Book of Life!

Chosen to Serve

Scripture: Exodus 2:1–10
Suggested Reading: Matthew 22:14; Romans 9

Having had no say in the circumstances of my birth and upbringing, I spent my youth as the son of devout Calvinists. In my old age I affiliate with the Wesleyans, mainly because Mary Ann is a Wesleyan, more by birth than conviction, and I enjoy a harmonious relationship with her that would be strained by a dispute over church membership. Fortunately, the fact that my parents have been gathered to our people has spared me the necessity of an unpleasant dispute with them on that matter. They would have scorned my claim that Wesleyans at least permit me the privilege of thinking.

The great saints of the Lord, John Wesley and John Calvin, didn't see eye to eye on what they considered some major points of doctrine, particularly the doctrine of predestination. Calvin insisted that in no instance could God deny his omniscience and omnipotence, and therefore both knew and determined everybody's temporal and eternal fate before he laid the foundations of the earth. Wesley, on the other hand, insisted with equal vehemence that God created people with the freedom to choose their own course, and in his self-imposed blindness allowed them to elect their own destiny. Both, of course, dug up plenty of scripture to support their conflicting views.

Unfortunately, pundits on both sides still perpetuate the opinions of the founders of their denominations, but generally with less venom and spite than the great reformers. My Wesleyan pastor knows my background, and on occasion we jest with little seriousness about the issues of predestination and free will. Though I have no expectation that the learned scholars on both sides will ever resolve the matter to their mutual satisfaction, I have resolved it to mine, and quite easily, too. I see no more conflict between the doctrines of election and free will than I do between creation and evolution.

Jesus pointed out that many are called, but few are chosen. Scriptures make it clear that whosoever will may come and that our Lord died to save any who would believe and call on his name. Joshua wasn't mocking the omniscience of God when he challenged the Israelites to "*Choose* you this day whom you will serve . . . ." But the same scriptures declare that almighty God picked Jacob to love and Esau to hate, Pharaoh for a vessel of destruction, and Judas to betray the Son of Man to the Roman guard. It is also obvious that God shouted from heaven and infused his Spirit into the heart of Saul, the ruthless persecutor of Christians, and shaped that lump of hard clay into the great apostle that he became through no real choice of his own. And I doubt if the disciples really had any option at all when Jesus looked into their eyes and whispered, "Follow me."

It is my guess that in what the Wesleyans are fond of calling "prevenient grace," God dangles the bait of salvation in the sea of humanity and allows most people to decide for themselves whether they will bite or not. But I'm equally convinced that God in his omnipotence created others strictly to serve his purposes. To me, that is why some of the great figures of scripture such as Jacob, Joseph, Moses, Samson, Samuel, and John the Baptist have their births recorded in the Bible. God decreed their births and destined those men to his service.

I'm convinced that God picked me and made me into what I am, mainly because I doubt if I'd been bright enough to take the bait. But I'm equally convinced that God, in his amazing grace, gave Mary Ann the good sense to consider all options and come to the wise decision that Jesus died for her sins and in gratitude she should give her heart to him.

The Prince of Egypt

Scripture: Exodus 2:11–20
Suggested Reading: Acts 7:17–29; John 15:5

In the late 1990's, Hollywood turned out a wonderful feature-length cartoon entitled *The Prince of Egypt.* The film spent a good deal of time and plot dramatizing a phase of Moses' life that God covered in just a few verses of scripture: his first forty years, most of which he spent in the court of Pharaoh. As the adopted son of Pharaoh's daughter, the young Moses gallivanted through the capitol on his steed, fun loving and a mischievous companion to the young heir to the throne. In those scenes he clearly established his identity as an Egyptian courtier, a youth of royal and arrogant mien.

We have no biblical or historical confirmation of such a disposition, but I believe that the screenwriters made a thoughtful and reasonable guess when they created the character they did. Luke gave us a hint about the nature of the young Moses when he narrated Stephen's defense before the high priest. Stephen testified that when Moses killed the Egyptian he "supposed that his brethren understood that God was giving them deliverance by his hand . . . ." Apparently, somewhere along the way Moses began to envision himself as the liberator of his people. And when he saw the Egyptian beating an Israelite, he thought that his moment had arrived. He charged up in his chariot and slew the offending Egyptian. He must have thought his people would respond by rising up in rebellion and hoisting him to their shoulders.

But his brethren didn't understand. Or better stated, God had not yet given them a mind to understand. How dejected Moses must have been when his people, rather than rallying around him, rejected him. He had a faint vision that God had spared him from a watery death for a divine purpose and had chosen him to be a man of destiny, a hero who would liberate his countrymen from the bondage of slavery. But now he had to flee from the sword of his brother princes and become an expatriate just as his ancestor Jacob had to flee from Esau. God's appointed hour had not yet arrived.

Abraham and Jacob also had a vision of their destiny, and they too were unwilling to wait for God's chosen moment to make that destiny come to pass. Abraham sired a son by Hagar and Jacob cheated his brother out of the birthright that God would have given him at the divinely appointed time. Now, true to the tradition of his ancestors, Moses stepped out on his own to grab the ring forty years before God's prescribed moment.

At that point in his life he was not a useful vessel. He was a brash young cavalier, strutting his palatial ego through the streets of Raamses and Pithom. The young man still had to die to self before he could be used of God. He had to give up his vision of being the heroic savior of his people and realize that without the help of God he could do nothing. He had to see himself as unworthy and incapable before God could work through him. He had to be reduced to nothing, become an empty vessel, before he could become the great man that God would make him. And what better way to become putty in God's hands than to grow old tending sheep on a foreign hillside.

The deliverance of the nation would not be Moses' deliverance, it would be God's. The victory over Pharaoh would not be Moses' victory, it would be God's, and what a victory it would be! It would not be a mere escape from the bondage of slavery and the drowning of an enemy army, but it would be a victory in the heavens, God's army of angels soundly defeating the evil forces of Satan. The gods of Egypt would be crushed, and the great *I AM*, not Moses, would get all the glory!

Go from Your Country

Scripture: Exodus 2:21–22
Suggested Reading: Genesis 12:1; Mark 8:34–35; 10:28–30

One Christmas Mary Ann and I went from store to store looking for just the right sweater for our daughter. We looked at several that we rejected because they "just weren't *her*." Finally we found the perfect sweater. It was truly "*her*," so we bought it.

It's funny how we are so closely identified with our "stuff." We decline purchasing a particular house because "it just isn't *us*." Most everything we own, from our car to our mailbox has a style that corresponds with our taste and character. Even the dog looks like he belongs in the family picture.

If the things we own seem to be extensions of ourselves, how difficult does it become to part with them? After we've spent a generous amount of time, money, and energy making the character of our house into something that reflects our nature, how easily can we pack up and move if the Lord calls us to go somewhere else? Or could we leave forever without even packing up all the stuff to which we so closely relate?

The fundamental principle of Christian discipleship is established early in the scripture: "Go from your country . . . ."

So far, just about all of the great heroes of faith that we have encountered have one thing in common: they were exiled from their homeland. In answer to God's call to "go from your country," Abraham moved from Haran to Canaan. His grandson Jacob fled from his home in Canaan and sojourned back in Haran. His son Joseph was sold as a slave and exiled from Canaan to Egypt, where he spent the rest of his life. And now Moses is forced to leave his home in Egypt and flee to Midian. Is it coincidence that all these people had to turn their backs on their families and all they owned in order to fulfill the destiny the Lord had planned for them, or is God trying to tell us something? Might there be a message here?

Jesus laid that message on his followers in several different ways. Once he made it quite simple. If you are to be my disciple, he said, you have to "deny yourself." In other words, deny your own nature, deny your needs, deny your identity, deny your own character, deny your very *selfness*, and find your identity in him.

In my library I have a book with the wonderful title, *Christ Esteem*, in which the author, Don Matzat, suggests that once we've denied our self and have found our identity in Christ, as he demands, we should have no self-esteem problems because Christ has replaced the self in us, and as a result, the esteem we can generate is much greater than before because it is Christ esteem rather than self-esteem.

Jesus also warned us that if we love the life that revolves around our own being, we are eventually going to lose it.

So, what's to motivate us to deny our self, to be willing to turn our backs and walk away from our land, our houses, our children and all that stuff that means so much to us? What's to move us to open our hands and loosen the tight grip we have on everything from our egos to our wallets and our automobiles?

Once we've declared that we love him more than we love anything else in this world, the affection we have for our loved ones and the joy we have in our possessions will become much more fulfilling than ever before. Making him first in our lives makes everything else much, much better.

Forsaken?

Do Not be afraid
I will never leave you

Scripture: Exodus 2:23–3:2
Suggested Reading: Deuteronomy 31:6; Joshua 1:5; Matthew 28:20;
Hebrews 13:5   *Also Deut 31 : 8*

*D*id you ever wonder what Moses must have been thinking as he sat on Mount Horeb in Midian day after day tending his sheep? Though he was on high ground, emotionally he must have been alone in a dark valley.

He was a very bright young man. His later writings prove that. But what was going on in his mind at the moment? Did he know his family history? Had his parents had time to teach him about Abraham, Isaac, Jacob, and Joseph? Had Joseph left a record somewhere in Pharaoh's court that he might have read? Had he lost the chance to become a leader in Egypt like his ancestor Joseph?

He was a Hebrew and the Hebrews were being persecuted by this new line of Pharaohs. He had identified with his people, and because he killed an Egyptian, had to flee the country. Now he was an alien just as his ancestors had been. Where was God, anyway? Had his God died in Egypt? Would God speak to his people only in Canaan? Why had he been silent so long?

Had he and his people been faithful to their God? As faithful as possible under the circumstances. All of the Hebrew boys had been circumcised in the tradition God gave to Abraham. Even as they built cities for their oppressors with insufficient materials, they passed on their ancient traditions and their belief in God to their children. What greater faithfulness could God ask?

But where was their God? He had spoken to Jacob over four hundred years before and no one had heard anything from him since. Had he forsaken them? Moses must have thought so. As he roamed those hillsides in Midian, he must have felt totally estranged from the God of his fathers. There he was, a stranger in a strange land among strange people. He was no longer a prince. He had gone to work as a shepherd for a foreign priest and had married one of his daughters.

And what about the traditions? Had he honored them? Although he had told his sons about his God, it must have been in less than optimistic terms, because for them he had abandoned the practice of circumcision.

He must have expected to spend the rest of his life there on Mount Horeb, apart from his God, apart from his people, living among strangers with strange gods. He probably expected to be buried there on the hillsides where his sheep were grazing. If any man ever needed a moon to pierce the darkness of his valley of despair, it was Moses.

Then it came! The fire in the bush! His God was alive and had come to him!

God knows that his people need the assurance of his presence. He promised Moses and Joshua that he would never leave them nor forsake them as they carried out the work he had called them to do. And, praise God, that promise extends to us.

Sometimes I have alienated myself from the presence of the Lord. Probably you have too. But although he has never called to me from a burning bush or spoken to me through the thunder, or even in a still, small voice, his wonderfully reassuring last words to his disciples have echoed through my mind wherever I've been, far or near, "Lo, I am with you always . . . ."

Afraid to Look at God

Scripture: Exodus 3:2–12
Suggested Reading: Exodus 2:23–3:5

*M*y mother always warned me that I should never go anywhere I wouldn't want to be found by the Lord, in case he returned while I was somewhere I shouldn't be.

I often thought about her words while I lingered in places a Christian boy ought not go. I've wondered what I would say to the Lord should he return at some embarrassing moment in my life. Would I make some lame excuse for being there or for doing that? What if I hadn't been to church lately? What if I hadn't given my tithe? What if I had let an opportunity pass to witness for him? What if he were to catch me at a time my life was misdirected and while he was the last thing on my mind?

I know just how Moses must have felt when God came to him there on Mount Horeb. I know why he was afraid to look at God. I would have been afraid too if I had wandered so far from his presence. I would have been afraid too if I had failed to pass the traditions of my faith on to my family and practiced the rituals God expected me to observe. I wonder if Moses had an excuse prepared. I wonder if he had an answer on the tip of his tongue if God were to ask him why he had not circumcised his sons.

But God didn't put him to the test. He didn't make him squirm. God knew what was in Moses' heart. He didn't have to ask him any embarrassing questions. He had saved him for this moment, and he got right to the point in laying out his plan for the work he was calling him to do. He didn't mention Moses' shortcomings or inabilities. He simply declared that he had seen the affliction of his people, knew their suffering, had heard their groaning under the heavy yoke of the Egyptians and had selected Moses to rescue them from their bondage.

But Moses' mind was on his own condition. "Who am I," he asked, "that I should go to Pharaoh and bring the sons of Israel out of Egypt?" He knew that he was not worthy of such a mission. He knew that he was not in right standing with God and was not spiritually qualified to be his agent.

But God ignored his question. Who he was, what he had done and what he had failed to do were irrelevant. God would take him as he was and make him into what he wanted him to be. "I will be with you," God simply said. In other words, "Have no fear. I will take care of you. I will give you everything you need to do the job I've chosen you to do. I didn't pick you because of your excellent qualifications, I picked you for what I would make of you. All you have to do is yield your will to mine, I'll take care of the rest."

I think my mother worried unnecessarily. Not because I never went where I shouldn't have gone, but because our God is not the kind of God who sneaks up on us in our weakness to chide us and make us account for our failures. He knows where we are all of the time, and he knows our shortcomings. All he wants to know from us, no matter where we are and what we're doing, is if we are ready to say yes to him if he were to call us for some task.

He won't entertain excuses. If we try to argue with him and avoid his call by claiming that we are not up to the job he's calling us to do, he will take our excuse away by simply promising that he will be with us and that he will provide the time, talent, and energy we need to get the job done.

And one of life's greatest blessings is finding that to be true.

Who Am I? Who Are You?

Scripture: Exodus 3:13–22
Suggested Reading: Romans 9

*J*ust yesterday I was rummaging through some old stuff that I've stored up in the attic. You know, those old things that have no use anymore, but are too precious to throw out. One box I opened contained some memorabilia from my professional days, awards and other mementoes of certain successes that once gave me great satisfaction. Among them was a file containing my resume.

At a time when I've spent the last decade doing menial chores, puttering in the yard, or pecking at a keyboard, that long outdated record of things I'd achieved in my youth and middle age seemed a mere relic of an almost forgotten past. I began to reminisce. What would I do if my office called and asked me to come out of retirement and take on a major project? Several years ago I might have welcomed the proposition, but today I'd shrink from it and suggest that they call Ron or Lois, or anyone who was younger and whose skills are not as rusty as mine. And when I ponder that possibility, I think I know how Moses must have felt when God called him out of retirement to resume his career as leader of a nation.

Barefoot and stunned, Moses clutched his staff and stood trembling before the flaming bush as God announced to him his surprise promotion from shepherd to liberator, a job he would have welcomed forty years earlier, but a task he would rather pass up at this point in his life. He had given up his ambitions. His princely arrogance had been drained from him. His vision of personal glory had been shattered by rejection. The skills he had acquired as a prince in Pharaoh's court had eroded. He no longer viewed himself as a Hebrew, instead raising uncircumcised sons and living in the tradition of the Midianites. And he was old. So, his question was a fair one, "Who am I that I should go to Pharaoh and bring the sons of Israel out of Egypt?"

God's answer was one we should all carefully note: "You're nobody." Oh, he didn't say it outright, he didn't have to. Moses implied it in his question. God said it by not answering directly, but rather by saying, "But [because you're a nobody] I will be with you." When Moses was a somebody, he volunteered for service, but at that time, God rejected his offer. However, now that he was a self-confessed nobody, God saw him as qualified and would empower him for the task.

Back in those days, names meant more than they do now. Moses was named Moses because he was rescued from a watery grave, spared from death because God had a mission for him. And now that God had established Moses' identity and qualifications, Moses asked the voice in the bush for some identification. "Who are you?" or, "What's your name?"

Was this a fair question for Moses to ask? Or had his streak of princely arrogance returned? "If you're the God of my fathers and if you're going to go with me to lead your people out of bondage . . . if we're going to be partners in this endeavor, shouldn't I know a little more about you? After all, you've never spoken to me before. I only heard about you from a mother I barely remember. So, who are you?"

God's answer comes crashing down through the scriptures in capital letters. "I AM WHO I AM!" I am the creator of the universe. I am the King of kings. Nations rise and fall at my command. The winds blow at my bidding. I am the Potter who made vessels of clay in my own image, breathed my life into them, and will use them as I choose. And who are you, a mere man, to question me?

At the Feet of God

Scripture: Exodus 4:1–9, 20

A cliché often tossed out by the chairman of the mission board during his little speech on mission Sunday is, "God does not call the equipped, God equips the called." And we accept that as truth more on the basis of scripture than on our own experience. After all, if God could turn the cowardly, foot-in-his-mouth Peter into an eloquent man of valor, he can do the same for any of us.

Buoyed by the simple faith that God would provide everything necessary, from fundamental needs to miracles, many missionaries have answered the call to go out into the world to preach the gospel to all creatures.

Moses didn't have the benefit of either scripture or stirring testimony to glue his faith to the sticking point, so God showered him with all the equipment one could hope for when setting out on a sacred dangerous mission. In return, God asked him for all he had.

At that moment, standing there quaking beside the fiery bush, Moses had in his hand only his shepherd's rod. He used it as a cane to traverse treacherous ground. It was his weapon to whack wolves and cobras. He needed it to discipline his wayward sheep. It was the tool of his trade, his Swiss army knife, the symbol of his entire identity. It was all he had.

And the commanding voice from the bush asked him to throw down all he had at the feet of I AM WHO I AM. And when he did, the miracle happened. The dead thing became alive! The rod turned into a snake! Of course Moses got scared and ran. If he'd had his rod in his hand, he would have sent that serpent to its final resting place. But without his stick he was unarmed, and the viper hissed and barred its deadly fangs.

Now God could have done a lot of different things to show Moses that he had the moment under control. He could have turned a rock into a mongoose to kill the snake, or he might have sent a tongue of fire out of the bush to burn it. But that would not have tested Moses' faith. So instead, God ordered Moses to pick the snake up by its tail. Not by its neck so it couldn't bite him, but by its tail!

Now I'm no expert on snakes. I've killed a few in my yard with a rake or a spade, harmless ones I'm sure, but better to err on the side of safety. Kraig, my fine veterinarian friend and expert on all of God's creatures, assured me that anyone who knows anything at all about poisonous snakes would never pick one up by its tail. It would be a sure ticket to the emergency room if not the graveyard.

Now Moses knew something about snakes too. With his rod in his hand he knew no fear, but he knew better than to pick one up by its tail. Yet, the I AM ordered him to do something that under normal circumstances could be fatal, since Moses had no hospital, only a graveyard. And Moses passed the test of faith!

At this point I'm ashamed. Sure, I've stuffed a few easy dollars into the mission envelope and prayed for brave souls called to serve the Lord in such places as Ghana or New Guinea, but I've never thrown all I am or all I have at the Master's feet, and my faith certainly has never emboldened me enough to pick up the serpent by his tail.

But I admire and envy those who have been blessed to see their lifeless talents come alive, and, as a rod in God's hand, open a path through the sea or draw living water from a rock!

Send Someone Else

Scripture: Exodus 4:10–17
Suggested Reading: Matthew 10:16–20; Numbers 12

When Moses picked up that snake and it turned back into a rod, I was sure that God had succeeded in convincing him that his mission would be much more than a mere task, it would be an adventure. Imagine having as a partner the great I AM, who could turn sticks into serpents, river water into blood, and a leprous hand clean. I can't imagine anyone turning down an opportunity to experience such thrills every day.

Yet Moses balked. Now God didn't get mad when Moses claimed exemption on the ground that he was unworthy. It's good to say we're unworthy. But God lost patience when Moses begged off because he felt inadequate. Lack of talent is not an excuse that God will accept, simply because God intentionally chooses the inadequate and provides the skills necessary to perform the task. That's one of the main reasons why God delayed his call for another forty years after Moses left the court of Pharaoh. God wasn't looking for an eloquent, dashing young prince. He wanted a stammering old shepherd. The God of the tongue would provide the words, the argument, and the rhetoric.

God is very clever with words. More clever than we are. Jesus out-parleyed the best lawyers of his day. The Holy Spirit's words in the mouths of uneducated fishermen awed the crowds in Jerusalem and changed the world. No one can beat God in a debate. Moses learned that the hard way.

Moses said, "Send someone else."

God said, "okay."

Moses meant, "Send someone *other than* me." He thought his meaning was clear.

God knew what Moses meant, but he took advantage of his ambiguous words. "okay," he said, "I'll send *someone else*, but not someone *other than* you, someone *in addition to* you. I'll let your big brother Aaron be your deputy and do the speaking for you." With those words, God snookered Moses, and when the fire in the bush flickered out, Moses knew he'd been had and went reluctantly home to give his old boss notice and to pack up his wife and kids.

Just as Abraham was chosen by God to father the nation, and just as Joseph was chosen to lead the family safely into Egypt and spare them from the famine, so Moses was chosen to liberate Israel from bondage under the Egyptians. But within the confines of their callings, each had the latitude to inject a little self into God's program. Abraham's faith faltered just enough to let him slip into bed with Hagar and sire a hoard of enemies. Moses' unwillingness back at Horeb not only cost him the gift of an eloquent tongue that God would surely have given him, but also saddled his command post with an older brother who built for the people the infamous golden calf and later committed treason by conspiring with sister Miriam to usurp the position of authority God had given exclusively to his servant Moses.

Our valley is dark with an array of human frailties: pride and unworthiness, arrogance and inadequacy, bravado and fear. And in giving us the long leash, God lets us suffer the consequences of our errors. But the glimmer of light in the valley is that in spite of our weakness and waywardness, God's will will be done. The Potter will shape the clay to suit his design, kings and nations will bow before him, and the paradise we lost will be regained.

A Little White Lie?

Scripture: Exodus 4:18–20

Until I gave this matter some thought, Moses' request to his father-in-law really baffled me.

His mission was clear. He was to quit his service to Jethro and go back to Egypt to deliver his people and become the leader of the newly liberated nation.

Why then did he say to Jethro, "Let me go back to my kinsmen in Egypt and see if they are still alive"? He knew they were alive. God told him so. He told Jethro a lie, or at best, intentionally misled him. Why? He didn't quit his job, he requested a leave of absence. And why was Jethro so willing to grant his leave and bid him, "Go in peace"?

The answer to the latter question seems quite obvious. The great I AM has the unquestionable right and ability to harden one heart and soften another. The great liberation, after all, was his plan in the first place, and Pharaoh will be obstacle enough without Jethro being cantankerous too. Once Moses was on board, God surely wanted the mission to begin without flaw.

But why did Moses mislead his father-in-law? Was he afraid that Jethro would not let him go if he knew the truth? Was Moses afraid that Jethro would not be willing to part with his daughter and grandsons? Was his mission so secret that he couldn't even tell his closest relatives?

Or, maybe there's another possibility.

What would you say if I walked into your house and told you that when I was out on my patio yesterday watering my plants, the rose bush caught fire and began talking to me? Would you believe me if I told you that the unconsumed burning bush ordered me to go to another country and engineer the liberation of two million political prisoners? And, oh yes, would you believe me if I told you that as proof of its authority and commitment, the bush asked me to drop my garden hose on the ground, and when I did it turned into a snake, and that when I picked it up again, it turned back into a garden hose? You'd probably humor me by telling me of the time you were abducted by aliens, then you'd call the men in the white coats to come and get me. And justly so.

So maybe Moses thought his experience was so rare that he would be mocked in the telling of it. Maybe episodes such as the one he'd just experienced are better left untold if the telling of it might invite ridicule. After the whole mission has been success-fully completed, that extraordinary scene on the hillside would become an acceptable tale.

Many new Christians have wondrous experiences as they meet God for the very first time. I've seen transformed souls so carried away by the encounter that they blurt their story without restraint to all they meet. And I've seen them crushed when the saints be-little the most glorious moment of their life.

Since even the clerics and the professors who write books about the quandaries they find in the Bible seem to have avoided the issue of Moses' little white lie, I suppose at this point my explana-tion is as good as any other. But if I'm searching the scriptures for lessons on how God wants me to live my life, my explanation not only works for me, but also instructs me that restraint is some-times the better part of wisdom.

A Bridegroom of Blood

Scripture: Exodus 4:21–26
Suggested Reading: Genesis 25:1–6

*P*oor Zipporah. One day she lived in a romantic dream, and the next day her visions shattered. One day while fetching water she was set upon by a gang of surly shepherds, and her proverbial knight in shining armor happened by and saved her from that fate worse than death. So, she brought her hero home to meet her father, and the rest of the story is the stuff of fairy tales. Her father gave her hand to him in marriage, and they lived happily ever after in a warm pastoral setting among the gentle lambs, raising lovely babies who romped on the hillside. Almost.

Life was comfortable. She and her hero husband were practicing the faith of the Midianites at the feet of her father, the priest, and happily ignoring the practices that her husband's God required. They were in her land living with her family; under those circumstances it made perfect sense for her husband to accept the traditions of her belief, or at least not interfere with its rituals. After all, the God of the Israelites was also the God of the Midianites, wasn't he? After all, they were all sons of Abraham and worshipped the same God, except that somewhere along the line the Midianites had ceased the practice of circumcision. But that was of no consequence. They were in Midian now and were doing things the way the Midianites did them with no objection from Moses.

But one day her prince came home from the fields with a strange look upon his face. She could tell that he was both happy and tortured. So he sat down and explained to her his encounter with the great I AM. And her life changed forever. She knew that soon they were to leave the pastures and go off on the mission that God had assigned him. She knew, too, that her husband had not been faithful to his God, and she knew that he was being driven by a spirit within him to change his ways, and that if he was going to return to his people, he had better begin to practice his religion as his parents had taught him.

Along the way the Spirit moved in her too, and suddenly she saw truth as she had never before seen it. Although she didn't see it clearly, she knew there was something right about the faith of her husband's fathers, and she knew what she had to do. She had to circumcise their son. It wasn't a pleasant task. After all, he was far more than eight days old. But Moses had neglected it, and now it had to be done if they were to walk in harmony with Moses' God. So, in accordance with tradition, she took a flint and cut off her son's foreskin. She used the foreskin to daub their son's blood on Moses' feet, and she called him her "bridegroom of blood."

Here, in a very mysterious way, God confirms to us that circumcision and blood is central to our relationship with him. Oh, we no longer practice circumcision as a physical ritual, but if we truly walk with Christ, we are circumcised in our hearts, and have spiritually separated ourselves from the flesh.

The blood that God demands as payment for our sins is not our blood, but it is the blood of Christ shed on the cross for us. And just as Zipporah daubed the blood of her son on Moses' feet confirming to him that he was now right with God and could go ahead and do God's business, we must apply Jesus' blood to our lives and become bridegrooms of blood to him. Being bridegrooms of blood to our Lord not only signifies our membership in his church, but also signifies that we are right with him and are available, without hindrance or reservation, to do his work.

... And the People Believed

Scripture: Exodus 4:27–31

$\mathcal{I}$'ve never had the privilege of standing among the spectators at Cape Canaveral and watching a giant rocket blast from its launching pad and thunder toward the sky. It must be a spellbinding sight. Only the people who worked on the project comprehend the amount of effort that has been expended to bring the rocket to the point of liftoff. And only the people involved know the amount of work that still lies ahead to bring the mission to fulfillment.

But the moment of liftoff is a moment to celebrate. In a mighty blast of smoke and flame, the thrust engines explode and the giant rocket begins to move slowly skyward. The fury of the propulsion makes the earth tremble as the massive ship sheds the bonds of gravity. In a few moments the rocket shrinks to near nothingness and disappears in the haze above. As the echo of the blast dies in the distance, the onlookers applaud and cheer the spectacle they have just witnessed. But at mission control and in the craft soaring high above, people are working intently on the mission's objective and will not rest until its goals have been met.

Prior to meeting Moses in Midian, God put a lot of work into mission "Paradise Regained." He sent Joseph to Egypt and manipulated the international power structure that allowed Joseph a seat in Pharaoh's court. Then, by governing the forces of nature, he caused a period of plenty and a period of drought. Then he touched the heart of the king and opened the gates of Goshen so the sons of Israel could safely and comfortably grow into a nation. Then he again turned the political tide and brought about a rebellion that ousted the Canaanite Pharaoh and replaced him with a son of Egypt who clamped the iron shackles of slavery on Israel's legs. And now he has chosen a liberator and has sent him to Egypt to assume leadership in the house of Jacob. The mission has begun, but there is still a long way to go before the second liberator touches down on the planet to complete the mission.

Moses conjured up a lot of worries as God outlined his mission there on the mountainside. His first fear was that the Israelites would not believe that God had sent him. There was some justification for such a fear because the last words spoken to him by an Israelite forty years earlier were, "Who made you a prince and a judge over us?" So God gave him signs as proof of his commission.

When he got to Egypt and met with the leaders of Israel, Aaron did the talking and Moses performed the signs. Now we don't know if the signs were the weight that turned the tables of belief for the people or not. Surely God could soften their hearts and make them believe, just as he would soon harden the heart of Pharaoh and make him reject Moses' pleas for deliverance. But whatever the cause, the people believed. They accepted Moses as their new leader and as a messenger from God. They believed that their Lord had visited them, had seen their affliction, and would lead them out of bondage. And they bowed their heads and worshipped.

We have liftoff! Oh, the mission has just begun and many perils and setbacks lie ahead, but this is a moment to celebrate. The sons of Israel have not yet broken the bonds of Pharaoh's grasp and the earth has not yet trembled with the fury that the great I AM will unleash on the gods of Egypt, but the countdown has finished and the mission has begun.

As I close my Bible after reading the fourth chapter of Exodus, I clap my hands and cheer!

You Have Not Delivered . . .

Scripture: Exodus 5

Last Sunday a friend in my church, the chairman of the missions committee, told me about a man who had recently volunteered to serve on the evangelism program. He had felt a great calling from the Lord to go out and win souls. The man had recently retired after a hectic and successful life in business, but had done little for God's kingdom except to plop a generous amount of money into the offering plate each Sunday. Now, with time on his hands, guilt in his heart, and his engine still racing, he felt a great need to use the gifts of persuasion with which the Lord had blessed him by going out and making converts for the church.

He attended the training sessions faithfully and earned honors learning the program. He amazed the other students with his skill and polish in presenting the gospel during role playing rehearsals. Finally the evening came for him to go out on a "two-by-two" as a trainee with a veteran evangelist at his side. He had learned his lines well and went out with a heart full of grand expectation.

He was not prepared for what happened that night. His potential convert, a backslidden former member of the church, scoffed at each of the points he made, and became more and more stubborn as the rookie evangelist went through his presentation with increasingly magnetic conviction. But at the end, rather than returning to Christ, the man ushered our evangelist from his home with a mocking laugh, thanked him for the lively debate, and told him if he ever came back he would be wasting time for both of them.

The Lord's fiery new salesman was crushed. He had never before been so severely rejected by anyone, either socially or in business. His ego was badly bruised, and he told my friend that maybe the Lord didn't really want to use him after all.

The veteran took him back to the church and reviewed with him the story of Moses.

Imagine what must have been going on in Moses' mind as he approached his task. The Lord had blessed him with miraculous powers, a collection of signs and wonders, and a silvery tongued assistant to do the talking for him. He was dedicated to doing what the Lord had called him to do. The Lord had said, "I will send you to Pharaoh that you may bring forth my people . . . out of Egypt." He had God's promise that he would be with him and would even put the words in his mouth. With all of that going for him, how could he possibly fail?

Yet he got booted out of Pharaoh's house with a derisive laugh. "Who is the Lord that I should heed his voice?" When he failed with Pharaoh, and the Egyptians put heavier burdens on the Israelites, even Moses' own people rejected him, and he turned angrily on the Lord and said, "You have not delivered your people at all . . ."

God has a method that is so simple that even the army understands it. No one is worthy to serve unless he first has had the ego crushed out of him. The army does it in basic training, but God does it on the battlefield of life. God used a reprobate to squeeze the ego out of the evangelist, and he used Pharaoh to squeeze it out of Moses. God wants us to know that when he uses us, we are vessels who have been emptied of self and filled with his spirit, and he wants us to know that when the victory finally comes, it is not a victory for which we can take a bit of credit, but a victory for which we must give all the glory to the Lord!

I Am the Lord!

Scripture: Exodus 6
Suggested Reading: Romans 9:9–24

Quit looking at yourself with such pity, Moses! Quit saying such things as, "Oh Lord, what have you done to your people?" and "Why did you ever send me?" Quit your grumbling! Stop there in your tracks and look at ME. You are about to learn the first thing a person has to know in order to serve as my instrument. You are nothing, and I am everything. You are merely the creature, I am the creator. I am the Potter, you are the clay. Now, listen up . . .

> I am the Lord.
> I will bring you out from under the burden of the Egyptians.
> I will deliver you from their bondage.
> I will redeem you with an outstretched arm.
> I will do great acts of judgment.
> I will take you for my people.
> I will be your God.
> I will bring you to the land I swore to Abraham.
> I will give it to you for a possession.
> I am the Lord.
> I am, I will, I will, I am.
> There!

One of the problems we seem to have as modern Christians is that we just don't know our place. Nor God's. We haven't come to grips with who God is and who we are. We discuss among ourselves the kind of God we are willing to believe in. One will say, "I can't believe in a God who doesn't love everybody," or, "My loving God would never send anyone to hell." All too often we presume to tell God his business. We ask him to quit letting those poor children in Africa starve to death. We tell him whom he should heal and what we think he should give us. In our offertory prayers, we even tell him how he should spend the few dollars we've so generously given to him. We presume that the great creator needs our money if his kingdom is to succeed on this planet.

When God acts in our lives, we sometimes, like Moses, tend to answer back to him, questioning his judgment, calling him to account, wanting him to explain to us just what he has done and why he has done it.

We can excuse Moses' reaction to God on the ground that he did not have the revelation we have about the nature of the Supreme Being. As Moses grew in knowledge of God, his respect also grew. And although he had such an intense relationship with God that they could converse as friend to friend, after he had made his point he always yielded to the word of the Lord.

But we have the revelation of the entire Word of God, from Moses through Jesus to the writings of the apostles. Because of the benefit of this broad revelation, our path through this valley is illumined a bit more brightly, and we should know that we are never to question God's wisdom or the actions that he chooses to take in our lives or in his world. We should know that we have no right to ask him why he made us the way he made us, and we should know that our duty is, as Paul hints, simply to submit to his will and keep repeating, "Have thine own way, Lord, have thine own way."

And when he has given us the grace to be as meek as Moses finally became, he will also confirm in our spirits that his way is best, assuring us that when we yield our lives to him completely, he will bless us in ways we cannot imagine.

Little Victories

Scripture: Exodus 7:1–14; 12:12
Suggested Reading: Revelation 20:7–10

*B*eing the curious sort, I sometimes raise questions that even the learned professors can't answer. I know how Aaron's stick turned into a snake: it was simply a miracle decreed by almighty God. But how did Pharaoh's magicians turn their sticks into snakes? There are many amusing guesses.

One guess is that they were never sticks at all, but that they were snakes all the time, paralyzed into stick-like rigidity by the pressure of the magicians' thumbs at the base of their skulls. They simply appeared to be sticks, and when the magicians released the pressure they regained their flexibility and began to wriggle on the ground. Another guess is that sorcerers created a clever and elaborate illusion, much as our stage magicians do today, to persuade Pharaoh that his gods were as powerful as the Lord. Yet another guess is that God actually turned the Egyptians' sticks into snakes just to harden Pharaoh's heart and set the stage for the fireworks to come.

Now I don't really like any of those guesses because they leave Satan out of the picture and depict our God as one who dabbles in trivia and deception.

The story behind the story goes far beyond the confrontation between Pharaoh and Moses, far beyond the liberation of a people from slavery and far beyond the birth of a nation. The real story here is the battle between God and the devil, and it is a fight to the finish, peaking at Calvary, and ending at the lake of fire.

The moment of beauty for me in this little story is not the wonder of sticks changing into snakes, but the fact that one snake, Aaron's, devours all the others. That tiny piece of the plot portends the end of the story that we don't read until we get to the last book of the Bible. As the millennia roll by, God will have his little victories over the forces of evil. One by one his angels will conquer the demons until the final day of judgment comes for their king and the Lord casts him into the everlasting fire.

The light that shines in the valleys of my life is that I get to witness many of those little victories along the way. And some of them were even won on my ground.

When an angry God cast the rebellious Satan from heaven, a multitude of demons fell with him, forming a force that has fought against God's army of angels down through time. Ever since, the spiritual realm has been a battlefield we can scarcely imagine, but if we look closely in the events of our own lives, we can visualize the scenes behind the scenes.

Through the eyes of the Spirit I've seen God's angels defeat the demons that lurk in liquor bottles, in sexual lusts, in business hierarchies, and social power structures, in our wallets, our possessions, our toys, and our pleasures. I've seen Aaron's snake eat up the serpents that Satan threw into the ring with it.

God's ultimate goal, of course, is to restore to us the paradise we threw away when we yielded to the lure of the serpent's lies back in the Garden of Eden. And we not only get to share the blessings of those great little victories along the way, but also, as he gave to the Israelites before us, God gives us the exhilarating experience of liberation from the broken spirit and cruel bondage that comes with triumph over the devils that enslave us.

Water, Blood and Wine

Scripture: Exodus 7:14–24
Suggested Reading: John 2:1–11; Ephesians 6:12;
Revelation 12:7–9

Sometimes we tend to shrug off those old pagan gods of wood and stone as nothing more than hand-carved idols that naïve people worshipped in ignorance.

The people of Egypt had a whole stable of gods, chief among them being Osiris, god of the Nile. The life embodied by the river was the life embodied by their god, and the life of the Nile was the life of Egypt.

Amusing myth? Certainly not! If the religion of Egypt had been nothing more than mere fancy, God would never have ravaged the land with those horrible plagues. Our God is not a Don Quixote who jousts with windmills or works miracles for mere convenience or pleasure; he is a warrior God who battles for us against the satanic forces that seem to dominate our world.

The battle for deliverance in the book of Exodus is not a war of diplomacy between Moses and Pharaoh. It is a war between the hosts of heaven and the angels that fell with Satan and became demons. There's no *abracadabra* here. When Aaron's rod turned into a snake and swallowed the Egyptians' snakes, the army of the Lord devoured some of those lesser demons, depriving the Egyptians of a few of their lesser gods. And when Aaron lifted his rod and struck the Nile turning it red, it wasn't simply a cute magic trick, it was God striking a death blow against a fallen angel.

In the Old Testament, we first met the nation of Israel struggling under the iron hand of the Egyptians. Thirteen hundred years later when we encountered them for the first time in the New Testament, they were struggling under the iron hand of the Romans. One of the things that the Egyptians and the Romans held in common was that their culture was controlled by the forces of Satan. The demons that ruled Egypt during Pharaoh's time ruled Rome during Caesar's time. Same bunch of fallen angels, just different names.

The first combative act of our angry God on behalf of the Israelites in Egypt was to strike a blow against Osiris, the god of the Nile. The first combative act of our angry God on behalf of the Israelites under Rome was to strike a blow against Bacchus, the god of wine. Jesus' miracle at Cana was not merely a trick of convenience to save face for an unprepared wedding host, nor was it only a sign to his friends that he had power over creation. It was a blow struck at a demon, letting him know in no uncertain terms that God is not only the God of wine, but that he is the master of all spirits. How that demon must have flinched!

So far in Exodus, God has taught us two very important things. First he has taught us, and we should never forget, that he is God over *us*. We are to assume a submissive role and recognize that he is the mighty Potter and we are the lowly clay, subject to be shaped in accordance with his will. Secondly, he has taught us that the world is full of evil spirits of which we must beware, but that he is master of those demons, is waging constant war against them, and that his ultimate victory is assured.

Why does he do all this? He wants to set us free from bondage. Not bondage to Egyptians or Romans, but free from bondage to sin, free from the control of the evil spirits of wine or lust or power or things or any of the demons that possess us. He wants to take the tasteless water of our sinful lives and turn it into the sweet communion wine of his blood, shed for us in the war against Satan.

Why Not a Blizzard?

Scripture: See section headings in your Bible, Exodus 8–11

When I was a very young teacher, I earned a little extra money teaching an evening class in world geography to high school drop-outs. Since I hadn't studied much geography in college, I had to stay one step ahead of the students by preparing the lessons very carefully before each class. I remember the unit on Egypt very well, because Melvin, one of the more "learned" students, found it personally fulfilling to challenge the faith of anyone who accepted the Bible as the Word of God.

The issue was the plagues. Melvin asserted that each of the first nine plagues was nothing more than an exaggerated description of common Egyptian phenomena.

The water of the Nile, he declared, often became red and bitter due either to silt being riled up during the flood season or to algae growing profusely during periods of stagnation. And hoards of frogs, flies, and locusts, he claimed, were not unusual consequences of climatic change or pollution. Field cattle often died of excessive heat. Epidemics of skin disease caused by lice were not uncommon. And late summer droughts often brought dust storms that obscured the sun.

I didn't waste class time arguing with Melvin for two reasons. First, it would have done no good, but second, to my low tech mind, his arguments might have had a sound scientific basis.

For the most part, Egypt is a desert country. Normal temperatures range from fifty degrees in the winter to over ninety in the summer, and its average humidity is in the arid category. Egypt has very little rain, and until modern Egyptians built the Aswan Dam and installed irrigation systems, the nation depended on the spring flooding of the Nile to water the farmland. Melvin was probably right about the river, the diseases, the dust and the pestilence, but he had a little difficulty with lightning and hail in a dry land and, of course, with the death of the firstborn. He explained the former as a very rare occurrence and the later as nothing more than myth.

In those days, I wondered why God sent plagues that could easily appear to be natural and common events occurring in the extreme. Why did he leave the matter open to dispute? Why didn't he do something really different and send a bitter cold spell that froze the river and killed all the crops and animals? Or why didn't he send a blizzard like those that paralyze Buffalo every winter? If he had done that, the Melvins of the world could make no logical argument, and God would have shown himself more powerful than any unrestrained natural force. But I was younger then and had less understanding of God's motives.

In my dotage, I accept the fact that the issue, as far as God is concerned, isn't whether twenty-first century thinkers see the plagues as miracles. The plagues were not events upon which God seeks to prove his omnipotence to the modern mind. Creation does that well enough. And the plagues were not simply attacks on the land or on Pharaoh or on the people of Egypt. Nature does that well enough. The plagues were attacks on Satan as represented by the pagan gods of Egypt, including the Pharaoh. They were one step in God's program to deal with sin in the world.

But to me the most salient point is that his battle against the devil is coupled with the liberation of his people from bondage. The two divine activities are inseparable. And every time one of God's arrows strikes a soldier of Satan, a shackle of sin drops off my legs!

Evidence

Scripture: Psalms 105:23–36
Suggested Reading: John 20:26–29

In a world that accepts no truth without proof, the notion that the plagues in Egypt were natural phenomena rather than miracles performed by the finger of God isn't the only event recorded in the Bible that fuels the imagination of the doubter and the cynic. God seems to have taken extraordinary precautions to hide substantive evidence that would tend to prove the miraculous truth of certain scriptural narratives.

Take the Exodus itself as an example. Archeologists who pride themselves in the fact that they found Solomon's horse stables and have even exhumed and examined enough manure to tell us exactly what those beasts ate, can't find a shred of evidence that two million Israelites camped at the base of Mount Sinai or roamed the area for forty years. They've combed the earth there for centuries hoping to find a bone, a bauble, a cooking pot, a tiny idol, or a stone column that would prove Moses and his people had been there, but they've come up empty. They've searched the northern reaches of the Gulf of Suez for mangled chariots, for armor, and for the bones of Pharaoh's horses and have found nothing. Some have given up hope of finding evidence of the Exodus in the Sinai Peninsula and have turned their attention to the mountains of Saudi Arabia, thinking that the Red Sea crossing might have happened at the narrow neck at the north end of the Gulf of Aqaba. But at this time the Saudi government forbids exploration of the area.

Then there's Noah's ark. Some super high tech photographers have enhanced aerial pictures of Mount Ararat that show a huge vessel nestled somewhere in its bowels. But clever photographers have also taken pictures of ghosts, flying saucers, aliens, and the Loch Ness monster; so what do those pictures prove? The only certain thing is that the government of Turkey forbids exploration of the Ararat area.

Funny how governments under God's control stand in the way of proving the truth of his Word.

There's also the shroud of Turin. Those who beg for proof of the Lord's resurrection find ample evidence on that piece of fabric that it served as Jesus' grave cloth and that some sort of radioactive flash etched his image into it as life leaped back into his body. But the shroud's detractors also find evidence that the whole thing is a monumental hoax.

Wouldn't it be great if our scientists could prove beyond a doubt that the stories in the Bible are true and that Jesus is the Son of God and that he died and rose again? And that there is a heaven to which all believers will ascend when they die? If we could only prove it, our churches would overflow, hatred and lawlessness would become things of the past, and we could raze our prisons and build seminaries to stock all those new churches with pastors.

But does the Lord want us to believe his Word because we can prove it is true? Is there a touch of sarcasm in Jesus' words to the doubting Thomas, "Have you believed because you have seen me?"

If we could prove the truth of God's Word, would there be any need for faith? And where would the heart be without faith?

Do we need the evidence of a burial shroud to testify to the truth that Jesus lives? I don't. I'm happier to be able to answer the question, "How do you know he lives?" by standing on the roof-top and singing at the top of my lungs, "He lives within my heart!"

Lots of Little Green Gods

Scripture: Exodus 8
Suggested Reading: Ephesians 6:10–18

Imagine having too many gods around! The Egyptian goddess Hekt was a frog, so every frog was sacred and Egyptians were not allowed to kill them.

As we modern Americans view God's plagues upon the Egyptians, we would say that they began more as nuisances than as plagues, but in the end grew to the magnitude of national tragedies. They were progressive in their impact. First the Nile became foul, so the people had to dig wells inland to get drinking water. Then suddenly billions of frogs began jumping out of the river and into their beds and mixing bowls. I imagine that at first many Egyptians got a good laugh when they found frogs between their sheets and in their pantries. They certainly lacked no opportunity to worship!

Then the frog population exploded out of control, and they began to die in such great quantities that the Egyptians had to pile them up in their town squares. Probably the closest we can come to comprehending the scope of that nuisance is to recall the garbage collector strike in New York when the foul kitchen refuse of millions of homes began to stack up on the street corners and spill out into the traffic lanes. Having played in the swamps as a child and collected frogs by the bucketful, I know the odor of dead frogs very well, and I know what the city of Raamses must have smelled like a week into the plague. The days of the frog will probably not go down in demon history as the best period of worship the goddess Hekt enjoyed during her reign in Egypt.

And when I look to the heavens with fanciful eye and tongue sticking in my cheek, I can even imagine God grinning a little and the angels slapping each other on the back as the little green corpses of the fallen devils began to litter Pharaoh's palace ground. The Lord was having his way with the gods of Egypt! The battle plan was beginning to fall into place, and little by little the Lord was determined to have victory over those rebellious spirits, beginning with the fouling of the river and continuing to the flight of the angel of death.

But the war didn't end with either the first Passover or the second. The battle rages even today. The demons that survived the days of the graven images attack us today in much more subtle forms. They lurk in our work places as passion for raises and promotions. They lurk in our churches as judgment and dissent. They lurk in movies as lust for power and pleasure. They lurk in our homes as anger and conflict. They lurk in our hearts as lust and greed. And because they're not green and don't croak, we often fail to recognize them as the angels that were banished from heaven and have infested this earth to turn our hearts away from our Lord.

It gives me great comfort to know that even though I often fail to sniff out some of those lesser gods that are odious to the Lord, he is keenly aware of their presence. Sometimes he lets them have their way with me for a little while and allows them to be a nuisance in my life in order to teach me a valuable lesson or to be a lesson for someone else. Sometimes he allows them to be like gnats buzzing in my ear or flies swimming in my soup so that in my weakness I might know his strength. Sometimes he warns me of their presence and equips me with the sword of the Spirit to do battle against them.

But I'm certain more than anything else, as I wander through this dark and fearsome valley, that my warrior God secretly intervenes to protect me from the vicious, snarling demons who are determined to destroy my spirit completely and deprive me of my salvation.

Fire and Ice

Scripture: *Exodus 9*
Suggested Reading: *Matthew 24; Galatians 3:29*

As Pharaoh stood on his palace porch watching the constant flash of lightning and the deadly deluge of hailstones that killed his slaves and his cattle, he must have thought the world was coming to an end.

In his poem, *Fire and Ice*, Robert Frost wondered which of the two phenomena would rain down final destruction upon this planet. Perhaps he heard, as I did, that any slight deviation in the alignment of the earth and the sun could plunge the earth into instant deep freeze or searing heat, both of which could destroy all life. But poets tend to see possibilities such as that with a more intellectual eye, and they turn events into symbols with a deeper meaning.

Frost equates fire with desire and ice with hate, both of which can be very destructive forces. Uncontrolled ambition has been the ruin of both people and nations, and hate has sprayed bullets into rival lovers and armies. Both extremes of emotion have started wars and slain millions, and both have the capacity to unleash forces that can leave our earth a smoldering, uninhabited planet if God chooses to use our atrocities to serve his ends.

We're taught in the Bible to expect an end of some sort. We're not sure how or when it will happen, but we do know that it is inevitable and that it will be horrible beyond words. Since the Father has kept the timing of the end a secret unto himself, we have no idea when it will be. Oh, we can make educated guesses based on how we interpret and comprehend the "signs of the times," as many a well-meaning scholar of prophecy has tried to do, but in the end we tend to look presumptuous trying to guess the plans of God.

The only people who were in a safe place when God poured out his wrath against Egypt were the people living in Goshen, God's chosen people, the heirs to the promise. There's a message in that for us as we anticipate the day when he will pour out his wrath against the nations of the earth.

If we are to be safe from the fire and ice of God's anger, we must be free from the fire and ice in our lives that makes God angry. We must, through the power of the Holy Spirit in us overcome the fire of the flesh that burns us with sinful desire, and we must overcome the ice of hate that alienates us from our neighbors, whether they live next door to us or on the other side of the world.

The latter is as formidable as the former. If we listen to some "Christian" radio and television today, and listen to the talk in some of our pulpits and Sunday school classes, it is evident that hate has filtered into our own circles. And if we listen to the gossip swirling around us, it becomes obvious that unbridled passions are as rampant in the church as in the world.

But the good news is that we have a Savior who provides a haven for us. We have a land of Goshen where we can be safe from both the wrath of God and the sins of the flesh. If we are truly in Christ and he is in us, we are Abraham's seed and heirs to the promise. If we claim Jesus as our Lord and Master, he will shield us from the wrath to come and will cleanse us from all of our iniquity.

Then, on that awful day of judgment we might hear the thunder in the distance, but we will stand in the light of his presence, fearless and sinless.

To God Be All the Glory

Scripture: Exodus 10:1–20
Suggested Reading: Genesis 29:31; 30:2; Exodus 13: 21–22; 14:21;
Hosea 13:15; Luke 8:24

*I*t's frightening how soon we can forget our God. I've seen brothers and sisters in Christ slip away and I've seen sons and daughters of saints sink into lives of sin and selfishness.

The sons of Noah had the privilege of watching God work his miracles. They stood by as God gave their father instruction in shipbuilding and as God led the animals two by two onto the deck of the ark. They watched as God kept his word and opened the fountains of the deep and the windows of heaven to pour out his judgment upon sinful man. They had great stories about their sovereign Savior to pass on to their children and grandchildren, but within a few short generations, the sons of Japheth had turned savage and the sons of Shem and Ham had forgotten the Almighty and were falling on their knees before figurines of frogs and snakes. Instead of remembering that Jehovah ruled the wind and opened and closed the womb, they gave the glory to little statues of birds and bugs. They traded the great God who made them for little gods they made for themselves.

The Lord makes a point of reminding us that he is still in charge of his creation. Into Egypt he blew his east wind bearing a dense swarm of locusts that the little clay images were powerless to stop. Later he used his east wind to stack up the waters of the Red Sea to let his people pass through, and neither plaster bugs nor golden snakes could stop the wall of water from covering Pharaoh's army.

Later, during Roman rule, Jesus showed the wedding guests that he, not Bacchus, was the real God of the vine and showed his disciples with a mere word that he was still God of the wind. All through history he shows us that he is the God who placed us here on this earth and will take us to our eternal home. He is the sovereign God of life and death, and of everything before, after, or in between.

Recently Margaret, a lovely saint from my Sunday school class was "gathered to her people." She loved that Old Testament description of the patriarchs' death because she looked forward to the day she would be reunited with her beloved Hank. Of all of nature's parables, she was most grateful for the wooly worm, whom God empowered to spin his coffin around himself and later burst forth as a butterfly. As cancer slowly devoured her, she grew anxious for the day that parable promised, when she, like Christ, would rise from her tomb, fly away, and live forever. Her family honored me by asking me to be a pallbearer.

The day after the funeral, Mary Ann and I went to visit Angi, a young friend whom God had just blessed with another baby girl to be sister to Rachel. The new mother placed little Paige Elizabeth into the same hands that had borne Margaret to her grave the day before. As those little fingers grasped mine, I was again convinced of the grace and greatness of our sovereign God who walks with us through the wilderness from the day we are born until the day we die, and who, as the song says, has "the whole world in his hands."

If we remember who made us and who saved us, he will give us the assurance that like the pillar of smoke and fire, his presence will go before us over the sun-drenched hills and through the dark valleys of our lives. But if we turn from him and begin to worship the things he has made, his wrath will descend upon us, our water will turn to blood, and devouring locusts will blanket the face of our land.

To God be all the glory.

The Power of Darkness

Scripture: Exodus 10:21–29
Suggested Reading: Luke 11:23; John 1:1–5

The plagues upon Egypt have escalated. The first were nuisances: bloody water, frogs, gnats, and flies. Then the Lord raised the level of intensity and struck the people and the animals of Egypt with sores, sickness, and death. Then he devastated their vegetation with locusts. Imagine the land after the eighth plague. Dead frogs littering the streets and courtyards, dead cattle in the fields, buildings pitted by hailstones, people scratching at their sores while they buried their dead, and finally every plant stripped of its leaves and fruit. It was truly a national disaster.

Then came the plague that was worse than the others, if you can imagine anything worse than the picture we've just painted, three days of darkness so thick that people couldn't see each other and dared not venture from their homes.

We don't often characterize darkness as the thing we fear the most. Maybe there is a spirit lurking about that discourages such fear in order to give us a false sense of security in the presence of evil. Children who have not yet learned that the world views bravery as a more desirable trait than honesty, fear the darkness and often ask their parents to illuminate their bedroom with a nightlight. They may be smarter than adults. When we visit caves, the guides often turn out the lights so we can experience darkness more profound than we can experience above ground, and when we come home we testify to our friends that it was a truly petrifying moment.

In the Bible, light and darkness are symbols of good and evil. Jesus is the light of the world while Satan is the prince of darkness. Light and darkness are also symbols of spiritual knowledge and ignorance. Those who walk in the light know Jesus as the Son of God who brings salvation to the world. Those who walk in darkness do not know Christ.

In our physics class, Mr. Selles taught us that darkness was merely the absence of light. That definition may be good enough for scientific application, but it is not good enough for the spiritual. The mere absence of light in our physical world leaves us nothing to fear but the possibility of bumping into things we forget are there. The light switch simply being off does not turn the room into a den of monsters that want to hurt us. There is nothing in that kind of darkness to fear.

But spiritual darkness is not merely the absence of Christ in our lives. It is the presence of evil. The absence of the light is a vacuum that attracts Satan. If the light of the Lord is not illuminating every path we walk, the demons that lurk in the shadows will pounce upon us. This might sound like mystical nonsense, but it isn't. Any aspect of our lives that is not bathed in the light of our Christian commitment is by definition evil. In Christ there is no such thing as lukewarm, twilight, or dusk. We are either for him or against him. There is no neutral. If we are not children of light, we are children of darkness. We belong either to Christ or to Satan.

What comforts me most about this is that right after he died, Jesus spent three days in the pitch black tomb on my behalf waging a war against the devil so I never need fear the powers of darkness again. Not because there is nothing to fear in his darkness, there is, but because when we come out of the darkness into Jesus' light he protects us from the evil that lurks in those shadows and assures us that we are safe with him.

A Distinction

Scripture: Exodus 11
Suggested Reading: Matthew 5:43–48

*M*oses told Pharaoh that the Lord made a distinction between the people of Israel and the people of Egypt. The Lord demonstrated that distinction when he unleashed the plagues. When swarms of flies filled the houses of the Egyptians, there were no flies in Goshen. When the cattle of the Egyptians died, the cattle of the Israelites remained healthy. When the Lord rained fire and ice upon the Egyptians, there was neither lightning nor hail in the land of Goshen. And when the Lord turned out the light in Egypt, the sons of Israel could still see their shadows.

Egypt is often used by Christian writers as a symbol of evil. When we read about the Lord warning the Israelites not to return to Egypt, we of the church take it as a warning not to return to the bondage of sin from which he set us free. For Israel before the Exodus, the land of Goshen represented the kingdom of God, a fertile and safe haven from a dry and thirsty world. If we accept his invitation to be called by his name, to be his people, we can dwell in the land of Goshen, protected from the plagues he heaps upon the citizens of Egypt.

We are now standing at the threshold of one of the greatest and most ancient of our theological quandaries: why don't the children of the light get a better deal in this world than the children of the darkness? Why doesn't the Lord make a clearer distinction between his people and those who reject him? Why do Christians suffer from the same diseases that the world suffers? Why are the people of the church subject to the same fickle forces that bring success or failure to the people of the world? Shouldn't Christians be visibly rewarded for their faith?

Think for a moment what might happen if the Lord gave clear and obvious physical rewards to Christians for believing in him. The same thing would happen that would happen if the supermarket on the east side of town always sold its goods cheaper than the supermarket on the west side of town. Everybody who wanted to save money would shop on the east side. If all of the members of Christ's church were healthier and wealthier than unbelievers, people would join the church just to get the visible rewards. We are not to be Christians for visible rewards. We are to be Christians out of gratitude to God for his sacrifice. We are to be Christians in order to restore the relationship with God that we had before Adam and Eve ate the forbidden fruit.

Then where's the distinction that God makes between his people and unbelievers? The abundant life is there, but unbelievers can't perceive it as a visible reward. Oh yes, we know that the people of the world sometimes look at the citizens of the kingdom of God and see that we have something that they don't have, such as inner peace or radiant joy, but that is the Holy Spirit working in them, graciously opening their eyes just a little and giving them a glimpse of what they will have when he begins his good work in them.

But if God makes the sun to shine on the wicked as well as the righteous, why bother being righteous? Simple when we think about it. We're supposed to be like him. He's our example. We're to love as he loves and let our sun shine out there in the dark world.

Only when we become like him, letting the warmth of his love fill our hearts to overflowing and letting his light shine through us, will we be able to comprehend the wonderful distinction that he makes between children of light and children of darkness.

Happy Birthday!

Scripture: Exodus 12:1–2
Suggested Reading: Galatians 3:29

*E*very Sunday in our church, the pastor asks those who are having a birthday in the next week to rise and be recognized. Then the congregation sings *Happy Birthday* in their honor.

I visited a Pentecostal church once where they did a similar thing. When the worship leader started down the aisle, an elderly gentleman in the front row excitedly raised his hand, took the microphone and joyously announced to the congregation that on that very day he was celebrating his first birthday!

Instead of celebrating biological birthdays, my Pentecostal friends celebrate the date of their spiritual rebirth, the anniversary of their being born again. To them it was more important to celebrate their liberation from the bondage of sin than to celebrate their liberation from the womb.

God must love celebrations. He commanded the Israelites to do something to commemorate nearly every major event in their journey from Egypt to the Promised Land and many other events that occurred during their history. As a result, the Jewish calendar has many sacred holidays which people celebrate by feasting, fasting, worshipping, and even making pilgrimages.

Undoubtedly, Passover is the most important of all Jewish festivals. It celebrates their deliverance from bondage, their birth as a nation, and the beginning of their passage to the Promised Land.

Passover is so important that the Lord ordered them to start a new calendar with the month of Abib or Nisan becoming the first month of the year rather than the seventh. The civil calendar remained the same to continue unbroken the measure of earthly time, but on that first Passover the Lord established a second calendar and rearranged the months so the festival of their deliverance would occupy the first page.

Although the church that raised me discounts the joy other members of Christ's family find in identifying and celebrating the day they came to know the Lord, I've always been rather envious. My testimony is one that begins with the rather common, "I've been a Christian all my life . . . ."

God arranged the history of the Hebrews so they had a specific day to look back on and say, "This was the day of my liberation from the bonds of slavery!" And I'm sure that God arranged the history of some of his saints so they could look back on a specific time and declare, "This is the day that the Lord delivered me from the bonds of sin and came to live in my heart forever. This day represents the beginning of my eternal life. This is my new birthday!"

But since I can't look back on my spiritual life and specify the day of my deliverance, each year as the snow begins to melt and the tulips pop up to promise me that a new season of life is about to begin on this blessed little spot the Lord has let me call my earthly home, I look at the calendar to find the date of Passover and join my Jewish friends by telling myself, "This month shall be for you the beginning of months; it shall be the first month of the year for you."

And when I do that, since I am in Christ and thereby an heir to the promise, I feel that in some way I am celebrating my own rebirth. So I not only shout "Happy New Year!" but also "Happy Birthday!" to myself.

To Eat the Lamb

Scripture: Exodus 12:3–32
Suggested Reading: John 6:52–56; Colossians 1:26–27

*I*once read a ditty declaring that a poem was a thing to be eaten, to be feasted on until the juice ran down your chin and you had completely indulged yourself in the fullness of its flavor. You had to ingest it until its substance became part of you. I've always liked that metaphor because it has a spiritual implication confirmed by Jesus himself.

I often ponder odd thoughts and raise what some call absurd questions. For example, how does the flesh of a dead steer, after any trace of life has been cooked out of it, revive after I've eaten it and become a collection of living molecules that compose my body and blood? I've never asked that question in any academic environment, not so much for fear of ridicule, but for fear that I might get some scientific explanation that would compromise the wonder of it all.

Before the Israelites could be liberated from their Egyptian captors, they had to survive the final plague. Their firstborn could be spared only of they killed an unblemished lamb, swabbed the blood on the doorposts of their homes, then cooked and ate its flesh. We focus much on the blood on the doorposts, but speak little of the killing and eating. Those rituals were also part of the command.

It's easy to sprinkle the blood on our doorposts. Many people do it in a symbolic way to tell the world that they are part of the redeemed community. I've seen people wearing little gold crosses on their earlobes or on chains around their necks, and I've wondered if they really had Jesus living in their hearts. Not to be judgmental, because that's God's job, not mine, but it seems that the gold cross might have become nothing more than a piece of costume jewelry or a talisman to bring good luck or ward off evil. But just the external show of faith will not keep the angel of death from entering the house. We also have to kill and eat the lamb.

Jesus said, "Unless you eat the flesh of the Son of Man and drink his blood, you have no life in you. He who eats my flesh and drinks my blood has eternal life, and I will raise him up on the last day."

Clearly we don't escape judgment by the mere outward appearance of faith. We escape judgment by feasting on Jesus, by ingesting him in every way until his very substance has become a part of us. We must sit at his feet, listen to him, absorb his words, know him, and make him the essence of our reborn selves.

The pundit who said, "You are what you eat," was, I assume, speaking biologically. I've often thought of that line as I've watched robins eat the fat juicy worms they dig up out of my lawn; the redbirds eat the nutritious sunflower seeds Mary Ann puts out for them. Though the robin didn't become a worm nor the redbird a sunflower, the robin got fat while the redbird remained slender.

Jesus, the Lamb of God, said, "He who eats my flesh and drinks my blood abides in me and I in him." In a sense, if we absorb the essence of Jesus into our being, we become him. That's the mystery the world can't solve: Christ *in* us, our only hope of glory.

And God established the principle way back in Moses' day when he ordered his people to kill the lamb and eat it as well as paint its blood on the doorpost. The angel of death knows a fake. He isn't fooled by a shiny cross around the neck of someone who doesn't have Jesus in his heart.

Blood on the Doorpost

Scripture: Luke 12:8–9

Remember my neighbor who has a sign on his gatepost that reads, "As for me and my house, we will serve the Lord," and my daughter who has the same quotation on a little plaque hanging just inside the back door of her home? My neighbor's intent is obviously to inform all who pass by that they who dwell within those gates are servants of God. Kyle's and her husband Tom's intent is to remind themselves and their children that every time they go out into the world they are going out to do the Lord's will.

On that first Passover the Israelites painted their doorposts with the blood of the lamb as a sign to inform the angel of death that they who dwell within that home are children of Abraham who have killed and eaten the Passover lamb. But that sign on their doorposts also served two other purposes. It informed the Egyptians who passed by that an Israelite lived there, and it reminded the Israelites who lived in that house that they were God's people, chosen for his purpose and destined to be delivered from bondage and led to the Promised Land.

Certainly we wear the blood of the Lamb on the doorposts of our hearts as a sign to God that we are his people. But is that enough? Not to the Lord. He does not tolerate secret admirers. We are told that if the blood of Jesus is not visible to the world as a testimony of our faith, he wants no part of us. We have to let the world know that we have chosen to serve the Lord.

But Kyle and Tom make a solid point too. In the busy and demanding world we live in, it is easy to neglect our testimony. As we struggle to secure what has become necessary for physical survival, it is easy for us to let our Christianity take a back seat to our secular business, and it might, therefore, be prudent for us to hang signs in our path to remind us that our service to the Lord must be the first priority of our lives.

The blessing here is that the lord knows that we are mere humans, subject to backsliding and lapses of faith. He knows our weaknesses and wants to help us overcome them. We shall see as we progress through the Bible that he often instructed his people to set up stones, to observe memorial events, and even to hang signs on their foreheads as reminders to themselves of their duty to serve him.

When we really think about it, we have to know that the Lord who "went forth in the midst of Egypt" to slay the firstborn, didn't need a bloody doorpost to tell him that one of the faithful lived in a particular house. The omniscient God who delivered the plague not only knew who lived in every house, but he also knew the heart and secret desires of everyone inside.

Then why the blood on the doorpost?

Luke revealed the reason. Jesus ordered us to proclaim to the whole world that we are covered by the blood of the Lamb. He wants us to mark the doorposts of our being in such a way that everyone who passes through our lives recognizes that we are pledged to serve him.

If we do, the angel of death will surely pass over us as our Savior confesses to the court of heaven on Judgment Day that we belong to him.

But if we don't . . .

The Gods of Egypt?

*Scripture: **Exodus 12:12–30***
Suggested Reading: Genesis 32:1–2; Exodus 20:1–6;
Mark 9:14–29; James 4:7; 1 John 4:4

*C*hristians who have not had the privilege of extensive Bible study have often asked if gods other than our God really exist. Some Old Testament passages seem to imply the existence of other gods that we may choose to serve at our own peril, while other passages declare that the Creator, the great *I AM*, is the lone deity in the universe.

We know from scripture and from history that people of other nations believed in their own gods and that those gods had names. Sculptors made images of those gods and people bowed down to them. Those gods were described as territorial, and when the nations who served them made war on each other, their various gods went to war with them. When a nation won a war, its gods were also victors, and when it lost, its gods were also defeated.

But were those gods real? Did those pagans just make them up? Or is there some other reason for their presence in the record of human events?

Different learned professors have proffered different answers. Some say those ancient heathen societies invented their deities. Some say they interpreted the true deity erroneously, with no revelation other than nature to guide their thinking. Still others define pagan gods as evil spirits sent by Satan to cause havoc in God's creation.

So, when God executed judgment on the gods of Egypt, did he simply destroy the vain imaginings of an ignorant people, or did he go to battle against a host of demons that had not only the nation of Egypt but much of the rest of the world in their grip?

Most ministers I've heard preach sermons on the Ten Commandments, interpret the term "other gods" in modern context to mean those priorities and desires in life that we place ahead of our commitment to our God, such as addictions, improper pleasures, or excessive fondness for possessions or wealth. Those gods are the gods we've created and empowered, consciously or subconsciously, to control the "Egypt" of our lives, those things to which we've enslaved ourselves.

But what if some of those gods are not of our own invention? What if some of the powers that possess us are dark spirits commissioned by Satan to fight in his war against the body of believers? Can our God vanquish them?

He has already answered that question. He told us that he has an army of angels out there that is more powerful than all the armies of Satan. Jesus Christ, the commander of that army, has authority over any demon that may try to possess us. The Spirit that lives in us is greater than the powers of darkness. If we resist the devil in Christ's name, he will flee from us. Martin Luther said it best:

And though this world with devils filled
    should threaten to undo us,
We will not fear, for God has willed
    His truth to triumph through us.
The Prince of Darkness grim,
    We tremble not for him;
His rage we can endure, for lo his doom is sure:
    One little word shall fell him.

Despoiling the Egyptians

Scripture: Exodus 12:31–36
*Suggested Reading: Genesis 15:13–14; Exodus 3:19–22; 25:1–9;
32:1–6; Malachi 3:6–12*

Despoil: to deprive of property or possessions by force; to plunder.

I raised my eyebrows in bewilderment when I first read the fifteenth chapter of Genesis. How in the world could a mass of people live for centuries in a foreign land as slaves and come out with great possessions? I continued to be bewildered as I read Exodus twelve and discovered that the Israelites simply asked their neighbors for jewelry and things, and in doing so acquired great possessions.

I have to conclude that the Egyptian neighbors didn't respond to the Israelites' requests by simply giving them a spare necklace or an extra pair of earrings. Their "gifts" were not the kind of "white elephant" gifts we sometimes give for fun at goofy office parties. When the Bible tells us that the Israelites *despoiled* the Egyptians, I've got to conclude that the compelling Spirit of God forced those neighbors practically to dump the entire contents of their jewelry boxes into the wagons of the Israelites. Thus the children of Abraham left the land of their captors with chests full of precious jewelry and left the Egyptians with little of anything. They plundered them.

Why? Oh, I'm sure it was a small measure of comfort to Abraham to know that his descendants would get some reward for the many years they slaved for their foreign masters. And maybe, since they might have needed "cash" for their trip through strange nations back to the land of promise, they could barter the jewelry for life's necessities. But what other reasons might God have had for filling their coffers with all sorts of precious metals as they left the land of Egypt? And if we figure that out, might we also comprehend why he sometimes blesses us with things of value?

I think that sometimes God gives us things to test the desires of our heart. At the beginning of an old television show, *The Millionaire*, they would visit select unsuspecting persons and bless them with a gift of a million dollars. The rest of the story described what the newly rich recipient did with the money. Some were benevolent, others selfish. Some used the money for good, others for evil. Some became happy, others miserable. It is fascinating to watch what people will do with newfound wealth.

Early in their sojourn in the wilderness the Israelites pleased God by voluntarily opening their hands and releasing their precious metals for the building of the tabernacle. Later they failed the test of faith by using their precious metals to make the infamous golden calf, a blunder that eternally altered the destiny of that nation. In general we know that they were more motivated by greed than by benevolence and thanksgiving, because God later accused them of stealing the temple tithe from him.

A major theme of the Bible from Genesis to the maps is the theme of openhanded living. Just as God loved us so much that he was willing to become one of us and to die for our salvation, he wants us to love him and to love our fellow man so much that to benefit a neighbor in need, we are willing to part with the earthly possessions he has so graciously given us. And Jesus continually told us that we are to give to the poor. Why? Because our giving generously might eradicate poverty? No. The simple reason God offers, through his prophet Malachi, is that when we open our hand to God and to man, the Lord is moved to open his hand of blessing to us.

As a Native of the Land

Scripture: Exodus 12:37–51
Suggested Reading: Exodus 23:23–24; Acts 10

One thing that must make us look like barbarians to God is the racism that pervades every institution man has ever devised. When we watch history we are sickened by the ethnic cleansing we saw in eastern Europe. From all over the world have come news stories of tribal warfare and genocide. People in Africa and Asia have murdered their racially different neighbors by the tens of thousands. Mobs of racists have burned the homes of refugees from other countries. Even policemen in some of our cities have joined hate groups.

As a nation we hope that God will not hold us guilty of the same sins we saw the Germans commit in the middle of the last century and the Serbs commit as the century coasted to an end, since our nation took a stance against the practice of ethnic cleansing soon after we cleansed "our" land of most of its native inhabitants.

Israel had a mean racist streak too. They somehow interpreted God's plan to use them to punish the wicked inhabitants of Canaan and his order not to mix with the people whose lands they invade as a sign that they were better than all foreigners. They took the fact that they were a special people chosen by God for a wonderful purpose to an evil extreme. They still do.

In the days of the early church, God had to teach even the apostles that his saving grace extended to people other than Jews, in spite of the fact that he had made a point of telling them that right from the days of Abraham when he declared that through the patriarch *all of the families of the earth* might receive a blessing. He made the point even clearer when he told Moses that any foreigner who wanted to become one of God's chosen people could do so by being circumcised, and that after he was circumcised he was to be treated as a native of the land.

Now, given the figurative nature of much of God's revelation, it is easy to understand why we have so many denominations in the body of Christ. There are many points of doctrine over which well-meaning people of good judgment and common sense might logically disagree. So, it's no wonder that groups separate themselves from others according to what they believe about the government of the church, the method or time of baptism, the nature of grace, the structure of the Trinity, the working of the Holy Spirit, the proper day of worship, or the free will of man. But in spite of the clear revelation given to Abraham, Moses, and Peter, we still divide ourselves on the basis of race and nationality.

Racism and nationalism are among the most volatile issues humanity faces. Ethnic separation and superiority have been the cause of great conflict, suffering, and atrocity. They are the fundamental evils of our time, more devastating than the sins we define as deadly.

Why then is the church of Jesus Christ separated according to race? To accept such separation on the ground that inherited and historic cultural differences is the way the races worship is to avoid the issue by begging the question. We don't alienate our children from the church because their music hurts our ears, rather we express tolerance and encourage their participation in worship services.

If we were to accept cultural differences with the same grace we accept generational differences and encourage membership and unique methods of participation regardless of race, we might eventually ease some of the tension in our very stressful world.

By Way of the Wilderness

Scripture: Exodus 13

*E*xodus thirteen is a pivotal chapter in scripture. Monumental things happen and monumental lessons emerge. In it Moses exhorts us to remember the day that the Lord, by a mighty hand, delivered us from the bonds of sin and death. He exhorts us to celebrate that day and to teach our children the meaning of salvation. He exhorts us to enter our spiritual promised land in the attitude of sacrifice, truly thankful for our redemption by the blood of the lamb. A preacher could easily spend a year on this chapter.

But after learning all those things and promising to put them into practice, my mind keeps going back to one of the seemingly lesser moments of this episode.

God could easily have led the Israelites directly to Canaan, skirting the tip of the Mediterranean Sea and heading north. It wouldn't have been a long journey, and certainly, though the country was full of Philistines, God could easily have tamed them or smitten them so his people could pass through unmolested. He could have taken them the direct route through hostile territory to show his power over his enemies, as he did in Egypt, and to show his love and his providential care for his people.

But he didn't choose to do that. Why? "Lest the people repent when they see war and return to Egypt."

God equipped the Hebrews for war when he led them out of Egypt, presumably by despoiling the Egyptian army of its weapons just as he despoiled the citizens of their jewelry. When God delivers us from the bondage of sin, he arms us with the double-edged sword of the Spirit and the Word so we may do battle against the powers of darkness. But just as he led the young nation of Israel away from hostile forces, he leads new Christians in their early walk toward the spiritual promised land on a route that avoids the haunts of Satan until he has properly trained those Christians to use that sword skillfully enough to contend successfully against the devil.

This is no myth. I've heard testimony from many people who have recently been liberated by the Lord, and one of the high points of their message is the absolute conviction that God has set a hedge of protection around them, keeping the howling demons at bay. And many decorated heroes of the wars of faith also recall those early days when God allowed them time to bask for a while in the joy of rebirth.

What a wonderful and loving God we have! He created us sinless and wanted our companionship. We cruelly rejected his affection and yielded to the serpent's siren call. Still, he loved us and sacrificed himself to get us back. Then, when we finally repented and came back home, he received us with a warm embrace and held the door tight against the evil influences to which we were so vulnerable.

But the detour away from the field of battle is only temporary. He has plans for our life that include conflict with Satan. On that wilderness trail he trains us for the battles that lie ahead.

So, new Christian, enjoy your little hiatus from the strife, but don't think this moment of tranquility is the Christian way of life. We are a church militant. Be aware of the battles to be fought and know that you will soon encounter the enemies God has called you to face.

How else will you ever know the ecstasy of victory and the joy of knowing that the Commander of the army of the Lord is fighting for you?

To Die in the Wilderness?

Scripture: Exodus 14:1–14
Suggested Reading: Genesis 12:2; 15:13–14; Philippians 1:6;
Hebrews 4:14–16.

Those Hebrews are beginning to get under my skin. They watched from the front row as the God of their fathers pounded Egypt with horrible plagues. They watched as the Lord slew the firstborn of their captors and spared the lives of his chosen people. They marched from the scene of their torment carrying a trove of treasures that their tormentors, hearts softened by the grace of God, heaped upon them as going away gifts. Their Protector stood behind them in a massive cloud of smoke and fire to guard them from their pursuers and went before them to mark the way. It should have been crystal clear to them that the God who unlocked the shackles of slavery from their legs had plans for them and would not let his chosen people perish in the desert.

Perhaps generations of slavery had driven from their corporate memory the promises that God made to Abraham. Perhaps Moses had not yet reminded them of their destiny.

What would have happened if God and Moses had just thrown up their hands and told the unappreciative mob to turn tail and run back to Egypt? There would have been no David, no Solomon, and, of course, no Jesus. Would God have found some other way to restore us to paradise? I hope so.

As we continue our journey from Egypt to the Promised Land, we are going to become more frustrated at the ungrateful horde than we are today. This rebellion is but the beginning. As time passes, they whine and complain more and more. God and Moses will almost come to blows over what to do with this herd of stubborn mules. Why are they so faithless? Shouldn't they have learned by now that the God who rescued them from Pharaoh would protect them from his armies? Shouldn't they expect miracle after miracle?

Now I don't want to spend a disproportionate share of my writing time being angry at God's people because of their obstinacy and distrust. Instead, I want to find a lesson in it that will make me a better pilgrim as I wend my way through the wilderness toward my spiritual promised land. And I can't be too self-righteous, because had I been one of them, I might have been as apprehensive as they.

But I have the advantage over them because I've read the end of the book, so I know what is going to happen both to me and to those Israelites. I'm going to find out that their continuing doubt and timidity finally cost them the opportunity to enter Canaan, and the entire generation of them did die in the wilderness, in what now seems to have been a self-fulfilling prophecy. It was the second generation of them who got to cross the Jordan and possess the promised inheritance.

Another advantage I have over the ancient Hebrews is that Jesus sent the Holy Spirit to dwell in me and give me courage to face the enemies that lurk in the shadows of this wilderness and behind the rocks that are strewn in this valley. And through the inspired apostles he promised me that he would never abandon me and that he would finish the good work he began in me the day he delivered me from the bondage of sin.

How then should I live? Since Jesus walked in my shoes and faced more daunting evils than I can ever expect to face, I have no choice but in gratitude to learn from the Hebrews' mistakes and have bold confidence that wherever he leads me I should "fear not, stand firm, and see the salvation of the Lord."

Stretch Forth Your Hand

Scripture: *Exodus 14:15–25*
Suggested Reading: 1 Corinthians 3:5–9

I don't know if the fancies of my youth are much different than anyone else's because for some reason we never speak much of them. If I were to tell you too much about some of the foolish thoughts that I enjoyed tinkering with in my childhood brain, you might never listen to a word I say, and probably with good reason. Some of the creations of our artless, infantile minds we remember with some embarrassment, and we are not inclined to reveal them to other adults for fear of being ridiculed. But there is one moment of my youth that I recall for which I will risk derision because it proves a cogent point.

The Monday morning after I heard the story in my primary Sunday school class about Moses parting the Red Sea, I borrowed one of my grandfather's canes and went "down the crick" to see if I could emulate that trick. To make my miracle easier, I picked a nice spot on the bank where the current wasn't very swift, and I stretched forth my hand just as I'd seen Moses stretch forth his in the picture Mrs. Hooker put up on the flannelgraph, raising the cane over the creek to see if I could make it stop flowing and let me pass over on dry ground. What a story that would have been to tell next week! But it didn't work. The obstinate stream kept flowing in spite of my command. And today I'm glad it did, because I'm afraid that success might have landed me in what we called in those days an insane asylum.

You're the only people I've told about this, but I tell it now because there is a lesson in it that can bless us.

Moses didn't have anything to do with the parting of the Red Sea. Oh, sure, we give him credit for that wonderful feat, and Mr. DeMille and Mr. Heston enshrined him to the everlasting glory of Hollywood and a nation of fawning moviegoers. But what Moses did on that historic day is nothing more than I did on that memorable Monday in the first grade. The only difference is that God parted the Red Sea for Moses but he didn't part Cedar Creek for me.

So why did God have Moses go through the motions of stretching forth his hand over the sea when his hand had nothing to do with the miracle? Simple. God just wanted Moses to step out and take action in faith, and he wanted to share the glory with his servant in order to strengthen the people's faith.

Again, here is an event of colossal magnitude that teaches us a multitude of valuable lessons about God's greatness and his love. Here is an event that spawns symbolic relevance to everything from baptism to resurrection and has been the subject of centuries of theological dissertation. Here is an event that forms the very foundation of our faith.

But my pleasure comes in simpler things. Our great, mighty and wonderful God, to fulfill his own purposes, wants to share himself and his glory with us. Just as I hoist my grandson up to the hoop on my shoulders so he can dunk the basketball, then applaud him for his magnificent slam, God lifts us up to do his work and lets us enjoy a share of the satisfaction. We take pleasure in leading others to the Lord when we know full well that no one can come to him unless the Spirit draw him. And those who come to know him through us celebrate us as their spiritual parents. How rewarding!

So let us continue to stretch forth our hands knowing that it is God's effort, not ours, that parts the waters, but humbly enjoying the bit of glory he wants to share with us.

King of Kings

Scripture: Exodus 14:26–15:1
Suggested Reading: Exodus 14:3–4; Daniel 4:17; Romans 3:1;
Revelation 17:13–14

The Lord has veiled the date of the Exodus from Egypt and the identity of the Pharaoh who "knew not Joseph" in a cloud of mystery. But some expositors believe that the Israelites may have served under the whip of Raamses II, a pharaoh recorded in Egyptian history as the builder of great monuments and breathtaking cities, and perhaps the pharaoh over whom the Lord triumphed gloriously in the waters of the Red Sea. But whatever his name, he stands as a testimony to the vainglory of man.

English romantic poet Percy Bysshe Shelley captured his futile arrogance in the sonnet *Ozymandias*, which is a corruption of the name Raamses II:

> I met a traveler from an antique land
> Who said, "Two vast and trunkless legs of stone
> Stand in the desert. . . . Near them, on the sand,
> Half sunk, a shattered visage lies, whose frown
> And wrinkled lip, and sneer of cold command
> Tell that its sculptor well those passions read
> Which yet survive, stamped on these lifeless things,
> The hand that mocked them and the heart that fed;
> And on the pedestal these words appear:
> 'My name is Ozymandias, king of kings;
> Look upon my works ye mighty and despair!'
> Nothing beside remains. Round the decay
> Of that colossal wreck, boundless and bare,
> The lone and level sands stretch far away.

King of kings he called himself, and it was not an idle boast. The Ruler of the Nations had made him dominant over other countries and their kings, just as in subsequent centuries he gave similar superiority to David, Solomon, the various emperors of Europe and Asia, the czars of Russia, the kings of England, and hosts of tyrants and dictators of all eras.

Raamses II was not in a class by himself except in his own eyes. The authority the Lord gives to those leaders is given solely to fulfill God's purposes as he rules over the kingdoms of men. Often, under God's watchful eye, that power is abused and serves also to fill a bulging ego. This Raamses saw himself as a king of kings, but the old Greek historian whose writings form the basis of Shelley's poem saw him as a decayed wreck whose splendor eventually got buried under the shifting sands of the desert.

Caesar, Caligula, Domitian, Hitler, Stalin and other tyrants gave their power over to the beast to be used for evil, but eventually our memory of them dims as their exploits are relegated to old library stacks and remembered only in academia. Moguls of enterprise build castles of sand that get washed away by the waves of history, and savage little men leave only scars on the backs of their children. Time erodes all monuments men erect to themselves.

But the one timeless and everlasting King of kings rules the universe, and someday all of history's tyrants and tycoons will bow the knee before him. The great and small will stand in judgment, and chariots and fortunes will not sway the verdict. When in the end the forces of good and evil meet for the final battle, all who made war on the Lamb will be conquered, but the faithful will stand secure at his right hand. Joshua challenged the Israelites of old, "Choose you this day whom you will serve." The same challenge goes out to us. Shall we serve a king who will bring us to ruin, or shall we serve the King of kings whose kingdom is forever?

Sing the Story!

Scripture: Exodus 15:1–21
Suggested Reading: Luke 15:7,10; Revelation 15:2–3

All during my youth I sang,

> There is a fountain filled with blood,
> Drawn from Immanuel's veins,
> And sinners plunged beneath that flood
> Lose all their guilty stains . . .
>
> (William Cowper, 1771)

I sang it with reverence and a great deal of gusto until my college Bible professor declared it to be one of the most repulsive religious metaphors he had ever heard. One of the grand old hymns of the church forever lost its charm, and I became aware that the glorious is not always beautiful.

The baptismal liturgy of my old home church contained a magnificent prayer that began, "O almighty, eternal God, thou who hast according to thy severe judgment punished the unbelieving and unrepentant world with a flood . . . thou who hast drowned the obstinate pharaoh and all his host in the Red Sea and led thy people Israel through the midst of the sea on dry ground by which baptism was signified . . . ."

The cleansing flood is a spiritual metaphor that has its origins in real events that occur in scripture. In baptism, when we are sprinkled or plunged beneath the waters we are crucified with Christ and die to sin and self. The sins that enslaved us lose their grip and, like the army of Pharaoh, drown in the deluge. When we emerge we are raised with Jesus in newness of life and are ready to begin our pilgrimage to the spiritual promised land where we can feed on the produce of the land, the fruit of the Spirit.

God foreshadowed our baptism as far back as the Flood, and reinforced the principle at the Red Sea when he scored a glorious victory and freed his people from the evil forces that enslaved them.

What strikes me is the dichotomy of feeling that attends such an event. It is indeed a great victory, but as in all victories, there is the agony as well as the ecstasy. I recall once during the Friday Night Fights on television a boxer landed a powerful uppercut that sent his opponent bouncing off the ropes and collapsing into a motionless heap on the canvas. The referee didn't bother counting. The loser's fans gasped in horror as the medics rushed into the ring, but the winner's handlers hoisted him to their shoulders as he waved his fists in the air and as his fans loudly chanted his name in celebration of a glorious victory.

On one hand the Red Sea was not a pretty sight the morning after. Limp corpses of men and horses bobbed in the surf and washed up onto the shore while the hills echoed with the joyous victory chant of the Israelites as the Lord led them on toward Sinai. In the spiritual realm the demons gasped in the agony of defeat while the angels filled the halls of heaven with thunderous applause, as they do whenever any sinner repents and is plunged beneath the cleansing flood.

Christians would do well to memorize the Song of Moses, because on the day of final victory over Satan and his hosts they will gather with the Lamb at the shore of the sea of molten glass, and as the demons are consumed in that lake of fire, the saints will join the white-robed chorus and joyously proclaim to all the hosts of heaven that the victorious Jesus Christ reigns forever and ever!

Will you be there to sing the story with us?

Their Healer

Scripture: Exodus 15:22–27

God had just revealed himself in a mighty way to the people he had picked to be his own. Right before their eyes he performed a miracle that completely annihilated their enemy. It was a stunning event, and when the sun went down that day they must have gathered around their campfires and told stories about the bodies of the Egyptian soldiers they had seen lying half submerged on the Red Sea beaches. It was an event so worthy of praise that the people burst into song, extolling the might of the great God who had saved them from certain disaster. And in the morning as they marched toward the mountain of God, the wilderness hills echoed with their inspired shouts, "The Lord will reign for ever and ever! The Lord will reign for ever and ever!"

But just a short three days later they ran short of water, only one day's journey from the lush plain of Elim where God had an abundance of sparkling springs and shady palm trees waiting for them. Now he could just as easily have ordered them to tough it out for only one day more and led them to Elim, but instead he directed them to Marah where he could teach them another important lesson about the kind of God he is.

What kind of people were they? What did they know about their God? What had they learned as they walked on the dry bed below the sea? Our scholars tell us that their knowledge of God was laced with pagan beliefs. Those gods didn't care about people. They were fickle, unreliable, and unpredictable.

The God they had experienced since the onset of the plagues was a God of terror and brute strength. He rained fire from heaven and inflicted boils and pain and death upon man and beast. He opened the sea to let some through on dry ground, but closed it again to drown others. He lived in fire and smoke. He was a warrior.

Now, after a jubilant day of victory and joyous celebration, they encountered a problem and turned with a vengeance upon their leader. They complained about their difficulty. What did they think? Did they think the God who opened the sea and destroyed their enemy might let them die of thirst in the desert? How much could they trust him? Did this God toy with humans as do the pagans' gods? They had a lesson coming, and Jehovah God was very patient in teaching them . . . this time.

At Marah they came to a pool, but when they tasted the water they found it undrinkable. What a great opportunity to look to their great God in expectation of another miracle. What an opportunity to learn that their deliverer was more than a sea-parter, more than a warrior, more than a God of hail, fire, and death. They had a chance to learn that their God was a healer, that he cared about their condition, and that he could turn their bitter water sweet.

But what was the price of learning? What was the cost of healing? Was it free? Of course not. God demanded that they "diligently hearken to the voice of the Lord," that they "do that which is right in his eyes," and that they "heed his commandments and keep his statutes."

Reasonable expectations?

Were they able to pay the premium he demanded for their health care?

Are we?

Our Healer

Scripture: Review Exodus 15:22–27
Suggested Reading: Isaiah 30:20; 53:6; 1 Peter 2:22–24

*G*od took great care to preserve the record of this event, not just for the Hebrews as they tramped through the wilderness and strove to establish themselves in the Promised Land, but for us as we struggle through the valleys that lie between us and our paradise. The lesson he teaches here is a universal lesson of great importance that transcends the momentary experiences of a group of grumpy people whose mouths were puckered from drinking dirty water.

As we progress through our spiritual pilgrimage, we sometimes get thirsty and our Lord seems far away. Sometimes he leads us to a pool of brackish water, not because he wants to offend our taste buds or make us sick, but because he wants us to remember Marah and know that no matter how bitter the water tastes, he can touch it and make it sweet.

Commentaries on this event tell us that there is no tree in the wilderness capable of purifying a polluted pond. If the water was transformed from bitter to sweet, it clearly was a miracle.

But maybe the water didn't change at all. Maybe the water remained sour but maybe the Lord altered their senses of smell and taste so the water just seemed sweet. And if it was diseased, maybe he made them and their animals immune to the germs that infested it. Maybe that's how he worked as their healer. Maybe he didn't alter the circumstances, but rather altered the people and gave them the fortitude to tolerate, and even appreciate, that which was bitter. Maybe.

Sometimes the Lord leads us to the distasteful water of life, that which Isaiah calls "the water of affliction," and we have no choice but to drink. Because it rains on the just and unjust alike, we often have to endure the same troubles the world has to endure. But for us the Lord makes the situation tolerable, not by changing the universal facts of life that surround us all, but by giving us the strength to stand firm in the face of adversity and the spirit to testify that the water he has given us is sweet.

But we often forget that he has put a price on sweet water. His healing is not free. He has put a premium on our health care that must be paid. That premium is obedience. He requires that we hearken diligently to his voice, that we do what is right, and that we keep his commandments. If we do all that, he has promised to be our healer.

But can we be obedient? Can we walk uprightly before him and do all that he has commanded us to do? Well-worn scriptures burn our ears: "Our righteousness is as filthy rags. . . . None is righteous, no not one. . . . All have sinned and fall short. . . . All we like sheep have gone astray . . . ." And on and on. If obedience is the price of our healthcare, how will we ever be able to pay our premium? How can we possibly be healed?

Fortunately, someone stepped forward and wrote the check for our coverage. The only person ever to have lived a perfect life, the person who drank the bitter water and didn't become embittered, the person who turns our brackish water sweet and turns our wash water into wine is the person who was betrayed, spat upon, beaten, scourged, and nailed to the cross to pay the price for our sin and render us innocent.

By his stripes we are healed.

That I May Prove Them

Scripture: Exodus 16
Suggested Reading: Deuteronomy 8:1–4; John 6:1–40;
Philippians 2:8

Another test. Why did God give his people manna in the wilderness? Because they were hungry? Because they murmured? Because he wanted to prove to them that he was their provident God? Because he wanted to establish the front end of the metaphor for the Bread of Life to come later?

None of the above is the best answer, although none of those answers is totally incorrect. He told us clearly why he gave them manna in the wilderness. It was simply ". . . that I may prove them, whether they will walk in my law or not."

We often forget the big picture. God made us good and gave us the choice whether to follow his orders or to violate them. When Satan tempted us, we failed and by our disobedience became alienated from our creator. From that point on he has given us many opportunities to restore ourselves to his favor by hearkening to his voice and heeding his commandments. He gave Noah that opportunity and now he has given Israel that same chance.

The bread from heaven is not the central theme of the story. The main point of the heavenly manna is not to show that a loving God cares for his people and works miracles in order to preserve them from starvation. The single issue here is what they do with the Sabbath Day. Will they obediently take for themselves just one daily ration for each of the first five days of the week and gather just enough on the sixth day to last them through the seventh?

Will they perform this simple task in trust to demonstrate their faith and their obedience to God?

God could have fed them any way he wanted to. He could have miraculously preserved their bodies on that trek through the wilderness by eliminating the need for food and drink. He could have had desert dwellers come out each day and prepare a table for the whole assembly. He could have had ravens bring them meat. He could have given each family a small supply of food that never ran out. He could have fed them all on five loaves and two fishes and they could have gathered enough leftovers to keep them for forty years.

But he didn't. He decided to rain down on them a special bread from heaven because he had a proposition for them. Do it my way to prove your faith and obedience. Do it my way to end the alienation caused by Adam and Eve. Come back to me in humble trust, and I will be your God and you will be my people. Do as I say and I will bring you to a new Eden, a land flowing with milk and honey. There I will be your protector, provider and healer. But the price is obedience. Do it my way.

As we watch the human tragedy unfold through the Old Testament, we learn that it is not in fallen man's nature to walk with his God in humble obedience. When offered the opportunity back there in the wilderness of Sinai to begin a new relationship with God, we failed again, and that failure was just the beginning of a long history of failure that didn't end until God gave us the true Bread of Heaven who would be obedient for us, obedient even to the point of willingly suffering the death we deserve.

Now we have a choice again. God offers us the opportunity to eat of the Bread from Heaven, who is Jesus Christ, and in doing so fill ourselves with his righteousness so we may walk in his light and never again hunger for the pleasures of sin.

Murmured . . . Again

✑

Scripture: Exodus 17:1–7
Suggested Reading: John 4:7–15; 1 Corinthians 10:1–5;
Galatians 5:22–23

I find it almost impossible to read Exodus without getting angry. And sometimes I find it very difficult to understand why the Lord would choose such an obnoxious and thankless group of miscreants such as the Israelites to be his chosen and beloved people, unless all the other people in the world were even worse.

Today we see a moment in their national life that gets repeated so many times that we just want to pick them up and shake the daylights out of them. What ingrates! The Lord has rescued them from terrible slavery, has destroyed their enemy, has turned their bitter water sweet, and has miraculously provided an all-you-can-eat buffet of manna and quail. Then they run out of water again.

After all this providential care, what should they expect? Should they expect that the Lord will provide? Seems logical, but what did they do? Complain! They can be thankful that I'm not God, because if I were, I think I would have been so mad at that point that I would have just let that whining bunch of cowardly rabble die of thirst out there in the wilderness.

And that is just the beginning of a long, shameful national history of faithlessness, distrust, and moral adultery. It's no wonder that in the end God scattered them like ashes to the corners of the earth.

What does it all go to show? If we think that we are any better than they, we are no different than the Pharisee who prayed, "God,

I thank thee that I am not like other men . . . ." We'd better get down on our knees, repent of our self-righteousness, and beg God to be merciful to us sinners.

We can never forget that in a very real sense, they were our agents, acting on our behalf. Just as "In Adam's fall, we sinned all," we are all guilty of Israel's moral crimes. The slaves that Moses led out of Egypt were humanity's representatives. What they did, we did. Their sin is our sin, and if we can't see ourselves in them, we can have no hope of salvation.

We too were led out of a life of slavery by a second Moses, Jesus Christ. We too were as unworthy and faithless as that band of Hebrews, and we certainly didn't deserve the love, patience, and forgiveness he lavished on us when we spat on him, whipped him, and nailed him to the cross.

As we journey through the wilderness of this life on the way to our spiritual promised land, we too need the sustenance he gives. We need the bread from heaven, and the water from the rock. We need to partake of his body and his blood so that he becomes alive in us.

The trip is not easy. Trouble and enemies lurk in the way. He told us that walking down his road would be difficult. He said it would be full of hardship. But we have one advantage the Israelites didn't have. We can eat of the Bread that will satisfy us forever, and never hunger again. We can drink the Living Water from Christ, our Rock, and never thirst again. And when we feast on the produce of the land, the fruit of the Spirit, we will never murmur again.

He hasn't given us heavenly sustenance because we deserve it, but only because he loves us.

The Fervent Prayer . . .

Scripture: Exodus 17:8–13; Matthew 7:7–12
Suggested Reading: James 5:16; Acts 12:1–17

My mother was fond of hanging scripture plaques on the walls all over the house. One little plaque that hung on the narrow strip next to the back door proclaimed, *"Prayer Changes Things."* Since she took that saying very seriously, I kept trying it, but as a kid I could never testify that it really worked.

I remember getting my bike out of the garage one morning, retrieving my hidden pack of cigarettes from the niche in the wall, peddling blindly down the street and crashing into the telephone pole in front of old Mrs. Doorn's house as I closed my eyes and quickly prayed that I would pass the first period algebra test. Studying would have been far more useful.

Moses' intercession during Israel's battle with the Amalekites proves the efficacy of prayer, but why did God respond so favorably to Moses' prayer and seemingly ignore mine?

Mrs. Hooker taught me that prayer changes things by showing our Sunday school class on the flannelgraph how Joshua's army prevailed when Moses held his hinged arms up toward the sky, but how the Amalekites prevailed when he let them droop. From far above the clouds, God reached down and moved the army of Israel over the army of the Amalekites when Moses raised his staff toward the sky, but reversed the momentum when he let it down. So why didn't God help me with my algebra test? Didn't he understand that I needed my hands to steer the bike?

Over the years I've found that one little saying cannot possibly convey the whole truth. James added essential ingredients to the simple plaque when he said, "The *fervent* prayer of a *righteous* man availeth much." My prayer for an assist with the test probably was less than fervent, and its source was far from righteous.

Fervent is easy to understand. One would have a hard time being fervent while trying to guide a bicycle to the schoolhouse balancing a bag of books on the handlebars. It should have been offered the evening before, without distraction, within the privacy of my room, and with all the intense pleading I could muster. Perhaps then instead of wasting my time and attention with fantasy and foolishness, I would have been led to concentrate on algebra, and perhaps God would have been my study guide and pointed out to me that the whole purpose was to learn the subject, not just pass the test.

Righteous is a bit tougher. Never could I claim to be a righteous person. I know any righteousness I may have is like filthy rags to God. But James explained by saying, "Confess your sins one to another." Righteousness is not being perfect. Righteousness is being forgiven. And righteousness begins with confession and repentance. A boy on his way to school with a pack of cigarettes hidden in his pocket cannot possibly claim to be penitent.

Jesus made the criterion for effectual prayer a bit tougher. His teaching in Matthew 7:7–11 gives us the illusion that God will always give us whatever we ask. But verse 12 is crucial to the equation. It begins with the word *so*, and includes obedience to both the Golden Rule and the Ten Commandments. That morning on my way to school with cigarettes hidden in my pocket I was bearing false witness, thinking only of myself, and dishonoring my parents.

Prayer does change things, but only if we come to the mercy seat with singleness of purpose, repentant, and seeking forgiveness of our sins.

Remembrance of Amalek

Scripture: Exodus 17:14–16
Suggested Reading: Leviticus 18:19–25; Deuteronomy 25:17–19

*I*suspect that even the most faithful among us have moments of doubt. The most honest of the faithful have even admitted it openly. If Satan sometimes enters your heart as he does mine, perhaps you say to yourself, "Did that fish story really happen?" or "The sun standing still is a bit difficult for me to accept." Sometimes when the devil fills us with an extraordinarily strong sense of logic and reason, we might even turn a disbelieving eye at the whole of scripture and wonder if the atheists might not be right after all. But then, providentially, the Holy Spirit leads us to a gem of truth that reconfirms our faith in the Lord and his Word.

While the Israelites were slaving in Egypt, the sons of Ham and Shem occupied the land of Canaan. Some of those Canaanites were closely related to the Hebrews. The Amalekites, for example, were descendants of Esau, Jacob's brother. Both God's Word and secular history reveal that the Canaanites were, by our standards, perverse and barbaric. Moses described some of their behavior in the book of Leviticus and warned us not to follow in their footsteps.

God told us in several scriptures that one of his purposes in leading his chosen people to Canaan was to purge the land of its evildoers. He gave Israel victory after victory and ordered Joshua to destroy the enemy completely. He ordered his people not to mix with the inhabitants of the land and not to spare them from the edge of the sword. That was his judgment on them for their sin. They, too, had an opportunity to worship the one true God, but they turned from him in favor of idols. They were taught by their ancestors to walk uprightly before the Lord, but they preferred perversion. So he used the swords of the Israelites to bring them to justice.

The sons of Amalek were a savage and sinful nation that roamed the land of Canaan and were a constant stone in Israel's sandal. Joshua, Gideon, Saul, and David all took up arms against them, and Samuel personally put the sword to one of Amalek's kings. The Lord gave them plenty of time to turn from their evil practices and plenty of opportunity to see the light and change their way of life. The survival of the nation of Amalek for a long period through Israel's early history is a perfect example of God's patience and his willingness to give people time to repent, yet he knew from the beginning that the Amalekites would not repent, and he declared that one day he would "utterly blot out the remembrance of Amalek from under heaven."

Archeologists digging in the Holy Land have turned up multitudes of objects that confirm the truth of scripture. Granted, they sometimes cause us to question some of the things we've always thought were true and sometimes force us to develop new understandings of God's Word, but all in all, the things they dig up generally confirm and enhance what we read in the Bible.

Usually logic demands that proofs be positive, but in this case a negative may be proof that the scriptures are true. A Bible dictionary's description of *Amalekites* ends with these words, "Archeology has thus far revealed nothing concerning them."

God has kept his promise. For their sin he utterly blotted out the remembrance of Amalek from under heaven. Not a bone or a coin or a shard of a chamber pot remains to testify that they once walked the earth.

And yes, that fish story really happened.

A Morning Kiss

Scripture: Exodus 18:1–12
Suggested Reading: Numbers 12:1; Ephesians 5:25–32

Marital relationships are funny things. Some people announce to the world all that is going on in their homes while others vigorously guard their domestic privacy. Some movie stars, for example, have highly publicized multiple marriages, their private spats having been a source of many a tabloid headline, while others have lived their whole life with one mate whose name is seldom if ever mentioned in the papers. Among Hollywood marriages there seems to be a relationship between publicity and vulnerability; the most public being the most frequently failed and the most private being the best preserved.

There is no doubt that marriage is the most important human relationship in our lives. What happens at home affects all that we do. Studies show that if we leave home without our morning kiss we are more vulnerable to bad things happening to us during the day such as auto accidents and failures on the job.

Although I sometimes mention Mary Ann in my writing, I am most inclined to protect and preserve our relationship by keeping the details of our lives private. I do tell the world that I love her and that she is my best friend and the most important person on my life, but you know I would be lying if I were to tell you that every moment of our time together is spent in perfect bliss and harmony.

Like other humans, we don't always see eye to eye. Then, if we start our day on a disagreeable note, everything I do until I see her again and set things right, I do under a cloud of discontent and distraction. Sometimes we even call each other on the phone during the day to make amends, then the glow of our restored affection drives the dark cloud away and the day is brighter for it.

I know how Moses must have felt from the moment God called him to lead his people. He had strayed from the faith by not circumcising his son, and along the way to Egypt he and Zipporah had a spat about that. In fact, it was more than a spat, it was a downright scene, with Zipporah slipping off in the dark of night, circumcising the boy and spattering his blood on the feet of her sleeping husband. And it wasn't a refreshing sleep either; some commentators believe that Moses had nightmares about it. Some suggest that might be why he sent his family back to Midian.

Though he mentioned her in his writings only on those very special occasions when mentioning her was of some importance, I suspect from what little he did say that she might have been the most important person in his life, because when Miriam and Aaron used the fact that she was a foreigner to degrade Moses and claim equality with him, God punished Miriam severely. I'm happy that God planned this reunion in the wilderness and that Zipporah and the boys went with him the rest of the way because I'm sure that God would want a good man like Moses to have the comfort of a loving wife, considering all the abuse he had to tolerate during the next forty years.

This chapter can teach us a lot; indeed, it has yielded a lot of wisdom regarding worship, sacrifice, recognition of the Lord as the one true God, delegating of authority, managing the affairs of a community, and setting up a system of justice. But on deeper reflection, it has taught me mostly about the importance of protecting and preserving the most valuable human relationships of my life, my relationship with my wife and children.

So, if you're blessed with a loving mate, treasure that blessing and don't ever leave home without your morning kiss.

Sharing the Load

Scripture: Exodus 18:13–27
Suggested Reading: Numbers 10:29–30; Deuteronomy 1:9–15;
Judges 4:11–22; 1 Chronicles 23:2–6, 15–17; Acts 6:1–4;
1 Corinthians 12:1–7; 1 Timothy 3:1–13

I've always believed that God spared the baby Moses and floated his little basket right into Pharaoh's household so he could be trained to be the leader of a nation. And obviously one aspect of such training has always been the delegation of the colossal responsibility of government to underlings of progressive rank. Either Moses forgot that aspect of generalship, or he was one of those people who had to have his finger in every pie.

Or maybe God made him that way to teach us a lesson.

When Jethro arrived from Midian, he found a son-in-law who was overworked, a nation of people who were being denied swift justice, and a lot of good, qualified people who were not being given the opportunity to use the gifts God had given them. So he gave Moses some good advice, advice that has filtered down to the church today.

The disciples who ran the early church were also unable to render the services their congregations required, so they appointed deacons to perform certain of the ministerial duties. Jethro advised Moses that his staff, from corporal to cardinal, not only was to be competent, but was also to be God-fearing and trustworthy. And Moses was to instruct them in "how they must walk and what they must do."

Likewise, the first deacons were to be "of good repute and full of the Spirit and wisdom." And as the church matured and grew, leaders developed a set of more detailed qualifications for the various offices.

But Moses didn't quite tell us the whole story here at the beginning of the journey. Forty years later in his farewell address he reflected on an additional feature: the democratic process. He allowed the people to select their leaders, and he screened the nominees to see if they met the qualifications. Is God telling us here that it is wise to give the governed a voice in their own government?

It's no wonder that Moses would have liked to keep an advisor of Jethro's wisdom in his cabinet, so he asked him to stay on. But Jethro had an enterprise of his own to manage, so he returned home.

Later we learn that his brother-in-law, Hobab, had also dropped by, and Moses offered him the job of reconnaissance point man, figuring that he had the qualifications to be a good forward spy. Hobab refused for a reason he probably didn't really understand: God had a use for his sons in the future as Israel was struggling to wrest the Promised Land from the Canaanites. A couple of generations later, God used Jael, the wife of Heber, a descendant of Hobab, to drive the famous tent peg that gave Barak his great victory over the Canaanite king Jabin.

After the gory business of the circumcision, Moses told us very little about his sons. But the chronicler Ezra revealed that as sons of Moses, Gershom and Eliezer were Levites, and in the Promised Land they and their sons served as priests in the temple.

The moral of it all? Be good husbands, wives, and parents. Heed good advice. Don't overburden yourself. Use your gifts wisely and recognize the gifts and qualifications of others.

On Eagles' Wings

Scripture: Exodus 19:1–4
Suggested Reading: Deuteronomy 32:10–14;
Psalms 19:1–4; 91:1–7

*W*hen I was young my catechism teachers taught me that God reveals himself to us in the scriptures, through the Holy Spirit, and in nature.

The Christian church has been fastidious about understanding the character of God by studying his Word. Bookstore shelves cannot stock all the work done by students of the scriptures, and Christians of all denominations buy study guides and flock to Bible classes to learn all they can about the wondrous ways of the Lord. Believers in some denominations more than others rely to a great extent on the voice of the Holy Spirit, whether spoken in their own hearts or the hearts of others and interpreted by someone gifted for that purpose. But we fall very short in our study of the deity when we fail to hear him tell us of himself through the natural world that surrounds us.

We are so certain of our understanding of the sacred scriptures that we often use them to contradict the messages God gives us in nature, and we prefer to see the creator of the universe more as a clever magician than a brilliant laboratory scientist. Sometimes we even have said that God deliberately planted contradictions in the belly of the earth to test our faith in his Holy Word. If we would only open our eyes to the messages he sends us through the lens of the microscope and the bray of the mule, we might discover that our God is far more than a wizard by whose incantations all heavenly bodies suddenly came into being.

Jesus used metaphors from nature to instruct us in the ways of God. He spoke of faith in terms of a mustard seed and rebirth in terms of a kernel of corn. He used the wind to teach us about the Holy Spirit, Jonah's great fish to reveal the sign of his resurrection, and the wings of a hen to describe his love for us. God used a docile lamb to describe his Son, a hard working ant to teach us about diligence, and a lion to teach us how Satan pounces on his unsuspecting prey. We could go on and on.

I close my Bible and go to my back yard to learn about the sneaky nature of sin from the cat lurking beneath the bird feeder, about grace from the swan tending its nestlings in my neighbor's pond, about being born again from the wooly worm and the butterfly, and about the omnipotence of God from the trunks of great trees twisted like pretzels by the tornado.

And now God tells me that he cares for me as an eagle cares for its young. He not only brought me food when I was hungry and swooped down with talons barred upon the enemies who sought to ambush me, but when I struggled in my maiden flight, he hovered beneath me so when I fell I landed on his back, and he carried me safely to his holy hill. When the vultures circled overhead, he hid me in the shadow of his wings, and in the chill of the night he gathered me to himself to keep me warm.

When I sit on my deck after sundown, how I wish that someone would give me a book that witnessed in detail to the words of David, giving me a hundred illustrations of just how the stars and the planets in the night sky declare their maker's glory, and a myriad of examples of how I might see the hand of God in the silent swoop of the bats over my head and hear his voice in the raucous babble of the creatures that inhabit the swamp. Nature has no words, but her language is sweet and she lectures without ceasing.

Please, Lord, give us ears to hear.

A Kingdom of Priests

Scripture Exodus 19:5–6
Suggested Reading: 1 Samuel 2:22–29; Luke 10:25–37

Throughout the history of the church, priests have had a very special role. They are the ones ordained by God to be intercessors between the creator and his creatures. They attend the seminaries and study the Word so they can clearly communicate God's truth to their congregations. They sit in the confessionals listening to sinners recount their evil deeds, and pray for their forgiveness. They have the special privilege of approaching the throne of God as agents of a fallen human race.

But it is God's will that we all become priests. He wants his church to be a whole kingdom of priests, each of whom can walk boldly through the torn veil and approach the mercy seat in person. He doesn't want any of us to be aliens from his grace who stand in need of an earthly intercessor wearing a clerical collar.

In death, Christ became the ultimate priest. Once and for all he made intercession for us to the Father, and in doing so reached down from heaven and tore the veil of the temple from top to bottom, opening the holy place, the place of God's abode, and making him accessible to repentant sinners. Now each of us can live in the presence of God by offering our bodies to be his temple. Our hearts can be the holy place where he sits and hears petitions. In prayer we can directly share with him our joys, our praise, our sorrows, and our needs. We can be the kingdom of priests he wants us to be, each confessing his own sins and pleading for others.

But throughout history, the church has had its corrupt priests. The sons of Eli were an abomination to the priesthood, and in Jesus' time the temple priests abused their office, abused their worshippers, and robbed even the poor of their meager sacrifices. Jesus told the story of a man who was beaten and left for dead by thieves. A priest and a Levite both passed him by, crossing over to the other side of the road and offering no help. Then the good Samaritan came along, and, having the mind of Christ, had compassion on him and tended to his needs. He was the real priest.

When we have a presidential campaign, candidates go from state to state in search of delegates. One of the differences among them often seems to boil down to the question of the poor. How much healthcare should we offer to the sick and the needy? Should we open our nation's gates to the ailing stranger? Should we offer to trade our work and our goods with the rest of the world or keep them for ourselves? Should we feed the children of the poor in our schools? How much should we care for the elderly and the underprivileged? The poor become the axis on which our attention turns. And suddenly I realize that we have become a nation of priests. The condition of our neighbor, whether across the street or across the sea, had become the focus of our interest.

But the big question is, what kind of priests have we become? Have we become the kind of priests who have the mind of Christ? Will we give our naked neighbor one of our coats? Will we share our bread with the neighbor who is hungry? Will we stop and bind the wounds of the poor unfortunate who has been robbed? Will we tend the sick no matter what their nationality or disease?

Or are we like the greedy and adulterous sons of Eli, living only to fulfill our own lusts and getting fat on the sacrifices of others? Do we, like the infamous priest of the Good Samaritan story, look upon the suffering of others and pass by on the other side of the road? What kind of priests have we become?

Prepare to Meet Thy God

Scripture: Exodus 19: 7–25
Suggested Reading: Exodus 3:1–12; Amos 4:11–12; 1 John 1:7;
Revelation 7:14; 8:8; 21:8

When Moses first met God on the mountain in Midian, the angel of the Lord appeared to him in a burning bush and called him to lead the nation of Israel from Egypt to the Promised Land. When Moses tried to beg off, the Lord promised to be with him and offered as a sign that when he had brought the people out of Egypt, they would return to that very same mountain to worship the God that had set them free.

It's hard to reconcile Midian with the Sinai Peninsula since researchers have had no luck finding any trace of some millions of Israelites camping for two years at the base of what they generally consider to be Mount Sinai, let alone any evidence of a consuming fire at the top of that mountain. Some scholars now think that the mountain of God might have been east of the Gulf of Aqaba.

The historical and geographical references are truly baffling, and archeology raises more questions than it answers, again pointing out to us that God does not intend his Word to be a history book or a geography book, but rather a manual on how we should live our lives, teaching us mainly by the positive and negative examples of the people who are featured on its pages.

When Moses stood in the presence of the Lord, the voice from the burning bush ordered him to remove his sandals because he was standing on holy ground. The fire did not consume the bush, nor was it accompanied by any terrifying natural phenomenon, just the authoritative voice of God speaking to a man and changing his life forever.

When the Israelites gathered around the base of that same mountain just a few months later, Moses ordered them to wash their garments, consecrate themselves and live in purity, all in preparation for gathering on holy ground and meeting God.

And when God did appear, it wasn't in the quiet of a few soft wisps of flame on the leaves of a bush, rather it was a jarring earthquake and a roaring fire that wrapped the entire mountain in smoke, all accompanied by thunder and loud blasts from God's trumpets, a picture reminiscent of the destruction of Sodom and ominous of God's appearance on the last days of the earth.

The geography and the timing may be different, but the message is always the same: prepare to meet thy God.

Moses had to prepare to stand in the presence of God by removing his sandals. The Israelites had to prepare by washing their garments, consecrating themselves, and forsaking their sinful ways. And God calls us to prepare to meet him by washing our garments in the blood of the Lamb.

God demands respect and purity. He abhors evil and will not tolerate it in his presence. Before we can stand on holy ground, he demands that we be cleansed. No amount of self-righteous behavior, penance, or consecration will suffice to wash away the deeply imbedded stains that blemish our robes and bear witness to the contaminated paths we've trod. The only detergent with the power to purge and sterilize is the blood of Jesus.

Prepare to meet thy God.

I Am the Lord Thy God . . .

Scripture: Exodus 20
Suggested Reading: Romans 8:1–2

When I was a boy in the old Dutch Christian Reformed Church, the dominie read the Law to us every Sunday, a habit that has disappeared from most of our churches since the middle of the last century.

Having moved from my hometown fifty years ago and returning to visit once or twice a year, I was able to watch the liturgy evolve to the point that the reading of the Ten Commandments became about as infrequent as baptism.

Recently, however, I returned for the celebration of the church's centennial, a Saturday dinner and program in the high school gym, and a nostalgic retro service on Sunday morning at which several former pastors played a part. A son of the church who grew up a generation after me and who had become a minister in another city, had the privilege of reading the Ten Commandments.

He began by reminiscing about writhing in the pew as a child during the service, listening to the Commandments, which he timed at two minutes, and the summary, which ate up another twenty seconds, then eating peppermints during the "long prayer," which usually lasted ten to twelve minutes, and finally surviving a sermon that droned on for thirty to forty minutes. With the hymns, the choir selection, the offering, and sundry other activities, the service usually lasted well over an hour and a half.

Then, as he prepared to read the Law as in the old days, he noted an amazing fact. He pointed out that God gave the Law to Israel *after* he had brought them out of the house of bondage.

He went on to explain that there would have been no point in giving them the Law before delivering them from slavery. It would have made no sense to require them to worship only him when all they knew was pagan gods. It would have been futile to expect them to honor the Sabbath when their Egyptian slave masters made them work seven days a week. Why tell them not to steal when sometimes that was the only way to get a crust of bread, or not to lie when often lying was their only protection? And it would not have been practical to expect them to remain chaste and faithful when the Egyptians used them freely for their sexual pleasure. The Law simply was not for an enslaved people.

He added that we always considered the Law as a standard of righteousness that God set before sinners so they could learn their failures, confess their sins, seek forgiveness, and resolve to do better. But that is not how it is set forth in the scripture. In God's order, the Law doesn't come first, it comes only after he has extended his hand of grace. It follows God's intervention and liberation of his people, only after he has set them free from the bonds of sin. God doesn't set the Law before us as a measuring stick to condemn us when we are powerless over sin, but rather it is set before us as a description of the freedom redeemed people have in the Lord who saved them.

Now that I'm free, I need no idols. Now that my Provider supplies all I need, I don't have to covet or steal. Now that I'm no longer in Satan's grasp, I don't have to lust. Now that I know how much I'm loved, I'm free to love my neighbor as I love myself.

So let's go back and read the Law anew and learn how the one who freed us from the bondage of sin empowers us to live, as wholesome and grateful citizens of the kingdom of heaven!

Slaves Forever!

Scripture: Exodus 21:1–11
Suggested Reading: Romans 6:15–22; Ephesians 6:5–9

*Y*esterday I sat on a bench in the shopping mall while Mary Ann browsed in the ladies' clothing stores. She browses better without me and I meditate and people watch better without her.

As I waited there, a man came over and sat on the bench across from me, a rather ordinary looking fellow about my age, conservative by comparison to the types of folks that generally hang out in the mall. I didn't notice anything unusual about him until his wife, a neatly dressed lady with coifed silver hair, sat down beside him and he turned to look at her. In his left ear lobe, which was obviously pierced, he wore a small gold cross.

Shortly after they left I forgot about him and began to meditate on the issue of slavery. In the history of man, slavery is more the rule than the exception. Only in modern civilized society has the idea of slavery become detestable. Even Christians raising cotton in Alabama years ago believed there was nothing wrong with subjugating black humans to the bonds of involuntary servitude. Reports still abound of people who live in bondage to others, not only in strange corners of the world, but also in the dark corners of our own cities.

Joseph's brothers sold him into slavery, but by the grace of God he rose to power and took charge of the Egyptian economy. During the later years of the famine, when the native Egyptians had sold all they had in order to buy food, he gave them grain in exchange for their lives, making them slaves to Pharaoh. Some generations later, his own descendants became slaves to Pharaoh.

Throughout the entire Bible, the concept of slavery is never condemned. When he instituted civil law, God included numerous provisions for slaves. He issued orders instructing them to be obedient to their masters and for masters to be kind to their slaves, a rule that persisted into the church age. Men were permitted to sell their daughters to other men to serve as cooks, maids, or concubines. Victorious armies, including the armies of Israel, rounded up the vanquished and marched the soldiers and the women and children off into lives of bondage. In the end, Israel too, for its faithlessness, became slaves to foreign rulers, even into the twentieth century.

It would seem normal for people to dislike slavery, but God made provision for the slave who loved his master and did not wish to go free. His master was to take him to the house of God and at the doorpost bore his ear through with an awl, and he was to serve him for the rest of his life.

Paul said that just as his ancestors were slaves to Pharaoh, by our first disobedience in the Garden of Eden we became slaves to sin. But just as Moses led the children of Israel out of bondage, so the second Moses, Jesus, led us out of bondage to sin and set us free.

But what if we don't want to be free? What if we love the one who redeemed us and want to become his slaves, slaves to righteousness? God thought of that long age. All we have to do is go to our master and offer him our lives. Then he'll put his sanctifying mark on us and we'll belong to him forever.

And now I wonder if the man who sat across from me in the mall had that little gold cross put in his ear to testify that Jesus had set him free from the bondage of sin, that he loved his redeemer, and had willingly become a slave to righteousness forever.

Internal Matters

Scripture: Exodus 21:12–23; Exodus 22
Suggested Reading: Matthew 5:38–48

When God's spokesman came down from the mountain to deliver the package of moral, civil, and ceremonial laws to the people of Israel, he confronted a nation of people who had just been delivered from the bondage of slavery. The only law they knew was the law of submission to the tyrant's cadre of bullies who whipped them and ripped nursing children from their mother's breast. They had no idea how to govern themselves as a free nation about to take its place among the other nations of the world.

There were internal and external matters facing them. In order to become a nation with land and borders they would have to attack and drive out the enemies who possessed the land that God had promised to them. At the same time they would have to have order among themselves. The oppressors who controlled their every move with whips were gone; they would have to become responsible for the way they related to each other.

As we shall see, God took care of the external business of possessing the land. He promised to send his angel before them to guard them on the way and bring them to the place he had prepared for them. He promised to fight their battles and subdue their enemies. All they had to do was to submit obediently to him in faith and do as they were told. Establishing their place in history was his business, and he would see to it that it was done exactly as he wanted it done. They just had to be obedient to him.

But he gave them extensive instructions for dealing with internal matters, the business of getting along with each other. That was to be their business, and they had better do it right. They didn't have to try to figure out for themselves how to relate properly with their friends and neighbors, their brothers and their sisters, God made the rules clear and plain. That was his covenant with them, and he fully expected them to obey.

The history of Israel and God's Old Testament covenant with them is a very valuable metaphor God has given us to guide us in this age. The same principles that applied to them apply to us as we relate to each other under the new covenant in Christ's blood.

The external matters fall to his care. All we have to do is submit to his calling and he will send his angel before us to guard us in the way and take us to the place that he has prepared for us. He has a work for each of us to do out there in his world. He has set aside some kind of ministry for each of us, a ministry with certain boundaries, a mission with certain goals. He may simply call us to that work, give us the tools to perform it, and send us on our way with the promise to go with us and fight our battles for us.

But in the matter of getting along with each other, God places the burden of responsibility squarely on us, just as he placed it on the Israelites. From beginning to end, the Bible repeats the command to be our brother's keeper, to love our neighbor as ourselves, to feed the hungry, to clothe the naked, to heal the sick, to care for the widows and the fatherless, to walk the second mile, to give to the beggar, to lend to the borrower, and even to love and do good to the enemy who persecutes us.

And in the end, when the goats are separated from the sheep, the judgment will not be based on the extent to which we made our place in history, but on the extent to which we served even the least of our brothers, and in doing so served our Lord.

A Desolate Land

Scripture: Exodus 23:22–33

After giving his people the laws he wanted them to follow, God made promises to them regarding the rest of the trip to the Promised Land. At this point, if we haven't yet read the rest of the story, we might think this new nation is just going to take a short journey to Canaan, walk right in and possess the land.

Of course, it's not going to be that simple.

We often use the story of Israel as a metaphor for all of life, beginning with our rebirth at the first Passover until the glorious day we cross the river of death and enter the eternal home that Jesus won for us on the cross. But another application of which I become more and more certain as I review my walk with the Lord is that he carefully preserved the story of Israel's journey for us because he intended it to be a metaphor of our spiritual journey from the day he rescued us from the bondage of sin to the day we are crucified with Christ, die to self in the waters of the Jordan River, and rise up to possess our spiritual promised land, enjoying the milk and honey, the produce of that land, the fruit of the Spirit.

It works beautifully. He promised to send his angel before us to guard us on our way and to bring us to the place he has prepared for us. His name is in him, that is, the angel is none other than the creator himself, in the form of the Holy Spirit, telling us which way to go and scattering our enemies before us. What enemies? The Hittites and Jebusites? No, the lusts of the flesh, ego, and the spirits of anger and hate that seem to plague us as we try to be what we should be and do what we should do.

Now comes the best part. He is going to conquer all those enemies for us. Eventually.

Every now and again we hear a story about a sinner who suddenly got converted and reborn all at once, like Paul on the road to Damascus. One moment he was an enemy of God, and the next he was a child of God, perfected in every way. I knew a man like that. On Saturday morning he was just another neighborhood drunk, but by the afternoon he had become a sanctified evangelist, fully purged of all his evil ways. The Lord touched him, healed him, and drove out of him in an instant all that was offensive. And it wasn't just a passing fancy; this brother has been a faithful witness now for more than a quarter of a century.

It didn't happen that way with me, but I'm not jealous. In fact, I'm glad that my conversion is a journey rather than a blinding moment in my life. The Lord didn't drive out all my enemies at once. I didn't become suddenly sanctified. Instead he lets me watch as day by day and year by year he scores victories over the sins that plague me. I'm afraid that if he had scored all those victories in a single blow, my land might become desolate. I need a regular diet of victories, and thankfully, he doles them out to me one at a time.

As he constantly enriches my life with daily victories over those enemies that battle to overcome me, I am gradually increasing in grace. With each step I take over the mountains and through the valleys, he shines his moonbeams on my path and gives me another new taste of the milk and honey that flow like rivers through the paradise that is never desolate, but ever alive and new.

And with every taste of victory, I come to possess a little more of this blessed promised land, the kingdom of heaven!

With One Voice

Scripture: Exodus 24

It's interesting to muse on the possibility that this chapter might have been nearly the end of the Bible. God has spoken. He has laid down his law and his ordinances. And now his people have answered. With one voice they have said, "All the words the Lord has spoken, we will do, and we will be obedient." This was the end of sin. They sealed their covenant with blood, and God led them to the Promised Land where they kept their word, obeyed all his commandments, and lived happily ever after.

Wouldn't it have been wonderful to end the Bible with the glorious picture of God that Moses painted there: a devouring fire on the top of the mountain, the God of heaven walking on a pavement of sapphire stone! Moses beheld God as no one has before or since, a presence so majestic that those who even hear of it are forever incapable of sin. A picture so compelling that all of God's children lived in perpetual obedience. Eden restored!

Of course, that's not how it turned out, and boy am I glad.

No, I'm not happy that man is incapable of a life of obedience to the spirit of God's law, and I'm not happy that the Hebrews stumbled and fell so far so often. But I am happy that the Lord saw fit to come up with his "final plan," his ultimate solution to the problem of sin in the world.

A pastor I knew used the words "fortunate fall" to describe the sin of Adam and Eve in the Garden of Eden. He didn't mean that they had done a wonderful thing by disobeying God, but he did recognize that if they had never yielded to temptation, the world would never have heard the Christmas story.

Now, we will never know what life for humankind might have been like had our first parents passed the temptation test. We can imagine that they might have enjoyed the blessings of paradise forever, basking in the sunlight, splashing joyously in the rivers and relishing eternal communion with their congenial creator.

But what might have happened had the children of Israel walked uprightly before their God? Would they have enjoyed the blessings of the Promised Land forever? We can only expect that they might have, because that is what God promised them if they would obey his law. There would have been no Diaspora, no exile, no weeping by the river of Babylon, and no Holocaust.

But what about the rest of us? The other sons of Shem? The sons of Ham and Japheth? Would there have been salvation for us? Or would God have been happy to save his chosen people while the rest of us lived without hope?

That's a mystery we'll never solve and an eventuality that could never have happened because the chosen people of God, using the same single voice with which they promised to be obedient, mouthed dissatisfaction with their lot and asked Aaron to make for them an idol they could worship while they thought God was away.

God promised Abraham that through him *all the families of the earth* would be blessed, and God knew me from before the foundations of the earth. I'm not happy that Israel did those terrible things and suffered as they did, but I'm happy that God's wonderful plan of salvation stretched far enough to include this poor son of Japheth!

A Willing Heart

Scripture: Exodus 25:1–9
Suggested Reading: Matthew 26:36–46

One Easter Sunday, my church had a groundbreaking ceremony for its new building. Three days earlier the pastor had used the episode of Christ praying in the Garden of Gethsemane as his Maundy Thursday message, reflecting on the willing heart Jesus demonstrated when, by praying, "not my will, but thine, be done," he submitted to the will of his Father and resigned his human self to the torment that lay ahead.

Three years earlier the pastor used today's scripture from Exodus and the generosity of the Israelites as the basis for his message to inspire the members of the congregation to make generous pledges to the building fund. As I contemplate these two services, it strikes me that the whole Christian experience relies on *willingness* as opposed to *willfulness*.

In the garden, Jesus confessed that as a man he had the potential for willfulness, but in his willingness to submit, he put off self will and yielded to the will of God. God too, as we shall soon see, suggested to Moses that the darker side of his will urged him to destroy the evil Israelites and pour out his blessing upon Moses instead. But Moses, putting his own self-interest aside, appealed to God to be forgiving toward his people and give them another chance. In response, God modeled for us by acting willingly rather than willfully, and continued to bless the sons of Jacob despite their evil ways.

In our Christian experience, the Lord has provided the perfect example of willingness over willfulness. He has shown us that both as a divine being and a human being he has faced the temptation of self will and has overcome its power. As our Lord and Savior he also demands that we emulate him, sacrifice self-gratification, and serve him with a willing heart.

The nation of Israel did not often stand out as a model that we should imitate, but in the building of God's sanctuary they set a marvelous example for us to follow. Enough of them opened their treasure chests, and with willing hearts gave Moses all the precious metals, timbers, skins, and fine textiles he needed to build a house suitable to be the dwelling place of God.

At the pastor's request, the members of my congregation did the same. Over a three year period they donated enough money to build a substantial and necessary addition to the church. They had to set aside some of their own willfulness and their own self-interest in order to pledge the amount necessary to begin construction.

In such projects, we humans might equal the willingness of the Israelites to open our treasure chests and give a portion of our wealth to God's service, but we fall far short of the degree of willingness that Jesus demonstrated when he gave his life for us.

Perhaps in our offertory prayer we should say,

Lord, as we bring our offerings to your altar today, we look up to the cross and reflect on the offering that you, our creator, brought to Calvary for us. And we simply ask you to give us the grace, the faith, the courage, and the willingness to imitate your sacrifice and give back to you all that we have, all that we are, and all that we ever will be. Amen.

... *I Will Meet with You*

Scripture: Exodus 25:10–40
Suggested Reading: Exodus 26:31–34; Matthew 27:45–51

*W*hat a wonderful moment in the history of the developing relationship between God and fallen man!

God told his servant Moses to build a special little room at the far end of the holy place, separate it from the rest of the tabernacle with a veil and call it the *most* holy place, or the Holy of Holies. He was to bring into that little room the holiest object that the Jews possessed, the ark of the covenant, and on top of the ark to place the mercy seat. There God would meet with Moses and give him direction for leading the people.

Let's savor the moment.

In Genesis we learned that Adam and Eve had a casual relationship with God before they sinned. They walked together in the cool of the day and talked. We have no record of what they talked about, and though knowing the subjects of their conversations would be fascinating, it doesn't really matter. They talked *with* each other as friends as they strolled together along the shaded paths of paradise!

But when Adam and Eve disobeyed God and ate the forbidden fruit, the casual conversation gave way to inquest, accusation, evasion, and judgment. The friendship ended and a strained relationship began. Later God talked *to* Noah, *to* Abraham, *to* Jacob, and *to* Moses. But now God changed the preposition and told Moses that their relationship would grow to a new level of familiarity, and that he would meet *with* him and speak *with* him.

Moses enjoys a special place in the history of man's relationship with God. Nowhere else in the Bible do we have any account of such intimate conversations as the talks between God and Moses. Oh yes, David poured out his heart to God, and other giants of scripture such as Samuel had brief conversational encounters, but no one else ever had the enduring intimate relationship and dialog that Moses had.

God saw to it that he and Moses had their privacy. He ordered that a veil be placed over the entrance to the Most Holy Place. And that veil did its duty throughout the whole of scripture. It guarded the Holy of Holies in the temple that King Solomon built. After Nebuchadnezzar destroyed Solomon's temple, Zerubbabel built a new one and King Herod remodeled it. The second temple, too, had a Holy of Holies that was separated from the rest of the temple by a veil, and only the high priest might step into that sacred place and represent the people to God.

But something wonderful happened when Jesus died. The veil of the temple was torn in two *from the top to the bottom*. It didn't just tear of its own accord or tear from the bottom up, as it would have had some human torn it. No, it tore from the top. God himself tore the veil and opened up that Most Holy Place so all who would might enter.

No longer would the people have to go to the high priest to gain second hand access to God. Now the creator sits on his mercy seat and invites all weary souls to,

> Come ye disconsolate, where 'ere ye languish,
> Come to the mercy seat, fervently kneel;
> Here bring your wounded hearts, here tell your anguish;
> Earth has no sorrows that heaven cannot heal.
>
> (Thomas Moore, 1816)

The Tent of Meeting

Scripture: Exodus 26
Suggested Reading: 1 Chronicles 28:11–19; Matthew 27:51;
1 Corinthians 3:16; Revelation 11:19; 21:22

I vividly remember the day when Mrs. Hooker, our Sunday school teacher, led us into that room in the basement of the church. There on a large table in the center of the room was an elaborate model of the tabernacle. On another table against the wall was Solomon's temple. Both structures were built by Elder Roosema, one of the pillars of our church

Mrs. Hooker, exuding praise for both the structures and their builder, excitedly explained how the Bible contained instructions from God which Moses, Solomon, and Elder Roosema followed explicitly in constructing their buildings. What struck me most, however, was that both models, the tabernacle and the temple, contained similar veils that separated the Holy of Holies from the holy place. Both were made of blue, purple, and red linen with cherubim woven into the fabric. The difference between the two was that the veil of the temple was "rent in twain, from the top to the bottom."

I have often wondered why God gave such detailed instructions for the building of the tabernacle. After all, it was a temporal thing, serving the nation of Israel only during their early years and giving way to two successive temples, both of which God saw fit to destroy in due time. Some pundits of prophecy interpret certain passages from Daniel and Revelation to mean that the temple will be rebuilt in the last days. John, in his vision, saw the temple in heaven, complete with the ark of the covenant. But even that heavenly temple did not survive in the New Jerusalem, because there God and the Lamb are the temple.

I doubt that God used two whole chapters of his Word giving such a detailed description of the tabernacle just so the good elder could build an authentic scale model. When we read the Bible we often skip over those sorts of descriptions much as we skip over the long list of unpronounceable names in the genealogies. So why did God bother to be so precise in his instructions to Moses?

When it came to building the temple, God didn't instruct Solomon in the same manner, although there is a suggestion that he secretly revealed the blueprints to David. Why didn't he instruct Moses as privately? Did he preserve the details of the tabernacle in durable scripture just for us? Why? Why is it important for me to have over fifty verses of detailed directions for the building of an old tabernacle that went to dust thousands of years ago?

Maybe it is important for me to know that the place God set aside for meeting with me is a place in which he has a punctilious interest. He cares very deeply about every tiny detail of the place where we meet. Every trifle of our common habitation is a matter of deep concern to him. And he wants it to be beautiful, made from the finest available substances.

Where is this place? Is it the building downtown? The one with the steeple and the beautiful stained glass windows? Does he wait for me there or does he meet me at my place?

My body is his temple. He dwells in me. My heart is his holy of holies. He loves me and knows every detail about me, each step my foot takes, everything my hand touches, every hair that grows on my head and every thought that races through my mind. He wants his habitation to be carefully maintained as a thing of beauty, as suited to his holy presence as I can possibly make it.

My Altars

Scripture: Exodus 27; 30

The model of Elder Roosema's tabernacle had two altars; an altar of incense inside the holy place and an altar of burnt offering out in the courtyard. Knowing the elder's piety and penchant for propriety, I have no reason to doubt the accuracy of his rendition.

In my youth I gave little thought to the two altars, but as the path of my life began to draw nearer to the gates of paradise, I began to ponder their necessity. Why two? And how do I translate the two altars from the context of the Lord making his abode in the center of an ancient material edifice to the context of the Spirit of God dwelling in the heart of an old man just stepping over the threshold of a new millennium?

Do I need two altars, one on which to burn fragrant incense to give pleasure to my God and another on which to offer up to him all of the failures, lusts, idolatries, and broken promises of my life?

My altar of incense is right inside the heart of the holy place, right next to the torn veil, right next to the mercy seat. It is a very special altar, most holy to the Lord. It is the altar deep within my soul, the spot he has purified to be his own dwelling place. There I can bring nothing unfit to be in his presence. There I can make no confession of sin nor entertain any unholy thought. On that altar only the sweetest incense burns. From that altar only perfect praise ascends.

When I am at that altar I am in ecstasy. I am in perfect harmony with my Lord. Beautiful hymns rise from the core of my being, and I experience the presence of God in a most delightful way. I tingle with the sense that God is pleased with me and enjoys my company. I feel like John must have felt when he leaned against the bosom of Jesus and knew that Jesus loved him like he loved no one else in the world.

But when I am at the altar out in the courtyard, I feel distant from God. I am away from the holy place, separated from his presence by my sin, alienated. There is no place to sit down, no place to rest until the offering is complete.

I kneel alone there with a heavy heart, mourning the error of my ways, yesterday's wrongs, the immorality of my youth, and the evil I expect to commit tomorrow. On that altar I heap the sum of my infirmity, the weakness of my flesh, and the iniquity of my soul. One by one I pile up the memories of each transgression, each failure, each moment of depravity, each lapse of faith. Then I confess, repent, and watch as the whole heap is engulfed in the flames of God's wonderful absolution. Some of the things on that altar don't burn very well. Certain sins seem impervious to the fire and remind me of old soggy logs that require several dousings of kerosene before they finally flame up and slowly turn to ash.

As the last of the foul embers dies I slowly rise. My knees hurt and my back aches, but the joy of forgiveness swells within my heart. I turn from the searing heat of that altar and feel the cool moonbeams of his grace on my face. Then with a smile of contentment that only divine pardon brings, I once again return to the mercy seat and the altar of fragrant incense, and there I again raise to the highest heaven my prayers of praise and thanksgiving.

No Fear!

Scripture: Exodus 28
Suggested Reading: 1 Samuel 16:7; Matthew 6:25–30; James 4:12

Each year my church designates one Sunday as Youth Sunday. The young people of the congregation take charge of the service. Last year guitars and drums substituted for the organ, and the youth chorus sang a contemporary gospel song. The special music was a Christian rap tune performed by a young man wearing a hip hop costume. The associate pastor for youth preached the sermon wearing blue jeans and a designer t-shirt proclaiming him to be a warrior for God and having *No Fear!*

I enjoyed the service, but I was glad that my parents were not there to see it. They would have been shocked. But then again, if they were able to watch from on high, maybe they did see it, and dressed in their new robes, maybe they were pleased. I hope so.

We've come a long way since my childhood. The first pastor I remember, Dominie Brink, always wore long tails and a high collar when he preached. In public, and even at the church picnic, he never appeared in anything but a suit and tie. His successor, Reverend Veltkamp, preached in a conservative suit, white shirt, and tie. Sometimes on the street during the week he wore casual clothes. The next pastor, Marv Beelen, broke all tradition by daring to preach in pastel shirts and sports jackets. During the week he often wore jeans. Many in the congregation spoke critically behind his back, opining that anything other than a white shirt and suit in the pulpit violated God's dress code for preachers, and that a man of the cloth defiled his calling by wearing denim in public.

I can understand why both old people and kids are confused about dress in church. Most old timers still wear suits and ties to worship while most of the teenagers wear jeans. Some of the adults find fault with what the kids wear, and some are tolerant. Most older people were brought up believing that when we enter the presence of God, we ought to be dressed in our Sunday best. But young people do not believe that God is impressed by an outward display of finery. Both have a point. We struggle with what appears to be a confusing message from God with regard to attire.

The Lord gave specific instructions for the design of clerical garb. Priests were to perform their sacred sacrificial duties wearing very exquisite garments, replete with gold clasps and precious stones. But the ultimate High Priest performed the ultimate sacrifice wearing only a loincloth; some contend he was naked. All Christians are called to be priests, but what shall we wear as we perform our priestly duties? Tuxedos or blue jeans?

There can be no doubt that clothing sends a message, or as some put it, makes a statement. The Levitical priests wore their robes, ephods, turbans, and engraved onyx to communicate a concept of great importance to their congregation. The Catholic church adorns its high-ranking clergy in classical attire as a statement to God and the world. My associate pastor for youth was also making a statement of obvious significance to the young people of the church and, he hoped, to the adults.

As long as the church is intergenerational, and I hope that is for all time, there will probably be conflict over dress. The modernists are no less obsessed than the traditionalists. I'm glad I don't have to referee that dispute, because there is no happy medium. But I'm content to conclude that the issue is of no real importance, because in matters of the heart, clothing becomes meaningless. And is anyone other than God qualified to judge the heart of man?

A Perfect World?

Scripture: Exodus 29
Suggested Reading: Leviticus 10:1–5; Luke 10:30–37;
Revelation 19:7–9

My pastor once lamented to me that the bishop had assigned him to a task he detested: screening candidates for the ministry. He agonized over the standards of judgment he was to use in determining whether the young seminarians were qualified to become pastors. Were they authoritative enough to run a church? Could they be compassionate? Did they have the necessary language and oratorical skills? Were they knowledgeable in matters of scripture and doctrine? Did they pass the tests of faith and belief? Would they submit to the bishop's jurisdiction? On the other hand, he questioned by what authority he could disqualify anyone who genuinely loved the Lord and felt called into the ministry. Once he and his committee put their stamp of approval on the candidates, they were deemed fit for ordination as pastors in the church and would be sent out to serve.

The gap between the Levitical process for ordination and the modern process in which my pastor participates reminds me of the gap between arranged marriages and modern courtship. In societies where marriages are arranged by families, there appears to be little question of qualification. Children are taught by their parents how to act as mates and an appropriate bride is simply selected and appointed to be the wife of the appropriate husband. By virtue of that training and by the vows of commitment, proper performance by each is expected to follow. In modern courtship, however, love is the benchmark, but we also have ways of testing our prospective mates to determine their suitability and compatibility.

In ancient Israel, God determined that the Levites should be set apart for service in the tabernacle. It seems that his selecting them and running them through an impressive ordination ceremony made them fit for such service. There is no evidence that he tested them individually to determine their qualifications, or had them parade their talents before a screening committee.

Did God choose them, equip them for their duties, ordain them, and presume that proper performance would follow? Should he have required them to submit to competency exams and tested their suitability and commitment to their calling?

Just as there are enough failed marriages and recorded divorces to prove that neither arranged marriages nor modern courting serve to ensure successful relationships, both the pages of the Bible and the annals of church history are strewn with the bodies of enough fallen priests to show that neither calling nor the rigors of ordination serve to make successful clergy. Passionate hearts, beautiful gowns, sparkling rings, and eloquent vows do not equip one to deal successfully with the many stresses of marriage. Nor do piety, elegant robes, advanced degrees, and anointing oil equip one to shepherd a congregation of wayward and headstrong sheep.

In a perfect world, love would conquer all, vows would not break, and a calling into the ministry would guarantee successful performance as a pastor. But God has shown us enough Nadabs, Abihus, and heartless priests and Levites to convince us that we are not living in a perfect world, and that all of our revered institutions, including marriage and the church on earth were tainted by our foolishness in Eden.

But, praise God, some day the perfect world will come and the Lord will usher his bride, the perfected church, to the marriage supper of the Lamb!

To All Able Men

Scripture: Exodus 31:1–17
Suggested Reading: Matthew 25:14–30; John 3:27; James 1:17

O Mary, Don't You Weep, Don't You Mourn
Go, Tell it on the Mountain
Were You There When They Crucified My Lord?
It's Me, It's Me, It's Me O Lord
There Is a Balm in Gilead
Lord, I Want to be a Christian
Every Time I Feel the Spirit
We Are Climbing Jacob's Ladder
Go Down, Moses
Nobody Knows the Trouble I See
Do Lord, Do Lord, O Do Remember Me
We Shall Overcome
This Little Light of Mine
Let Us Break Bread Together
Swing Low, Sweet Chariot
Steal Away
My Lord, What a Morning
We Shall Not Be Moved
Deep River
Give Me Jesus
I Got Peace Like a River
Ezekiel Saw the Wheel
Dry Bones
Roll Jordan, Roll
Let My People Go
Little David Play on Your Harp

The tunes and the words to these songs are well known and loved, not only by Christians who appreciate such music, but by the secular world as well. They all have one thing in common. If you haven't guessed it already, they are all listed in my hymnbooks as African-American spirituals. Many are songs that were first sung in slavery, but they have survived more than a century after slavery was officially abolished.

The words, melodies, and rhythms of these great spirituals are pure art. Though they are earthy in substance, they transcend the stuff of which they were formed, and they soar to grand, heavenly heights. They lift the soul far above the mundane and transport it to the ethereal. Though they were born in the soil of the cotton field, they were conceived in paradise.

Who fills the human mind with ability, intelligence, knowledge, and craftsmanship? Who gives the soul the skill to devise artistic designs, to mold precious metals, to cut stones, to write poems, to make music? Who can take a lump of clay whose only visible molding influence is the brutal curse of slavery, whether in Egypt or in Alabama, and engender in it the delicate spirit and sensitive touch needed to shape a work of fine art?

Let there be no mistake. God loves good music and good art, gives us our creative talent, and appoints us to our tasks. Even though some of us misuse our gifts, making golden calves instead of Pietas, and some of us use our gifts in the service of Satan, those gifts come from our Creator!

He knows our names, keeps an inventory of the skills he has bestowed on us, and gives us access to the power of the Holy Spirit to enable us to accomplish the work he wants us to do.

And someday he will call us to account for the way we have used his holy gifts.

The Finger of God

Scripture: Exodus 31:18
Suggested Reading: James 1:17

Speaking of gifts, we usually tend to think of them in terms of an extraordinary skill that sets one person apart from the rest, such as nimble fingers that have mastered the keys of a piano, a soprano or tenor voice that can lift our souls to heaven, or oratory that can bring sinners to their knees. But as I look carefully around the church, I see gifts that almost go unnoticed, such as the patience and commitment to tend the nursery every Sunday morning, to mow the church lawn and edge the sidewalk every Saturday afternoon, or to go up and down the rows of pews after the service picking up scraps of paper and even feeling under the seats for a sticky wad of gum that some thoughtless sinner might have stuck there.

One such gifted saint has served our church for as long as anyone can remember. Every Sunday, long before services begin, even when many people stay home because the freshly fallen snow is a foot deep, Wilma unlocks the door to the church kitchen and begins brewing several urns of coffee, pouring juice into little cups for the children, and laying out trays of cookies. During fellowship time she draws cup after cup for the long line of worshippers, and at the start of the Sunday school hour she delivers decanters of coffee to all the adult classes. Her gift may have been cultivated in rural Indiana, but just as all good and perfect gifts, it came from above, wrought by the very hand of God, workmanship as sacred as the greatest tenor voice, the Grand Teton mountain range, or the tablets of stone carved for Moses by the finger of God there in the thick darkness of Mount Sinai.

Sometimes my mind wanders beyond the bounds of theological and historical practicality and I fantasize that the ark of the covenant might someday be discovered and brought forth from some ancient secret cavern in Ethiopia or the bowels of Temple Mount.

After scientists had completed the myriad of tests intended either to prove or disprove the authenticity of the find, the ark would be brought to the museum in Jerusalem and placed in a climate controlled glass showcase. Crowds of pious believers and curious skeptics would stand in line for hours, or maybe even days, to pass by the shrine and see the cherubim, Aaron's budding rod, the jar of manna, and the two tablets of testimony written in Sinai stone by the finger of God.

Some perceptive and thoughtful people, such as my wife, don't have to cross the sea to view such marvels. We stand amazed at God's craftsmanship when we view the majestic snow-capped peaks of the Rockies and the deep gorges of the Grand Canyon; we stand in awe of his might as we watch thunderbolts leap from cloud to cloud over Lake Michigan.

And we really don't have to leave home at all. We can come into the presence of God and see his handiwork just by going out into the back yard in the springtime and looking at the blossoms on the magnolia bush or watching the butterflies land delicately on the daffodils. The bumblebees tell the continuing story of creation as they buzz from one blossom on the apple tree to another, and the robins tell their version as they gather grass to build their cradle in the crotch of the big old blue spruce. The finger of God paints its wonders wherever we look.

But when Wilma delivers that pot of coffee to my Sunday school class, I see the hand of the Lord at work as vividly as if I were standing before the original tablets of stone!

The Service of the Lord

Scripture: Exodus 32
Suggested Reading: Ecclesiastes 11:1; Matthew 10:37;
Luke 18:28–30; Acts 2:41

The sad story of Aaron making that golden calf was carved into my memory by my first grade Sunday school teacher, Mrs. Hooker, long before I had any understanding at all of the horribly pervasive nature of sin.

I understood the anger Moses felt and the bitterness that gripped his heart as he threw down those tables of the Law and smashed them on the stones on the side of the mountain when he saw the orgy of idolatry going on in the valley below. I understood the passion that drove him to grind that idol into powder, scatter it on the water, and force the Israelites to drink it. I understood, somewhat, why the Levites took up their swords and massacred three thousand of the guilty revelers. But I didn't understand how those brutal slayings ordained them for the service of the Lord and earned them a blessing from on high. And, if we are to be a nation of priests, how does the shedding of our guilty brothers' blood ordain us to that holy priesthood and earn us a holy blessing?

Not until I began to understand death in more than a literal sense, did I begin to comprehend the true meaning of that awful incident. Yes, if we are to become true priests, we must be willing to put the sacrificial sword to those we love the most.

How so? A young friend who recently became a pastor confided to me that his decision to enter the ministry was as much of a monumental moment as was his decision to give his life to Christ.

When he decided to become a pastor he had to put aside all personal interests and submit his whole life to the calling of the church.

For example, he had to set aside all financial interests and have faith that the Lord would provide for his material needs. He had to have faith that if it were God's will that his children be educated, he would provide a way. He had to give up any expectation that his children could be raised in an environment that contained grandparents, since the location of his service was totally at the will of the bishop, who had absolute authority to assign him anywhere in the world. In accepting ordination into the service of the Lord, he figuratively had to put a sword to his parents, his children, his sisters, and his brothers. He had to be willing to give up everything, including the family he loved, in order to be fit for the priesthood.

But the ordination ritual doesn't stop with those who don the clerical garb. It extends to us as well. We are all called to be priests, and like the disciples of Jesus, we must be willing to sacrifice our ties with those we love the most in order to be fit for his service.

But don't stop there. With the sacrifice required of the universal priesthood of believers, the Lord makes a wonderful promise: he assures us that we will receive blessings many times over in this life, and in the age to come, eternal life.

How does he prove that promise? The three thousand people those first priests of Israel slew at Sinai were the first fruits of God's judgment under the law of Moses. A dozen centuries of Pentecosts later, again at the time of the harvest, the apostles, the first priests of the church, reaped the first fruits of grace, the three thousand souls who were redeemed, baptized, and added that day. At Sinai, the bread was cast upon the waters, and in Jerusalem that bread began to return to the church of Jesus Christ, and manifold more sinners were to come in the years that followed. God is good!

Mercy

Scripture: Exodus 33
Suggested Reading: Romans 9:9–24

*M*oses had an enviable relationship with God. He had the privilege of standing toe to toe with the Creator and arguing about whether that stiff-necked generation of Israelites was his responsibility or God's.

When God threatened to disown his people, Moses dared to chide God and cause him to "repent of the evil he had thought to do." He had the courage to engage in hard bargaining with the Almighty about the level of "presence" that God would lend to the efforts of the people to migrate toward the Promised Land. In some of the exchanges, Moses seems to have almost treated God as his equal.

We speak of coming boldly before the throne of grace with our prayers and petitions. When we say that, do we mean that we can come before God with the boldness of a Moses? Do we have the privilege of treating God as an equal?

Sometimes I shudder when I hear fellow Christians making demands before God, as though God is in some way obligated to them. They come to God and seemingly order him to honor the promises they claim that he made to them in the scriptures regarding blessing and healing. Is this the kind of boldness with which we should approach the mercy seat of God? Dare we go head to head with him as Moses did? Or should our approach be made in humility?

In all of this give and take with Moses, God made a point of saying, ". . . I will be gracious to whom I will be gracious, and will show mercy on whom I will show mercy." Why did he make that statement at that particular moment? In his letter to the Romans, Paul makes the meaning clear. While allowing Moses the privilege of a *tete-a-tete*, he warns the rest of us that we cannot presume to have a similar relationship. He reminds us that he is God, and as God has the absolute right to relate with anyone in any way he chooses to relate. And he makes it clear that if he wants to allow Moses to speak with him as an equal, he has the right to let him do that, but he is under no obligation to allow any other human being the same privilege.

God, says Paul, is the Potter, we are the clay. God can do whatever he wishes with any of the lumps of clay he has created. The clay has no right to demand that all lumps be treated equally. If the Potter wants to make of one lump a priceless vase, he has the right to do so. If he wants to make of another a chamber pot, he may do that too. The clay has no right to limit the Potter's sovereign authority to do with his clay whatever he will.

Whatever God does with any of us, he does by the authority inherent in being the Creator. If he did not have that unfettered power over us, he would not be God. If he were limited in any way, to the extent he is limited we would be empowered. If we were empowered, we would have certain rights over him, and he would have certain obligations to us. And if he had obligations to us, there would be no such thing as grace and no such place as the mercy seat of God. Thank you Lord for your omnipotence.

> Have thine own way, Lord, have thine own way.
> Thou art the Potter, I am the clay.
> Mold me and make me after thy will,
> While I am waiting, yielded and still.
>
> (Adelaide A. Pollard, 1906)

A Terrible Thing

Scripture: *Exodus 34:1–28*
Suggested Reading: Revelation 20:15

*M*oses petitioned God to "pardon our sin, and take us for thine inheritance."

God responded by saying, you "shall see the work of the Lord; for it is a terrible thing that I will do with you."

The fall and rise of the whole human race is contained in that one monumental exchange of words. Let's look first at Moses' prayer.

Note that he did not ask God to pardon *their* sins, referring just to the wayward Israelites who had just offended God and profaned themselves by worshipping the golden calf. But by the use of the first person pronoun, he included himself in the request for forgiveness. Why? He didn't bow down to that idol or violate God's laws as the people had done. Why should he include himself?

His prayer was not just for the Israelites, including himself. His prayer was for the whole human race. When Adam and Eve disobeyed God in the Garden of Eden, they plunged the whole of humanity into a state of sin, including good people like Noah, Abraham, Moses, Paul, and all the saints. By their disobedience, the human race lost its relationship with God and became estranged. Moses asked not only that the sins of humanity be forgiven, but that the relationship between God and man be restored.

God answered Moses' plea positively, but warned that fulfilling that petition would not be simple. Forgiving the human race for its sin and restoring its inheritance would become "the work of the Lord," and most certainly would be a "terrible thing."

From the day we fell from grace, it has been God's purpose to restore us to himself, to make us heirs to his kingdom.

The work of the Lord included cleansing the world with a flood, preserving Noah and his family, selecting Abraham to be the father of a special nation, bringing that nation into and out of slavery, guiding it through the wilderness, establishing it as a world power, scattering it to the four corners of the earth, returning it to slavery, fathering the baby of Bethlehem whose destiny was to die on a Roman cross, saving repentant sinners, and bringing the nations of the earth to final judgment.

When, on behalf of all mankind, Moses made his plea for forgiveness and restoration, God declared that his work of salvation would be a "terrible thing."

What could be more terrible than God himself descending upon the earth that he had made? What could be more terrible that the creator of the universe being despised and betrayed by the very people he came to save? What could be more terrible than the Lord of heaven and earth being nailed to a cross and suspended between heaven and earth, rejected by both? What could be more terrible than immortal God dying an agonizing death for the sin of mortal man? What could be more terrible than deity bursting the bonds of death and rising from his grave to claim his own?

And what could be more terrible than an unrepentant sinner refusing God's offer of salvation and plunging headlong into the flames of eternal damnation?

The Face of God

Scripture: *Exodus 34:29–35*
Suggested Reading: 2 Corinthians 3:12–18

*M*oses had a special relationship with God that no other saint was privileged to experience. He was invited to the mountaintop to stand in the very presence of God and absorb the splendor of deity. When he returned to the people his face was aglow with godly radiance.

Now one would think that the people of God, especially the priests, would gather around him in awe to witness that remarkable sight, and in the hope that the glow was contagious, to catch a bit of it themselves and take it out into the world to share it with others who needed a little light in their lives.

But sadly for the people of the old covenant, the divine plan was not yet ready for the Spirit to be poured out upon all flesh; the only response the people could muster was fear. And in response to their fear, Moses had to cover his face with a veil to hide the glory that radiated from him.

But such veils have no place in our New Testament world. When Jesus died, the Father reached down from heaven, tore the veil of the temple in two, and removed forever the barrier that separated us from God. Now, as Moses, you and I have the privilege of entering into the holy presence of our Creator and communing with him face to face.

And when we come down from our mountaintop experience, our faces too should glow with the radiance of God, but unlike Moses, we should not veil the luster of our joy, but should let our faces gleam before the eyes of others as though we are mirrors reflecting the brilliance of the countenance of God.

As children in Sunday school we sang such wonderful little songs as,

"This little light of mine, I'm going to let it shine."

or,

"Jesus wants me for a sunbeam to shine for him each day."

and

"Brighten the corner where you are,
brighten the corner where you are . . . ."

At that time we were just innocent children who had no idea what we had to do to absorb the light with which we were promising to illumine our dark world. But the Holy Spirit preserved the songs in our minds and the promise in our hearts until he taught us that we had to take a trip to the mountaintop and stand in the presence of the Lord to behold his glory and be transfigured into new creations that were ablaze with his splendor.

If only we could remain on that mountaintop and enjoy his presence forever! Sorry, not just yet. Until he sounds his trumpet and gathers us to his holy hill, we've got work to do. People are wandering in the dark valleys of despair and sailors far from harbor need guidance to the shore. As long as we live it is our privilege to let our light shine, to reflect God's sunbeams and moonbeams into dark corners and to mirror the bright face of Jesus in a dreary world.

A Dwelling Place for God

Exodus 35–40 Scan chapter headings
Suggested Reading: 1 Kings 8:1–30; Acts 2:1–4; Ephesians 3:14–19

The very idea of God having a dwelling place drives me to the brink of mental exhaustion. We know that the omnipresent deity is everywhere at once, and we know that it is impossible to confine God to any one particular location. Yet the scriptures abound with references to the house of the Lord and the dwelling place of the Most High God.

When Moses built the tabernacle in the wilderness of Sinai, he sensed that he was building a house for God, a place where he would come to meet with him and disclose his plans for the destiny of his people.

David had a lofty aim to build a habitation suitable for the Most High, but God refused his offer. Instead God directed Solomon, David's son, to build a temple "for my name." But even though Solomon built a magnificent temple, an "exalted house, a place for thee to dwell forever," in his great wisdom he realized that God was too great to be confined within any structure that man could build, and he said, ". . . will God indeed dwell on earth? . . . the highest heaven cannot contain thee, how much less this house which I have built!"

Scripture shows the presence of God occupying many places. Moses found him in the flames that engulfed the burning bush. Elijah looked for him in the earthquake, wind and fire, but found him in the still, small voice that spoke to him after the storm. Paul found him in a great light beaming down from heaven. Wherever he appeared, God chose his own form of manifestation, declaring that every atom of the entire creation can reflect the likeness of God.

One of the most common manifestations of the presence of God in the Bible is fire. God was present in the pillar of fire that went before the Israelites and filled the tabernacle at night. He descended on Mount Sinai in fire, he appeared in the fire that incinerated Nadab and Abihu, his fire consumed the sacrifices and the altars built by Aaron and Elijah, his chariots of fire swooped down to transport Elijah to heaven, and finally he signified the entrance of his Spirit into the being of man by placing little tongues of fire on the heads of the apostles at Pentecost.

Even though the giants of scripture always wanted to build God a house, God distained their plans and declined to be permanently enclosed in any of man's structures. The Lord expressed his intent to go from tent to tent and dwell *with* man, but he never confirmed that anything man had built could truly be called the exclusive dwelling place of God. He had other plans that he held close to his chest as a mystery yet to be unveiled, leaking vague suggestions of his purpose to prophets such as Jeremiah and Elijah.

Until Pentecost that is. On that great day God announced to the world the place he had chosen for his holy habitation. The wind blew and the tongues of flame descended on the heads of the saints as the essence of God penetrated human flesh, and deity made his dwelling place in the heart of man.

And though the mystery of *God in us* defies our understanding, when we are born again we sense that the fullness of God inhabits our very being. We sense that our body has become the temple of the Holy Spirit and that we have become one flesh with our Lord! Hallelujah!

A Generous Heart

Scripture: Exodus 35–40

Three times during my life my pastors have been led to preach sermons from Exodus 35. Each such Sunday morning was kickoff day for the gathering of pledges to pay for the construction of a new building, and the theme of each message was, "a generous heart."

Invariably after each "generous heart" message, a discussion arose among the congregation regarding the new building's appointments. "Why do we need such a fancy kitchen? Why do we need such expensive carpets? Why do we need stained glass windows? Why do we need such fancy woodwork?" Debating those issues usually resulted in divisions in the church, and on more than one occasion a family has packed up its membership papers and left for a more modest or debt free worship environment.

One courageous pastor was brave enough to tackle those questions right from the pulpit, and told the congregation that what they were really asking was, "Why does God want so much of my money? Why can't I keep more of it for myself." You guessed it. That is when at least one of those families fled from the church.

Today's reading answers all of those questions. Simply put, God wants our best. Or rather, he wants us to be willing to return to him the finest fruits of what he has given us. He wants our precious stones and rare metals, our finest fabrics, and our sweetest oils for fragrant incense. He wants us to be willing to part with the things we hold dear to build an edifice suitable to be called the dwelling place of God. He wants his house to reflect the generosity of our hearts.

When visitors come to my church the first thing they see is the blacktopped parking lot, which is usually overflowing. They can't help but notice that we have cars of every vintage, from new luxury sedans to "beaters," as my kids used to say. They can't help but conclude that our people come from every station in life and from every income category. Yet, when they look around at the lovely oak woodwork, the gorgeous chandeliers, and the beautiful stained glass windows that portray the major events in the life of Christ, they can't help but conclude that the people who worship there are people of generous heart and open hand who want to return to the Lord the very best of what he has given them. Figuratively speaking, some of them have brought gold while others have brought a pair of turtledoves, yet all have brought the best they could, and each has brought it with a heart overflowing with generosity.

We cannot read this scripture and fail to conclude that the tabernacle the Israelites built as a habitation for the Lord was an incredibly beautiful place, marvelously crafted and overlaid with artistic designs, cut stones, precious metals, and carved wood, a model for us to follow as we build our sanctuaries. God appointed the builders by name and gave them the proper spirit and the skill necessary to create that masterpiece for him. God also placed in the hearts of that congregation a spirit so magnanimous that Moses had to go to the people and ask them to stop giving because the builders had more than enough materials to complete the work.

When the building was finished, the glory of the Lord filled the tabernacle. My talent is not grand enough to paint a word picture of what that house must have looked like when it was filled with the glory of the Lord. But I get a faint impression of what it must have been like on Easter Sunday morning when the sun shines through the resurrection window and illumines the faces of the children carrying lilies to the altar while the choir makes those big oak timbers shiver as they sing, "He arose, He arose, Hallelujah, Christ arose!"

The Law

Suggested Reading: 1 John 2:1–2

The human race seems to be at odds with the business of law. I was raised to have respect for the law, but as I've watched the law in action, respecting it has become as difficult as respecting crime.

From top to bottom, the law of man has become corrupt.

By their behavior, those who make the law have traded their esteem for gratuitous gain and pleasure. Presidents have abused the power of their office, broken the law, flaunted their crimes, and made themselves sad spectacles of public derision. Legislators have engaged in the politics of personal destruction, have openly and brazenly committed crimes, and have traded their integrity and their votes for campaign contributions and graft. Miscreants in the Congress of the United States have created evil laws designed to injure the vulnerable and, self-serving laws meant to pad the treasuries of the patrons to whom they are beholden.

Those who administer the law have administered it in a manner that has resulted in the term *honest lawyer* becoming as much an oxymoron as *painless dentist*. Judges, attorneys, and juries have given in to the evil manipulations of crooked lawyers and clever criminals.

And those who enforce the law have become as soiled as those who break the law. Horror stories abound of policemen who abuse citizens, strut arrogantly before the television cameras, refuse to assist people in need, and take bribes.

How can a citizen respect the law when the law can't respect itself?

Is the Law of God any different? It was authored by a perfect deity for perfectly good reasons, but when it fell into the hands of men it became tainted with abuse.

From Genesis on, those entrusted with the solemn duty of applying the law were as corrupt as their counterparts in civil law today. Old Testament priests applied God's laws in a manner that served their own gluttonous appetites. New Testament rulers, judges, and advocates in the halls of "justice" suborned perjury, and perverted the law to condemn the innocent.

Until Jesus comes again to rule the world, the headlines will continue to shout the shortcomings of the law and of those who make it, practice it, and enforce it. Sinners will continue to enact evil laws and other sinners will continue to be arrested by a corrupt constabulary, tried by tainted tribunals, condemned by perverse juries and incarcerated with convicted policemen, judges and legislators. The tragedy goes on.

Is there any sliver of moon casting a small gleam of hope on this muddy picture?

Fortunately, one guiltless defendant, Jesus Christ, was found guilty by corrupt courts of violating the laws of God and man. He fulfilled the law and served the sentence that sets us all free from the law's condemnation. But regardless of the spurious nature of the charges against him, his punishment was meted out by the only court capable of dispensing true justice: the court of heaven.

All defendants, no matter what their moral crimes, who choose Jesus as their honorable intercessor will be found guiltless of any violation of the only truly honorable law, the Law of God.

Thou Shalt Not . . .

Scripture: Scan chapter headings in the Book of Leviticus
Suggested Reading: Romans 8:1–11

Most of us are like a mule between two bundles of hay when it comes to the law. We hold the concept of the law itself in high esteem, but we have little respect for lawmakers, judges, lawyers, and police officers. Jesus, too, loved the law, but he despised the judges, loathed the lawyers, and pitied the ignorance of the constables who parted his garments among themselves as they carried out the sentence of the court. How does something inherently wonderful become so sullied upon application? Why are we inclined to break it?

When I was a boy, the Law of God was rigidly enforced at our house. We didn't dance, go to movies or drink beer. We didn't play with devil cards. We didn't listen to the radio, play ball or eat out on Sunday. We didn't do as million things, or at least we weren't supposed to.

One hot Sunday afternoon late in August when I was nine and my parents were sound asleep, lured by the siren call of Abner Doubleday's ghost, I sneaked out back with my ball and glove to toss myself a few popups behind the garage where no one could possibly see me. But somehow my mother picked me up on her instinctive sonar and sent Dad out to apply the Law of the Lord to my behind. Now I believe to this day that by whipping me he was more in error than I was, but little good it ever did to argue the point.

About six weeks later on a Sunday afternoon when I thought the folks were asleep, I wandered out to the garage and discovered Dad, bent over at his workbench with his ear to radio and a big grin on his face as the muffled voice of Harry Heillmann aired the good news that Hammerin' Hank had belted three doubles to lead our Tigers to victory over the Cubs in the fifth game of the World Series. "One more win and we'll be champs again!" he whispered. "But don't tell your ma we heard it on the radio," he winked. "We'll pretend it's news to us when we hear it in the morning." Sinning with dad was okay.

Even today my conscience quivers a bit, and I glance around to make sure mother isn't looking as I fill my plate at the Big Boy buffet after the service on Sunday morning, and glance up at the television to watch the Lions fumble away their playoff chances again. Then I sit with my church friends and boast a bit about my deprived childhood, all the time giving thanks in my heart for the parents who laid down the law to me and did their best to hold me to it.

I love that old law. I'm a Methodist now, and they make a big point of telling me I'm not under it anymore, but I'm truly grateful that something in me deeper than denominationalism still holds me subject to it and stings my conscience when I break it.

I tell my Sunday school class about old Elder Douma who hid his beer behind a side of beef in the cooler of his meat market, but prohibited Uncle Pete from taking communion because he spied a Sunday paper in his house during a surprise inspection visit. In those days you always had to stay clean because you never knew when an elder might drop by, an elder you knew broke the rules himself.

Having once lived under the old law it is clear to me how righteous God is, how perfectly Jesus lived, and how totally incapable we are of keeping it, in letter or in spirit. Having tried and failed to keep the law not only convicted me of my unrighteousness, but also gave me an uncommon appreciation for the fact that Jesus bore my punishment for me, a punishment not administered by an outlaw elder, but by a righteous judge. And now, praise God, I'm a sinner who's been set free!

The Fat of Rams

Scripture: Leviticus 1
Suggested Reading: 1 Samuel 15:22; Micah 6:6–8; Mark 12:33

Once it fell to me to go to the supermarket without supervision to do the week's grocery shopping. I was further blessed to have the companionship and assistance of Collin, my four-year-old grandson. At the meat department I selected a few packages of skinless chicken breasts and a nicely marbled rump roast for a Sunday dinner. As Collin helped me by taking the packages from my hand and dropping them into the shopping cart, I was struck by what he was missing in his young life.

When I was four years old, there were no supermarkets with packaged meat. If we were to have a chicken dinner, dad or grandpa would go to the henhouse with hatchet in hand, select the appropriate bird, and dispatch it in the old fashioned way while the children danced around in gleeful imitation as the headless chicken flopped around the yard, violently protesting the sacrifice it had to make to become our feast. The image of those moments still lives vividly in my memory.

Sometimes we would help pluck the feathers from the lifeless bird just so the business of making dinner could be a project in which the whole family participated, children included. My grandchildren will probably never be party to such a ritual. The closest they may come as children to having a hand in the preparation of a meal will be dropping bundles of prepackaged meat into the shopping basket, setting the dinner table, or at best helping to skewer the roast on the barbeque spit. It's not a giant leap of thought from my childhood memory of chickens to the sacrificial altars of old Israel. When those folks made a sacrifice, they made a sacrifice! Not only did they have to give up a valuable piece of livestock, but they also had to watch a bull or a lamb writhe in agony as its life slipped painfully away and as the aroma of its burning fat rose as sweet incense to the Lord.

The closest I come to genuine sacrifice is dropping my numbered envelope into the offering basket as it passes painlessly through the rows of pews on Sunday morning, in sharp contrast to the Jews of antiquity who should have been able to sense through the suffering of a lamb the pain their Messiah would endure as the ultimate sacrifice for their sin. I have no such reference in my experience, except for the poor chickens in grandpa's henhouse.

In the old days, the Lord required a sacrifice consistent with the blessings the worshipper had received. The wealthy would have to offer a bull as a burnt offering, the middle class a lamb or a goat, and the poor, a pigeon or a turtledove. I have often wondered how often a rich man tried to get away by offering only a bird.

In every case however, the worshipper was required to kill the animal himself and watch it give up its life as a substitute for the life of the sinner. Today we know that the Lord still expects those he has blessed the most to return the most to him, and he respects the poor widow's mite as much as the tycoon's bundle. But because Jesus went to the cross as the final sacrifice for our sin, we no longer are required to bring our burnt offerings to the altar. The Lord has had his fill of blood and suffering.

Is there an aroma that can ascend to heaven which would be more pleasing to the Lord than the fat of rams? Of course there is. More than anything he wants us to love him and worship him, to pray, to obey, to love others as we love ourselves, and to show it by being fair, generous, honest, and humble. That aroma smells good to him.

No Pain, No Gain?

Scripture: Leviticus 2
Suggested Reading: Hebrews 9:15–28

Yesterday, as I was struggling with my childhood memories of butchering chickens, Mary Ann came into my study and brought me a little gift she had fashioned from trinkets she had purchased at the Christian book store: a little fish symbol with Greek letters on it that I can wear around my neck to Emmaus events.

Jokingly I asked her if she was giving me the gift out of guilt, as a sort of peace offering for some infraction she had committed against our relationship. "No," she said, "I'm giving you this just because I love you and I'm glad you are my husband." Gratefully I smiled, hugged her, thanked her and got on with my meditation on the book of Leviticus.

The second chapter of Leviticus contrasts sharply with the first. God began his instruction in the business of sacrifice by ordaining offerings of blood. Animals had to be killed by hand, their blood splashed about the altar, and their flesh burned by fire. Those were sacrifices of anguish and death that accomplished atonement for sin and ultimately symbolized the death of Christ on the cross as the final payment to God for the sins of mankind.

In comparison, the grain offering was clean and painless. There was no blood, no agony, no death, no gore, just some flour, oil, and incense baked on the altar to send a pleasing aroma up to the halls of heaven.

The animal sacrifice, though brutal, makes a lot of sense in that it reminds us of our guilt, God's hatred of sin, his uncompromising sense of justice, and the bloody sacrifice of his Son. But what is the purpose of the bloodless offering of grain?

We don't burn things on altars anymore, but we often speak of the sacrifices we feel obligated to make. We sacrifice our money by bringing our tithes into the storehouse of the Lord and by making charitable donations to the Salvation Army, the Red Cross, the Disabled American Veterans, and other charitable organizations. We sacrifice our talent by teaching Sunday school, playing the piano, singing in the choir, or maintaining the church grounds. We sacrifice our time by visiting the sick or serving on church committees. But are these sacrifices to be equated with sin offerings or to serve as grim reminders that our Savior sacrificed his all for us? Does everything we do for the Lord have to be done out of guilt? Or can we sacrifice simply out of gratitude?

Not to diminish the necessity of blood offering as atonement for our sin, but simply to salvage a smile of satisfaction for the fulfillment that our walk with God brings us, the grain offering can signify the simple act of gratitude. We give our first fruits to our Lord just because he loves us, just because we are thankful that he walks with us and provides abundant nourishment for our bodies and our souls, just because we have the pleasure of sitting and meditating on the blessings that surround us, and just because we love him and are glad that he is our God.

So the next time I have the privilege of bringing an offering to the altar, I'm not going to approach that holy moment groaning under the weight of a spirit heavy with guilt for the many sins of my life, but rather I'll step into his presence with a happy heart, setting aside for a moment the torment he had to endure to redeem me, and basking in the joy of his fellowship, grateful that he stoops to love an old sinner like me.

Peace

Scripture: Leviticus 3; 7:11–21
Suggested Reading: John 14:27; Revelation 19:9,17

*W*hen I was in high school, our athletic league consisted of several other local schools. Our contests were often spirited and sometimes quite contentious. When the season ended, we crowned the champion at a citywide banquet. At the dinner, members of opposing teams were intermingled at the tables, and a carefully selected speaker used his persuasive gifts to erase whatever residual animosity might have remained among us after the battles, and to restore an ambiance of peace and brotherhood.

After we shared a family-style dinner, with the rivals we had spiked, elbowed, and tripped during the season, the speaker asked us to stand up, to look into the eyes of our foes, and to extend the hand of fellowship. As we reluctantly followed his directive, we subconsciously sacrificed the hostility we prized so much and replaced it with a brittle peace that was certain to break the next time the whistle blew and we met each other with a ball in our hands.

In later years, I have had the opportunity to reflect on the process by which we make peace with our adversaries. In the course of doing business we sometimes offend a colleague or treat a competitor unfairly. After the fray we might arrange lunch with our adversary in order to resolve our differences. Sometimes there is a mediator involved, and often we sit at a table and share food and wine. There is something about breaking bread together that contributes to the making of peace. And there is something mutually celebratory about a feast. Usually we leave the table with a smile and a handshake, at peace until greed and competition make us foul again.

The peace offering of Leviticus stands apart from the other sacrifices in that worshippers and the priests, in fellowship with each other, ate the flesh of the sacrificial animal. In a sense, the parties to the meal had been foes. The man bringing the sacrifice had engaged in unseemly conduct toward his God, who was represented by the priest. Their relationship had become contentious because of man's sin, and the offering was designed to renew the peace between the believer and his Lord, at least until the next time the devil entered the scene and tempted the sinner.

In this fallen world we often find ourselves out of harmony with our God. Discord with men may result in the loss of a contract, the collapse of a business deal, or at worst, the loss of a friend. But discord with God may have eternal consequences. Fortunately, Jesus periodically calls us to his altar where we break bread together on our knees and make peace with God. His peace is not the same peace the world offers, for how can peace with man compare to peace with God? He extends his hand of forgiveness and offers us a peace far deeper than the peace we make at sports banquets and business luncheons.

But as long as we wallow in a world filled with competition and a striving after things, our peace with God is fragile and breaks each time we commit a new offense against him. And as the Hebrews of old, we return to the altar of sacrifice and repent, seek his favor, and restore the proper relationship between the Potter and the clay.

But the best part, the bright moon in our valley, is that we don't have to butcher any bulls or birds. All the blood that had to be shed was shed at the altar of Calvary. The food on the table is his body and the wine is his blood. That is the feast we share until the trumpet sounds and he calls us to dine at the marriage feast of the Lamb!

A Pure Heart

Scripture: Leviticus 4–5
Suggested Reading: Psalms 24:3–4; 1 Corinthians 6:19

*I*n the days of our youth, parents didn't have to worry as we do today about keeping the hearts of the children pure. On Sunday we went to church and read a book or took a nap. During the week we went to school and studied decency as much as arithmetic. On Saturday mornings we swam at the YMCA and watched Tom Mix and the Lone Ranger cleanse the world of bad guys. The most evil outside influence in our lives was Fibber McGee's cluttered closet.

The only censorship in our lives came when dad read the Bible. Although in the interest of presenting to us the entire Word of God he dutifully read and mispronounced all the names in the endless genealogies, he often omitted the gory passages of Leviticus and other narratives in which blood is spilled or immoral acts committed. Our parents had prohibitive ratings on certain passages in the Bible just as parents today use prohibitive ratings to protect their children from smut and carnage in music, on television, in the movies, or on the internet. From then to now, Christian parents have done all they can to sanitize the environment so their children can have clean hands and a pure heart, and qualify to ascend to the holy place of the Lord.

But the children of the ancient Hebrews were not so protected from the sludge of life. Moral decay surrounded them in the form of licentious pagan religious practices as well as the lusts that drove the behavior of the people around them. The Bible does not mince words when it describes the conduct of Lot or Onan, the sins of the Canaanites, the fate of Agag or Jezebel, or the details of the offerings.

Israel's children watched as animals were slaughtered for sacrifice, and I'm sure they were not strangers to lewdness. Even today orthodox Jewish children memorize the first five books of scripture, including those passages my father omitted in the interest of my purity of heart. Much of what we know only from the stories we read in the Bible was the brutal reality of life for the people who lived in those days. It's no wonder that the Lord directed Moses to institute a very detailed purification process for the Israelites.

Scholars tell us that other sacrifices served mainly to restore a right relationship between man and God or between people. The main purpose for the sin offering, on the other hand, was to purify the tabernacle so it would be a dwelling place fit for God. The house of worship was polluted simply because sinful priests and sinful worshippers had entered it, and the Lord could not stand to dwell in such an unclean place.

Something wonderful happened shortly after Jesus ascended to heaven: he returned to live in our hearts. We speak figuratively now and then when we refer to the church as the house of God, because we know that it is only a building dedicated to his worship and service. Fortunately, we no longer have to kill any animals and spread their blood on the curtains in order to make the building a suitable habitat for the Most High. He lives in us.

But that doesn't mean that the day of sacrifice is over. Far from it. The Lord still requires a clean place to live, and in order to provide that for him, something has to die. It's not a bull or a goat or a turtledove. It's a self. It's an ego that gorges itself on vanity. It's a heart that seeks its fulfillment by loving possessions more than God. It's a body that satisfies its lusts in the world of fantasy or in the world of reality.

Who can stand in the presence of a holy God? Only one who has clean hands and a pure heart.

Don't Drink the Blood!

Scripture: Leviticus 6–7, 17
Suggested Reading: John 6:53–60

My mother cooked a beef roast every Sunday as far back as I can remember. It happened as regularly as going to church, in fact it seemed to be a part of going to church. When we woke up on Sunday morning, we always woke up to the succulent smell on beef roast being seared in her big iron pan. Then she added salt and water and put it into the oven to cook for several hours while we attended services and Sunday school.

When dinnertime came, the meat that started out red had cooked to a dark brown, and the juices that remained went into the making of gravy. At the table we talked as we ate, mostly about church stuff, the sermon, the Bible stories, and, of course, the people. But the conversation never quite made it to sharing the essence of the Christ who was supposed to be living in us. That was too private, too personal. I've forgotten a lot of things since those days, but in the dusty corners of my memory, I recall that well done beef roast as the finest I've ever smelled or tasted.

Very well done beef was one of the last vestiges of my youth to yield its place to tastes more modern and more socially acceptable. At lunch, my business acquaintances ridiculed me as the waiter served my black steak next to their quivering red filets. I felt alienated, sort of "cut off from my people." At first I was repulsed as I watched them savor the blood, but they seemed to enjoy it so much that in time my dry morsel seemed to become less and less tasty. Then I got a little braver and began to order my meat medium well, then just medium until I finally graduated to rare. Today there's nothing to me as succulent as the taste of red prime rib or rare filet mignon.

My mother would have been a good Old Testament woman. Had she lived back then I'm sure she'd have earned honorable mention along with the likes of Sarah, Ruth, Hannah, and Dorcas. Maybe her name would have appeared as a model of obedience for refusing to eat blood. In her memory I sometimes go to the market and buy a nice rump roast, cook it until it is black, then nostalgically feast on is as though it were a Sunday afternoon fifty years ago. But I never order it that way in restaurants.

I understood how Jesus' disciples felt when he told them that they were to eat his flesh and drink his blood. That was indeed a "hard saying," a gross violation of Moses' law, an idea as repulsive to them as rare steaks were to me when I was twenty-five.

Before the very first communion, the price for eating blood was alienation. Anyone who dared to eat "any manner of blood" was to be cut off from his people, shunned the way my Amish neighbors shun one of their own who violates their basic principles. The very life of that sacrificial lamb was in its blood and was not to be ingested. But Jesus made a practice of turning Jewish principle on its ear. After that first communion, the price for *not* eating his flesh and drinking his blood is alienation, being cut off from the people of the kingdom of God.

Since old tenets die hard, it probably took the disciples as long to become comfortable with the idea of eating Jesus' flesh and drinking his blood as it took me to become comfortable with the idea of rare meat. And, come to think of it, some of us took a long time to become comfortable testifying to others about the life of the sacrificial lamb that lives in us because we have eaten his flesh and drunk his blood. But just as there's nothing as pleasing to the palate as a rare steak, there's nothing as fulfilling to the soul as being filled with the lifeblood of Jesus and sharing that satisfaction with others.

As the Lord Commanded

Scripture: Leviticus 8–9
Suggested Reading: John 13:34–35; 14:15; 15:17.

I'm glad I live in the Christian era. I would have made a lousy Old Testament saint. As we read Leviticus, we have to wade through a mountain of minutiae about exactly which animals were to be killed for which sacrifice, how they were to be divided, how their parts were to be distributed, and exactly what one could or could not do with the sacrifices. Unless the Lord had given me a different kind of spirit than the one I have, I probably would have rebelled against the myriad of rules, and I probably would have been stoned by the community.

During my lifetime I've read most of the Bible several times and have read a number of commentaries about most of the books. My father read us a chapter every day, starting with the first chapter of Genesis and ending with the last chapter of Revelation about 1189 days later. I say about, because I recall that he read more than one short psalm at a sitting, but to make up for it, he divided Psalm 119 into several readings. Every three and a quarter years he finished and started over, so I calculate that during my sojourn in that home, I had the Bible read to me about five times.

But, to be honest with you, though I enjoyed much of his reading, I never paid much attention to the book of Leviticus, and in most of my adult life, I've rather intentionally avoided reading it. The reason is probably obvious. You may have done the same.

But in reading this book essentially for the first time now, I'm less struck by the gore than by some of the sparkling little things that leap out along the way. One of those little gems is the fact while wading through the heaps of tiny details God required of him, Moses always did "as the Lord commanded." Those words appear in today's chapter no less than nine times. And when something is repeated over and over again in the Bible, we'd better sit up and take notice. The Lord doesn't engage in redundancy just to hear himself talk. Maybe today the fact that Moses was obedient to the detail of the Lord's commands is more of a message than the detail itself.

We are no longer obligated to comply with rules of sacrifice set forth in the book of Leviticus. But unfortunately, in this age of amazing grace, we no longer feel much obligation to comply with God's commands in general. Although Jesus said he came to fulfill rather than abolish the commandments, we don't punish anyone anymore for adultery or idolatry; but rather we accept such sins as moral lapses for which we can be forgiven. It's far less popular today to be obedient to the Lord's commands than it is to be grateful that he poured out his blood on the altar as an offering for our sin.

Just before he went to the cross, Jesus sat down and taught his disciples what they were to do after his departure. He told them that he wanted them to love one another just as he had loved them. They were to love each other enough to sacrifice their lives for each other just as he was about to sacrifice his life for them. And he didn't say this in the form of a recommendation—it was a command!

Moses was a good example of obedience. Fortunately for most of us, we don't have to be obedient to a multitude of weighty details of sacrifice in the same manner as Moses, but we are required to be as obedient as Moses to the new command Jesus gave us, the command to love one another.

And, as we shall soon see, it means loving those who do not merit our love just as he loved us and gave his life for us when we in no way deserve to be so loved by him.

Bewail the Burning

Scripture: Leviticus 10

The football team from a rival school used to practice in the field near my home. Their coach, Oscar Fikens, was the most exacting man I've ever known. Any player who missed a block, missed a tackle, dropped a pass, or fumbled a ball suffered severe chastisement at his hands. Laps and pushups were only for first offenders. He often ordered the other players to pummel teammates who consistently made errors. He demanded perfection and inflicted painful punishment on anyone who did not meet his expectations. And he even punished those who committed no error because he was angry at those who did. Imagine that! That's how he prepared them to become what he wanted them to become.

I thought of him when I read about what God did to Aaron's sons, Nadab and Abihu.

The side of God we see when he's called his people into the desert to prepare them to become his chosen nation in the Promised Land is a side we're often unwilling to recognize. Today we tend to focus on the graciousness of God and blur out such attributes as jealousy, hate, and justice. I've even heard Christians say, "My God is a loving God, he'd never condemn anyone to hell." Little do they know.

When God commanded, yes *commanded*, Moses to prepare the altar and organize the sacrifices, he insisted on a painful attention to detail. He tolerated no error. He even demanded that the sacrificial lamb be without blemish. Like Coach Fikens, he demanded perfection and inflicted painful punishment on any of his priests who did not meet his expectations—and even on the One who did.

The moon that brightens our valley here is the knowledge that Jesus came and perfectly performed his sacrificial role as flawlessly as the Father demanded. He was the model prophet, communicating God's Word without equivocation. He was the consummate priest, preparing a fit offering for his Lord. He was the ideal sacrifice, the Lamb without blemish, sufficient propitiation for the sins of all humankind. And when we play out the final chapter of our saga, he will be the mighty king at whose feet every knee will bow. In every way, Jesus met the standard of perfection God demands.

The sons of Aaron who offered unholy fire were themselves consumed by fire for the error of their ways. Sinners who do not repent and accept the redemption that Jesus offers will suffer the fires of the eternal hell we all deserve. The tradition in which I was raised included in their rendition of the Apostle's Creed the line, "He descended into hell." They accepted the doctrine of the Heidelberg Catechism which declares that the "Lord Jesus Christ, by his inexpressible anguish, pain, terrors, and hellish agony in which he plunged during all his sufferings, but especially on the cross, has delivered me from the torment of hell." In other words, he went to hell to save me from it.

Every day I offer up unholy fire before the Lord. Like Cain's, my sacrifices are tainted by a multitude of imperfections; considering God's demands for absolute purity, I deserve no less than Nadab or Abihu, to be devoured by the flames of hell.

But thanks to the love and grace of One willing to suffer my punishment for me, I'm able to stand before the altar of God unscathed, but with head bowed to bewail the burning of the innocent Lamb.

If She Can't Afford . . .

Scripture: Leviticus 11–12
Suggested Reading: Matthew 25:44–46; Mark 10:29–30;
Luke 2:22–24

One of the most inscrutable ironies of the Christian faith is that when the Lord wishes to open heaven's treasury and pour down blessings on some deserving soul, he sometimes blesses them with wealth. But almost in the same breath he commends those who scorn wealth.

The Lord certainly has a soft spot in his heart for the poor. Recently, a guest speaker in my church warned us that the surest road to hell is to abuse a poor person. He based his assertion on the statement by Jesus that anyone who fails to feed the least of the hungry or clothe the least of the naked is failing to minister to the Lord himself and thus earns eternal damnation.

As I sit in my relatively spacious home either working on a quality computer or watching a game on the big screen television, I sometimes think of myself as exceptionally blessed. I give thanks to God that he has seen fit, for some unfathomable reason, to open those celestial windows for me. I don't think I deserve to abound as I do, and I wonder why he has treated me so well.

But sometimes I look around and feel awfully guilty. I'm aware of much suffering, not only a half world away, but also just a few miles away. And I ask what right have I to enjoy all of these material gifts while so many are hungry, cold, or homeless. I could do much more than I do to relieve some of the suffering of the poor in this world.

When almighty God decided to come to this earth to live as a man for a while, he could have chosen any lifestyle he wished. He could have come as a king or an emperor and used his miraculous power to expel sin and greed out of the heart of man and redistribute the wealth of the world in equitable lots. Instead he chose to be born into a poor home and live the life of a servant.

In his ministry he extolled the blessedness of being poor and he railed against the pitfalls of riches. He told us that wealth could be a stumbling stone on the road to heaven. He told an affluent but law-abiding young man who was seeking to enter the kingdom to go out and sell everything he owned and give the proceeds to the poor. He praised the poor widow who dropped her last farthing into the offering basket.

And through the Holy Spirit he paid highest tribute to his poor mother by reminding Luke that when Mary went to the temple to make a sin offering to atone for the defilement she incurred by giving birth to the unblemished Lamb of God, she could not afford to offer a lamb and instead offered the sacrifice the Lord would accept only from the poor: a pair of pigeons or turtledoves.

Jesus voluntarily rejected the glory of heaven to become a lowly servant in a poor nation oppressed by a tyrannical emperor. Through the centuries many believers have followed his example by spurning earthly comforts and devoting their lives to serving the multitudes of needy people throughout the world.

When the Son of Man comes in his glory, those obedient disciples will not have to squirm in discomfort, wondering if they will be counted as sheep or as goats.

But what about the rest of us?

Unclean! Unclean!

Scripture: Leviticus 13–14
Suggested Reading: Matthew 7:1–2; 8:1–3; John 9:1–3

During a recent presidential election, I remember grimacing as I read a letter from a nationally known television evangelist who had organized a political action movement. He recommended voting for a particular group of candidates because, among other things, they would deny immigration privileges to foreigners who were suffering from AIDS. I wondered how a man so grounded in the teachings of Jesus could possibly advocate such a position.

By contrast I know of a nurse from one of our local churches who volunteered to work in the hospital with AIDS patients because many other nurses refused, and she felt called by the Lord to fill that desperate need. By accident she contracted the disease from a contaminated needle and eventually died. Although she left behind a husband and children, she never complained of her suffering, condemned anyone for her fate, or regretted her decision to serve as she did.

Maybe that evangelist took his ideas solely from the Old Testament which sometimes suggests that leprosy was punishment for sin, and from Leviticus in which the leper is instructed to go around shouting "Unclean! Unclean!" and to dwell alone in a habitation outside the gates of the camp. But the nurse learned her duty from studying the kind acts of Jesus who healed the lepers by reaching out and touching them. Again he set an example for us by loving the unlovable and touching the untouchable.

Now I don't know, as some suggest, whether or not such awful diseases as leprosy and AIDS are God's condemnation and death sentence upon people he finds guilty of committing abominable sins. That is a matter for theologians. And I don't know why he allows good doctors, nurses, and innocent children to become contaminated. But I do know that he has not instructed me or any pastor or evangelist, famous or not, to pass judgment on other sinners and to slam the door of healing in their faces.

All I know is that he wants me to leave the judging to him and to fulfill the job description he's laid out for me, which is to love him above all and to love my neighbor as myself. And loving my neighbor as myself means doing unto others as Christ did unto me, loving me when I didn't deserve his love and stretching out his hand of mercy to me when I was foul with sin.

Jesus' disciples asked him if a man's blindness was caused by his own sin or the sin of his parents. They knew that sin was the antecedent for all human maladies, and they assumed a direct link between a person's disease and a specific sin. Although not denying a cause-effect relationship between sin and infirmity, Jesus did point out that one reason for disease might be to permit the manifestation of divine power. Jesus then healed the man who quickly became a witness to the mighty works of God.

We err when we see God more as a God of affliction than a God of remedy. Our behavior, not God's, caused the corruption of his perfect creation, but he is the redeemer of his people all over the world and wants to restore us to incorruptibility.

Our task, then, cannot be to slam the gates of redemption shut in the face of the defiled, but to view every appearance of contamination as an opportunity that God may use to manifest his glory.

He works in mysterious ways.

. . . And Led Him Away . . .

Scripture: Leviticus 15–16
Suggested Reading: Matthew 27:31; Hebrews 13:10–16

I've lost track of the gentle lady who was my eighth grade teacher, but if she's still alive I hope she doesn't read this because if she does, she'll lose whatever respect she might have had for me, if in fact she remembers me at all. At any rate, she could never forget Henry, the boy who sat beside me in the second row.

Henry had freckles, a shock of unruly red hair, wide, round eyes, and a big foolish grin. He never said much. When he tried to talk he turned red and stammered, especially in the presence of adults. In a tense situation, if he opened his mouth, only gibberish would come out.

Once, when Mrs. Page was writing on the blackboard with her back to the class, two of the more disorderly boys whose seats flanked Henry's, which included me, tore our ink blotters into bite-sized pieces, chewed them up, and launched blue spitballs that stuck to the ivory ceiling directly over Henry's seat.

Alerted by a wave of general giggling, Mrs. Page turned and discovered the prank immediately. She asked the responsible party to confess, but instead of owning up, we perpetrators pointed accusing fingers at Henry, who could only stare, grin, and babble incomprehensible sounds which she interpreted as admissions of guilt. Then she called in the hall monitor who led the innocent Henry out of the classroom to the principal's office for the administration of justice.

During the summer Mrs. Page and her husband and moved away, and Henry transferred to an institution that could better meet his special needs. But as we progressed up learning's ladder in our Christian school, we began to study such esoteric theological concepts as atonement, and inevitably encountered that famous scapegoat described by Moses in Leviticus and applied to the forgiven Christian by the writer of Hebrews.

Our rude treatment of Henry served as a poignant object lesson in atonement. I had no doubt what it meant to have my sin heaped on another's head and to stand happily by as the one bearing the burden of my guilt was led off to suffer the consequences that should have befallen me.

Now I don't hold Henry in high esteem for absorbing the responsibility for my misbehavior because he didn't do it voluntarily. And Henry cannot suffer the guilt of my inhumanity to him. That was a millstone I carried around my neck until God granted me the grace to confess my sins at his mercy seat and come to him begging forgiveness. Then the innocent Jesus became the scapegoat for me too, as in my spirit's eye I watched him led out of Jerusalem to Golgotha for the administration of divine justice.

The whole idea behind the laws of Leviticus seems to center on purification: purification of the tabernacle, of the priesthood, and of the people. God demands purification. He can't tolerate a single smudge of dirt. The sacrificial lamb, too, had to be without blemish.

Even in my old age, I'm far from pure. The fact that I recall my wretched treatment of Henry with a twinkle in my eye proves that I'm not one hundred percent contrite.

None of us can ever be perfect in our penitence or in our sacrifice. But thankfully we have an unblemished scapegoat to carry our sins out to the wilderness of God's forgetfulness.

When in Rome?

Scripture: Leviticus 18
Suggested Reading: 2 Corinthians 6:17–18

*B*ut dad, everybody's doing it! is a plea we made to our parents and a plea our children made to us. So, if everybody's doing it, it must be okay. Right?

The difference between us and them is a most difficult concept to teach. Our whole world opposes it.

When we welcome people of a different culture into our community, the courteous among us find it proper to accept the differences they bring us. We try to pronounce their names as they pronounce them, when invited to their homes we try to eat the food of their choice as they have prepared it, and we try to honor their customs, even if we find them strange, or perhaps offensive. We do our best to accommodate them in every way.

The discourteous among us, however, mock and ridicule them. And the intolerant torment them because of their differences, and try to drive them away.

When we travel to foreign lands, we often get a little handbook warning us that certain of our customary and usual behaviors might be offensive to the people whose country we are visiting. In some places, we don't offer to shake hands, look people in the eye, or get too close. The byword is, "When in Rome, do as the Romans." Fit in.

Often we hear that immigrants preserve their cultural identity for a time, but gradually assimilate into the culture that surrounds them. Japanese people, for example, might eat sushi in their own homes or when they dine in a Japanese restaurant, but sooner or later we're just as likely to find them eating hamburgers at a fast food chain.

One of my neighbor ladies who came from India wore a sari for several years, but now usually wears jeans and a sweatshirt. Parents I know from Mexico pronounce their name *Mar TI nez*, but their children say *Martin EZ*, because that's how their American friends pronounce it.

My folks were second generation Dutch and had given up wearing wooden shoes, but my neighbors back home in the Dutch ghetto were straight from the old country, and we ridiculed poor Albertus because his parents still wore *klompen*. Yet, once a year or so, we still cook hutsput from grandma's recipe, and our decorative wooden shoes still adorn the doorstep. Not only is it tempting to try to blend in with the people around us, it is uncomfortable not to. If we don't fit in, we run the risk of being ostracized, and we all seek the approval of the people in whose midst we live.

The old Hebrews left one culture and went into another. God told them not to behave the way the Egyptians behaved in the land they came from, and not to behave the way the Canaanites behaved in the land he was going to give them. He called them out to be separate from the world, and if they committed the abominable acts either the Egyptians or the Canaanites committed, they would not be fit to inhabit his kingdom.

He calls us to give up any ancestry we claim in this world, and in exchange he offers to be our Father and invites us to be his children. And even though we might suffer barbs of distain from the intolerant, he promises us that we will inherit a new and glorious kingdom.

God's Greatest Gifts

Scripture: Leviticus 19
Suggested Reading: Review Leviticus 18

Once when I was a young man trying to live as I thought God wanted me to live, I was invited to dine at the home of an elder in my church. Before dinner he prepared himself a Manhattan and asked me if I wanted a drink. Fearing some underhanded effort to test my godliness, I respectfully declined with the comment that I didn't care for alcohol.

As we sat and talked, he sipped. He told me that alcohol was one of the many things he thanked God for every day. He was serious. He declared that alcohol was one of God's greatest gifts, and that his daily nip not only promoted good physical health, but also helped his mind to be at peace. He pointed out, however, that alcohol, as is the case with most of God's greatest blessings, is easy to abuse and that abuse has severe consequences.

Beyond the black cloud of abomination that hangs over Leviticus 18, glows a moon of blessing.

In some places, the Bible is a very sexual book detailing acts of perversion and opening the closets of the patriarchs and the heroes of faith to reveal the skeletons rattling inside. From beginning to end it warns us that adulterous and unnatural acts are abominations on which God will not fail to render harsh judgment. Yet it points out very clearly that the pleasures of marriage are pleasures that he has ordained, and that the sexual union of man and woman is not only the means by which his creation progresses, but also stands as a metaphor describing his love for us. Jesus is the groom and the church is his chosen bride. Sex is a wonderful gift, and to abuse it is hateful to the one who gave it. He will not let such abuse go unpunished.

Those of us who have given nice gifts to others and have watched those gifts abused know exactly how God feels when we abuse the gifts he has given us. Sex is a blessed gift, but its abuse ruins young lives, destroys happy homes, and inflicts mortal illness. Certain substances that God created in plants and animals can be processed into drugs that cure diseases, relieve pain, and bring peace to troubled minds, yet the improper use of drugs has resulted in destructive addictions, rampant crime and a whole underground economy. Alcohol, according to my elder friend, is a gift from God, yet its abuse lands many on skid row, tears up families, and causes fatal accidents. Many Christians have found wealth to be a blessing, while others have turned it into a ticket to hell. Political power can be used to ease human suffering and bring peace to a tense world, but it can also corrupt those who wield it. We could go on and on citing the blessings of God's good gifts and the hellish consequences of their abuse.

It's a mystery to me why God made his greatest gifts so vulnerable to abuse and gave their abuse such grave consequences. Maybe he didn't do it. Maybe we did it back in Eden when we profaned the gift of righteousness and brought down consequences on ourselves that ultimately resulted in an evil world taking another great gift and nailing it to a cross.

But thanks be to God, the gift that he gave us on Christmas, Good Friday and Easter is the gift that can overcome the consequences of abusing the others. It is the one final gift that restores us to his favor and restores our squandered citizenship in the kingdom of heaven. It is the one final gift we dare not abuse, because he guarantees us that its abuse will result in an eternity in hell.

Children for Molech

Scripture: Leviticus 20

The sons of Israel were a bit confused about the business of placing their children into the hands of God. Moses had made it clear to them that their children belonged to God, but the process of committing them to God became blurry in their minds when they became too friendly with their pagan neighbors.

The pagans, too, believed they should give their children to their god Molech, and they did so by hurling the infants into the mouth of a fiery furnace. Apparently some well-meaning but misguided Israelites thought they should do the same. Hence the prohibition.

When I first began to study this chapter, I understood quite clearly the prohibitions against adultery, incest, and consulting with mediums and wizards. I've never been interested in horoscopes or psychics, and at my age I've quit worrying about getting caught up in sexual sins. And we're way past the point in history at which we have to be admonished not to offer our children to Molech. Or are we?

Perhaps giving our children to the pagan gods is one of the sins we've been committing all along without knowing it. There was a commercial on television showing a father and his young son eating breakfast together in silence, then each going his own way for the day. The spot ended with the comment, "Another missed opportunity to talk with your child about drugs." Was that father unwittingly offering his son to Molech? Have we offered our children up to the pagan gods of this world by keeping silent about things we should talk to them about? Do we offer them to the god of the furnace when we fail to anchor them securely in Christ?

When God issued the Ten Commandments at Mount Sinai, his first rule was, "Thou shalt have no other gods before me." The Israelites took that to mean they were not to worship the heathen gods of the Egyptians and the Canaanites. But now that those gods have gone the way of all mythology, has the first commandment become obsolete?

Pastors who are true to the Word recognize that the first commandment is still valid if we broaden the definition of idolatry to include those things that might become gods to us today. For adults, idol worship might include the love of such things as money, jobs, status, cars, clothing, or sports. It can even mean excessive adoration of a spouse or a child.

What do our children idolize? The vague, haunting memories of my own adolescence abound with images of singers, movie stars, sports heroes, and cars, mostly youthful versions of what people still idolize today. Do children learn their infatuations from adults, or do adults preserve their childhood fancies and extend them, in modified form, into adulthood? Do they pass the penchant for such idolatry down to their children?

One burden that accrues to us as adults is responsibility, not just for our own attitudes, but the responsibility to rear our children properly. And rearing them properly is not limited to assuring their education and physical well being, but assuring their spiritual welfare, moderating their attraction to rock stars, and educating them to the dangers of drugs.

If we don't raise them to love God and treat their bodies as his temple, we are offering them to Molech.

Role Models

Leviticus 21–22
Suggested Reading: 1 Corinthians 8

A noted professional basketball player once misbehaved in public and was chastised by the media for being a bad example to the youngsters who admired him. He retorted that it was not his job to raise other people's children and that he had no intention of being a role model.

He was right, of course, in asserting that it was not his duty to raise other people's children, but how could he possibly avoid being a role model for kids who admire sports superstars? Not only did this hero plaster his name and number on jerseys and jackets that hung on racks in department stores, but he also endorsed other products that had more to do with lifestyle than with basketball. How could he claim not to be a role model when he openly asked people to emulate him by wearing his number and using his deodorant?

When the Lord instituted the priesthood, he made it clear that the priests had to behave in an exemplary manner. Not only was their office a sacred trust that demanded proper deportment before God, but as they walked among the people they inadvertently set standards of conduct. If a priest was found engaging in certain acts, the people might assume that such acts fell within the bounds of propriety.

Most clergy today recognize that they set standards of conduct for the members of their congregations and other people who live in their community. Some pastors I know decline to take a drink in a restaurant because it might be a stumbling block, or bite their tongue when they miss a short putt because the use of an expressive earthy term might imply that such terms are generally acceptable. They are aware that by virtue of their position they are inevitably role models for others.

When I was a young teacher, members of the school board held me to a standard of behavior higher than was expected of others in the community, including themselves. They asserted that by their very title, teachers were role models whose conduct should serve as an example for others, especially children. In our teachers' lounge someone hung an antique poster that enumerated the rules of conduct expected of teachers a century earlier. The policy delineated conditions of employment that included the duty to attend church regularly and prohibited smoking, drinking, dating, and even marriage without permission. When we looked at those standards, we didn't think ours were so harsh.

It's easy to glance around and conclude that people in certain positions need to behave in a respectable way because they are role models for our children. Certainly pastors, teachers, and athletes are automatic role models. But what about the rest of us?

As I reflect on the people whose traits most influenced me, I look far beyond pastors, teachers, and superstars. At one time or another, I found myself emulating the mailman, my basketball coach, the church custodian, or the butcher down at the meat market. Whenever we see in someone else a trait we either covet or admire, we tend to copy that person's actions whether that person be saint or sinner, baker or candlestick maker.

We never know when our conduct induces similar conduct in others. And even though by our own standards we might not be sinning, we might unwittingly cause someone, even a little one, to stumble. So, from young pastors to old pew warmers, we should all behave as though we are role models.

Feasting and Fasting

Scripture: Leviticus 23
Suggested Reading: Proverbs 24:13; Matthew 6:16–18

*M*y church is famous for two things: its faithful preaching of the Word of God and its potluck suppers. I understand why the Lord inspired my pastors to be true to their calling, but I don't understand why he inspired so many great cooks to join my church. You can go to the world's biggest cafeteria chains, but you'll never find the vast array of sumptuous dishes like the ones that grace the tables at the United Methodist potluck suppers. We always begin the feast with prayer, thanking God for blessing us with the abundant life.

We have a potluck every month and a rummage sale every spring. People donate to the rummage sale last year's duds that don't fit anymore, and members of the community come in and get good deals on slightly used clothing. Then, after we notice that we've stepped up a size or two, we repent of our gluttony and start counting calories and fat grams. We go on a diet of bland, tasteless food and sugarless everything until we cease to strain at the buttons of our newest shirt or blouse. Then we start all over again.

We've coined the expression, "If it's good, it's fattening," and we ask each other if God put fat on beef and planted sugar cane just to torment us. We have a difficult time understanding a God who fills our lives with a bounty of wonderful food, then punishes us for eating it by making us fat and vulnerable to consequent diseases. Or is it really God who is to blame?

I've got to believe that God put good food on this earth for us to enjoy. After all, it was he who put the calories and the fat grams into the food and it is we who process them out. If he didn't want us to consume the fat and the calories, why didn't he process them out himself?

When we look at the scriptures, we find that God instituted both feasts and fasts. We don't have to look far into the history of God's people to realize that he fully intended to bless their lives with an abundance of good food. A glance at a concordance reveals column after column of such words as honey, oil, fat, sweet, and savory. He told us flat out that he wants to fill our mouths with good things. On the other hand, there are times when he has told us to abstain from food, mainly for spiritual reasons and as an indication of submission to him rather than slavery to our own appetites. God wants us to celebrate his goodness by enjoying the delicious foods he has given us, but he also wants us to discipline ourselves, deny ourselves, and focus on him through fasting.

The wisest man of all said it best. In one breath he said, ". . . eat honey, for it is good," but in the next he added, "it is not good to eat *much* honey."

As we pointed out a few days ago, God's greatest gifts are most easily abused. Food is no exception. If we overindulge or let food become our idol, it can be the death of us. Literally. Our doctors tell us that obesity is one of the main causes of death and disease in our country, and it is amazing to note the vast number of obese people we meet every day.

You see, God gave us blue cheese, meat, potatoes, gravy and apple pie. But he also gave us the wisdom of Solomon. He gave us the feelings of hunger and fullness. He gave us our potluck suppers and the good sense to put our forks down before we have to loosen our belts.

Coals of Fire

Scripture: Leviticus 24
Suggested Reading: Matthew 5:38–39; Romans 12:19–20

Leviticus 24:20 is one of the Bible's best known passages, quoted by saints and sinners alike, each for their own reasons. It's a verse that even Jesus quoted.

Most gentle Christians think that the eye-for-an-eye form of justice is severe. But scholars point out that the rule was intended in Moses' day to limit the punishment to equal the severity of the crime. No person was to be punished to a greater extent than a crime against a fellow human warranted.

Blasphemy is akin to killing God, so the proper punishment is death. Jesus was put to death after being declared guilty of blasphemy in accordance with the law of Leviticus. If a person killed another, the proper punishment was death, but if a man broke a neighbor's leg, the proper punishment was to have his leg broken, not a sentence more severe.

We humans have a long history of punishing malefactors out of proportion to their offense. The hero of *Les Miserables*, Jean Valjean, was sentenced to five years in the galleys for stealing a loaf of bread. Such punishment was not uncommon in nineteenth century France. Black men in Mississippi were castrated for ogling white girls. Such punishment was not uncommon in twentieth century America. And even after our collective conscience told us to free our slaves, we still condoned the hanging of horse thieves in the heroic Old West. And the nightly news proves that we have not outgrown that mentality even today.

When Jesus declared, "You have heard it said, ' . . . an eye for an eye and a tooth for a tooth,' but I say unto you . . . if anyone strikes you on the right cheek turn to him the other also," he was arguing for justice tempered with mercy. It would be foolish to suggest that Jesus favored letting all kinds of dangerous and defective people run the streets free to do their harmful business. But he was ordering us to replace the old law of retaliation with the law of love.

Paul cast further light on the notion by ascribing to God the sole right of retaliation, and by quoting the proverb that says rendering to an enemy mercy in place of vengeance "will heap burning coals of fire upon his head."

Jean Valjean learned about the law of love from the good bishop, Monseigneur Bienvenu, whose silverware he had stolen. When he was arrested for his crime and returned to the bishop for identification, the bishop turned the other cheek by telling the police that he had given Valjean the silver and by handing him a pair of valuable candlesticks, which he told him he had "forgotten." Without an accuser, Valjean went free.

All the punishment all the prosecutors in France could pour out upon Jean Valjean would not reform him. Slavery in the galleys and rejection by the people only made him bitter. His life was not transformed until Monseigneur Bienvenu heaped coals of fire on his head by showing him uncommon love and mercy.

His final words to Valjean were, ". . . my brother, you belong no longer to evil, but to good. It is your soul that I am buying for you. I withdraw it from dark thoughts and from the spirit of perdition, and I give it to God."

May God give us the grace to go and do likewise.

... *For the Land Is Mine*

Scripture: Leviticus 25:1–24
Suggested Reading: Psalms 24:1

*M*ary Ann feeds the birds. Because she keeps several feeders full of seeds and sugar water, we have warblers enough to drown out the Mormon Tabernacle Choir. Even in winter while I'm plowing the snow out of the driveway, she is busy shoveling paths and hauling her suet cakes and bags of sunflower seeds out to the various feeding stations. Then we sit in the sunroom and watch her birds enjoy their feasts.

In the big old cedar tree, flickers peck as they hang upside down on the suet cages while the house finches take turns nibbling at the thistle tubes. Cardinals and blue jays dine together in the big feeder on the post while juncos gather below to munch on the leftovers that fall on the snow. I enjoy sharing my land with God's creatures.

Except the moles, that is. All summer long I battle those contemptible little underground varmints that tunnel through my lawn, killing the grass and ruining the carpet of green I work so hard to keep up. After chemical warfare fails, I set traps. Every now and again I nail one, but mostly they escape the poison and the smoke and the prongs of my iron assassin. I don't enjoy sharing my land with the evil critters that God, in my opinion, should have denied passage on the ark.

Mary Ann and I disagree on the rabbits. She thinks they're cute, especially the little ones, and gives them names like Flopsey,

Mopsey, and Thumper, but when they trespass into my garden and pilfer my carrots and my lettuce, I tend to side with Mr. Fudd.

Then I read Leviticus 25 and become aware how really worthless my land deed is in the greater scheme of things. God has granted me the temporary privilege of sojourning on these premises, and the government he empowered has reserved the use of the land solely for me to the exclusion of other human beings. But I'm obligated to share it with all the other creatures that God, in his mercy, saw fit to spare from the Flood.

Years ago my uncle Abe had his farm condemned because it stood in the path of the new highway. Although they compensated him, in their opinion fairly, for it, the relatives all bemoaned the fact that the government could step in and usurp the property rights of its citizens. But then again, we understand that God institutes governments and gives them authority over people. And he uses everything from moles to governors to remind us that the land really belongs to him. We belong to him too, and are really no more than strangers and sojourners on his land, just like the birds, the rabbits, and the moles.

Land is a funny thing. In 1944, warring armies wrung lifeblood from each other just to possess a tiny barren mound of it that stuck up above the surface of the Pacific Ocean. Then in 1994, survivors from both armies gathered at the posh hotel that now occupies that mound to celebrate the fiftieth anniversary of that great battle, to dine together, and to remember the fallen heroes from both sides. Old soldiers from Japan and the United States played golf together on the same ground they fought over a half century before. The ultimate folly of it all reminds us once again that the land and the governments he ordains to manage it all belong to God.

The older I get, the more aware I become that I'm no more than a stranger and a sojourner on this land and that he has reserved an eternal habitation for me in glory!

Proclaim Liberty!

Scripture: Leviticus 25:25–55
Suggested Reading: Revelation 11:15–16

In the coffee shops during my college days, I listened to the young intellectuals rant about "the greedy excesses of unrestrained capitalism." Though they offered no evidence that state communism had successfully liberated the masses from the oppression of the power mongers, those students of politics and human character had already discovered that man by nature sought to accumulate all he could, even at the expense of his neighbor.

Man's innate avarice was not discovered by sophomores in college coffee shops. God was keenly aware of it when he fashioned the rules by which he expected his people to live. In developing a social and economic order, he gave latitudes to the ambitious while protecting the less capable from the cruel shackles of poverty. His rules serve two purposes: to protect his people from each other, and to declare once again that the earth and all who dwell therein belong entirely to him.

Unfortunately there is no evidence that the Israelites or anyone else ever fully implemented the concept of jubilee. Unfortunate because I'm sure that if they had given it an honest try, it would have worked. I think God would have seen to it. Those who had lost their inheritance would have got it back, and I'm sure God would have found some way to bless those who willingly relinquished the wealth they had gained. But the priesthood of the day was corrupt and self-indulgent. They were probably beholden to the successful capitalists, and together they probably conspired to see that jubilee never came.

In the end they paid dearly for it.

I don't know that when God ordered them to blow the trumpet of jubilee to proclaim liberty throughout the land he was actually looking ahead to the day the seventh angel would blow the trumpet of consummation, proclaiming the eternal kingdom of the Lord. But it works wonderfully well for me.

Some of the pundits who make educated guesses about the end times see a grand total of seven thousand years in the age of man, six before the millennium and then a time of jubilee when those who have lived for themselves will have their gains stripped away, and those who have lived for the Lord will receive their reward. I don't know if their projections are on the mark or not, and I really don't care.

But what I do know and what I do care about is that at the end of the devil's rule God will proclaim liberty throughout the land. He is letting us have our way for a while, but at the end of his time he will ring the bells of freedom, liberating those who love him from the clutches of sin and greed.

And his bell won't crack like ours did. He will proclaim a jubilee for his people and will set us free from the dominance of the oppressor. We will be renewed as spiritual beings, free from the fetters of the flesh, free from lust, and free from conceit.

How then should I live?

With the help of God, I should live as though that trumpet will sound tomorrow. I should read Matthew 25 very carefully and know what separates the sheep from the goats. I should look into the face of each man I meet and see the face of Jesus Christ. And if he is lost, hungry, sick, or cold, I should look deep into my heart and see my duty very clearly.

Then Shall the Land . . .

Scripture: Leviticus 26
Suggested Reading: Psalms 137; Romans 11:1; Genesis 12:2–3.

A just God can be a cruel taskmaster.

In the shadow of man's proclivity to sin and the horrible consequences that God promises, where can we find a little moon glow? Where is the comfort in this vale of misery?

After the last king, the time for obedience had long past. God executed the horrible sentence. The Israelites' happy song ended and they sadly hanged their harps on the willows by the river of Babylon. Their enemies reaped their harvest, had their women, and enslaved their children, just as promised. What chance for a little joy was left?

What did they do that was so horrible? The books of Kings and Chronicles detail their idolatry, a violation of the very first commandment. Their history shows that they had only sporadic moments of faithfulness and they failed to take proper care of the land God had given them.

Adam and Eve sinned by eating the forbidden fruit, but the Israelites sinned by gorging themselves on the whole tree of it.

Among other rules, God made it clear to them that the land, as well as the people, was to enjoy its Sabbaths. The people were to rest every seventh day, and the land was to rest every seventh year. Except for the Pharisees of Jesus' day, there is little evidence that the people held the Sabbath in very high regard. And there is no evidence at all, even during their moments of righteousness, that they gave the land its Sabbath rests. When the Lord evicted the people from the land, he saw to it that the fields lay desolate, finally able to enjoy all at once the rest they had been denied for so many years.

If we don't take care of the things God has given us, he will see to it that those things are cared for in some other way, even at the hands of our enemies. The land belongs to him, and what he ordains for it will come to pass, regardless of the quality of our stewardship. God is in charge, and his will will be done.

But what about the people? Will they ever enjoy their rest? Will the guilty get as much compassion from God as did their innocent and abused land? Yes, and more.

Yet for all that, when they are in the land of their enemies,
I will not spurn them, neither will I abhor them so as to
destroy them utterly and break my covenant with them;
for I am the Lord their God; but I will for their sake
remember the covenant with their forefathers . . .
Leviticus 26:44

After God had driven the people from the land because of their sin, how much of the covenant was left to remember? Abraham's name had become great, his sons had already become great nations and their numbers were enormous. But, in addition, God had promised Abraham that through his descendants, all the families of the earth would be blessed. That had not yet happened.

Had God forgotten his people? By no means! He loved us so much that he restored the land to his people long enough to bless the whole world by sending his Son to serve the death sentence for our disobedience.

And when Jesus returns as King of kings and Lord of lords, all who love him will finally enjoy their eternal Sabbath rest!

Vows

Scripture: Leviticus 27
Suggested Reading: Ecclesiastes 5:4–6

The making of vows is a painful subject for me, having once been party to the breaking of one of the most important vows one can make in the presence of God and the people.

There is little comfort in the fact that vow breakers far outnumber vow keepers. Members of the clergy have broken the vows they made to God and their church. Husbands and wives have broken more vows than they have kept. Children have failed to keep promises they made to their parents. Employers have failed to keep promises to employees. But there's no solace in that.

We promise payment and deliver a bogus check. We promise faithfulness and deliver infidelity. We promise till death do us part and deliver abandonment. If we dig right to the bottom of it, we would probably find that no one alive has kept all of the vows he has ever made. But still, that does not assuage the guilt.

The making of vows is a serious business, and we ought to be very circumspect before we commit ourselves to a promise we are not absolutely certain we can keep. Often we rush into vows hastily, before we know what keeping those vows entails. Sometimes we make promises we cannot keep simply because we lack the capability.

Often we have good intentions before we pledge ourselves, but later things change and we regret that we ever made the promise. Some people glibly make vows on the spur of the moment for their own convenience and forget them in an instant. Others make vows under duress and when good times return forget their commitment. The words of our mouths have been a great source of grief, for both ourselves and others.

Vows made to each other are very important, and failure to honor them is a sin. But vows made to God fall into a different category entirely.

God takes our vows to him very seriously, and failure to honor them could be disastrous. We promise God service and deliver sloth. We promise obedience and deliver rebellion. He tolerates neither tardiness nor excuse and may punish a renegade by destroying the work of his hands. That is serious. He warns us that it is better not to make a promise to him at all, than to make one and fail to keep it.

Yet in the face of all the advice the Bible gives us about vows and all the importance we place on the value of our word and the keeping of our pledges, we scatter more broken promises in the dust than we honor.

What if God were as irresolute about his promises as we are with ours? What if he promised us heaven and delivered hell?

Because we are fallen sinners, our vows are suspect from the start. But God can do no wrong. When he makes a promise, he keeps it! If he promises to punish us, you can bet the paddle will land, and if he promises to destroy, you can count on ruin.

But when he promises a blessing for all the families of the earth, we can be assured that he will deliver that blessing, and when he promises eternal life to those who repent of their sins, praise God, we can take that promise to the bank!

In the Wilderness

Scripture: Scan section titles of the book of Numbers

Sometimes we old people look in the mirror at our gray hair and wrinkled faces and ask, "Where did the years go?" We remember details of our youth as though they happened just last week, but what about all those years in between. Where did they go?

If the book of Numbers is the saga of Israel's life in the wilderness, those leathery-faced old Hebrews who survived to the end of that story might well look back at the text and ask where the years went. The book opens with a census, a few specifics about the march from Sinai to Canaan, the selection of the twelve spies, and the tragic decision not to cross the border at Kadesh-Barnea and go forward to claim their inheritance in the Promised Land. For their faithlessness, God sentenced them to forty years in the wilderness, a year for each day of the spy mission, until every last one of the adults who left Egypt died there in that barren waste.

All of that happens within two years after the flight from bondage. The pages representing the rest of the lives of the freed slaves are practically blank. Little happens between the shameful departure from their outpost at Kadesh and the battles with their cousins on the plains of Moab thirty-eight years later

Lately I came across an anonymous tract entitled, *The Dash Between the Dates*. Some thoughtful scribe had taken note of the fact that our tombstones declare the year of our birth and the year of our death, and that a mere dash separating those two numbers represents our entire life. He asks us to reflect on that dash and contemplate the story it might tell if it were a book. Would it tell the story of a life worth living? Would it tell of a miserable and useless life? Would it describe a life lived for Christ? Or would it be blank?

For the Israelites that dash between Kadesh and Moab represented thirty-eight years of misery. Since being banned from their inheritance for forty years for their refusal to go forward in faith and claim the promise, their fate was to suffer and complain until their "dead bodies fell in the wilderness." They struggled through that hot, dry desert, surviving on the daily ration of manna that rotted before the next morning. They had no goal except to fulfill the forty years, bury their loved ones, wander like nomads in search of a few green shoots of grass for their animals, and die so their children might have a second chance. Talk about a life without hope!

Their fate forces us to ponder what we do with our lives. After we've been set free from the bondage of sin by the blood of Christ, do we devour the Word of God in a sincere effort to determine how he wants us to live our lives? Do we then march to the border of the kingdom of heaven and reconnoiter the land? And what do we report to ourselves? Do our eyes behold a land that devours its inhabitants, a land of demon giants? A land of terror? Or do we behold the land that flows with spiritual milk and honey, a land abundant with rich produce, the fruit of the Spirit, a land whose inhabitants we can easily defeat with the Lord fighting at our side?

When we come to know the Lord's story of salvation, we have choices. On one hand we can decide not to walk closely with Jesus, but rather to wander in the dry wilderness of life until we die. We can choose to live, as some of the Israelites did, just outside the boundary of the Promised Land, vulnerable to pagan temptations, going to church regularly but never truly giving our lives to Christ. Or we can make the wise choice and walk boldly over the length and breadth of the land, claiming every inch of it as our own!

Every Man Able . . .

*Scripture: **Numbers 1***
Suggested Reading: Leviticus 18:24–30; Romans 13:1–5

Make no mistake here. This is not a census for sociological or demographical purposes, nor a process for satisfying the need to know how many people survived the trek through the wilderness. This census is for military conscription, or in more familiar terms, a registering for the draft. Moses was to register every man able to "go forth to war." And we see no exemption for conscientious objectors.

In our time, many men have had to register for the draft. Some were never called. Fortunate ones such as I were called during peacetime and enjoyed pleasant duty either here or overseas. Others went forth to fight our country's wars. Many were killed, wounded or taken prisoner. Some still bear scars. Some fought proudly, convinced that they were on a righteous crusade against evil. Others fought for an unappreciative nation of people who believed the war was unnecessary, unwise, or unjust.

We welcomed the veterans of the world wars home as heroes. We forgot the veterans of Korea. We shunned or abused the veterans of Viet Nam. And we denied responsibility for the infirmities incurred by the veterans of the Gulf wars.

God uses governments and armies for a multitude of reasons, some of which elude our understanding. He promised the Jews that if they served him and obeyed his law, he would bless them and bless their land, but if they disobeyed, he would drive them to the ends of the earth and ordain other nations to persecute them.

Before the Israelites fled from captivity in Egypt, Canaanites inhabited the land God had promised to the children of Abraham. They were wicked people, defiling the land with unspeakable abominations. Thus, God ordered the young armies of Israel to cleanse his holy land of those evil nations, telling the sons of Jacob that if they defiled the land as the Canaanites did, they would be cast out in the same manner.

They did and they were. When Israel failed to live as the Lord commanded, he used pagan empires to disinherit her and other evil nations throughout history to torment and abuse her people, just as he had promised.

In the twentieth century, the government of Germany treated the Jews with a savagery that still appalls rational humanity. Then, as many believe, God used the allied armies to punish Germany for what it had done to them, fulfilling the promise to Abraham, "I will bless him who blesses you, and him who curses you, I will curse."

War among nations is the rule rather than the exception. America was born in war, and in her short history has sent her soldiers out more than a dozen times. My conscience cries out against war. War is barbaric. War is mankind at its savage best. It is not easy to see God's hand in war, much less his design. But in the Garden of Eden we chose to eat the forbidden fruit, and now we must suffer the consequences. It is ironic that God uses man's depravity to execute his judgment against sin.

Is there any moon glow in all of this? Only the knowledge that God is in charge of all nations, the good ones and the evil ones. In his Word he gives us no right to tell our governing authorities that we object to their using us to execute the Lord's will. We must submit.

War, as the general said, is hell. But we should have thought of that six thousand years ago when we still had a choice.

Numbers

Scripture: Numbers 2

At face value, a book named Numbers would appear to be very boring reading for a person who likes drama, and quite appealing for an accountant. Surprisingly, there is a lot of drama in the numbers.

Reuben is a case in point. Logically, he should have more descendants than any of his brothers. Being the eldest, he had time to get a head start on the other eleven. And he was a lover. As a child he gathered mandrakes for his mother and as an adult he took his father's wife to bed. Not being a man of violence, he did not instigate the killing of the Shechemites, but left Dinah's revenge for the next two, Simeon and Levi. It was Reuben who intervened when the other nine were conspiring to kill Joseph, and he saved his life. Yet, when Father Jacob dispensed "blessings" upon his boys, he stripped Reuben of the double share typically reserved as the birthright of the firstborn and prophesied that he would not have preeminence.

True to Jacob's prophecy, Reuben's tribe numbers far fewer than the average of the twelve, and not a single *Who's Who* of the Bible traces his heritage to the tribe of Reuben, no great soldier, no prophet, no judge, and no apostle.

Judah, on the other hand, had a slow start in the business of propagation. God struck his eldest two sons dead for their sins, and Judah protected his youngest, Shelah, from marriage to Tamar. His own adulterous relationship with Tamar produced the twins, Perez and Zerah; Perez being the forebearer of Jesus. Even with such a slow start, Judah led the others by a substantial margin in producing offspring. Dan is a distant second, almost twelve thousand behind Judah.

And speaking again of *Who's Who* in the Bible, it is interesting to note that with the exception of Judah and Levi, none of the other sons of Leah or the concubines produced any Bible personages of note. The descendants of Rachel, on the other hand, Benjamin and Joseph's sons, Ephriam and Manasseh, were ancestors to *all* of the rest of the great Bible characters.

Other amusing numbers:

Dan had only one son when the family moved into Egypt, but, at the start of the Exodus four hundred years later, that one son had produced sixty-three thousand descendants.

Dan's little brother Benjamin had already sired ten sons before they left Canaan, but during those years in Egypt, those ten only produced an average of thirty-five hundred each, a small enough output to be considered least among the tribes.

Judah's sons numbered but three, putting him nearly in last place before the move to Egypt, but when they came out, his tribe was by far the biggest, numbering nearly seventy-five thousand.

What does all this mean?

The Lord told us that the first shall be last and the last shall be first. He alone determines a place for each of us in the grand pattern.

We glibly toss around such terms as "the survival of the fittest," and "natural selection" as though we have the tools and the wisdom to comprehend and calculate the destiny of all things. Wrong. God may or may not use these evolutionary devices to manage his universe, but at any time he is ready to step in with new twists such as "survival of the meekest," or "divine selection."

God, not the whim of chance, is in charge of all things.

The Hub

Scripture: Numbers 3–4
Suggested Reading: Exodus 14:4; 2 Peter 1:10–11

When the Lord told Moses to number the tribes, he specifically told him not to number the Levites. He set them apart as separate, directed them to encamp around the tabernacle, and declared that anyone else who came near must be put to death.

All males twenty years old and upward in the twelve civilian tribes were counted for the purpose of military conscription and arranged in a regimental square, with the tabernacle, surrounded by the Levites, in the center. From Judah at the head to Naphtali at the rear, they were ready to march off to war and seize the land of promise from the Canaanites. But when they were encamped, Levi and the tabernacle were at the hub.

The sons of Levi were numbered apart from the others for the purpose of service to the tabernacle rather than to the army. Their census was never mixed with the numbers of their brothers. Their count was by far the smallest, only twenty-two thousand, but their work was by far the most important. They were called out to be separate in every way, and placed at the very center of the nation's activity.

The men enlisted under martial banners totaled a little over six hundred thousand. Their job was crucial to the destiny of the nation. The relatively small band of raw recruits was to march against a far greater force of seasoned Canaanite soldiers. The census reveals how badly the Israelite armies were outnumbered as they clashed with the heathen hosts who occupied the land. Yet we find no recorded formula for the manufacture and use of weaponry, no directions for training soldiers, and no manual for making war.

The Levites numbered a mere twenty-two thousand. They got a clergy's exemption from military service. While their brothers were standing by for war, their job was to remain in the camp and serve the church. And God gave them a job description that consumes two long chapters filled with meticulous minutiae. Every move of the priests conducting the service was carefully choreographed. Every sacred relic was described in detail. Every task was precisely assigned, from the pounding of the tent pegs to the setting of the pillars. Every jot and tittle of the work of the church was set forth in exact particulars.

Why does the work of the church merit so much more attention to detail than the work of the armies? Why are we given such a fine description of our sacred obligations and a dearth of detail about our military service? Why so much about the altar and so little about the sword?

Perhaps the key to our understanding lies in the pattern of the encampment. The tabernacle is the center of attention. The war machine gathers at the perimeter, focused on the hub. The soldier's first general order is to stand before God and do his will.

We don't have to worry about our enemies. We don't have to be concerned about their strengths or their strategies. If we tend first to the business of the kingdom, God will lead us in our battles. Our task is to confirm our election and to ensure our entrance into the kingdom of our Lord Jesus Christ. If we are diligent in that work, our Lord assures us that we will never fall to our foes. If we seek first the kingdom of God and his righteousness, if we make him the hub of our lives, he promises that all other things will be added to us.

Caste Systems

Scripture: Numbers 3–4
Suggested Reading: Matthew 19:30; 20:25–25;
Philippians 4:11–13

One evening Mary Ann and I watched a television documentary about the caste system in India. We were appalled to see the untouchables cleaning public latrines with their bare hands, a duty handed down from generation to generation. The untouchables perform servile tasks for meager wages. They work in fields, clean the city streets and carry garbage under threat of harm from thugs employed by the upper classes. Although the Indian constitution now forbids such caste discrimination, its practice continues unabated, ignored by the government and condoned by the religious hierarchy. Children inherit their parents' duties and station in life.

I expressed gratitude that we do not live in such a society, that we and our children are upwardly mobile, free to develop our careers in accordance with our skill, ambition, and, as some would say, luck. But Mary Ann was quick to point out that our heritage is not entirely free from the caste mentality.

My father was limited by an eighth grade education and spent most of his adult life serving as the custodian of our large church. Before I went off to college, I assisted him by sweeping floors, mowing the lawn, shoveling the sidewalks, and dusting the pews on Saturday morning. After high school I went to college, earned a master's degree, and eventually established myself professionally in a distant city. When my father retired after about forty years of joyful service, the congregation honored him with a grand reception, which the whole family attended. As we sat in circles of chairs sipping punch and eating a fine cake baked especially for the occasion, the head elder came and sat beside me and after a brief bit of chit-chat, offered me the position of custodian at a salary substantially below what I was then earning. He not so subtly suggested that I had a duty to carry on my father's tradition, and that it wasn't really right for me to step out of the class into which I was born.

Mary Ann was similarly cast. Her father had a business in a neighboring city, so she didn't have a niche in the social hierarchy of the city in which they lived. Because she didn't fit into the circles of the youngsters whose parents owned businesses downtown or otherwise had status in the community, she lived her teen years on the fringe. Like me, she had to leave her hometown to "rise above" the class to which the locals had consigned her. We agreed that the people of our hometowns would forever limit us to the social status of our birth, and that a caste system, formal or informal, unfairly restricts the use of one's talents and ambitions.

But then we read of the caste system that God imposed on the Levites. The sons of Aaron were to be forever priests, while the sons of other Levites were to serve the sons of Aaron in the tabernacle, performing the more menial functions such as polishing the precious chalices and carrying the ashes from the altar. Sons inherited their fathers' duties and their station in life. The boy who hauled trash could not aspire to shining golden goblets or offering sacrifices, regardless of his hopes and dreams. God consigned them forever to the status of their birth.

How does this make any good spiritual sense? Simple. Getting ahead should not be our ambition. Jesus was a willing servant and commands us to be willing servants too. He wants us to step voluntarily into the lowest class and become untouchables for him. If we humbly submit our destiny to him, if we serve him willingly and heartily, without regard for class and status, as my father did, he will reward us with a measure of joy the upper crust can't imagine!

The Spirit of Jealousy?

Scripture: Numbers 5

Generally, when I meditate on a passage of scripture and apply it to my daily life, a blessing is not long in coming. When I sit and ponder the inferior size and inadequate weaponry of the Israelite army, for example, it doesn't take me long to understand that it is not our strength that wins our spiritual battles, but rather the army of angels surrounding us that wins our battles for us. I conclude that we can rest in the blessed assurance that God is our security system, and that in our weakness his strength shows. But when I try to contemplate the business of trial by ordeal as outlined in today's chapter, I wander down all sorts of trails of thought before coming to any spiritual enlightenment.

If the issue of fidelity would arise today in a Christian household, and if a similar trial by ordeal under the laws of Moses were still in effect, how might we update the procedure for determining the truth and visiting chastisement upon the offender?

First, to avoid any charge of sexism, I would reverse the roles. The spirit of jealousy would come upon the offended wife, who would charge her husband with a breach of faith. He would, of course, plead not guilty, and, in accordance with the law, she would escort him to the church where, for a small fee, the pastor would order the husband to declare his innocence and swallow a prescribed capsule. If he were blameless, the capsule would have the effect of an aphrodisiac, but if he were lying, the capsule would have the effect of a poison, rendering him impotent and afflicting him with a horrible genital disease. Absurd, you say. Well, so do I.

Nowhere else in the Bible do I find an example of such trial by ordeal. In certain other instances, God judged guilt and innocence without a trial. In the case of Ananias and Sapphria, for example, once they lied, God simply struck them dead.

Trial by ordeal is an ancient procedure once used for determining guilt or innocence when there was only suspicion and no evidence upon which to convict. The accused was subjected to some prescribed torment and God was expected to be the judge. In the Middle Ages a man accused of a crime might be tortured, and if the wound healed quickly he would be considered innocent, but if it became infected and the accused died, he was considered guilty.

The practice of trial by ordeal was abandoned long ago by civilized societies, I presume because as man became more refined, the less he relied on God to make judgments for him. I'm happy that we no longer practice that ancient form of justice. I've always wondered how many innocent people died from snakebites or oil burns because God declined to suspend the laws of nature so someone could be found innocent of the false charges made against him.

I'm happy that our system of justice requires proof of guilt, and I'm happy that we are finding new scientific ways of proving guilt and innocence. I'm more concerned about innocent people being wrongly punished than I am about the guilty going free. We are all guilty sinners who deserve the death penalty anyway, and in the end, God will do the judging.

But I still wonder why the Lord instituted trial by ordeal to test marital infidelity, but for no other crime. Could it be that he is a jealous God, and that faithfulness of his bride, the church, is very important to him?

And could it be that he reserves judgment on that matter solely to himself?

The Law Is the Law

Scripture: Numbers 6
Suggested Reading: Matthew 5:17–22

My father taught me never to lie under any circumstances.

As a child I loved to bait him by asking such questions as, "If a Nazi knocked on the door and asked if you had a little boy, wouldn't you lie to save my life?" I'll never forget his response, "Son, I'd let them kill me for refusing to answer, but I'd never lie. It's always a sin to lie. Bearing false witness is a violation of the Ten Commandments. The law is the law. Period."

In later years we sometimes talked about situation ethics, and occasionally we each had a hard time of it. "Killing in war is okay," he'd say, "because God gave the government the authority to order me to do it, and he ordered me to submit to my government. And God uses some nations to subdue others, all for his own purposes." But he struggled when I asked, "What if the government ordered you to lie?"

In my youth I tried to build a case for situation ethics, arguing that sometimes it was necessary to commit a lesser sin in order to prevent a greater one from happening. But I struggled when I recalled Daniel's faithfulness to God's law, and when I remembered Jesus' declaration against relaxing the law just a jot or an iota. Then confusion would set in when we remembered how Jesus defended his hungry disciples for doing a little harvesting on the Sabbath.

I never appreciated the notion that "the law is the law." Once as the corporal of the guard during military service, I appeared for inspection with mud spatters on the back of my pants leg. When the captain dressed me down, I explained that I had to walk on muddy paths from my barracks to headquarters and that I really couldn't help having those spots. He sternly dismissed me from my post with a reprimand, allowing no excuse for my "sloppy appearance."

Even worse was the time the policeman stopped me at dusk one evening for driving with just one headlight. I explained that both of them were working the evening before and that I was unaware of the malfunction. Merciless, he gave me a ticket and ordered me to appear at the police station within twenty-four hours with my light repaired in order to avoid a fine. The law, apparently, is the law.

My willful attempt to defend situation ethics suffers another setback when I read the sixth chapter of Numbers. Here people have the freedom to take Nazarite vows and voluntarily devote themselves to the service of the Lord. During the time of their devotion, they must remain pure, even to the extent of not coming near a dead body, even if the deceased is a member of the family. Proximity to a corpse renders them unclean. So far, so good. But even if someone dropped dead unexpectedly in their presence, the Nazarites still became defiled and had to purify themselves and start their vows over. The law was the law. Period. There were no exceptions for any reason. Just like the army and the police.

Where is the joy of the Lord in all this? Is there any moon glow in this valley?

Yes, there is. I've come full circle since my youth. I'm glad my God isn't flexible. I'm glad that he never changes. I'm glad that he is the same, yesterday, today, and forever. I'm glad that when he says something he means it, and that what he ordains *will* come to pass. I'm glad that the law is the law.

But I'm also glad that he understands my willfulness and offers to forgive.

The Bookkeeper

Scripture: Numbers 7

When I began my career, electric typewriters had just replaced manual ones. We stood amazed as that little ball with letters on it spun around so quickly to turn the keyed letter toward the page. On the fancier machines, built-in correction tape rendered erasures and white outs obsolete.

When I dictated briefs, Maggie, my secretary, typed them triple spaced, then I edited and changed the text by making notes in the margins and between the lines. Then she labored to retype the entire document on fresh paper. Sometimes she had to type it several times before I was satisfied with the final product. Even though she didn't complain, I knew that she wasn't thrilled to retype the entire brief over and over just because I wanted to make a few minor changes every time I reread it. Sometimes I think she believed I made the changes just to torment her.

Later in my career we replaced typewriters with word processors. Maggie's job became much easier when she had to type the brief only once and simply insert my changes into the text and press the button to reprint the edited document rather than to type it all over again.

I thought about her and those old days when I read this chapter about the offerings each tribe made to the Lord. If she read this chapter I know that she would empathize with the poor scribe who had to handwrite the same paragraph a dozen times over with some antique stylus, changing only the days and the names of the tribes and the leaders at the beginning and end of each paragraph.

How much easier his job would have been if he had had a word processor.

Why, I asked, since every tribe's offering was the same, didn't God just list all the silver plates and basins and gold dishes and sacrificial lambs just one time and state that each tribe brought an identical offering? Did he have no heart for the poor scribes who must have suffered severe writing cramps? And for the scribes in later years who had to copy all of the scriptures? Why all of this repetition?

Each of the tribes brought a valuable offering to the Lord. Even though their gifts were identical, God recorded them separately in the eternal scriptures to identify each of the givers with their contribution. Our God is a God of meticulous detail and deep concern for individuals. He doesn't lump the collective gifts of his children into one pile and issue a general proclamation of appreciation. Just as a bride sends notes to each of her wedding guests thanking them individually for their specific gifts, our God keeps a careful record of each person's contribution.

Our Sunday church bulletin records the number of people in attendance the prior week and specifies the total amount received in the offering. But in January the treasurer sends me, mainly for tax purposes, a statement of appreciation specifying the contributions I made over the past year. When I read it I get the feeling that God is thanking me. Not that I deserve his thanks since his generosity to me is far greater than I could ever repay, but that's just the kind of God he is. The book of Numbers teaches me that.

God's record books are accurate and detailed. On the debit side he has recorded every transgression and on the credit side every good deed. So I'm especially grateful for one book, the *Book of Life*, which records my name and his most generous gift to me, forgiveness of my debts and my inheritance in the kingdom of heaven!

This Little Light of Mine . . .

Scripture: Numbers 8:1–4
Suggested Reading: Exodus 25:31–40; Matthew 5:14–16; John 8:12;
Revelation 21:22–23

*M*iss DeVries taught us that little song way back in Sunday school kindergarten. We marched around the room pointing our little candle-fingers toward the sky and vowing to let our little lights shine all over our world and never to let Satan blow them out. It was a classic of the church ages ago, and yet today my grandchildren sing it with the very same motions we used. I have the song in my record library sung by a gospel quartet, and I also have it on a secular album by a Dixieland jazz group. Is the tune so good, or is God preserving its message for a particular reason?

God gave Moses very specific instructions for the forming of the lampstands. They were to be made of very ornate hammered gold with branches, flowers, and cups shaped like almonds. God was very particular about their shape. They had to be perfect. And when the lamps were lit, their light was to shine forth in the midst of the congregation as God's people marched through the darkness toward the land he had promised them.

I'm not sure that Jesus had Moses' lamps in mind when he told his disciples that they were the light of the world, but the metaphor works for me and teaches me a lot of things about how I'm supposed to let my light shine. For example, how should I appear to someone who comes into my beam? How can my witness be like hammered gold with finely wrought features?

Moses' lampstands were works of art, fashioned by craftsmen whose talents were gifts from God. Should the presentation of my witness be any less than all the art I can muster? I used a number of arts to make my way in the world for my own gain. Should I do any less for God's gain?

I also find it instructive that God used seven lamps, seven being the number of fullness. How brilliantly should my light shine? How many watts? Should I turn my switch up to maximum, letting my light shine at full beam? To do less would be hiding my light under a bushel.

Just what is the nature of my light? Is it a candle glow? An incandescent bulb? A fluorescent tube? A halogen lamp? Something newer and better yet? The light that I'm supposed to let shine from my lampstand is a much brighter light than that which pours from any lamp man can make. It is Jesus himself, the light of the world, the lamp that will illumine paradise for all eternity, the light that renders the sun obsolete.

God must have inspired the songwriter to pen that precious little tune. I memorized it at a point in my life further back than my memory goes. And when I hear little ones sing it in Sunday school today, the song, like the light it memorializes, seems eternal.

Jesus made me his lamp bearer. I am to shine the light of his glory everywhere I go, lighting the path and pointing the beam so others will know the way to the kingdom of heaven.

Along the way I can expect Satan to blow as hard as he possibly can to extinguish this little light of mine, but long ago I promised to let it shine until Jesus comes again. Although many times over the years I've allowed my light to grow dim, now is the time to renew the vow that with God's grace I'll let it shine, let it shine, let it shine, let it shine. . . . How about you?

. . . And Serve No More

Scripture: Numbers 8:5–26
Suggested Reading: Exodus 19:5–6

One of the goals I set for myself when I finished college was to work hard, get ahead, put away a respectable stash, and retire early. I was only a nominal Christian then and didn't give much thought to a life devoted to the Lord's service. I was very happy to let others do the work of the Levites while I went out to change the shape of the world. About thirty-five years later I met my goal and retired at the age of fifty-seven.

During those years of work, God shaped me. He melted me down, cooled me off, and hammered me into what he wanted me to become, sometimes against my wishes. Although I entered my profession intending to serve mostly myself, along the way God convinced me that he had chosen my path in life and that I was really serving him. I always knew that I was a spiritual child of Abraham, a sometimes wayward heir to the Promise, but I started out as a son of Simeon and ended up a son of Levi. And like the Levites, God blessed me with an early retirement, at least from the job that paid me a salary.

Sometimes we kid our clergy about their soft jobs and short hours. Anyone who was as little involved in the life of the church as I was in my twenties and thirties, might think that pastors only work one day a week and for just enough hours to preach a sermon and count the money. Only after I retired did I really begin to realize the amount of work our pastors really do.

During my years on the job, I worked an average of sixty hours a week. On a forty-hour job, I would have had to work more than fifty-two years, or until I was almost seventy-five, to get in the same total number of hours. So, I never felt I had to apologize for retiring at fifty-seven.

But our pastors work longer hours than I did. Early bird Bible studies at five in the morning. Breakfast meetings with trustees at seven. Staff meetings at nine. Visit the sick at ten. Counsel a distraught mother at one. Make an emergency run to the hospital at two. Comfort a grieving family at three. Counsel a pregnant teenager at four. Listen to the whining of a disgruntled parishioner at five. Meet with the worship committee at seven.

Then at home, when everyone else is in bed, start preparing Sunday's sermon. The next day throw in a wedding rehearsal, youth programs, a broken copy machine, an offended organist, an angry trustee, a treasurer who is pulling her hair out trying to meet budget, and a dozen other little things, and you begin to comprehend a little of what the pastor's life is like.

God knew all of this when he drafted the job descriptions for the priests and Levites who served in the temple. Maybe that is why he let them retire at fifty. He knew that the work of the church would demand twice the effort, time, and stress of a normal job, and that between the ages of twenty-five and fifty, a Levite would probably put in more hours than a person who worked until he was over seventy.

But just a minute. He has called us to be a nation of priests. On our secular jobs we are to view ourselves as working in his service, doing what he has called us to do, and doing it his way. Then after we punch out and go home, we are still priests, serving him in the church or in the kingdom as he calls us, not as trouble makers and critics, but ministering to the brethren in the tent of meeting, and . . . keeping the charge.

Divine Rain Checks

Scripture: Numbers 9:1–14
Suggested Reading: Exodus 34:6–7; 2 Peter 3:8–10

It was drizzling the day my dad took me to my first Detroit Tigers baseball game. We didn't have much money, and I knew that he and Mother had made significant sacrifices in order to buy the tickets. If the game were to be rained out, I didn't know if we could afford to come back.

Our heavy old black rubber raincoats dripped water into our shoes as we sat in the left field bleachers wondering whether or not we would get to see Hank Greenberg play ball that afternoon. Finally, after what seemed like hours, the man announced on the loudspeaker that the game had been postponed due to rain. What a letdown!

As we splashed through the puddles on our way back to the car, Dad comforted me with the fact that we still had our rain checks and could come back another day. When they issued the tickets, they issued rain checks right along with them, and they were good for the season. He showed them to me and tucked them into his pocket.

The expression "rain check" has spread from the ballpark and is used in a variety of settings, even when it isn't raining. When Mary Ann clips a coupon for a special bargain being offered for a "limited time" at the supermarket, and they run out of the sale item, the cashier offers her a "rain check" so she can come back when they get a new shipment and buy the item at the sale price even though the "limited time" had expired. And sometimes when friends invite us to some event, we decline by saying, "I'll take a rain check on that," even though it isn't raining. Once I invited our neighbors to go to church with us. They politely declined by saying, "Thanks, but we'll take a rain check on that." With a wink of understanding, we assured them that we would honor the rain check after the weather improved.

Had Abner Doubleday invented baseball before the Exodus, Moses might have told the unclean men who appealed their exclusion from the Passover not to worry because God had issued them rain checks for the feast. After a month had passed and they had performed the required purification rituals, they could come back and celebrate the Passover even though the "limited time" had expired.

I'm very thankful for God's rain checks. As a foolish young man I declined many invitations to attend the marriage feast of the Lamb. The Lord stood at the door of my heart and knocked, and I politely answered, "Thanks, but I'll take a rain check on that." I fully expected that at some day in the future, when the climate was better and I didn't have so many important and fun things to do, I would find my way to the feast. I tucked the rain check into my pocket, and for the time being went my self-indulgent way, hardly noticing the cloud of guilt hanging over my head. Then somewhere along the line I noticed that time was passing swiftly, that the season would someday end. Time might expire on me, and my rain check might not be valid.

We should all be thankful that our God is loving and patient, long suffering, slow to anger, and abundant in loving-kindness. We should be grateful that he wants us all to repent and that he wants none of us to perish. We should be thankful that when Jesus knocks on our heart's door and doesn't get a positive response that he will leave a rain check and that he will call again another day.

But we should also remember that the season will not last forever. Time will expire. The day of the Lord will come like a thief, and along with the rest of the elements, our rain check will be destroyed in the fire.

Learning to Ride

Scripture: Numbers 9:15–23
Suggested Reading: Exodus 40:38

When my daughter Kyle began the transition from the tricycle to the bicycle, I taught her the same way my dad taught me: by walking beside her and holding on to the back of the seat. If the bike began to lean too much one way, I would straighten it up, and if it veered too far off the path, I would guide it back again.

In time she began to pedal faster, and I had to run to keep up. My grip on the seat lightened as she became less dependant on my help. Finally one day she took off and left me puffing with exhaustion but beaming with pride as I watched her solo down the street and around the neighborhood.

In the early days she fell a few times and I had to pick her up, treat her wounds, dry her tears, and encourage her to try again, but in the end, she mastered the skill. Then I would watch inconspicuously from the window, and although she was out there alone, my spirit was with her, and in a way my hand was still on the seat of that bike, holding her up and keeping her on the right path.

As I watch her now, being a blessing to the world, practicing her profession, mothering her family, living in the will of the Lord and fulfilling her duty to serve in response to God's calling, I can still sense my hand in her life. And in a remote sense, I am still holding her up and keeping her on the right path just as the unseen hand of my father has remained with me throughout my life.

God has been a loving and caring father to the Israelites. When they began their transition from a life of slavery to a life of freedom, he taught them how to take their place in the world by walking beside them in a pillar of fire and smoke. He held them up very carefully, standing between them and their pursuers, opening the sea so they could pass through, providing water from the rock and food from the sky, and defeating their foes before them.

As a parent trains a child to face the challenges of life, God trained his child to face the challenge of becoming a nation called to live in his will and to fulfill his promise to be a blessing to the world. He walked very close with them at first, but as time passed he loosened his grip and emancipated them. When they fell, he picked them up, bound their wounds, and encouraged them to try again. Eventually he stepped back and let them go it alone, but from the windows of heaven he kept his eye on them, and throughout their history his unseen hand has pointed the way they should go.

Many new Christians have testified to the amazing presence of the Lord in their lives. They tell of moments when Satan attacked them, and the Lord's army of angels came to their defense. They tell of times in the spiritual desert when the Lord provided a sparkling spring of water to revive their thirsty souls. They tell of times when they veered from the path and felt his hand on them, showing them the way. They tell of times they fell and he picked them up, dried their tears, and encouraged them to go on.

My memories of being a new Christian are as cloudy as my memories of learning to ride a bicycle. I vaguely recall some of the traumatic moments of being wobbly on my wheels, but years ago God put me out there on my own with an assignment to learn his will and do his bidding. And now as I travel the path of life, I can still feel his grip on my shoulders, steering me in the direction he wants me to go and keeping me from falling.

Reveille

Scripture: Numbers 10:1–10
Suggested Reading: Joshua 6:1–20; Psalms 22:27–29;
Daniel 2:21; 4:17; John 19:8; Romans 13:1;

When I was in the army, some young soldier from the guard detail went every morning to the battalion headquarters, turned on the camp's public address system and played reveille on a phonograph record into a microphone to rouse the troops at the start of the new day. Now if the United States Army had followed God's instructions for sounding an alarm to rouse the troops, the manual would not have assigned the task to a member of the combat unit, but rather to the chaplain's office.

Isn't it fascinating that God assigned the priests, rather than the generals, to the duty of calling the soldiers to battle? Can you imagine in today's world the declaration of war being issued not by the government, but by the church?

In our political system, war is the province of the state, not of the church. Our founding fathers saw fit to separate the business of state from the business of the church because they wanted to prevent the government from meddling in God's affairs.

Today, however, the purpose of that separation has been twisted to try to prevent God from meddling in the affairs of state. Our courts have ruled against the Almighty.

Now I'm not going to get angry about that and march to Washington carrying a sign of protest. God hasn't called me to do that, and I'm sure God wouldn't want me to do that. The simple fact, whether the governments want to acknowledge it or not, is that God still has dominion over the nations, just as he had in Daniel's day and in Jesus' day. The Congress can pass bills, the president can make proclamations, and the courts can rule to the contrary, but those authorities can do nothing outside the will of our sovereign God.

Someday the whole world will remember how we won the battle of Jericho. God didn't send in the first division of archers followed by a battalion of slingers, a platoon of swordsmen, and a two-ton battering ram. He sent in the choir boys, the organist, the praise band, and buglers who blew the trumpets. Why? Simply to show the nations for all time who is in charge of the affairs of mankind.

People who take money to tell us how God accomplished his miracles have suggested that the steady rumble of six days of rhythmic marching weakened the walls of Jericho to the point that a few high frequency blasts of the trumpet would knock them over. But someday we'll all look back and confess that it was God who knocked down those walls, and for all of the centuries that have followed it has been God sitting on his unseen throne ruling over all petty tyrants, all savage dictators, all arrogant judges, and all bumptious lawmakers who have tried to legislate him out of business.

The trumpets that rouse soldiers and move armies to action are not the trumpets men have fashioned in factories and sold to governments. The laws that govern nations are not the laws that are passed by legislatures, signed by heads of state, and reviewed by courts. The trumpets that have moved all of history's great empires and the divine laws that have driven the destiny of man have all been fashioned in the fires of heaven.

And the final trumpet that will drive both the proud and humble to their knees to confess that he rules the kingdoms of men is the trumpet which God will blow to call his people to begin a new day, a day that will last forever.

The Trumpet of the Lord

Scripture: Review Numbers 10:1–10
Suggested Reading: Exodus 19:12–19; 20:18; 1 Corinthians 15:52;
1 Thessalonians 4:16

When that scratchy, tedious version of reveille reverberated through our barracks in the morning, we quickly jumped into our fatigue uniforms, and with boots still unlaced scrambled to assemble out front to meet our commander, who scanned the ranks and, if every soldier was in place, shouted to his commander, "Third platoon all present or accounted for, sir!" But if any soldier hadn't returned to camp after a night of carousing or was unable to get out of his bed, his report was, "One man AWOL, sir!"

After my tour of duty was over, I declared that I never again wanted to wake up to the blare of a brass horn, particularly one recorded on a warped vinyl disk and played too slowly over a crackly loudspeaker. When I got my first civilian job I bought a clock radio I could set to wake me up to the strains of some classical masterpiece being played clearly on our FM station. And not until I began to write these meditations did I give another thought to waking up in the morning to any sound other than the melodies of violins.

But as I searched the scriptures, I discovered that blasts from a horn do more than rouse soldiers from their groggy slumber and call them to assemble in the presence of their commander. When the Israelites set up camp below Mount Sinai, the Lord used a trumpet to call them to assemble at the foot of the mountain to meet their God. And it wasn't a recorded horn played over a public address system. It was a heavenly trumpet played by a heavenly being.

On the journey from Sinai to the Promised Land, God's people moved to the sound of the trumpet. The trumpet called them to assemble, the trumpet called them to break camp, the trumpet called them to march, the trumpet called them to war, and the trumpet called them to celebrate days of gladness.

But their lives were not filled with gladness. Had they served the Lord in happy obedience all the days of their lives, the Lord would have surrounded Israel with a hedge of protection from the empires that surged around them, but they failed and, as he had promised, he gave them up to their enemies. The Assyrians eventually captured the ten northern tribes and scattered the people over the face of the earth, not to be forgotten forever, but to suffer until God blows his heavenly trumpet and calls them to assemble once again in the land of promise to worship at his holy hill.

Now I repent of my wish never again to waken to the sound of the horn, because some day the trumpet of the Lord shall sound once more, calling believers to rise from their long slumber and assemble, not with shabby clothes, unlaced boots, and groggy minds, but in new and glorified bodies and radiant faces, ready to meet their God. Those who have spent their lives carousing will not hear that trumpet blast, but will remain asleep until they are called to account for themselves in the final judgment.

Can we sing that grand old hymn of the church with confidence? Can we testify to the world that . . .

> When the trumpet of the Lord shall sound
> and time shall be no more,
> When the morning breaks, eternal, bright and fair,
> When the saved of earth shall gather
> over on the other shore,
> When the roll is called up yonder . . .
>
> (James M. Black)

we'll be there, ready to meet our God?

Talent Scouts?

Scripture: Numbers 10:11–36
Suggested Reading: Judges 4:11; 1 Corinthians 3:5–10

Years ago when I was a young school teacher, an enterprising young fellow who taught in the room next door invited me to join the Junior Chamber of Commerce. Apparently he saw in me some virtue that warranted my membership in that worthy body, because when he invited me he said, "The organization surely can use a man with your talents." His praise was persuasive.

During our brief friendship as Jaycees, I returned the honor by inviting him to join the new and growing church that I attended. He was an excellent fundraiser, a gift that I believed warranted his membership in our needy congregation. When he declined, I was more disappointed for our church than I was for his soul. Soon thereafter he finished his master's degree and left town to launch a successful career as a leader in a major charitable organization. I never heard from him again.

We don't know why Moses asked his brother-in-law, Hobab the Midianite, to join the congregation of Israel. We do know that Hobab had talents that might be useful to the tribes as they navigated into dangerous territory. But did Moses need his talents when he had the pillar of fire and the presence of God to guide and protect them?

Did Moses suffer a lapse of faith, or did God inspire him to ask Hobab to join the pilgrimage to Canaan for practical reasons? Was Moses' praise of Hobab just sugarcoating to make the invitation attractive, or did Moses think he needed Hobab's skills? Did Moses invite him because was convinced the new nation needed Hobab's talents, or did Moses invite him so he could experience the blessing of adoption into the family of God? Since Hobab's descendants appear again later in Israel's history, some commentators guess that he must have accepted Moses' offer to cast his lot with the sons of Israel.

Now we know that the kingdom of God doesn't need our gifts in order to survive on this planet. And we know that we should never credit our skills and our labors for the successes that accrue to the church of Jesus Christ. As I've matured I've come to the realization that God doesn't need to exploit the talents of man in order to take the gospel to the ends of the earth. Without the persuasive jargon of a fundraiser to motivate me, I've felt the Spirit of God urge me to return to him a measure of the substance he's given me. I give, not because God needs my gift, but simply because it's required of me, and because he promised to bless me for it.

On the other hand, we know that God calls and equips people to serve him. We know that he is the giver of gifts and that he expects us to use the talents he's given us for the work of his kingdom. But does God use us as talent scouts to recruit players to his team?

I feel I was wrong in inviting my friend to church because I believed the church needed his skills. I believe I should have invited him simply because I was concerned for his soul and wanted to share with him the blessings of membership in the family of God. If God wanted to use his skill as a fundraiser, it would be the Spirit's business to motivate him to use his abilities for the increase of the kingdom and to give all the glory to God if the Lord blessed his work.

Unlike Moses and Hobab, I have no record of my friend ever accepting anybody's invitation to join the caravan marching to the promised land.

I hope I'll see him there.

How's the Food?

Scripture: Numbers 11:1–9
Suggested Reading: Psalms 78: 17–31

We're just not ready for this. For a year now God's people have been model citizens. Ever since the fiasco with the golden calf and subsequent bloody punishment by the Levites, they have been obedient to God and submissive to Moses' leadership. On at least a dozen occasions they unquestioningly obeyed the directives God had given their leader. What happened? What finally got their goat?

Now I'm not at all sure we want to place all the blame on the rabble. After all, the rabble had been there all along. The rabble's voice will not become the voice of the majority unless a substantial number of the majority side with them.

The rabble had to be pretty upset. For a year their voice had been nothing but a murmur. They were probably part of the rebellious voice that conned poor Aaron into making the golden calf and were fortunate to have escaped the swords of the Levites who avenged that evil, but in spite of that bloody warning, they rebelled again and again until the masses were finally swayed by their complaint.

What was the problem? Of course, it was the food. Food is one of the things we complain about the most when we're not eating in our own dining rooms.

When people come home after a hospital stay, the first thing they talk about is the food. When you go to a jail and talk with the inmates, the first thing they complain about is the food. Ask a soldier what he hates most about the army, and he is sure to say the food. Kids in school complain about the cafeteria food, and after a week at summer camp, what will the little campers complain about most? Of course, the food.

Now the manna could not have been all that bad. It could be prepared several different ways. Moses recalled it as tasty, especially if it were baked like a cake, in oil. The psalmist called it the grain of heaven and the bread of the angels. It was so good that it even became the metaphor to describe the Messiah, the Son of God. But only manna for a whole year? No variety?

I had a little taste of that once. I invited a group of people over to watch the football marathon on New Year's Day. The price of admission to my party was a contribution to the buffet table. My contribution was a massive heap of shrimp and the sauce for dipping.

But on New Year's Eve the Lord saw fit to bless us with more snow than all the plows in the county could handle, so Mary Ann and I were stuck with six football games and a mountain of costly shrimp all by ourselves. Before the Rose Bowl was over, I was feeding shrimp to the cat. After the Orange Bowl I was so sick of shrimp declared I would never eat another one again. So I can understand how the rabble felt about the bread of the angels after a whole year.

Now the cooks in the schools and the nutritionists in the hospitals are proud of their efforts. They work hard to provide tasty meals and are rightfully offended when people whine about the food. God made sure that the manna he made was tasty, so I can understand his anger when the rabble complained. In his righteous anger he punished them for their dissatisfaction. Oh, he gave them what they wanted all right, but he made sure it was bitter to the taste and made them sick unto death.

Is there a lesson here for us?

Take Your Burdens . . .

Scripture: Numbers 11:10–25, 31–35

Several years ago a young man in my church was called into the ministry. A powerfully persuasive evangelist had made a great impact on our kids and many made pledges to serve the Lord. The young man who received the call finished high school, completed college and seminary and became a pastor.

While he was in school he made several visits home and I had the opportunity to talk with him and give him words of encouragement. When he was in seminary we invited him to speak one Sunday morning, and in his message he thanked the people of the church for helping him. He declared that he was excited about going into the ministry, to stand in the pulpit and preach God's Word, to shepherd a flock, and to serve the needs of a congregation.

Several years later we learned that he had taken a leave of absence from the ministry and was working temporarily as a juvenile probation officer. When we contacted him he told us that he was suffering from pastoral burnout. He had worked hard to do a good job, but the pressures of the work drove him to seek escape.

Preaching to unhearing ears and serving a congregation of complaining and demanding ingrates had discouraged him to the point of wondering if he had truly received the call from God or if his brain had been addled by the fast talking evangelist. He said that he might have been better off had he chosen some other profession.

His family has since moved away, the friends of his youth no longer stay in touch with him, and no one knows where he is. So I don't know if he ever returned to the ministry or not, and I'm in no position to judge his motives or the merits of his call. But I will not join the chorus of voices who complain that we "wasted our money" helping him gain his education.

I've been around pastors long enough to know that theirs isn't always the happiest job in the world. They work hard on sermons only to be told that their words were not appreciated. They struggle thanklessly with the miseries of managing a church only to be criticized for doing it wrong. Conflicting forces within the congregation tear them apart. Their paychecks often reflect the ingratitude of the people they serve. I understand the torment and the disillusion that drove our young friend from his pulpit.

Moses suffered similar grief. God called him from a quiet pastoral life and heaped on him the daunting task of leading a horde of thankless slaves out of captivity and shaping them into a nation. There is no doubt about the authenticity of his call, and there is no doubt that God equipped him for his task. But it's easy to understand his reaction when those complaining ingrates turned on him. I'm sure he would have liked to take a permanent leave of absence from his calling and returned to the tranquil grazing lands of Midian.

But let's take our lesson from what happened next. He went to the Lord, and very honestly, without mincing any words, laid his burden at God's feet. Did God desert him? No, God listened to his pleas and helped him through his problem.

I don't know if our discouraged young friend followed Moses' example, but from Moses' experience I have learned what to do if I ever face such discouragement doing the work God's called me to do.

If we take our burdens to him, somehow he will provide relief.

Christ Divided?

Scripture: Numbers 11:26–30
Suggested Reading: Joel 2:28–30; Mark 9:38–41; Acts 2:1–4;
1 Corinthians 1:10–13; 1 John 4:1–3

Before I was able to conduct myself in accordance with the standards my parents had set for a young boy sitting in church, one of the family members used to stay home and take care of me on Sunday evening. During morning services they took the little ones to the nursery so we wouldn't disturb the sermon, but in the evening we stayed home.

One warm Sunday evening my grandfather, an elder in the church, took me for a walk while the others went to worship. A few blocks down the street we came near a Christian church of a different denomination which also held services on Sunday evening. We soon noticed that the doors of the church were open and the sermon was spilling out on to the street. Abruptly grandpa took my hand, turned around, and went back to the house. When my parents got home, he related the incident to them and assured them that I hadn't heard enough of "that drivel" to be hurt by it.

We were "of John Calvin," and the church down the street was "of John Calvin" too, but they differed on small points that no one alive today even remembers. Members of my church insisted on one point of doctrine while "those liberals" in the other Christian church took the same words of scripture to have a different meaning. That was my first taste of sectarianism.

And God forbid that a boy who was "of John Calvin" date a girl who was "of John Wesley" or "of Martin Luther." They called that unequal yoking together.

I'm grateful that the evil spirit of sectarianism isn't as rampant today. The mood of the era forced my parents to believe that if anyone's views differed from theirs in any way, we were to separate ourselves from them and not even listen to their thoughts lest we be tainted. Today our borders are much more elastic. We know that the Holy Spirit has been poured out upon all flesh. We are willing to accept the fact that reasonable people of good intent have had different experiences and therefore may see things differently.

Even Joshua and Moses had different notions about sectarianism. Joshua wanted Moses to issue a gag order to forbid the preaching of Eldad and Medad. But wise Moses tested the spirit of the men who were prophesying in the camp, found it to be of the Lord, and rather than viewing other Spirit-filled brothers as the competition, he viewed them as allies. Even Jesus' territorially minded disciples were so very full of themselves that they viewed as competition allies who were casting out demons in Christ's name. But Jesus set them straight with a few simple words, ". . . he that is not against us is for us."

In this ecumenical age we really don't need warnings against sectarianism. Competition between churches is pretty much limited to the basketball court or the softball field. John admonished us to accept the brother who confesses Jesus Christ as the Son of God incarnate. But in the same breath he warned us to be aware of the antichrist which does not confess the deity of our Lord.

Satan uses our willingness to accept as brothers those Christians whose doctrinal views vary from ours as a disguise to infiltrate Christ's church. So we must also remember that the words of Jesus might be easily restated, "he that is not for us is against us."

The Rules of Checkers

Scripture: Numbers 12:1–2
Suggested Reading: Revelation 17

Grandpa taught me how to play checkers. Away from the board he was a gentle man, but when contemplating his moves, he was merciless. "In checkers," he would say, "your only aim is to sweep across the board, get crowned king as often as you can, lure your opponent into a deadly trap, and devour him completely."

I learned well, but one day the age of checkers ended. Along with the checker board Grandpa had made with carefully cut slate squares, the Duncan Fife table moved from the corner of the living room into the attic and was replaced by . . . the television console.

Grandpa's favorite show was Perry Mason. He loved it when the world's cleverest lawyer lured the guilty witness into a deadly trap of logic, snapped the jaws, squeezed the truth out of him, and devoured him. The rules of checkers were the rules of the courtroom.

Grandpa didn't make up those rules. He learned them on his lunch break at the shop, and if he wanted to play the game, he had to live by the standards of competition that came naturally with the red and black disks.

I've since learned that the rules of checkers my grandpa taught me apply as well to most worldly endeavors, from taking a wife to making a living. You've got to wade into the fray, climb the proverbial ladder of success, blow away the adversary, and secure your prize. You've got to aspire to possess what the other person has or wants. If you succeed you'll be able to afford a big house with a two-car garage and a den to hold your television and all your trophies.

I've watched those rules of the game practiced by everyone from labor negotiators to insurance salesmen and politicians. The successful players squeezed money and rights from employers, lured clients away from the competition, and swept votes from the constituencies of opposing candidates. The object of the game of life is to use whatever strategy necessary to get all you can get. To deny that sad truth is to be monumentally naïve.

It's tragic enough that the strategies for winning at checkers are the same as the world's strategies for succeeding in life, but what's sadder yet is to see those strategies used for succeeding in the church. What began with Aaron and Miriam coveting the position Moses held continues in church government today. I've been there. I've watched it, and I've been a part of it: leaders of the laity competing with each other for higher positions, associates squeezing pastors out of their pulpits, and pastors trying to topple bishops. I don't know, but I've read that the politics of the Vatican are no different than the politics of the church in the valley by the wildwood. The same forces that drive business tycoons drive some deacons: ego, greed, and lust for power and recognition. In the world they are honest enough to call him the competitor, but in the church they call him brother and sweep him from the board.

The whore of Babylon is alive and well in the church. She began her abominations at the foot of the infamous tower, continued through the times of the patriarchs, the Levites, the rabbis, the apostles, the popes, and the reformers, and she will continue her evil fornications until the church becomes the *church* and those she seduced turn on her, devour her, and cast her into the everlasting fire.

Then finally all of God's people will wear a crown of righteousness.

Moses the Meek

Scripture: Numbers 12:3–16
Suggested Reading: Psalms 37:11; Matthew 5:5; Colossians 3:12

*B*ible commentators have written many chapters on this event. The focus of their thought ranges from Moses' marriage to Miriam's arrogance, to Aaron's weakness, to Moses' meekness and to God's intervention. The incident touches on both social and spiritual issues.

Since Miriam was the one God punished, she is considered by most to have been the main perpetrator of the attack on Moses, while Aaron is generally viewed as an accomplice.

Miriam's attitude toward Moses' Cushite wife has been used as a weapon against racism and segregation in our churches and to reconfirm that in Christ there is neither Jew nor Greek, male nor female, white or black. All confessing souls are seen as the same by our Lord.

Miriam's unwillingness to take a seat behind Moses has been used to teach us not to be arrogant about our baptism in the Spirit. If we sense a special touch from God or a particular calling, we should be humble about it, not parade it before the family of God, and certainly not use it to elevate ourselves above our Christian brothers and sisters.

Aaron's failure to defend Moses' special calling has been used to teach us to be openly submissive to the servants God has chosen to lead us, both secular and ecclesiastical, and not to project ourselves as their superiors or even their equals. And when other of the family of God speak unwarranted evil against the people he has put over us, we are to come to their defense in compassion, kindness, lowliness, meekness, and patience.

I'm grateful that God inspired some later editor to add the note about Moses being the meekest man on the face of the earth. Certainly the meekest of men would not even consider writing such a thing about himself. In he had, he couldn't have been very meek. No one who is truly submissive in every way to the will of God congratulates himself for it. But the point had to be made to confirm what I perceive to be the message here for me.

When Eldad and Medad began to prophesy in the Spirit, Moses took no offense. He was willing to share the presence of the Lord with others. When his own brother and sister openly challenged his spiritual leadership and made an overt incursion into the role to which God had appointed him exclusively, Moses had reason to rise up in his own defense. But he didn't.

Moses knew that if God had wanted him to share the leadership role with others, he somehow would have told him so. Just as God directed him to appoint the seventy elders, he might have told him to appoint his brother and sister to more significant roles in the hierarchy of authority. And, more importantly, he knew that if they were sinning against God by demanding a higher place, God would set the matter straight.

I am aware that God has appointed me to certain tasks in the kingdom and has denied me certain others. If he wants me to share the duties to which he has appointed me, somehow he will let me know. If others try to usurp the place to which God has appointed me, I'm confident that he will intervene.

But most importantly, I hope he has given me the grace and the meekness to know my place and to stay in it.

" . . . *Stronger Than We* . . . . "

Scripture: Numbers 13:1–31
Suggested Reading: Deuteronomy 1:1–25

I have often wondered how the Hebrews of the Exodus could be so blind about the presence of God in their lives. From the day Moses came back from Midian to the day they stood at Kedesh, God had maintained an awesome display of power over their foes and concern for their well-being.

They watched as he rained down plagues on the Egyptians, as he stood between them and their pursuers, opened the sea, drowned their enemy, spoke to Moses on the mountain, gave them water to drink, and manna to eat. How could people who had witnessed such divine control over their destinies now suddenly think that the God who had brought them this far would not continue to go before them into the land he had promised would be theirs? Yet, I'm inclined to be easier on them than God was.

The Bible contains sixty-six books and covers the entire history of God's creation from the first "Let there be . . . ." to the last blast of heaven's trumpets and the pronouncement, "Behold, I make all things new." We have the entire Word to give us a thorough understanding of who God is and what he plans to do with his creation. That band of escaped slaves had nothing but legend and the recent mighty acts of a powerful God on which to base their understanding. How did they know for sure that they could trust him?

True, they had seen divine things happen that we can only read about and accept by faith, but they had also seen evil spirits at work in ways we can only imagine. They witnessed the Egyptian priests mimic some of the plagues, and surely they had seen other "evidence" of the power of the gods of Egypt.

They also believed that the gods were territorial, and maybe thought that this new "I AM," although he had defeated the gods of Egypt, might not be strong enough to take on the many mighty gods of Canaan. After all, every nation had its gods who led them into battle and to whom they ascribed their victories. They were fearsome and savage gods who demanded awful sacrifices. And if they lost a battle, their fate might lie in the hands of a new and angrier god.

So, let's go back to Egypt. Maybe things have changed there now that Pharaoh is dead and his gods defeated. Maybe now they will respect us and our God. Life was good there before this new dynasty arose, and maybe the good old days will return and we can once again tend our sheep in Goshen rather than build cities. Besides, those giants in Canaan might kill us. Why take chances? After all, our God forgot us for several generations and maybe he'll forget us again.

At that point in history, they could make a lot of excuses for their faithlessness. Moses had faith because he had seen God face to face and had spoken to him man to man. The Spirit of God rested upon Joshua and Caleb, giving them the gift of faith far beyond the comprehension of their brother spies and the average citizens of Israel. How could the others know for sure that God would go before them and bring their enemies to submission?

But we have no such excuses. The Spirit of God has been poured out upon all flesh and his revelation to us is complete. We know there are no other gods except the gods we create for ourselves. We know that the name of Jesus gives us victory over evil. We know that our omnipotent God has already won our battles for us. We have no excuse for not girding up our loins and taking full possession of the wonderful land he has given us.

The Giant Weed

Scripture: Numbers 13:32–33
Suggested Reading: 2 Corinthians 12:1–10

When I started high school at the age of fourteen, the older boys taught us freshmen the art of smoking. During our lunch hour we would walk a block down from the school, turn the corner at the church, slip into a cove and light up. That habit lasted for four decades.

During those forty years I would never have confessed that my addiction was an impediment to a closer walk with God. I believed that I was walking the length and breadth of the promised land and fully enjoying its milk and honey. I was aware of other spiritual enemies lurking in the bushes, some of Satan's henchmen seeking to inhibit my spiritual growth, but I felt that smoking was nothing more than a harmless habit. And I enjoyed it.

Only in retrospect do I realize that a fraction of an ounce of tobacco, either wrapped in a paper or stuffed into a pipe, was really a Goliath that kept me from possessing the land as God wanted me to possess it. Over the years I sometimes forgot my briefcase or my wallet, but I never forgot my cigarettes or my pipe. I often forgot where I parked my car or where I put my keys, but I never forgot where I put my smokes. Sometimes I would call a recess in a meeting so I could go out and feed my habit. I always made sure that I was seated in the smoking section of the restaurant or the airplane. Anyone looking for me at a convention knew they could find me in the section where smoking was permitted.

Once when my son Cameron was a child we went canoeing on a pretty sporty river, and when our little boat capsized at a swift hairpin bend, I came to the surface and saw my tobacco pouch floating off in one direction and my son in another. For one brief horrible moment I couldn't decide which to rescue first. After I had secured Cam in my arms, I watched as the tobacco pouch disappeared in the white foam around the turn. When we docked at the end of the trip, the first thing on the agenda was to find a store that sold tobacco.

Thankfully the Lord has set me free from that bondage, and only as I recall such moments from the past do I realize how big an idol I had carved for myself. And though I haven't smoked for many years, I still smoke in my dreams, as if to be reminded by my deliverer that but for the strength he gives me day by day, I'm still a weak sinner who must keep a watchful eye out for the tempter. Though I've prayed for the dreams to end, God reminds me that some addictions last forever, and even though we stop bowing to an idol, we can't banish it to oblivion. It lurks in the shadows of our mind, taunting us and warning us that at any time it might appear again in our temple.

My habit was more important to me than things that rate a much higher priority. It was an idol, a giant in the land that mocked me and clouded my relationship with God. It was a master I served with more devotion than I had to the master whom I had pledged to love with all my heart. And I loved it more than I loved my wife and children.

God defeated that monster, but I can still hear it howling in the darkness. And with that howling comes the knowledge that I'm still dependent on God's grace, that in my weakness his power is made perfect. I decline to boast of either my frailties or my victories over them, but I will boast that I serve a Lord who can hold all giants at bay. And does.

Into This Land

Scripture: Numbers 14:1–4
Suggested Reading: Numbers 11:7–8; John 6

Our journey from the slavery of sin to the spiritual promised land is not a leisurely stroll through a lovely garden; it is a difficult climb over rocky terrain with a multitude of impediments. We may even complain and wonder why the Lord is leading us into this land because we perceive that the trip is dangerous and the benefits few. We may even long for the good old days that were filled with self-serving pleasures.

Perhaps the greatest impediment between us and the territory God wants us to possess is our fear of the giants that appear to inhabit the land. Now I'm not sure that the giants which the ten pessimistic spies reported to have seen were as much real as they were imagined. We aren't sure who the Nephilim or the sons of Anak were. Some commentators suggest that they may have been genetic freaks of nature, and still others surmise that they may have been descendants of Cain or even surviving remnants of a prehistoric subspecies. I think God purposely leaves their identity a mystery, because knowing who they are is the first step to our developing a strategy for dealing with them.

There are also unidentifiable giants in our spiritual promised land. As we die to self, cross the Jordan, and nail our lives to the cross of Christ, we can expect those spiritual giants to rise up and try to drive us from their territory. Satan's armies might attack us frontally, and his fearsome warriors, like Goliath of the Philistines, might taunt us and intimidate us, and try to force us to retreat to the wilderness.

Some of the giants we recognize, and perhaps two of the most recognizable are our fear of the unknown and our contentment with things as they are. We have our jobs and our homes. We are forgiven sinners who go to church most Sundays and even sing in the choir or usher one month out of the year. We bowl on Tuesdays, dine out with friends on Thursdays, and spend Saturdays with the children. We have our comfortable routine and don't want it changed.

If we listen to the words carefully, we should cringe when we sing Charles F. Weigle's song, "I would love to tell you what I think of Jesus, how I've found in him a friend so strong and true. *I would tell you how he changed my life completely . . . .*" Whoa! There's a red flag, the biggest giant yet. We dread the prospect of change.

If the Holy Spirit doesn't compel us to quit our jobs, sell our businesses and go to Mexico as missionaries, he might urge us to host a Bible study in our homes on Tuesday evening instead of bowling in the league. Then maybe cars will pull into our driveways and people will get out carrying Bibles! What will the neighbors think? And if anyone looks in the window and sees us sitting in a circle holding hands and praying, we'll become the laughing stock of the block. And heaven forbid that the Spirit might urge us to start a Bible study at the office on our lunch hour. Now there's a giant we don't want to face.

But God has told us we need not fear those giants. He has promised to protect us, give us courage, and fight our battles with us, assuring us of victory. He has shown us that we don't even have to put on ungainly armor, carry heavy weapons or devise strategies for defending ourselves. Like young David, all we need to do is hurl a small stone in the right direction and God will guide it to its target.

The Lord guarantees that the giant will fall!

If the Lord Delights in Us

Scripture: Numbers 14:5–9
Suggested Reading: Genesis 34:2–4,19; Deuteronomy 21:10–13;
Psalms 119:16,24,35,47,70,77; Proverbs 11:1,20; 12:22; 15:8

*I*n describing the word *delight*, the dictionary uses such terms as pleasure, gratification, joy, and enjoyment. The Bible uses the word in several different contexts.

The word is first used to describe Shechem's feelings for Dinah. Setting aside the abuse to which he may have subjected her, in the final analysis he delighted in her. She must have gratified him and given him pleasure and enjoyment. In Deuteronomy the word is again used in a sexual setting, suggesting that a man may delight in the affections of a woman. But if she does not respond to him in a way that brings him pleasure and satisfaction, he may not delight in her.

As I search my memory, I have heard of only one couple among my friends who have delighted in only each other all their lives. Back in the third grade, Doug sneaked up behind Shirley and planted a kiss on her cheek. She giggled, and ever since, they have loved only each other. Now they are great grandparents.

But most of my friends have dated a number of different people, and some have been married more than once. Although one person may have feelings for another that are not reciprocated, most of my friends tell me that delight is a two-way street. One person can hardly be delighted by another unless the other is delighted as well.

Love and delight are not synonymous. As many of us know, one can love and not be loved in return. There is no delight in such love. In fact, such love causes great anguish.

I find it very enlightening that the Holy Spirit inspired the writers of the Bible to use the word *delight* to describe the ideal relationship between us and our Lord. The psalmist tells us over and over again that we are to delight in the Word of God, and Solomon tells us that the Lord delights in people who are obedient to his Word. This is not the same as love. God can love us, but if we do not love him in return, he cannot be delighted in us.

The Lord uses the sexual metaphor to describe his relationship with us. It is he who calls us his bride and himself our groom. But I have known brides and grooms who did not delight in each other. One may have loved the other but may have suffered great pain for that love if there was no mutual delight. Sometimes such pain causes divorce, and sometimes brutality and murder.

God promised to love Israel and he held true to that promise. But as they stood at the gate of the Promised Land, they did not respond to God's love in a way that delighted him. Joshua and Caleb urged their brothers to return God's love, knowing that if they did, God would delight in them and give them the land flowing with milk and honey.

I know married couples who let Valentine's Day and anniversaries slip by without celebration. I thank God that Mary Ann and I celebrate our delight in each other by giving gifts and professing our love. We are truly grateful for that love. We are also grateful for God's love for us, and we try to return that love by our obedience.

And I think he delights in us, because he has given us a wonderful spiritual land to live in, a land flowing with milk and honey and abundant with the fruit of the Spirit.

The Power to Resist

Scripture: Numbers 14:10–23

It's a good thing that I wasn't the Israelite God tapped to lead the nation out of bondage and into the Promised Land. Had I been Moses the whole course of history would have changed because I'd have taken God up on his offer to disinherit the ungrateful mob and make me the son of promise. And sometimes I wonder if Moses might have yielded to that temptation had he known the misery that was to plague him for the next forty years.

But here is the humblessed and the wisest man to appear thus far on the pages of scripture. Does he realize what God has offered him? God has offered to relieve him of the awful responsibility that he never wanted in the first place, the responsibility of leading this mob of malcontents through the desert and the impossible task of shaping them into a functional nation. They've only been free for a brief time, and already they've challenged his leadership, rejected his directives, and told him that they want to go back to Egypt. We certainly couldn't fault him had he accepted God's offer.

But Moses was too wise for that. In bold humility he explained to God why it would be a bad idea to destroy the people he had redeemed from captivity and make him the father of a new nation, the nation of Moses. Moses reminded God that he had already developed a reputation among the surrounding nations as a God of power and might who had promised to be a just but loving and forgiving God. If he were to slay these people here in the wilderness, he would lose his standing among the nations. Humanly speaking, against that argument God had no chance. He relented and pardoned the people at Moses' request. But he also punished them.

I've often wondered if God really meant it when he made that offer or if he was just testing Moses to see if he was truly humble and obedient. And I wonder if he made the offer just as a warning to the people that they had better straighten up or they might face grave consequences. And I've also wondered what might have happened had Moses accepted the offer. Would God really have slain the whole nation and given Moses and his children the land that he had promised to Abraham? If he had, the whole wonderful metaphor of redemption and salvation would have been lost.

Personally, I doubt that God really meant it, and I'm certain that Moses never truly entertained the possibility, no matter how attractive. But none of that really matters. What does matter is that Moses did not yield to temptation. He knew his calling. If God is showing us anything here, he is showing us what power we can generate if we allow the Holy Spirit to take up residence in our hearts.

He showed us that power when Jesus rejected Satan's offer to rule the world. He showed us that power when Peter preached Christ to the Passover celebrants in Jerusalem. He showed us that power when Paul turned from his wicked ways to become the missionary without peer. He showed us that power when Stephen forgave the thugs who were hurling the fatal rocks at his head. He showed us that power when Joshua and Caleb urged their brothers to be bold and to march into the land God had promised them. And now he is showing us that power in Moses as he turned down the offer to retire and become the father of a great and mighty nation.

In our times he has shown us that power in the mighty works of Billy Graham and Mother Theresa. And as we gaze at the parade of saints, God is telling us that the same power can strengthen us to do the work he has called us to do.

A Different Spirit

Scripture: Numbers 14:24
Suggested Reading: Isaiah 62:3–5; Revelation 21:9–14

Our God is a God of beautiful metaphors, and I'm glad that the Holy Spirit inspired the prophets to envision our relationship with the Lord as that of a bride with her bridegroom. It is a metaphor that survives from the Exodus through eternity.

The church of my youth prescribed simple vows for a couple entering marriage. To the groom, the pastor said, "Do you promise that you will, with the gracious help of God, love, honor, and maintain her, live with her in the holy bonds of marriage according to God's ordinance, and never forsake her as long as you both shall live?"

And to the bride the pastor said, "Do you promise that you will, with the gracious help of God, love, honor, and obey him in all things lawful, live with him in the holy bonds of marriage according to God's ordinance, and never forsake him as long as you both shall live?" Back then they smiled and said, "I do."

Now I realize that in our human frailty, self-centeredness, and lack of desire to be submissive, we have abandoned some of the principles contained in those vows, but the very tenants we have rejected always were and always will be the cornerstone of our marriage with God. As his bride, we, the church, must promise to love, honor, and obey him and never forsake him. He corresponds by promising to love, honor, and maintain us, and never to forsake us.

For either the new bride or the redeemed church to keep those vows, a special Spirit that will sustain love, honor, and obedience over self-will must possess her soul. That Spirit will supply an unshakable conviction that God will always maintain his church and will never forsake her. When the Holy Spirit invigorates the relationship, the lovers will always delight in each other. There will be no fear of rejection or unfaithfulness, and they will live together in a restored paradise, a land flowing with milk and honey.

Of all the adults that Moses led from the bondage of Egypt, none but Joshua and Caleb possessed that Spirit. The others didn't love, honor and obey, and they certainly weren't faithful to God. He kept his vow to maintain them and preserve them as they wandered in the wilderness, but it was a relationship without fulfillment. They never set foot in the Promised Land, they never shared the delights of love with their Lord, and they never tasted the milk or the honey.

But Joshua and Caleb were another tale. They followed the Lord *fully*. They loved and honored their Lord. They were obedient. They had faith that the Lord would keep them and never forsake them. They believed in the Promised Land, and, as with Father Abraham, God reckoned it to them as righteousness, and as a reward they feasted on the milk and the honey of that good land.

I'm grateful that there is a promised land that we can inhabit, both in this world and in the next, and I'm grateful that God has shown us that land through the metaphors of scripture. But I'm mostly grateful that he has given us the Spirit to comprehend these great truths, the grace to submit obediently to his will, and the faith to accept without condition the wonderful promise that he will never leave us or forsake us.

With those vows spoken, our groom will lift the veil and kiss the bride, and we will delight in each other eternally!

Death in the Wilderness

Scripture: Numbers 14:25–38
Suggested Reading: Exodus 20:5–6; Numbers 14:2; Galatians 6:7

 haven't met anyone yet who has much sympathy for the faith-less Israelites whose bodies fell in the desert. When they said, "Would that we had died in the land of Egypt! Or would that we had died in this wilderness!" they passed sentence upon them-selves. Their tongues prophesied their own destiny.

They lost trust in the God who had revealed himself to them through many mighty works, and they lost the courage to live as children of promise. God judged them harshly and sentenced them to forty years of suffering, not only the hardships of no-madic life, but also plagues, diseases, hunger, internal dissent and military defeats.

But what about the children? Should they have to suffer for the sins of their parents?

God has always made it quite plain that we do not sin in a vacuum. Innocent people may suffer the effects of our evil deeds. Innocent children inherit diseased contracted by their sinful par-ents. Innocent people get cancer from second-hand smoke. Inno-cent people are injured by drunk drivers, thieves, rapists, and murderers. The innocent have always suffered as a result of the sins of others.

As children of Adam and Eve, we are all sinners, and the sin of any one of us affects the whole creation. And we can't blame it on God. There is no escape from the sad spiritual fact that we are reaping exactly what we sowed back in the Garden of Eden.

But God is not only just. He is also merciful. Although the children of the ungrateful Hebrews had to suffer for forty years in the wilderness until the last responsible adult dropped dead, in the end they led the new generation into the Promised Land. They could have gone in as children had their parents trusted the Lord to be faithful to his promises. But because their parents lost faith, they had to postpone their joy until the forty-year sentence was complete.

But this ugly fact of history has a beautiful application. The old sinful man whom the Lord has led from the bondage of sin is not fit to enter the spiritual promised land. Because by nature he is rebellious and faithless, he must die to self and be born again. He must become a second generation to himself, dead to the flesh but alive in the Spirit.

God reveals this wonderful truth not only in scripture, but also in nature. In the fall when I clean out the eaves trough for the last time, coil up the hoses and put the lawnmower away, some old, misguided wooly worm inches his way into my garage where the environment just is not conducive to his rebirth. When I touch him he curls up as if to play possum. So I pick him up, carry him to the abandoned woodpile out behind the garage, roll him into a crevice in the stack and tell him that if he has any sense at all he'll stay there until winter is over.

Then in the spring when I'm out raking up winter's debris, I look up and see a beautiful butterfly gliding past and dipping his wings as if to thank me and show me that he did have enough sense to stay put until God raised him up and made him a new creation.

The most amazing grace God can give us is the grace to let ourselves curl up and die in the wilderness of sin with the full expectation that he is faithful to raise us up and carry us on gossamer wings to the land he has prepared for us, the land that flows with milk and honey.

A Mighty Fortress

Scripture: Numbers 14:39–45
Suggested Reading: John 3:3; Galatians 2:20; Luke 18:22–30

Martin Luther's great hymn speaks pointedly to the ancient Israelites and to me. Our God, mighty in battle, crushed the Egyptians and the Amalekites and promised to destroy all of the enemies that possessed the land he had sworn to give them. And in my life, amid my flood of mortal ills, he is able to conquer addictions, obsessions, and any other foes that prevent me from fully possessing the kingdom of heaven. All victories are his and his alone.

But on that awful day at Hormah, the Israelites learned that when "we in our own strength confide, our striving would be losing." And without the "right man" on their side, they were struck down before their enemy.

When I tried to get God and my family to delight in me by overcoming my tobacco addiction all by myself, I fell flat on my face in embarrassing defeat. And it happened more than once. That enemy did not taste defeat until the Lord took up the battle. Then it fell like the famous walls of Jericho.

But the essence of Luther's inspiration lies in the last sentence of the song, "Let goods and kindred go, this mortal life also . . . ."

The key to possessing fully the kingdom of heaven is dying to self and being born again. As old sinners simply set free from the bondage of sin by the blood of Jesus Christ, we do not have the power within ourselves to conquer all the giants that seek to keep us from inhabiting the spiritual promised land. We have to camp for a time at the base of Sinai, studying the Word of God and learning how our Deliverer wants us to live. And those instructions for living righteously before God include being crucified with Christ, loosening our grip on earthly things, including our loved ones, and following Jesus in true and committed obedience.

I heard a story once about a man who squirmed in his pew all during a sermon on the necessity of letting goods and kindred go and loving God above all else. In a conference with his pastor he declared that he loved his wife so much that it would be impossible to put God before her. And he loved his children so much he would, without hesitation, die for them. Besides, he had worked hard for many years to build a fine home and fill it with all the things that made his wife and children happy. And he loved his work and his life, and how could he possibly be willing to sacrifice all that he loved so much and put God above it all? Sure, he loved the Lord, lived a good Christian life and served the church well, but his home and family was his first priority and he couldn't really understand how such a commitment couldn't please God.

Then one night he heard a persuasive evangelist preach a powerful sermon on the rich young ruler and the necessity of owning Christ as the one Rock on which to build his life, and of seeing goods and kindred as sand sifting through his hands. The Holy Spirit spoke to him, and he symbolically opened his hands, letting all the sand of his life filter through his fingers and fall into the hands of God.

The next day he met his pastor early in the morning and joyfully testified to him that he had finally put his love for God above all else, and had built his house upon the Rock. And now, having put all things in their rightful place, he was able to love his wife, his children, his home, and his work far more than he ever could before.

God is so good!

The Sovereignty of God

Scripture: Numbers 14
Suggested Reading: Deuteronomy 1:41–46

Every now and then, God uses some human act to remind us that he is a sovereign God and has every right, as the divine Potter, to use the vessels he has made as vessels for a glorious purpose or for menial use.

When Moses told the Israelites what their punishment would be for refusing to march at God's command, they were, to say the least, unhappy.

But why were they so unhappy? Were they unhappy because they realized that they had sinned against their faithful God? Or were they unhappy because they felt their punishment was harsher than their life would have been had they been obedient in the first place? Were they sorry for their sins, or sorry for their punishment?

I think they reconsidered their decision in view if its consequences and decided that it would have been a better choice to gird their loins for a foray into the land of promise.

I remember acting like the Israelites once when I was a child. I played in the basement one rainy morning, but at noon my mother came downstairs and told me that the rain had stopped and the sun had come out, so I could go outside and play with my friends.

But she ordered me first to help her pick up all the toys I had left strewn in the basement. Since I had left quite a mess, I whined that it was too much work, and didn't want to help her pick them up. She simply turned, went back upstairs, and said, "Okay, then you can't go outside."

After a few minutes I regretted my decision and went to her and offered to help her pick up the rest of the toys before going outside to play. She asked me why I had changed my mind, and I said, "Because I want to go outside."

"Sorry," she said, "too late. You made your choice."

I really wanted to go outside, and I knew that I wouldn't get out there until all the toys were picked up, so I went downstairs and quickly put the basement in order. Then I went up and told her that I had taken care of all the toys and was ready to go outside.

She looked at me again and said very crisply, "Sorry, too late. You made your choice. You're staying in for the rest of the day. Think about it."

I learned two things the hard way that day. First, that my mother was the boss and that I was not to toy with her. Second, that I had to be sorry for my waywardness, not just for its consequences.

I think the Israelites learned the same lesson, and they learned the hard way too. They learned that God was sovereign, and that when he ordered a march, their only response could be obedience.

They also learned that true repentance was being sorry for their sins rather than for the punishment their sins incurred. Their ultimate choice was not for God's pleasure, but for their own, a feeble effort to avoid a sentence already rendered.

God give us all the grace to be humbly submissive to his calling.

Tassels of Remembrance

Scripture: Numbers 15

Another thing I learned on that day of my incarceration and hard labor was that my mother was unflappable. Although I was crushed by her edict forcing me to spend the rest of that sunny day imprisoned in the house, she went on about her work as though nothing had happened, except that now she included me in her daily grind.

It was Monday, and as she prepared the clothes for washing, she handed me the old dull paring knife and assigned me to whittle the bar of Fels-Naptha soap and drop the shavings into the kettle of boiling laundry water. Then she had me sort the colored clothes from the whites and the linens from the cottons. Then I had to peel potatoes and snip beans for supper while she seared the meat and lit the oven. She calmly gave directions and seemed not to even notice my constant sobbing.

When the people of God refused his order to march into Canaan, God issued them a scathing punishment, then turned and continued his business as though nothing had happened, dictating to Moses the mundane, detailed instructions for preparing the sacrifices. As they sobbed and whimpered and mourned their forty-year sentence and the comrades who had fallen by the swords of the Canaanites, God was undeterred from the purpose of that first year out of Egypt, the business of making the rules for the nation to live by.

But was my mother totally oblivious to my devastation? Was God blind to his people's pain? Certainly not. A mother is keenly cognizant of her child's suffering, even though that suffering is self-inflicted. And God's heart ached because his people had to die in the desert rather than live in the land he had prepared for them. But God and Christian mothers are also just. And both had to teach their children a lesson.

So God educated his children, not only by going about his business as usual while they fumed and fretted about their fate, but also by instituting "tassels of remembrance" which they were to wear on the corners of their clothes to remind them of the commandments of the Lord.

Some devout Jews to this day wear tassels of remembrance on the corners of their clothes as reminders of this sad moment in their history and to remind them not to follow wantonly after the desires of their own heart and eyes.

Today on my antique shelf is a bar of Fels-Naptha soap, its wrapper yellow and brittle with age. Each time I look at it, it brings to memory the day of my obstinacy when I dared tell my mother I would not do as she directed me. It is my tassel of remembrance. Whenever I see it, I think not of those simple and quaint old days, but I think of the day of torture when I spent the morning sorting clothes, whittling soap, peeling potatoes and snipping beans while the sun shone brightly on my friends playing outside.

But then I see the picture of my mother on the table and I thank her for that tassel of remembrance that reminds me that God ordered me to conquer the enemies that inhabit the spiritual promised land that he has prepared for me. It reminds me that if I follow after my own heart and my own eyes, and fail to step out and challenge the giants of the land, he will deny me the privilege of citizenship in his kingdom of heaven, and will force me to spend the rest of my days in wilderness living.

Near to Himself

Scripture: Numbers 16:1–14
Suggested Reading: Psalms 84:10; 1 Corinthians 12;
Philippians 4:11–12

Sometimes I wish that God would give each of us, as a reward for decent living, a razor blade and allow us to excise from the scripture a few verses that perturb us, verses that smart, verses that cut a little too close to home. If God were to allow such a thing, I'd slice out the verses that chastise us for seeking upward mobility in this world, but I'd highlight in bright yellow the verses that encourage us to seek the higher gifts.

When we were children, the most common question adults would ask us was, "What are you going to be when you grow up?" Sometimes when I was feeling mischievous, I would answer, "garbage man" or "street sweeper" just to see them wrinkle their noses and look at me out of the corners of disbelieving eyes. But if I wanted to impress them, I would answer, "doctor" or better yet, "minister." Then they would give a nod or an approving smile. The desire for upward mobility was good. So we were encouraged to do well in school, go to college, and make something of ourselves.

Our society has often put limits on what people are permitted to achieve. In India the lines are clearly drawn and, until recently, generally accepted. People are born into a caste and stay there all their lives. In the past few years though, the lower caste has begun to rebel and has tried to escape the bonds of the oppressive system.

In our own country, we have put unwritten limits on what certain groups of people were allowed to become. Blacks could not become major league baseball players until Jackie Robinson broke the color barrier. Aspiring women today testify to the "glass ceiling" that prevents them from becoming top executives. We protest against such barriers. Godly people want everyone to have the right to be all that they can be.

So, why were Moses and God so upset when Korah desired the priesthood? All he did was to protest the ceiling that prevented him from achieving his aspirations. They had gone too far. Didn't he just desire the "higher gifts?" Wasn't the system discriminating against him because of his birth? Isn't that against the constitution? Wouldn't he win his case in an American court today? Wouldn't we all support his claim?

The problem, I believe, is not aspiration. The problem is discontent. It's not wrong to want to be all we can be, but it is wrong to be discontent with what God has called us to be. God called Korah and his sons to tend the ark of the covenant, the table, the lampstand, the altars and the vessels of the sanctuary. He didn't call them to be priests. If God had called Korah to be a priest, it would have been wrong for him to want to tend the ark.

God called my father and equipped him to be the custodian of the church, not a doctor, a minister, a lawyer, or a street sweeper. He was content to serve the Lord in that capacity. No, he was more than content, he was happy, because for him there was more joy in being a doorkeeper in the house of the Lord than in being a "high muckety muck" in the world. He felt honored that the Lord had separated him from the congregation and had brought him near to himself to do service in the tabernacle and to minister to the congregation.

So when we aspire to be something, let's aspire to become all the Lord wants us to become, and if we seek his will, he will draw us near to himself, and there is greater contentment in that than in dwelling in the tents of greatness.

Angry with All?

Scripture: Numbers 16:15–24
Suggested Reading: Genesis 18:23; Matthew 25:31–33;
James 1:2–3

If I were God, I'd do things differently. I surely wouldn't give all the sinful and worldly people all the blessings he gives them. I see a lot of people who don't care at all for God, yet he pours out for them such an abundant measure of joy, health, and success that many of the righteous are tempted to covetousness.

On the other hand, I watch as many God-fearing saints labor under awful burdens, struggling painfully against poverty and disease while some mellifluous preacher murmurs, "The rain must fall on the just and unjust alike."

Now I'm far from the first to question God's apparently arbitrary treatment of the just and the unjust. Far greater folks than I have challenged him on that point.

Abraham pointed an accusing finger at the almighty when he threatened to destroy the entire population of Sodom for the sins of some. And Moses incredulously asked, ". . . shall one man sin and wilt thou be angry with the whole congregation?" Our human comprehension of fairness just doesn't allow a righteous God to treat good people badly.

But then I think about it and conclude that the world is far better off that I am not God, because if earthly blessings were to accrue only to believers and burdens befall only the heathen, there would be such a run on righteousness that the churches couldn't handle the crowds. Then there would be no hurting brother or sister for me to help and no unchurched neighbor to invite to worship, and missionaries would have no purpose. With everyone investing their lives in some religious scheme that paid great dividends, the whole world would go topsy-turvy. So, I guess I'll just let God go on being God and do my best to stick to the work he has assigned me to do.

I find comfort in the fact that eventually he will see things my way. In the end he will separate the sheep from the goats and give all people the rewards they have earned. But until then he wants me to see things his way and live the way he wants me to live.

We've read Matthew 25 enough to know what he expects of us. He has allowed Satan to afflict some members of the family of God, but he's spread out an abundance of blessings among other brothers and sisters so those who are blessed may serve those who suffer. He's permitted needs to exist in his church and in his world, and he has endowed his saints with gifts enough to meet those needs. He's called each of us to a service, whether it is to visit the lonely, tend the sick, sing in the choir, serve the coffee, go to committee meetings, or teach the Word.

Nor let any of us judge hastily between good and evil, justice and injustice. The rain that falls on us all may be the rain that causes disastrous mudslides or the rain that makes flowers grow. The sun above may give us life or scorch our lawns and burn our skin. And often that which we judge to be evil is really good. The fire that rages in a forest, say the environmentalists, spares the forest from turning itself into a wilderness, and actually nourishes new growth.

God's inscrutable ways are best, and I'm glad he's given himself the job of separating the sheep from the goats, because in my blindness, I couldn't tell one from the other. And I just hope he gives me the grace to see his face in even the least of my brethren.

Like Father, Like Sons?

Scripture: Numbers 16:25–35
Suggested Reading: Psalms 42; 46; 84

*P*lease once again be tolerant of my frequent ramblings back to my childhood, but my early years greatly influenced what I have become as a senior citizen.

I remember vividly the flannelgraph Mrs. Hooker made in Sunday school to illustrate the story of Korah, Dathan, and Abiram. The flat paper figures of the major characters stuck to the flannel background and faced each other as the confrontation unfolded. The perpetrators of the rebellion stood toe to toe with Moses while their friends, wives, and children stood grimly behind them.

Suddenly at Moses' command, the earth opened up and the evil men tumbled headlong into the deep crevice as their families watched in horror. I especially remember watching the children turning their backs and running from the gaping hole as their fathers fell, screaming, into the depths of Sheol. Then the hole slammed shut and the voices of the errant men were heard no more.

Like Moses and Aaron, Korah was a Levite. But only Aaron and his sons held the office of priest while other branches of the family of Levi served the tabernacle in other roles, from musicians to servants of the priests. Korah's sin was the sin of discontent; he wanted to elevate himself and others to the priestly roles that God had reserved for the sons of Aaron; for that he and his followers paid the ultimate price.

At dinner that Sunday noon, I performed the regular ritual of retelling the Sunday school story to my parents so they could be sure that I had listened to Mrs. Hooker rather than letting my mind wander to the ball yard or some other place it shouldn't be on the Lord's Day. Then as I went upstairs for the traditional Sunday afternoon nap, I began to wonder what Korah's sons did after they watched the earth swallow their father. Did they spend the rest of the day in agonizing and bewildering grief? Moses thought it best not to tell us.

We do know that when they grew up they followed Joshua into the Promised Land as Levites in the service of the Lord. When Joshua divided up the land, he assigned branches of the Levites, including the sons of Korah, to serve in the midst of the various tribes.

Would God visit the sins of the father upon the sons? Would the evil perpetrated by Korah place his descendants under the heavy hand of God's lingering punishment? Would these boys grow up to be rebels like their father? Would they live their lives in resentment toward God for his judgment of their father? Would they become enemies of the state and conspire to overthrow the order?

I waited for many years to have my questions answered. Recently a Bible study guide referred me to several psalms attributed to the sons of Korah, and it blessed me mightily to see how the cleansing power of God had worked in their hearts.

Their psalms attest that as they grew, they became keenly aware of the emptiness of separation from the Lord. They learned that they could rest on the bosom of a mighty God when they were afraid. And they professed that there are greater blessings in being servants in the house of God than in seeking the pleasures that Satan offers.

Thank God that he is willing to wash away the evils of the past and give us life anew, reborn from the lusts of the flesh into the joys of the spirit.

Human Shields

Scripture: Numbers 16:36–50
Suggested Reading: Romans 8:34; Hebrews 7:25; 1 John 2:1

As I read about the people in the Bible, I am repeatedly shocked that they could experience the terrible judgments of the Lord over and over again and still not repent and turn from their evil ways. From the Flood to the Tribulation, people stood and watched as the Lord poured out his wrath, then simply shrugged their shoulders and continued in their disobedience.

Now I've always considered our pastors to be special friends of God, people he has called to serve as his representatives. I have never viewed them as soldiers dug in at the front lines, warding off God's attacks against a horde of despicable sinners. But this episode in the life of Israel shows us a side of the priesthood we seldom notice.

When God punished Adam and Eve, they had no intercessor to stand up to the Judge and try to bargain their return to Paradise. And when God visited the earth in Noah's day and found it corrupt, there was no mediator there to beg God to withhold the torrents of water that destroyed the whole earth. Abraham started something when he dared come face to face with the Lord and bargain with him in an attempt to spare Sodom from the fierce fire of God's wrath.

So now Aaron, in the tradition of the bold intercessor, grabbed his censer and raced out to the congregation where people were collapsing in waves, and he stood as a human shield between the plague and the people who were still alive. And the plague was stopped.

If I were a pastor I might sometimes see myself as Aaron. After preaching to deaf ears, enduring abuse at committee meetings, struggling vainly to save eroding marriages, counseling adulterers and addicts, and burying both saints and sinners, I might go to God and beg him to end the human carnage I see swirling around me. And when the nice people of my congregation come to me and commend me for my good work as a gentleman of the cloth, I'd like to look them in the eye and tell them what I really do for a living.

Sometimes we see Jesus as good old Parson Brown, teaching his disciples by the seashore, feeding hungry followers, touching the eyes of the blind and telling the lame to rise and walk. We see him in pictures breaking bread with his friends, holding children on his knee, and knocking gently at the door of our heart. We see him on the hillside considering the lilies and talking of treasures laid up in heaven. But we seldom see him as a priest in the tradition of Aaron, dressed for battle, standing between an angry God and a sea of sinners who deserve nothing better than to be cast alive into the pit.

While we murmur and complain, Jesus is defending us, wading into the fray and standing up to our accuser. While we daily offend our God by whining about our ailments, wanting more than he has given us, wallowing in discontent and going about our business as though the children of the world were not dying of hunger, abuse, and deprivation, Jesus is shielding us from the plague of God's justified wrath just as Aaron shielded the murmuring Israelites as the angel of death swept toward them.

And our good pastors are imitators of Christ, part of the nation of priests. We see them on Sunday morning serving communion, baptizing babies, and smiling graciously when we heap platitudes upon them as we exit the sanctuary. But we don't see them after they close the doors, hang up their robes, clutch their Bibles to their bosom, and fall on their knees between the living and the dead in a heroic effort to turn the tide of God's wrath from us sinners.

A Sign for the Rebels

Scripture: Numbers 17
Suggested Reading: Hebrews 5:4; 9:3–5; Revelation 11:19

Back in Aaron's day, the rod that budded had a pretty simple meaning. After Korah's rebellion and the plague that killed the people, God had to show the Israelites with certainty that he had picked Aaron to be their priest, and that only upon pain of death should one dare challenge that appointment.

Delegates from each of the brothers' houses were to bring their walking sticks into the tent of meeting, leave them till morning and come back to see what God had done to them. Lo, and behold, in the morning they found that Aaron's rod had budded and brought forth fruit while the rest of them remained bare sticks.

Aaron was indeed God's chosen priest, and now the rod was to remain in view of the people as a sign for the rebels that they were not to challenge the divine authority by challenging Aaron's exclusive right to the priesthood.

But God's signs have a way of growing into new meanings and far-reaching applications. God's confirmation of the priesthood of Aaron by the budding of his rod has grown into the confirmation of Christ's priesthood. The wooden cross on which Jesus was crucified has become an Aaron's rod, covered with the fresh buds of resurrection, and the church is the fruit that has grown from that stick of wood and has become the parish over which the Great High Priest presides.

Now I don't know how long Moses and Aaron expected that blooming staff to serve successfully as a sign for the rebels and stave off their rebellion. We hear of no murmurings as long as the people lived in comfort. But when they got a little thirsty at Meribah, again they sang their old song, "Why have you made us come up out of Egypt to bring us to this evil place?" Perhaps by this time Moses and Aaron had stashed that old rod into the ark of the covenant, out of the sight of the people, and they either forgot about it or its familiarity had deprived it of the value of its message.

The sign for the rebels abounds. Ornamental crosses grace the throats of ladies behind the counters at the malls and the models in the catalogs. Little gold crosses might dangle from the earlobes of men and raise the eyebrows of other men. White wooden crosses stand in neat rows in cemeteries and are pounded into the ground by the roadsides to remind us of death. Crosses scare away vampires in our horror movies. And crosses tower atop tall spires, signifying that the church below is still alive in the shadow of Calvary.

But do the rebels notice? In spite of the signs all around us, the headlines of our newspapers still blare out news of lust, depravity, greed, hate, and brutality. Unlike the crosses in the movies, the crosses we wear scare no one, especially the most evil among us. The cross has become a familiar trinket and a stage prop, and the people look at it and still murmur against God.

So, where is our moon? Where is there any ray of hope in a dark world so full of itself that it has become completely insensitive to the priest who stood between the living and the dead for it?

The blessing is this: the rod confirming the priesthood is still there. Though the box the Israelites carried has been lost, the presence it symbolized is at home in God's temple. And if we could peer inside, we'd see it teeming with beautiful blossoms and savory almonds!

Bearing the Iniquity

Scripture: Numbers 18
Suggested Reading: Isaiah 53:6; Daniel 7:14: Philippians 2:8–11;
1 Timothy 5:17–18;

As I mentioned before, my pastor once served on a committee that examined candidates for the ministry. In addition to noting such obvious factors as scholarship and other measurable abilities, the committee probes into intangibles such as the nature of God's calling and the level of the candidate's commitment to the Lord and to the work of the church. Often he anguishes over the prospect that he might have been party to excluding someone the Lord has genuinely called, or approving someone who was not fit.

He took very seriously his duty in connection with the priesthood, knowing that the wrath of God might descend upon the people he has ordained to be priests, that they might have to bear the burden of iniquity that God finds in the sanctuary.

As I noted a few days ago, the priesthood is a burdensome office. Not only do pastors bear the wrath of their congregations, as Aaron did, but also the wrath of God, as Aaron did. In addition, the sins of their congregations hang like millstones around their necks because they share the opinion that if they do their jobs well, their work will show it, and their congregations will be composed mainly of alabaster saints.

God paid his priests well. Although as a tribe they had no land to call their own, they were free to eat well, dress well, and accumulate wealth from the tithes the people brought to God.

If we take God's Word to heart, we should feel the sting of remorse when our pastors go to the bank to cash a pittance of a pay-check. Whenever I review the church budget for the upcoming year, I cringe at what the finance committee is willing, or able, to pay the preacher. Most of them, it seems, take generous salaries from their employers or substantial profits from their businesses. I know because I've been in their homes, I've seen their cars, and I've seen the clothes they wear. Some of them spend as much on their golf clubs and their annual country club memberships as their pastor spends on his car. And they're half as educated and work half as hard.

Yes, God paid his Levitical priests well as compensation for the grief and iniquity they had to bear, and his Word strongly suggests that we do the same. So, instead of "muzzling the ox at the threshing floor," we should go and do likewise.

Jesus, our great High Priest, also bore many burdens. While he walked this earth, the Pharisees constantly reviled him. Even one of his own plotted against him. In the end, the elders of his church subjected him to torture and killed him.

But that was only the beginning of what he bore. The priests of Moses' day had to bear only the iniquity connected with the priesthood and the sanctuary, but Jesus bore the iniquity of us all. When God poured out his wrath against all of the sin ever committed by the human race, he poured it out on the one priest he had ordained from eternity past, the priest of whom all other priesthood is but a shadow.

And for all of the grief he suffered, did God pay him well? Oh yes! Because he obediently bore the sins of mankind on the cross, he earned his reward: the right to be the king of the universe forever. He will have his robe, his crown, his throne and his scepter, and every knee shall bow in humility to him. The angels will shout and a great feast will be prepared to welcome him into his kingdom. And if we've let him bear our iniquity, we'll be there too!

Serious Soap

Scripture: Numbers 19
Suggested Reading: Isaiah 53; Hebrews 9:11–14

Acomedian once began his routine by saying, "My mother always told me not to play with dead animals." He explained, amid laughs, that he grew up poor and had few toys. Dead cats, rabbits, and other road kill often served as bases for a ball game, or even as Frisbees if they were flat and stiff enough. If he admitted playing with dead animals, his mother bathed him from head to toe with the same kind of serious soap she used to launder soiled clothes. So he did his best to keep his disobedience a secret, though odors sometimes gave him away.

Sometimes I have to touch dead animals. Though I have no extraordinary fetish against it, I feel compelled to wash my hands afterward, as though to wash off the taint of death. I enjoy petting animals when they are alive, but a mild repulsion grips me once they've died, and I'm reluctant to touch them.

Sometimes birds fly into the glass windows of our sun porch. If they are alive, I take them in and nurse them, hoping they will get well. But if the crash kills them, I pick them up with a stick and a shovel and bury them out back without touching them.

I've had to bury house pets that I've stroked and cuddled while they were alive, but once they died, I tried to avoid touching them. And if I did, I was careful to wash my hands afterward. And I've never touched a dead person. I've seen others stroke the hands or even kiss the brows of loved ones lying in a casket at the funeral home, but I've never been able to do that.

Maybe my repugnance stems from the fact that from my earliest childhood to the day I left home, my father read aloud a daily chapter of scripture, from Genesis to Revelation and around again. Maybe my subconscious stored up all those all those prohibitions that God piled on the Israelites about touching dead bodies. And maybe I took to heart, as did the comedian's mother, the need to be cleansed from the defilement that resulted.

Some suggest that many of the rules God laid down, he did for hygienic purposes; the Israelites had little education on the subject while they were in Egypt. It is certainly wise to avoid touching things that may carry disease, and it is a healthy thing to bathe after getting dirty, especially if the dirt may contain germs. But how does killing a perfectly good heifer cleanse one from the impurity of death? Could it be that God's intent was to set them to thinking about another kind of death, another kind of contamination, and another kind of cleansing?

It would have taken an awfully perceptive Israelite to make the mental leap from hygienic defilement to moral defilement, and from animal sacrifice to the perfect sacrifice to come. In fact, I believe that such a leap is beyond the mind of man. That is why the Holy Spirit had to inspire a prophet such as Isaiah to conceive of a Lamb of God that could take away the sin of the world, and a theologian such as the author of Hebrews to connect lambs and heifers to Jesus Christ and to express those ideas in ways we could understand.

Unless we hide in our houses, we come into touch with moral decay every day. And since it is contagious, we can hardly help being contaminated by it. But, thank God, Jesus has secured for us the eternal redemption, and once plunged into his cleansing fountain, we are purified forever!

Perfect Obedience

Scripture: Numbers 20:1–13
Suggested Reading: Deuteronomy 34:1–8; Psalms 106:32–33;
Matthew 17:1–8; 1 Peter 2:22

When I was young and rebellious, I didn't like God a lot. After all, any God who would punish a giant of faith as severely as he punished Moses surely didn't deserve a lot of praise and worship.

What, really, did Moses do that was so bad? He was in grief over the loss of his sister, Miriam, and that mob of miscreants was testing his patience again by whining just as their fathers had done. He was old, tired, and exasperated. So, he made one little mistake. Couldn't a loving God forgive him for that and reward him for forty years of faithful service by letting him lead the new generation of Israelites into the Promised Land?

Bible expositors have thoroughly analyzed Moses' sin. He hit the rock instead of speaking to it as God had commanded him to do. He desperately needed credibility with the people, so he and Aaron took credit for the flow of water rather than pass the glory up to the God who provided the miracle.

He made an error in judgment, and although everything he had endured for the past forty years seemingly earned him the right to ride at the head of the column as it marched into Canaan, his punishment was to have the door of the Promised Land slammed shut in his face. As the multitude of sinners he had tolerated for a generation prepared to claim their inheritance, he was denied his share. He stood atop Mount Pisgah and surveyed the land from which he was alienated. Then he died, and God buried him in a secret place.

What was his eternal fate? Did he go to heaven? Surely God would not forbid his entrance into heaven! And praise God, we learn from Matthew that Moses not only went to heaven, but also that he did get to tread on the promised sod after all, in the company of the prophet Elijah when together they met Jesus and his friends on the Mount of Transfiguration!

His fate was better than it would have been had he not sinned. Instead of fighting more battles with both the pagans and his own people, and struggling to divide the land among the thankless and greedy tribes, he got to retire, to sit in the throne room of God and watch from the portals of heaven as future generations of Israelites suffered the fate they earned. But best of all, God let him in on the big secret, the mystery hidden for ages, the mystery of the salvation he had promised to Abraham. And from the lofty heights of paradise, he got to sit and watch the patterns of that gracious plan unfold.

Still, the question remains, is perfection one of God's requirements for the man who is to lead the people into the Promised Land? The answer, of course, is a clear and resounding *yes!*

And when we switch our metaphorical gears and see Israel become the church and see the sinless Son of God, the Lamb without blemish, the second Joshua, leading his body of redeemed sinners through the Jordan and upward to the New Jerusalem, we understand why God said to Moses, "You shall not bring this assembly into the land which I have given them." Moses' disobedience disqualified him to serve as a model for the Messiah. As the righteous judge, God required a sinless sacrifice to atone for the sin of the world, and by living a spotless life, Jesus met God's demand for perfection and also earned him the right to usher the church into paradise.

A Greater Strictness

Scripture: Review Numbers 20:1–13
Suggested Reading: Review Exodus 3–4; Leviticus 10:10–11;
Deuteronomy 4:1; Matthew 10:32–33; 22:14; Romans 9:17;
James 2:14–18; 3:1

*I*am a Bible teacher. I don't know if God in his sovereignty determined that I would be a Bible teacher, or if he offered me the opportunity and I voluntarily accepted. Should I go by my Calvinistic upbringing, I would have to believe that he predestined me to do what I do. But should I subscribe to the thoughts of Wesley, in whose church I now teach, I would believe that by his grace he inspired me, but gave me the choice to accept or decline.

When I get to heaven, one of the first things I'm going to do is get to the bottom of the mysteries of predestination and free will, of the difference between being called and being chosen. One thing is certain: our sovereign God has exercised his right as the Potter to determine the destiny of at least some of his clay pots. Pharaoh is the prime example. Clearly God appointed him to play his evil role in the drama of Israel.

And it also appears that under the same authority, God elected Moses and Aaron to lead the descendants of Jacob out of bondage and commissioned them to teach his people how they should live. He intentionally spared Moses' life and raised him in Pharaoh's court to prepare him for his role.

But within the confines of predetermined destiny, did Moses have the free will to make vital decisions? When he and Aaron went to the rock to bring water, did they have the choice of speaking to the rock or striking it? Did they have the option to obey or disobey? A good Calvinist would have no choice but to argue that God predisposed them to disobey for a divine purpose, but a Wesleyan might disagree. Someday we'll see clearly and understand the mysterious ways of God.

God ordained them to be teachers and held them to a higher standard of obedience than he holds others. Does he also hold me, a Bible teacher, to a higher standard than those members who fashion the church budget or set rules for the use of the building? The idea scares me. With how much greater strictness might he judge me?

God ordered Moses to *speak his word* to the rock so the rock would bring forth water and the people would know that the miracle came from the mouth of the Lord. But the angry and grief stricken teachers shouted to the mob, "Shall *we* bring forth water for you out of this rock?" By striking the rock, they robbed God of the credit he deserved and failed to honor him in the eyes of the people. And God either let them or made them do it.

If I take credit for an idea inspired in me by the Holy Spirit, if I fail to confess the works of Jesus before men, or it I fail to give God the honor and obedience I owe him, might I lose my inheritance in the kingdom of heaven as Moses lost his in Canaan?

Taught as I've been about the assurance of salvation as a gift that derives from faith rather than from works, I cannot be arrogant enough to presume that my conduct, especially as a teacher, is without consequence. Moses was a hero of faith, yet one lapse in his conduct cost him the privilege of entering the Promised Land.

Whether God has chosen me or I have chosen him, I pray that he doesn't let me make the same mistake or suffer the same punishment.

A Twice-Smitten Rock?

Scripture: Review Numbers 20:1–13
Suggested Reading: Exodus 17:1–7; Daniel 2:31–45; John 12:13;
1 Corinthians 10:1–4; Hebrews 9:25–28

At two separate turns in his life, Moses encountered a rock that yielded water. The first time, shortly after the escape from Egypt, God ordered him to smite the rock to secure the life-giving flow, but the second time, shortly before the Israelites' entrance into the Promised Land, God directed him only to speak to it. We all know the story by now. In anger, Moses struck the rock instead of speaking to it and God punished him by denying him entry into Canaan.

Why did God require Moses to strike the rock the first time and forbid it the second time? Was it necessary to strike the rock the first time? Why was God angry when he struck the rock at Meribah instead of simply speaking to it? Was it only because Moses disobeyed a direct order? Was it only because Moses denied God the glory of the miracle? Or does the episode have a larger implication?

Perhaps when we view the historical event as having a metaphorical meaning that defines our walk with Christ, we can gain some additional insight into the significance of Moses' action.

The Rock of our salvation makes two special appearances in our lives, once when we are liberated from the slavery of sin and begin our pilgrimage to the Promised Land, and once again as we stand at the edge of the wilderness and view our eternal home from this side of the border.

The first time we met our Rock, he had to be smitten; smitten just once as atonement for our sin. He had to be humiliated, whipped, spat upon, and nailed to the cross as the ultimate sacrifice for mankind's guilt. And once smitten, the living water began to flow.

But the second time he appears, there can be no smiting. The second time he comes, he comes not to deal with sin, but he comes in glory to claim those who eagerly await his return. The second time he comes, he brings living water just for the asking—there is no more need for stripes, nails, or blood. And the second time he comes, he comes in power and might to establish a sovereign eternal kingdom that will crush all other governments, which will fill the entire earth and never be destroyed.

Having been born in sin, we are all guilty of Christ's blood. When he went to the cross, we all shouted, "Crucify him! Crucify him!" and we all pounded the nails in his hands and his feet. But once redeemed, we trade the hammer for the palm branch. When we ride with him we are reborn into a new, Spirit-filled life. We become his disciples and are on speaking terms with him.

But if we reject his flow of living water and live in disobedience, we continue to smite the Rock of our salvation, and, as Moses, we too will earn the wrath of God. What will then be our punishment? God makes that clear also: just as he denied Moses entry into the Promised Land, he will deny us entry into glory.

But if we are obedient, if we eagerly await his return with palm branches in our hands rather than hammers and nails, and if we shout, "Hosanna! Blessed is he who comes in the name of the Lord, even the King of Israel!" instead of shouting, "Crucify him! Crucify him!" he will pick us up in his hand and carry us to the Promised Land where we will enjoy an eternal flow of his living water!

... *Your Brother Israel*

Scripture: Numbers 20:14–21
Suggested Reading: Genesis 25:23; 27:38–40;
Genesis 33; 35:27–29; 36; Obadiah; Matthew 5:39

So far we have not witnessed a lot of brotherly love among the members of the patriarchal families. Abraham and his nephew Lot parted company over the use of the land. Jacob conned his brother Esau out of his birthright. Joseph's brothers sold him into slavery. And now the descendants of Esau, the Edomites, deny their cousins passage through their land, even though Moses gave them full assurance that they would cause no damage.

Their refusal is hard to understand. One of the major arteries of international trade, the King's Highway, passed directly through their territory, right up the Jordan valley. The road was their main livelihood, and the Edomites made a good living robbing, selling to, protecting, and collecting tolls from the caravans that passed through their country. So, why didn't they treat the Israelites as any other group of travelers?

Moses would happily have paid to use the road. And since the Israelites left Egypt wealthy, they certainly could have traded with the Edomites and bought provisions. The Edomites might have even permitted passage and ambushed the Israelites, stealing their wealth. That certainly would have given God another opportunity to rise up in defense of his people and bring distress to their attackers. There were many unused options.

When Jacob returned from Haran and reunited with his brother Esau after many years of separation, it seemed that they had made peace with each other. Jacob told Esau that he would follow him to Edom, but when Esau went on ahead, Jacob turned and went instead to Succoth. The only recorded time they met after that was when they met at Mamre to bury their father Isaac. Did latent animosity smolder for five hundred years and finally manifest itself at this moment in their troubled history?

The rebuff on the highway was only the beginning of a long legacy of feuding between the two nations. King David conquered the Edomites and used them as slaves in fulfillment of the Lord's promise to Rebekah, but many years later, during the reign of Jehoram of Judah, the Edomites revolted in fulfillment of Isaac's prophecy to Esau. From then on, the Edomites were always allies to Israel's enemies, a pattern that reached its zenith when Herod, an Edomite who was put into power as a puppet king by the Romans, sentenced Israel's Messiah to be crucified.

So why did this event occur as it did, and why did God see that it was recorded in the scriptures? Can it in some way be moonlight on our path as we pass through our valleys?

Perhaps the answer lies more in Israel's response than in Edom's offense. What were Moses' choices? He might have argued with the king of Edom for the privilege of passing through his territory, or, since the Israelites were equipped for battle, he might have even forced his way into their land, relying on God to intervene as he did with Pharaoh and the Amalekites. But he didn't. He simply turned away from him.

In the grand finale of it all, Edom has disappeared from human history without a trace, while Israel stands victorious with the Lamb on Mount Zion. So much for revenge. So much for turning the other cheek.

Defrocked

Scripture: Numbers 20:22–29
Suggested Reading: Exodus 39:1–31; John 19:23–24;
Hebrews 7:23–25

When members of our congregation die, we have funeral services to celebrate their lives. Often we sing their favorite hymns and quote their favorite scriptures, but the best part is when their friends stand and reminisce about special or humorous moments they shared together. We remember outstanding qualities and praise the deceased for their virtues, but never do we mention their bad qualities, or remember events that are better forgotten.

So, when we eulogize Aaron, we are going to say nothing about his blunders at Sinai or at Meribah, or criticize him for condemning Moses and trying to usurp some of his authority as a prophet of God. We are only going to mention the good things.

We will praise him for his faithfulness to Moses and his courage in standing before Pharaoh. We will remember how he stood meekly beside the altar and held his peace as God torched his reprobate sons before his eyes. We will remember how he stepped back as Korah, Dathan, and Abiram confronted him and Moses, and declared themselves to be of equal status. We will remember how, after the earth opened and swallowed the rebels, he strode bravely with his censer into the middle of the contentious congregation to make atonement for them and to purge them of the contagious plague that God had sent to consume them. And we will remember how his rod budded, confirming him and him alone as God's chosen High Priest.

Someone at the funeral is sure to mention how splendid he looked, all decked out in his priestly garb, and how magnificent was his wardrobe of finely woven blue and purple and scarlet fabric, of woven gold thread, and the twelve precious stones on the breastplate. And the mourners are sure to mention that those garments are very becoming on Aaron's son, Eleazar, and how proud he must be to follow in his father's footsteps.

And after the funeral is over and the mourners have gathered around the tables in the church parlor to drink coffee, eat cake, and chat, they may talk about his defrocking and shake their heads and declare that the punishment was unfair, that his sentence didn't fit his crime, and that God should have been more sympathetic to him. After all, he was in mourning for his sister and he had a right to be angry with the insensitive rabble that was harassing him.

The discussion among those who gather at one table might take a different direction from that at another table. They might say the same thing they say about pastors. Some might whisper that it was about time God made a change, and that a new and younger man might bring more energy and new ideas into the pulpit.

Then those of us some thousands of years removed, who have the benefit of hindsight, might look back and see another defrocking. We might see that Jesus, like Aaron, was also stripped of his garments and taken up a hill to die, and we might remember how Jesus bravely walked into the midst of the congregation of humans that were dying of the plague of sin, and made atonement for them and saved them from eternal death. We might allow that Aaron deserved his punishment because of his sin, but we would be sure to declare that Jesus was sinless and that it was our sins that brought him to that hilltop.

And certainly we will note the contrast that when Aaron went up Mount Hor, he lost his temporal title, but while dying on Mount Calvary, Jesus earned his eternal priesthood!

Waterloo

Scripture: Numbers 21:1–3
Suggested Reading: Numbers 14:39–45

Years ago an old country song had us crooning, "Where will you . . . meet your Waterloo . . .?" That song, reflecting on Napoleon's famous defeat, suggests that someday we'll all meet our match and limp home a loser. If I were ever to write such a song, I'd write it about Hormah rather than Waterloo.

My Waterloo, or rather my Hormah, was tobacco. I got hooked when I was fourteen when smoking cigarettes was the thing that separated the brave from the cowardly.

For the first twenty years it was cigarettes, but when I decided that a responsible father ought to set a good example for his son, I switched to a more refined form of self-abuse, the pipe, with the expectation that one day I would quit entirely. In the next twenty years, I must have burned out a hundred pipes and burned up five hundred pounds of tobacco. Although I no longer smoke, I have several shelves of tobacco cans that I use for storing everything from nails to mole pellets and all the other small things a man keeps in his workshop.

Over the years I tried to quit several times, usually on a birthday. Once, on the night before my fortieth birthday, I sat up late and smoked my pipes "for the very last time." Before finally going to bed with a sore tongue, I put on my boots, trudged through the snow to the barn out back and safely deposited my pipe collection and my can of tobacco in a cabinet next to my workbench.

On my birthday the next morning I got up, showered, poured a cup of coffee, took a few sips, and, missing my smoke horribly, put on my boots and trudged through the snow back to the barn to retrieve my pipes and tobacco. As I sat there sipping and puffing, I confessed that in my own strength I couldn't quit. I had met my Waterloo.

Then one December 7, several years later when other Americans of my vintage were remembering our country's great defeat at Pearl Harbor, I visited an acupuncture clinic that advertised a sure cure for smoking. I was apprehensive because I was sure the treatment would fail, and I also discovered that a part of me didn't really want to quit. My pipe had become both my best friend and my worst enemy. I believed that it gave me great comfort and satisfaction as I fought the stresses of life, yet I knew it threatened to kill me.

As I stretched out comfortably on the cot and the Oriental doctor painlessly slipped little needles under the top layer of skin on my hands and feet, I was suddenly caught up in the feeling of being crucified, and I sensed an extraordinary closeness to Jesus. Then I realized that I was not fighting the addiction alone. The Lord was there with me. I felt I was being crucified with him, and the evil that had possessed me for forty years was being transferred from my cross to his. By his stripes I was healed. My worst enemy had died and I had a new best friend.

Many years have passed since I left that clinic, and I have not had the slightest urge to smoke since that memorable December 7. But it was the Lord, not the acupuncture, that won the battle for me. Like the soldiers of Israel at their first Hormah, I had presumed to go into battle by myself and leave God safely back in the home camp. But without him I experienced only defeat. Tobacco was my invincible enemy until the Lord joined the battle.

Now on December 7 we don't remember Pearl Harbor or Waterloo, we celebrate our final victory at Hormah together.

A Snake on a Stick

Scripture: Numbers 21:4–9
Suggested Reading: 2 Kings 8:1–4; John 3:1–15; 2 Corinthians 5:21

Those awful people are at it again, whining in the wilderness about their "worthless" food! Why couldn't they be content with the bread God sent them from heaven?

But who am I to criticize them? I who enjoy watching the snow fall while lounging next to a warm fireplace and looking through a big picture window? I who have more delicious food stored in my pantry than ten people need? No, I'll leave the judging to God, as I should.

And he did judge them, very harshly . . . again. This time he infested their camp with swarms of deadly venomous snakes, and, of course, the people repented . . . again. They had repented often, but this time repentance wasn't enough to rid them of the plague of fiery serpents.

Now God could have done a million different things to heal them and teach them a lesson. He could have had Moses whip up a batch of paste made of manna from the sky and water from the rock to rub on their snakebites as a healing balm. That would have been a wonderful lesson for them and for us.

But God had a different idea. He ordered Moses to fashion a bronze snake and hoist it up in a stick. What a strange thing to do. A brass image of a snake must have rekindled memories of Egypt, where their pagan taskmasters worshipped such things. And worse than that, Moses must have taught them that back in the Garden of Eden, Satan took the form of a serpent and tempted Eve to take a bite of the forbidden fruit. A serpent was the very essence of all that was evil. Yet when the people looked upon it, they were healed!

From that day on, the Israelites worshipped the snake on the stick. They even burned incense to it. Good King Hezekiah might have thought he destroyed all traces of the idol when he broke it to pieces, but somehow the thing survived, and yet today its image graces the cornerstones of our hospitals and gleams on the brass insignia worn by military medics.

The Israelites, of course, had no idea that the serpent Moses set on a stick signified the healing that was to come, the ultimate antidote for the serpent's deadly venom. And I doubt most members of the medical profession or the military really know the true meaning of their emblem, since neither acknowledge the crucified Christ as the real remedy for what ails the human race.

How can a snake on a stick possibly symbolize the healing work of Jesus? We know that Jesus told Nicodemus that he had to be lifted up just as Moses lifted up the snake in the wilderness. Now I don't know if that teacher in Israel understood what Jesus was saying, since this teacher in America understands only because Paul told the Christians in Corinth that Jesus *became* sin for them.

When he was lifted up on the cross, Jesus absorbed all of the world's sin. All of the venom that the fangs of the serpent ever injected into the heart of humankind entered into the being of our Savior, and he became the embodiment of all that is evil. And when he died, sin died with him.

Now when I see the snake coiled around the stick on the sign at the medical clinic, I remember that Jesus is the one great physician, and that he alone can heal.

A New Day

Scripture: Numbers 21:10–35
Suggested Reading: Deuteronomy 2; 3:1–11; Genesis 15:12–16;
19:30–38; Leviticus 18:20–25; Numbers 14:20–35

*I*magine being a child on the day Moses raised his staff over the waters and the sea opened up to let the people pass through. Imagine walking beside your father as the water stood up in massive walls on your right and on your left. Imagine standing on the eastern shore and watching those walls of water slam shut and consume the chariots of the Egyptian hosts as the sun set behind you. And imagine singing to the top of your lungs the next morning, ". . . and he shall reign forever and ever!" What a memory it must be, now that you are in your forties or fifties!

Your faith was sealed when you were young, but your life has been difficult ever since. For nearly forty years you have suffered for the sins of your fathers. Because they rebelled back at Kadesh and didn't have faith enough to march into the land, you have been forced to live as a nomad, gathering your jar of daily manna, and just waiting for the old ones to die so the punishment would be complete and God would allow your generation to claim its inheritance.

Now the day you have longed for has dawned, and your heart shouts with joy as you sense that you are about to burst into your destiny. And again you sing songs of joy and praise as you begin your march toward Canaan.

You slip around Edom without incident, taking care not to provoke your cousins or damage the land God gave to the sons of Esau. With equal caution you skirt the eastern border of Moab and the southern tip of Ammon, remembering that God gave those lands to the boys the drunken Lot conceived with his misguided daughters after God burned Sodom.

Then you try to make a deal with the Amorites simply to follow the King's Highway northward. You offer to buy food and water from them, but they are belligerent and not only refuse you passage, but come at you with their swords drawn. For a moment you tremble, but as you raise your sword you feel the presence of the Lord surge through your body. As you lunge, the Amorites fall before you, and soon you have annihilated their entire army and slain their king. You wonder why it was so easy, but then you remember that Moses taught you how the Amorites had dispossessed the sons of Moab and were terribly evil. And you remember that God had promised Abraham that your generation would return to this land and punish them.

The sons of Reuben and Gad stay behind to occupy the cities of the Amorites, but the rest of the company continues the invasion northward, singing songs of joy all the way to Bashan. Og's army confronts you, but the power of God is still in your hand, and after a brief fray the king falls and not one of his soldiers remains alive.

Old memories of the dead Egyptian soldiers floating in the Red Sea leap into your mind. In one short campaign the Lord has slain your enemies and has delivered into your hand the entire east bank of the Jordan. The disorderly multitude of cowardly slaves has been reborn into a nation that is poised to cross the river and claim its inheritance.

You have been used by God to cast out those who have defiled the land. The debt has been paid for the sins of your fathers, and you have been restored to a right relationship with the Lord.

It is a grand new day!

A Gift Misused

Scripture: Numbers 22:1–20
Suggested Reading: Deuteronomy 2:9

So, what do you think of Balaam so far? Doesn't he sound like a nice, reasonable man? Now, I spent over twenty years at negotiating tables and learned not to take people at face value. I've met many ravenous wolves who were wearing the wool of sheep, people who would smile at you with a friendly twinkle in their eye and snatch the wallet from your pocket as you turn to leave.

I learned over the years, sometimes the hard way, that when I face a new person on the other side of the table, before I allow myself to trust him, I should consult with a friend who has had experience with this fellow and who might have some insight into his character. So, let's check out Balaam . . .

Suggested Reading: 2 Peter 2:15; Jude 11; Revelation 2:14

See? It pays to consult. Peter tells us that Balaam is untrustworthy, that he puts profit above morality. Both Jude and John confirm Peter's opinion. So, as we continue to deal with this man, let's be fully aware that behind that pious smile and righteous attitude lurks a selfish and evil mind.

Balaam is a seer, a psychic whom either God or Satan has endowed with the power of divination, a hired gun who, for a price, will put a curse on your enemy. But God always has the final say.

As any good negotiator, Balaam listened to the offer made by the people on the other side, consulted with the Lord and returned to tell them that he couldn't possibly meet their demands.

But the king of Moab knew Balaam. He had dealt with him before. So he sent another delegation with more money to bargain with him for a curse. Balaam again rejected the offer, but this time he told them that he would consult with the Lord again to see if he has changed his mind. If so, he might be willing to meet Balak's demand.

Now, God had already told Balaam that he would not allow him to put a curse on Israel, so Balaam's persistence was offensive to him. It was a sin, and Balaam had to be taught a lesson. So, God allowed Balaam to meet with the princes of Moab, but gave him strict parameters and set him up for the remarkable educational experience he was to have along the way.

Before we get all caught up in the drama that follows, we should note what might have happened had Balaam not been so motivated by personal gain, and had been more concerned with the best interests of both the Moabites and the Israelites. Had he had any standing with God at all, he might have gone to him and asked whether or not Israel was a threat to Moab. He might have learned that God had blessed Moab too, and was not about to let Israel do battle against them. That might have allayed Balak's fears and resolved the matter to everyone's benefit. Unfortunately, he was more selfish than circumspect, and terribly in need of a lesson on how to exercise his gift.

We cannot be arrogant with God or try to use his gifts for our own personal gain. Many so-called servants of the Lord today find their ministry to be very profitable, and their profits lead to a level of greed that transcends the purpose of their calling, becoming the sole aim of their work. We have seen God humble such ministers and teach them very painful lessons.

From the Mouths of . . .

Scripture: Numbers 22:21–41

I can still see them on Mrs. Hooker's flannelgraph, the big white angel with his huge feathered wings and a fiery sword blocking the path, and the mule with his swivel head turning and speaking to Balaam sitting on his back.

The story is quite memorable and instructive, but the only lessons I gleaned from it in my childhood was that I should not mistreat animals that don't mistreat us, and that maybe they see things that we can't see and know things we don't know. None of the subtleties of the story got through to me back then.

Now I know that if I were riding on the back of a cantankerous mule who wouldn't stay on the path, and who would lie down under me instead of going forward, I just might be tempted to use the switch on his behind to teach him who's boss, just as Balaam did. But if the creature started talking to me, I would be off his back and a mile down the road before my churning feet hit the path.

But Balaam didn't seem to be taken aback at all by the talking mule. He answered him just as though a conversation between them was a common occurrence. Perhaps he was so engrossed in enchantments that a talking mule didn't shock him in the least.

How strange it is that a silver-tongued man such as Balaam could be outtalked by an animal. The man who could hold his own with kings and princes and who dared debate God, could not win an argument with a mule. If Mrs. Hooker said that it was God talking through the mule, I didn't catch it. I don't know how it escaped me, because I knew that Satan spoke to Eve through the snake, and that God talked to Moses from a burning bush. Perhaps I just couldn't see God in a donkey costume.

I know God has a sense of humor. Much in the Bible makes me laugh, and I think God wants it that way because he made laughter such great medicine. This is one of the funniest stories in the Bible, but perhaps the funnier the story, the more serious the message.

There was once an old time television series that featured a talking horse, Mr. Ed, who was wiser than his master, Wilbur, and sometimes uttered profound statements, lessons for the audience. In the story of Balaam, just as with Mr. Ed, the animal is more perceptive than his master, Balaam. He sees what the seer can't see and knows what the psychic doesn't know. And the irony is poignant. Balaam said that if he had a sword, he would smite the mule, but the mule knows the angel has a sword and could use it to smite Balaam.

The lesson that both Balaam and I learn from this amusing event is that God is sovereign and can use any part of nature to do anything he wishes to do. He can make water stand up in a wall, he can make bread fall from the sky, he can multiply little loaves and fishes enough to feed a crowd, he can put prophecy in the dreams of infidel kings, and he can use the mouths of mules and charlatans to bring his word to the world.

Sometimes when I hear spiritual words uttered, I tend to assess the character of the speaker and so assess the validity of the words. But the story of Balaam and the mule reminds me that God can speak to me through any means that will get my attention, and that I had better be attentive to all possibilities, including messages that come through dumb animals. My favorite message is the one from the wooly worm who reminds me that one day I, too, will be wrapped in death's box and emerge a new creature, winging my way to heaven!

The Lure of Gold

Scripture: Numbers 23; 24

*B*laam is an astonishing character indeed! Gifted as a prophet, he seems equally comfortable sitting with God in the spiritual counsels of heaven and with the demons in the gates of hell. He understands the power of the Lord to issue a blessing or a curse upon an entire people, and he understands that God has ordained the sons of Jacob to prosper in ways he can barely comprehend, yet he is willing to conspire with Israel's enemies to tempt them to sin against that God and bring his wrath down on them and upon himself.

Does he feel immune to God's anger, even when he has just confronted an angel with a sword in his hand who said he would have killed him had the mule not turned aside? How can he bow his head, confess his sin, and fall on his face before God one day, and the next day try to strike a deal with the devil? Does he truly have a contrite heart, or is he just putting on a show of contrition in a futile effort to deceive an omniscient God? How can a man so intelligent, so gifted, and so intimate with deity, be such a fool?

Perhaps at this time he has a clearer picture of Israel's future than even Moses has. He knows that God has brought this legion of people up out of Egypt and that this nation has a divine destiny. As he stands on the top of Mount Pisgah where Moses will soon stand, he can survey the Promised Land and through prophetic eye see that God will make Israel a grand and splendid nation that will totally annihilate its neighbors.

Through the power given him, he comprehends that the King to come is a heavenly star whose kingdom will transcend earthly bounds. This pagan has prophesied the coming of Jesus! How can a man whose eyes have been so opened, who has become so intimate with the counsels of almighty God, insidiously conspire with a pagan nation to bring harm to the chosen people?

And what's the lesson here for me?

Balaam's first love, it seems, is money. Perhaps he repeatedly ordered the construction of altars and persistently offered sheep and oxen to Israel's God in the hope that his sacrifice would change God's mind and allow his people to be cursed so he could exact an exorbitant fee from Balak. A man can be driven blind by greed even though his eyes are open to spiritual wonders that other humans can't perceive, and even though the very hand of God has reached out and touched him. Standing today in the presence of God is no guarantee that one might not bow tomorrow in the presence of Satan.

In our time we've known other people who have borne mighty witness to the power of God in their lives, but who have yet yielded to the lusts of the flesh and the lure of gold. Like Esau, they have sold their birthright to satisfy their own desires.

Whatever the meaning of the long and detailed story of Balaam might be, it certainly must be telling me to put up my defenses against the temptations Satan hurls at me. Even though I do my best to walk with God and serve him today, since I am subject to all human weaknesses, tomorrow might present an entirely different picture.

Immersing myself daily in his Word is not enough. I must continually pray for the presence of the Holy Spirit in my life to keep me walking in his way, or I too may find myself trading my eternal inheritance for a mere pot of gold.

Sneaking into Camp

Scripture: Numbers 25; 31:16

When we were kids just beginning to sense the urges that biology lavishes upon the young, we used to go to church camp for a week in the summer. During the day we would have a Bible class, then swim, do crafts, and play games. In the evening we would gather around the fire for singing and devotions, at the end of which we would inevitably renew our commitment to the Lord.

After campfire when the counselors were asleep, instead of staying in our cabins, the more daring of us would sneak down to the dock, quietly untie the boats and slip across the moonlit lake to visit the girl scouts, who somehow knew we would be coming and were waiting for us in the shadows behind their boathouse.

Our church was very strict and old fashioned. They didn't believe in coed camping. The boys camped one week and the girls camped the next, for the same reason that we don't carry dynamite and blasting caps in the same truck. That way our church fathers felt they could harness nature and prevent an explosion.

At our campfire we sang church hymns and Bible choruses, and if we turned our ears to the south and listened carefully, we could hear the girls across the lake singing girl scout songs and secular camp rhymes. Sometimes the girls sneaked over into our camp, and once a counselor caught one of our boys smooching with one of them behind the chapel. He was punished severely.

So, I understand the Israelites.

God's people set up camp in the land of the people they had dispossessed, the Amorites and the Bashanites. There they erected their tent of meeting and gathered to worship and offer sacrifices to the Lord. Outside the boundaries of their camps the pagans worshipped their gods in ways the Israelite men could imagine only in their wildest dreams. Sometimes the foreign girls slipped into their camp, and anyone caught with one of them was punished severely.

Today we remember our romantic camp forays as nothing more than innocent mischief, but there were sinister forces at work in Israel's camp. Balaam, who couldn't make a nickel by putting a hex on God's people, found a new way to satisfy his client, Balak.

He urged the Moabites to invite Hebrew boys to sneak over into their camp and join their religious rituals, which usually were sexual orgies performed as praise to the gods of fertility. Since their natural urges had been repressed by the strict morality of Moses, they found a new way to unleash their vigor. And soon they were dancing with the Midianites and the Moabites, and inviting their new friends into their camp to flaunt their pleasures right in the face of Moses himself. Balaam and Balak thought they would achieve their goal by making the Israelites so odious to God that he would revoke his blessing.

But God didn't simply turn his face and wink away their mischief as I hope he did ours. He was angry. He recorded for all posterity the names of two offenders, Zimri and Cozbi, as well as the names of their fathers. And he raised up as a national hero the man he ordained to punish them, Aaron's grandson, Phinehas. Then he sent Israel's army into Midian to execute his vengeance upon the sirens who seduced his children. The five kings of Midian died in the battle, and the fickle Balaam also fell by the sword of Israel.

God punished the sons of Jacob severely for their adultery, but he didn't rescind his blessing. He didn't go back on his promise. He never has and he never will.

Scattered

Scripture: Numbers 26
Suggested Reading: 1 Corinthians 10:1–11; Genesis 49;
Exodus 1:7–20; Numbers 1; 14:26–35

I have never been much of a numbers man. One of my golfing friends seems to remember the yardage and score of every hole he has ever played, as well as the clubs he used. Before he retired he was in charge of a parts department and is reputed to have known the item number and inventory of every part in the bins. Being a baseball fan, he also knows everything from batting averages to box scores. He loves the book of Numbers. He finds meaning in numbers.

Why did they call it Numbers? The Hebrews call it "In the Wilderness," which is a far more accurate description of its contents. The only numbering occurs in the census at the beginning of the book and the census in chapter twenty-six. The rest of the book consists of narratives of the events that occurred during the forty years in the wilderness and of various commandments. Maybe whoever was inspired to name it Numbers, wants us to be sure to take a close look at the before and after censuses and glean from them a lesson.

Being somewhat of a sports fan myself, numbers interest me. Numbers often tell the story behind the outcome of the game. Commentators for all sports bombard us with numbers reflecting time of possession, turnovers, assists, bases stolen, yards gained and a host of other measurable factors in an effort to help us understand the game more clearly. And if we look closely at the numbers in the Bible, maybe we can understand more fully the message that God is giving us here.

While in Egypt, the sons of Jacob were "fruitful and increased greatly." God blessed them during the early time of plenty and the later time of oppression until their numbers had grown from the original fifty-one sons to over six hundred thousand.

During the forty years in the wilderness their numbers declined, but only by a negligible fraction. Eight of the tribes increased and five of the tribes decreased, most by just a few thousand. But there were two notable exceptions: the tribe of Manasseh increased by sixty-four percent and the tribe of Simeon decreased by nearly the same margin. Why?

Before he died, Jacob prophesied that Joseph, though he had only two sons, Ephraim and Manasseh, that he would be a "fruitful bough by a spring (whose) branches run over the wall." He promised him "blessings of the breast and of the womb." And since no one from the tribe of Manasseh ever distinguished himself in any way, Jacob's prophecy was fulfilled simply because God blessed the family of the man whose "bow remained unmoved" even though "the archers fiercely attacked him, shot at him, and harassed him sorely."

An elder son, Simeon, was not so blessed. He was a violent man and his father promised that he would be scattered in Israel. The bodies of many of his descendants were scattered in the desert, and we wonder how many of his offspring were among the twenty-four thousand who died of the plague when Zimri, a Simeonite, polluted the camp by his debauchery with the pagan woman. The tribe of Simeon never had an inheritance of its own, but was scattered among the people of Judah.

The bottom line? God punished them severely for their sin at Kadesh. He scattered in the wilderness the dead bodies of all adults who left Egypt except Joshua and Caleb, yet he preserved an equal number to populate the new nation. The gates of hell had not prevailed.

Two Sides of God

Scripture: Numbers 27:1–11
Suggested Reading: Exodus 20:5–6

I was raised in a tradition that taught an angry and vengeful God. One of the things that kept me in line during my youth was the notion that God was always up there in his heaven keeping an eagle eye on me and ready to punish me for any villainy he might catch me doing. My mother even posted scary plaques here and there that read, *Be Sure Your Sins Will Find You Out*. Puritanical fervor had all but blinded them to the loving side of God, and it took me many years to discover that our just and righteous God could also be charitable.

So, I can understand these Israelites. When they left Egypt they knew the same God I knew as a child. They watched as their angry God assaulted the Egyptians with a salvo of plagues, and they came to know him only as the fearsome God of fire, hail, disease, and death. It took the sweetened pool at Marah, the shade of Elim, the manna in the wilderness, and the fountain of Rephidim just to begin to persuade them that God cared, that he was their healer and provider as well as their judge and executioner.

Mary Ann, on the other hand, was raised in the tradition of a warm and benevolent God. The plaque on her wall read, *God is Love*. She was taught that she should be a good girl and not get into mischief, but if, in her weakness, she should yield to temptation, God would understand and forgive. Until she began to study the Bible, she just couldn't understand that her loving God would ever consign any sinner to hell.

Over the years, I've given some thought to the question of whose error was the least damaging. Were my parents better off trembling in fear of the wrath of an angry God, or did her parents benefit more by resting comfortably in the warm bosom of the amiable Father? Who is better off in the long run?

Schoolteachers learn in college, or at least they used to, that they should first establish their authority over a classroom full of students before beginning to show a soft side. Army officers, at least those of the "old army" of which I am familiar, learn first to be harsh leaders and instill the fear of the brass in their soldiers before letting them know that they are made of anything less than acid and iron. Teachers and officers learn that it is easier to let up a little after they've asserted control than it is to regain control after they've lost it. And children and soldiers have no respect for weak leaders, but admire strong leaders who know when to be gentle.

I think it no accident that God revealed himself first as an almighty God who demanded absolute obedience and who condemned to death anyone who violated a command so seemingly trivial as "Thou shalt not eat of the tree in the midst of the garden." I think it no accident that when he gave the law he first declared himself to be a jealous God who "visits the iniquity of fathers upon the children to the third and fourth generation." And after he had established himself as the just judge, he added that he shows "steadfast love to thousands of those who love me and keep my commandments." Only by knowing him as the former, can we truly appreciate him as the latter.

A sonless Zelophehad who died in the wilderness for his sin knew a God of wrath. But his daughters, by pleading for mercy, discovered an amazingly gracious heavenly Father who was willing to restore their fortunes. Their plea became the basis for the refinement of the inheritance laws, and from that day on, no orphan girl had to worry about her future. God is just, and he is merciful.

Beyond the River

Scripture: Numbers 27:1–11
Suggested Reading: Joshua 17:3–4; Ecclesiastes 12:1–8;
Matthew 25:1–13; 1 Peter 1:3–4; 2 Peter 1:10–11

*T*he great hymns of the church echo the many biblical euphemisms for death. From the stormy banks of Jordan we "cast a wistful eye to Canaan's fair and happy land where our possessions lie." Life departing from this body is described as the loosening of the golden cord or the breaking of the golden bowl. The dust returns to the earth, but the soul takes flight to the Promised Land and finds, as the Israelites finally found, rest beyond the river.

In his Word, the Lord continually encourages us to make preparation for that inevitable day when our pitcher breaks at the fountain and our bodies can no longer hold the life-giving water. He warns us to keep our lamps trimmed, filled with oil, and burning bright because we do not know when the groom will return to claim his bride.

Why is the story of Zelophehad's daughters in the Bible? Simply to show legal historians that the Mosaic code was far ahead of its time in recognizing the rights of minorities and women? Simply to show the ancients that the one and only true God, unlike the capricious and unreliable pagan gods, genuinely cared for human beings, especially the downtrodden, the vulnerable, the disenfranchised, and the orphans who have no one else to champion their cause? Simply to comfort those among us who are hopeless and needy with the knowledge that our heavenly Father knows our grief and heals our pain?

Or does the story reveal more to us than that? Is it a mandate for us, while we are still walking on this side of the river, the wilderness side, to stake our claim to our inheritance in the Promised Land?

Zelophehad's daughters were five wise virgins indeed. Undoubtedly they were born after the spies returned from Canaan with tales of monsters in the land that made a majority of Israelites fainthearted. They were probably children of the wilderness who knew nothing more than the nomadic life, wandering from grassy glen to grassy glen with the hope in their hearts that someday their weary souls would find rest beyond the river. But they can teach us one of life's most valuable lessons.

Peter urged us to be zealous in confirming our election into God's eternal kingdom, our imperishable heavenly inheritance. Zelophehad's daughters went zealously to Moses to claim their inheritance in the Promised Land and to set an example for us to go and do likewise, because . . .

Someday the silver cord will break,
    and I no more as now shall sing,
But O the joy when I shall wake
    within the palace of the King.

Someday my earthly house will fall;
    I cannot tell how soon 'twill be
But this I know, my All in All
    has now a place in heaven for me.

Someday . . . 'til then I'll watch and wait,
    my lamp all trimmed and burning bright,
that when my Savior opens the gate,
    my soul to him may take its flight.

(Fannie Crosby, 1893)

The Torch Is Passed

Scripture: Numbers 27:12–23
Suggested Reading: Matthew 17:1–3; Revelation 11:1–13

I remember listening intently and tingling as President Kennedy delivered his inaugural address. The first president born in the twentieth century electrified us with his words about the torch being passed to a new generation of Americans. We had come under the leadership of a man who had experienced war and depression, and was dedicated to taking us to a chivalrous and peaceful land where even the least among us would be able to get a good taste of the American dream.

The Lord never told us how the children of Israel received their new leader. He must have had an impressive inauguration ceremony, taking his vows before Eleazar the priest, bowing his head under the hands of Moses, and receiving his commission to lead God's people through the Jordan and into the Promised Land.

Maybe the new generation that had been born in the wilderness and had no memory of either the fleshpots of Egypt or the lash of the slave master rejoiced as the bold-spirited son of Nun accepted the staff of leadership from the ancient lawgiver. Maybe those who had known only the hardship of the hostile wilderness tingled as the torch was passed to a new generation of Israelites, to a man they knew would lead them to their inheritance, the man who would take them to the land flowing with milk and honey.

At present, we are on a wilderness sojourn, more than a generation beyond the inauguration of President Kennedy. Well over forty years have passed. We have stepped over the threshold of the twenty-first century. Our Camelot went up in the fire and smoke of riots, assassinations, and a confusing and horrible war; most of the rest of the century was characterized by scandal, licentiousness, and greed. Then came September 11. The dream turned into a nightmare.

We know the story of the Jews. The generation that marched under Joshua's flag captured the land. They were the generation of conquest, and they lived to see their promised inheritance finally parceled out. Their sons after them took a firm grip on the territory and eventually lived in splendor under the leadership of David and Solomon. Then that dream also ended in scandal, licentiousness, and greed. Then came a horrible attack from the outside.

The torch, it seems, is a thing to be passed. The beginnings and ends of historical eras are punctuated by the passing of torches. We never speak of leaders raising the torch or lighting the way, only passing it to their successors. But what our leaders do while they hold the torch determines what we remember them for, and it's time to remember Moses.

At the end of his forty-year tenure as the leader of Israel, he fell into disrepute. The man who bellied up to Pharaoh, commanded the plagues, opened the sea, made water gush from the rock and met God face to face, became irritable, rebelled against the Lord and smote the rock he was supposed to address with God's words. And though his sentence was to pass the torch, climb the mountain for a solitary panoramic view of the land he could not enter and there be gathered to his people, his work was not ended. He entered eternity chastised, but commissioned to confer with Jesus on the Mount of Transfiguration and to appear once again as a powerful witness for the Lord during the great tribulation.

And I expect to watch those final events from the banks of the river that flows by the throne of God!

Once for All

Scripture: Numbers 28; 29
Suggested Reading: Hebrews 9:23–28; 1 Peter 3:18

A few weeks ago on Laity Sunday, one of the brothers of the church was asked to preach the sermon. He put a great deal of effort both into the content and the presentation, and afterward one of the sweet ladies from the congregation declared to him that he had missed his calling, that he most certainly should have been a pastor. He responded, "Mrs. Hargrove, Balaam's ass could preach a compelling sermon, but I doubt if he would have been a good pastor."

That brother knew whereof he spoke. A pastor's moment in the sun comes every Sunday morning when he has the privilege of preaching, but his schedule of duties for the rest of the week requires the exercise of every gift and fruit the Spirit has to offer.

And if it is tough to wear the robe of a priest today, think of what it must have been like in Bible times. Accountant types who like to sift through little things can tell us how many times each year the priest had to kill an animal and burn it on the altar. I don't know the number, and I have no interest in counting or even reading a book by someone who has counted, but from scanning the scripture it is clear to me that a priest needed more than just vitamins to give him the energy required to slay all the bulls, lambs, goats, and rams necessary to please God and atone for the sins of the people.

And besides all that slaying for all those offerings and feasts and other rituals, those priests had to learn all the laws and procedures that God had ordained for the priesthood. And if we think that today's overworked pastor takes a lot of abuse from the people who think their weekly dollar in the offering plate entitles them to a pound of pastoral flesh, just page through the Pentateuch and count the number of times the people rebelled against Aaron.

Though the life of a pastor has never been easy, pastors in the church age are grateful that they did not serve before the Common Era. Not just because their work doesn't center around altars, burnt sacrifices, and the blood of animals, but because they have the privilege of representing the Priest who offered his own blood once and for all as the eternal sacrifice that would never have to be repeated. And that's just the beginning. They have the privilege of preaching the gospel of the Lamb who will come back one day to claim as his own all who eagerly await his return.

I doubt if the priests of Bible times found much joy in their work. Maybe that's why so many of them went bad. Maybe they compensated for the drudgery of the ceaseless killing and the incessant whining of the people by gorging themselves in pot roast and debauchery. They had to make a perpetual offering to a God who would never be satisfied with a people who would never be content. Where's the reward in that?

Maybe many of today's parishioners will also never be satisfied, but God has been satisfied. The single sacrifice of the unblemished Lamb has atoned for all of the sins of all of the people for all time, and that is the glorious message that today's priests get to preach! But more glorious still is the message that the Lamb has become a King who welcomes his subjects to come and enjoy his kingdom forever.

Most pastors need only a small wallet, but the moon in their valley gleams brightly when the blessing they receive for telling the story of the risen Christ, who died once for all, fills their hearts to overflowing!

As Good as His Word

Scripture: Numbers 30
Suggested Reading: Matthew 5:33–37

One of the first bits of advice I received from an old professional negotiator about to retire was, "Never take them at their word. Make them give it to you in writing."

The advice was sound. Coming into the world of collective bargaining as a neophyte who by nature trusted everybody, I was burned over and over again in my early days because I believed people would honor their word. Unhappily, I found that most people in my business tended to lie . . . a lot.

Apparently the propensity to lie is not a trait limited to the folks of our day who strive in tough businesses. God found it necessary as he formed his nation to devote a set of laws to the subject of telling the truth. In fact, mendacity was such a big problem that it warranted even more than a slot as one of the Ten Commandments; in addition, it had to be addressed by numerous collateral scriptures, even by Jesus himself. It seems that people of all eras just can't be trusted.

When dealing with people of the world, it is prudent to "get it in writing." Although I'm somewhat sloppy in that regard, Mary Ann, who made her living as a librarian, has a propensity for collecting and organizing all the tidbits of paper that infest our lives, such as receipts, guarantees, advertisements for the things we buy, and, of course, the contracts into which we enter. I'm grateful to her because so often people and companies go back on their word and have to be compelled to perform as they promised.

Falsehood is so common in our society that we are often assumed to be lying unless we can prove that we are telling the truth. The manager of the supermarket won't believe that we purchased a defective item at her store unless we can show her a receipt. And the vice president of the bank won't believe we gave our money to the teller unless we can produce a deposit slip. When it comes to our word, we are guilty until proven innocent.

Even in the most honorable of the venues in our society, honesty is suspect. When people are elected to public office they must swear to carry out their duties in accordance with all applicable statutes. When one becomes the treasurer of service club, he must be bonded and vow to handle the money with fidelity. When we testify in court, we must swear to tell the truth. Man, it seems, is by nature assumed to be full of guile.

Even the heroes of faith were caught lying. Abraham and Sarah lied to Pharaoh about their relationship. Isaac lied to Abimelech about Rebekah. Jacob lied to Isaac by pretending to be Esau, his brother. Judah lied to Tamar. Moses lied to Pharaoh. Aaron lied to Moses. Peter lied about knowing Jesus. All through the scriptures, the very best of God's people let false words slip through their lips.

So how can we expect anyone to be telling the truth unless we get it from them in writing or make them swear an oath?

Jesus had the better idea. The need to swear or get it in writing is, in itself, a creature of evil. It is proof of the deceitful nature of fallen man. The answer is not to conform to that nature and feed it by taking vows and getting written confirmations. The answer is to transcend that nature by being a person who is known as one who always tells the truth.

I've always figured that the highest compliment that can be paid to me as I pass by is, "There goes a man who is as good as his word."

To Weed the Garden

Scripture: Numbers 31
Suggested Reading: Matthew 13:24–30

*I*don't like chapters like this, but I know people who do. Don't get me wrong, I'm glad God included it in his Word because it teaches me a lot. But I'm afraid some people learn the wrong lesson.

God will not tolerate iniquity. That is plain. God punishes sin. He said that the wages of sin is death and he meant it. It still is. God hasn't changed.

The people who occupied Canaan before the Israelites got there were so evil that God used the Israelites to destroy them. Some passages suggest that the soldiers sent out to do the destroying didn't think it was the most enjoyable experience in their lives because they often didn't do the job as completely as God wanted it done. Sometimes they spared people they thought were innocent or who could be useful to them in some way.

Some of the Christian brothers and sisters today want to succeed where past exterminators failed. They've joined what they believe to be God's army of avengers, and they think he's commissioned them to swagger through the world and root out the evil that is in it. With McCarthy-like fervor they attack individuals and institutions they judge to be sinful. And they celebrate like school children when they've brought an evil doer down. But in the process, like McCarthy, they've hurt a lot of innocent people. They simply call it collateral damage.

Now I don't know if God still uses people to punish sinners today. Those who believe he does cite Hitler's persecution of the Jews as fulfillment of God's promise in Deuteronomy that the sons of Jacob would be cursed for their disobedience by being treated as they were treated during the Nazi era. They believe, as Moses prophesied, that the Jews became "a horror, a proverb, and a by-word, among all the peoples where the Lord will lead you away." And they further cite the Allied victory over Germany as evidence that God used us to punish those who abused his chosen people. They might be right, but if they are, I get no pleasure from it.

The first time Christ came to earth, he came to deal with sin. God's wrath was poured out on him with as much fury as it was poured out on Sodom, on Egypt, and on Midian, showing us once and for all that rooting sin out of the world is at the top of God's agenda. Sometimes we think it is our job to root sin out of the world. That is wrong. God has reserved that job for himself, and he doesn't want us to play God.

Jesus told us very plainly that we are not to go out into his field and pull weeds, lest in pulling the weeds we inadvertently pull up some of the wheat along with them. Instead, we are to let them grow together, and in the end when we join him on the judgment seat we'll help him separate the good from the bad. Then he will carry off the bad to be burned, but will bring the good into his storehouse.

What then is our work? We've cited chapter and verse so often in these meditations that it's getting tiresome, but yet we can't re-peat it enough. Our commission is to love God above all, and our neighbor as ourselves. Our work is to feed the hungry, clothe the naked, see to the needs of the poor, tend the sick, give comfort to the sorrowing, and bring peace to those in turmoil.

If we do all that, maybe we are doing more to root sin out of the world than we can possibly imagine.

East Bank, or West?

Scripture: Numbers 32
Suggested Reading: Genesis 19:22–26; 49:3–4;
Deuteronomy 33:6, 13–17, 20–21; Psalms 60:6–7; Acts 20:32

The division of the land is a fascinating study, fraught with more questions than answers, yet very revealing in its spiritual applications.

Both Jacob and Moses blessed the sons of Joseph very generously, prophesying that God would deliver to their descendants the choicest fruits of the land. And God kept his word.

Manasseh is most to be admired. Manasseh's domain was twice the size of any other tribe's, stretching from the Mediterranean Sea on the west to over forty miles east of the Jordan at its farthest point. His branches truly ran "over the wall" of the Promised Land, deep into Gilead. Machir and Jair, descendants of Manasseh, invaded Gilead, and as a reward Moses gave them the land they conquered. So, Manasseh inherited a vast territory inside the boundaries of the Promised Land west of the river, and an equal sized plot outside, to the east, known as the half-tribe.

We have Manassehs in our church, people who have laid full claim to their eternal inheritance and who have also been blessed in the secular world. They have conquered Satan and live sanctified lives. They are models of Christian discipleship, serving the Lord and their church with all their heart and all their possessions. They have also conquered the world beyond the borders of the church and have been blessed with wealth. Their two worlds meet at the river, and their inheritance, though divided, is one.

Reuben and Gad are least to be admired. For his sin against his father, the firstborn Reuben was denied preeminence and, by his own choice, preferred not to have an inheritance among his brothers in the land of promise, but settled in the nation's remotest regions, on the east bank of the Dead Sea. His numbers declined during the forty years in the wilderness, and as Lot, he opted for the rich grasslands that neighbored the territories of Baal.

Jacob promised Gad a life of strife, and the warrior lived up to that prophecy, earning a portion of Gilead by the edge of his sword and preferring to dwell beyond the Jordan, his flanks exposed to the Ammonites. The ten brothers who homesteaded inside the boundaries of the land God promised to Abraham had natural protection from their enemies: mountains to the north, a desert to the south, a sea to the west, and a river to the east. But those who chose to live outside the boundaries were the first to vanish when the armies of the great eastern empires carried their vanquished foes off to slavery.

We have Gads and Reubens in our church too, people who dwell on the fringe of the Promised Land and who have never laid full claim to their inheritance in the kingdom of heaven. They attend worship irregularly, give little, serve less, and never attend Sunday school or Bible study. During the hymns they open the book but don't sing, during the sermon their cruising eyes bear witness to their bored minds, and at communion they drop a perfunctory knee at the altar and devour the Eucharist as though it is their midmorning snack. They claim to be Christians, though they never carry a Bible, and their neighbors only suspect that they go to church because they see them drive off dressed up on Sunday mornings.

Don't settle for an inheritance on the fringe. Claim your eternal abode among the sanctified.

To a Large Tribe...

Scripture: Numbers 33
Suggested Reading: Numbers 36; Genesis 49;
Deuteronomy 33

A Christian brother who had amassed a substantial fortune was asked to reveal the key to his material success. "Tithing," he answered. "From my youth I've always given the first ten percent of my income to the Lord, and in return, he has blessed me abundantly." Another brother who lived on modest means but always wore a smile was asked to reveal the key to his happiness. "Tithing,' he answered. "From my youth I've always returned the first fruits of my labors to the Lord, and in return he's blessed me with more than material things. He's given me a wealth of contentment, the assurance of salvation, the grace to endure adversity, a wonderful wife, and a happy family. What more could I want?"

The Lord has blessed me with a nose for quandaries. All my life I've looked for problems simply for the pleasure of solving them. I enjoy crossword puzzles, game shows, and mystery stories. But in reading this chapter of Numbers, I thought I had found a puzzle I couldn't solve, until I remembered the story of the tithing brothers.

I understood that the tribes of Israel were to have the size of their inheritances determined by populations. A small tribe was to receive a small inheritance and a large tribe a large inheritance. But by putting one eye on the numbers in the census and another eye on the map, it is easy to see that it didn't quite work that way, at least to my original understanding, except for the large tribe of Judah, which got its fair share, and the large tribe of Dan, who finally got two tracts.

When I compared population to square mileage, I found that Zebulun and Issachar, the largest of the remaining tribes, inherited the smallest tracts of land. On the other hand, Ephraim and Gad, two of the smaller tribes, inherited large tracts. I found a problem that needed solving, but by searching through the Bible and consulting other sources, I could find no reason for the apparent discrepancy. That is, until I remembered the story of the tithing brothers.

The true measure of wealth is not found in quantity, but in quality. Numbers of dollars or acres cannot tell us how blessed a person truly is. The same is true of the tribes of Israel. Asher had access to the sea and his land featured fertile olive groves, but his energy, as Naphtali's, was consumed by constant battle with the Sidonians to the north. Manasseh, Ephriam, and Benjamin lived on rocky soil, but controlled the famous Jericho Road, the crossover between two major trade routes, the Via Maris and the King's Highway. Simeon, the smallest tribe, was scattered in the wasteland south of Judah. The lower half of the tribe of Dan enjoyed coastal lands, but were constantly harassed by the Philistines, and the northern half fought perpetually against foreign invaders.

But Issachar and Zebulun are special. Moses blessed them together. He said they would "suck the abundance of the sea and the hidden treasures in the sand." Though their estates were small in terms of acreage, their fortunes were as vast as their populations. They bordered no enemies, their soil was fertile and productive, they enjoyed river access to the sea and they controlled the Mediterranean ports. They became rich by commerce as Jacob and Moses predicted.

The Lord wants our first fruits. Not just ten percent of our earnings, but also the best of our time, energy, thoughts, and talents. And in return he has promised to bless us, perhaps not in measurable quantities of material goods, but in the immeasurable joys of the fruit of the Spirit and an invaluable eternal inheritance in the kingdom of heaven.

From the Euphrates to . . .

Scripture: Numbers 34
Suggested Reading: Genesis 15:18; Exodus 16:35

*W*hat the Bible doesn't say is often more remarkable than what it does say. I find it most interesting that back on the first day the manna fell, Moses pointed out that it continued to fall for the entire forty-year period of their sojourn in the wilderness, when they hadn't as yet been doomed to that punishment. Of course, that little tidbit was added later, but here, when the borders of the Promised Land were defined, Moses didn't point out that the nation of Israel would never actually conquer and inhabit the entire tract because of their sin. He could have, since he was a prophet, but perhaps God didn't find it useful to give Moses that bit of insight into the future.

If we look at good historical maps of the Holy Land, we can see that even in David's reign, the Philistines inhabited the Gaza Strip and the Phoenicians occupied the costal lands from Tyre northward. Although under Solomon, kingdoms south of the Euphrates paid tribute to Israel, the Israelites never occupied any land within a hundred miles of that great river. The sons of Jacob never received all of the territory that God promised would be theirs. Why not?

Could it be because some of the brothers were content to live outside the promised boundaries? If we could push on the east side of our maps and force the Gilead tribes of Reuben, Gad and Manasseh westward across the river, the tribal perimeters would have to bulge to the farthest reaches of the promised northern boundaries in order to accommodate all twelve tribes. But three of the brothers looked to the east, saw the fertile grasslands of the plain and decided to settle there while the northern portions of the Promised Land remained in the grasp of pagans.

I also find it remarkable that the Lord addressed in detail the manner in which the land west of the Jordan was to be divided, but ignored the division of land among the sons of Gad and Reuben. He personally appointed overseers from each tribe settling between the Jordan and the Mediterranean to supervise the drawing of lots for the division of land among the families of those tribes. But in that list of leaders chosen to divide the land, no leaders from Gad or Reuben are named. Didn't God care how the east bank was divided? Didn't he care about those people?

Is there a lesson here for us? When we enter our spiritual promised land, God wants us to inhabit it fully, to walk the length and breadth of it, as he instructed Abraham. He wants us to take every bit of our baggage across the Jordan, giving him total control of our lives and bringing every aspect of ourselves into the confines of our new habitation: our work, our families, our possessions, our recreation, our habits, our interests, and even those things that cause us grief. If we commit everything to his control, he is sure to divide it in an orderly manner. Whatever we leave outside the borders may have to exist with a lesser level of divine protection.

But as we shall notice next, God appointed Levitical cities and cities of refuge even in those tribes that settled east of the Jordan. So, he doesn't ignore those aspects of ourselves that we leave outside his prescribed boundaries. But when the enemy empires came in later generations, the tribes who preferred to remain outside were first to fall and become slaves to the foreign invaders.

The lesson is clear. When we commit ourselves to him, let's leave no aspect of our lives on the wrong side of the line that separates us from the rest of the world.

'Til the Storm Passes By

Scripture: Numbers 35
Suggested Reading: Psalms 46; 57:1

Everybody needs a place of refuge. Down in hilly Park County, Indiana, travelers in open buggies used to find shelter in one of the many covered bridges when the hard rains came and torrents flooded the gullies. Chicks scurry for cover under their mothers' wings when the thunder roars, and my old dog Duke, hides in the basement when the sound of the shotgun echoes from my neighbor's woods during hunting season. All living things need a place to go when life gets troublesome.

I was fortunate when I was a child that my grandmother lived just a half block away. When my playmates became ogres or my parents scowled at me in disapproval for something I'd done, I sought sanctuary at Grandma's house. She would lift me to her knee, cuddle me in her soft bosom, talk with me and fill me with the courage I needed to go back and face my persecutors.

In my living room today, I still have that treasured old chair where I took refuge on Grandma's lap when my troubles became more that I could bear.

God knew there would be times in our lives when we needed asylum, and he wisely provided cities of refuge in which we can hide until the perils pass.

Shortly after the Israelites left Egypt, God led them through the hot desert to Elim, an oasis of seventy palm trees and twelve springs, numbers I suspect symbolically tell us that there was enough shade and water to give comfort and relief to the entire company. But after a short stay, they were back on the road, heading for Sinai. The refuge at Elim was only a place where they could stop long enough to be refreshed for the rest of the journey.

When they arrived at God's mountain, Moses found refuge in the cleft of the rock, in the hollow of God's hand, unwittingly providing metaphors that became the epitome of refuge both in succeeding scriptures and in the great hymns of the church.

David needed refuge often. Early in his life he was chased by the armies of Saul and found refuge in the caves that dot the rugged hillsides of the Judean wilderness. Later his own son, Absalom, raised an army and drove David from the palace. But even in the wilderness, God provided food and comfort for David and his army. No wonder he could exclaim, "He prepareth a table in the presence of my enemies. My cup runneth over."

If we scour the Psalms, we find frequent reference to God as the shelter in time of trouble. Over and over again, the beleaguered king found refuge in the Lord where he could hide 'til the storm passed by.

Mosie Lister captured it beautifully in the great gospel classic:

In the dark of the midnight have I oft hid my face
While the storms howl above me and there's no hiding place.
'Mid the crash of the thunder, precious Lord hear my cry;
Keep me safe 'til the storm passes by.

'Til the storm passes over, 'til the thunder sounds no more,
'Til the clouds roll forever from the sky,
Hold me fast, let me stand in the hollow of thy hand.
Keep me safe 'til the storm passes by.

A Sweeter Song

*N*owhere did the writers of the scriptures recommend a refuge from the perils of life other than in the bosom of the Lord. He alone is our hiding place, our refuge, and our strength.

But that doesn't stop Satan from chartering his own cities of refuge, which give the illusion of comfort but only mire us deeper in the trouble he has brought upon us in the first place.

We all know people who make poor choices in seeking shelter from life's stormy blasts. They seek comfort in alcohol, drugs, or other vices that appear to be oases, but turn out to be sinkholes in disguise which seduce them into torments worse than the ones they are trying to escape.

Literature and mythology are full of false sanctuary.

Old German lore tells of the Lorelei who sat atop a towering rock at a bend in the Rhine River luring lonely sailors into the shoals at the base of her rock where they wrecked and drowned. Greek and Roman mythology tell of the sirens, beautiful women who sang lovely songs, luring sailors to their death. And there's wisdom in those tales.

In his travels, Ulysses and his brave sailors found themselves approaching the Island of the Sirens. Ulysses was a bold and curious but bright fellow who had heard of those ladies and just *had* to hear their song. So he stuffed wax into the ears of his sailors to deafen them, but bound himself to the mast of his ship so he could hear their song but couldn't dive overboard and swim to them.

As they passed the island, he could hear the music and was so tempted that he strained with all his strength at the ropes that bound him, but was unable to get loose. Out of earshot, his sailors removed the wax from their ears and untied Ulysses. They had passed successfully, and Ulysses was the only man to have heard the sirens' song and survived.

Jason and his Argonauts also passed the Island of the Sirens, but that hero had a different plan. As they approached the island he had Orpheus play on his lyre, and the song Orpheus played was so sweet that the sailors didn't even hear the fatal voices of the sirens. They too, passed by successfully and survived.

The wisdom, though pagan, is still wisdom. What should we do when we are lured to a false refuge that is really a trap that will bring us nothing but torment? We have several choices. We can stuff our ears with wax so we can't even hear the siren call. We can strap ourselves to the mast and ride it out 'til the storm passes by. Or we can do as Jason did and tune our ears to a more beautiful song.

I like Jason's remedy best. Ulysses tempted fate by listening to the sirens. Jason turned to a sweeter song and never heard the temptress sing. We should not test ourselves by toying with false places of refuge. What if the bonds don't hold? We could easily find ourselves overboard and dashed to pieces on the rocks.

David was a poet and a musician who, through the inspiration of the Holy Spirit gave us beautiful songs. When we need refuge from the storms of life we need only turn to his psalms and discover the sweeter song, the same safe haven he discovered, the God who will hide us in the cleft of the rock and cover us there with his hand.

And I'm sure that the same heavenly Muse who inspired the great poets whispered words into the ear of Mosie Lister who added more sweet songs to the divine repertoire.

The Second Reading

*W*hen God gives us instructions in the scriptures, he is often repetitious. He does not say things over and over because he enjoys hearing himself speak. He knows if his important messages are to get through to us he has to pound them repeatedly into our thick skulls. I think that if we enjoyed listening to God's instructions as much as we enjoy listening to our favorite music, the Bible just might be a considerably thinner book.

The book of Deuteronomy is a second reading of the law, which Moses composed nearly forty years after the first reading. The first rendition was given at the base of Sinai, and the second was delivered to the people of Israel on the plains of Moab nearly forty years later. Although the contents of Deuteronomy are similar to passages in Exodus, there is much that is different.

The first difference concerns the author. When Moses first laid down the law to his people, he was their chief, their authority under God, their commander, their warlord who fully expected to lead them northward from Kadesh-barnea into the Promised Land.

The Moses of Deuteronomy was a man with a far different perspective. He was forty years older, the retired commander of the forces, the professor emeritus, the dethroned leader whose only destiny was to climb the Mount Pisgah, take one panoramic view of the Promised Land, and die.

Thus, the first rendition was written mostly in the legalese of the day, a product more of intellect than of spirit. Deuteronomy, on the other hand, flows from Moses' heart.

But the most interesting difference is that of audience. The first reading was delivered to a generation of people who had spent their lives in the bonds of slavery, who had practically no understanding of the great I AM, who mingled with pagans, who feared the giants in the land, and who were destined to die in the wilderness.

The second was delivered to a people who had spent their lives under God's hand of protection in the wilderness waiting for forty years to pass and for the last of their elders to die, to a people destined to drive the pagans out of the land God promised to them. This was a generation anxious to claim its inheritance in the Promised Land. To each generation the law had a totally different meaning.

So it is with us. Before our rebirth, when we dwelled in the wilderness of sin and had no hope for a life in the land flowing with milk and honey, the law was a prison of thou shalt nots. It was the standard by which we were judged and condemned. It was a myriad of rules that were impossible to obey. The law was a thing to be circumvented when at all possible and to be disobeyed in the darkness. It was a burden imposed by a jealous God who demanded unquestioning submission.

But when we became new creatures in Christ, the law also became a thing reborn. Our Lord had delivered us from its condemnation, the price had been paid, the law had been fulfilled. It lost its heartless, despotic character and became a law of love enabling us to love the Lord our God with all our hearts and our neighbors as ourselves. Jesus told the Pharisees who were obsessed with such trivia as picking grain or rescuing beasts from the ditch on the Sabbath that they should pay attention to the weightier matters of the law such as justice, mercy, and faith.

If we live under the law, obedience is a burden, but if we are in Christ, obedience is a joy. "Trust and obey" said John Sammis, "for there's no other way to be happy in Jesus, but to trust and obey."

Farewell Address

Scripture: Deuteronomy 1:1–18
Suggested Reading: Micah 6:8; Scan Matthew 24–25

*I*t was a tradition in my home church for a departing pastor to preach a farewell sermon. I remember that many of them were filled with the tears of departing, but they always contained a commission to the church to continue its faithful service to the Lord.

The greatest farewell address I ever heard was the one General Douglas MacArthur delivered to a joint session of Congress after President Harry Truman relieved him of his military command in Korea and Japan. He encouraged America to be vigilant and to continue its fight against communism. He concluded by citing an old expression, "Old soldiers never die, they just fade away" and declared that like those old soldiers, he too, would "just fade away."

Well, the old soldier didn't exactly keep his promise. He allowed his hat to be thrown ceremoniously into the ring for the Republican Presidential nomination in 1952. Then he served as chairman of the board of Remington Rand. Later he addressed my college graduating class, and in addition to still claiming, a decade after the fact, that Truman's China policy was wrong, he encouraged the graduates to use their gifts to serve their country well and to maintain the American ideals of democracy and free enterprise.

Two of the most famous of all farewell addresses are in the Bible: Moses' Deuteronomy and Jesus' Olivet Discourse. In the fifth book of the Bible, Moses reviewed the Israelites' forty years in the wilderness, reminded them of the law, with numerous footnotes, and commissioned them to walk in humble obedience with the God who rescued them from bondage, bore them through the hazards of the wilderness on eagles' wings, and brought them to the brink of the Jordan from where they could view their promised inheritance.

Finally he revealed to them the many blessings God had waiting for them if they would just be obedient, but he also warned them of the consequences of disobedience. Then he blessed them and climbed Mount Pisgah for a final talk with the Lord and a view of the Promised Land before being gathered to his people.

When Jesus knew that his end was near, he gathered his disciples about him on the Mount of Olives and encouraged them to be faithful and not to be led astray. He told them what signs would signal the end of time and warned them of the antichrist and the Tribulation. He promised that he would return in power and glory to gather his church unto himself, but until then urged them to be faithful and vigilant, to use their gifts wisely and to be sure to take care of the poor and the needy. Like Moses, he warned of the consequences of disobedience, and just before he returned to the Father who sent him, he commissioned his followers to go out into the world and preach the good news to all people.

Now I'm no biblical figure or even remotely an American hero. And I don't plan to stand behind a podium and deliver a farewell address before I'm finally gathered to my people. But if I did plan to do that, I wouldn't concern myself with politics or economics, but rather I would be sure to tell my children and my grandchildren and anyone else who would listen just how the Lord has borne me on eagles' wings through the wilderness of this life and has brought me to himself. I would encourage them to use wisely the gifts God has given them. I would encourage them to trust and obey. I would warn them to be wary of the demons that lurk in the path and want to trip them, and I would encourage them to do justice, to love kindness, and to walk humbly with their God.

The Tree of Knowledge

Scripture: Deuteronomy 1:19–46
Suggested Reading: Genesis 2:15–17; Numbers 13–14

*W*hen God uses the word *knowledge* in the scripture, he generally means much more than understanding or acquaintance, or even scholarly insight. He's talking about a level of familiarity based on intimate interaction, as the knowledge that people have of the mates to whom they are married.

When Adam and his wife ate of the tree of knowledge of good and evil, they didn't merely experience the flavor of the fruit on their taste buds. They experienced the terror of disobedience to their Maker in the depths of their souls. They experienced the loneliness of alienation from the loving God who had given them a paradise for their home. And they knew the sting of evil as well as they knew each other as they cowered naked in the bushes, hoping that God would pass by and not notice them.

When Moses chastised the Israelites for their cowardice and faithlessness forty years earlier at Kadesh-barnea when they refused God's command to take possession of the land he had promised them, he reminded them of the intimate knowledge they had of evil. Their lack of mettle had not only deprived them of residence in the land of olives, figs, and giant grape clusters, but sentenced them to a lifetime of dusty nomadic life in a dry and barren land. And from the lice in their hair and the grit in their eyes to the blisters on their feet, they also had intimate knowledge of the consequences of sin.

As promised, the dead bodies of that first generation fell in the wilderness and only the descendants of the adults God brought out of the house of bondage crossed the Jordan and occupied the Promised Land. Though those children experienced the miseries of life in the wilderness, they did not have the knowledge of good and evil that their parents had, or as their original parents, Adam and Eve had. They were innocent of the sins of those who gave them birth.

God also delivered me from the house of bondage. As a slave to sin I had carnal knowledge of its consequences. Like our first parents, I too was disobedient. And like the Israelites, I too had turned my back on the promises God makes to those who are righteous, and I found myself estranged from the Lord and surrounded by the terrors of the night. Maybe it's coincidence that the wilderness is called the Wilderness of Sin, but it's appropriate because the wastrels who tramp through it are far removed from God and are on intimate terms with the consequences of their waywardness.

But when I finally yielded and climbed on the cross to be crucified with Christ, I could feel that tired, aching, and infested old body drop into its grave. I died to self, and at the moment of death a new spirit came to life in me. Like a butterfly emerging from a cocoon, I sensed a new freedom, a childlikeness, an innocence of that intimate knowledge of sin that sentences the unrepentant to a life of guilt and shame.

As the cool waters of the Jordan soothed my weary feet and I caught a glimpse of my spiritual promised land, I knew that the Lord had cast my sins into the sea of forgetfulness.

He forgave my transgressions and remembered them no more, but he left me with scars and memories enough to remind me what happens when I go my willful way and disobey his Word.

Cousins

Scripture: Deuteronomy 2:1–3:22

$\mathcal{S}$ometimes I search my television program guide for old movies, movies that I've seen many times before, but which are so good I never tire of watching them. And almost every time I see one, something new leaps out at me that I didn't see the last time I watched. Sometimes they edit the rerun, and in a new release they add snippets of film that were cut from the original production.

The Bible is something like that. When we finish reading Matthew, we read Mark. Essentially it looks like an edited rerun of Matthew with some cuts and some additions, but we read it anyway because it is so good and it tells us something new each time. Then we go on to Luke and start all over again.

Deuteronomy is like that too. Essentially, it is Moses' review of everything that has happened to the Israelites since they left Egypt forty years before, most of which is contained in Exodus, Leviticus, and Numbers. But he left out certain memories that he must have figured didn't bear repeating, and added some new facts here and there that he didn't tell us in the other books. And we read it again and see something we didn't see before. And being somewhat of a rerun made it easier for young Jewish boys, including Jesus, to memorize.

In the Bible we learn a lot about the Edomites, the Moabites, the Ammonites, and the Amorites. Esau, the father of the Edomites, was Jacob's twin brother. God disinherited him of any portion of the Promised Land, yet he made him Jacob's neighbor and ordered the Israelites to leave him alone. For generations he was a constant thorn in Israel's side. Eventually, an Edomite became the king of the Jews and ordered the crucifixion of Jesus. Then they ceased to exist.

Ammon and Moab were sons of Lot conceived in a drunken stupor in a cave near Sodom. I've never ceased to wonder what might have happened had Abraham been totally obedient when God called him to "go from your country *and your kindred,*" and had left his nephew Lot in Haran. Whatever sons he had might have played a totally different role in the life of God's people, but then again, Ammon and Moab would never have been born, the Ammonites would not have been neighbors who intermarried with the Israelites and brought in terrible spiritual corruption. They would not have been there to taunt Nehemiah when he set out to rebuild the city that the Babylonians had destroyed. And the Moabites would not have been around to plague David or soak up the sons of Reuben.

I've always wondered if the Israelites ever looked back and wished that some of their cousins had never been born. But if Lot had never sired Moab, there would have been no Ruth to say, "Whither thou goest I will go . . . ." Some other lovely woman might have been David's grandmother, but what would the line of Christ be without Ruth in it?

Ammon and Bashan were not relatives, but their sin was so great that the Lord used Israel to destroy them. Bashan fell to Moses and the tribe of Manasseh took his land, and in the course of time the Amorites completed their iniquity and finally fell to Solomon.

Recently one of my cousins published a family tree, going back to the seventeenth century. I scanned the branches and to my amazement found the names of people I knew both as allies and competitors, but not as relatives. Beyond my name were the names of my children and grandchildren, and I wondered if their descendants, another few hundred years down history's road, might look at their family tree and wish that some cousin had never been born.

Speaking to the Rock

Scripture: Deuteronomy 3:23–29
Suggested Reading: Numbers 20:1–13; Matthew 17:1–3;
1 Corinthians 10:1–4

Currently there is a debate going on about the merits of capital punishment. One governor in a state that has the death penalty is so against it that he has commuted the sentence of everyone in his jurisdiction who has been convicted of a capital crime.

Some judges seem to have no problem imposing the death sentence, while others refuse to do it. Philosophers argue whether the state has the moral right to take life. Journalists point out the number of convicts who have been exonerated after the executioner has pulled the lever as well as the number who go to their death protesting their innocence.

On the other hand, some people get away with murder. One defense that has justified killing is extreme provocation. One person has vexed another enough to incite justifiable homicide. Judges and juries sometimes find such inducement to be exculpatory and find the defendant not guilty. Some accused argue that they didn't know their actions would result in the death of another and are either found innocent or have the charge reduced to involuntary manslaughter.

I suppose Moses felt he was not guilty of a wrongdoing sufficient to send him to his death without setting foot in the Promised Land. He had to know that he violated a direct order by striking the rock at Meribah, but did he believe that the provocation from the Israelite rabble justified his actions? He had struck the rock to get water once before, and may have had no idea that his disobedience was of sufficient magnitude to warrant the punishment he received.

In his farewell address he confessed to the people that he had pleaded with God to commute his sentence and allow him to go over and see the good land that lay beyond the Jordan. And he declared that it was on their account that the Lord was angry with him, that it was their fault that he struck the rock, that their constant whining and complaining drove him to lose his temper and provoked his disobedience.

But God would not listen to any excuses. Moses had to take complete responsibility for his actions, regardless of his state of mind or the events that precipitated his rage.

I wonder how many people get to their final judgment and make all kinds of excuses for striking the Rock of their salvation right up to the end of their sojourn in the wilderness of this life. I wonder how many stand in the dock and blame their mothers for the offensive lives they've led and plead with God for admission to paradise on the ground that they had no idea that what they were doing was so terrible it would keep them from heaven.

I've always felt sorry for Moses. Had I been a juror in God's court, I would have argued for leniency, swayed by the fact that the frazzled man was sorely provoked by a rebellious mob of ungrateful people. But God would have rejected my argument on the ground that all of us, including Moses, have to be accountable for our behavior, regardless of extenuating circumstances.

God executed his final judgment against all sin at Calvary, and now his amazing grace has tempered his sense of justice and he has turned my eyes toward the top of a high mountain and has allowed me to see a transfigured Moses standing face to face with the Rock of his salvation, and this time *talking* to him!

Never Too Old

Scripture: Deuteronomy 4
Suggested Reading: 2 Chronicles 7:14; Matthew 20:1–15;
Romans 9:14–15, 19–21

Recently our Sunday school class discussed the parable of the householder and asked if it were really fair to pay a worker who had toiled all day the same as one who had worked just one hour. There was little agreement.

Some argued that those who had worked more hours deserved more pay, and some said that they had no complaint because they got what they had bargained for at the beginning of the day. Others said it was nobody's business how much the boss paid any of the other workers as long as each got what was promised. But in the end, we generally agreed that the parable had a spiritual meaning and shouldn't be taken to apply to a worldly work force.

After we read the words of Paul, we added a different twist to the application of the parable. We as humans have no business trying to hold the sovereign God to our standards of fairness. We are not his judge. God's law requires us to love him above all and to love our neighbor as ourselves. He imposed his rules on us because we need guidance, not to set a standard of behavior for himself.

For us to hold God to any standard of conduct is an act of monumental arrogance on our part. What constitutes fairness in the relationships between human beings is irrelevant in setting a standard of fairness between us and God. The only basis for any such standard is for us to recognize that he is the Potter, the sovereign Creator of the universe, and we are the clay, the creatures that he has created. Be still and know that he is God.

When we understand fully who he is and who we are in relation to him, we can finally begin to comprehend that anything he gives us at all is given in a great act of kindness that we do not deserve. If he rewards us in any way for the work we do for him, we should accept that reward with nothing but gratitude, and least of all without any complaints or jealousy toward others for the reward he gives to them.

So it was pure grace that moved the Lord to promise the Israelites that no matter how long they served the gods of wood and stone, when they repented from their sins and turned to him, he would be merciful to them and honor the covenant he had made with their forefathers. Any time they would humble themselves and turn from their wicked ways, he would be ready to forgive them and heal their land.

And the promise he made to Israel holds true for the church as well. A saint who has been a Christian all his life and has served the Lord through the heat of life's long day has no right to expect a greater reward than the eleventh hour convert. To expect more is akin to the clay telling the Potter how to mold his vessel.

The work of the lifelong believer is to go to the wayward brothers and sisters and reveal God's wonderful promise of forgiveness. And when they say that they've been sinners all their lives and have no right to expect that God will forgive them in their final hour, the day workers should be humble and grateful and should show the errant ones that the owner of the vineyard has set only one wage—eternal life in paradise with him—for anyone who has accepted employment as a servant of the Lord, whether it be for an hour or a lifetime.

Alive Here This Day

Scripture: Deuteronomy 5
Suggested Reading: Matthew 5

When we first considered the law of God as given in Exodus, we noted that modern Christians pay little mind to it, preferring to emphasize the new covenant in Christ's blood which declares that as sinners saved by grace and reborn in the spirit, we who dwell in Beulah Land, are a new generation of God's people and are no longer slaves to the law of Moses. But we might want to review that position in light of Moses' admonition to the new generation of Israelites who stood poised to claim their inheritance in the Promised Land.

First we must remember that the Israelites who listened to Moses' farewell address were either children at the time of the Exodus or were born along the way during the forty years in the wilderness. Those over forty-five or so may have been able to recall that awful day when God descended upon the mountain in fire and smoke, earthquake and thunder, to deliver the Ten Commandments to the budding nation. But at that time they had not yet achieved the age of accountability and were not expected either to understand or to apply the law.

But as Moses spoke to them on the plains of Moab, he went out of his way to emphasize the concomitance of the past and the present, and declared that the Lord did not issue the commandments only to the adults of the Exodus who perished in the wilderness, but also to the generation about to cross the Jordan, even though they may not even have been born when God made his appearance at Sinai. In other words, the law is timeless in its application and bridges the gap between the generations. It applies to all of us who are alive here this day.

As young Isaac's trip up Mount Moriah with the wood for the offering on his back signified Christ's carrying his cross up to Calvary, and as Jonah's stay in the belly of the big fish signified Jesus' temporary interment in the tomb, so Israel's journey from the house of bondage to the land of promise signifies our pilgrimage from the tents of wickedness to our dwelling place in the righteousness of Christ. And the obligation to love the Lord our God with all our heart and our neighbors as ourselves is as much an obligation of the church today as it was of the nation of Israel before the age of grace.

And even more so. Once I polled my Sunday school class and asked how many had never bowed down to a graven image. All hands went up. I went through all Ten Commandments, and with each one someone claimed innocence. No one had murdered, no one had perjured himself on the witness stand, a few had never stolen and most had never committed adultery. We had a little trouble with taking the Lord's name in vain, keeping the Sabbath day holy, honoring our parents and coveting things our neighbors owned, but generally speaking we agreed that it was entirely possible for a very good person to keep the Ten Commandments as a Pharisee might.

But Jesus is not satisfied with a literal, Pharisaical keeping of the law. He told us that he wouldn't accept us as citizens of his kingdom unless our righteousness *exceeded* the righteousness of the Pharisees. Jesus didn't negate the law, he amplified it. Anger became murder and lust became adultery. Not living up to the name *Christian* became taking our Lord's name in vain.

Put in those terms, we're all guilty of violating God's law and can be exonerated only by the cleansing blood of Christ.

Teach Them Diligently

Scripture: Deuteronomy 6:1–7

 I stand condemned. I know the Ten Commandments by heart and I'm generally aware of the other principles of Christian living that the Lord laid out for me in his Word. In the face of some of those rules I can claim a reasonable level of innocence, while in the face of some of the others, I'll admit fault, but when I'm charged with the sin of failing to teach God's Word diligently to my children, I'll plead guilty and throw myself on the mercy of the heavenly court.

Most men I know want to be successful on three fronts. They want to do their jobs well, they want to be good fathers, and they want to be good husbands. Since men in our culture are more likely to be identified with their work than with any other endeavor they undertake, that which they do for a living becomes their first priority. To be sure, their wives and children are very important to them, but since the family's bread and butter comes from the employer or the business, and since success at work is a dominant need of the male psyche, the demands of the job usually dominate life's schedule.

Oh yes, we are careful to set aside time for parent-teacher conferences, dance recitals, and Little League games, because our appearance at those events secures our reputation as parents and provides a basis for bonding with our spouses and our children. And after the occasion we take the family to the ice cream parlor and talk about progress in math, the lovely pirouette, or the fundamentals of baseball, all in the name of good parenting.

But when it comes to teaching the children the fundamentals of faith, I for one, bear a heavy burden of guilt. Yes, I took them to church and Sunday school, bought them Bibles, taught them to tithe, and listened to their bedtime prayers, but I never came close to instructing them in the faith of the fathers as the Lord prescribed.

I was supposed to give them spiritual instruction whenever we sat in the house, walked along our way, lay down, or rose up. The words *sitting, walking, lying,* and *rising* strongly infer that we make teaching the sovereignty of God and the saving blood of Christ our full-time activity whenever we are together with our children, that we make it the main topic of every conversation, the first priority of our relationship. I did not do that. I was too busy doing a good job of putting food on the table and building a good reputation as a professional. I taught a good work ethic, scholarship, and sportsmanship, but left spiritual matters to the church and my wife.

By the grace of God, my children grew into spiritually responsible adults. My daughter Kyle and son-in-law Tom read Christian books to their children, and take advantage of every opportunity to teach them the way. When my son Cam marries and has children, I expect he'll do the same.

So today my grandchildren, Collin, Caleb, and Krista are well taught in the faith. Their parents fulfill honorably the mandate to teach the Word diligently to their children. But it wasn't my example that motivated them to that level of obedience. The credit for that goes to their mother.

Perhaps one of my subliminal motives for undertaking to write these meditations is to atone for my failure as a father. That is the moon in my valley, and I hope in the long run my children will remember me more for the education and inspiration they find in this book than for the nights I spent away from them working diligently in my office.

Between Your Eyes?

Scripture: Deuteronomy 6:8–12
Suggested Reading: Joshua 5:12; 10:7–13; Luke 2:52;
2 Timothy 2:15

I didn't do much to make my parents proud of me when I was a boy, but the one thing I remember being praised for was my knowledge of scripture. Now I can't say that I went out of my way to fill my mind with facts from the Bible or that I put any great effort into it. Mostly I was coerced into filling my mind with scriptural facts, both by my sweet tooth and my ego.

Dad read a page from the *Daily Manna* every noon and a chapter of the Bible at supper, between the main course and the dessert. To make sure we were paying attention, he would stop and ask us to repeat the last three words that he had read. If we passed his test, we could have our chocolate pudding, if not, we went to bed with the sour taste of meat and potatoes lingering in our mouths.

My earliest memory goes back to about the age of four, and I left home at eighteen, so I figure that Dad read the Bible to me out loud at least four times, and as he read, I listened intently so I wouldn't miss the pudding. Besides that, I went to Sunday school and catechism every week and attended a Christian school where my teachers made sure I knew the names of all of Jacob's boys as well as the twelve apostles, and could recite the Ten Commandments.

Both at home and at school we played Bible games. We had trivia cards that asked questions about obscure biblical people, places, and events. I knew what God created each day of that first busy week of the earth's existence, I knew how old Methuselah was when he died, and I could list, in order, the names of the cities

Joshua conquered in the conquest of Canaan. The plaques and certificates on my bedroom wall boasted of my knowledge of scripture. I had grown in favor with man, but what about with God? His words were written in pencil on my mind, they were as frontlets between my eyes, but they were not engraved on my heart. That came years later.

Long after I had ceased being a child, my adult Sunday school teacher asked me a question I couldn't answer. We were reading the book of Joshua and came to the chapter where the sun stood still over Gibeon so the Israelites could finish routing the army of their enemy. Almost as a casual afterthought, Joshua mentioned that the moon also stopped in its path over the Valley of Ajalon. The teacher asked me why the moon stood still, and why Joshua found it necessary to mention that seemingly insignificant fact. For the first time in my life I had no answer for a question about the Bible. I was ashamed.

So, I began to study. I bought a big concordance and I started reading both scholarly and popular commentaries. I began to meditate and pray over what I read, asking the Holy Spirit to give me understanding so I could "rightly divide the Word of Truth." Then I began to understand the profitability of scripture. I discovered a God who not only controlled the great light in its flight, but also fixed the beams of the gentler light on the valleys of my life so I would not stub my toe or stumble over the rocks.

Now I find boasting to be vain. It's nice to be in favor with my fellow man, but it's far more important to have grown in favor with God, to have studied and shown myself approved, a workman unashamed. The daily manna has stopped now and I am eating the produce of the land, the milk and honey of the kingdom of God, the fruit of the Spirit.

And it's better than chocolate pudding!

A Defense Against Satan

Scripture: Deuteronomy 6:13–25
Suggested Reading: Matthew 4:1–11; Hebrews 4:11–12

Most of the adults who grew up in my church have been fed an overdose of grace at the expense of obedience. Probably as a 1950's reaction to the austerity of the Depression and the self-sacrifice of wartime, they began to indulge themselves in the new fat of the land. Preachers began to derive their sermons mainly from the gospels and the epistles. Former staples of liturgy such as the Old Testament reading ceased and the weekly reading of the Ten Commandments was generally abandoned. Praise and thanksgiving blossomed as confession and repentance faded.

Fortunately for my church today, new people of more fundamental practice moved in and seasoned the new programs with flavors of the old. One lady started a highly motivational children's program that included the lost art of memorization. The kids learn the books of the Bible, valuable scripture verses, the law and the parables. They program a great deal of valuable knowledge into their memories.

I teach Sunday school to adults, most of whom are much closer to their death date than their birth date. They are attracted to my Old Testament curriculum with its regular connections to Jesus and Paul primarily because they are comfortable in their retirement, the stark past no longer threatens to return, and they have become nostalgic for the scenes of their youth, which have grown pleasant with age.

When the lesson in my class one Sunday was the twentieth chapter of Exodus, I invited one of the young disciples from the children's program to come in and recite the Ten Commandments. As he spoke, the faces of my mature students glowed with the joy of remembrance. They had not heard the Law read in decades. When the youngster finished, the class applauded with great appreciation and respect.

Then we discussed the usefulness of such an exercise. Children of the church who learn their required assignments receive rewards such as treats, badges, and special privileges, but they are also taught that their learning will some day bring far greater rewards. God commanded the Israelites to lay the words of the Lord upon their heart and to teach them diligently to their children. They were to use every spare moment of their lives, while sitting in the house or walking down the street, to instruct them in the laws of God.

Joseph, the father who raised the boy Jesus, must have done a good job of teaching those words to his sons. Following his baptism, Jesus went to the wilderness to fast and to contend with Satan. Every time the devil tempted him, he responded with scripture he had memorized. When Satan suggested that the hungry Jesus turn the stones to bread, he replied, "It is written . . . ." and quoted Deuteronomy 8:3. When the devil cited Psalms 91:11–12 and challenged him to leap from the pinnacle of the temple, Jesus again responded, "It is written . . . ." and quoted Deuteronomy 6:16. And when Satan offered him an earthly crown and an escape from his crucifixion, Jesus said again, "It is written . . . ." and quoted Deuteronomy 6:13. Then the devil left him and angels came and ministered to him.

The children of Israel carved the words of the law into their hearts, wrote them on their doorposts, and carried them on scraps of paper in their purses as a weapon against temptation.

Would that our children do the same.

A Special Treasure

Scripture: Deuteronomy 7:1–16

Years ago I had an old Christian friend who had a special treasure: an old baseball. He kept it on an oaken pedestal, under glass, vacuum sealed, and out of the sunlight in his family room, near his easy chair and right beside the door to the garage.

"Where did you get that old baseball?" I asked when I first visited his home.

"My dad took me to a St. Louis Browns game in 1922," he answered, "the year they won the pennant. I was just a little kid. A ball got hit into the stands near us and I scrambled in the aisle, tussled with a few other kids, and ended up with it."

"Wow! Was it a homerun off the bat of Gorgeous George Sisler?" I asked, remembering that he was a Hall of Fame slugging first baseman who hit over .400 for the Browns.

"No, it was a foul ball off the bat of Frank Ellerbe," he laughed.

"Who's Frank Ellerbe?"

"A journeyman infielder with a short, undistinguished career in baseball. Played for three teams in six years."

"So why have you enshrined the foul ball that he hit into the seats?"

"I decided that I needed a small memorial to remind me constantly what God has done for me," he answered. "Like me, it has no intrinsic value. It's just another old baseball. But I chased after it, fought for it, rescued it, and made it my own. And to remind me that God chased after me, fought for me, rescued me, and made me his own special treasure when I was foul, I just decided to make it my special treasure, to love it, and to give it a special place in my home. I wouldn't part with it for anything."

Then he added, "I made the oak pedestal and sent for this bell jar and vacuum sealing kit out of a science magazine. Every time I look at this old ball I'm reminded not only of how God rescued me and made me his own treasure, but how by grace he has put me on a pedestal and how he protects me and preserves me.

"Every time I leave the house the sight of it inspires a little prayer of gratitude. I always wonder what might have become of it had some other kid grabbed it, and I wonder what might have become of me had the Lord not reached out and saved me. Maybe both this old ball and I would have ended up on the trash heap."

The Lord had no special reason for choosing Israel as his own special people. They did nothing to earn his favor. He easily could have picked someone else. He didn't select them because they were better than any other nation, in fact, they were quite undistinguished among the peoples of the earth.

And he chose me the same way. God is no respecter of persons. I'm not like a homerun ball off the bat of some famous slugger, I'm more like a foul ball off the bat of some obscure infielder.

But he chased me, fought for me, rescued me, and took me home to be his own special treasure. And I'm grateful.

Wild Beasts

Scripture: Deuteronomy 7:17–26

The idea of the Lord driving the enemy nations out of the Promised Land slowly has always intrigued me. It seems to me that different strategies could have worked more efficiently to implant the new nation of Israel into the territories inhabited by the pagan Canaanites, one of which might have been for God to send a plague of epidemic proportion that would have wiped out the entire evil population and allowed the sons of Jacob to enter the land and possess it without launching a single arrow or shedding a single drop of blood, including their own.

There are at least two reasons why the Lord chose not to do that. First, he clearly wanted them to fight for the land. They had to put forth an heroic effort to make the land their own, in a small sense, to earn it. Sure, he would be on their side, fighting for them as no other ally could; but still, they needed to step out in faith and attack the enemies on whom God was bringing judgment.

The second reason is more interesting. If God had by some miracle caused all the Canaanites to drop dead in their tracks, all of the vicious animals that inhabited the land might have multiplied without control, and, having fed on human flesh, might have become a rabid force more formidable than an enemy army. General Joshua knew how to fight against human armies that fought with swords, slings and arrows, but those military tactics would be ineffective against legions of ravenous or diseased mountain lions or wolves. So, the Lord went with them, battle after battle, until most of the enemy armies fell to their swords.

As I have stated, my pilgrimage from the bondage of sin to the spiritual promised land was not accomplished in the blink of an eye as with the apostle Paul and some Christian brothers and sisters I know. And I still have not conquered and possessed the entire land. The Lord has been a strong ally in my battles against lust, pride, ego, envy, hatred, idolatry, and all of the other enemies of godliness that the redeemed have to overcome in their quest for sanctification. The Lord wants us to confront those enemies and, with his help, defeat them one by one. The Lord wants to share with us the wonderful victory celebrations that can be ours whenever we win a battle against the evil in our own flesh.

Some few of the saints who have enjoyed the incredible experience of having all of their evil human frailties wiped out in one blinding moment have a wonderful testimony to share, but that is not how God has chosen to work in most of us.

Maybe if I had become an instant saint, demons I don't know how to fight would have fed on the carcasses of my dead sins, multiplied, and set out to haunt me. The first rule of warfare is to know your enemy, and I can know him if he is of my own psychological and physical composition. But if he is composed of inhuman forces such as the dark powers of Satan, I can't understand him and wouldn't know how to fight him.

I thank God that he has let me homestead here in Beulah Land. I thank him for the many victories he has given me over the sins of the flesh. But I also thank him that he has let some of those enemies survive to plague me, so, like Jesus in the wilderness, I can take the sharp, two-edged Word from its sheath and do battle with some of the lingering forces of pride, greed, and envy that have survived the previous battles and live to fight again.

My land is not desolate. Some of my enemies are still lurking there in the shadows. But I know victory lies ahead.

The Sword and the Cradle

Scripture: Deuteronomy 8
Suggested Reading: Numbers 14:26–35; Matthew 6:25–33;
Luke 12:4–7

When I was a brash young soldier in occupied Europe after World War II, I put on my civvies, slipped into the eastern sector of Berlin and visited a Russian military cemetery.

Unlike the rest of the sector, it was beautiful and well maintained. The mausoleum housing the remains of their most decorated war heroes had a gigantic stained glass replica of Russia's highest medal of honor for its domed ceiling.

But the most thought-provoking sight came as I stood on a hill in the center of the classical gardens and gazed at a massive statue of a Russian soldier brandishing a sword in his right hand but cradling a baby in his left arm. The symbolism was obvious.

Today I remembered that giant statue of the soldier who both slays and protects as I read this chapter in the book of Deuteronomy. We have a God who does the same. Back in the wilderness he not only wielded a sword against the Amalekites, but he also wielded a sword against his own people, the ones who refused to invade Canaan forty years before. Their dead bodies fell in the wilderness, smitten by every heavenly avenger from sickness to snakebite. Yet those who neared the banks of the Jordan and looked over into the Promised Land were reminded of the miracles that had preserved them. God had given them food and water, had protected them from their enemies, and had even prevented their shoes and clothing from wearing out. During the long marches over rocky terrain and hot desert sands, their feet didn't even swell. Their God held a sword in one hand and cradled his baby in the other arm.

The same God reigns today and carries the same two-edged sword. I've stood in awe as I've watched that sword lash out and slay my enemies, those within and those without. By his might he has set me free from demons of my own making that enslaved me. By his might he delivered me from the grasp of the tempter when I was too frail to defend myself. And by his might he held back the hosts of Satan as I trudged through the wastelands of my life.

But I've also felt his blade on my own neck. When I sinned he made sure that I suffered the consequences of my evil deeds. Though he eventually removed my guilt and spared me from the eternal damnation I deserve, he punished me as a father would punish a child he loves. But as I look at the cross of Christ, I realize that the full force of his rage fell on his own Son for my sins the day he smote him there on Calvary. Yes, our God is an angry God who hates sin and executes his wrath against it.

I thank him for that anger. If, like an indulgent parent he had just turned his face and ignored our wickedness, we would still be wallowing in the slough of our transgressions instead of marching into our spiritual promised land. We would be worshipping the world's idols and worrying about what tomorrow would bring. Without his anger there would have been no Calvary, no forgiveness, no life in the spirit, and no expectation of a heavenly home.

As I stand near the banks of Jordan and survey my eternal promised land, I thank him for punishing me and protecting me. I thank him that he has given me daily manna and water from the Rock, and I thank him for the clothing he put on me when I was a child, the fabric that my parents wove for me as we sat in the house and walked by the way. It has never worn out.

When You Are Full . . .

Scripture: Deuteronomy 9
Suggested Reading: Psalms 51:2–3; Isaiah 43:25; Micah 7:19

*I*n this wonderful land to which God has led us, the land flowing with milk and honey, there is enough delicious spiritual cuisine to puff us up with pride. But the Lord warns us against overindulging in the bread of our sanctification, growing obese, and forgetting that it was he who bore us on eagles' wings and brought us to this fair land, and that it was he who devoured our enemies and made us to dwell here securely. And that brings us to one of the Bible's most fascinating anomalies.

God is omniscient, omnipotent, and omnipresent. He has a mind that encompasses all knowledge. He knows our names. He numbers the hairs of our heads, and not a sparrow falls from the sky without his knowledge. His memory bank makes our most powerful computers look like toys. Forgetting anything seems totally inconsistent with his omniscience. Yet he tells us that he will forget the things we do that rile him the most: He will forget our sins!

We, on the other hand are frail human beings. We have serious memory problems, especially as we get older. We walk from the living room to the kitchen and forget why. We forget people's names. We forget appointments if we don't write them on the calendar. We forget where we put things. Our minds are more like sieves than traps. Yet God tells us to remember our sins, including the sins of our youth. And we do.

Though we are creatures of clay, about the only things that seem not to escape our memories are our sins. They seem to linger forever in some dark pit within us. They haunt us. They torment us in our dreams and come out in some of the behaviors we are powerless to explain. Even after God has forgiven them, the sins of our past prey upon us, robbing us of sleep and disturbing our tranquility. Sometimes we even obsess over them.

But God casts our sins into the sea of forgetfulness. As the grand olds hymns of the church declare,

> He'll forgive your transgressions
> He'll forgive your transgressions
> He'll forgive your transgressions
> And remember them no more
> And remember them no more.
>
> (Fannie J. Crosby)

and,

> My sins are blotted out, I know
> My sins are blotted out, I know
> They are buried in the depths of the deepest sea,
> My sins are blotted out, I know.
>
> (Merrill Dunlop, 1927)

Yes, he'll forget our sins for his own sake, but he wants us to remember them for our sakes, and he makes sure we do remember them by giving us a psyche and a subconscious that keep our sin ever before us.

In this goodly land our Lord sustains us, satisfies our thirst with living water, fills us with the bread of life and the fruit of the Spirit. He gives us rich gifts and multiplies our blessings. But to keep us humble and obedient, he makes sure we don't forget our sins.

Loving the Sojourner

Scripture: Deuteronomy 10
Suggested Reading: Exodus 32:25–29; Deuteronomy 18:1–8;
1 Samuel 2:12–15, 22–24; Daniel 4:27; Luke 10:30–34

Why does the Lord hammer the same commandment into our heads over and over? Presently I'm leading a Bible study on the book of Daniel, and I find the prophet advising King Nebuchadnezzar to "break off your sins by practicing righteousness, and your iniquity by showing mercy to the oppressed . . . ." Kindness to suffering people is a theme that echoes incessantly through scripture, jumping out at us at the most unexpected times.

The sons of Levi did not get a geographical inheritance. They were spread throughout the other tribal lands to serve the priests, staff the cities of refuge, maintain the Levitical cities, and minister to the people. Their inheritance was spiritual. Their inheritance was the Lord himself. What a blessing!

Now that is a very great inheritance, surpassing anything material. The Levites were chosen from among all the tribes in Israel for special service to the Lord. They were the finest jewel in God's special treasure. Their destiny as a tribe was to walk hand in hand with the Lord, standing before him on behalf of the people and serving as God's agents to their brothers. They were exempt from military service. They ate the best food. Their parishioners gave them the first fruits of their grain, wine, and cattle. They were especially blessed. Why?

Forty years earlier in the wake of the golden calf fiasco, Moses asked the people. "Who is on the Lord's side? Come to me." Without hesitation, the sons of Levi gathered behind him. And when Moses ordered them to draw their swords and execute God's judgment on their sinful brothers, they obeyed, therefore ordaining themselves for the service of the Lord. For that God blessed them and set them aside as a chosen tribe from among his chosen people.

But their service included more than executing God's judgments, tending the altar of sacrifice, preaching, and praying. They were also to go out into the streets and minister to the needy, to find the hungry and weary sojourners and give them rest. They were to imitate the God who sought them out when they were sojourners in a strange land and set them free, bound up their wounds, protected them, fed them and brought them to himself. They were to serve him as his angels of mercy.

But they failed. They became self-indulgent, perverse, and sinful, gorging themselves on the fat of the sacrifices and fornicating with the women of the temple. Jesus represented their backsliding in his parable about the Good Samaritan, portraying them as people who had failed to minister to the needy and who failed to follow the Lord's command to reach out and extend the hand of mercy to the beleaguered sojourner.

Jesus had a reason for telling that story; it was not simply to cast a judgmental eye on the priests and Levites who were derelict in their duty. His main reason was to point out to us that as his church we are a new nation of priests who are to practice righteousness by showing mercy to the oppressed.

Where the priests of Israel failed, we, the foreigners, the Gentiles, the Samaritans, the church, have inherited their duties, and their blessing!

Not Like Egypt!

Scripture: Deuteronomy 11
Suggested Reading: John 14:15; Scan 1 John 3,4,5

The Israelites knew Egypt's inhospitable climate all too well. Their taskmasters forced them to make bricks and construct buildings under the blazing sun of that hot, dry land. Their only breeze was the dusty, burning wind that blew across that land from the Sahara. If they were to eat, they had to carry water by foot to their vegetable gardens and drive their flocks to the well.

Light showers occasionally watered the northern coast, far from where they labored under the whips of their captors.

Israel's climate, on the other hand, is far more friendly, enjoying cooler temperatures and much more rain. Except for the Negev south of Beersheba and the Judean wilderness, the land is well suited for raising cattle, farming, olive orchards and vineyards. Other natural resources allow its inhabitants to be largely self-sufficient. The land that the Lord gave his chosen people was not at all like the land of Egypt!

And the spiritual promised land that the Lord has given to those who love him is not at all like the land of bondage from which he rescued us. Back there we lived in slave shacks without privacy. There we raised our crops among the thistles and harvested them by the sweat of our face. There we laid up treasures and lost them to rust, decay, thieves, and inflation. There our enemies marched against us constantly, destroying our homes and our marriages, and taking our children captive.

But the land to which he has called us is a land that is secure. Here we dwell safely in the mansions that he has prepared for us from the beginning of time. Here we eat the produce of the land, the fruit of the Spirit, and drink the living water that flows freely from many springs. Here our treasures are safely locked in the impregnable vaults of heaven. Here no man can stand against us. Wherever the sole of our foot treads, our enemies cringe in the shadows, and our children are safe.

Because he loves us, the Lord wants us to abide in this good land and enjoy all the milk and honey and spiritual fruit that he lavishes upon us. The choice is ours. Between us and the land of our slavery stands the wilderness of sin, and if we wander outside our borders and stray into that wilderness, our dome of security is lifted from us and we become prey for the demons that lurk there.

As long as we show our love for God by doing what pleases him, he promises to give us whatever we ask in his name. As long as we walk in his way, he assures us that the power residing in us is greater than the powers that prowl the wilderness. As long as we obey his commandments, he guarantees us that he will give us the faith that overcomes the world. He assures us that his sun will glisten on our mountain tops and his moon will light our valleys.

And how do we demonstrate our worthiness to dwell in this wonderful land? First, we must love him with all our being. And that is not the kind of love we are capable of generating in our own hearts. That is the kind of love we can know only by knowing him. It is the perfect love that emanates from heaven above and that can be ours only if we open ourselves to it by willingly submitting to him and accepting him in faith. And secondly, we must share that pure love by loving others as he loved us, by reaching out as Jesus did, loving the unlovable and touching the untouchable.

And by his grace, we can be worthy.

No Amendments Allowed

Scripture: Deuteronomy 12
*Suggested Reading: Leviticus 25:4; 26:34; 2 Chronicles 36:17–21;
Psalms 19:7; 119:97; Matthew 5:17–22, 27–28; 12:1–13*

The colonists who first settled on our shores came here to escape the unfair laws of England. They soon rebelled against the crown and established a new law: the Constitution.

Realizing that both the government and the governed were imperfect, they provided in their new law a judiciary empowered to interpret it and a process for amending it. Only thirteen years after adopting the Constitution, we amended it for the first time and have done so regularly ever since.

And today legislators in Washington and in the various states add to the existing laws of the land. Politicians run for office vowing to change those laws, and people circulate petitions in an effort to repeal old laws or create new ones. Unlike the laws of God, our imperfect laws change with the times.

Before he left them and climbed Mount Pisgah to die, Moses warned the wilderness survivors to be careful to do all that the law of God commanded, and not to add to it or subtract from it. And before he climbed Mount Calvary to die for all lawbreakers, Jesus warned us to submit to that same law and not to presume to change it in any way. Anyone arrogant enough to alter the law would be called least in the kingdom of heaven.

The law of God is perfect and requires no amendments to accommodate the changing times. But we who are required to obey the law are imperfect in our understanding and need the law interpreted to us. Jesus Christ serves the law of God as the Supreme Court serves the Constitution of the United States. In our human ignorance we are unable to apply it as God intended, so he taught us by lesson and example.

One of the most difficult statutes for us to interpret is the law of the Sabbath. The Pharisees erred on the side of conservatism, developing rigid Sabbath rules, even to the point of counting the steps one might take before walking constituted prohibited work. In interpreting the law, Jesus pointed out that the Sabbath was made for man, not vice versa, and that it was within the parameter of the law to pull your ox from the ditch, heal a sick person, or pluck grain to eat.

In the old days my church was very strict, but now allows most any activity, so long as one makes it to worship service for an hour or so in the morning. Today we probably err on the side of liberal interpretation. To keep things in perspective, we should not forget that one of the reasons God allowed the Babylonians to destroy Jerusalem and take its people into slavery was that the people ignored the Sabbath law and that the length of their exile was measured by the number of years the Israelites failed to accord their land its Sabbath rests.

Because we got mired down in disputes about the letter of the law, Jesus had to interpret it to us. He told us that if we wanted to be truly obedient, we should look beyond the letter to the spirit of the law. And if we conform our lives to the spirit of the law, we need not be concerned about keeping it to the letter.

What it all boils down to in the end is love. If we love the law as the psalmist did, obedience becomes a joy. The Lord loved us so much that he sacrificed himself for our disobedience. And if we love him, we will keep his commandments and love others as he loves us.

A Heart of Love

Scripture: Deuteronomy 13
Suggested Reading: Ezekiel 11:13

Our God is indeed a jealous God. He formulated a multitude of rules forbidding his people to worship other gods or even to tolerate anyone who does. And he designed additional laws to keep his people pure and to preserve them unto himself. More than anything else, he wanted them to be faithful to him, and in return he would bless them in ways that were beyond their imagination.

And each time I review those laws, I seem to remember an occasion on which they violated it. Every page of their history testifies to their continual infidelity. And their treachery, of course, did not escape God's riveting attention. He reacted in two ways: anger and love.

In his anger over their faithlessness, he punished his people by raising up the empires of Assyria and Babylon against them, destroying their dwelling places, uprooting their crops, devouring their herds, scattering them to the ends of the earth, and allowing their captors throughout the world to enslave them and their children.

When their punishment ended, in an act of reconciliation he touched the heart of Cyrus, King of Persia, who let the Judeans go back home to rebuild their city and their temple and to resume practicing their faith and offering their sacrifices. But again they disappointed God; most of them preferred to remain in the lands of alienation worshipping foreign gods and bowing to foreign princes.

A tiny remnant of Hebrews returned to Israel and rebuilt the city and the temple, but soon they fell into disobedience once again, and God allowed the Greeks to dispossess them and to desolate their holy place with a horrible abomination.

When a core of them demonstrated faithfulness to God and love for their homeland, he again deposed the invaders and gave his beloved people another chance to serve him. But once free, the Israelites again forgot their God and his laws, so he smashed them with the iron boot of Rome. But before he ground the city and the temple to dust, he reached out one final time in the most beautiful act of love the world has ever seen.

He loved his people so much that he became a humble but perfect man, living among them, teaching them obedience by example, and finally offering himself as the ultimate sacrifice for the sins of the whole human race. Then in his final act of anger he gave his holy city and everything in it, including his dwelling place, over to the destructive war machine of Rome, ending forever the sacrifices and the Levitical priesthood.

The day had finally come that his law on a tablet of stone vanished from the face of the earth and he carved his law on new stones, our hard hearts, turning them to flesh and giving us an opportunity to live in grateful and humble obedience. And since the old temple had burned to the ground, God made for himself a new dwelling place, the heart of man, and filled it with his Holy Spirit.

Whenever we go to our churches, sing hymns of praise, offer our tithes at the altar, taste the bread and the wine, and hear the Word of God taught and preached, we should do so with an understanding of the pain and horror that made it all possible. As fundamentally evil beings, we should prostrate ourselves in repentance for all the grief we have caused our God throughout history, and in gratitude for the pain he suffered to make our hearts his holy temple.

The Work of Our Hands

Scripture: Deuteronomy 14
Suggested Reading: 1 Samuel 8:10–18; Malachi 3:6–12;
Matthew 23:23; 25:31–46; 2 Thessalonians 3:6–12

*E*very election year, it seems, politicians wrangle over whose job it is, and whose it isn't, to feed the poor. One side boasts about the welfare programs they've established, and the other side complains that all it does is breed sloth and dependence. Then they migrate philosophically toward each other and agree that welfare recipients ought to work, if possible, and they establish training programs and set rules requiring that one work in order to eat.

Then the Christian brothers and sisters carry on the argument, one side citing Malachi and the words of Jesus on the Mount of Olives, and the other side citing Paul's admonition to the Christians in Thessalonica. Then they set party politics aside for a time and join in on committee deliberations about stocking the food pantry so they can continue their annual project of distributing food baskets every Thanksgiving.

Whenever some pious soul ponders aloud about whether the government or the church should be in the business of feeding the poor, the chairperson of the church finance committee points out that the government spends billions on welfare, and that it would be mathematically impossible for the people of the church to raise enough money, even by tithing, to pay the pastors, pay the utilities, pay the interest on the mortgage, fund the usual programs of the church, *and* feed the poor as well. Besides, the church does its share with the thanksgiving baskets.

When God established the theocracy in Israel, the church *was* the government, so there could be no debate about who should feed the poor. The tithe had to be sufficient to pay the Levites, support the needs of the temple, and provide bread for the storehouse of the Lord, where those in poverty could find nourishment for their bodies as well as their souls.

Then came the separation of church and state. The people of Israel wanted a king, and in spite of Samuel's arguments against the idea, the people prevailed. And before long the church and the government each demanded their tithe. The government had an army to enforce its tax laws, but the church had to rely on the obedience of the people.

And that's where it is today. If we don't send our income tax forms in by April 15, the IRS agent will soon be at our door threatening to take us to jail. But if we fail to meet our obligation to the church, the chairperson of the finance committee has to make an emotional plea to the congregation.

The committee gives each parishioner a copy of the budget showing how much goes to salaries, utilities, loan payments, apportionments, and insurance, leaving just a little for Sunday school supplies and mission work, including the food pantry.

And after going home and reviewing the household income, after taxes, and the household budget for mortgage payments, car payments, insurance, utilities, medical bills, college tuition, the retirement account, food, clothing, gasoline and miscellaneous, there might be a little left for the church. Not ten percent, of course, but what does the church need ten percent for anyway?

Will the Lord open the windows of heaven and bless the work of our hands?

No Poor Among You

Scripture: Deuteronomy 15

*S*ssh . . . I think I hear an aeroplane . . . someone would say, and we would all stop clanging our spoons in our cereal bowls and listen carefully for the drone of the engine. And if it sounded as though it were coming near, we would run outside and shade our eyes with our hands as we searched the skies for the wonderful machine. Sometimes one flew so low over the house we could see "the guy," and we would wave wildly, and sometimes, unless our imaginations deceived us, he waved back.

"You'll never get me up in one of them things," Grandpa would vow. "If the Lord wanted us to fly he would'a gave us wings. Too dangerous for my blood." And he kept his word. But a few years later he lost his youngest son, my Uncle Johnny, to those very perils when his bomber went down in World War II.

When we were young and poor, the flying machine was a marvel, and none of us dreamed we'd ever ride in one, let alone stand in long lines, suffer delays, and lose our baggage. Now we are frequent fliers. Even my son, Cam, is a career pilot.

We were poor, but didn't know it, and that made us rich. It didn't matter that we didn't have a car because Grandpa had one and sometimes he let us take it to Lake Michigan to go swimming. On Sundays, the whole family, Grandpa, Grandma, Aunt Catherine, Mom, Dad and old Annie down the street, piled into the big old Buick with the wooden steering wheel and rode to church, four in the back and three in the front.

I have rich memories of poverty. My old hand-me-down wooden wagon was more than a toy, it was the family trailer. Every Saturday during the summer I pulled it to Sternberg's grocery store with a list in my hand, and Mr. Sternberg boxed the order and loaded my wagon for the trip home. Once he packed the groceries in an old Fels-Naptha carton and my mother was mad because the butter tasted like soap. That is a priceless memory.

I also made frequent trips to Ed's Filling Station and Lubritorium for a block of ice for the icebox. I had to hurry home because the ice melted and left a trail of drops on the sidewalk. The closer I got to home, the closer the drops got to each other. That's another priceless memory that comes flashing back over the years every time the ice dispenser on my state-of-the-art Maytag refrigerator goes on the fritz.

Poverty is relative. In the black hole of Calcutta, one is wealthy if he has his own cup for his daily handout of gruel, a sleeping mat, and a cardboard roof over his head at night. In America a family is poor if it has only one car.

Though we were poor, we were wealthy because we all lived with an open hand. My dad inherited an old set of extension ladders, so everyone in the neighborhood had extension ladders simply because we shared. Only one boy in my neighborhood had an electric train, but we all had an electric train because he shared.

In one verse the Lord tells us that if we are obedient there will be no poor among us, and in another he tells us that the poor will always be with us. Is that a contradiction? By no means.

Today the poor family in town may only own one car, but they are rich because when they are in a bind I let them borrow one of mine. And the Lord blesses me richly because I open my hand and share my blessings with my neighbor.

Remember the Day . . .

Scripture: Deuteronomy 16

I once knew of a rather eccentric old one-armed man who eventually made a lot of money as a portrait artist. I say eventually, because he struggled for a long time before he finally struck it rich. He wasn't a particularly religious man, in fact I doubt if he was religious at all. But he was humble and he was kind.

He got his start during the Great Depression drawing portraits of homeless people on the back streets of Detroit. His specialty was pencil art, and on grocery bags and sheets of wrapping paper begged from merchants he portrayed the face of every emotion, capturing the very essence of despair, dejection, desperation, and fear, but with an occasional glint of hope or courage.

He lived on the streets with his subjects, not because he chose to, but because he was one of them. They shared duties, some of them scouring the alleys behind the stores for anything combustible, some tending the fire in the barrel, others out begging for coins or somehow turning their talents or wares to profit, in his case, selling his art. Those who begged for nickels and dimes and those who sold goods bought food and commodities for the others. He sketched during the week, and on weekends hawked his drawings to shoppers on the street corners downtown.

One day a businessman, apparently unscarred by the Depression, sought him out and commissioned portraits of his wife and children. The rest is the stuff of a storybook.

His business grew and he abandoned the pencil for the paintbrush. As wartime prosperity drove hard times away, he rented a studio and began painting portraits of the prosperous. He became famous for his ability to capture the character of a person's soul in the lines of his face. By the 1970's he was wealthy, and his work hung in the drawing rooms of America's finest homes.

Most people would have been so happy to get out of the slums and into the suburbs that they would never want to go back. But he always remembered the day when he was a slave to poverty, and he celebrated his deliverance by regularly putting on his old clothes and going back to hang out with the unfortunates who still inhabited the back streets of the city. Without flaunting his wealth or acting superior, he quietly provided food, clothing, and opportunity to those who were victims of their times.

Some of the people he helped had once been successful managers, engineers, or executives who lost all they had when they became the waste products of corporate downsizing and mergers. And there were others who never had the mettle to succeed in modern commerce. Without judgment or preference, he offered companionship and succor to the lost souls who, a generation before, would have been his comrades. He always remembered the days of his own bondage.

As we now enjoy the blessings of life on our spiritual mountaintop, let us remember our days in the valley. And as the bright light of God's favor gives splendor to our days, let us never be too grand of spirit to go back and walk through those valleys from which God by his grace liberated us, and offer a moonbeam of hope to those who languish where we once languished. Sin is a slave master from whose irons we could never have been ransomed unless a merciful God and a loving Savior had not set us free.

Let us always remember the day we came out of Egypt.

No Foreigner King!

Scripture: Deuteronomy 17
Suggested Reading: Genesis 27:39–40; 2 Kings 8:20–22; Mark 3:6;
Luke 23:11–24; John 19:15; Acts 12:1–3; Romans 13:1–2

The Word of the Lord is full of ironies and his ways are very mysterious. Before the Israelites entered the Promised Land, Moses gave them a library full of laws and rules to obey. He gave directions for selecting a king. Anyone on whom they bestowed a crown had to be a blood brother, a descendant of Jacob, one of their own, not a foreigner. Moses also gave orders regarding the sacrificial lamb. It had to be perfect, without blemish. But they broke both rules.

Until the Gentile empires began to exert their influence in the area, the Jews always had a Jewish king. All of Judah's monarchs descended from the line of David, and before the Diaspora, all of the crowned heads of Israel had come from the tribes, but by their abominations they led the people down the road to destruction.

And during those kingdom days, the priests offered defective sacrifices. The people brought their very best goats and lambs, and the Levitical priests would inspect them, claim to find a flaw, keep their offering for themselves, and sell them instead an inferior animal to lay on the altar. No wonder God exiled them and abolished them as a nation until the "latter days."

When the remnant of Judah returned from Babylon during the times of the Persians to rebuild the temple and the city of Jerusalem, God placed new governors over them, men of his choosing, who supervised the reconstruction until the Greek tyrants invaded the land and desecrated the house of the Lord. Loyalist Jews rose up in opposition and eventually succeeded in ending the reign of terror and crowning one of their own king again, a loyalist priest whose family remained in power until the iron monster of Rome crushed them and tainted their royalty. Then, for the first time, God's chosen people claimed foreigners as their king. One was Caesar, the Roman emperor, the other Herod, a Roman sympathizer loyal to Caesar.

King Herod "converted" to Judaism by being circumcised, not by his own initiative, but by being forced to the knife by Jews loyal to Moses' laws. To add to the irony, he was an Edomite, a descendant of Jacob's estranged brother, Esau, of whom his father prophesied that even though he was destined to serve his brother, he would one day break loose and slip from his neck the iron yoke of Israel. And though that prophecy had been fulfilled once during the reign of King Jehoram, it was fulfilled again during the time of the Romans.

Sure, Herod and Caesar weren't exactly kings that the Jews had anointed and set over themselves, so technically they were not in violation of Moses' law, especially since all authority comes from God in the first place, and since God used all the powers that he raised up, from the Pharaohs to the Caesars, to rule and to punish his wayward people. God even appointed Herod to build him the splendid temple in which Jesus worshipped. And pious and influential Jews, the Pharisees and the Herodians, played politics with these outsiders, claimed them as their king, sympathized with them, supported them, and conspired with them to crucify the real King of the Jews and to persecute his church.

And it was Herod, the foreign king forbidden by Moses, who unwittingly obeyed Moses and offered up the Lamb without blemish, the perfect sacrifice for sin, the sinless Son of God, Jesus Christ.

Yes, the Lord moves in mysterious ways his wonders to perform.

Abominable Practices

Scripture: Deuteronomy 18:1–14
Suggested Reading: Exodus 22:18; 1 Samuel 28;
Matthew 24:11; 23:25

When I sit down to watch television, I'm bombarded with commercials for psychics who want to tell our fortunes. When I pick up the newspaper, the daily horoscope stares me in the face. When I drive through town I see the sign on Mother Margaret's house, advertising spiritual readings and séances. When I go to the movies, I see previews begging me to attend films about people who are in league with demons or children who communicate with the dead. Abominable practices are alive and well.

From Moses to Paul, the Lord issued strong prohibitions against fraternizing with any spirits other than those he sends us. Evil spirits are not to be toyed with. They are real, and they are our enemies. They are at enmity with God and want only to harm us.

Now I'm sure that most of the people who want to take our money in exchange for information they claim to receive from spiritual sources are nothing more than shysters operating their scams. But since we can't distinguish the con artist from the genuine sorcerer, we're well advised to keep our distance from anyone who even appears to be involved with the occult.

To the best of my knowledge, I've never entertained demons, unless it was unawares, and I've never paid any attention to superstitions. But I know people, right from my own church, who buy lottery tickets and trade stocks on the day their horoscope claims will be their lucky day. Now I know that isn't quite the same as going to the witch of Endor and asking her to raise a prophet of God from the dead to tell you what the winning numbers will be or what stock to buy, but are they, though peripherally, dealing in the same black art?

Fascination with prophecy is nothing new. Biblical figures seem to have been far more involved with oracles than are modern folk. From patriarch to king, they sought to know the future, and multitudes of prophets, from Moses to John, have laid it out in detail. I have a shelf full of books which admit to my interest in biblical prophecy and the end times. I've studied and taught the major and minor prophets, the epistles, and the book of Revelation. And if I draw a tight circle around *biblical* prophecy and confine my interest to the future God reveals in his Word, even though I don't understand it very well and have little faith in those who claim they do, I believe I'm safe. But when I begin to poke into the secular world of mysticism, I'm stepping into quicksand. It is a world populated with demons who have evil intentions.

I raise this point now because interest in the future usually heightens in the decades bracketing the turn of a century. We are at the point in time when the sixth millennium of recorded history has ended and the seventh has begun. It is a time when Christians are paying closer attention to the signs of the times in the expectation that the end may be near. God tells us that in that day a brilliant and persuasive antichrist, a master of the black arts, will arise and do everything he can to deceive us. We have no idea when he is coming. All we suspect is that he will be a very likeable character at the first, and when millions fall for him, he will destroy them.

Jesus warned us to be wary of the false prophets who arise and claim to speak in his name. Their signs and wonders may astonish us, but unless we see him coming on the clouds of heaven with our own eyes, hear the trumpet blast and see the angels, we are to turn a deaf ear and quickly walk away.

A Prophet Like You

Scripture: Deuteronomy 18:15–22
Suggested Reading: Exodus 23:20–21; Joel 2:28; Matthew 8:27;
John 8:28; 12:49–50; 14:15–26; Acts 2; 1 Corinthians 10:4

*A*nyone with even the most basic grasp of scripture cannot help but understand that Jesus Christ was present with the Israelites as they journeyed from Egypt to the Promised Land. He was their rock, their source of water, he was their bread from heaven, he was their guide, and he was their protector. His Spirit was in Moses, the man God chose to confront and confound Pharaoh and to lead the children of Israel to the land of milk and honey. Just as the winds and the waves obeyed him at the Red Sea, they obeyed his will on the Galilee, and just as he supplied water for Jacob's sons in the desert, he supplied living water for the woman at his well. The Spirit who moved on the face of the deep, piled up or flattened out the seas and forced subterranean streams to flow through rock, also moves in the hearts of people and guides them safely to their home in heaven.

The most incredible thought that can occupy the human mind is the notion that the same almighty power that called the universe into being makes its home in the human heart. The concept so stretches our capacity to think that it has to be fed to us in bits and pieces. God is the omnipotent essence who started it all by speaking light into instant existence, harnessing its boundless energy, transforming it into spheres of substance and floating them on their precise paths through the immense vaults of space. Then that infinite power selected a tiny speck of insignificant celestial dust to populate with billions of seemingly insignificant specks of life in whose hearts he would someday dwell.

All through the scriptures, God took on form and appeared in the lives of people. Sometimes he came and walked among us, sometimes he sent his angels, and sometimes he sent his Spirit to penetrate the being of a person, and to speak and move through the one he inhabited.

During the Exodus the Spirit of the creator God was in Moses, Joshua and Caleb, and later in David, the prophets and the apostles. Those men were still fully men, clay forms molded into shape by the Potter and prone to fall short of the perfect standard of righteousness, but nevertheless, their bodies were the dwelling place of God.

But there was one to come who would be different from all the rest, one incomprehensible and perfectly righteous creation of God who was God and was with God from before the beginning, a creature who made all creatures and for whom all creatures were made. Our Creator became our brother and lived among us. The Word that went forth and called everything into being became a being itself. The Potter became a vessel for menial use. God had raised up a prophet like Moses and had put his Word into him. And he spoke, not of his own will, but of the will of the one who sent him.

But before that vessel could fulfill its intended purpose, it had to be broken. And after it was broken, its spirit returned to the realm from whence it came. Then that Spirit that hovered over the deep, the Spirit that scrambled the tongues of those who built the infamous tower in Babel, the Spirit that opened a path through the sea and sent water gushing from a rock, the Spirit that filled Moses and Elijah and John the Baptist and spoke through the mouth of Jesus, stood poised for its finest moment, Pentecost! Then that Spirit was poured out on all flesh, flowing from the lips of the apostles and melting the hard hearts of sinners.

And the same spirit that gave Peter utterance can live and work in us all!

The Avenger of Blood

Scripture: Deuteronomy 19
Suggested Reading: Exodus 21:14; Revelation 12:9; 20; 21

In Israel it was the nearest male relative. In merry old England, it was the hangman; in the military, it was the firing squad; and in states that have capital punishment, it is the executioner. From the time of Moses to the present, civil laws have provided for an avenger of blood, a person designated to end the life of a person who has committed willful murder.

Of course, through the history of mankind, capital punishment has been meted out for crimes other than murder. In New England as well as in old Israel, sorcerers were put to death. In the old west, horse thieves were hanged. The military has been known to execute deserters. And in the Garden of Eden, death was the punishment for disobedience.

So, since "By Adam's fall, we sinned all," we are all capital offenders. We are all on death row, awaiting the clink of the key in our cell door that will open for the last time when we are called to walk that last mile to meet our executioner. Can we make a final appeal before the sword of justice falls on our necks? Will anyone save us from eternal death?

We all know the story. In a very extraordinary way, Jesus Christ stepped in to take the punishment we deserved. The guilt of our disobedience was heaped on him, and he was executed in our place. He carried his cross to the top of the hill where the Roman soldiers crucified him. The anguish he suffered there was an anguish we earned when we ate of the fruit of the forbidden tree. Since we triggered the chain of events that ended in Jesus' death, we are murderers too, as guilty of his blood as any high priest, Roman soldier, or Edomite king.

But there's still more to the story. He went to the cross of his own accord, but he was also the victim of a conspiracy by the sinners, the high priests, and the politicians who wanted him out of the way. He volunteered to die for us all, but he was murdered nonetheless. And since he was willfully murdered, his blood must be avenged. Who will be the avenger? And whose blood must flow to avenge the death of Christ?

His next of kin is God the Father. Will the Father avenge the blood of his Son? And who is the guilty party? Who plotted our transgression by tempting us in the garden? Who caused the murderers of our Lord to conspire to crucify him? Who is the deceiver of the whole world? At whose instigation did it all happen?

The questions, of course, are rhetorical. Every believer knows that Satan is the tempter who brought sin and death into the world. He organized the conspiracy. The blood of the innocent Jesus is on his hands, as well as on the hands of all sinners. And that blood will most certainly be avenged! John revealed to us the sentence the Judge handed down to the devil who took his Son's life: he will be cast into the lake of fire to suffer torment day and night for ever and ever.

But the fire that devours Satan will also devour every sinner who has not confessed his part in the chain of events that ended in Christ's going to the cross. Confession and repentance bring pardon, and only the names of the pardoned are written in the Book of Life.

And pardon is not simply the offer of a lifetime, it is an offer and a promise for all eternity!

Back to His House

Scripture: Deuteronomy 20:1–9
Suggested Reading: Judges 7; Psalms 44:3–8

Although there are exceptions, throughout the history of warfare, larger armies have generally defeated smaller. As the Assyrian empire grew and acquired more territory, it conscripted additional soldiers from the armies it defeated, and as its forces grew in number, its victories increased until it controlled vast areas of land.

Then when the Assyrian power flagged, the Babylonian multitudes built a new empire, followed by the Meads, the Persians, the Greeks, and finally the Romans. Except for instances of exceptional strategies, brilliant leadership, and innovative weaponry, the size of a military force had always been its greatest asset. In the days of the great empires, any man who could brandish a sword, throw a javelin, or twirl a sling was forced into service.

When greetings came from Uncle Sam calling our soldiers to arms, there were very few excuses that would suffice to exempt one from service. If the need for warriors was great, as in World War II, deferments for any reason were rare. Back then, the main thing that distinguished the potential conqueror from the potentially vanquished was numbers. The Allies eventually overcame the Axis forces because they had more ships, more tanks, more planes, more bombs, more guns, and more men.

Though we still give credit to spirit, tactical superiority, strategy, and morality of cause, until the advent of the atomic bomb, the size of the military was its most important quality. The soldiers had always won the wars, and the heroes were the men who raised their flags on the enemies' hilltops and the generals who led them.

The age of technology changed all that. In the war against the invader of Kuwait, Allied fighter planes, missiles, smart bombs, and super tanks reduced the Iraqi hordes to a colony of ants under the foot of a giant. The well-equipped volunteer few destroyed a multitude of poorly armed enemy draftees. Because of high technology there was no need for a general call to arms. For the first time in the history of battle, comparative numbers of troops had become irrelevant.

With one outstanding exception.

When Israel went to war against the nations that occupied Canaan, God made a point of reducing the number of soldiers in his army to less than the enemies' numbers. Any soldier who didn't want to fight or who had an excuse was dismissed and sent back to his house. No longer would the hero be a clever general who could outthink the brass on the other side, or the fearless swordsman who dared attack an entire squad of charioteers. No, the hero of the fray would be God, and there's a good reason for that.

When men win wars, the grateful people turn their victorious commander into a president and the heroic leatherneck into a movie star. They give the glory to those who fought. They commission sculptors to carve statues of generals atop prancing steeds, they honor their heroes with parades and medals, and they build war memorials to remember the brave warriors who fell in battle.

And in the war against the demons that occupy our spiritual promised land, God is telling us that he alone will give us victory, not by our own courageous struggles against Satan's rabble nor by our own cunning, but only by the powerful, conquering blood of the only war hero who truly defeated Satan's army, Jesus Christ.

Only the Trees

Scripture: Deuteronomy 20:10–20
Suggested Reading: Genesis 1:26–30

Mary Ann is very sensitive about nature. At home in the summertime she catches insects in paper cups and releases them outside to carry on their brief existences. When we drive through the country, she mourns the encroachment of civilization into the habitations of rabbits, skunks, and squirrels. She even winces when I set traps for the moles that lay waste my lawn. But she is particularly testy about the cutting of trees, whether it be for timber to build houses or to clear the land for expanding the suburbs or even for growing crops and protecting electric wires.

Years ago when the city declared war on a row of stately oaks that grew close to the road and posed a danger to wayward motorists, she joined in the protest to protect God's beautiful creation from the chainsaw massacre. She declared that it was the automobile that was endangering the trees, not the other way around. And now she sends money to organizations dedicated to preserving everything from equatorial rainforests to pandas.

It's a good thing that she wasn't there during the invasion of Canaan when the warriors of Israel laid their axes to the woods all around in order to build siege works against the pagan cities. She and General Joshua would never have agreed on such tactics. She probably would have protested. Now it wouldn't surprise me a bit to learn after I get to heaven that in some mysterious prenatal sojourn back into the far reaches of eternity past, she put the bug in God's ear to tell Moses to lay down the law about the fruit trees. In fact, I'm convinced that she had something to do with getting the question put into the Bible, "Are the trees in the field men that they should be besieged by you?" It sounds just like her. Either that, or her mind works amazingly like God's. If only God can make a tree, how can we cut it down?

It's hard to maintain a moderate view of nature. When we contemplate the miracle of a blade of grass poking up through the asphalt, and when in our poetic mind a sprouting plant dwarfs the majesty of a rocket soaring into space, every particle of nature becomes hallowed. Gnats, mosquitoes, and fruit flies are more wondrous than the Concorde, and the seed of the cottonwood tree floating in the breeze is more astounding than the Goodyear blimp. When we see God in everything that grows, even the least of living things takes on a sacred dimension. Even weeds demand respect.

But when we fail to see the hand of God in the world around us, insects become bothersome little things that need to be swatted, and the marvelous little helicopters that spin down from the maple trees become nothing more than scum plugging up our rain gutters. Moles become the enemy of man, and even the birds lose their splendor and become the little rascals that leave white stains on our redwood decks.

Somewhere between the extremes is the place where God wants us to be. He expects us to appreciate the beauty of the blossom and the song of the bird, but we must never forget that he has given us nature for our use, timber with which to build our homes and cattle and plants for food on our table. He even put the lowly earthworm to good use for both farmer and fisherman.

God has given us dominion over all living things, but as we exercise that dominion and cut the timber, till the soil, slaughter the fatted calf and enjoy tasty meals in our lovely homes, we must always remember to be good stewards of the world that gives us our breath and our sustenance.

A Rebellious Son

Scripture: Deuteronomy 21

Now I was never what you would call a stubborn and rebellious boy, but there were times when the devil had his way with me. I remember coming face to face with this passage one day after I had caused my mother some awful grief. She lamented my wrongdoing to my father when he came home from work, and he sentenced me to what seemed like a lifetime at hard labor.

That evening at dinner, the scripture reading was the twenty-first chapter of Deuteronomy. I'll never know if it happened that way by God's grace or if my dad gerrymandered his progression through the Bible, but in the discussion that followed, they made sure I knew that I was greatly blessed by having been born in twentieth century America rather than in ancient Israel. Had the latter been the case, I'm sure I would have been stoned to death for my misdeeds.

Since the Israelites seldom obeyed the rules God set for them, I don't know of any parents who actually ever took a rebellious lad to the city gates to be stoned. In our culture, we can't imagine any mothers and fathers doing that. I was a juvenile probation officer once back in the sixties, and I had frustrated parents call and ask that I put their rebellious son in jail for a night or two to be taught a lesson, but no one ever asked me to take their boy to the electric chair, though, knowing how some of those boys behaved, some parents might have given it some thought.

In our Sunday school study of the Pentateuch, people rebel at the brutality that characterized early societies. In the age of juvenile justice systems bent on rehabilitation, they find it hard to believe that God would order a misbehaving son to be stoned to death. And they find particularly abhorrent God's order to go into the land and destroy every living thing: men, women, children, and beasts.

Since the modern mind cannot comprehend ancient thinking, I find it profitable to contemplate those events in the light of metaphor. The release of the Israelites from bondage and their entrance into the Promised Land compares figuratively to our release from the bondage of sin and our entrance into the promised land of life in the Spirit, walking hand in hand with the Lord and dining on the produce of the land, the fruit of the Spirit. We are to cross Jordan symbolically by being crucified with Christ, dying to self and being raised with him, born again as a new creation into a new paradise.

When I transpose myself from the historical realm into the spiritual, I can begin to understand that the Lord wants me to keep our relationship pure, that he has given me a beautiful land in which to dwell together with him, and that he will be angry if I defile our habitation with the sins of the old life. So I must put the pagan powers to death and cast all the darkness out of my being.

But I have also accepted the fact that when I crossed the river, I did not become magically or instantly sanctified. Evil habits of the past, like rebellious sons, have infiltrated my new life and are doing all they can to reclaim their lost inheritance. Lust, envy, pride, and covetousness do not, like the cast out demons, go thankfully into the bodies of swine when they learn they are no longer welcome to inhabit this body. They resist eviction and try to reclaim their old haunts with renewed conviction.

So, I learn that I must be brutal with any remnant of sin that arises in me after I've claimed my inheritance in this new and wondrous land, and like the old Jewish father of the rebellious son, I have to take those old sins to the city gates and stone them to death.

For He Is Your Brother

Scripture: Deuteronomy 22–23:23
Suggested Reading: Matthew 12:46–50

A bloc of warped politicians who advocated saving the government money by making English the official language of the United States used to send me propaganda and requests for donations. I responded, rather sarcastically, that my pet project was the passage of legislation to limit the amount of snowfall in our cities and guarantee a minimum of snowfall each year in our winter recreation areas. And I suggested that we work together to achieve our respective goals.

One of their staff who apparently didn't have much of an eye for ridicule actually called me back to inform me that snowfall was an act of nature, and that no legislative effort could possibly change that. I thanked him and advised him that the language used by a people was also a natural phenomenon impervious to government control, and I even recommended a book about the history of language that would prove the point.

I didn't let him off the line without pointing out that the obvious purpose of his plan was to disenfranchise the non-English speaking people of our country, and that if he were really interested in saving the government money he should try to do something about Medicare fraud. He didn't come right out and say that the people who benefited from Medicare fraud were his congressman's constituents, he didn't have to. But before he hung up he knew for sure that in my opinion his efforts were being masterminded by racists who abhorred all ancestries other than their own.

Now I can understand God not wanting his people to abhor the Edomites. After all, the sons of Esau were not only their brothers, but Esau was the brother their father Jacob defrauded in the first place to get the inheritance in the Promised Land. And even though the Edomites got some small measure of revenge by refusing them passage along the King's Highway, they were still not to hate them, for they were their brothers.

But I struggle a bit with the prohibition against malice toward the Egyptians. After all, the Egyptians made them slaves and abused them terribly, so why not detest them for it? Sure the Israelites were sojourners in the land of Egypt, but they certainly didn't owe their slave masters any respect for their brand of hospitality.

But think back. When Jacob and his sons were suffering from famine, the Egyptians not only invited them to come and live in their country, but gave them the choicest of lands in which to raise their cattle and their crops. And the way most scholars count the years, the Israelites spent far more time enjoying the lush grasslands of Goshen than they spent building cities under the barbed whips of Pharaoh. Anyway, God had already punished the Egyptians for abusing his people, so they still owed their hosts for their many pleasant years of sojourning in their country.

So, what's the point?

We don't have to work very hard to find an excuse for abhorring people. We might begin by abhorring people who have harmed us. But God knows that such feelings would do nothing more than make our psyches fester with acrimony and would do nothing to hurt the one who hurt us. Or we could abhor people of another color, people of another heritage, or people who speak a different language.

But God is careful to point out to us that we are not to abhor others, after all, as creatures of one Creator, we are all brothers.

All You Can Eat

*Scripture: **Deuteronomy 23:24–25***
Suggested Reading: Exodus 16:11–27; Deuteronomy 8:1–3;
Matthew 6:25–34

The area in which I live is famous for its food. People come two days' drive just for the pleasure of eating some of our Amish cooking. The buffets are heaped with the tastiest fried chicken, roast beef, mashed potatoes, stuffing, gravy, biscuits, glazed carrots, pies of all flavors, and if I continue to dwell on it, I'll be driven to leave my desk and go out for an early dinner.

There's always that big sign hanging out over the road that lures you in by proclaiming, *"All You Can Eat."* But once you get inside, there's that little sign hanging over the cash register that says, *"No carry outs."* My favorite restaurant has a small sign over the buffet that reads, *"Take All You Want; Eat All You Take."* They don't want you to eat your fill today and pack a lunch for tomorrow.

Now, I've watched people piously give thanks for the food they were about to receive, rise and make several trips to the counter, heap their plates with chicken breasts and roast beef, return to their table, gorge themselves over and over again as at some Dionysian feast, and slyly rake huge portions of food into plastic bags hidden under the table inside a lady's purse, which is more the size of a suitcase than a handbag. And after they've eaten their fill, they pay for one meal and leave with bulging satchels. I've often wondered if they give thanks for it again the next day, or if they feel that the one prayer, like the one check, covered it all.

If you talk to them, they'll either tell you rudely to go away and mind your own business, or say that they're just being good stewards of the resources with which God has blessed them, being frugal and making their money stretch as far as possible. But we know, and so do they, that they are gorging themselves with stolen food. But they will forever refuse to admit that God looks with great disfavor upon such ravenous appetites.

I have more antipathy for the gluttons than I have for their victims. After all, the people who own the restaurant are millionaires many times over. I know, because they live in a mansion not far from my home. And they are good people. They willingly give to the poor, care for their neighbors, and do their share to stock the food pantries of our churches and soup kitchens.

I think God is less concerned about the bank account of the farmer who owns the vineyard than he is about the heart of the gleaner. He wants the farmer he has blessed with bounty to live with enough of an open hand to welcome his poorer neighbor's snagging of a few grapes as he takes a shortcut through the field. And he wants the pedestrian with an empty stomach to feel free to help himself to enough of the divine abundance to assuage his hunger pangs. But God allows no doggie bags, because to take more than you can eat is gluttony.

In fact, it's worse than gluttony. It is faithlessness. There is no way we can honestly ask God to "give us this day our *daily* bread," then go to his buffet with a plastic bag hidden in our purse and fill it with tomorrow's lunch. It's sinful to sit there and stuff ourselves so full of roast beef that eating the piece of raspberry cream pie for dessert is more chore than pleasure. We are seeking first to fill ourselves, not seeking first the kingdom of heaven. And like the Israelites who gathered manna for the morrow, we are testing God and failing to rely on him, the giver of all good things, to give us the ration of bread for which we pray.

Stewardship or Greed?

Scripture: Deuteronomy 24

As long as God has set our minds on the subject of our greed and his generosity, he takes the opportunity to tell us a second time to control our appetites and concern ourselves with the hunger of others. This chapter has its redundancies for a reason. We can't simply nod our heads in understanding and move on to the next topic. Sometimes God stops us and says, "Let's cover that again just to be sure you understand." And that reminds me of a story.

Many years ago I was with a church group having a picnic at a public park. I noticed an indigent man ride up on his bicycle, stop at the nearby trash bin and pick out the returnable ten-cent aluminum beverage cans that people had thrown away. I saw him glance over toward our picnic area and cast a wistful eye on a box at the end of our table marked with a felt pen, "*CANS*" that a thoughtful lady had put there to keep us from littering. At least, that's why I thought she put it there.

As we were cleaning up after the picnic, with the pauper in mind and when the lady wasn't looking, I picked up the box, carried it to the trash bin and dumped the cans inside. Now I wasn't being particularly saintly, I simply remembered my college days and the week before my GI check came in the mail. My wife and I sometimes had to walk along the highway next to our trailer park and pick up pop bottles and cans to return to the store for a two-cent refund so we could buy a small box of noodles and a can of tuna. Experiences such as those remain locked in your memory forever.

But the lady who marked the box became indignant. She gave her young son the box, and with a blistering glare at me that I'll remember forever, ordered him to retrieve those cans from the trash bin so she could return them for a refund. The lad obeyed his mother, salvaged the cans, and loaded the box into the trunk of their Lincoln Town Car that had an unexplainable "handicapped" tag hanging from the rearview mirror.

I know that lady quite well, and if she reads this before I die, there will probably be one less mourner at my funeral. But I can live with that. We were both children of the Great Depression and knew what it was to be poor. But poverty had a far different impact on her than it had on me. Her memories took a negative turn, and she vowed to do all she could to avoid penury for the rest of her life, including going to garage sales looking for bargains, clipping grocery store coupons and, of course, returning empty pop cans.

But there's a fine line between stewardship and greed. Now I have nothing against good stewardship; I do my best to practice it, but not at the expense of open handed living. And although I don't pray for a return to the days of want, I'm grateful for that experience, not only because it taught me the value of the dollar, but because it taught me compassion for the poor.

After she drove away, my conscience compelled me to drift over to the trash bin and wedge a five-dollar bill under the latch of the lid; then I went back to the picnic table and waited for the pauper to return. I tingled with joy and my eyes grew teary as I watched him glean the cash and ride away, a happy man.

On the way home we passed the supermarket and saw her big black Lincoln parked in the place reserved for the handicapped. And I knew, as I pictured her pocketing the cash from those discarded cans, that my blessings far surpassed hers.

Humility First

Scripture: Deuteronomy 25
Suggested Reading: Proverbs 15:33; 18:12

*N*ot too many pastors preach sermons from the book of Deuteronomy, but every now and again when pledge time makes its annual appearance in the church, the people from the finance committee are bound to make their rounds of the adult Sunday school classes with Bibles open to the verse that prohibits muzzling the ox as it treads out the grain. It's probably the one time of the year that the pastor doesn't mind being seen as a beast of burden.

I'm not at all sure that God put that text in the scripture simply as fodder for advocates of higher pastors' salaries, nor even as instructions for grain farmers. I think he intended it as a precept for any entrepreneur who benefits from the labor of another. Pay the employees an honest wage for an honest day's work! And I don't think it's too much of a stretch to read it as a message to the ox that if he doesn't tread the grain, there will be nothing for him to eat.

But the message reaches its fullness of meaning near the end of the chapter. We are obliged to be honest and fair in all our dealings, whether we are the oxen who tread the grain or the farmers who harness them to the mill.

Had this chapter been the basis for more sermons, perhaps we wouldn't have had television evangelists turning huckster to sell non-existent condo space or cheap religious trinkets for far more than they're worth, the deacon putting the old tires back on the car after he sold it, the farmer putting the lean ears at the bottom of the bushel, the saleswoman padding her expense account or the factory worker padding his overtime. The expression, *caveat emptor* would be a byword only in the world of secular enterprise, and the people of the church could be trusted to conduct their business fairly.

Pastors preaching funeral sermons have to do a lot of fancy footwork when officiating at the services of a parishioner with a reputation for guile, but they dance for joy when they have the opportunity to eulogize one with a reputation for integrity. Why is it that one brother can go to his grave with a plastic smile on his face because he successfully tricked another in his pursuit of wealth, while another would gladly suffer loss if profit demanded deceit?

Had Solomon asked for something other than wisdom, we might never know.

The great insight that God gave to the author of Proverbs bends the entire focus of thought to one human attribute: humility. Humility is the well from which all decent qualities flow, while haughtiness is the primary source of evil. If one reveres self less and loves others more, many rich blessings will flow, including contentment, honor, and respect.

The humble people are free to live honest lives because self-aggrandizement is not on their agenda, while the haughty are fettered to lives of treachery because coming in second hurts so much. For the deceivers, success is hollow because it derives more from others' loss than from their own gain. Truly humble people can enjoy second place because it affords them the opportunity to congratulate the victors, but if they win, victory is sweeter because they have earned it honestly.

Victory over self is the greatest triumph of all, and until we have conquered the forces of ego, humility is a mere forgery and contentment but a mirage.

The Windows of Heaven

Scripture: Deuteronomy 26
Suggested Reading: Malachi 3:10

My good friend Jim who owns a hardware store framed the first dollar he ever took in, and hung it on the wall behind the cash register. Since the day he opened the store many years ago, millions of dollars have passed through his hands, but that first dollar will always be special. His first customer was a man named Roy Carr who bought new lantern battery for ninety-eight cents.

Handwritten just above that framed dollar on a photo of Roy handing Jim the dollar is a note indicating that the store's first sale happened on November 8, 1968. A note just below the dollar has a quotation from Psalms, "*We give thanks unto thee, O Lord.*" He says that the remembrance of that first dollar is important to him because it reminds him how much God has blessed him over the years, and because it reminds him to give his tithe regularly to the Lord.

His confession is not unlike the confession Moses required of the people of Israel after they entered the Promised Land. They were to gather the first fruits of their very first harvest in their new land and make a declaration celebrating God's initial blessing to them. They were to continue to tithe, but that first tithe stood apart from the rest.

I have not kept very precise records, but I remember my first earnings from my first job when I was twelve years old: a little brown envelop containing four one dollar bills and a fifty cent piece. I had worked for twenty hours at the celery farm that week in April of 1948 for twenty-five cents an hour. I expected to receive five dollars, but that reduction of fifty cents was my first brush with the IRS. When I got home my dad took the fifty cent piece and set it aside as a tithe which went into the offering plate the next morning; he divided up the rest into categories such as Christian school tuition, savings, and room and board. When he was finished sorting, I had a dollar left to spend as I wished, and a word of advice, not to waste it or spend it all in one place. After President Truman took his cut, the first fruits of my first fruits went to the Lord.

For the next several years, my parents had charge of my finances. Every payday they made sure I first paid my tithe, then my other obligations, then I could spend what was left at my own discretion, which was not always very good. But I always got by. Until I left home, that is. When I turned eighteen I went to seek my fortune in the great city of Detroit, but I didn't fare nearly as well as Horatio Alger's heroes fared. But that's probably because I wasn't the kind of moral giant that those boys were.

The first adjustment I had to make on my budget was to strike the tithe. I wasn't living with my parents anymore so what they didn't know wouldn't hurt them. At first my conscience bothered me a little bit, but I soon got used to it. I don't know how I could have afforded to tithe anyway, because after I covered my necessities, the deductible for the fender bender I had, the traffic ticket, and the increase in insurance premiums, there wasn't a tenth left. In fact, fate forced me to visit my friendly neighborhood financier whose high interest rates kept me in the red for several months.

Later in life I came crawling back to the Lord, made up for my missing tithes, got my books right, and began seeing the blessings from heaven pour down upon me. But I know for a certainty that if I had kept a remembrance of my first gift from God as my hardware friend did, and if I had continued to return my first fruits to the Lord as my parents taught me, I would have avoided many costly errors in my youth.

The Little Brother

Scripture: Deuteronomy 27

The most memorable sporting events of the twentieth century took place in the empty lot behind VanBruggen's house on Oak Street when the neighborhood boys gathered to choose up sides for their baseball games. Red's tape measure home run went all the way into Albert Bush's junkyard, Johnny hurt his arm trying to tag me out at second base, Marv hit a fly ball that wedged in a crotch of the mulberry tree so high up that we couldn't reach it, and we argued for the rest of the day whether it should have been a home run or a double. The vote was a tie, and the matter was never settled.

About the only boy who isn't remembered in our neighborhood hall of fame for some outstanding feat is Sonny, Alan's little brother, who, because of his lesser sporting skills, never got picked to be on a team when there was an odd number of boys to choose from. Usually he was designated to fetch water from home in milk bottles on hot days or to shag the ball when someone hit a long foul or if a wild throw rolled all the way down the hill to the celery farm below.

Sonny only got picked to play if we needed him, or if Rolly, Alan's big brother came out, which wasn't very often because his skills were less than Sonny's, which I'm sure was the result of obesity. Besides that, Rolly knew we held his vile temperament against him, and didn't like to play with him. I've lost all track of Rolly. He moved away and everybody says he never amounted to much. But Sonny did okay; he got an education and became a biology professor at the university.

Unlike parents today, our elders never meddled in the games of our youth. They just let us play. I don't know if that's good or bad, but had they intervened, Sonny might have got to play more, and Rolly might have learned a little sportsmanship and responsibility.

I thought of those grand old days when I read today's chapter, because Israel had both a Rolly and a Sonny, neither of whom distinguished himself in any positive way. Reuben, the oldest, never did much to get written up in the Bible except to avoid war, gather love apples, or to slip into bed with his father's concubine. For his folly, Jacob disinherited him and he ended up pitching his tents beyond the Jordan, the first to fall victim to the armies of the east. And Zebulun, the youngest of Leah's children, was never picked to play any major role in any of the nation's events. Except for the littlest brother of all, Benjamin, Zebulun got the smallest piece of land. But to his credit, he made the best of it and prospered.

Just before the nation crossed over the Jordan, Moses "chose up sides" for the recitation of the blessings and the curses. The six brothers he chose to bless the people were, of course, the two sons of the beloved Rachel and four of Leah's six boys. The two omitted were the oldest, the vile Reuben, and the youngest, little Zebulun, who went on the side of the curses with the four sons of the concubines. Sociology hasn't changed much in the three thousand years that separate the sons of Jacob from the boys of Oak Street.

Today I sometimes sit on a lawn chair and watch my grandsons and their neighbor boys and choose up sides for a game of soccer. Dutifully, as I did with my own children, I meddle in their sociology and insist that young Collin or Caleb get an equal chance to play, I upbraid the big neighbor boy for being a bully, and I do what I can to encourage fairness, decency, and mutual respect. I'll never know if my intrusions will alter the destiny of any of the boys, but I do know that if any of them suffers any of the twelve curses of Mount Ebal, the guilt for it won't be on my head.

Almost Persuaded

Scripture: Deuteronomy 28
Suggested Reading: Acts 26:28 (KJV)

When my father read a chapter from the Bible every evening at dinner, sometimes he would omit certain graphic passages that might cause blushing, snickering, or nightmares. When he got to Deuteronomy twenty-eight he would read slowly, looking ahead to the next verse and omitting it if it might offend tender ears. This has to be the vilest chapter in the entire Bible. It's a challenge to call it the inspired Word of God.

Now it doesn't take a Ph.D. in Hebrew studies or in world history to know that all the curses mentioned here actually came to pass. When Israel's kings led their people astray, foreign armies invaded their land, stole their crops, ravaged their daughters, scattered their children to the four corners of the earth, and repopulated their land with foreigners.

During the Babylonian siege, starving Israelites ate their own children, and those who survived were carried off by Nebuchadnezzar as slaves. Empire after empire battered them until at the end there was little, if anything, left to identify them as a nation. Their holy temple lay in ruins, their city demolished, their land occupied, and their monarchy and priesthood crucified. And, as the Museum of the Holocaust testifies, for the next two thousand years they suffered under bigoted tyrants and were abhorred by their neighbors. The prophecy of Deuteronomy twenty-eight has been fulfilled, even in our own time.

I knew an old Jewish man who was raised on the Torah. Obedient to Moses, his father taught him the Law and the nation's history as they sat at dinner, walked by the way, and went to bed at night. He knew this chapter by heart and confessed that the prophecy had come to pass, yet refused to ascribe it to the disobedience of his people. To him the guilty parties were the evil empires and any Gentiles who considered Jews as less than their equals.

The warning of Moses outlining the destiny of the nation if they did not obey the voice of the Lord is so accurate that it appears almost to have been written as history rather than prophecy. The writings of Daniel were not discovered until the period of Greek domination, and they predicted events so accurately that critics assert that they were actually written after the fact. If we didn't have proof that the Pentateuch is an ancient document, those same critics would, by the same logic, assert that Deuteronomy was composed after the events chronicled by Josephus, Ezra, and more recent historians. But since it obviously looks forward in time rather than back, secular historians avoid it because they think they would look foolish ascribing the woes of modern Jews to the idolatry of ancient kings.

My Jewish friend, just for the sake of argument, asserted that even if I was right, the body of law laid down by Moses was impossible to keep. In the first place, he pointed out, pagan religions were so close and so attractive that it was impossible for normal human beings not to be seduced into participating in their rituals. Even the wise Solomon yielded to their temptation. Besides, the laws were so restrictive they were bound to be disobeyed.

And, for the sake of argument, I agreed. But I was quick to add that God provided a way out, even for the vilest offender. No matter how grievous the disobedience or how painful the punishment, he made redemption possible through the blood of the Messiah. Then I could see the war in his soul as he looked up and said with his eyes, "Almost thou persuadest me . . . ."

A Mind to Understand

Scripture: Deuteronomy 29:1–15
Suggested Reading: Genesis 9:27; 12:3; Romans 10,11

I was raised a disciple of John Calvin, the champion of the doctrine of predestination. Among Christian denominations we were a minority, but it was very comforting, especially for a youth of questionable conduct, to believe that we were chosen by an omniscient God from before the foundation of the universe and irrevocably destined to spend eternity in paradise.

With maturity, of course, came inquisitiveness and doubt, and the whole business of divine election has become more of a haunting mystery than a comfort. Awe for the inscrutable ways of God has replaced the complacency of youth.

God promised Japheth that his sons would inhabit the tents of Shem. God promised Abraham that his descendants would bless all the families of the earth. God told Moses that the covenant was not only for the offspring of Jacob who were gathered there on the banks of the Jordan, but also "with him who is not here with us this day," meaning us. Salvation for us Gentiles was part of God's plan well before the creation of the earth.

For a long time I was astonished that the children of Israel misbehaved so badly. How could they watch the Red Sea close up and swallow the chariots of Pharaoh and not love and obey God forever? How could they gather the bread from heaven and not be eternally grateful? The question is enigmatic, but the answer is simple, God had not given them minds to understand.

Equally inconceivable is the heart of Pharaoh in the face of the plagues. His closest advisors begged him to relent and the entire population of Egypt gave up all they had just to shoo God's chosen people out of their country. But even as his nation lay in ruins, Pharaoh's heart was hardened and he refused to let the people go. How could he be so stubborn? Answer: God hardened his heart.

And the same God hardened the hearts of the Israelites so they sinned and made him angry and moved him to open the door of salvation to the Gentiles. Their trespass meant salvation for us. And it sounds as if God planned it that way all along. Why else would he have made those promises to Japheth and Abraham?

But just as we think we have the mystery solved, the solution turns to mystery again. Why save the Gentiles? Again God gives the answer: to make the Jews jealous. The Jews whose hearts God has hardened will look on us and see the riches we have in Christ, will see the blessings we have in the spiritual promised land we inhabit, will covet our blessings, will turn from their trespass, will cease to reject their Messiah, and will reestablish themselves as inheritors of the kingdom of God.

The skeptics among us chuckle at the apparent foolishness of it all, but it is no more foolish than injecting one with a tiny dose of the flu to stave off the ravages of the epidemic, or setting a back-fire in the forest to stop the inferno from spreading.

Paul found the solution to the mystery in the revelation of nature. The branch was broken off from its tree and a wild branch was grafted on in its place and bears fine fruit. Then the natural branch was restored to its original tree and it too bore fruit.

God hardened the hearts of those Jews of old for one reason: that I might be saved! And today this son of Japheth dwells happily in the spiritual promised land God swore to give Abraham's children.

Where's Dan?

Scripture: Deuteronomy 29:16–29
Suggested Reading: Genesis 49:16–18; Joshua 19:40–48;
Judges 1:34–35; 5:13–23; 17; 18; Ezekiel 48; Revelation 7:5

The destiny of Dan is another of the Bible's mysteries. As a son of Jacob, he didn't distinguish himself in any particular way. He is not recorded as a man who led his brothers, either as a malefactor or as a benefactor. It seems he simply went along with any plot they hatched. On his deathbed Jacob envisioned something satanic in Dan's future. After leaving Egypt, Dan's tribe maintained anonymity until the time came to claim territory in the Promised Land.

We know that Israel's armies didn't conquer Canaan in their own might. The Lord went before them and drove out their enemies. All that was required of them was faith, courage, and obedience, and God promised to do the rest. Many stories of their battles, recorded both in scripture and in history, show how God routed the pagan nations that should have easily defeated the inferior Israelite forces.

But Israel also suffered some losses. Why? There is but one answer: faithlessness. Several of the tribes, including Dan, failed to drive the pagans from the land. While the loyal Ephraimites, in God's strength, succeeded in wresting their allotment of land from the enemy, Dan, their neighbor, failed. And when their brothers called them to fight by their side, the Danites instead went to sea in ships. And because the Lord didn't fight for them, they lost to the Philistines the valuable coastal plain that had fallen to them by divine lot. So, the tribe of Dan turned its back on its God-given inheritance, migrated to the north, massacred the inhabitants of a defenseless city, and dwelled there until Shalmaneser's Assyrian hordes swept down and blotted them from the pages of human history.

But the Danites did more than desert their brothers in their time of need, they also deserted their God. When they failed to take possession of their inheritance and migrated northward instead, they began to worship idols they had stolen from a foolish Ephraimite, and they lured an apostate hobo Levite into becoming their pagan priest. From the day they established the city of Dan as the northernmost city of the nation, they were a stumbling block to Israel, causing them to abandon the God of their fathers. They welcomed the evil King Jeroboam to set up a golden calf in their capitol and to draw worshippers away from the Lord.

Perhaps that was the kind of behavior Moses foresaw when he uttered the warnings to any family or tribe whose heart turned away from the Lord and went to serve the gods of the people they failed to conquer. He prophesied that not only would they become victim to the curses described in "this book," but also that God would blot out their name from under heaven.

Most popularly read commentators avoid the question, "Where's Dan?" when expounding on John's vision. Most attribute his absence as a scribal error or note that generally one tribe is omitted from a list to maintain the number twelve, but a few brave scholars are willing to suggest that God may have disinherited Dan's descendants from being named among the hundred and forty-four thousand sealed elect because of their apostasy back in those early days. But then to offset that thought, some point out that in his apocalyptical vision, Ezekiel saw a place for Dan in the New Jerusalem.

If it is true that Dan's name has been blotted out from under heaven, it is a stern warning for us. To preserve our inheritance in the spiritual promised land God has willed to his church, we must faithfully serve him and him alone.

He'll Gather You Again . . .

Scripture: Deuteronomy 30:1–10
Suggested Reading: Revelation 7

*M*oses seemed to know that the people of Israel would violate the laws he had laid down for them. He knew that God hadn't given them a mind to understand, that they would disobey, and that for their disobedience they would be evicted from their land and would suffer horrible curses. But Moses also knew that after their punishment was complete, God would call them back to the land they were about to enter.

From the times of the Romans until 1948, the Jews had no homeland. As he said he would do for their disobedience, God had scattered them to the ends of the earth and made their lives miserable wherever they lived. But even though the Jews were as oppressed as the early church, they preserved their identity as the children of Jacob and dreamed of the end of persecution. But when the doors of their Promised Land reopened for them, as when the Babylonian exile ended, only a smattering of the Jewry ever returned, most preferring to remain where they were. Has the prophecy of Moses been fulfilled?

One researcher has traveled all over the eastern world looking for the "lost tribes" of Israel, and claims to have found them. From Ethiopia and islands in the Mediterranean to mountain passes and city enclaves in India and in China, he has found small groups of people claiming to be Jews. Though their appearance is similar to the natives in whose land they live, they follow old Jewish customs and tell of a longing deep in their hearts to return to the land

God gave their father Abraham. Even the names of their groups resemble the names of the twelve sons of Jacob. Is another miracle exodus possible?

When the new state of Israel was founded after World War II, Jews from all over the earth made their way to the new nation, joined the compatriots who had never left or had immigrated earlier, and, as in the days of the Old Testament, fought amazing wars, scoring victories over more powerful armies and expanding their borders to their original configuration.

And today Israel has earned stature as one of the most significant nations in the world. Her cities bustle with commerce, the Lord has blessed the fruit of her ground, reclaimed from the wilderness, and has made her abound in prosperity. Have her fortunes been restored as Moses prophesied?

One thing is clear. God has not yet circumcised her heart. The majority of her citizens are secular Jews, caring nothing for their spiritual heritage. Among the religious there are various sects, some studying the prophets and praying fervently for their Messiah to come, others just casually observing the traditional Jewish holidays. Very few have come to an understanding of the fulfillment of their heritage of salvation through sacrifice: salvation through the sacrifice of the final Passover Lamb, Jesus Christ, their Messiah.

But the day of the great awakening will come, unfortunately not until the Tribulation at the end of time. The sealed servants from the twelve tribes will witness to the multitudes in Israel, and throngs of new saints, Jew and Gentile alike, without distinction, will stand before the throne, clothed in clean robes made white in the blood of the Lamb.

And finally God will have gathered his chosen people into the New Jerusalem!

The Power to Choose

Scripture: Deuteronomy 30:11–20
Suggested Reading: Isaiah 30: 19–22

I have two friends who are alcoholics. Art is a happy husband, father and grandfather who serves his employer and the Lord well and hasn't had a drink in over thirty years. Joe, on the other hand, seems to be a hopeless sot who can't stay sober for thirty days. Though a brilliant, educated man with a warm heart and great potential, Joe is estranged from his family and is chronically unemployed, while my sober, successful, born again friend Art walks closely with the Lord, studies the Word, and lives happily in our spiritual promised land. With God's help he defeated the giant that stalked him in his younger years. His car passes all liquor stores without any urge to stop and make a purchase.

But that same giant still controls Joe. He seems to place his huge hand on Joe's car and forces it to turn into the liquor store parking lot, then it propels him into the store to buy the biggest, cheapest bottle of whiskey the proprietor has to offer. Joe drinks for several days until he is nearly comatose, then he retches in agony for another forty-eight hours, unable to eat a morsel of food or drink another drop of alcohol. Finally he stumbles into the emergency room of the recovery clinic, gets his vital signs stabilized, and struggles through the lingering effects of his trauma until he is feeling well enough to go back to work. Sometimes he goes to jail for drunk driving or for causing a disturbance, and sometimes he loses his job. When he recovers, he stays sober until the next time that giant hand turns his car into the parking lot of the liquor store.

When he's sober, Joe attends church, goes to Sunday school and sings in the choir. But all the goodness of sobriety holds low priority in his life compared to the god he really serves. The Word of the Lord is very near to him; it is in his ears and on his mouth, but another spirit owns his heart. And as long as that other spirit dwells in him, Joe will hear the voice of his Teacher behind him telling him the way, but he will not shout, "Be gone!" to the idol he worships.

Just as the Lord wanted Israel to possess Canaan, he wants us to possess his spiritual promised land. He wants us to walk the length and breadth of it hand in hand with him, peering into every crevice and cranny, and, with his help, defeat every enemy who wants to deny us any square foot of that hallowed ground. Possession of that land is blessed life, and failure to possess it is cursed death.

And the same rules that Moses laid out for the Israelites apply to us today: loving the Lord our God, walking in his ways, and following his commandments. If we do that, we shall flourish in that good land, enjoying its produce, and the fruit of the Spirit; but if we are drawn away to serve other gods, we are bound to perish. God sets before us the option of life or death, the blessing or the curse. The choice is ours.

God has given Joe, and all of us, the power to choose. The Word of the Lord surrounds him, but he does not allow it to penetrate to the core of his being to drive out the enemy. I pray daily that Joe will choose to open his heart and let God give him a glimpse of the glory that can be his as an unfettered citizen of the kingdom of heaven. I pray daily that God will give him the determination to twirl the sling and fire the deadly stone that God promises to guide to the vulnerable spot in the giant's armor.

But as long as Joe chooses to love the other god, the one who cannot love him back, he is cursed to dwell in that dismal, moonless valley beyond the border of God's blessed promised land.

He Will Not Fail You . . .

Scripture: Deuteronomy 31:1–6
Suggested Reading: Ephesians 6:10–20

He Will Not Fail You Or Forsake You was another of the plaques that my mother hung on the walls of our home, and I'm sure she hung it there with godly purpose and innocent intent. There was one problem: it gave rise to a false sense of security, a sense that we could just go on our own merry way in any direction we chose and that God, like a good guardian angel, would always hover over us to keep us from any danger, physical or spiritual, and that when we got into any kind of trouble, he would always be there to bail us out. Today I wish that plaque had been a little bigger, had included the command to be strong and of good courage, and had contained the warning to be cognizant but not fearful of the enemies of faith.

In my naïve, youthful wanderings back and forth over the borders of the promised land, I dallied in the tents of the enemy much more than I should have, without any awareness of their devious nature or evil purpose, comfortable in the illusion that God was solely responsible for my spiritual security and preordained destiny. I made sure my mother never found out about my exploits because she was far more judgmental than God, and certainly would never have understood that my dalliance was totally harmless. The part of our Calvinistic belief about God being in total control of our lives was an opiate that obscured the need to be wary of the demons lurking in the bushes that edged our aimless path.

Be strong and of good courage. Anyone with muscles knows that being strong requires long and strenuous workouts with fitness equipment. To have good courage in the presence of an enemy is to know that enemy and the damage he can do if you drop your defenses. And good courage is far more than simple bravado. It is not foolish abandon. That is bad courage. Good courage comes from knowing your strength and your enemy's weakness.

Our inheritance, our promised land, is the kingdom of heaven, a spiritual state in which we can live in close harmony with our Lord, enjoying the blessing of his company and the fruit of his Spirit. It is a state of secure contentment that is achieved only by overcoming the evil forces of our carnal nature and maintained by constant vigil against counter attack once, with God's help, we've experienced victory over Satan's evil forces.

As we face the enemies that lurk in the shadows of our land of promise, with what intelligence and weapons should we arm ourselves? Paul, inspired by the spiritual military tactics he learned from the prophet Isaiah, outfitted us for our war against Satan. If we are arrayed with salvation, righteousness, faith, spirit, and the Word of Truth, then God assures us that with him at our side we can stand against the wiles of the devil.

Salvation is citizenship in the kingdom of heaven and a commission to serve in the Lord's army. Righteousness is having our robes cleansed by the blood of the Lamb and our passion to keep them clean. Faith is confidence that our Commander has given us wise leadership and effective weapons. Spirit is the zest we take into the battle against sin and the godly instinct for strategy. The Word of Truth is the gospel, the sword that can slay the serpent and the stone that can fell the giant.

So armed, we can truly be strong and of good courage. So armed, we need not be in fear or dread of our spiritual enemies. So armed, we can be sure of our inheritance in the kingdom of heaven.

Slaves to Righteousness

Scripture: Deuteronomy 31:7–8
Suggested Reading: Matthew 5:17–20; Romans 6–7

As God's chosen people prepare to enter their Promised Land, we should notice two very important features of their makeup that give us direction in our lives as we prepare to grow in grace and sanctification.

First, a new generation of Israelites is encamped on the plains of Moab, ready to cross the river. The old identity is gone, and a new identity looks toward the future. Those who were slaves in Egypt have died in the wilderness, and a generation born to be free is ready to claim its inheritance. So with us. When we make our commitment to leave the old life behind, in the wilderness of sin, we look forward to a new life in the Spirit, a new generation of self, dead to the old, alive in the new.

The second thing to notice is the change in leadership. Moses is out and Joshua is in. Respect and admiration for the devoted man of God forbids us to say anything bad about Moses. He was a great hero of faith and a great leader. But his identity was with the law, and the law condemns us by convicting us of our sin, and conviction of our sin is the first step in our conversion, the last act of a life lived on the unsanctified side of the river. When we are crucified with Christ, we cross the river, die to sin, and are reborn, raised with him in newness of life, freed from the curse of the law.

Once across the river, we are in our spiritual promised land, forgiven of our sin and unfettered by the law. Jesus has conferred upon us a permanent pardon, and the law of Moses is no longer the master of our lives. Our new master is Joshua, or Jesus, the leader who has guided us through the waters of the Jordan, ushered us into our new habitation, and led us in victorious battle over the foes who would keep us from enjoying our full inheritance in our new land.

But freedom from the law is not freedom to break the law. The law is still the law. Those tablets of stone are still with us, every jot and tittle securely lodged in the ark of the covenant, and we are the guilty, but forgiven, violators of that law. But just as Joshua was innocent of the sins the majority of spies committed at Kadesh, so Jesus was innocent of the sins we committed at Eden and of the continual wickedness of man that grieved God and moved him to initiate his plan of salvation. And Jesus' willingness to pay the price for our sin puts us forever in his debt.

As the Israelites were slaves to the Egyptians before the Exodus, so we were slaves to sin before we accepted Christ as our savior and made our exodus from the bondage of sin. As the Israelites camped at the foot of Mount Sinai to learn the law and rules for godly living, so we sit at the feet of our teachers, study the Bible, and listen to the Holy Spirit to learn how God wants us to live. As a new generation of Israelites crossed the Jordan under the leadership of Joshua, so we cast off the old self, die to sin, become born again, and lay claim to our inheritance in our spiritual promised land under the leadership of Christ, our savior.

We are free from condemnation under the law because the Righteous One redeemed us by paying the penalty for our sin. Now we are free to live righteously. Our commitment to the Law of God is not diminished by that freedom, it is increased, and the only way even to begin to fulfill that commitment is to return to slavery, not slavery to sin, but slavery to righteousness.

Thanks be to God, our master!

Write This Song . . .

Scripture: Deuteronomy 31:9–30
Suggested Reading: Psalms 90

Although I can't play an instrument, sing, whistle, or even hum on key, I love music. And I've always sung my favorite songs at the top of my lungs, declaring that if God didn't appreciate my discordant caterwauling he could either strike me dumb or transform my voice into a heavenly tenor. But even if he were to choose the former, he couldn't silence the song in my heart.

When I was a young man courting the girls, as the wonderful old song goes, the popular tunes of my day wove themselves into the fabric of each of my romantic relationships. With each love of my life, I associated a song that we called, "our song." And even today when I feel nostalgic and play my "golden oldies," the music reminds me of the joys of my youth and the sweethearts with whom I shared tender moments.

I love the grand old hymns of the church. On my eighth birthday my wonderful Aunt Catherine, the one with the gnarled fingers who knitted mittens for the neighborhood children, gave me my own copy of the *Psalter Hymnal*, the songbook that is still used by the church of my youth and to which I owe a great debt for many of the spiritual blessings I've enjoyed in these later years. As our memory work in junior high school, we engraved the verses of the psalms and the hymns on our minds, and even now I can sing all the stanzas of many of those hymns with the book closed. Today that old, battered *Psalter Hymnal* is one of my prized possessions.

I have no doubt that the Holy Spirit inspired many of the song writers much as he inspired Moses, the prophets and the apostles to write the holy scriptures. The poetic words penned by Fannie Crosby, Isaac Watts and Charles Wesley, among many others, convey the truth of the Word of God in such a compelling way that the gift of music they possessed seems to have emanated from the same source as the gift the Spirit gave the psalmists.

Music records itself on our hearts and seems to outlast the knowledge we store in our brains. I remember the song and the girl from a particular year, but I struggle to remember who was president or what car I owned at the time. I changed churches, and songbooks, many years ago, but though the music resounds in my soul, I struggle to recall the names of the pastors and even some of the Sunday school teachers for whom I recited those verses. The melody lingers on while most of the events of those bygone days have sunk, like my sins, into the sea of forgetfulness.

Many of the world's greatest songs were recorded by various artists over long periods of time. Songs composed by country rustics and made famous on the stage of the Grand Ole Opry have not only climbed to the top of the pop charts after being rearranged and re-released by pop artists, but have also been recorded by "high brow" orchestras. And recently I even heard a vintage country tune done in rock 'n roll.

The Song of Moses didn't fade into oblivion after the first wave of Israelites made it into the Promised Land. Several psalmists, including Moses himself, have included phrases from that song in at least ten different psalms. And those ten psalms have been set to music and incorporated into twenty songs in my old *Psalter Hymnal* by more modern writers.

Thank God for music and the memory of the heart!

Oil and Honey

Scripture: Deuteronomy 32:1–47
Suggested Reading: 1 Kings 17:8–16

The Song of Moses is rich with imagery that has deep significance not only for the Israelites but also for us.

The Lord found the vagabond Jacob wandering in the wasteland with nothing on which to lay his head but a pillow of hard stone. But, true to his promise to Abraham, God turned that wilderness into a fertile land, a land in which farmers could grow verdant groves of olive trees, fields full of flowers and humming bees brewing combs of savory honey.

And he peopled that land with poets and prophets whom he inspired to see beyond the mundane and envision a spiritual country founded on the Rock of Truth in which humankind could find forgiveness for their sins, balm for their suffering, salvation for their souls, and sweetness for their lives.

Our God is a creative genius who teaches us his ways through the wonders of nature. He gave us the caterpillar and the butterfly as symbols of our rebirth in Christ. He cast himself and his Son as the Rock of our salvation, a firm, timeless, and enduring foundation on which to build our house. He moved the poets to see the blood of Christ in the wine they drank, to see the Light of the world in the oil they squeezed from the olive, and to taste honey in a life spent walking the paths of obedience that our Savior walked.

People looking at us from the outside may see the Christian walk as a hard journey characterized only by sacrifice and self-denial, but their vision fails to penetrate the shell and view the soul of the matter. The true substance is on the inside. In various ways, our Rock gives us a peace, a joy, and an understanding far beyond the world's comprehension.

Olive trees grow best in soil laced with limestone. Hence oil from the rock. Olive oil had many uses, among them fuel for the lamp, tasty shortening for the cakes and the bread, unction for anointing, a base for ointment, a balm for healing, a medium of exchange, a tithe for the offering, and a sign of prosperity. The widow of Zeraphath had as cruse of oil that could not be depleted, just as the symbolic oil of our anointing in Christ is of endless supply, as the eternal light on our path is the sun by day and the moon in our valley by night.

Only nature produces genuine honey. Bees sip nectar from the plants, carry it to their hives, add their own secret enzyme ingredients, and guard their brew with their lives until it transforms into the thick, savory substance we spread on our dinner rolls and pour on our sweet potatoes. We use it as a cough medicine, as a laxative, and the ancient Egyptians even used it in embalming. It is the only sugar food that requires no refining, and made of simple sugars it provides quick energy. Just as honey from the comb is a perfect food for our bodies, honey from the Rock is a perfect food for our souls, giving us zest, keeping us spiritually healthy, taking us beyond this life to the next, and filling our spirit with sweetness.

But as with all rich blessings, it comes with a warning. We must not yield to the temptation to hoard the oil and the honey unto ourselves or to get fat from overindulgence. Our job as citizens of the kingdom of heaven is to share our honey with those who have only a bitter taste in their mouths, and to share the light of our lamps with those who walk in darkness.

No Hard Feelings

Scripture: Deuteronomy 32:48–33:29
Suggested Reading: Review Genesis 48–49; Numbers 12:3

This is the second "deathbed" speech recorded in the Bible. Oddly, both cover the same subject, but differ greatly in mood.

When old Jacob, the father of the nation, lay dying in Egypt, he slipped "into the spirit" and began to "bless" his sons with the visions God had given him of their future. During Jacob's lifetime, his sons had dealt him a generous measure of both grief and joy. They tore his heart from his breast when they sold his favorite son, Joseph, to the slave traders, and they grieved him deeply when they took his youngest, Benjamin, to Egypt to see "the man." Yet, when he grew old and needed their protection, they cared for him and finally began to honor him as children should honor their parents.

But in his final hours when he prophesied their future, he called them into account for the evil they had done and predicted the misfortune that would befall them for the error of their ways and for their sin against him. He foresaw good things for Judah, for the sons of Joseph, and for the less unrighteous of the brothers, but he didn't spare his wrath for those who had it coming.

Moses had far greater cause to chastise the sons of Israel than Jacob did. Practically from the moment he met them in Egypt they grumbled. And for the next forty years they complained constantly about their food, their water, their accommodations, their social structure, and even about their destiny. Any lesser man would have accepted God's offer to destroy the lot of them and give their inheritance to Moses. Had I been Moses, the level of my frustration with them would have exceeded my threshold of tolerance, and I would certainly have abandoned them in the desert.

And now Moses has to face his punishment for breaking faith with God at Meribah. He is to climb Mount Nebo, take a long look at the Promised Land he is forbidden to enter, and die while his successor, Joshua, prepares to lead the people across the Jordan River. And the reason he broke faith and struck the rock instead of speaking to it was his frustration with the very people who were poised on the riverbank to claim the inheritance God has denied to him.

If ever a man was entitled to lash out, it was Moses at this moment in his life. It would have been entirely appropriate for him to chastise the thankless rabble who, by their constant whining, had caused him forty years of grief. But no, in the true spirit of Christ, the meekest man on the face of the earth rose to bless those who had persecuted him, reviled him, and uttered all manner of evil against him, falsely.

There's an old saying among educators that if you treat a child as though he were what he ought to be, he will become what he ought to be. I've seen that old theory of motivation work some of the time, and I've seen it fail.

I think at this time the Holy Spirit has taken all hard feelings from Moses' heart and has led him to bless this people in the hope that they will become what they ought to become, a nation of priests standing at the crossroads of the continents as beacons of light, by word and example persuading the pagans who pass through their land to become obedient servants of the one true God.

But sadly, Moses' blessings didn't take. Those whom God had entrusted with the greatest truth of all time despised their inheritance and ended up being cursed for their unbelief.

A Better Country

Scripture: Deuteronomy 34
Suggested Reading: Exodus 2:1–10; Matthew 17:1–3;
Hebrews 11:8–28; Jude 1:9

On a clear day, the old song goes, "you can see forever." It must have been a very clear day when Moses climbed to the top of Mount Pisgah and viewed the Promised Land. Maybe God lifted the haze that usually hangs over the area, or maybe God gave Moses' eyes a touch of divine acuity so he could see as far northward as Dan, southward to Beer-sheba, and westward from the palms of Jericho to the surf of the Great Sea. Then he died, and God buried him in a grave so secret that no man could ever find his bones.

I used to wonder why Moses didn't argue much with God over his fate. After all, he didn't hesitate to stand toe to toe with the Creator and dispute with him over the destiny of the people of Israel. Often he and the Lord had serious disagreements about the events in the wilderness, and sometimes Moses won those arguments and caused God to repent. So when his own fate hung in the balance, why didn't Moses come to his own defense and claim the right he earned over forty miserable years to lead the chosen people to their inheritance?

As he stood on Mount Pisgah looking over the land, did his view of the land transcend normal ocular limitations? Did he see beyond the temporal into the spiritual? As he faced death, did God give him a prophetic eye so as he gazed at Melchizedek's little town of Salem he actually saw the foundations of a new and glorious city whose builder and maker is God? Did he consider the forty years of suffering in the wilderness as suffering for Christ? Did he envision himself standing one day with Elijah on the Mount of Transfiguration conferring with Jesus and the apostles? Did he greet from afar a better country, a heavenly one? Did he comprehend the promise made to Abraham that through that miserable, complaining rabble that Jacob spawned, God would eventually extend the blessing of salvation to all the people of the earth?

Moses is one of the heroes of faith who witnessed the full scope of human history before it happened. God chose him from the beginning, gave him life, plucked him from certain death at the hand of Pharaoh, educated him in the palace of a king, trained him in the wilderness, equipped him with extraordinary powers for his mission, and by the power of the Holy Spirit guided his hand to pen the most profound piece of literature ever written so that we, thousands of years later, might come to believe the whole story, that Jesus is the Christ, the Son of the living God who has gone on to prepare a place for us in a better country.

The same Spirit prodded William Walford to reflect:

Sweet hour of prayer, sweet hour of prayer
May I thy consolation share
'Til from Mount Pisgah's lofty height
I view my home and take my flight.

And Sanford Bennett to understand that

There's a land that is fairer than day,
and by faith we can see it afar,
For the Father waits over the way
To prepare us a dwelling place there . . .

The Beginning of the End

*T*he word *end* has two meanings. The first meaning suggests the termination of something, such as the end of life or the end of the war. The second meaning suggests achievement, such as the end result or the purpose for which we do something.

For the Christian there are two ends, both of them achievements. The second end comes when we "drop this robe of flesh" and enter into life eternal. When we achieve that end we ascend to the New Jerusalem, don the white robe that we've washed in the blood of the Lamb and take our place beside Jesus on his throne to live with him forever. That end is the focus of our effort, our ultimate hope, our grand desire.

But before we can achieve the second end, we must achieve the first. Jesus said that unless we are born again, we cannot enter into the kingdom of heaven. The first end comes when we die to self and spend the rest of our days on this earth living the Spirit-filled life, walking constantly with Jesus, the second Joshua, and dining sumptuously on the produce of that good land that is profuse with milk and honey and the fruit of the Spirit. It is living in the kingdom that Jesus said exists in the present time, the kingdom that is within us, the kingdom in which we can gain citizenship before we reach the second end.

Achieving the Spirit-filled life is not easy. The book of Joshua is the metaphorical guidebook for gaining residence in that kingdom. It pictures for us as a series of battles, a conquest, with ultimate victory over the evil forces that do everything in their power to keep us from taking possession of that spiritual promised land.

The first end is the goal that we achieve when, by the grace of God, we summon up the courage to die to self, as signified by stepping into the swollen waters of the Jordan, the symbol of death. It is a blind step of faith, not being able to see the bottom of the river, but believing, as Peter did, that the Lord will hold us up. We emerge on the other side, baptized in the Spirit, cleansed, robed in white, and reborn to life anew.

Then, as we shall see Joshua do, we turn control of our lives over to Jesus, the commander of the army of the Lord, the army of angels. Turning control of our mind, our will, our loved ones and our possessions over to the Lord is not an easy thing to do. It is a step that demands trust.

These acts of courage and faith remind me of the day my dad urged me to jump off the deep end of the raft at Stony Lake, where the water was over my head. He was there to catch me, but fear had a tight grip on me as I slowly edged my way over the boards toward the far end, one part of me wanting to prove my pluck, another part of me terrified that I may never breathe again. But dad held out his arms and smiled and nodded encouragement. In childlike trust I leaped from the raft, and as the water began to close over me his strong arms scooped me up, and he held me, and I knew I was safe.

The Lord asked Joshua to take courage and do as he was told. He obeyed and soon the Lord began to work wonders. The walls of Jericho came tumbling down, the enemy turned tail and fled, hail-stones rained from heaven and the sun and the moon stood still at his command. He scored victory after victory and soon possessed the entire land.

We can possess our spiritual promised land, defeat giants and demons, and have eternal joy in the Lord if we, like Joshua, simply trust and obey, for there's no other way to be happy in Jesus but to trust and obey.

Arise, Go Over . . .

Scripture: Joshua 1:1–3
Suggested Reading: Luke 17:21; Hebrews 11:8–31; 1 Peter 1:4

The torch has been passed to a new generation of Israelites. And as the generations of faith surge through the branches of that great family tree, the land we are called to inherit takes on a new and more spiritual meaning. And if we become transfixed at any point along the way we fail to comprehend the ultimate truth that our inheritance is not simply a heap of stones in a dry and thirsty land, but a green valley that produces fruit, a land flowing with milk and honey, a promise imperishable, undefiled, unfading, and preserved for us by God in heaven.

The patriarchs and the early leaders of the nation constitute the root system of our faith. The early history of Israel must, as time passes, become a metaphor that gives meaning to our spiritual journey from the bondage of sin to our eternal home in glory. But if we view our pilgrimage as nothing more than forty years of wandering in a treacherous wasteland until we finally die and enter the promised land of heaven, we find little fulfillment in living the Christian life.

It's no accident that the name *Jesus* is the Septuagint spelling of the name *Joshua*. The Joshua of the Old Testament who led his new generation of Israelites into the Promised Land becomes the Jesus of the New Testament who leads the next generation of chosen people, the church, into another promised land, the kingdom of heaven. No, not the heaven we go to when we die, but a promised land that exists in the present, a lofty promised land of life in the Spirit, a life spent walking with Jesus and feeling his presence in us as we face the moment to moment events of our earthly existence. He is with us as we confront the enemies that would keep us from fully possessing the land, and he is with us as we celebrate the victories he gives us along the way.

The promised land, the kingdom of heaven that is at hand and present within us is of special value to me. I was raised by godly parents in the puritanical Old World tradition that life is meant to be harsh, and that the children of God are called to endure hardship with stoic determination until they are called to their heavenly home. So awakening to the notion that the kingdom of heaven is a present reality that exists in the hearts of believers hit me like the light that hit Paul on the road to Damascus. It was a blinding flash that illumined the entire Word of God, gave the scriptures new meaning, and gave my life new dimension. I could enjoy a land flowing with milk and honey *before* I die!

How do we enter that land? The same way Joshua's tribes entered at the Jericho crossing and the same way we enter our eternal abode. We must cross the Jordan River. Crossing that river has long been the Christian symbol for death. At the end of our sojourn on this earth we stand on Jordan's stormy banks, take our final breath and cross those waters into our heavenly home. But we can also cross the Jordan and enter our spiritual promised land before we take that final breath. We can reject the life of sin, be crucified with Christ, die to self, and be raised with Jesus in newness of life.

The kingdom of heaven is a multi-dimensional reality. It existed for a time on the eastern shore of the Mediterranean Sea, it exists today as Jesus reigns in his church, in the hearts of believers, and it will exist forever when he comes in glory and takes the throne his father gives him.

So arise, go over . . .

Only Be Strong

Scripture: Joshua 1:4–9
Suggested Reading: John 13:34

*P*ossessing our spiritual promised land is a daunting task that we must approach with wisdom and courage. It is a land where angels fear to tread, it is a land where fools rush in only to be befuddled and crushed. It is a land we can capture only by battling the very demons of hell.

Our first job is to get to the other side of the river. Dying to self is not easy. We cannot see the bottom of the river we have to cross, the water is cold and the current is swift. The land we are leaving has many enticing features we are reluctant to abandon, and we are unsure what lies on the other side. Our spies have reported, but the report is mixed. We waver on the bank.

There are giants in the land that have to be conquered. Soldiers of Satan's army lurk behind every rock. Our "ancient foe," said Martin Luther, "doth seek to work us woe. His craft and power are great and armed with cruel hate." The last thing Satan wants is for us to inherit the kingdom of God, and he will do everything he can to thwart our campaign to enter that promised land.

Given that picture, is it any wonder that so many of our church friends are content to dwell on the east bank, enjoying the view but never possessing the land? The saddest sight in the world is the glum Christian who brings nothing to church but prayer concerns and an attitude that life is nothing more than a joyless journey from the cradle to the grave, a Christian who has no idea that Jesus offers a life of joy and contentment that transcends the mundane concerns of mortal existence. What is the secret to possessing the land? God laid it out very clearly in his message to Joshua.

First he said, "I have given [it] to you." A done deal. A thing already accomplished. Oh, we must still put forth the effort to win the land from the enemy, but it is a land promised to us and given to us by the One who already wrote the end of the story. Victory is sure. We have the deed for the land in our hand; we can claim ownership, but we must first evict the trespassers squatting there.

Then he said that we don't go in alone. He is always with us, going before us, never failing us or forsaking us. Sometimes in our lives we've all felt lonely. And when we are lonely we are afraid. Having a strong friend with us always gives us the mettle to face the unknown, and having Jesus as our friend and constant companion removes all fear. With the Lord going before us, we can be strong and of good courage.

But the main ingredient is obedience. God commanded Joshua to be careful to do according to all the law of Moses, to turn not to the right or the left, to meditate on it continually and to speak it with his mouth. And as a reward for obedience, the Lord promised success.

How does God's command to Joshua translate into the new covenant in Christ's blood? It's simple, but it's hard. We must love the Lord our God above all, and love our neighbor as ourselves. We must see Jesus in everyone we meet and live with an open hand. The new commandment he gave us is to love one another to the point of being willing to lay down our lives for each other as he loved us and laid down his life for us.

And when we get to that point, we are ready to take the plunge, cross the river and possess the promised land.

A Place of Rest

*Scripture: **Joshua 1:10–18***
Suggested Reading: Matthew 11:28–29

God dropped many hints along the way that the land in which he established his earthly kingdom was not the final goal of his dealings with the fallen human race. That little strand on the eastern shore of the Mediterranean Sea with its ranges of rocky hills and its network of lush valleys held strategic importance when it was the crossroads of the continents, when caravans from Europe, Africa, and the Orient crossed paths there. But God, in his omniscience, looked far beyond that moment in history to a future those old-world inhabitants couldn't begin to imagine.

The Lord intended the land of Israel to be a place of rest for his obedient servants who courageously cleansed the land of its pagan inhabitants and established a new nation, a kingdom of priests whom he would protect from the savage empires that stormed around it, a kingdom of holy people who were to love him above all and their neighbors as themselves, a kingdom of light who would be a beacon to all who passed through, a kingdom of witnesses who could bless all the nations of the earth by bringing them eternal life.

For all of that, the land has served its purpose. God has fulfilled his ageless plan to rescue the human race from damnation. He used the land as the altar on which to offer the final sacrifice and as the launching pad from which the apostles carried the good news of the kingdom to the remotest reaches of the globe. Today we have transcended rocks and wells and tamarisk trees. Today we enjoy our inheritance in the spiritual kingdom that Jesus promised to those who are born again, and whom he wants to stand obediently at the new crossroads of the world and let our light shine.

One of my good friends has an old Chevy in his garage, the car he drove to school and to work when he was a teenager, the car he drove to the drive-in restaurant and the drive-in movies, the car in which he courted his old girl friends. That old car knows secrets only my friend knows and bears marks that testify to memories only he understands. He probably paid a hundred dollars for it a half century ago, but he wouldn't part with it today at any price. Although it is no longer useful, it is a precious relic of his past.

The Promised Land today is like that old Chevy. It is precious to the Israelis because God gave it to Father Abraham to pass along through Isaac and Jacob as an inheritance, and because it is where David reigned and where Solomon built his temple. It is precious to Christians because that is where Jesus walked, taught, healed, died, and rose again. It is precious to the Arabs who believe God gave it to Father Abraham to pass along through Ishmael as an inheritance, and because that is where Mohammed is said to have ascended to heaven. It is a relic that Jews, Christian, and Arabs have shed their blood to possess, a holy relic of their past that they wouldn't part with today at any price. It is clear that the land will have no rest from hatred and conflict until Jesus returns and brings his kingdom of peace.

I've been to that restless land of constant strife. I've tripped over the rocks on its sun-scorched hills, and I've sat under the palm trees of its moon-drenched valleys. It is a wonderful place to visit during rare periods of respite from bombs and gunfire, but I'm happy that my promised land, my place of rest and service, is not a fragment of geography on the map of an ancient continent, but that my country lies over another river in the heart of the kingdom of God, in the land of rest that only Jesus can give to those who have accepted his invitation to "come unto me," and who are committed to letting their light shine in whatever part of the globe God has put them.

A Brothel in Jericho

Scripture: Joshua 2:1–7
Suggested Reading: Joshua 6:22–25; Matthew 1:1–6; Hebrews 11:31;
James 2:25

*E*ver since in my youth when I discovered what a harlot was, it has been both amusing and curious to me that Rahab's house was the first stop the spies made upon entering Jericho. Was it natural for young men away from home to seek her out for carnal reasons? Did they have some reason to believe that her home was a safe haven from the enemy? Were they led there by the power of the Spirit?

Most commentators avoid exploring the reason for their stopping at her house, and some even suggest that she was not really a harlot in the modern sense, but rather the keeper of a rooming house for travelers. But since the word *harlot* is usually attached to her name whenever she is mentioned in the Bible, I'll accept the common definition and try to be less curious and amused that the young Hebrew spies sought out the local brothel for their lodging place.

As I mature, my interest shifts from their motivation to God's. Obviously God intended that they visit her house, not simply to rouse the idle curiosity of an inquisitive teenager, but to make a statement profitable for doctrine and righteous living. Though nowhere in scripture is she chastised for her occupation, she is always labeled a harlot. But even so, her good and brave works on Israel's behalf not only saved her life, but also earned her a niche among the heroes of faith and a bough on Jesus' family tree.

Just how it came to pass that Salmon, Boaz's father, had a relationship with Rahab the harlot of Jericho is a question for some bored theology professor to tackle when all of the more useful subjects of scholarly inquiry have been exhausted. But we do know that when Jericho fell, because of her heroism, she was spared, and that she and her entire family were granted citizenship in Israel. We learn from the story of Ruth that Rahab's son, Boaz, became a wealthy landowner near the little town of Bethlehem. Undoubtedly, Rahab's efforts gained her celebrity status in her new country, and she passed her newfound faith down to her son, who in turn passed it down the line to Obed, to Jesse, and to David the king. The harlot of Jericho must have become a powerful witness for the God of Israel.

Two things leap out at me.

First, the business of judgment. We humans are inclined to judge people by their behavior and to exclude them from our fellowship even though we are told over and over again that judgment is God's business and that we, the unworthy saved, are called simply to witness to others and to love them. And since we don't do our work nearly as well as we should, we have no business trying to do the work that God has reserved for himself.

And second, there is the business of inclusion. Look who's included in Jesus' family tree. We find there not only the names of patriarchs and great kings who did what was right in the sight of the Lord, but also Tamar who played the harlot and seduced Judah, Rahab the harlot, the wife of Uriah the Hittite whose name Matthew couldn't bring himself to mention, and a long line of kings who did what was evil in the sight of the Lord.

How then should I live? Can I exclude?

Without condoning sin, I am compelled, with God's help, to be charitable to sinners, to treat sinners as citizens of God's kingdom who don't yet have their papers, to reach out and love the unlovable and touch the untouchable. Nothing less will do.

Who'll Clean the House?

Scripture: Matthew 25:31–46
Suggested Reading: Matthew 13:24–30

*Y*esterday's meditation reminded me of a story.

Once my mother volunteered to open our home to a group from the church on a Sunday evening after services so members of the congregation could meet the new pastor and his wife. Her task was to prepare and serve light refreshments, and Dad's was to greet the guests, introduce newcomers, and moderate the gathering.

Mrs. Heethuis, the saintly wife of one of our church elders, offered to spend Saturday cleaning our house so mother could devote herself to making sandwiches, preparing a salad, and baking a sheet cake. Mother accepted her gracious offer, then spent all day Friday cleaning so Mrs. Heethuis would have a nice clean house to clean when she arrived on Saturday. It made sense to my mother.

Many Christians are like that. They are awaiting Christ's return and are doing their best to see that when the trumpet sounds Jesus arrives to clean up a nice clean world.

Jesus ordered us to let the tares grow in the wheat field lest we, in the process of pulling them up, pull up the good plants by accident. Switching metaphors, Jesus promised us that someday he would return to separate the sheep from the goats. When he returns in judgment, he will clean the house that he made for us here by shooing the goats out the door into eternal flames, but he will gather up his sheep and take them home to live with him forever.

He reserved for himself the job of separating the goats from the sheep, and told us to prepare for his coming by providing nourishment for the hungry, giving clothing to the naked, and tending the sick and the sorrowful. His job description for himself is perfectly clear, and so is his mandate to us.

Why then do we find so many Christians trying to do Christ's job and ignoring their own duties? Why are so many Christians trying to judge the Rahabs of the world and rid the world of sin instead of making sandwiches and baking cakes for the poor?

I find prominent people in clerical garb and other people of standing who bear the banner of Christ trying to run the government the way they think God should run it, passing severe judgment on sinners they deem less holy than themselves and ranting about the evils of taxes on families, especially taxes the government uses to provide school lunches for the children of idle sinners and medical treatment for sinners with diseases they think only sinners get.

It was once a tradition in my church to read the Ten Commandments every Sunday and to recite the Apostles' Creed. Those old customs have fallen in the path of less intimidating and more self-righteous homilies. I've since come to think that every Christian church should include as a regular part of its worship the reading of the last part of Matthew twenty-five. Perhaps if we were fed a regular dose of the duties Christ expects us to perform as we wait for his return, we might be less inclined to do God's work at the expense of the work he's assigned us to do.

It will be an awful thing to get to Judgment Day believing that we have done righteously by shooing the goats out the door, only to have the shepherd look us in the eye and ask where we were when he came to us hungry or sick. Will we have failed to recognize his face as we glared with contempt into the faces of those we judged to be undeserving sinners?

A Forked-Tongued Saint?

Scripture: *Joshua 2:8–24*
Suggested Reading: *Matthew 5:33–37*

*M*ost of the heroes of faith had one thing in common: they could tell a lie to an enemy when their loved ones were in danger. Abraham, Isaac, Jacob, and now Rahab all lied when their lives were at stake or deceived their adversary when it was profitable to do so.

Now I know that those people were not perfect and that through the years they grew as any Christian should on the road to sanctification. And I know the Ten Commandments forbids bearing false witness. But in a moment when the truth would bring disaster and a lie would save the day, what choice does one have?

I have always struggled with the axiom that we should always tell the truth. Does the thief, the rapist, the murderer, or the molester deserve the truth from our lips when his aim is to harm us or to harm someone we love? And I have trouble accepting the ploy of dancing in the gray area of circumvention by saying something deceptive which is neither a lie nor the truth.

When President Clinton was under oath to tell the truth, he, in the strictest sense of the word, probably did not lie, but he made such a mockery of the truth that no matter what good he did while in office, his legacy will always be obscured by his conduct in the witness box. I've found that in the world of business and politics, being evasive causes as much harm as lying, but that sometimes telling the truth can be dangerous.

Our government declines to tell us the truth when the truth might undermine national security or public safety. And in international politics as well as in local law, people play roles specifically designed to deceive other governments and lawbreakers. Does that mean that a Christian can't be a spy or an undercover narcotics agent because the whole essence of such activity is by its very nature a lie?

Rahab lied to the authority that God had placed over her. Members of the Nazi resistance lied to their governing authority and its law enforcement officers. And all decent human beings applaud them for their lies. Is it okay to lie to bad people? If we are caught in a bind between the law of man and the law of God, might we sometimes be compelled to compromise our rigid values?

We've all been in situations in which we've had to choose between the lesser of two evils. When the king's men banged on Rahab's door, she found herself having either to lie to them or to bring disaster on both herself and on God's chosen people. She chose to lie. And if she hadn't, she would not have been spared in the invasion and Jesus' family tree would have a bough lopped off.

Thankfully I'm retired from a business that was rife with falsehood, evasion, and manipulation of truth. Thankfully, I don't have to deal anymore with people who lie and with people who don't deserve to be told the truth. I did my job well, but not perfectly. I was never classed among the evil people in my business, but there were decisions I made then for which I've had to repent. And sometimes I withheld the truth for the greater good.

I doubt if my evil colleagues look back on their careers and find great joy and contentment in their lies, but I am blessed that at my retirement banquet one of my adversaries honored me by saying, "He not only did his job well, but he was an honest man, a man of his word." I hope he was telling the truth.

Taking the Plunge

Scripture: Joshua 3
Suggested Reading: Exodus 14; 2 Kings 2:6–15

Commentators have all written extensively about Joshua lead-ing the Israelites over the dry riverbed into Canaan. They've pointed out that when Moses parted the Red Sea, he did it by stretching his hand over the seas to divide it, that Elijah and Elisha smote the Jordan with a rolled up mantle, and that the water stopped flowing when the priests carrying the ark stepped into the swollen river.

Each crossing of water on dry ground was a little different from the others, but each served at least three common purposes: to demonstrate the powerful presence of the God of all the earth, to show that God selects certain humans in whom to invest his au-thority, and to declare to all those standing by that the Spirit of God and the accompanying power had flowed into his servant.

Each time the Israelites crossed over on dry ground, God re-quired of them the faith to go over at his command. When they crossed the Red Sea, they went through "the midst of the sea . . . the waters being a wall to them on their right and on their left." So escaping from their slave masters through a miraculous corridor of water must have demanded a massive amount of faith. I would have been scared half to death that the God who slew all those firstborn might just be upset enough about something we did to collapse those walls of water upon us and drown us right there. And especially after I got through and turned and saw the Egyp-tians being crushed under the torrents, I might have had a difficult time risking such a crossing again.

Perhaps that is why God caused the water to pile up at Adam, ten to fifteen miles upstream and out of sight. There were no walls to walk through this time. Most of the people who crossed the Jordan at Jericho were born in the wilderness, but those over forty-five or so probably remembered the day their parents carried them or pulled them along between the two mountains of water and remember seeing the Egyptian soldiers perish as those mountains cascaded over them. And those who remembered told their children and grandchildren, so everyone in the camp knew how terrifying it was.

I've been to the Jordan in the winter when the temperature was about sixty-five degrees. It was not intimidating. Even at my age, I could have easily swum across it several times. But the Israelites crossed it during the height of the flood season when the river had overflowed its banks. They saw "the mighty Jordan roll" as they waited on the east side. But then they saw the wonder that Joshua had promised. When the priests bearing the ark of the covenant stepped obediently into the water of the swollen river, knowing that if they stepped in too far they would step beyond the bank, plunge to the bottom and be swept away and drowned; but that mighty river simply dried up, and the priests stood on dry ground.

We use the term "taking the plunge" to refer to stepping courageously into one of life's new ventures, such as a business or a marriage. And "taking the plunge" into a born-again life with Christ required courage because it was something new. Because we had never passed this way before it was a bit scary. Because we had to step in blindly, not knowing where the bottom was, it was somewhat intimidating. But those of us who have crossed this Jordan to claim our inheritance in the kingdom of heaven can testify to those who wait on the east bank that the water didn't return and sweep us away, that we felt the presence of God as we passed over, and that as he promised, he has been with us wherever we've gone.

So go ahead, take the plunge.

Memorials

Scripture: Joshua 4
Suggested Reading: 1 Peter 2:4–10

Our lives are saturated with memorials.

At church we have a memorials committee whose job it is to record gifts given to the church in memory of the dead and to assure donors that those gifts are used as requested.

Some of the brothers and sisters question the propriety of such gifts, particularly if the stipulations attached to the gifts tend to magnify the person in whose honor it was given. Names of the departed are liberally spread throughout our churches. They are inscribed on Bibles and hymnbooks, painted on stained glass windows, carved in the concrete bases of cornerstones and bulletin boards, and engraved on brass plates that are attached to doors and pews or hang on the walls. All to inform everyone who passes by that an otherwise forgotten saint once served there, was loved by someone who served there, or that someone seeking to assuage a guilty conscience bequeathed money to that church.

As I sit here at my desk, memorials surround me. Three cloth pennants celebrate the World Championships that the Detroit Tigers have won during my lifetime. Framed photographs keep the faces of my beloved family members always fresh in my mind. Wooden plaques, cast trophies, needlework, printed diplomas, book spines, and even chiming clocks with pendulums and engraved plates memorialize my personal achievements. Treasured pieces of artwork that my children and grandchildren made for me in elementary school grace my office walls. Cherished icons keep precious memories of the past alive and remind us of the ones we love.

All those things are made of paper, cloth, wood, and metal and will eventually rot, burn, melt, or tarnish. They will probably survive little more than a single lifetime, and serve only to massage my nostalgia and my pride.

We love memorabilia, but the stuff that celebrates our lives is transient. My 1945 Tiger pennant has already been nibbled by mice and might be again when some disinterested heir someday stows it in a box in some far-off attic.

But God's memorials are intended to last forever. He didn't tell Joshua to paint a picture or weave a tapestry portraying the crossing of the Jordan. He didn't tell him to plant a commemorative tree or engrave a metal plate. He told him to erect a monument of stones, the most enduring of his creations. Cloth and canvas would decay, a tree would eventually die, and metal would corrode or rust, but stones, which are as old as the earth, will still be there when Christ rules the world from his throne in Jerusalem.

God did not ordain his monuments simply to stand as memorials to past events, but to be inspirations for future generations. The miracle of the river crossing was not just to be remembered by those who experienced it as a wondrous act of a loving God, but as a witness to all who passed that way, that the God of Jacob is the one and only God of all the earth and that he is our deliverer and our refuge.

And we are called to be monuments too. Not monuments of wood and cloth, but indestructible monuments of stone whose testimony will survive forever by being passed on to our children and our children's children, not so meaningless as to be tucked away in boxes in attics but to be treasured in the sanctuaries of our hearts.

The Art of Vulnerability

Scripture: Joshua 5:1–9
Suggested Reading: Genesis 34; Deuteronomy 10:16;
2 Corinthians 12:5–10; Romans 2:29

In business as in war, when the "brain trust" is plotting its strategy, the back room is flooded with opinions. When militant union officials design their plans to squeeze another dollar from the hands of frugal employers, leaders gather at headquarters and bang heads until a consensus develops. When corporate heads meet to lay a plan for increasing productivity and profit, vice presidents gather in conference rooms and bounce ideas until a generally acceptable plan emerges. When armies stand at the brink of war, the top brass gathers at central command to assert various plans of action and settle on one strategy that best suits the moment. In all cases, consensus and power merge into plan.

It was probably the same in Joshua's day. The Israelite men of war stood poised at Gilgal for battle, ready to make their first incursion into the Promised Land. Caleb and the captains of the thousands might have gathered in the command tent to discuss various strategies for attacking Jericho. They probably discussed the reports the spies brought back. Most may have agreed that the Canaanite kings were cowering in fear after having seen and heard of the miracles the Lord wrought in bringing Israel to the border of their land. But a few might have disagreed, suggesting that the fear might be feigned, a ploy to make Israel overconfident. Pharaoh saw miracles too, they recalled, but yet he hardened his heart against them. So they probably sat around in small groups and talked of catapults, battering rams, and siege ramps.

Then Joshua entered the tent, and instead of listening to their strategy discussions handed them all flint knives and told them to go out and circumcise their men of war. The officers must have shuddered in disbelief. Militarily it made no sense. The enemy was bound to find out. This was sure to be Shechem revisited, but with Israel on the victim end of the treachery. An army on the brink of war rendered totally vulnerable!

But maybe the wiser among them were beginning to understand. Maybe when they warred against the Midianites and slew every enemy soldier without losing a single one of their own, they began to realize that victory did not come to them because they were strong or clever, but because the Lord was on their side. And soon they would understand it even better when their mighty men of valor would trade their swords for trumpets, march around the walls of Jericho, and watch the city fall without slinging a single stone or throwing a single spear.

The key to inheriting the kingdom of heaven is voluntary vulnerability. When we step into our Jordan, are crucified with Christ and die to self, we must remove the brass from our collars and stack the weapons we have crafted with our own skill and wisdom. When we emerge from the river, reborn and raised with him in resurrected life, we must circumcise the foreskins of our hearts, separate our flesh from our spirits, and look forward to our first conquest completely disarmed and vulnerable.

When we are totally without strength, we have no choice but to put all our trust in God, and no choice but to submit to him in total obedience, even if his strategy makes no sense to our human way of thinking. He accepts nothing less from us than complete surrender.

And if we go forth into our spiritual inheritance following our High Priest and sounding God's trumpets, the walls of Satan's city will crumble before us!

The Produce of the Land

Scripture: Joshua 5:10–12
Suggested Reading: Exodus 16:4; John 6:31–35; 16:4–15;
Galatians 5:22–24

Upon being circumcised, the Israelites were released from the reproach of Egypt. God lifted from them the degradation of slavery that the nation had carried for forty years in the wilderness. And as they prepared for war, God also lifted from them the curse of cowardice they had carried since their rebellion at Kadesh. Now it was time to celebrate the Passover as they had never celebrated it before.

They first observed Passover in Egypt at the end of their captivity. There they slaughtered the lamb and spread its blood on their doorposts of their houses to avoid the wrath of God and spare the lives of their firstborn. The next time they celebrated Passover was at Mount Sinai, this time in thanksgiving for their deliverance from bondage. And as they received the law, they pledged themselves to lives of obedience. Most scholars believe that they did not observe Passover again until they reached the plains of Jericho. So, the third time they celebrated, it was in thanksgiving for their safe transport from the hostile wilderness into the land of promise, into the land flowing with milk and honey.

And when they did, the manna ceased and *they ate of the produce of the land*!

Passover is for Christians the symbolic representation of the Lamb of God being slain as the final sacrifice for sin and our deliverance from the bondage of sin. We continue to celebrate it as the Lord celebrated it with his apostles, with the bread that signifies his body and the wine that signifies his blood. We celebrate it as we sit at his feet and listen to him teach us how we should live, and we continue to celebrate it with new and special meaning as we cross over into our spiritual promised land, the kingdom of heaven.

What does this moment mean for us? Clearly Jesus is our manna, our Bread from heaven, our Bread of Life. He is our Rock that yields living water, and if we eat his bread and drink his wine we will never hunger or thirst again. When God rained down manna for his people in the wilderness, unworthy as they were, he intended it as a sign for us, far removed in time, that we too would receive bread from heaven. But does our manna cease when we are born again and enter the kingdom of heaven? Does Jesus cease to be with us?

As we wandered through the wilderness of sin, as unworthy and insufferable as the Israelites, God lavished on us the blessing of his only begotten Son. The Bread from heaven came to us in our sin and misery, and as a man walked with us, taught us, fed us, bound up the wounds inflicted on us by those who held us bondage and attacked us in the desert. He claimed us as brothers and finally died for us, opening the gates of paradise and stopping the flow of the river of death way back to Adam so we might cross over and claim an inheritance in the spiritual promised land as adopted sons of God.

God gave manna to the Israelites in the desert as a test to see if they would gather it obediently, in the manner he prescribed. When we lived in the wilderness, God gave us his Bread from heaven as our test, and when we crossed the river, died to sin and self and rose with him in new spiritual life, the period of testing ended. We no longer have to go out and gather the cupful of spiritual sustenance that spoils in a day. We now dwell in the promised land with Jesus living *in* us, sustained by the wheat fields, orchards, and vineyards that surround us, *the produce of the land*, the fruit of the Spirit!

Holy Ground

Scripture: Joshua 5:13–15
Suggested Reading: Genesis 32:1–2; Exodus 3:1–5;
2 Kings 6:15–17; Matthew 4:11; John 14:2–3;
Hebrews 1: 13–14; Revelation 19:11–16

*O*nce we begin our crusade to occupy our spiritual land of promise, Jesus takes on a whole new identity for us. He becomes the Commander in Chief of the army of the Lord, a warrior on a white horse whose eyes are like a flame of fire and from whose mouth issues a sharp sword with which to smite the principalities of evil. He is the King of kings, the Lord of lords.

When we meet generals we need only salute, but when we come into the presence of this Commander of the army of the Lord, we need to remove our shoes and fall on our faces to the earth. We stand not only in the presence of supreme authority, but, like Moses on the mountain of God, we stand on holy ground!

God's army of angels serves many purposes as we strive to take full possession of our spiritual promised land. When we score great victories over temptation and the devil, as Jesus did in the wilderness, the angels will come and minister to us, nourishing us, sustaining us, encouraging us. But then they set aside their servant's garb and don their battle gear to continue the war against the many forces of evil that stand in our way.

Before they crossed the Jordan, Joshua's officers reminded the people to keep their eyes fixed on the ark of the covenant and to follow it because, "you have not passed this way before." As it was new territory for them, our spiritual land is new territory for us.

We have not passed this way before. We have never stood on holy ground. We have never experienced the presence of the Lord so intimately within us. We've never felt such a surge of almighty love coursing through us.

At this point in our walk with Christ, it is important to keep our eyes focused on him or the many distractions all around us could divert our attention from him. It is important to follow our leader closely because he knows the territory, he knows where the dangers lurk because he has passed this way before.

"I go," he said, "to prepare a place for you." His meeting with Joshua on the Canaan side of the river with his sword drawn is proof sufficient that he got to our promised land long before we did and that he has been busy battling the enemy at the border, preparing a place so our landing would encounter no resistance. Our enemies' hearts had melted, their courage had flown. They were fainthearted because our Lord had prepared the way. He is the king of hearts. He can harden hearts as he hardened Pharaoh's and he can make them wilt.

But now that we have landed safe on Canaan's side we cannot yet raise the flag of victory. There is much land to conquer, many enemies to defeat. Satan lurks behinds every rock like a roaring lion. His "craft and power are great," and he's "armed with cruel hate." Sometimes he's a wolf in sheep's clothing trying to deceive us and tempt us to sin. Sometimes he storms our position from his fortress in the hills, and sometimes he sneaks up quietly from behind.

But if we keep our eyes focused on our Lord and do not turn to the right or the left, with the Commander of the army of the Lord leading us into battle, we can be strong and of good courage because he promises that we will have success wherever we go.

We are standing on his holy ground!

From Within and Without

Scripture: Joshua 6:1
Suggested Reading: Leviticus 19:33; Deuteronomy 28:15–68

When I came to this chapter, the first verse literally leaped out at me. I was there. I saw Jericho "shut up from within and without."

In Joshua's day the Canaanites who lived there secured their gates for fear of the Israelites. Today the city is under Palestinian control, but the Israelis have surrounded it and closed its gates. The Jews claimed that Arab terrorists were based there and laying siege to the city was a military necessity. Palestinians claimed that the Jews were angry because Jericho had attracted tourists, both Jewish and foreign, who came there to enjoy its glitzy nightlife.

In 2001 when Mary Ann and I visited Israel, we were permitted to see Jericho only from a distance. We passed by on the highway and saw the barbed wire and the blockades that kept Palestinians from leaving and visitors from entering. Only a few were allowed in and out, trusted men with families to feed, and others who had jobs essential to Israel's interests. The rest were confined behind the fences and minefields. Israeli soldiers guarded the checkpoints and routinely searched vehicles attempting to exit or enter.

All my life I had empathy for the Jews. They were God's chosen people who had been persecuted all through their history. Their hearts had been hardened and their eyes blinded to the truth that salvation might come to me, a Gentile, and because of their sin they had become a curse among all nations. But by 1948 they had paid for their sin and God redeemed them from their oppressors and gave them back their land. But what of the Palestinians, Abraham's other children, who had inhabited the land far longer than Israel ever did? What should become of them?

In Israel we visited the Holocaust Museum. Vivid life-sized pictures on the walls portray life in the Warsaw ghetto when the Nazis herded the Jews into a small section of the city and surrounded it with guards and barbed wire fences. When we drove past Jericho, images of the Warsaw ghetto came quickly to mind. The Jews had learned well from the Nazis how to deal with "undesirable elements" of the population. The only thing missing from Jericho was the sign declaring that *Arbeit macht Frei*. And I wondered then if the Jews have ever considered a "final solution to the Palestinian problem."

Had the Israelites remained faithful to the God who commanded their armies against the Canaanites, they would have been invulnerable. But their victories quickly turned to defeat when they began mixing with the pagans who worshipped gods of wood and stone, whose worship practices consisted mainly of sexual orgies to honor the gods of fertility. The lust of the flesh turned them from the God who had delivered them from the house of bondage, and his judgment on them was to deliver them back to persecution from one end of the earth to the other.

The nations God ordered Israel to purge from the land were pagan nations. They were sinful but had been given plenty of time to repent. When they didn't, God's judgment on them was total eradication. But the Palestinians who possessed the land prior to 1948 do not worship idols. They are sons of Abraham, Ishmaelite monotheists who worship the God of their fathers. They are not even strangers, they are brothers sojourning among them who should be loved and treated as natives of the land, but their distress has led them to do terrible things.

Pray for the peace of Israel. Shalom.

Who Fit What Battle?

Scripture: Joshua 6:2–25
Suggested Reading: 2 Corinthians 10:1–6; Hebrews 11:30

Contrary to the old song, Joshua didn't "fit" anyone, and there was no battle. At least what we understand a battle to be. The first thing commentators note about this event is its unconventional nature, prompting them to confirm the scriptural truth that God works in mysterious ways and that God is not dependant upon man's service to achieve his purposes.

If the only reason for the conquest of Canaan had been to possess the land, victory in any manner over the pagans would have sufficed. But behind the objective and historical lies the spiritual, and the true understanding of the extraordinary events of the conquest goes to those who have been crucified with Christ and raised again to a new way of living.

As we stand on the western shore of our Jordan and survey the enemy strongholds we have to face as we set out to possess the kingdom of heaven fully, the first thoughts that enter our minds are of strategy and tactics. What objectives should we set for ourselves, and what means should we employ to achieve those objectives?

What sins in our lives should we attack first? The inordinate attraction to television? The inappropriate sexual desires? The gluttony? The addiction to nicotine? The egocentric passion for fame and recognition? The lust for wealth and worldly goods? Our idols? Our anger toward those who have abused us?

And just how should we deal with those strongholds of Satan? Should we pick one show a night to watch? Should we destroy those offensive videos? Should we start a diet and exercise program? Should we stop smoking? Should we visit that person who offends us and try to make peace? Should we give away some money just to see how good it feels? Should we make some sacrifices we wouldn't ordinarily make? What should we do?

When Joshua finished celebrating Passover, he may have climbed a hill and surveyed Jericho, contemplating his military options. Should he attack now or lay siege to the city? Should he attack the east wall or go around to the west side? Should he build a ramp to the top of the wall? Should he catapult boulders over it? Maybe he should batter the gates. Maybe he should. . . . Maybe he should. . . . Maybe he should . . .

But then the Commander of the army of the Lord came to him and he realized who really was in charge of the battle. It was not up to him to determine the objectives or methods of his warfare. It was his place simply to prostrate himself before his superior, to go forth in faith and humbly obey his Lord's commands no matter how strange or mysterious his tactics may seem.

Our strongholds will not crumble because we devise some ingenious scheme, engage in some self-righteous act of contrition, deprive ourselves of something we enjoy or make some pious resolution. Our enemies will fall only when we have circumcised our hearts, accepted Jesus as the Lord of our lives, and bound ourselves to him in humble obedience, willingly to step out and do as he demands, no matter how extraordinary his plan may appear.

It was faith and obedience that toppled the walls of Jericho, and it is faith and obedience that will defeat the enemies that stand in the way of our fully possessing the kingdom of heaven.

. . . *And Expect a Miracle*

Scripture: Joshua 5:13–6:7

If we may be permitted to speak in modern parlance, Joshua was a general, a four star general at least, maybe five, like Eisenhower. He was also the head of state of the nation of Israel, a theocracy under martial law. Under the Lord, of course, he was commander-in-chief of the armed forces, which consisted of about six hundred thousand fighting men. Below him in rank were lesser generals and colonels and majors, down to corporals and privates. No one outranked Joshua.

He had been trained for his office by Moses. Remember that Moses grew from infancy to manhood as a son of the king of Egypt. As a prince he was certainly well trained in the art of war and served in one of the greatest military forces of the age. One of his last acts was to plan the successful war against Midian before he commissioned Joshua to lead the invasion of Canaan.

As a good leader, Joshua certainly allowed his subordinates to participate in the planning. Probably some brigadier general suggested smashing the gates of Jericho with battering rams. Another may have proposed shooting flaming arrows over the walls. The commander of the artillery division most likely recommended catapulting boulders over the walls into the heart of the city. The infantry may have wanted to storm the battlements. Some were sure to have insisted on a siege before taking offensive action. After listening to all of their ideas, Joshua may have gone off to a place by himself just to look at Jericho and ponder the variety of options.

That's when he met the Commander of the army of the Lord.

When the stranger confronted him with his sword drawn and identified himself, Joshua may well have asked, "Are you here to replace me? Moses appointed *me* to be the commander of this army. Why are you here?" But he didn't. His spirit told him that he was in the presence of the Lord, so he humbled himself in obedient submission and listened carefully as his Commander laid out the plan for the conquest of Jericho. Then he went back to his people.

First he called the priests together and told them that they would lead the army in its march around Jericho. Then he called a meeting of the military minds. Imagine Joshua returning to command headquarters and explaining the battle plan for conquering Jericho. If a modern commander brought back such a strategy to his subordinates, they wouldn't be subordinate very long. They would mutiny and usurp his authority.

Now we aren't told how those generals reacted when Joshua revealed the plan, and we'll never know if he divulged to them his meeting with the mysterious stranger who called himself the Commander of the army of the Lord and who laid out the strategy to him. But if they are anything like people today, there had to be some among them who wondered if the old man had gone daft. But, as good soldiers, they obediently submitted and hoped that the scheme, silly as it seemed, would work. But Joshua didn't question his orders. He carried out every detail as directed, and expected a miracle to happen. And it did!

And therein lies the lesson. Sometimes the Lord's plan for his church might seem strange. Sometimes the direction the Holy Spirit delivers to our church administrative bodies makes no sense to our secular minds. But the Lord is not bound by secular convention, so we should just humbly submit, and, as Joshua, expect a miracle!

A City Cursed

Scripture: Joshua 6:26–27
Suggested Reading: Exodus 22:20; 1 Kings 16:34

I don't presume to know if God's curse on Jericho holds to this day or if he lifted it when Jesus cried from the cross, "It is finished!"

When Heil of Bethel had the gall to rebuild the city in spite of God's curse, he lost his youngest son at the start and the eldest at the finish. Some commentators even suggest that during the rebuilding of the city, the sons in between also died.

Perhaps God intended Jericho to remain forever as nothing more than a mound of ruins.

When I saw the city under siege by the Jews, it certainly appeared to be cursed. Prior to the siege, we were told, Jericho abounded with nightlife. Neon lights attracted the gamblers to its casinos and the lusty to its bawdy houses. Money poured in from the world's tourists and from the wealthy of Tel Aviv. Times were good until the government of Israel found reason to shut it up again, "from within and without."

But the lasting application of the curse upon Jericho is not to be found in the punishment of Heil or in the conditions that exist today. The lasting application is the question, what have we done with the spoils of our spiritual wars? If God has defeated a particular force of Satan, say, inappropriate sexual desires, have we destroyed those offensive videos? If God has purged us from alcoholism, have we emptied the liquor cabinet? If God has removed some personal animosity from our heart, have we turned an old enemy into a new friend? If God has curbed our pride, have we found a place to serve in true humility? If God has removed our lust for worldly gain, have we sacrificed any of our gold for the good of the poor?

We cannot keep trophies of war. Those vanquished strongholds and all within them must be devoted to the Lord for destruction. If we keep the trophies, they only serve as remembrances of the past and may be used again by Satan to undo our victories in moments of weakness. And if we return to our old ways, we may bring trouble down on ourselves and again become vessels for destruction.

But there is a second dimension to trophies of the war against the sin in our lives. They are not trophies we choose to keep or to destroy. Since God won the victories, the trophies belong to him. If we keep any for ourselves, we are stealing from him. Anything that is in the city must be devoted to him for destruction, with two grounds for exception. First, if anything in the context of our sin is innocent, it should be preserved. Second, if anything is found to have intrinsic value if properly used, it should be turned to good use.

There are many examples. If the Lord has given us victory over abuse of alcohol, we may do well to celebrate by pouring our liquor into a hole in the ground. But, if he has given us victory over abuse of our bodies by gorging ourselves on food, do we throw good groceries into the garbage? Most churches have food pantries and would gladly accept our contributions. If the Lord has given us victory over the love of money, do we burn our dollars? That would be foolish. Food and money in themselves, unlike alcohol and tobacco, are innocent. The Lord didn't tell the rich young ruler to destroy his wealth, he told him to give it to the poor.

But if we can't turn evil into good, we must curse the booty before it leads to our destruction.

The Curse Reversed?

Scripture: Review Joshua 6:26–27
Suggested Reading: 2 Kings 2:1–22; 2 Chronicles 28:1–15;
Mark 10:46–52; Luke 19:1–5

*J*ericho is a city with fascinating geography and history. It is situated in the deepest rift in the earth's surface. Depending on who is doing the measuring, it is, more or less, a thousand feet below sea level and over three thousand feet below Jerusalem, only fifteen miles away. Jerusalem, built on Mount Zion, is among the world's highest capital cities. Jericho, in the Jordan valley, on the other hand, is among the lowest cities on earth.

An oasis in the Judean wilderness, Jericho was known as the city of palm trees and was one of the oldest fortified cities in the world. It was also known as *moon city*, a name which suggests that its inhabitants worshipped a pagan deity, a moon god, and which also suggests one of the reasons for its accursed fate.

The Jericho whose walls came tumbling down at the sound of Joshua's trumpets was not the first Jericho, nor was it the last. Earlier cities on that same site were destroyed by invaders, by earthquakes, and other catastrophes. It has known both luxury and want, at times blessed by an abundance of fresh water and at other times destroyed by drought. In recent years it has been an attraction for tourists and pleasure seekers, and when I saw it in 2001 it was under siege by the Israeli army.

After Heil the Bethelite rebuilt the cursed city at the cost of his sons' lives, Jericho blossomed. The prophet Elijah moved there and established a school for prophets. In the hills beyond the city,

God's chariot of fire raptured the old prophet to his heavenly home as his successor, Elisha, watched. Then Elisha took up his mentor's mantle, parted the waters of the Jordan, and went to his new post in Jericho.

In that day the city of palms was a pleasant place to be, but soon the water turned brackish and the land unfruitful. When the sons of the prophets reported those conditions to Elisha, he threw a bowl of salt into the water and it became fresh again. Speaking through his prophet, God said, "I have made this water wholesome; henceforth neither death nor miscarriage shall come from it." And the chronicler reported that "the water has been wholesome to this day." Was that the lifting of the curse?

Less than a hundred years later the wicked King Ahaz of Judah engaged in a brutal war against King Pekah of Israel. Pekah defeated Judah and took two hundred thousand of its citizens to Israel to be his slaves. But the prophet Oded and some of the leaders of Israel intervened on their behalf and convinced their king to release his captives. Then Oded and his friends clothed and fed the refugees, anointed them, and carried them to Jericho. The city of palms became their city of refuge.

Little is heard of Jericho again until the time of Christ. Just before his triumphal entry into Jerusalem, Jesus preached there. When he entered the city a great crowd followed him, and wee little Zaccheaus, a loathed tax collector, climbed a sycamore tree just to see him, and ended up hosting the Lord at his home. And when Jesus left the town, a blind beggar, Bartimeaus, cried out to the Lord for mercy and was healed.

It's a long drop from the Holy City to sinful Jericho, but the love of the Lord knows no limit. It can make foul water fresh, turn a curse into hospitality and healing, and shine moonbeams of grace into the deepest valleys.

The Anger of the Lord

Scripture: Joshua 7:1

When we were in the eighth grade, Jack Rooker dropped several pieces of candy-coated chocolate into Mrs. Page's goldfish bowl. The whole class snickered as the water slowly turned yellowish red and gradually changed to a deep brown. When the teacher noticed it, she snatched up the bowl and ran from the room to change the water and save the life of the fish. She returned and said nothing about the incident the rest of the day, but when the closing bell rang and we prepared to leave, she instructed us to remain in our seats with our heads down and our mouths shut. After fifteen minutes she broke the silence and asked the perpetrator to come forward. We all raised up and watched.

Jack sat at his desk and gave no indication of coming clean. Instead he shot each one of us an intimidating glance that clearly conveyed the message that if we ratted on him, there would be consequences. So no one ratted. Mrs. Page declared that unless the culprit was identified, we would sit there all night while she graded our test papers. Finally fidgety Ruthie Ann Wagonmaker went up to the teacher's desk and tattled on Jack.

Mrs. Page let Ruthie Ann go home and declared to the rest of the class that since we all knew who polluted the fishbowl we were all guilty of the crime and therefore she was justified in keeping the whole class after school. After another fifteen minutes she dismissed all of us but Jack, further detaining him for more severe punishment, as God did with Achan.

Some members of our church belong to accountability groups. They meet regularly and share quite honestly with each other their foibles, their propensities to sin, their faults, their failures, and their obsessions. They take very seriously God's implied answer to Cain's question, "Am I my brother's keeper?"

Shared guilt is a difficult concept for one to accept who considers himself innocent. As we have previously noted, the oldest reading primer used in America's public schools in teaching the letter *A* declared, "In *A*dam's fall, we sinned *A*ll." When our first parents disobeyed the command of the Lord, we all became heirs to the guilt and the punishment. When Achan took to his tent some of the booty that belonged to God, the anger of the Lord burned against all the people of Israel. Like my eighth grade class, they were all guilty of the sin of their misbehaving brother.

We are our brother's keeper. When any of our members fall, the rest of us are duty bound to identify with them, to share their guilt and their punishment. It is not our responsibility to judge the conduct of our friends, but to help them bear their burdens, and that includes the burden of their sin.

Why? Just because God *said* so? No, but because God *did* so! He became one of us. He became our brother. He joined us in an accountability relationship. He asked us to confess our sins to him, and he took our sins upon himself. He became the guilty one in our place and suffered our punishment for us. No man has greater love than this, and he commanded us to go and do likewise.

We are always willing to share each other's blessings, and we are willing to share each other's sorrow. But is there any better way for us to show our love for each other than to share our guilt and our punishment?

Jesus did it for us, and we should do it for others.

They Are But Few

Scripture: Joshua 7:2–12
Suggested Reading: Joshua 9:14; Proverbs 3:5–7;
Ephesians 6:11–20

*D*on't send the whole army, Joshua, just send a battalion of bowmen and a company of slingers. Ai's army is weak, and a small force can easily subdue it.

Such was the advice Joshua got from his spies at the intelligence briefing. It sounded logical. No use gearing up a whole army for just a small battle. No use wasting the time of the Commander of the army of the Lord for a petty operation. No consultation necessary. Just do it.

Though Joshua only cited one reason for the military failure at Ai, the sin of Achan, there really are two. Before attacking the city, Joshua did not ask direction from the Lord. Had he sought the Lord's leading, God could have warned him that there was a serious problem in the ranks that had to be resolved before he would assure any more victories. But seeking the will of the Lord just didn't seem necessary for such an apparently minor conflict.

Each time we face an enemy that would prevent us from fully possessing our spiritual promised land, we need to seek direction from our Commander. No enemy is so insignificant that we can enter the fray single handedly and expect to win. And, the Lord may just hand us a loss merely because we thought we were strong enough and righteous enough to go it alone.

We must remember who the enemy is. Our enemy is not flesh and blood. If our enemy were nothing more than bone and muscle as we are, we might match up, pound for pound. But our enemy cannot be weighed and his reach cannot be measured. He is spirit. He is the Satan we may encounter either as a roaring lion or as a wolf in sheep's clothing. He has in his arsenal all of the demons and devils of hell, and in our own strength and wisdom we are severely overmatched. We are out of our league.

Another enemy that can lead us down the road to defeat is self. Ego. Especially male pride. We love to compete. We play bridge, we play battleships, we play football. We love to devise strategies, we love to contend, we love to win. We love the battles of wits, finesse, and muscle.

The wise Solomon knew and understood well the male ego, and the Holy Spirit told him to tell us not to be wise in our own eyes, not to rely on our own insight, but to trust the Lord in all things, seek direction in all matters, and have faith that he will provide the right outcome for all of our efforts.

Paul told us that in order to achieve victory over those hosts of wickedness we have to don the whole armor of God, the helmet, the shield, the breastplate and the sword to do spiritual battle against the demons. But that isn't all. We not only have to be well armed to contend against Satan's forces, but we must also be well advised. That's why Paul added that we must pray at all times and make supplication, not only for ourselves, but for all the saints. In addition to going against the enemy with all the weapons of spiritual warfare, we are to humbly entreat the Lord to go into battle with us, to lead us, and to give us the victory.

No conflict with Satan is insignificant. The temptation may be to take only a small bite of a lovely forbidden fruit, but the consequences can be catastrophic.

Up! Sanctify Yourselves

Scripture: Joshua 7:13
Suggested Reading: Matthew 5:6; John 13:3–10

For some reason, sanctification is not a popular topic among Christians. And when we do speak of it, we seem more anxious to confess that we have a long way to go rather than to testify about how far we've come. We turn very humble and seldom witness to the gains the Lord has given us in our striving for holiness.

Cleansing has almost vanished as a ritual of the church. My Methodist congregation has a foot-washing service but once a year, on Maundy Thursday. At one time it was a common ceremony.

The ancients had elaborate purification rites. I recently had the privilege of visiting Qumran in Israel where the Essenes of Jesus' time had a commune that contained a ritual bath. The spirit was powerful there. I felt a strong urge to descend the steps into the pool and climb out at the other end, but I couldn't because the Israeli Parks Authority had set fences around the ruins. Besides, the pool had long since dried up.

But when those pious brothers entered the bath, they were confessing their defilement, and when they emerged at the other end, they were confessing their purity. Their baths were mainly symbolic, but the symbolism begins with contamination and ends with absolution.

When Jesus washed his apostles' feet, it wasn't just because their feet were dirty from walking down the dusty Jerusalem streets nor simply to demonstrate servant hood, as is the theme of foot washing as practiced in some churches today. He did it as a ritual of cleansing from sin. And when Peter finally understood Jesus' purpose and asked for a full body bath, Jesus pointed out to him that he had already been cleansed from head to ankle and that only his feet were soiled from treading in the dirt of a sinful world.

Before Jesus died on the cross, people desiring to be pure needed a ritual head-to-toe cleansing. Not just once, but regularly. But having once been plunged into the fountain of Christ's blood, we sinners have permanently lost our guilty stains and stand unsullied in a grimy world, needing only to wash our feet at the door to keep from tracking its dirt into our homes.

Once, long ago, when my feet were very badly soiled, I behaved in a manner a Christian ought not to behave. A saintly lady called me to account, saying, "I thought you were a Christian. If you are a Christian, how can you act like that?" I responded, "You are right. My behavior was dreadful, but do you have any idea how badly I would have acted were I not a Christian?" I've come a long way down the road of sanctification since that day, and my greatest insight from that moment is that regularly cleansing myself has resulted in greater victories over my propensity to sin.

We should celebrate our holiness. The fact that we are still not perfect should not be the main theme of our testimony on sanctification. Our main theme should be how far we've come, not to glorify our evil past but to glorify the power of the Holy Spirit that gives us the grace to walk uprightly and be victorious over sin.

Yes, we should look at our feet and take the scrub brush to our soles at the back door of our house, but when we stand on the front porch we should stand as monuments of purity, not boasting in our self-righteousness, but humbly, with thanksgiving, testifying to the world that the blood of Jesus has made us clean.

Down in the Valley

Scripture: Joshua 7:14–26
Suggested Reading: Psalms 94:12–13; Proverbs 3:12; 13:24

This is the saddest chapter in the book of Joshua, but it could be the most instructive and the happiest. Sometimes we gain the most by losing and succeed the most by failing. The sad story of Achan is such an anomaly, but for any Christian a full moon illuminating one of life's darkest valleys.

Though the family of Israel had crossed the Jordan into the Promised Land, it still had flaws. It still had, among its members, at least one who was not fully obedient. This in itself is a great message for us. We don't have to be perfect to be crucified with Christ, born again and heir to the kingdom of heaven. We may still have a propensity to sin, but we have to *want* to be obedient and promise to *try* to be obedient. Jesus taught us to hunger and thirst for righteousness, he doesn't demand that we achieve it in a day.

Our entry into the kingdom of heaven is an early step in the process of sanctification, not the final step, if in this life there is such a thing, which I doubt. But we can be certain that once we cross over, the effect of our transgression is magnified. One self-serving act of disobedience brings down the wrath of God. He will root out sin and order the destruction of the offending member. But then he will turn from his anger.

Many of us who were strictly raised wince when we see permissive parents turn blind eyes to their children's misbehavior, either because they don't want to "strangle their creativity," or simply because they lack the will to challenge their erring children. We shake our heads and pray that such parents aren't "sowing the wind." Then we offer a quiet prayer of thanksgiving that our parents had the will and intelligence to train us in the way we should go and were not afraid to discipline us whenever it became necessary, sometimes even perhaps in public.

God is not a permissive parent. He allows us to make our mistakes and commit our sins, but because he loves us he chastises. Had God not loved the wayward Israelites, Achan's sin would have gone unnoticed, and all future military conflicts might simply have gone to the superior army.

But thankfully, God loved Israel, so he saw to it that the men of Ai won the first battle after the fall of Jericho. But he didn't stop there, as many parents do. He didn't simply punish without explanation and follow-through. He saw to it that Achan's sin was exposed and that Achan was removed from the congregation. He gathered his erring children about him and taught them all about obedience. He examined their conduct, purged the cause of their sin, and gave them a second chance.

The church of Jesus Christ is an extension of old Israel. We are grafted shoots to the family tree, adopted heirs of the kingdom of God. And the same rules apply. When we err, God is sure to punish, and sometimes his punishment spills over to the less guilty. Then he takes us aside, gives us a lesson in obedience, and turns us loose to do it again and do it right.

After the loss to the army of Ai, Joshua led Israel into many conflicts but didn't lose another battle.

Had God been a permissive parent, Israel could never have become a great nation, and we could never have inherited the wonderful kingdom of heaven.

Learning from Mistakes

Scripture: Joshua 8:1–29
Suggested Reading: Psalms 27:11–14; Joshua 6:2; 7:2–4;
Isaiah 30:19–23; 2 Corinthians 6:17–7:1; Philippians 1:3–11

And so our record stands at two wins and one loss. The victory over Jericho was totally God's victory. We simply marched around the city blowing our horns and shouting as God ordered us to. Then those walls came tumbling down just as God promised. We didn't raise a sword, sling a stone, or shoot an arrow before the walls collapsed. Then we just went in and, as they say in the army, "mopped up."

We lost our second battle for the two reasons already addressed: Achan sinned by taking as personal booty some of the spoils of war that God ordered destroyed, and Joshua summarily implemented the suggestion of the spies without seeking the face of the Lord. And the battle was lost.

The return bout with the soldiers of Ai started in a completely different manner. The Lord took the initiative to devise the strategy and order the attack. But unlike the victory at Jericho, God won the battle of Ai by involving Israel's men of war in the military action. The *soldiers* lay in ambush. The *soldiers* set fire to the city. The *soldiers* smote the men of Ai with the edge of the sword. And this time the soldiers earned their booty in combat with the enemy.

Both the victory over Jericho and the victory over Ai were predestined. God told Joshua before each battle that he had given the enemy into Israel's hand. Victory was an accomplished fact before

Joshua's soldiers even engaged the enemy. It was prophesied in the past tense, a promise for the future already fulfilled.

We have the same promises. God will live and move among us, devising the strategies and providing the miracles to defeat the forces of Satan in our lives. He began the good work in us and will bring it to completion by giving us victory after victory until love abounds and we are filled with the produce of our spiritual promised land, the fruits of righteousness.

But we must take a lesson from Joshua. As he learned from his mistake in the first attempt to conquer Ai, we too ought to learn from it. We are never to devise the battle plan ourselves or to judge the strength of the enemy as anything less than a roaring lion seeking to devour us. We must never proceed into battle until the Commander of the army of the Lord has designed the strategy and ordered us to arms. If we advance on our own, the results may be disastrous.

How do we consult with the Commander? Not the same way Joshua did. The Lord spoke directly to him, and I suppose our battles might be easier to win if we could talk with him as Moses and Joshua did. But in a different way we can consult with him.

We have God's revelation in his Word and we can have the Holy Spirit in us, directing us. The prophet Isaiah looked forward to our time and saw a vision of our Teacher walking behind us, whispering in our ears, telling us the way to go.

The Bible is packed full of direction for winning the battle against sin and possessing the rich and plenteous land. And as we sit in quiet prayer, waiting on the Lord, he makes his will known to us through the prompting of the Holy Spirit. The secret to success and miraculous victory is in submission, patience, and a willingness to do whatever God asks.

Carved in Stone

Scripture: Joshua 8:30–35
Suggested Reading: Deuteronomy 27; Judges 9:51–54;
Jeremiah 31:33; Ezekiel 11:19; 2 Corinthians 3:2–3

Anyone traveling through the Holy Land cannot help but be stunned by the incredible number of rocks. In the cities, in the hills, and even in the fertile valleys, the land is covered with rocks.

The rocks have a multitude of purposes. At Masada, the Jews rolled rocks down the mountain into the camp of the Romans below. In defense, the Romans built rock fences, which still stand today, to stop the volley from above. People built houses and walls of rocks, hurled them at each other, and, of course, set up monuments.

As we journeyed through the country, we saw many heaps of rocks, small and large, and we wondered if one of the patriarchs had piled them up as a remembrance, if soldiers had stacked them as military emplacements, if some zealot or romantic had gathered them for a memorial, or if some tourist had decided to do something to emulate the father of the nation and just leave something to be remembered by. And we too, made a little heap of stones and took a picture by it to memorialize our treasured moment on holy ground.

I think the Lord intended rocks to be primary features in the lives of his people. The rock is one of his favorite metaphors. He calls himself the Rock of our salvation from which flow rivers of living water. Rocks provide a variety of allusions, from Genesis to Revelation. Someday, God willing, I hope to write a book just about the meaningful rocks found scattered throughout the Bible.

God uses rocks in scripture to symbolize both good and evil. The wise man built his house upon the rock, Peter represents the rock of truth, altars are made of rock, Jesus is the cornerstone, and God engraved his law on tablets of stone. On the other hand, people stoned each other with rocks, hung them around their necks and cast them into the sea, and flung them from towers to kill evil tyrants. And after Joshua took the king of Ai down from the tree on which he was hanged, he threw his body down at the gate of his ruined city and raised over it a great heap of rocks.

Joshua built his altar of uncut stones, as the Lord commanded, offered burnt offerings upon it, wrote the words of the law upon those altar stones, then read from the book of Moses all the words of the law, the blessings of obedience, and the curses of disobedience while the tribes stood divided, six on the mountain of the blessings, six on the mountain of the curses. It is a picture that we must carve into our minds as we begin our conquest of the Promised Land.

Our hearts must become altars upon which we sacrifice our entire beings as offerings to our God. We must decide to take our stand on the sacrificial side of the mountain of obedience rather than the self-serving side of the mountain of disobedience. As Joshua wrote the commandments on the rocks of the altar, so we must write them on the altar of our heart and pledge to live our lives in submission to the Lord's will.

But there is one difference between us and the Israelites. They pledged obedience in an effort to earn salvation and the good will of God. They failed because they had hearts of stone. So Jesus came and earned salvation for all of us by living a life of perfect obedience and dying in our place. So why do we pledge to live holy lives since our salvation has already been earned? For two reasons: gratitude for what he has done for us, and because we can't help it since the Holy Spirit lives in us and has carved the Law of God on our hearts.

In Sheep's Clothing

Scripture: Joshua 9:1–15
Suggested Reading: 1 Peter 5:8

You probably know Andy. He went to my church. Once in a while. His wife and children came regularly, and perhaps once a month or so, or if the kids were in a program, Andy would appear at the service and act as though he attended every Sunday, glad-handing the pastor and nodding at everybody. Every church has an Andy.

But then a miracle happened. Andy went on a weekend retreat and God smacked him over the head with a timber. Andy was born again and filled with the Holy Spirit. He became very active in the church, serving on committees, singing in the choir, teaching Sunday school, and witnessing at every opportunity. Every church has that kind of Andy too. There aren't enough of them.

A lot of things changed in Andy's life after he "crossed the Jordan" and became a new creature in Christ. Like Joshua, with God's help, he conquered enemy strongholds. He quit drinking almost entirely, quit smoking, quit his Friday night poker club and took a new and vibrant interest in his family, paying more attention to Helen, his wife, and getting involved in his children's activities. He even became Kevin's soccer coach and helped Jennifer with her 4H projects. There aren't enough fathers like Andy.

He had a good job as a research chemist for a pharmaceutical company. Perhaps two or three times a year he and a few colleagues had to spend a few days in a distant city on business. They would fly in the company jet, and if it were summer or if they were going south, they would take their golf clubs along. They would stay at fine hotels and enjoy good food and luxury accommodations, all at company expense. For him it seemed like a bonus from his employer for all his hard work and overtime.

There was one small problem. After hours the guys usually went out to one of the local bars for an evening of entertainment. And I don't mean bingo. Away from the constraints of home, they indulged in pleasures they didn't talk about with their wives.

It was, to them, only harmless fun, a little strip tease, table dances and the like. And the next day it was all in the past, forgotten, as though it never happened. Harmless and almost innocent. No one would ever know.

But one night while they were at one of those clubs, Andy got caught up with a lady he should have left alone. She told him a pitiful story, and out of the goodness of his heart he gave her companionship and money. And to make a sordid story brief, she gave him AIDS.

Satan toyed with the conquering Andy just as he toyed with Joshua at Gibeon. He came to him clothed in innocence, told him a sad story of depravation and assured him that a little departure from accepted practice, a little liaison in a distant town, would be harmless and would never come back to hurt him.

Now Andy's life is in ruins. He is disgraced, alone, and dying . . . somewhere.

The devil is not always a roaring lion. Sometimes, as the cliché goes, he appears in sheep's clothing, looking sad and playing on our Christian sympathies.

And all we can say in closing is, brother and sister beware! We are all fair game.

Fake 'Em Out?

*W*ay back in elementary school we discovered that we could read a comic book in class if we hid it inside a notebook so the teacher would think we were studying our lesson. Later we learned that we could wrap a forbidden book in the dust jacket of a proper book and no one would be the wiser. On the playground we discovered that we could fake right, go left and score quite easily. From early childhood it was obvious to us that deception was common in daily life.

If the good guy tricked the bad guy, we applauded. If the bad guy tricked the good guy we not only condemned the bad, but, in recognition of the fact that deception is the norm, we criticized the good guy for letting himself be faked out. The world, on one hand, says that the seller must represent his product honestly, but on the other hand says, "Buyer beware," as if to say, "If you are deceived, it is your own fault. Maybe this will teach you a lesson."

Early on in Sunday school we learned that the crafty old serpent deceived Adam and Eve. We hissed back at the serpent, but we criticized the parents of us all for falling for his scam. A few chapters later, Abraham tricked Pharaoh about his wife, Sarah, and later taught that very trick to his son Isaac who used it successfully on Abimelech. Then Jacob deceived both his brother Esau and his father Isaac in stealing the birthright. He fled to his Uncle Laban who quickly deceived him by giving him the wrong daughter as his wife. We hissed. Then he got even by deceiving Laban in the breeding of the flocks. We applauded. Years later Jacob's sons deceived him by dipping that famous coat of many colors in sheep's blood and lying about Joseph's fate. And after that, Joseph, in concealing his true identity, used his appearance as an Egyptian to deceive his brothers.

After four hundred years of silence, deceit again emerged as the strategy of the day. Moses tried to deceive Pharaoh about taking the Israelites out into the wilderness for feast. Rahab deceived her king. Joshua lured the fighting men of Ai into his trap by pretending to retreat. We applauded that clever deception. Then Joshua himself was deceived by the Gibeonites. We hissed at them, but upbraided Joshua for falling for such a ruse.

Life and the Bible are rife with stories of deception. Both good people and bad trick their enemies with false impressions. How do we judge such behavior? If the evil person deceives the good person, we are inclined to throw the tablets at him and convict him for bearing false witness. But when the shoe is on the other foot, we often justify the deceit by saying that the victim had it coming or give the credit for the deceptive strategy to God as in Jacob's case with the cattle or Joshua's with the battle of Ai.

Does God condemn deceit in any form? Does all deceit violate the Law of God? Does the end justify the means? Is it okay to trick sinners in defense of a righteous cause? Here again we fall into an ethical and theological abyss, unable with our small minds to comprehend the thoughts of the Almighty. And we rely on a moral fad: situation ethics.

So, where is the safe ground? Obviously we are not to lie when we are sworn to tell the truth. Obviously we are not to act treacherously for personal gain. And obviously we are not to make deceit so habitual that it becomes our second nature, and we, like Jacob, earn the label of deceiver. To be known as an honest person is a high compliment.

But perhaps the best application is to understand that since deception seems to be fundamental to human nature, we should not only strive to avoid the practice of it, but we should also be vigilant so as not to fall victim to the treacherous practices of others.

Victim's Rights?

Scripture: Review Joshua 9:1–15

An Acquaintance, Jim, recently confessed to me how he had been deceived by a slick used car salesman. One day while driving down "Automobile Alley," he glimpsed a shiny, black, five-year-old Mercedes on the front row of Honest Eddie's lot. He stopped for a closer look. The body was perfect and the upholstery spotless. The odometer registered only thirty thousand miles. He opened the hood and stood amazed at the clean engine that ran like new.

Honest Eddie bragged that he had just bought the car from a rich widow for a paltry sum and was willing to pass on the good fortune to a buyer who would really cherish such a fine automobile. Her husband, Eddie said, bought it new and drove it gently for less than two years before he died. The widow wouldn't drive it because it was too big, but she just kept it in the garage for the last three years as a remembrance of her husband.

Jim fell in love with the car at first sight and went into Honest Eddie's office, wrote a check for the down payment and signed a sales agreement. Within an hour he was at his credit union doing the paperwork to finance his beautiful new acquisition.

Then the surprise. One of the loan officers at the credit union, a friend from his church, saw him filling out the papers and stopped to say hello. When Jim explained happily what he had done, his friend shocked him by saying that he lived next door to the previous owner of the shiny Mercedes on Eddie's lot.

The car, he said, had been driven furiously for five years and had run up over two hundred thousand miles. It had been smashed twice. Before selling it, the owner had turned back the odometer, had it bumped out and painted at a cheap makeover shop that specialized in eye washing cars, steam cleaned the interior and the engine, and sold it to Eddie for quite a reasonable price, considering the car's new good looks. "Honest" Eddie made up the story of the car's history.

Jim was not only crestfallen but he was embarrassed. He consulted an attorney who told him that if he could prove that the salesman had seriously and intentionally misrepresented the vehicle, Jim would undoubtedly be released from the sales agreement he had signed. The attorney suggested that if Jim not only threatened to sue but also to expose him and report him to the Better Business Bureau, Eddie might back down. So Jim put on his angry face, did as the attorney suggested, and Eddie reluctantly relented.

Now Jim might not have been legally bound to honor his agreement since Eddie misrepresented the car, but was he morally bound, even though he had been duped? Was Joshua morally bound by his sworn agreement to spare the Gibeonites?

We might be quick to say no, but what does God say? He answered our question in 2 Samuel 21:1–2. King Saul, in his zeal for Israel, refused to be bound by the agreement that Joshua was tricked into making and set out to kill the Gibeonites. But because Saul didn't honor Joshua's contract with them, God punished Israel with a famine. God held his people to their word even though it was obtained by deceit.

Had Jim sought the Lord's direction before agreeing to buy that car, he may have saved himself a lot of grief.

In all thy ways acknowledge him and he will direct thy paths. Good advice for Joshua, for Jim, and for us.

Turning Evil into Good

Scripture: Joshua 9:16–27

The Lord has always had a way of turning evil into good. Some old Calvinists described the disobedience of Adam and Eve as the "fortunate fall" because its ultimate result was the saving work of Jesus Christ and eternity in heaven for those predestined to go there.

Joseph's sale into slavery eventually resulted in the salvation of Jacob and his sons from famine and the growth of the nation of Israel. Israel's defeat at Ai was the catalyst by which God purged his chosen people of an evil influence; it also formed the basis for the strategy that eventually defeated that pagan city. In the New Testament, the persecution of the early church was the very force that caused its phenomenal growth. Most everything in the Bible, it seems, has both a dark and a bright side.

And God has extended that principle far beyond the boundaries of scripture. For generations Christian missionaries labored in China, making converts by the handful. With the Cultural Revolution, missionaries were sent home and the communists slammed the door in the Lord's face. When a somewhat less restrictive Chinese government reopened that door a few decades later, Christians emerged from underground by the thousands. Again the church of Jesus Christ had flourished in the face of persecution, and again the Lord had turned evil into good.

When Constantine imposed Christianity as the official religion of the Roman Empire, he decreed the destruction of the idols displayed in the niches of the pagan temples and ordered that they be replaced by images of the holy family and of Jesus' disciples, converting those temples into houses of worship for the Lord. And when those "converted" pagans needed a new celebration to replace the annual spring festivities for the gods of fertility, the Christian church gave them Easter to commemorate the resurrection of Jesus from the grave. The bunnies and the eggs have survived as reminders of the pagan origins of our happiest Christian holiday. Evil put to good use.

And when the "converted" pagan Norse tribes needed a new holiday to celebrate the return of the sun god from his trip so far south that he all but vanished for a few days, the Christian church gave them Christmas to commemorate the birth of the baby Jesus. Again, evil put to good use.

Joshua blundered by letting the Gibeonites trick him into thinking that they had come from a far country. Had he probed into their story, he could have uncovered their lie and saved himself and his nation a lot of embarrassment. Had he gone to the Lord in prayer and sought direction for dealing with them, he certainly would have avoided a humiliating predicament. But their ruse was so convincing that the great servant of God fell victim to their treachery and swore a sacred oath to let them live. Then he had to suffer the consequences of his error and decide what to do with them. But that dark story has a sunny side. The Israelites gained a manpower asset by condemning them to a life of forced labor, in the house of the Lord.

From scripture and history we learn a great principle: evil can be turned to good. When I was a child, Brother Pierce, the pastor of our local rescue mission, came annually to our church seeking financial support. And he always had in tow a ragged tippler whom he had, with the help of the Lord and our money, rescued from the gutter. He turned evil into good by using a life of intemperance as evidence of the saving power of God. We are not to boast of our sins, but as forgiven sinners we can use the error of our past to boast of the goodness of God, turning our evil into good.

In All Things . . .

Scripture: Joshua 10:1–11
Suggested Reading: Deuteronomy 20:10–18; Proverbs 3:6

So we won one battle simply by marching around the town, blowing our horns and shouting. Then we lost one because of Achan's disobedience and because the Commander of the army of the Lord took a calculated furlough. When we attacked a second time we won because we had repented and so the Lord was with us once again. Then, before we even girded our loins to march against the Gibeonites, they duped us into a peace treaty by claiming to have come from a far country, and hence they became our slaves. They must have somehow learned about Moses' directions to the Israelites regarding sieges and such.

And now, instead of being the attacker on the offensive, we have found ourselves in a defensive mode because the kings of five Amorite cities have banded together to punish Gibeon for desertion. So we marched all night and at dawn hit them with a surprise attack, scattering our panicky foes all across the countryside. God was with us again and handed us the victory by bombarding those fleeing men of valor with deadly hailstones.

How many ways does God have of defeating his enemies? So far he's drowned them twice, battered them twice with hailstones, zapped them with lightning, aggravated them with drought, frogs, and bugs, swallowed them up in an earthquake, and plagued them with diseases. And if his generous use of the forces of nature isn't enough to convince us that God has an inexhaustible supply of weapons and strategies at his disposal for routing our enemies, he reminds us that he is also the great master of psychology who has uncanny ways of making men's hearts melt with fear. He is our commander, our strategist, our tactician, and keeper of our armory.

So why do we sometimes get on our high horse and try to evict the demons from our lives without God's help? We take satisfaction in pointing out that Abraham, Moses, Joshua and other great heroes of faith in moments of weakness took matters into their own hands, so why aren't we entitled to such moments as well? We sometimes forget that until the writings of Moses were published, the giants of scripture didn't have each other as examples of what to do and what not to do. Since we have them as examples to emulate or to learn from, and since we also have the presence of the Holy Spirit in our hearts to show us the way, their excuses hold more water than ours.

Joshua's first battle against Ai and his experience with the Gibeonites should be a lesson to us that we are never to leave God out of life's struggles and never try to fight our battles against Satan without his leading. If we try to go it alone, he may see to it that we lose the battle just to teach us a lesson.

But are we to include him only in our struggles against sin and temptation? Are we to pray only when we face trauma, dilemma, death, and disease? Or does he want to be a part of all of life's decisions?

I'm going to try something. In addition to committing the day to him when I get up in the morning, I'm going to involve him in other ways. I'm going to ask his blessing on my meal before I select from the menu or put my order in at the restaurant. Maybe then I'll make better decisions about what to eat.

He has all the weapons. He has all the answers. Maybe I should have more questions.

Awesome

Scripture: Joshua 10:12–15
Suggested Reading: Genesis 1:14–19; Habakkuk 3

One day a big flatbed truck stopped across the road from my house and a thin young man stepped casually from the cab and climbed into the seat of the biggest piece of earthmoving equipment I had ever seen, started the engine with a deafening roar, and backed it down a set of steel ramps.

Belching black smoke from its vertical exhaust, the huge contraption rumbled to the hill where surveyors had planted stakes a few days before, and in moments its mammoth scoop had moved half the mound and smoothed the ground for my new neighbor's walkout basement.

As I stood there amazed, I remembered the hot summer a generation ago when I watched my sweat-soaked father and a few helpful friends spend several days digging our basement by hand, slinging the dirt, shovel full by painful shovel full, out of the hole while I played with my toy bulldozer on the top of the pile. The overpowering thought was not the evolution of construction equipment during my lifetime, but the awesome power that we have harnessed in our quest for a more comfortable life, and how matter-of-factly we use that power.

In less than an hour the operator had loaded that colossal machine back on the flatbed, climbed into the cab of his truck, and clattered away to his next job. At this rate, I figured, he might move as many as six or eight mountains a day.

As I walked back up my driveway I kept repeating that overused word, *awesome*. And soon I had made the transition and was humming that song we often sing at church, *Our God is an Awesome God.* . . . Then it struck me. I was using the same word to describe the power of God that I used to describe the power of man. Then, as I contemplated the majesty of God's creation, the lofty mountains, the roaring rivers and the violent storms, that piece of earthmoving equipment shrank to the size of my toy bulldozer.

Sometimes we treat the power of God very casually. Even as a child, when I sat in the front row of my Sunday school class and watched Mrs. Hooker put up her hand and block that big yellow sun in its track while her assistant, Miss DeVries, maneuvered the sword-wielding Joshua against the enemy below, I failed to comprehend the mighty hand of the Lord, not so much in the battle, but in the stopping of the sun. It seemed no more extraordinary than a car coming to a halt at a stop sign. And even today when I read about that moment in the Bible, the true wonder of it escapes me.

I'm no scientist, so I can't talk numbers. But I know that the sun is many times the size of the earth and the explosions that occur in one moment on the face of the sun reduce the total sum of civilized man's atomic blasts to an almost imperceptible pop. So stopping the sun in its course probably required much more energy than we would generate if we could harness the power of all of our bombs and all of God's hurricanes combined.

But even more amazing to me was the fact that God saw fit to stop the moon in its path over the Valley of Ajalon. And while he held back the great light that rules the day so his chosen people could finish their battle on the field at Gibeon, he also stayed the light that rules the night so some poor wandering shepherd might find one of his sheep lost out there on the rocky hillside.

Our God *is* an awesome God!

Moon Over Ajalon

Scripture: Joshua 10:12–15

Our almighty God created the heavens and the earth. When we take our trips to the spectacular places of the world and see the oceans in winter, the mighty rivers in the spring, the devastation of tornadoes, the deep canyons, the majestic mountains, and the spewing volcanoes, we see but a tiny fragment of the power of God.

Astronomers with giant telescopes stare light years into the distance and see black holes with gravity so strong even light cannot escape. They see swirls of energy so potent that the terms they need to define them have no use in normal human vocabulary. Our God unleashed all of those forces, and probably other forces so powerful we can't begin to imagine them. And yet this mighty God numbers the hairs of my head, knows my innermost thoughts, loves me, and wants to make my heart his dwelling place.

Scientists have scorned the idea that the sun stood still. Even Christians of the modern era struggle with the idea. We know that the sun doesn't actually travel across our sky, but as the earth turns, it only appears that the sun moves. And if the earth were to stop spinning and give the illusion that the sun stood still, we'd all certainly go flying off into outer space. Wouldn't we?

Now consider the sun. We know what time it will rise each morning and set each night. We set our clocks by it and measure the seasons by it. From one year to the next it never changes. Every Christmas morning it will rise at just about the same time it rose the previous Christmas morning, and will for every Christmas morning in the future. We declare that the sunrise is the one certain thing in life, so certain we are of its regularity.

So, I just have to accept by faith that somehow God intervened in his established pattern of nature during that battle over three thousand years ago and made his sun to shine longer on that one day than it did on any other so that Joshua could have more hours of daylight to fight his war against the Amorites at Gibeon.

Now Ajalon is just a short drive from Gibeon, so naturally, when it is high noon at Gibeon the sun is also directly overhead at Ajalon. So why did God inspire Joshua to point out that when the *sun* stood still at Gibeon, the *moon* stood still over the Valley of Ajalon? By some miracle did God make it daytime in one place and nighttime just a few miles down the road? And why did he even bother mentioning the moon since the sun's standing still is the only significant part of the story? Or is it? If God saw fit to tell us that the moon stood still, he must have done so for a reason.

It's clear that God stayed the sun in its course to aid the nation of Israel in its invasion of the Promised Land. The longest day is the headline story here. But let's turn to the second page. The moon's standing still also had a purpose. If it hadn't, God wouldn't have made a point of it. Could he be revealing to us that he will extend the glow of his nightlight in the valleys of our lives as we fight to possess our spiritual promised land, the kingdom of heaven?

While major events are taking place under the bright lights on the center stage of the world, millions of smaller dramas are being enacted on the little stages where you and I play our roles, where the lesser lights shine. And as the creator of the universe is managing the destiny of the nations, he is also keeping his heavenly eye on each one of us who love him, especially as we struggle to find our way through the dark valleys of our lives.

Sealing Stones

Scripture: Joshua 10:16–27
Suggested Reading: Matthew 27:57–66; Revelation 20

Jesus, our Savior, the very epitome of all that is good, died; and when Joseph of Arimathea had securely lodged his body in a cave, he rolled a great stone over its mouth and Pilate secured it by sealing the stone and setting a guard so no one could steal the body.

The five Canaanite kings, Israel's enemies, the symbol of all that is evil, fled and hid in a cave; and when Joshua captured them, he rolled great stones over the mouth of the cave to secure it and set a guard so they could not escape.

A forced and fanciful comparison? I think not, less because of the similarity of the events, more because of the difference.

If we view Canaan as a type of our promised land, the kingdom of heaven, that we can inhabit in this life, the evil kings represent our propensity to sin. They are the enemies we have to conquer in order to possess fully that pure and wonderful land. Our sinful inclinations, insecurities, bad habits, addictions, and general lusts of the flesh are complex and deeply ingrained into our human nature. They are not easily overcome. With God directing the battle, we can defeat those adversaries and capture their territory little by little, assuring ourselves of an endless series of small victories. And when God's army of angels has successfully vanquished Satan's army of demons, we open the cave in which he has hidden the crown symbol of that evil, extricate it, slay it, and bury its corpse forever under a pile of monumental rocks, never to face that foe again.

In order to possess the kingdom, we must destroy the forces of evil that corrupt our bodies. We must barricade their remains in a cave of forgetfulness. We do that by nailing our old self to Jesus' tree and burying it in his grave. Then our purified being escapes from that cave of sin that entombs us, raised with Christ, a new creation.

On our trip to Israel we visited the garden tomb. It may or may not be the actual tomb of Jesus, but as a representative sample it reaches out and touches the visitor in a most compelling way. One can sit there on a bench and meditate for hours. It is a lovely and peaceful place.

We stepped inside the tomb and saw the place where he might have lain. While gazing at that spot, we contemplated the moment of our crucifixion with Christ, the moment we died to self and were laid in the grave with him. Then we stepped back through the opening and away from the tomb, smitten to the depths of our heart with a new sense of our own resurrection.

We sat on the stone bench a few feet from the tomb, bathed in a spiritual glow one can only feel after being raised with him incorruptible, reborn to begin life anew in the kingdom of heaven. It was a moment beyond the telling.

The thought of dying to self in this life can be so scary that many of our church friends never do it. They are content to dwell, like Reuben and Gad, east of the river, never willing to take the plunge and commit their lives to the kingdom. They never come to grips with the reality of dying an eternal death and being trapped forever in a hellish cave, under a monumental pile of rocks with the enemies they didn't even try to conquer. To me, that is a far more terrifying prospect than a dip in the Jordan.

Are we to languish behind the rock in a sealed cave forever? If we but ask, angels will come and roll our stone away.

My Heart's Desire

Scripture: Joshua 10:28–11:20
Suggested Reading: Exodus 4:21; Deuteronomy 2:25; 29:2–4;
Joshua 2:9; Psalms 37:4; Ezekiel 11:17–20; Romans 9:18

Once when I was wishing for something, one of my ecstatic friends pointed out to me the psalmist's promise that if I just delight myself in the Lord, he will grant me the desires of my heart.

I assured her that I do take great delight in the Lord, and asked if David meant to tell me that if I simply delighted myself in the Lord, he would grant me the new car and the new set of golf clubs that my heart desired. She rationalized that my heart's desire had to be something God approved of, not something facetious or self-serving. Well, I have since pondered that brief conversation and have come to a far different understanding of the intent of that promise.

God is the king of hearts. For whatever holy purpose he might have, he controls the heart of man. He is omnipotent. He has the power to determine what our minds think, what our tongues say, what we like or do not like, what we feel and what we desire.

Ample proof that he not only has that power but that he uses it lies in the fact that he hardened Pharaoh's heart, that he melted the hardened hearts of the Canaanite kings, and that he closed the minds of the Israelites so they couldn't understand the significance of all the wonders he wrought in their presence. Paul confirmed that as the supreme authority over his creation, God can harden the heart of whomever he will, and that we have nothing to say about it. We'd just better accept the fact that he is the Potter and we are the clay.

God promised that if I delight myself in him, he would give me the desires of my heart. But he certainly didn't mean that if I did what pleased the Lord, and if in my heart I were to desire a new motorcycle and a new computer, he would deliver those things to my doorstep as though he were the driver for a catalog company.

What I think he meant is that if I delight in him, he will determine what the desires of my heart will be. And if I truly delight in him, he will see to it that my heart's desire will not be for temporal things of personal convenience or pleasure that I do not have, but that I will long for more heavenly, spiritual things.

Now I consider that a wonderful promise. While I live in the flesh, my heart craves things of the flesh, unnecessary luxuries, and personal fulfillments. And as long as my heart yearns for things of the flesh, I am shackled to the flesh. I am in a prison of personal want, sometimes obsessed by a desire for things I do not have, unhappy and jealous of those who have what I do not have. But if I put my delight in the Lord he will free me from that prison, take away those longings, and fill my empty heart with pure and righteous desires.

He promised Israel that someday he would gather them from the four corners of the earth and restore them to their land. But better yet, he told them that he would remove from their breasts their stony hearts and replace them with hearts of flesh so their eyes would see and their minds understand that he alone is God, that they are his people, that their Messiah has come, and that he is their King who reigns over all the earth.

And I take that as a promise to me, a citizen of the kingdom of heaven living on the produce of the spiritual promised land, a guest at his great banquet, that he will remove my heart of stone and give me a heart that delights in him and desires only what he wants me to desire. All I love and all I think will be a gift to this vessel of clay from the Potter who made me.

Only in Gath

Scripture: Joshua 11:21–22
Suggested Reading: Genesis 6:4; Exodus 23:27–30; 1 Samuel 17:4;
2 Samuel 21:15–22

Joshua was on a roll. God had commissioned him to scorch the entire land and to destroy everything that breathed. And he did. Almost. Among the remnants of the Canaanites who survived Joshua's wars were a few giants, perhaps descendants of some mysterious race of ancient Palestinian aborigines who found refuge among the Philistines in the city of Gath.

We don't know exactly who they were or where they came from. Some scholars think they have the answer, but in the end they are mostly guessing. Some think they are descended from fallen angels, others from Cain. The Bible refers variously to the Nephilim, the Anakim, and the Rephaim, and Genesis describes them as mighty men of old, men of renown.

Why did they survive the conquest? Was it because Joshua was not diligent in fulfilling his calling? Was it because some members of his army were slack in discharging their duty? Or was it because God allowed them to survive for some purpose he had in mind a little later in the story? Though God may have used the sloth of the Israelites for his greater ends, I think he permitted the giants to survive because he had some potential use for their descendants. And when we look about two hundred years into the future, that use becomes clear: God demonstrated his love and protection for his people by empowering them to slay the giants who wanted to prevent them from fully possessing their Promised Land.

The story of David and Goliath is the perfect case in point. The giant's ancestors survived Joshua's carnage and allied with the Philistines. When the time came for God to design an event that would show his people that they could do all things through the Lord who strengthens them, he sent a child on a mission with a slingshot, and the heavily armed giant fell dead at the young shepherd's feet. When David became king he went to battle against more of the surviving giants, and later when he grew weary of war, God gave David's friends the strength to slay them.

We have giants who want to keep us from claiming our inheritance in the kingdom of heaven. Sometimes we question God for having allowed them to survive our release from the bondage of sin, the victory of the cross, our baptism by water and the spirit, and our fervent prayers, but we must understand that God has permitted them to survive for some divine purpose.

Now the lessons I've learned so far from studying his Word lead me to expect that in his good time he will give me victory over those monstrous forces of evil. He will choose the time and he will choose the place to shine the light of his grace into my valleys. I may, like David, become a great example of how God can use one little human being to sling one little stone that will fell a mighty demon, or he may let me, Also like David, step aside and watch one of my friends hurl the stone into the vulnerable chink in the giant's armor.

But until he gives me the final victory, I must remain patient and courageous, with a wary eye in the direction of my Gath. I must remember that in my own strength I'm no match for those monsters, and that I must wait on him to call me to arms and empower me to gain the victory, or to call my friends to carry the battle for me.

But this I know: the Lord has promised me the kingdom of heaven and he has promised that he will drive my enemies out one by one, little by little, until I am increased and possess the land.

The Whole Land

Scripture: Joshua 11:23a

I have a friend, Les, who confided to me years ago that when he was about fourteen or fifteen, his neighbor and playmate, Mike, took him into his garage one day and showed him a tool box in which his father kept an eight millimeter movie projector and a collection of the kind of old one reelers you didn't tell your mother about.

Mike knew where the key was hidden, and one day while his parents were away, Les, Mike and a few other neighborhood boys sat on the dirt floor and watched those sexually explicit old silent black and white films as they flickered on the wall of that old garage.

Les is a perfect example of how interests developed during one's formative period survive through the years. Try as he might, he just couldn't banish those images from his mind. As he grew, his fixation on pornography grew, and even after he was married and had a family he would slip off when the opportunity arose and would patronize an adult theater. Sometimes he had to go on overnight business trips, and when business was finished, for his evening's entertainment he went to the adult movie house.

Then one weekend during a revival in his church, Les went forward and made a commitment to the Lord, plunged into the Jordan and emerged a new creature in Christ. Everything went along beautifully until about two months later when he had to go out of town on business. The first night after dinner at his hotel, Satan went to work on him like never before, and Les was compelled to drive the few blocks to the adult entertainment section of town that he had frequented earlier. But when he got there, he had a shocking experience. The place had been torn down. Only rubble remained.

Les was absolutely convinced that the Lord had a hand in the destruction, and when he returned to his hotel he opened his Bible, which "just happened" to open to the sixth chapter of Joshua and the story of the destruction of Jericho. Then he knew that the Lord's army had been there, reducing the walls of that theater to dust and preventing him from losing his first big battle with Satan since crossing his Jordan. Sometimes we refer to a disastrous event in our lives as our Waterloo, but Les refers to that event his Jericho.

As I review Joshua's conquest, I cannot help but notice the declining level of Jehovah's overt involvement in Israel's military conflicts. At Jericho the battle was entirely the Lord's. The people did nothing but march and shout. God appears almost to have destroyed the city all by himself. Then at Ai, God instructed Joshua in the strategy and infused courage into the hearts of the soldiers, who went on to slaughter the enemy, burn the city, and hang its king. At Gibeon, after Israel's dauntless army attacked the fainthearted and panicky coalition of pagan soldiers, God bombarded those who fled with hailstones, and stayed the sun in the sky until the last fleeing coward was caught. In subsequent conflicts the hand of God is less obvious, apparently limited to giving fortitude to Israel and striking the hearts of its enemies with timidity.

In our battles against the evil forces in our lives, the Lord first defeats Satan with miracles. Then as we grow in faith we grow in courage, and as God deprives the devil of his valor, he empowers us to greater tenacity, until, like Joshua, we've taken the whole land.

I'm blessed to report that my friend Les spends a lot of time on his computer, but has never logged on to a pornographic website. Since the miracle at his Jericho, Les has grown in grace, and God has removed the evil desire from his heart.

Rest from War

Scripture: Joshua 11:23b

When we were little children we prayed that old standard bedtime prayer, "Now I lay me down to sleep . . . ." But the prayer didn't end with the "Amen." We added a postscript.

It was wartime, so we lengthened our prayer by adding, "and God bless Uncle Abe, Uncle Johnny, Ed Medendorp, Charlie Frye, Joe Klein, Hank Greenberg . . ." and on and on until we had blessed every relative, friend, neighbor, church brother, and baseball hero who was serving in the military. When others were drafted, we added their names to our list, and when someone was killed we prayed for comfort for his family.

Every evening we gathered around the radio and listened to Gabriel Heatter read the news. He always began the program by saying, in his deep, sonorous voice, "There's good news tonight," or "There's bad news tonight." If the news from the front was good we rejoiced and praised God for the victory, but if it was bad, we bowed our heads and asked God to give General Eisenhower wisdom and our boys courage to turn the tide of battle.

The war dominated our lives. At the door of the church hung a large bronze plaque engraved with the names of our servicemen, and when one was killed, they put a star next to his name. Every family with a man in the war had a little banner in the front window with a blue star for each soldier. When one was killed, the blue star was changed to gold. We had two stars in our window, and when Uncle Johnny was killed, we changed his star to gold.

The most dreaded person in town was the Western Union boy who carried telegrams to families announcing that their sons were wounded, missing, or killed in action. When he approached on his bicycle, we begged God that he would inform us that our soldier was only wounded or that he had been taken prisoner.

The back page of the daily newspaper had maps with lines and arrows showing the fronts, the advances, and the retreats. We followed the battles as well as we could, trying to pinpoint the place where our uncle or neighbor was serving, but their letters home were so cut up by the censors that we rarely knew where they were.

Some of our boys were in the Pacific, and whenever they fought for an island, we knew that we had suffered great losses, and we would gather and pray with the families who had sons at sea.

At the stores, ration books were more valuable than money, and we needed special stamps to buy everything from sugar to gasoline. Cars stood on concrete blocks for lack of tires. Before the war we were just beginning to come out of the Depression. Things were just beginning to look better, but when our boys went to battle, we gave up the few meager luxuries we had. On the home front we grew victory gardens. Women traded their skirts for slacks and went to work in defense factories or drove busses. Children collected newspapers, tin cans, worn out tires, and even milkweed pods to help the war effort. Boys wore GI haircuts. The whole nation, even our baseball players and comic strip heroes, had gone to war.

One glorious day the factory whistles blew and the sirens shrieked announcing victory in Europe. We all rushed downtown and spent the evening hugging strangers and dancing in the streets. Joy abounded. Our land had rest from war. Soon the survivors and the prisoners would come home, families would be reunited, rationing would end and we could buy tires and take our cars down from the blocks. Life would be good again. Or would it?

There Remains Yet Much

Scripture: Joshua 12:13–1
Suggested Reading: Exodus 23:29–30; 2 Samuel 3:1–3

All in all, the army of the Lord has defeated thirty-one kings in addition to those who dwelled east of the river. It is an impressive record of victory, and all the glory goes to God. Though the land has essentially been purged of its pagan inhabitants, pockets of enemies remain. If we fail to eradicate them, they will become a snare to us.

When we come under conviction and give our lives to the Lord, he gives us the strength to claim victory over many of our greatest sins, yet he leaves other foes out there yet to be defeated. He does not rout our enemies before us all at once, lest our land become desolate. He knows that we need to celebrate new victories over evil from time to time so we continually have a fresh testimony.

The Christian life is a constant struggle against the forces of Satan. Even if we were to eradicate all the enemies that inhabited the land, new ones would arrive on our shores or make their way into our territory via our trade routes on a regular basis. The land is never fully secure. There are enemies within and without, seeking whom they may bring down.

Probably smugness and self-satisfaction are the greatest impediments to sanctification. At some point in our walk with the Lord we may think we have grown enough, that we are good enough, that there are enough stars in our crown, and that we're content to be where we are in our spiritual growth. That's when we are most vulnerable to the wiles of the devil.

The Israelites may have looked around and said to themselves, "A few Philistines in Gath, Gaza and Ashkelon. A few Geshurites north of Galilee . . . no problem. They can't harm us."

How wrong they were. A few generations later those very pagans not only slew their first king and made constant war with his successor, but even married into Israel's royal family and mothered Absolom, the renegade son who usurped the throne from his father David. Just as those early Israelites relaxed their guard in the face of what seemed to be insignificant adversaries, we too might consider some of our lingering "little sins" to be harmless or petty. But what may be the consequences?

Dan is a fine Christian man who for years enjoyed an occasional trip to Las Vegas to play blackjack and the slot machines. He knew when to quit. He never won or lost much, a few dollars here, a few dollars there, certainly no more than any of us waste on life's little frivolities. He served the church well and has always been a good husband and father.

When his son Danny turned twenty-one, he took him along on one of his trips for a little fun and some father and son bonding. Danny enjoyed the city immensely, but didn't have the self-control his father had. Las Vegas became his obsession. He seldom won, and often lost large sums of money. And now that casinos are a widespread phenomenon in America, Danny gambles as often as he can. He is an addict, and his addiction has cost him his house, his family, and at least one job.

Those little sins we should have driven out when we first gave our lives to the Lord can grow into monsters that rob us of our inheritance. As we are scoring victories over the enemies that would keep us from possessing our land, we should do our best to honor the command to destroy all that breathes, so we don't have to hear God say, "There remains yet much to be possessed." Ominous words.

The Constant Thorn

Scripture: Joshua 13:2–6
Suggested Reading: Genesis 9:27; See Bible maps

Old Philistia, known today as the Gaza Strip, has always been a thorn in Israel's side. The original Philistines are thought to have migrated by both land and sea from Eastern Europe through Crete and Turkey down to the fruitful, well watered coastal strip on the south-eastern shore of the Mediterranean Sea. Having descended from Japheth, they were more closely akin to us westerners than are the Jews, and to the extent that his descendants "inhabited the tents of Shem," old Noah's prophecy was somewhat fulfilled even before Israel became a kingdom.

The Philistines were a daunting military power. Their technology had surpassed that of the Israelites. Their culture had advanced into the iron age, while most of the rest of the Middle East remained in the bronze. Though they forged superior weapons, spears, and chariot wheels of iron, God often gave his people miraculous victories over their more powerful forces. Yet the Philistines remained a constant threat, and the strip they inhabited has most always remained beyond Israel's grasp.

The Philistines were strong for other reasons as well. They were reputed to be big, strong specimens of humanity, and the Bible often refers to them as giants. Though the word *philistine* has slipped into the English dictionary as a common noun meaning someone who is crass or ignorant, and who has materialistic rather than intellectual values, the original Philistines were anything but philistine. Excavations show their artwork to have been sensitive and thoughtful.

The five great Philistine cities allied in a common cause against their enemies. The kings of Gaza, Ashdod, Ashkelon, Ekron, and Gath not only formed a common army but also allied with some Canaanite kings in their wars against Israel. They were a formidable foe.

History transformed the word *Philistia* into Palestine, and though the word has endured, the people it first represented haven't. The great empires overwhelmed them as they did Israel, and the Philistines passed from the pages of history as a definable group of people. A group of Arab descendants of Ishmael adopted their name, mainly because the whole world called the entire area Palestine until the nation of Israel reemerged in the twentieth century. But the inhabitants of that strip of land remain as much a problem to Israel today as their namesakes were to Joshua and to Israel's kings.

So what does all that have to do with us citizens of the kingdom of heaven today? Even though we've crossed the Jordan and with divine help have generally defeated the forces of sin that have tried to prevent us from gaining our inheritance in the kingdom as children of God, the Philistines are still living right next door and launch surprise attacks on us whenever our back is turned. One of their cities is right on our border, and they remain a thorn in our side.

The Bible uses such terms as *sanctified* and *saints* to refer to those who have claimed their inheritance in the kingdom of heaven. But that is not to suggest that those who have entered the land have defeated all of their enemies and are, by any stretch of the imagination, perfect. Far from it! Satan's forces have allied themselves in a powerful effort to undo the great victories God has given, and they watch from their strongholds just across the border for any opportunity to attack.

We must always remain vigilant. Our past sins remain a constant thorn in our flesh.

In the Midst of Israel

Scripture: Joshua 13:7–14

The land had rest from war after many years of conflict. The miraculous crossing of the Jordan and the glorious march around Jericho had become memories of a distant past. The sordid story of Achan and the embarrassing defeat at Ai were remembered only in Joshua's diaries. Moses' successor had grown old and the generation now in its prime knew nothing but war and victory. How would it handle the peace?

Joshua's armies had conquered most of the land, but yet the Israelites did not possess it fully. Not only did the Gaza Strip still belong to the Philistines and the north and east extremities still belong to the Sidonians and the Lebanese, but many Canaanites had survived the wars and now lived in the midst of Israel.

The Israelites whose inheritance lay in the conquered territory went to work dividing up the land, building cities, and planting farms. They begrudged military assistance to their brothers whose inheritance had not yet been fully wrenched from the pagans. They tolerated the presence of those foreigners in their own towns, having turned their attention from military to material gain.

When our war ended in 1945, our lives changed. Soon we had plenty of food on our tables, plenty of gasoline in our tanks, and plenty of money in our pockets. We built modern homes, bought new, sleek cars, and took up golf. Tired of war, we paid little attention to the conflict in Korea, taking notice only when we heard that someone we knew had been killed. We wouldn't even call it a war, but rather a "police action." But by whatever name, it was deadly. Still tired of war, we turned our backs on our soldiers in Viet Nam, preferring rather to protest than to serve. And all the while we inflated our economy, raised our salaries, and watched the stock market grow and become our primary source of personal wealth. We changed our hairstyles, our fashions, and our music, forcing ourselves into a new age of freedom, prosperity, and equality for all.

When we first gave our lives to Christ, we rejoiced that we had died to self and had been reborn. We had a honeymoon with the Lord. Our enemies fell before us and we suffered no wounds. We served happily on church committees and even gave up Sunday afternoon football for the jail ministry. We studied the Word, enjoyed the fellowship of our brothers and sisters in Christ, and served the Lord, each other, and our church with joyous abandon. We had rest from our war with Satan.

Then someone in the church did something that offended someone else. Maybe the music director changed the types of songs we sang at the opening of the service. Maybe the administrative council shortened the Sunday school "hour" by fifteen minutes. Maybe the education director tied up the all-purpose room for six weeks with play scenery, temporarily canceling the volleyball program. Maybe the worship committee changed hymnbooks. Or maybe someone started complaining about the pastor. Soon everyone was talking about the issue and choosing sides. The church divided into three camps: the pro, the con, and the apathetic.

And we all started talking. We lost some old friends and made some new ones. Some people left the church. We whispered in church corners and on telephones. We got angry. Some of those "Canaanites" we should have slain and who are living in our midst began meddling in our spiritual affairs.

And we found ourselves at war again.

The Eastern Front

Scripture: Joshua 13:15–31
Suggested Reading: Genesis 4:8–16; 1 Chronicles 5;
2 Kings 18:9–12 Isaiah 30:21–26

After Cain murdered his brother Abel, God evicted him from his home and he went "out from the presence of the Lord and dwelled in the land of Nod, east of Eden." The prospect of such alienation terrified Cain, and as he wandered into the land of giants, the Anakim and the Nephilim, he feared for his life and needed special protection from God in order to survive.

From the dawn of human history, "the east" has been known as a place of peril, a place of separation from the presence of God, a place where survival requires a divine shield.

Gilead, the land east of Canaan, was the land of Nod for Reuben, Gad, and the half tribe of Manasseh. Because they saw that the land was well watered, a good place for cattle, they preferred to dwell east of the Promised Land rather than cross the Jordan with their brothers. They were unaware of the peril that lay ahead.

As long as they were obedient, they were blessed, and the Lord was present with them. Though they warred constantly with their idolatrous neighbors, God gave them a series of victories, "for they cried to God in the battle and he granted their entreaty because they trusted in him."

But they did not remain faithful. They mixed with the pagans and began to worship their idols, so God removed their hedge of protection and sent the Assyrians against them, from the east. We don't know what gods they cried to in their battle against Tiglath-

Pileser, but we do know that those gods were as deaf as stone, for the Israelites who dwelled on the eastern front were the first to fall and be carried off into exile, erased forever from the pages of history long before the Assyrians invaded mainland Israel.

I have friends who live across the river, east of the kingdom of heaven. Some of them go to my church. They have not crossed the Jordan. They are reluctant to be crucified with Christ and be born anew because the land where they live is well watered and pleasant. They look over the river and see giants, but they fail to see the enemies who lurk beyond their own eastern border. They have a false sense of security. They enjoy pagan pleasures and are unaware that their eternal destiny is in mortal danger.

But can we who live as children of the kingdom within the borders of the spiritual promised land be certain that God will preserve us from the invaders? Pagans dwell in our midst and tempt us to serve other gods. What will happen if we transgress the covenant? Will we become casualties of God's battles against the powers of hell? Will we fall by Satan's sword? Will God evict us from our promised land, our kingdom of heaven, our paradise, and banish us to eternal exile? History's message seems quite clear.

Is there any moon glow in this dark valley? Do we mainlanders have protection from temptation that others don't have? Yes. We have our Teacher, the Holy Spirit, who walks behind us and whispers in our ear, "This is the way, walk in it." He is our hedge of protection, the strength in our lives, the power for obedience, the grace to withstand. Through his might we can scatter the unclean things that defile our lives and say to them, "Be gone!"

Then the light of the moon will be as the light of the sun, and the Lord will bind our wounds and heal our pain.

Better Than Land

Scripture: Joshua 13:32–33
Suggested Reading: Matthew 6:19–21; 25:34; 1 Peter 1:3–4

From time to time our church council wrestles with the parsonage question. The church owns two homes, one for each of the pastors. Because the buildings are old and only meet the denomination's minimum standards of adequacy, we've considered tearing them down, using the space for increased parking, and offering the pastors a housing allowance.

We've talked with pastors who like the idea. With a housing allowance they would have the option to rent or to purchase property of their choice. If they were to purchase property, they could build equity, and they could be in a better financial position to provide for themselves in their retirement years, or even accumulate an estate for their children to inherit.

But other pastors with whom we've talked scorn the idea. One of them identified with the Levites. He said that he had devoted his entire life to the Lord's work and confidently believes that the Lord will bless him and meet his material needs, both now and in the future. He and his family are content to live in a house which is below the standard that most of the parishioners have set for their own dwellings, and he is unconcerned with equity or accumulation of wealth. The management of property would be nothing more to him than an additional burden. His only burden, he says, is his congregation, and his only inheritance is the Lord.

The other tribes possessed the land, but the Levites had no territory of their own except for Levitical cities. Absent such political responsibility, they could devote their entire attention to the service of the sanctuary while their sons would inherit nothing more than their father's duties. While the secular tribes were busy laying up treasure on earth, the Levites could focus on laying up treasure in heaven.

But is the privilege of heavenly bounty reserved only for clergy? Can we who sit in the pews share that spiritual wealth? Jesus answered that question for us.

Moth and rust consume our earthly treasures and thieves deprive us of them. Decay erodes the value of our homes and property, while taxes, inflation, a shaky stock market, and an uncertain social security system cast long shadows on our future. But in spite of that, we still keep our financial advisor's phone number in our automatic dialing system and our investment house's email address on our easy click list, while we have to hunt for the church directory to call the pastor or the church office.

Do we invest more heavily in transient treasures than in the inheritance that is imperishable, undefiled, and unfading? Do we pay more attention to the up again, down again stash that sends us a monthly report on slick paper than on the fortune that has been stored up for us in heaven from the foundation of the world? When we meet with family and friends, do we spend more time discussing the vicissitudes of the stock market than the firmness of the Rock of our salvation? Have we, like the tribes of Israel, worshipped idols of wood and stone rather than the one true God? A quick inventory of our priorities will reveal where our heart truly is.

Would that we took our priesthood more seriously and thought like the pastor who clearly understood that the best investment one can make is in eternal securities. It's better than land!

Bring on the Giants

Scripture: Joshua 14
Suggested Reading: Genesis 13:10; Numbers 13:6, 28–33; 14:24;
Joshua 15:14

At the onset of the conquest, the Lord reminded Joshua and the people over and over again that as they advanced against the enemy, they were to be "strong and of good courage." And with good cause, because Canaan was a land that "devours its inhabitants." There were giants in that land.

Giants are a thing to fear because they are bigger and stronger than we are, and therefore we should assume that they can defeat us in a physical confrontation. Unless, of course, the Lord is on our side. The Lord is bigger and stronger than giants. But it takes a special spirit to comprehend that.

When Caleb and the other eleven members of the reconnaissance team spied out the land from their headquarters near Kadesh-barnea forty-five years earlier, they brought back reports of huge people who lived in an area known as Kyriat Arba, or the city of Arba the giant. Arba was a descendant of Anak and was a mighty warrior of legendary stature, a man to be feared and avoided.

But Kyriat Arba, later known as Hebron, had a special place in Caleb's heart. It was the city where his ancestor Abraham had settled and sat under the oaks of Mamre. It was where Abraham, Isaac, and Jacob were buried; those patriarchs were the giants of faith he held most in awe, not the Anakim. And that was where he wanted to settle in spite of the giants that still lived in the land. Why? Because he had a "different spirit."

Caleb did not sit on the same limb of the family tree that David and Jesus sat on, he was of the tribe of Judah and therefore entitled to an inheritance in the southern section of Israel that included the city of Kyriat Arba. Moses himself had promised him an inheritance there, and Caleb justly laid that claim before Joshua. With no fear in his heart, he relished the prospect of a homestead in a land filled with giants.

Today in modern Israel, Hebron, a West Bank city, is under Palestinian control. But a small, embattled enclave of Jews still survive there and have named their suburb Kyriat Arba, as it was known in Old Testament times. Perhaps they claim spiritual descent from Caleb, and perhaps they see themselves as giant killers because they have a "different spirit," and because they are confident that the Lord is on their side. They too, have chosen to dwell in a land that devours its inhabitants, where survival demands that one be "strong and of good courage."

As we reconnoiter our spiritual promised land looking for a place to settle and serve, do we, in the spirit of Lot, look to the lush, well-watered valleys of the plain where life is easy and work is guaranteed to be fruitful? Or do we, in the spirit of Caleb, ask our commander to assign us to a Hebron? Isaac Watts asked the same question:

> Am I a soldier of the cross, a follower of the Lamb,
> And shall I fear to own his cause or blush to speak his name?
> Must I be carried to the skies on flowery beds of ease,
> While others fought to win the prize
>   or sailed through bloody seas?
> Since I must fight if I would reign,
>   increase my courage Lord,
> I'll bear the toil, endure the pain, supported by thy Word.

Their Real Lot?

Scripture: Joshua 15:1–12
Suggested Reading: Genesis 49:8–12

Somewhere in nearly every family's safe box is a piece of paper that describes the property they own. Perhaps the property is described as commencing a certain number of feet from the centerline of a particular road, then turning a certain number of degrees and minutes and progressing so many feet to the southwest and continuing, as my property did, "to the high water mark of the old millpond," thence so many feet to the northwest so many degrees and minutes, and so on, and so forth until every boundary is fully described and fathomable only to a surveyor.

Though the official property description may define for the probate court the exact boundaries of a survivor's legal inheritance, it can't begin to describe the true character of that piece of land and all it represents to the people who live there.

It will not say, for example, that there is an old two-story frame house, a vintage Chevy in the garage, a big oak tree with a tire swing, a creek with a bridge a father and his son built, a path through the woods, a pet cemetery, a swing on the front porch, and, above all, memories of parents, brothers, sisters, friends, unforgettable Christmases, courtships, blessed events, sicknesses, and deaths. No official document can record the laughter and the tears, the joys and the heartaches of the people who lived within the bounds it defines. Those memories are the true inheritance of a family.

So it is with "the lot for the people of the tribe of Judah." Brooks, seashores, cities, valleys, springs, and mountain peaks define the lines that compose its borders, but no such description can define its true inheritance. Joshua needed twelve verses to detail Judah's geographical boundaries, but Jacob needed only five to describe Judah's real heritage: the King of Israel, the Messiah, the cup of blessing, the washer of garments, and the Lord of lords.

I sometimes wonder what the man Judah understood when Jacob described his inheritance. As a son of Leah, he must have known from his youth that he would never be one of his father's favorites. His ire must have risen when the brash young Joseph paraded around in his colorful coat and shared his self-serving dreams. It was probably more fear than empathy that led him to spare Joseph's life when the other brothers wanted to kill him. He certainly had no sense of social responsibility when he married a Canaanite woman or when he "went in unto" the daughter-in-law who was masquerading as a harlot, and through her sired Perez, the illegitimate son who would be the progenitor of King David and Jesus.

As Judah gathered with his brothers around his father's death-bed to receive the final blessing, could he have possibly understood why his brothers would bow down to him or praise him? Could he in any way have begun to comprehend what Jacob said about the scepter, the ruler's staff, or the one who was to come?

And now as his seventy-six thousand, five hundred heirs and their families receive their plot of land, can any of them understand their true place in history, their real lot?

I am unaware of any legitimate prophecies about the destinies of my heirs. I pretty much know what their material inheritance will be, but do I have any understanding at all of what their spiritual destiny will be?

But more importantly, have I done all I should to assure it?

Springs of Water

Scripture: Joshua 15:13–62
Suggested Reading: Judges 3:7–11; 1 Samuel 25

Caleb was a very special man. He was the ultimate optimist. As a young man with a "different spirit," he was able to look beyond the clouds and see the sun. When the other spies saw defeat in the future, he saw victory.

Caleb was patient. When he was forty God promised him an inheritance. For the next forty-five years he lived by the sword, helping his brothers secure their land. Then he received his legacy at the ripe old age of eighty-five.

Caleb sought challenge. When he sought a dwelling place, he chose a city in the heart of the Negev that the Anakim occupied, and he drove the giants out.

Caleb was generous. When his daughter asked for a supply of precious water in the dry Judean desert, he gave her two oases.

Caleb was far sighted. After he established himself in the land, he made provision for his descendants. He did everything a man who "wholly follows the Lord" should do.

The character of Caleb as reported to us by Moses and Joshua is rife with spiritual symbolism and serves as a model for any Christian. The part I like best is his giving springs of water to his daughter. When I read that, I think of Jesus being our source of living water, and of our duty to share that precious water with our children.

But there is another principle here as well. Caleb is a model of a man who lived a godly life and raised his family well, sharing with them the springs of living water from the depths of that different spirit. He was a wonderful model for his daughter and her husband, Othniel. But he cannot be held accountable for the behavior of his descendants farther down the line. After several generations, Caleb's influence apparently waned, and from his genes emerged a notable scoundrel: the irascible, cantankerous Nabal.

Now the story of David, Nabal, and Abigail is a story that stands on its own merit and provides lessons for us completely independent of the story of Caleb. But Samuel does point out to us that the villain of his episode is descended from the hero of an earlier time. I'm not sure why he took the trouble to point out Nabal's heritage, but it does confirm that bad people can descend from good ones.

That truth bothered me a little until I realized that the opposite is also true. Good people can descend from bad ones. The genealogy of Jesus is proof of that. Though our Lord had God-fearing parents, he also carried in his human genes the same substance of which many evil men and worldly women were made. To maintain his righteousness, he not only had to overcome the temptations his environment offered, but also the propensities to sin that he may have inherited from his wicked ancestors.

God, in his Word, obligated our parents to pass on the good news of salvation to us and to raise us in the faith. Yet it is up to us to take our parents' teaching to heart and to live up to the standards they set for us. We can thank our parents for bringing us up according to the Word, but we cannot blame them if we fall from the faith and are lost. We are responsible for ourselves.

We have a God-given duty to share the springs of living water with our children, as Caleb did, but we cannot take the blame if they refuse to drink that water. They are responsible for themselves.

Could Not . . . Did Not

Scripture: Joshua 15:63; 16; 11:14–20
Suggested Reading: Romans 7; 2 Timothy 3:16

Hold it right here. Are we a little confused? After the conquest of the southern portion of Canaan, Joshua reported that he had done as the Lord God had commanded, that he had "utterly destroyed all that breathed." And after the conquest of the north he declared that he "did not leave anything that breathed." With the exception of the Hivites from Gibeon, who had become slaves, he had "exterminated" the pagans who had infested the land. But now we read that Ephraim failed to drive out the Canaanites from Gezer and that Judah could not drive the Jebusites from Jerusalem.

Some commentators are quick to point out the apparent contradiction and declare Joshua's account of the conquest unreliable. Some say that Joshua, as commanders are wont to be, inflated the body count to make himself look successful, and that later, when sizeable groups of Canaanites embarrassingly emerged from the heaps of the dead, he shifted the blame to the tribal leaders who could not or did not destroy them.

Now I was raised with the firm belief that the Word of God doesn't contain any contradictions, and that our failure to understand and make sense of some of his revelation derives only from the frailty of the sinful human mind. But in my old age I've learned that it is profitable for doctrine and instruction in righteousness to grapple with those quandaries of inspiration and apparent contradictions and to try to apply them in some way to our walk with the Lord in the spiritual promised land, the kingdom of heaven.

We testify that we have crossed the Jordan, that we have died to self, that we have been crucified with Christ and raised with him in newness of life, born again. We say we are filled with the Holy Spirit, that Jesus lives in our hearts. We claim to live victorious lives.

So then, why do we still covet? Why do we lust? Why do we still get angry and say things we shouldn't say? Why do we do things we shouldn't do? Why do we think things we shouldn't think? Why do some bad habits still survive in our flesh? Do we contradict ourselves? In light of the conquest of Canaan, I think not.

Some of those old Jebusites still dwell in my Jerusalem, and some of the pagan Canaanites still dwell in my Gezer because I could not or did not drive them out. Some of my evil deeds serve as examples for others of how not to live. Some of the residual evil that dwells in me is doing slave labor, like the Gibeonites, but some of it is still running free, like the Jebusites and the Geshurites.

Perhaps there is a subtle symbolic distinction between the force of angels under the leadership of the Commander of the army of the Lord, God's spiritual army, and the forces under the command of the Joshua and the tribal leaders, the armies soldiered by the Achans of the nation. When Jesus cried "It is finished!" he declared that his army of angels had achieved total victory over the forces of evil. Satan and his army of demons were sentenced to the eternal flames. That victory is an accomplished fact, a done deed, earned at Calvary. But though he has won the land for me, I am still carnal, still living in the flesh. Like Paul, I do the bad things I don't want to do and I don't do the good things I want to do. The members of my body war against my mind, and contradictions appear. My sin has been banished forever by the blood of Christ, yet the residue of evil dwells in me, wretched, thorn-in-the-flesh man that I am!

Who will deliver me? I *am* delivered, thanks be to Jesus Christ our Lord for his victory on the cross!

Those Girls Again

Scripture; Joshua 17:1–6
Suggested Reading: Numbers 27:1–11; 32:39–42; 36:10–12

When historians showcase famous women whose heroic actions altered the course of human events, they should not omit the daughters of Zelophehad.

While the nation was encamped east of the Jordan, some of the sons of Manasseh didn't just sit around waiting for the ferry to Jericho. They practiced their military arts by capturing cities in Gilead and Bashan and destroying their inhabitants.

A quick look at the map will show that their conquests were no small achievement. In fact, the land that Manasseh occupied northeast of the Jordan was larger than the territory possessed by any other tribe, even though in population they were just above the average. So, why did they also inherit such a spacious tract of land *west* of the river? All because of Zelophehad's daughters.

All of the tribes were entitled to an allotment of land between the Mediterranean Sea and the Jordan river. The sons of Reuben and Gad were beguiled by the good grazing land to the east, so they voluntarily waived their rights to their birthright among the other sons of Jacob. And the men of war that Manasseh sired were happy to dwell in the northeastern outposts and live a life of constant battle against the Midianites, the Hittites, and later the Assyrians.

But the daughters of Zelophehad, of the tribe of Manasseh, demanded an inheritance west of the river. And because Moses had promised them an inheritance with their brothers, they were entitled to territory within the boundaries of the Promised Land.

Thus the territory given to the tribe of Manasseh west of the river was cut into ten parts rather than the smaller number it would have been divided into had Zelophehad's daughters not claimed their right.

In the end, two and a half tribes east of the Jordan were the first to fall to the invading Assyrian Empire. And for a time, the river served as God's hedge against the invaders, but eventually the northern kingdom fell too. Mainly because of their sin, God gave them up to their enemies. Yet there is a point worth noting.

Many great Christians have testified that their mothers were the spiritual influence in their family. While Dad was absorbed by his job and golf, Mom taught the kids about Jesus, took them to Sunday school and told them Bible stories. Many have testified that the power of a praying mother preserved them from the life they may have led, and that the hymns she sang to them while they were ill helped heal their diseases. When fathers fail, God uses mothers to claim his children's inheritance in the kingdom of heaven.

The story of Zelophehad's daughters demonstrates to errant men that if they choose to live a life outside the boundaries of the kingdom of heaven, their women can rise up and right their wrong. And it also demonstrates that if men abdicate their spiritual responsibilities in favor of greener pastures or a more exciting life of slaying dragons and chasing golf balls, that God will honor the intervention of women who fight for the salvation of their children.

So when we pay tribute to the Sarahs, the Ruths, the Deborahs, the Esthers, and the Marys of scripture, we should also remember that the daughters of Zelophehad not only changed a nation's boundaries, but also stood firm to assure their children an inheritance in the land of promise.

Chariots of What?

Scripture: Joshua 17:7–18
Suggested Reading: 2 Kings 6:14–17; 1 John 4:4

Sometimes a warrior of the world to whom God has given very powerful personal qualities becomes a Christian. Usually that new convert doesn't abandon those worldly traits and mellow into a passive pew warmer, but rather uses the old character in a new way to advance the cause of God. I'm thinking of my old friend, the powerful and successful beer salesman whom God transformed into an equally powerful and successful missionary, selling repentance and the forgiveness of sins, and so enlarging his portion in the kingdom of heaven.

The sons Ephraim and Manasseh were not mild-mannered men either. As they waited on the east bank for orders to cross the Jordan, they didn't just sit around. They went to war against the Midianites who dwelled there, and claimed the conquered country as their own. And when they got into the Promised Land, they were not content with the amount of territory that fell to them by lot, they wanted more.

They went toe to toe with Joshua and claimed to be a great people. And Joshua said, "If you are such a great people, carve out a bigger piece of land for yourselves. Carve our more territory from the forests, and if that is still not enough, drive the Canaanites out of the Valley of Jezreel." And with God's help, they did.

So, as that new Christian used his old worldly traits to enlarge his portion of the kingdom of heaven, Joshua told the sons of Joseph to use their old traits to enlarge their holdings in the Promised Land. But there was one problem: the Canaanites had chariots of iron.

The early stages of the iron age had crept from Asia Minor into the north of Canaan and the pagans had weapons that were superior to those of the Israelites. Or did they?

When Joshua stood pondering his strategy for attacking Jericho, he met his superior officer, the Commander of the army of the Lord. Now the army of the Lord also had chariots, but they were not made of wood, or even of some inferior metal. They were chariots of fire, and we all know what fire can do to iron.

When a seasoned veteran of the world's battles puts on the uniform of the Lord's army, he trades in his old weapons for new. He no longer drives a chariot of wood, and his sword and shield are not of bronze. When Christ comes alive in him, God transforms his weapons from the substantive to the spiritual, and now he drives a chariot of fire, is protected by the shield of faith, and wields the Sword of the Spirit, the Word of God.

When we wage wars in the temporal world, in order to win we have to settle for the encouragement and confidence that comes from knowing our strategy is good, our skills are sharp, and that we have fortitude. The resources for victory come from within our own flesh.

But when we enlist in the army of the Lord, we have more than encouragement and confidence, we have the assurance of promise. God promised us that the hill country of his kingdom *shall* be ours and that we *shall* drive out the forces of evil even though they have powerful weapons. We are assured that we will overcome them, for Christ lives in us, and he who lives is in us is greater than he who is in the world!

How Long Are Ye Slack?

Scripture: Joshua 18:1–10
Suggested Reading: 1 Kings 19:19–21; Luke 9:57–62

Apparently after many years of battling to subdue the land, some of the people of Israel had not yet come forward to lay claim to their inheritance. Joshua took exception to their indifference and chastised them, urging them to get on with their business of possessing their portion of the Promised Land.

Jesus leveled a similar rebuke to the people who wanted to be his disciples but who had not yet made him the first priority of their lives. He said, "No one who puts his hand to the plow and looks back is fit for the kingdom of God."

Preachers have delivered many sermons about putting one's hand to the plow and looking back, the most memorable one I heard being about plowing a crooked furrow. A good plowman keeps his eye on a fixed point at the forward end of the field in order to plow a straight line.

Now that's a good sermon in itself, but I don't think Jesus was thinking about straight lines when he laid down the maxim about looking back. He was saying that he didn't want as a disciple anyone whose life was burdened with business other than kingdom business. Jesus has to be the primary commitment of the life of a true disciple. Anyone who gives Jesus less than full attention is not fit for citizenship in the kingdom.

Elisha is a good example of committed discipleship. When Elijah "cast his mantle upon him," declaring him to be his successor, Elisha left his oxen and ran after the prophet. He thought to go home and kiss his parents goodbye, but Elijah upbraided him, as Jesus would have, so Elisha severed any ties he had to his previous life by slaying his oxen, celebrating his departure with a feast, and rising up and following his new master.

What an example of not being slack in staking a claim to an inheritance in the kingdom of heaven! What an example of taking up the handle of a new plow and peering forward into the new field! What an example of plowing a straight furrow!

Putting Jesus first in our lives is no easy business because we must be willing to sacrifice other priorities. But *keeping* Jesus first requires continual sacrificing. Old priorities creep in, sometimes on an emergency basis, and demand attention. And new, very attractive priorities arise. Grandchildren come into our lives and worm their way into our hearts. Loving them deeply and giving them red carpet treatment is natural. I would sacrifice my flesh for my grandchildren, yet I must fight the desire to make them idols that compete with my love for the Lord.

Sometimes other new attractions appear. I know because I got a new computer with power and gadgets to spare. I've had to accomplish a set amount of work for the Lord before I allow myself to play with my new toy.

Our promised land is not governed by a master who smiles on cluttered or indistinct priorities. The price of citizenship in God's kingdom is to relegate everything in life to second place and to put Jesus first.

Anyone who does less is not fit to possess the land.

The Beloved of the Lord

Scripture: Joshua 18:11–28
Suggested Reading: Genesis 28:18–22; Deuteronomy 33:12;
Judges 19,20,21; 2 Chronicles 6:1–10

When Joshua apportioned the rest of the land to the seven remaining tribes, he did so by "casting lots before the Lord." That did not mean that territory fell to a tribe simply by the luck of the draw, but that God somehow decided which tribes were to receive which parcels of land.

When the lot for the tribe of Benjamin came up, the territory allotted to it fell between Ephraim and Judah. Joshua described his inheritance as going up from the "shoulder" north of Jericho, southward to the "shoulder" of Bethel, and back down around the Valley of Hinnom to Jerusalem, the "shoulder" of the Jebusites.

Long before the nation of Israel crossed into the Promised Land, Benjamin's father, Jacob, fled from his home and found himself alone and afraid in the rocky hills of the Judean wilderness. He first sensed the presence of the Lord at a place he named Bethel, and where he erected an altar and stones of remembrance. He called the place "God's house."

And after Israel became a powerful nation, King Solomon built, in Jerusalem, a great temple that he called "the house of the Lord, the God of Israel." So, in accordance with the prophecy of Moses, God dwells on the two "shoulders" of Benjamin, Bethel and Jerusalem, and Benjamin dwells safely between the "shoulders" of God.

What a beautiful family picture: the youngest son, the beloved son of the beloved wife, sitting high on the shoulders of his father and nestled between his full brother, Joseph, and his honored brother, Judah, whom God had chosen to sire great prophets, great kings and the Savior of the world.

We're never told why God loved Benjamin so. Perhaps it was because Jacob loved him. Benjamin never did anything to distinguish himself. God rejected the only king that came from his tribe, and the apostle Paul was his only other descendant of note. So why was he beloved of the Lord and given the honored seat on his shoulders?

Jacob prophesied that the tribe of Benjamin would be a ravenous wolf, devouring the prey and dividing the spoil. And if the story of the men of Gibeah defines the general character of the Benjaminites, Jacob knew whereof he spoke. Because the men of Benjamin acted more like Sodomites than like God's chosen people, the tribe was nearly wiped from the pages of history. But for some reason, God preserved them from oblivion.

It's a mystery why God loved and protected Benjamin. Benjamin didn't merit that love. Quite to the contrary, Benjamin did all he could to fall from favor with God, but God wouldn't let him. Benjamin was chosen. God, in his grace, decided to love Benjamin in spite of himself. Maybe God loved Benjamin *because* he didn't deserve to be loved.

It is equally mysterious why God loves me so. I never did anything to merit such love. Like Benjamin, I did much to fall from favor with God, but God wouldn't let me fall. I didn't deserve his care and protection, but God chose to love me in spite of myself and chose to make his holy dwelling between my shoulders, in my heart.

And now I am compelled to love others as he loves me.

As He Had Sworn . . .

Scripture: Joshua 19
Suggested Reading: Genesis 12:7–8; 22:1–2; 28:13; Exodus 6:2–5;
Psalms 27

I wonder what sort of thoughts flashed through Abraham's and Jacob's minds almost six hundred years before Joshua's time, when God visited them and promised that the land on which they stood would someday belong to their descendants. I wonder if they envisioned their grandchildren or great grandchildren playing hide and seek among the rocks at Bethel. Could they have possibly imagined that God would take half a millennium to fulfill that promise?

And after their mortal bodies took their last breath, were they able to look from heaven and watch the centuries pass? Did they, as they sat in the presence of the Lord, also hear the groaning of their children as they buckled under the heavy hand of their Egyptian slave masters and wonder when God was going to honor his promise? Did they hang their heads in shame as their faithless descendants rebelled in the wilderness and began to bend their knee before the idols? Did they pump their fists in joyful victory when the walls of Jericho came tumbling down and when the army of Ai fled before the Israelites? And did they heave a sigh of relief when Joshua finally finished dividing the land? At long last, the ancient promise was fulfilled.

If Abraham and Jacob had to wait over five hundred years for God to deliver on his pledge to them, how can we justify becoming impatient when God doesn't respond to our petitions in a day or two?

At the beginning of our Sunday school class we share our joys and concerns. Then we pray, praising God for his blessings and asking for healing, for comfort, for relief from oppression, for guidance, or for whatever our need might be. The next Sunday, we report our progress and on the progress of the loved ones for whom we prayed. Some praise the Lord for being with them during the week, some thank God for healing and answered prayer.

But sometimes disease persists and trouble lingers, and it seems that God hasn't heard us or has turned a deaf ear to our plea. Then we confess that he is the Potter and we are the clay, that sometimes his will for our lives might not be the same as our will, and we reluctantly submit and say, "Have thine own way, Lord." Then we smile a sad smile and hang our heads with the expression of martyrdom smeared all over our face.

We can look back at the history of the Jews and infer meaningful messages for the church. We know that God had a purpose in allowing several generations of his chosen people to suffer under the scourge of slavery. We know that God had a reason for blinding their eyes to his truth and hardening their hearts to pagan idolatry. We know the significance of the first generation dying in the wilderness and the second generation crossing the Jordan and spending its life fighting to obtain its inheritance in the Promised Land. As we study them we learn of God's sovereignty, his sense of justice, and his compassion. And we learn how he wants us to live.

So today as we live the victorious lives of citizens of the kingdom of heaven, we know that it is improper for us to make demands on our King. It is improper for us to exalt ourselves and look on him as our servant. We can learn from Abraham and Jacob that we are to be patient. David learned that lesson well. Evil men, including his king and even his own son, sought his life, but even as he begged God to deliver him from his enemies, he could, in faith, pray for understanding, be of good courage, and wait patiently on the Lord. How blessed we are to have men like Abraham, Jacob, and David to serve as models of patience for us.

Providing Asylum

Scripture: Joshua 20
Suggested Reading: Exodus 19:6; Romans 12:19; Revelation 1:4–6

So far in these meditations we've blessed ourselves with the understanding that we have a city of refuge, a place to hide when the going gets too tough for us to tolerate, a place to rest and regain our strength to continue the battle. And we've noted that the Lord is our refuge and our strength, our hiding place in time of trouble. But we have not yet undertaken to address the responsibility God places on us to provide refuge for the brothers and sisters who are being pursued by the devil.

The six cities of refuge that Joshua established in accordance with the command of God given through Moses were run by the Levites, the tribe God commissioned to be the priestly order. But God Also told Moses that someday his chosen people would be transformed into a kingdom of priests. The church of Jesus Christ has inherited that commission. We have been anointed by the blood of Christ to serve as his priests here on earth.

Such service requires, among other things, that we provide a city of refuge, a safe haven for the accused of Satan. We are to stand at the open gate of the church and admit into our community the strangers who are seeking asylum from poverty, disease, hunger, abuse, or any of the darts the devil hurls. We are especially to provide protection for sinners who have clouds of guilt hanging over their heads, and we are to treat them as innocent until the day God brings their cases to judgment.

During the old kingdom years, the avenger of blood was a near relative of a murder victim. He was commissioned under God's rules to hunt down the culprit and to slay him to avenge the death of his kinsman. But if the alleged offender considered himself to be innocent, believed the death to be accidental rather than intentional, or could argue that he acted in self-defense, he could flee to the city of refuge, a safe haven, and the priests there were obligated to take him in and protect him from the avenger. They were to hear him out and deliver him safely to the authorities for trial.

The whole process foreshadows the role of the church and its members. Our just God is on a mission to avenge the violation of his law, a crime of which all sinners are guilty. But the offender can seek sanctuary in the church. For the sinner, we are the priests who hold open the gates of the city of refuge and welcome the accused to seek shelter in fellowship with us. We are to hear him testify, to "explain his case," and we are to "give him a place."

We are now living in the kingdom age, the kingdom of heaven that Jesus said is within us, the kingdom of the saints who have been crucified with Christ and raised to newness of life in him, the age foreseen by the prophet Joel, the age of born again. Our High Priest is Jesus Christ, and he commissions us to usher the accused safely to the bar of justice where he will intercede for them.

In the old kingdom, the death of the high priest liberated the accused. The avengers had to abandon their case and the accused could return safely to their homes. In the new kingdom, the death of our High Priest absolves the sinners of their guilt, permanently pardons the iniquity they have committed, and assures them safe passage to their heavenly home.

The death of our High Priest has satisfied the Avenger's demand for justice.

. . . With Its Pasturelands

Scripture: Joshua 21
Suggested Reading; Joshua 13:33; Exodus 19:6; Matthew 6:19–21;
Luke 17:21; 1 Peter 1:3–4; Revelation 5:8–10; 20:6

*J*oshua doled out tribal lands to the descendants of all the other brothers, but to the sons of Levi he gave specific towns and their adjacent pasturelands within the boundaries of the other tribes. There they were to serve as clergy, performing the duties of the priesthood and the rituals prescribed by law, serving as shepherds to both their human and animal flocks, eating the food brought to them for sacrifices and enjoying the protection of the laity. The Lord was their only inheritance.

When I picture those Levitical towns in my mind, I recall a quaint little village in the Rhineland of Germany that I visited as a soldier after the war. It was a clean little town with narrow cobblessedone streets and picturesque stucco buildings. Rich green pasturelands encircled the village, and beyond those meadows lay the vineyards, extending all the way to the river. German ladies swept the streets and cared for the children, and men either tended the sheep or worked in the vineyards. It was a peaceful and charming place to be.

When I want to picture the Levitical towns of those ancient days, I reach back in my memory and recall that little village. Then I see Levite women sweeping the streets and watching the children, and the men tending the sheep in the pasture lands, serving in the places of worship, meeting the spiritual needs of their brothers in the surrounding cities, and seeing to the physical needs of the widows, the sick, the poor, and the orphans.

All we have to do is look up a few related scriptures and substitute in this passage *the church of Jesus Christ* for *the house of Israel,* and the whole inheritance of the Levites will take on a new significance. By accepting our salvation and freedom from the shackles of sin through the death and resurrection of Christ, we, the church, have become God's adopted children, his new nation, his chosen people, the citizens of the kingdom of heaven that Jesus founded here on earth.

And when we have been crucified with Christ and raised with him, we become priests, holy unto the Lord, living as shepherds and servants in the Levitical cities of the new kingdom.

Like the Levites, we have inherited the duties of the priesthood. It is our job to do the work of the church, to see that the gospel is preached throughout the world, to see that the hungry are fed, the naked clothed, the prisoner of sin freed from bondage, the sick tended, and the sinner prayed to sainthood.

We have not only inherited the Levitical cities of the kingdom of heaven, but the pasturelands as well. Those green lands of fellowship surrounding the church are our inheritance. There we find our sustenance, the produce of the land, the fruit of the Spirit, and the living water. There we find our hedge against Satan. There we find the paths of righteousness. There the Lord makes us to lie down in the grass and look up and see the wonders of the heavens. There he leads us beside the still waters, restores our souls and fills our cups to overflowing. There we find our comfort and our rest.

Then some glorious morning, as the old hymn says, Jesus will come and give his church a new task. We will shed the servant rags and don the robes of royalty to reign with him over the whole earth. Then we too will be able to look back and say, "Not one of the good promises which the Lord made to the church of Jesus Christ has failed; all has come to pass."

A Charge to Keep I Have

Scripture: Joshua 22:1–93
Suggested Reading: Numbers 30:2; 32:16–18; Matthew 22:37

God kept his promise to the children of Abraham and gave them possession of the land. During the long process of obtaining that promise, the beneficiaries of that promise made promises themselves, both to their God and to their brothers.

At their own request, God gave Reuben, Gad, and the half tribe of Manasseh an inheritance east of the Jordan River. They settled there after they wreaked God's punishment on the pagans who defiled those lands, and before their brothers crossed over into their inheritance west of the river.

Moses gave the two-and-a-half tribes their separate inheritance only on the condition that their fighting men pass over with the other ten tribes and fight by their side to annihilate the pagans who lived in Canaan. When the conquest was complete, Joshua commended them for keeping their promise to their brothers, and further urged them to keep their charge to the Lord their God by loving him, walking in his ways, keeping his commandments, cleaving to him, and serving him with all their heart and soul.

During the course of this life we all make many promises to our spouses, our children, our employers, and to others whose lives entwine with ours. We keep some and we break some. Most of the regret that haunts us until the day we die is the wreckage of broken vows that litters the road of our past and the injury we've caused to people we love. And sometimes the victims of our broken pledges are loathe to make personal commitments of their own because they've experienced the misery our faithlessness has caused.

Fortunately, God has promised to forgive our sins even when those we've sinned against can't. He never has and never will break that promise.

But, even knowing our weakness, God asks us to make a pledge to him just as Joshua asked the tribes of Gilead to promise to love the Lord, to walk in his ways, to keep his commandments, to cleave unto him and to serve him with all of our heart and soul.

And in the New Testament, Jesus reconfirmed that obligation when he answered the slick lawyer who tried to trick him into prioritizing the Ten Commandments.

When we accept his forgiveness, we also accept the charge to do all within our power to love him, and serve him as we should. We cannot do that in our own strength. We need God's help.

And so we should pray as Charles Wesley prayed, that God would give us the heart and the will to keep that sacred promise.

A charge to keep I have, a God to glorify
Who gave his Son my soul to save, and fit it for the sky.

To serve my present age, my calling to fulfill,
O may it all my powers engage to do my Master's will!

Arm me with jealous care as in thy sight to live;
And O thy servant, Lord, prepare, a strict account to give!

Help me to watch and pray, and on thyself rely;
And let me ne'er my trust betray, but press to realms on high.

A Witness Between Us

Scripture: Joshua 22:10–34

For the first time, we see a distinction develop between the people of the Promised Land and their brothers living in Gilead. Both sides seem to understand that the Jordan is not a river that runs through their common land, but that it is a boundary, a dividing line that separates one group of God's people from the other.

The eastern tribes built a massive altar on the west bank as a token of unity, but the western tribes mistook it as a token of separation, a symbol suggesting to them that the Gileadites were autonomous. That simple misunderstanding nearly led to civil war.

There was much to cement the tribes together. They shared a common belief in the one true God. They descended from a common ancestor and shared a common history. As a single nation, they were God's chosen people. They were brothers.

Yet there was much to drive them apart. Tribal delineations separated the sons of Jacob from each other. Rivers, valleys, and mountain ranges formed boundaries that divided them geographically. Tribal occupations and varying levels of wealth and prosperity led to class distinctions. And as each tribe developed its separate economy and politics, conflicts arose that eventually did lead to civil war.

When I was a boy we lived in the ghettos. I lived in a Dutch ghetto that abutted the Negro ghetto, the Polish ghetto and the Italian ghetto. Streets, celery farms, valleys, hills, and creeks separated one ghetto from another and formed boundary lines. Though we went to separate schools, we knew the kids in the other neighborhoods and even crossed the boundary lines to play ball against them. But athletic competition was the extent of our somewhat cordial relationship. Getting friendly with each other's girls was an act of provocation that could lead to war.

Certain things unified us. We all loved the Detroit Tigers and we all believed in God. We all had family and friends who went to war for a common cause. We were all Christian Americans.

Yet there were many stumbling blocks that we used as grounds for conflict. One ethnic group was Roman Catholic, one Baptist, and another Dutch Reformed. One was Republican, another Democrat. One was poor, another, by comparison, rich. One was black, one tan, and others white, a distinction that eventually triggered riots in the old neighborhoods.

How many of our churches are separated by artificial boundaries? Christians divide over the issues of papacy, baptism, language, ethnicity, and wealth. Sunday morning is the most segregated time in the United States.

During the week we all go to school together, learn the same lessons, cheer for the same teams and work together on common projects. But on Sunday we divide into the cell groups that emphasize our differences.

And even in our individual churches we segregate ourselves according to the style of worship and music that best suits our personal tastes. Often these differences lead to serious conflict.

But in spite of all the things that separate us, we Christians do have an altar, a symbol, a monument that stands as a witness between us testifying that the Lord is God and that his Son died for the sins of all of us: the cross of Jesus Christ.

Till You Perish

Scripture: Joshua 23

As I mentioned earlier, I didn't begin college until I was twenty-two years old. Being "of age" as a freshman, I had the privilege of sitting in on the bull sessions at Louie's with seniors and seminarians who also attended that Christian institution. One of the many topics of frequent discussion was the unanswerable question, "Once saved, always saved?"

Our Calvinistic elders had declared that the Lord predestined every name enrolled in the Book of Life and that no man had the power to alter his divinely appointed destiny. And they backed up that tenet of the church with selected scriptures.

But in the blue, intoxicating haze of the back room at Louie's, some of the bold ones took the liberty to differ with the elders, and backed up their dissent with other selected scriptures.

Now I'm an old man, much less sure of many things I knew for a certainty in my youth, more sure of some things I didn't quite understand back then, but still struggling with that mysterious question, "Once saved, always saved?"

I don't waste much time thinking about that quandary these days, because I know for a certainty that no one can ever be absolutely certain of the answer, no matter how educated he is or how much scripture he conjures up to prove his point. But I suppose that the boys in the back room at Louie's will debate the issue as long as that venerable building stands in the neighborhood of the college.

I am assured of my salvation. I can claim with unbridled assurance that if the Lord returns today, I will be caught up with him in the clouds, and that if I die tonight I will rise from my grave to meet him when the great trumpet sounds.

But I'm also keenly aware that pagans lurk at my elbow, sometimes with siren charm, urging me to turn and worship gods of wood and stone. They continually set a snare for me, and unless I take good heed to love the Lord my God with all my heart, I fear that I could surrender to their song and forfeit my inheritance in the kingdom of God. If Israel did it, why can't I?

The history of Israel contains a message for all believers. They lived in a covenant relationship with God. He always kept his end of the bargain, but often they failed, and when they did, he exiled them from their land and turned it over to their enemies.

In the twentieth century they returned as prophesied, and they obviously have a role to play in the latter days. Many pundits make many presumptions about their role and their destiny, but I think that had those same pundits lived in Joshua's time they might have expected the nation of Israel to last forever, protected by God's mighty hand from all their enemies and living comfortably on milk and honey, figs, grapes, and olives. God promised that destiny—if they lived obediently—but he also promised to banish them from their inheritance if they failed to keep their end of the covenant.

When I view the history of Israel as a symbol of the Christian's life story, I can't dismiss the fact that they were evicted from their inheritance for disobedience. I have to take that as a warning that I, too, may be evicted from my inheritance for the same reasons. But as long as I walk the paths of righteousness, I have the edge over the enemies who are trying to seduce me. But Joshua warned me that if I turn my back, the anger of the lord will be kindled against me and I shall "perish quickly from off this good land" he has given me.

As for Me . . .

Scripture: Joshua 24:1–27
Suggested Reading: Deuteronomy 28:30–34; 1 John 1:9

I suppose that it would have been an unforgettable experience to have stood in the wilderness beyond the Jordan and listened as Moses delivered his farewell addresses to the people of Israel. Then again, I don't know how they stood for so long and listened to him recount their every move over the last forty years, review all the laws, and prophesy a wonderful life as a consequence of obedience but misery for failure. It must have taken hours, or even days.

I wonder if the youngsters had to listen, or if they had the option to go to "children's church." I'm thankful that I have it all in a book so I can pick it up and read a chapter or two at my leisure. I doubt if I have the attention span to listen to that lecture all at once.

In Joshua's farewell address, on the other hand, he covered their essential history going back to Abraham, reviewed the fundamental commandment to worship only the Lord, and even held a dialog with the people in which they pledged to serve God and obey his voice. And he did it all in only four minutes. At least that's how long it took me to read it aloud. I timed it.

Joshua was a man of action, a man of few words. But the words he did speak are monumentally important. They are words that we should engrave on our doorposts.

I've always been touched that my neighbor down the road posted the words, *As for me and my house, we will serve the Lord*, on his gatepost by the road as a witness to all who pass by, and that my daughter Kyle posted those same words inside her back door as a witness to herself every time she left the house. But Joshua didn't mouth those words as a witness to anyone; he mouthed them as a promise to the Lord, and he honored that vow until the day he died.

The people of Israel made the same pledge and set up a stone as a witness. At the moment they were absolutely certain of their commitment, using such unqualified language as "far be it from us that we should forsake the Lord and serve other gods." But we don't have to read very far to learn that their solemn oath was nothing more than a hollow boast.

With a mighty hand, the Lord led his people out of Egypt, and with a mighty hand he brought them into Canaan. They dwelled in cities they had not built and ate fruit from vineyards they had not planted. But in the end they came full circle, just as Moses had prophesied. God evicted them from their land and gave their cities to invaders who raped their wives, took over their houses, ate the fruit of their vineyards, and took their children to be slaves.

I have watched couples come to the altar of the church to dedicate their children to God. In the ritual they promised to raise them in the faith and to teach them the ways of righteousness. Then I never see them in church again. I have seen young people consecrate their own lives and pledge to serve the Lord with their time, their talents, and their gifts. Then I see them stray from the faith.

Joshua's words are still true today. The Lord is a jealous God, and if we forsake him and serve the idols we make for ourselves, he will turn and do us harm after having done us good. He will give our inheritance to others. But the good news is that if we repent of our sins, he will forgive us and cleanse us from all unrighteousness.

Hear O Israel! Hear O church of Jesus Christ!

Joy in Heaven!

Scripture: Joshua 24:28
Suggested Reading: Luke 15:7

When I come to the moment when Joshua "sent the people away, every man to his inheritance," I cannot help but fantasize how the patriarchs might have celebrated as they might have watched from heaven.

Over five hundred years earlier, God spoke to Abraham and promised that his descendants would someday inherit that land. But as he watched his grandsons, Jacob and Esau, flounder in faithlessness and dissipation, I wonder if he began to question the truth of God's promise. And as old Jacob saw his sons settle with their flocks in the lush delta of Egypt, I wonder if he thought the promise God made to his grandfather might never come true. Then when the brutal hand of Pharaoh came down on later generations and forced them into hard labor, I wonder if the lore of that promise became to those slaves nothing more than a disheartening fiction.

But then as I envision Abraham, Isaac, Jacob, and Moses viewing the wars of conquest from heaven's grandstand, I wonder if they leaped up and shouted with the people as they marched around Jericho. I wonder if they stood up and shouted unheard warnings to Joshua when the con artists of Gibeon stood before him with their moldy bread and cracked wineskins. I wonder if they cheered wildly as God unleashed his deadly volley of hailstones from heaven and stayed the sun in the sky as Israel's army chased the remnants of the coalition back to their homes. And I wonder if they celebrated each victory and rose in standing ovation when the land finally had rest from war and Joshua sent each heroic soldier to his inheritance.

Now I don't think that my fantasy would constitute, as my Dutch grandparents might suggest, "sputting." I do not intend to make a mockery of solemn spiritual matters. But a cursory glance at the book of Revelation reveals that heaven is a place of great bliss. The white robed saints sing and shout at every opportunity, especially as they watch the Lamb don his battle gear and score great victories over the forces of evil. Even Jesus noted that when one sinner repents, ecstasy breaks out in heaven. So it seems quite logical to think that the patriarchs leaped for joy when God's promise was fulfilled and their descendants defeated their last enemy and finally claimed their long-awaited inheritance in the Promised Land.

We debate a lot about what those who have gone before can or cannot see from their celestial vantage point. Heaven probably wouldn't be heaven if Grandma could watch one of her boys slip into the maelstrom of sin and lose his inheritance. She cried when she saw it happen while she was still living, but since there are no tears in heaven, we expect that she can't see such things when they occur down here now, and we certainly can't accept the notion that she no longer cares. Yet we know she sees the rejoicing that goes on in heaven when one of her children scores a victory over sin and when the Good Shepherd finds that sheep that was lost.

Sometimes in my youth when I did something especially bad, my dad would say to me, "Boy, I'm glad your grandpa isn't here to see you do that." But if I did something especially good, he would say to me, "If your grandpa could only have seen that, it would have made him very happy."

Well, Dad, if you and Grandpa are watching, and can see all the good things your "young 'uns" do down here, I know that you are happy and proud. I'm sorry for the times I've failed you, and I hope you don't even know about them, but I'm happy for the joy I can give you in heaven.

... *All the Days of Joshua*

Scripture: Joshua 24:29–33

What higher compliment can be paid to a man than to declare that the people he led served the Lord all his days?

In succeeding generations, kings will come and kings will go, and in the recorded history of those kings, scripture notes whether or not the people of Israel served the Lord during the span of their reigns. Inevitably the character of the king was reflected in the hearts of the people. If he was a righteous king, the people served the Lord, but if he was a wicked king, his subjects followed his example and bowed their knees to idols.

The eulogies could have gone on and on at Joshua's funeral. Old timers may have looked back on his youth and recalled the courage he showed at Kadesh-barnea when he dared disagree with the majority of the spies. Soldiers who bore arms with him at the front lines during the battles in the wilderness might have recalled his heroism in the war with the Midianites. Those who served under his command in the conquest of Canaan might have praised his skill as a leader. But the best that can be said of a man is not necessarily said in reflecting on his skills or even his courage.

Since imitation is the highest form of flattery, his good friend Caleb might have eulogized him as an outstanding role model, declaring that he lived his life in such a way that others sought to emulate him. Joshua was such a man. As Caleb, he "wholly followed the Lord." He served the Lord all the days of his life, and the people he led followed his example and served the Lord as well.

Had I been offered an opportunity to speak at that final celebration of Joshua's life, I would not have remembered him for his bravery or for his heroic deeds, though he was certainly worthy to be remembered for such things. Rather, I would have testified that the single most significant moment in his life came when he fell on his face before the Commander of the army of the Lord.

The thing I admire most about him is the quality he must have acquired from his long association with Moses: his meekness. Though he was a war hero, the commander-in-chief, and the head of state, he did not hesitate to prostrate himself in humility the moment he recognized his Lord. To me, that was his finest moment.

My daughter Kyle and her husband Tom paid me one of the highest honors of my life when they named their son, Caleb Robert, after me. I'm especially blessed that my name is mentioned in the same breath with the namesake of the other hero of Kadesh-barnea, the man with a "different spirit," a man fully obedient to the Lord. We named Kyle Kathryn in honor of the aunt I admired, the crippled rose on our family tree who knitted mittens for the neighborhood children. My parents named my sister Carol for my grandmother, my shelter in the time of storm, and my sister Wilma for my Aunt Billie. And we named our son, Paul Cameron, in honor of the great apostle who devoted his reborn life to bringing others into the kingdom of heaven, our spiritual promised land.

If parents honor people they respect by naming their children in their honor, God must have admired Joshua because he named his only begotten son in his honor, the name Jesus being the Greek form of the name Joshua.

Did Joshua ever meet the Son of God who was named for him? Oh yes! When he lifted his head there on that hillside overlooking Jericho and looked into the face of the Commander of the army of the Lord, he saw his namesake, Jesus, his Messiah!

The Rest of the Story . . .

Scripture: Genesis 28:10–19; Deuteronomy 33:12;
Joshua 18:11–28; 1 Corinthians 3:16; Galatians 3:29;
Revelation 21–22

Are you in Christ? Is Christ in you? If so, you are children of Abraham and heirs to the promise of a land flowing with milk and honey. If so, you are beloved of God and joint heirs with Christ to the eternal kingdom of heaven!

Our inheritance is best exemplified in the legacy that fell to Benjamin, Jacob's youngest son born of his favorite wife, Rachel. Moses revealed that Benjamin was beloved of the Lord and that the Lord made his dwelling place between Benjamin's shoulders. That metaphor became reality when Joshua defined Benjamin's tribal territory as the high ground in the middle of the nation with its great hills, most notably Bethel to the north and Jerusalem to the south.

Jacob had a vision of the ladder of angels at Bethel, and there the Lord appeared to him and reconfirmed the promise he had made to Abraham. Jacob declared that awesome place to be the house of God, the very gate of heaven.

Several centuries later Solomon built his splendid temple on Benjamin's southern shoulder, the brow of Mount Moriah in Jerusalem where Abraham had brought his beloved son Isaac to be offered as a sacrifice. Solomon declared that magnificent edifice to be the eternal habitation of the God of Israel. Just as Moses prophesied, the Lord's dwelling place was upon the shoulders of Jacob's youngest and most beloved son.

But that inheritance at the crossroads of the ancient world lasted only a few brief years. A series of brutal empires ravaged the land, and finally, just a short time after Christ's resurrection and ascension, the Romans destroyed the city of Jerusalem and burned the Lord's dwelling place to the ground. As Jesus prophesied, not one stone was left upon another. The nation of Israel had ceased to be, and the age of the church began. At Pentecost the Holy Spirit became the essence of God living in and moving among us as he had promised; the Lord took up residence in his new temple between *our* shoulders, in our hearts.

Though our temporal inheritance had been turned to rubble, our eternal inheritance is under construction. Jesus has gone to prepare a place for us where we will meet him at the end of time. And there he waits, as a groom waits for his bride, and there the angels are preparing the grandest wedding ever!

The great consummation of salvation's story comes when the bride, the church of Jesus Christ, takes up its residence in Benjamin's eternal inheritance, the New Jerusalem. The old Jerusalem needed its Gibeon sun to illumine its streets and its Ajalon moon to light its valleys. It needed its strong gates to keep its enemies out. But the New Jerusalem needs no "moon or stars by night or sun to shine by day" because its streets are lit by the radiant glory of God, and its gates are thrown open because all of our satanic enemies have been vanquished to the lake of eternal fire.

As we walk today in the land of promise, the present kingdom of heaven, enjoying the produce of the land, the fruit of the Spirit, living the born again life in Christ, the beloved Son of God, we still know fear and grief and suffering. But some glorious morning when we walk the golden streets of the new, eternal Jerusalem, there will be no sadness, no pain, no tears.

My fervent prayer is that you will be there to enjoy it with me.

A Jewish Easter?

Scripture: Exodus 4:22; Deuteronomy 29:2–4; Hosea 1:10;
Luke 23:34; Romans 4:16; 9; 11:7, 11–16, 25–27

Sometimes when I ponder the Word I get distressed and call God into question, challenging the propriety of his actions. But then I reconsider and admit that he is the Potter and I am the clay, and confess that I, a mere man, have no right to answer back to God.

When he said, for example, that he loved Jacob and hated Esau, I thought he was being unfair. But then I console myself with the thought that the errant Esau would probably have earned God's wrath anyway. And even if God had not programmed Pharaoh to be evil, his immense power probably would have corrupted him.

But the eternal destiny of the Jews gives me pause.

A slightly biased reading of the scripture leads me to conclude that they were what they were because God determined that they should be that way. In B.C. times, he closed their eyes and hardened their hearts to all the great signs and wonders he wrought to bring them into their Promised Land and to preserve them there. That is why they bowed the knee to idols and that is why God destined them to deportation and centuries of persecution.

But what bothers me more is the reason for their stumbling: my salvation. In A.D. times God hardened their hearts and blinded their eyes to their Messiah so that the apostles would be forced to flee from Israel and take the gospel to the Gentiles of Asia Minor and Europe.

So, in a sense, God's wayward son, Israel, was also wounded for my transgressions and bruised for my iniquities. God gave the Jews a Good Friday of their own. Will he also give them an Easter?

As I write this we are just getting over Passion Week and the resurrection. On Maundy Thursday we shrouded our chancel in black, hung a crown of thorns on the cross and celebrated the Last Supper. Then on Sunday morning we sang *He is Risen* and the children paraded down the aisle with the lilies and transformed the sanctuary from a scene of sobriety to one of gladness. But even in the joyful glow of knowing that Jesus is alive and I am alive in him, I felt some sadness and shame because generations of Jews may have gone to their graves destined for eternal damnation because God had hardened their hearts for my sake.

And so I went to the scriptures looking for some consolation, and made what was to me a delightful discovery. Paul said that the promise of God's grace was guaranteed to *all* of Abraham's descendants, and that righteousness was *reckoned* unto them as it was to the father of their nation. And Hosea said that God would call all of the "sands of the sea" his sons again. And Paul further spoke of their *full inclusion* and said that *all* Israel will be saved, that the holiness of the dough rendered the whole lump holy and the holiness of the root made the branches holy as well.

For me, Good Friday took on a new and brighter glow. When Jesus interceded on behalf of those who "know not what they do," did he extend the blanket of his forgiveness beyond the men who drove the nails? Did he, with those words, pardon all of his compatriots whose hearts God had hardened and whose eyes God had closed?

That prospect made my Easter happier. And as I sat and pondered the Rapture and the resurrection of the dead in Christ, I smiled because in my reverie I saw my grave open and I saw myself rise to meet Jesus as he stood amid the whole nation of Jacob's sons!

To order additional copies of

MOON OVER AJALON

Have your credit card ready and call:

1-877-421-READ (7323)

or please visit our web site at
www.pleasantword.com

Also available at: www.amazon.com

Printed in the United States
16588LVS00002B/22-102